India Studies in Business and Economics

The Indian economy is considered to be one of the fastest growing economies of the world with India amongst the most important G-20 economies. Ever since the Indian economy made its presence felt on the global platform, the research community is now even more interested in studying and analyzing what India has to offer. This series aims to bring forth the latest studies and research about India from the areas of economics, business, and management science. The titles featured in this series will present rigorous empirical research, often accompanied by policy recommendations, evoke and evaluate various aspects of the economy and the business and management landscape in India, with a special focus on India's relationship with the world in terms of business and trade.

More information about this series at http://www.springer.com/series/11234

Utpal Kumar De · Manoranjan Pal
Premananda Bharati
Editors

Inequality, Poverty and Development in India

Focus on the North Eastern Region

Springer

Editors
Utpal Kumar De
Department of Economics
North-Eastern Hill University
Shillong, Meghalaya
India

Premananda Bharati
Biological Anthropology Unit
Indian Statistical Institute
Kolkata, West Bengal
India

Manoranjan Pal
Economic Research Unit
Indian Statistical Institute
Kolkata, West Bengal
India

ISSN 2198-0012 ISSN 2198-0020 (electronic)
India Studies in Business and Economics
ISBN 978-981-10-6273-5 ISBN 978-981-10-6274-2 (eBook)
DOI 10.1007/978-981-10-6274-2

Library of Congress Control Number: 2017950277

Printed on acid-free paper

This Springer imprint is published by Springer Nature
The registered company is Springer Nature Singapore Pte Ltd.
The registered company address is: 152 Beach Road, #21-01/04 Gateway East, Singapore 189721, Singapore

Foreword

The book entitled "Inequality, Poverty and Development in India: Focus on the North Eastern Region" has certain distinctive features. First, it approaches issues in human welfare from a multidimensional perspective. It is now well recognized that the traditional income-based poverty measures judge human welfare only partially. The various chapters in this book go beyond considering deprivation of income dimension and judge social development from several non-income dimensions such as education, nutrition, environment, and social stability. Second, as the subtitle indicates, the book especially focuses on the north-eastern part of the country which has remained relatively under searched. Hence, the chapters in this book have potential to draw attention of academic community and policy-makers interested in the development of the northeast India. Third, the authors advocate an integrated approach to address the economic, sociological, political, and anthropological factors related to the issues of social development. In this respect Profs. Utpal Kumar De of North-Eastern Hill University, and Manoranjan Pal and Premananda Bharati of Indian Statistical Institute have done a commendable job by bringing out this volume.

The papers included in this volume address a number of issues related to Millennium and Sustainable Development Goals. They cover a number of issues related to government and private institutions, corruption, rural–urban disparity, financial inclusion centering on inequality, poverty, and development. Advanced tools like Benson's splitting technique, cointegration, vector autoregression, and panel data techniques have been used. The volume thus deals with state-of-the-art techniques to examine problems of inequality and poverty. It is also encouraging to note that environmental issues have occupied a substantial place in the volume. An entire part out of the three parts in the volume is devoted to the environmental questions. This is as it should be in a book that focuses on the northeast.

I congratulate the authors and the three editors for their joint effort for a timely publication of such an important volume. It enhances our understanding of several issues related to poverty and inequality. I do hope that it will be helpful for further research as well as policy formulation.

Manoj Panda
Director
Institute of Economic Growth, New Delhi, India

Preface

United Nation's Millennium Development Goals (MDGs) are the stepping stones of developmental efforts in the new millennium. It sets eight goals to be achieved by the end of 2015. Amelioration of extreme poverty comes in the forefront of this declaration. The other goals range from promoting gender equality and empowerment of women, reducing child mortality, improving maternal health, and preventing the spread of HIV/AIDS to ensuring environmental sustainability. In these UN Millennium Development Goals, targets were set to achieve each of these goals by 2015.

The increasing inequality in income, wealth, and consumption is a great concern not only for India, but also the entire developing world is afflicted with this problem. The growing inequality often hinders achieving the developmental goals according to its full potentials.

Though there is significant improvement in the poverty reduction in both rural and urban areas, there is a significant rural–urban variation in the achievement across the states. The rural–urban gap in the poverty ratio varied from 1% in UP to 29% in Mizoram during 2011–2012. Also, there is significant variation in male female poverty ratio. We have to search for ways and means to tackle the issues of inequality to improve the welfare across all sections of the society. Lack of entrepreneurship and sluggish manufacturing growth are some of the important obstacles of generating employment and that in many ways lead to social disorder and sectarian movements, which further impedes development activities.

So far as amelioration of poverty is concerned, a significant reduction in the percentage of population living under poverty has already been achieved in India. The incidence of poverty in India came down from about 51% in 1990–1991 to 37% in 2004–2005 and thereafter to an overall figure of 22% in 2011–2012. The head count ratios of rural and urban poverty percentages were about 26 and 14, respectively. Though a remarkable progress in this respect has been achieved so far, there are about 250 million people living below the poverty line of which more than 200 million are in rural areas. Even now about 1 in every 5 persons in India is below the national poverty line.

In the world scenario also, the progress is commendable. According to the most recent estimates, in 2011, about 17% of the people in the developing world lived below \$1.25 a day, which is significantly lower than 43% figure of 1990. This means that, in 2011, just over one billion people lived on less than \$1.25 a day, as compared with 1.91 billion in 1990 in this world. Despite significant progress, we observe hunger, malnutrition, and starvation death in many parts of the world particularly in a number of countries in Asia and Sub-Saharan Africa. This is associated with the disturbances in social order including terrorism in West Asia and parts of Africa rendering many people homeless and also suffering from the lack of adequate survival materials and opportunities. This phenomenon is also observed, though in smaller scale, in many parts of India. One may recall the recent past incidences of rampant terrorism in Kokrajhar district of Assam in 2012 and 2014.

Problems are there with the method of identifying the target population. Several methods applied in the estimation of the extent of poverty and its gravity make the authorities confused on the process of eradication mechanism. Defining poverty measure as the percentage of people with income less than US\$ 1.25 a day represents an example of income-focused approach to poverty. In recent past fixing of 32 INR per capita daily in India as poverty line ushered huge debate, which is about half of a USD. The poverty line defined by the Tendulkar Committee did not reflect the changing times and aspirations of the people. Under the growing income, expenditure and the economic structure of the country in the previous decade with consequent changes in people's perspective led to the setting up of the Expert Group headed by Dr. Rangarajan. The committee has re-computed the average requirements of calories, fats, and proteins on the basis of the 2010 ICMR norms, rural–urban gender distribution of population as per 2011 Census and employment distribution status. People's capability to save is also considered. The new poverty lines were worked out as the monthly per capita consumption expenditure of Rs. 972 in rural areas and Rs. 1407 in urban areas. Estimation of poverty line by Rangarajan Committee is based on an independent survey of households by CMIE. As per their method, a household is considered to be poor if it is unable to save and this yields results that are remarkably close to those derived using the NSSO data. This provides additional evidence in support of the poverty line derived by them. Health and health care, gender inequality, and environmental sustainability are also the other important issues related to the overall development of a nation.

The aforementioned goals are, however, closely interlinked or interdependent and cannot be tackled only through the development of economic activities. Just addressing issues partially without an integrated approach may lead to imbalances in the development of various dimensions. Simultaneously, the allocation of resources and inclusiveness of all sections of the society and across both the gender are pertinent to the all round progress of the society. Deprivation of people from the growth process, exclusion from the decision-making process even in this decentralized institutional setup, is found to create several bottlenecks for the progress. Some forces always operate in the society to counter such progress and preserve poverty and inequality. Market mechanism and service delivery systems failed to completely eradicate poverty, reduce inequality even after so many commissions and strategies undertaken by the governments. Various societal and political forces also play important roles in matters of development. For example, superstitions, particularly in the rural areas in many cases, cause social disorder and take societies backward even today. Lack of education gives more chances to such forces to operate successfully. Despite matrilineal systems in some tribal societies of northeast India, women rarely participate in the political decision-making process. Thus it needed a concerted effort to address the sociological, political, anthropological and economic factors related to those issues. It is also needed to identify the relevant issues, suggest possible measures as well as delivery mechanism, etc., by re-examining the earlier measures and delivery systems.

Under these circumstances, we decided to have a fresh look into the matter and see how far the Millennium Development Goals have been achieved by the target year of 2015 in India and its adjoining areas, and more particularly in northeast India. The region has been almost disconnected from the mainland India over decades since Independence and deprived of several opportunities. Despite being the zone of one of the 18 hotspots of biodiversity in the world, and having rich mineral, forests, climate, heavy rainfall, etc., the region is yet to observe noticeable growth of manufacturing industries, tourism, sustainable resource management practices for the removal of poverty and promote the crippled regional economy.

However, there is a recent effort to integrate India with its eastern neighbors, particularly the ASEAN and form a bigger subregional cooperation through better connectivity under India's Look/Act East Policy and provide the region ample scope of socioeconomic development vide social, economic opportunities. Yet, there was a need to see the loop whole in the achievements and suggest measures for meeting the targets and go beyond the Millennium Development Goals.

In the context of climate change, agricultural sector faces serious challenges to meet the sustainable livelihood of the people especially for the vulnerable groups. Due to faulty strategies of single goal in the early stages of planning, farmers in many cases lost their indigenous techniques of production. Indiscriminate use of hybrid seeds, chemical fertilizers and excessive use of groundwater resources are largely responsible for the environmental pollution and worsening of soil quality. There is an urgency to explore the strategies in order to address such burning issues. The initiatives taken by the Government of Sikkim to ban the chemical fertilizers in agricultural sector are no doubt appreciable steps toward environmental sustainability.

Quality of environment is also directly and indirectly linked with the growth process. Thus achieving sustainable progress is another target and remains elusive. In terms of reduction in pollution, carbon dioxide emission, deforestation, etc., India is far behind the expectations. The growth of agricultural production has been decelerated substantially in recent decades and whatever institutional attempts have been undertaken, the benefits do not reach to all sections of the society.

From the above discussion, it is clear that we could not achieve the MDGs in all targets and there are also significant spatial variations. Thus it is high time we review our achievements and lapses incurred in comparison with the targets of the MDGs.

Thus the book discusses the fundamental issues of inequality, development, environment relationship focusing northeast India and we believe that it will be helpful toward policy formulation and further research in various lines. The research outputs presented here will also help the planners, politicians, and the social workers.

Shillong, India Utpal Kumar De
Kolkata, India Manoranjan Pal
Kolkata, India Premananda Bharati

Contents

Part I Inequality, Growth and Development

1 **Does Economic Growth Increase Inequality?: An Empirical Analysis for ASEAN Countries, China and India** 3
Partha Gangopadhyay and Biswa Nath Bhattacharyay

2 **Does Institutional Quality Affect Foreign Direct Investment? A Panel Data Analysis** 31
Girijasankar Mallik and Mamta Chowdhury

3 **An Empirical Verification of Kuznets Hypothesis in India** 49
Aadil Ahmad Ganaie, Sajad Ahmad Bhat and Bandi Kamaiah

4 **An Inquiry into the Dynamics of Inequality from the Perspective of Caste** 81
Anoop S. Kumar and P Yazir

5 **Can Horizontal Inequalities Explain Ethnic Conflicts? A Case Study of Bodoland Territorial Area Districts of Assam** 97
Rupan Boro and Rajshree Bedamatta

6 **Selection and Performance of Self-Help Groups in West Bengal: A Case Study** 127
Archita Ghosh and Tithi Bose

7 **Financial Inclusion Through Kisan Credit Cards in Arunachal Pradesh—The Truth Behind Aggregating Numbers** 145
Samir R. Samantara

8 **Insurance and Banking Habits Regulating Economic Stability of the People of Char Areas (Riverine) in Lower Assam** 159
Kishore K. Das

9 **Institutional Barriers to Development in the State of Nagaland** 175
Chothazo Nienu

Part II Poverty at State Level with Focus North-East

10 **A Study of Multidimensional Poverty in Northeast India** 189
Supravat Bagli

11 **Poverty, Inequality and Relative Deprivation Among Northeastern States of India: Evidence from NSS** 207
Mohammad Kashif Khan and Balakrushna Padhi

12 **Deprivation of Women in Northeast India: An Exploratory Study** 223
Papita Dutta

13 **Levels of Living in the North Eastern States of India** 237
Anika M.W. Kshiar Shadap

14 **Urban Poverty Reduction Through Local Governance in Nepal** 265
Dil Nath Fuel

15 **Rural Poverty and Employment Guarantee Scheme: Reflections from West Bengal** 301
Manjima Mandal and Amal Mandal

16 **Poverty in Rural West Bengal: Trend Over Four Decades** 321
Arindam Chakraborty

17 **A Study on Spatial Statistical Method of Poverty and Sustainable Development of North-Eastern States of India** 337
Manoshi Phukon and Rajeshwar Singh

18 **Hunger, Governance Failure and Its Outcome: An Analysis of the Historical Experience of the Mizo Hills District of Undivided Assam** 351
Malabika Das Gupta

19 **Conflicts Leave a Trail of Poverty and Malnutrition: Evidences from Assam** 363
Kalyan Das

Part III Agricultural and Environmental Perspectives

20 Integrating Management for Land–Water Ecosystem for Augmenting Productivity, Income, and Sustainable Livelihood 385
A.M. Puste, S.K. Gunri, K. Jana, B. Ray Pramanik, S.K. Acharya, M. Dasgupta and T.K. Maity

21 Family Farming in Amazon: Solution to Food and Regional Competitiveness 407
Alex Rotta Romani, Flávio de São Pedro Filho, Jeoval Batista da Silva, Janilene Vasconcelos de Melo and Jayashree Patil-Dake

22 Farm Growth in Northeast India and Its Effect on Poverty 423
K.U. Viswanathan and Anannya Gupta

23 Socio-Economic and Environmental Performance Across North-Eastern States of India 443
Rakesh Saxena

24 Adaptability of Farmers in Assam Towards Extreme Climate Effects: An Empirical Investigation 465
Utpal Kumar De and Kamal Bodosa

25 Dynamics of Forest Resources: Some Empirical Testing on Assam's Forest Cover 501
Gunjan Kumar

26 Is Indian Agriculture Shifting Towards Feminisation? A Study on Recent Trend in Indian Agriculture with Reference to the Selected States of Northeast India 513
Banjul Bhattacharyya and Udaybhanu Bhattacharyya

Editors and Contributors

About the Editors

Utpal Kumar De is currently Professor of Economics and also the Head of Department of Economics at the North-Eastern Hill University, Shillong, India. Professor De has been engaged in teaching at postgraduate level since 1994. His research interests include agricultural economics and rural development, issues on environmental and natural resources, climate change adaptation, and empowerment of women. Professor De has visited Europe and Asia for his various research projects and delivered keynote and invited lectures at a number of conferences. Besides presenting over 60 research papers in various international and national conferences, he has published seven volumes, completed a number of research projects, and published over 75 research articles in reputed national and international journals. The Marquis Who's Who Publications Board certifies that Utpal Kumar De is a subject of biographical record in Who's Who in the World 2013 Pearl Anniversary Edition, inclusion in which is limited to those individuals who have demonstrated outstanding achievement in their own fields of endeavor and who have, thereby, contributed significantly to the betterment of contemporary society.

Manoranjan Pal is currently Professor in the Economic Research Unit (ERU) of the Indian Statistical Institute (ISI), Kolkata. At the institute, besides teaching graduate and postgraduate courses, he is also engaged in carrying out projects of the Government of India and other organizations, while also guiding doctoral students. He was Head of ERU and Professor-In-Charge of Social Sciences Division (SSD) of the ISI. He worked as Member Secretary, Board of Directors, International Statistical Education Centre (ISEC), Kolkata, for more than 10 years starting from February 1999. Professor Pal has held the post of a Visiting Professor at many international institutions. He has published more than 100 papers in reputed national and international journals and books. His research interests include the measurement of poverty, inequality and segregation, applied econometrics, health and nutrition, and so on. Professor Pal's name is included in the World 2013 Pearl Anniversary Edition in Marquis Who's Who, inclusion in which is limited to those individuals who have demonstrated outstanding achievement in their own fields of endeavor.

Premananda Bharati is currently Visiting Professor at the Biological Anthropology Unit of the Indian Statistical Institute (ISI), Kolkata. He was Professor and Head of the same unit before his retirement in 2016. He served at the institute for more than 30 years. His fields of interest include human biology, physical anthropology, growth, nutrition, poverty, gender issues, and demography. He has taught at the Center of Statistics, Human Sciences Research Council (HSRC), Pretoria, South Africa. Professor Bharati was awarded the International Man of the Year (1993/94) by the International Biographical Centre, Cambridge, England; and Man of the Year 1994 by the American Biographical Institute, North Carolina, USA. He is a fellow of the Human Biology

Association, Michigan, USA. In addition to teaching, he has published more than 100 research papers in journals of national and international repute and completed a number of research projects. He has visited America, Europe, and Asia extensively in connection with short-term courses and has delivered invited lectures and presented papers at various international and national seminars and conferences.

Contributors

S.K. Acharya Department of Agricultural Extension, Faculty of Agriculture, Bidhan Chandra Krishi Viswavidyalaya, Mohanpur, Nadia, India

Supravat Bagli Presidency University, Kolkata, West Bengal, India

Biswa Nath Bhattacharyay Asian Development Bank, Manila, Philippines; CESIfo (The Center of University of Munich and Ifo Institute), Munich, Germany; McGill University, Montreal, QC, Canada

Rajshree Bedamatta Department of Humanities and Social Sciences, IIT Guwahati, Guwahati, India

Sajad Ahmad Bhat School of Economics, University of Hyderabad, Hyderabad, India

Banjul Bhattacharyya Department of Agricultural Statistics, Bidhan Chandra Krishi Viswavidyalaya, Nadia, West Bengal, India

Udaybhanu Bhattacharyya Department of Rural Development & Management, University of Kalyani, Kalyani, West Bengal, India

Kamal Bodosa Department of Economics, Kokrajhar Government College, Kokrajhar, Assam, India

Rupan Boro Department of Humanities and Social Sciences, IIT Guwahati, Guwahati, India

Tithi Bose Department of Economics, Haldia Government College, Haldia, India

Arindam Chakraborty S.R. Lahiri Mahavidyalaya, Nadia, WB, India

Mamta Chowdhury School of Business, Western Sydney University, Penrith, Australia

Kalyan Das OKD Institute of Social Change and Development, Guwahati, India

Kishore K. Das Department of Statistics, Gauhati University, Guwahati, Assam, India

M. Dasgupta Department of Animal Sciences, Faculty of Agriculture, Bidhan Chandra Krishi Viswavidyalaya, Mohanpur, Nadia, India

Malabika Das Gupta Tripura University, Agartala, India; Institute of Development Studies Kolkata, Kolkata, India; Department of Economics, Centre for Urban Economic Studies, Calcutta University, Kolkata, India

Utpal Kumar De Department of Economics, North-Eastern Hill University, Shillong, Meghalaya, India

Papita Dutta Gushkara Mahavidyalaya, Burdwan, West Bengal, India

Dil Nath Fuel Economics Education, Tribhuvan University, Kirtipur, Nepal

Aadil Ahmad Ganaie School of Economics, University of Hyderabad, Hyderabad, India

Partha Gangopadhyay School of Business, Western Sydney University, Penrith, NSW, Australia; CEPM, University of the South Pacific, Suva, Fiji

Archita Ghosh Department of Economics, University of Kalyani, Kalyani, West Bengal, India

S.K. Gunri Department of Agronomy, Bidhan Chandra Krishi Viswavidyalaya, Mohanpur, Nadia, India

Anannya Gupta NABARD, Assam Regional Office, Guwahati, India

K. Jana Department of Agronomy, Bidhan Chandra Krishi Viswavidyalaya, Mohanpur, Nadia, India

Bandi Kamaiah School of Economics, University of Hyderabad, Hyderabad, India

Mohammad Kashif Khan School of Economics, University of Hyderabad, Hyderabad, Telangana, India

Anika M.W. Kshiar Shadap St. Edmund's College, Shillong, India

Anoop S. Kumar Department of Economics, BITS Pilani KK Birla Goa Campus, Goa, India

Gunjan Kumar Department of Humanities and Social Sciences, Indian Institute of Technology, Guwahati, India

T.K. Maity Department of Vegetable Crops, Faculty of Horticulture, Bidhan Chandra Krishi Viswavidyalaya, Mohanpur, Nadia, India

Girijasankar Mallik School of Business, Western Sydney University, Penrith South DC, NSW, Australia

Amal Mandal Political Science, Tufanganj College, Cooch Behar, WB, India

Manjima Mandal Central Bank of India, Cooch Behar, India

Janilene Vasconcelos de Melo Federal University of Rondônia, Porto Velho, Brazil

Chothazo Nienu School of Economics, University of Hyderabad, Hyderabad, India

Balakrushna Padhi Centre for Study of Regional Development (CSRD), Jawaharlal Nehru University, New Delhi, India

Jayashree Patil-Dake KPB Hinduja College, Mumbai, India

Manoshi Phukon Department of Statistics, North Eastern Hill University, Shillong, India

A.M. Puste Department of Agronomy, Bidhan Chandra Krishi Viswavidyalaya, Mohanpur, Nadia, India

B. Ray Pramanik ADA, Department of Agriculture, Government of West Bengal, Kalyani, Nadia, India

Alex Rotta Romani Research Group in Management of Innovation and Technology (GEITEC/UNIR), Federal University of Rondônia (UNIR), Porto Velho, Brazil

Samir R. Samantara National Bank for Agriculture and Rural Development (NABARD), Assam Regional Office, Guwahati, India

Rakesh Saxena NABARD Chair Professor, Institute of Rural Management, Anand, Gujarat, India

Jeoval Batista da Silva Research Group in Management of Innovation and Technology (GEITEC/UNIR), Federal University of Rondônia (UNIR), Porto Velho, Brazil

Rajeshwar Singh Department of Statistics, North Eastern Hill University, Shillong, India

Flávio de São Pedro Filho Research Group in Management of Innovation and Technology (GEITEC/UNIR), Federal University of Rondônia (UNIR), Porto Velho, Brazil

K.U. Viswanathan NABARD, Assam Regional Office, Guwahati, India

P Yazir School of Economics, University of Hyderabad, Gachibowli, India

Abbreviations

ACI	People Republic of China and India
ADB	Asian Development Bank
AFO	Anti-famine Campaign Organisation
ANOGI	Analysis of Gini
ANOVA	One-way Analysis of variance
APRB	Arunachal Pradesh Rural Bank
APSCAB	Arunachal Pradesh State Cooperative Apex Bank
ARCH	Autoregressive Conditional Heteroscedasticity
ARDL	Autoregressive Distributed Lag
ASCARD Bank	Assam State Cooperative Agricultural & Rural Development Bank
ASEAN	Associations of Southeast Asian Nations
ATMA	Agricultural Technology Development Agency
BPL	Below Poverty Line
BTAD	Bodoland Territorial Area Districts
CAGR	Compound Annual Growth Rate
CHIP	China Household Income Project
CPI	Consumer Price Index
CRP	Community Resource Persons
DEBTGDP	The ratio of debt to GDP
DoLR	Department of Land Resources
DRDC	District Rural Development Cell
ECM	Error Correction Model
EHI	Economic horizontal Inequalities
EHII	Estimated Household Income Inequality
ENERGYO	Energy Output
FAO	Food and Agriculture Organisation
FDI	Foreign Direct Investment
FE	Fixed Effect
FGLS	Feasible Generalized Least Squares

FGT	Foster–Greer–Thorbecke
FMS	Farm Management Studies
FOODP	The Index of Food Prices
GA	Geographical Area
GCA	Gross Cropped Area
GDI	Gender-related development index
GDP	Gross Domestic Product
GEXP	Government Expenditure
GSDP	Gross State Domestic Product
GSDPA	Gross State Domestic Product from Agriculture and Allied sector
HCI	Cultural status horizontal inequality
HD	Human Development
HDI	Human Development Index
HDR	Human Developments Reports
HEI	Horizontal Economic Inequality
HPI	Horizontal Political Inequality
HR	Human Rights
ICAR	Indian Council of Agricultural Research
ICDS	Integrated Child Development Services
ICM	Integrated coastal management
IHD	Index of housing deprivation
IIM	Indian Institute of Management
IMR	Infant Mortality Rate
IPM	Integrated Pest Management
ISCED	International Standard Classification of Education system
KCC	Kisan Credit Cards
KVKs	Krishi Vigyan Kendra's
LFEY	Live fish Equivalent Yield
LSGA	Local Self-Governance Act
MANAGE	National Institute of Agricultural Extension Management
MDGs	Millennium Development Goals
MDPI	Multidimensional Poverty Index
MGNREGA	Mahatma Gandhi National Rural Employment Guarantee Act
MNC	Multinational Corporations
MPCE	Monthly Per capita Consumption Expenditure
MPI	Multidimensional Poverty Index
MRP	Mixed Reference Period
MSME	Micro, Small, and Medium Enterprises
NABARD	National Bank for Agriculture and Rural Development
NCO	National Classification of Occupation
NDC	National Development Council
NER	North-eastern Region
NFHS	National Family Health Survey

NSA	Net Sown Area
NSSO	National Sample Survey Office
NSSO	National Sample Survey Organisation
OBC	Other Backward Classes
OLS	Ordinary Least Square
PAB	Planning Advisory Board
PCA	Principal Component Analysis
PC-EPI	Planning Commission-Environmental Performance Index
PCGDP	Per Capita Gross Domestic Product
PCNSDP	Per Capita Net State Domestic Product
PCTE	Per Capita Total Expenditure
PEG	Poverty-equivalent Growth
PEI	Poverty Elasticity of Inequality
PIP	Participatory Identification of Poor
POPG	Population Growth
PPG	Pro-poor Growth
PPP	Purchasing power parity
PPS	Probability Proportional to Size
PQLI	Physical Quality of Life
PRC	People Republic of China
RCH	Reproductive and Child Health
RHS	Rural Household Survey
RRB	Regional Rural Bank
SBI	State Bank of India
SC	Scheduled castes
SEP-HRD	Society for Environment Protection and Human Resource Development
SGSY	Swarnajayanti Gram Swarojgar Yojana
ST	Scheduled Tribes
TFP	Total Factor Productivity
TO	Trade Openness
ToT	Transfer of Technology
TPE	Total Poverty Elasticity
UBI	United Bank of India
UNDP	United Nations Development Programme
URP	Uniform Reference Period
WCED	World Commission on Environment and Development
WDIW	Weighted Deprivation Index for Women
WECD	World Commission on Environment and Development
WPR	Work Participation Rate

Introduction

Utpal Kumar De, Manoranjan Pal and Premananda Bharati

This volume is not just a compilation of some chapters on the concerned aspects of inequality poverty and development issues. The chapters included in this volume address a number of issues related to two important aspects of MDGs, namely, poverty and inequality.

Poverty in earlier days used to be considered as an incidence of income deprivation. However, in the discourse of new development, paradigm poverty is considered as an acute case of capability deprivation and it is multidimensional in nature. It has been reflected in the studies of the researchers that there is no such straightforward relationship between Multidimensional Poverty Index (MPI) and official income/consumption-based poverty estimates. Hence, it is strongly recommended to incorporate the other aspects of human life such as education and health in the estimation of poverty.

The book covers a wide range of issues related to inequality, poverty and development, role of government and private institutions, corruption, etc. Development and poverty alleviation is examined in relation to environmental resource management as well as institutional arrangements. A large number of chapters address the issues in northeast India besides some cross-country and national analyses.

Besides introducing some new questions on development, sophisticated tools have been used like Benson's splitting technique, cointegration, vector autoregression, panel data technique like fixed effects and the system generalized methods of moments (SGMM), qualitative content analysis, for examining growth-inequality relationship, public–private investment and growth relationship, corruption–development relationship, etc. Other nonlinear techniques have also been employed by some authors. Further, Oaxaca Blinder decomposition method in consumption expenditure to show the endowment and return to endowment effects, spatial correlation-regression to analyze regional variation, diversification and adaptation index to check farmers' response to climate change, etc. have been used to find out socioeconomic complexities, and their impacts on poverty, human development.

We have divided the volume into three major parts: (1) Inequality, Growth and Development; (2) Poverty at the State Level with Focus Northeast; and (3) Agricultural and Environmental Perspectives.

Studies on reinvestigation of growth-inequality relationship, relationship between public and private investment in the process of national income growth, and the role of corruption in affecting economic growth are included in Part I.

The first chapter of Part I examines the relationship between economic growth and inequality in Asian countries. Using a panel regression analysis and Benson's splitting technique, the chapter reaffirms the inverted-U shape relationship. After the threshold limit of FDI, the relationship takes the form of a sinusoidal curve that has significant policy implication.

The second chapter investigates the effects of the institutional quality along with socioeconomic factors on foreign direct investment (FDI) across the countries using Ordinary Least Square (OLS) and Fixed Effect (FE) method. The study suggests that while corruption lowers FDI significantly, democracy, government stability, law and order, civil liberty, and political rights have significant positive effects on FDI inflows. Results of the study also indicate that increased levels of educational attainment and openness in a trade regime lead to a higher level of FDI. Thus the policy prescription to attract higher FDI requires focussing on ensuring better institutional quality with lower level of corruption along with raising the skill base of the labor force in an outward looking external trade regime.

Impact of corruption on economic growth has been examined in the second chapter in a nonlinear framework by using a cross-country data set. In general, corruption is not found to prohibit growth. But after a threshold level of corruption, a rise in it has adverse impact on the growth process. The results obtained after controlling for fixed effects and endogeneity biases by utilizing the system generalized methods of moments (SGMM), the most advanced, robust, and well-recognized technique in the literature.

The third chapter is devoted to the empirical examination of Kuznet's Hypothesis for India using some time series techniques for the period 1964–2007. Results reveal no relevance of Kuznets Hypothesis, instead the relationship is U-shaped in nature, implying that initial increase in GDP per capita leads to decrease in inequality, later on as GDP increases, inequality tends to increase. Among the control variables CPI (price level) is found to be positively and government expenditure negatively related to inequality, while trade openness showed no significant relationship.

The next chapter by Anoop S. Kumar analyzes two rounds of NSSO data, viz., 61st and 66th, to compute Gini coefficient and estimated overlapping index for the whole as well as the subgroups using ANOGI methodology. The analysis reveals that the level of overall inequality as well as the intergroup inequality is on the rise in Kerala as well as India during the period of analysis. The study also identifies the possibility of stratification among the group "Others" for both India and Kerala. Further, it finds that SC's and ST's (in particular) bear the burden of the increasing inequality. The indication is that the various welfare measures initiated by the central as well as state governments might not have reached the majority of these downtrodden communities.

Chapter 5 also examined horizontal economic inequalities as a cause of rising ethnic conflicts in Boroland areas of Assam. Standard inequality measure like Group Gini index of asset holding and opportunity is explained in the chapter and linked with rising violence in the area.

The study of Archita Ghosh and Tithi Bose (Chapter 6) examines different factors playing determining role in generating benefits under MGNREGA, the largest rural employment guarantee scheme in India. Household-level study in two districts of West Bengal with econometric analysis reveals that besides a few social factors, political patronage plays a vital role in generating benefits. Economic factors have almost no role in the whole process.

A district-level study on financial inclusion through Kisan Credit Card in Arunachal Pradesh and its convergence pattern is presented in Chapter 7. The chapter focuses on the questions of (a) whether there has been a catching-up tendency (β-convergence) of slow-growing districts with fast-growing ones; and (b) whether there has been a tendency toward convergence (σ-convergence) in agricultural productivity during 2000–2010 over a representative cross section of Arunachal Pradesh districts. The chapter also tests the operation of Galton's fallacy through growth-terminal level regressions for robustness of the results. The tendency of low-KCC concentration districts to catch up with high-KCC concentration districts is studied through the unconditional β-convergence approach, and the operation of Galton's fallacy through growth-terminal agricultural productivity-level regressions. The diminution of variance in productivity levels is tested by using the σ-convergence approach and the robustness of the results is tested by using alternative test statistics.

Chapter 8 by K.K. Das examines the insurance and banking habits of the people of Char areas (riverine) in lower Assam and how it regulates their economic stability. A log-linear model and contingency table have been considered in this study. It is observed that the proportion of insured households in the low-income group is nil; it rises to a small in the lower middle group and then goes up in the upper middle group and after that steadily increases to the high-income group.

Thereafter, Chapter 9, the final chapter of the part describes the institutional barrier for investment and development in Nagaland. In his opinion, Nagaland's economy from the usual economic indicators like Gross State Domestic Product (GSDP), Per Capita Income, Human Development Index (HDI), economic growth rate, etc. provides a misleading picture about the progressive performance of the state. There are other indicators which show the weak side of the state's economy: the service sector, the public administration contributes nearly a fifth of the state's GSDP, the industrial sector is rather very small, the infrastructure is poor, and the state is dependent heavily on the central government assistance. The state's economy has these ills because of the political problem that it is stuck in, resulting in the existence of many nationalist groups and a consequent weak government. Unless this is solved, Nagaland will continue to have the same economic problems it is having.

Part II deals with the regional analysis of poverty and inequality with a special focus on north-eastern region of India.

District-level multidimensional poverty index (MPI) has been computed for northeast India and presented in Chapter 10 by S. Bagli. The MPI has been computed measuring the normalized inverse Euclidian distance of the actual vector of deprivation indicators from the worst situation of deprivation. The disparities among the states and among the districts in terms of the indicators under consideration have also been revealed. However, there is no straightforward relation between MPI of the states and percentage of population live below poverty line income.

Chapter 11 examines poverty, inequality, and relative deprivation among north-eastern states of India during 2004–2005 and 2011–2012 by using the 61st and 68th Consumer Expenditure Rounds of NSSO data. This chapter used head-count ratio to measure poverty, relative deprivation index to understand the level of deprivation among the north-eastern states of India. Gini coefficient is used for understanding inequality prevalence. Oaxaca Blinder decomposition method in consumption expenditure is used to show the endowment and return to endowment effects. Significant interstate and rural–urban variation in poverty and inequality have been observed. Oaxaca Blinder results show that sector, state, and education play key role in differences of mean expenditure of poor and nonpoor for endowment as well as return to endowment impact.

Chapter 12 entitled "Deprivation of Women in Northeast India: An Exploratory Study" by Papita Dutta critically examines the degree of inequality in some indicators of deprivation of women across the states of northeast India. In order to have an interstate comparison, a weighted deprivation index for women (WDIW) has been computed at the state level following Sen and Anand (1997). Only the relevant principal components of the indicators have been replaced in place of the indicators and weights are generated from Principal Component Analysis.

Chapter 13 analyzes state-wise level of living by a wide range of indicators like employment, per capita consumption expenditure, nutritional intake, educational attainment, demographic structure, literacy rates, household amenities, consumer durables, and summary of health indicators from the NSSO data. In this chapter, each of these indicators has been combined into a composite index called the standard-of-living index.

Effect of fiscal decentralization on the welfare of urban population in Nepal is addressed in Chapter 14. Urban poverty and growing urban (municipal) population pose the major concern in the development process there. From the association between fiscal decentralization and poverty reduction in the municipalities of Nepal, the author prescribes for the formulation of policy strategy for the better life of such rapidly increasing urban population is to be done as early as possible. Here, the poverty measures and fiscal decentralization variables are used for the study from 1983 through 2010. The comparison in the state of poverty and fiscal decentralization before and after the enactment of Local Self-Governance Act, 1999 (LSGA) in Nepal is also analyzed.

Chapter 15, however, tries to find out the efficacy of MGNREGA in a part of northern West Bengal. Analysis of the aggregate official data evinces that MGNREGA has fallen short of offering the envisaged number of person-days, and thus has not catered to the subsistence demands of the poor. In other words, clear relationship between the outreach of MGNREGA and the proportion of the poor households seems to be missing and this is likely to have little impact on the poverty eradication effects. Together with such disconnect, the chapter also highlights a few procedural dimensions which hold up the general fruition of MGNREGA.

In Chapter 16, Arindam Chakraborty tries to focus on the changing nature and extent of rural poverty in West Bengal during the period 1974–2012 with the help of different poverty estimates of various Expert Groups. Using growth-distribution decomposition analysis of the changes in rural poverty in West Bengal, the author shows that during 1958–1997 both coefficients of growth and distribution are highly significant, and growth effect on rural poverty in West Bengal is found to be stronger than inequality effect. This implies that rapid economic growth can be the best measure for eradicating poverty in India.

Chapter 17 analyzes spatial distribution of poverty levels from the viewpoint of several poverty indicators and looks into mitigation of poverty and sustainable development in north-eastern states of India through three important pillars of development, viz., economic, social, and education. Technique of spatial correlation of Moran (1950) is used with weights assigned by generalized weighting matrix W_{ij} to analyze the spatial relationship among education, income, and employment. All the selected poverty indicators have a high degree of positive autocorrelation among the states of northeast except Sikkim.

Using Census data, Prof. M. Dasgupta in her chapter (Chapter 18) finds that the failures of governance in providing relief to the starving Mizos were proximate causes of the 20-year-long insurgency and social unrest in the Mizo Hills from 1966 to 1986. On the other hand, Chapter 19 tries to capture the malnutrition and starvation of children in relatively backward and conflict prone districts of Assam. Children in country like India are affected by certain indirect factors such as poor governance, corruption, and poor implementation of rule of law (prime determinants of conflicts!). At the same time, in addition to these, there are direct impacts from ethnic conflicts, violent crimes, and sexual assault on women and children. All these cause unpredictability and uncertainties at home and in the local economy, even leading to loss of livelihood. The final outcomes are dehumanization of people trapped in unemployment and poverty, lack of schools (reasons for dropouts are mostly economic), and lack of access to healthcare services (poor public provisioning). All are significant determinants, which affect well-being in the families.

Part III includes chapters dealing with the agricultural and environmental resource management in relation to the maintenance of livelihood and economic prosperity.

Chapter 20 analyzes the integrated farming system for proper utilization of waste wetlands in different agro-zones (new alluvial, old alluvial, and coastal and saline) on a wide sector of downtrodden resource poor to marginal farming communities in

West Bengal. TOT-based research projects of low-cost updating agro-techniques were implemented at farmers' fields on the integration of aquatic food crops—cum—fish culture (sweet water, life fishes, etc.) following improvised INM system (organic, inorganic including micronutrients applied with proper dose and time) for enhancing productivity and economic viability (exhibited even >3.0-folds than that of farmers' practice) at sustainable level. From the study, it may be concluded that this improvised farm practice is imperative to utilize this vast unused wetland, particularly north-eastern part with impetuously for food, livelihood, engagement of household labors and ultimately, economic sustainability of rural people, who are inextricably linked to the system as well.

Another qualitative Content Analysis based on "Theory U" has been presented in Chapter 21 for suggesting best practicable way of sustainable resource use. The epistemological conceptual elements for implementation of strategies required for sustainability in generating competitive advantage in family farming activity can be done through competitive advantages models adaptations extracted from classical literature with the Triple-Bottom Line Sustainability precepts, which models the sustainable development throughout the relationship of social, environmental, and economic aspects.

The content analysis denotes that the indicators linked to family farming and sustainability have been used more frequently than those related to competitive advantages; this is due to the difficulty of finding specific content addressing sustainable competitive advantages for family farming.

In this sense, it was raised the basic competitive strategies for family agricultural activities as the Strategy for Value Creation which works the interaction between suppliers, farmer, customer, and the transformation of potential value; in another way, it was identified the Environmental Competitive Strategy formulated by Orsato (2012) that generates connections between the economic sector where the farmer operates, his position, the types of market, and his abilities to acquire resources and implement innovative strategies, that allow induce competitive advantage either by costs or through environmental cost leadership or eco-efficiency of processes is by differentiation through eco-differentiation processes or by the environmental brand consolidation. These factors raised should guide the farmer's market positioning that can be in operational excellence, innovation in product or customer relationship.

Growth of agricultural farm and its effect on poverty has been addressed in Chapter 22. High farm growth is associated with reduction in poverty in Sikkim, Tripura, Meghalaya, and Assam and the effect is reversed for Manipur. High growth of agriculture was noninclusive, and hence could not have impact on poverty in Arunachal Pradesh and Nagaland. Chapter 23 on the other hand analyzes the socioeconomic and environmental performance of north-eastern states. Land use, demographic pattern, growth of income and sectoral composition, inequality in income distribution, housing pattern and other amenities and livelihood and Planning Commission published environmental index have been analyzed. Correlation among poverty, per capita income, and environmental index has been computed, and the result reveals positive correlation between per capita NSDP and environmental performance, while negative correlation is observed between poverty and environmental performance.

In Chapter 24, De and Bodosa examine the farmer's adaptability toward extreme climate behavior for sustainable progress in agriculture in northeast India. The important contribution of the chapter is providing a suitable index from the heterogenous ways followed by the farmers in the region to counter the adverse impacts of extreme climatic behavior. An adaptation index and diversity index are constructed and related to various determining factors to understand the factors responsible for adaptation for survival by the poor peasants in the region. Crop diversity is used as an adaptation technique followed by the farmers. Through decomposition technique the trend in contribution of diversification to the farm income has been examined. Also, panel data analysis has been adopted to find the effect of various factors on adaptability.

Dynamics of forest resource depletion in Assam is examined in Chapter 25. Estimation of exponential growth function shows that a slight depletion of stock would have series effect on depletion of such resources. He opined that a small decline in regeneration and a small increase in consumption may lead to notable deforestation. Impatience (discounting the future utility with higher rates) in planning may result in lesser consumption and lower stock in future.

The last chapter of the part by Banjul Bhattacharyya & Udaybhanu Bhattacharyya, however, shows the increasing role of women in the agriculture of northeast India.

Part I
Inequality, Growth and Development

Chapter 1
Does Economic Growth Increase Inequality?: An Empirical Analysis for ASEAN Countries, China and India

Partha Gangopadhyay and Biswa Nath Bhattacharyay

Abstract Even though 10 member countries of the Associations of Southeast Asian Nations (ASEAN), People's Republic of China and India (ACI) have adopted polices for archiving more pro-poor or inclusive growth. However, income and non-income inequality in ACI have witnessed an increasing trend in recent years. In view of rising inequality in fast growing Asian developing countries, it is important to study the relationship between economic growth and income inequity which could assist policy makers to adopt appropriate policy action for more inclusive growth. This paper undertakes an empirical analysis to examine if economic growth increases income inequality for ACI. The objectives of the paper are: (i) to develop a simple model of policy-induced growth which shows a nonlinear and wave-like relationship between growth and inequality; (ii) to provide an empirical support to the above model to establish that the intention to use economic growth and inequality as policy instruments to shape economic development can backfire since the possibility of a wave-like function receives an empirical support from ACI data; and (iii) to exhibit that the nonlinear relationship between growth and inequality

---

An earlier version of this paper was prepared as a background paper for the Asian Development Bank (ADB) Institute/Asian Development Bank's (ADB's) study on 'Role of Key Emerging Economies—ASEAN, the People's Republic of China, and India—for a Balanced, Resilient and Sustainable Asia, Tokyo' and was released as a CESifo Working Paper Series, CESifo Group Munich (see references for details).

P. Gangopadhyay (✉)
School of Business, Western Sydney University, Penrith, NSW, Australia
e-mail: p.gangopadhyay@westernsydney.edu.au

P. Gangopadhyay
CEPM, University of the South Pacific, Suva, Fiji

B.N. Bhattacharyay
Asian Development Bank, Manila, Philippines

B.N. Bhattacharyay
CESIfo (The Center of University of Munich and Ifo Institute), Munich, Germany

B.N. Bhattacharyay
McGill University, 845 Sherbrooke St W, Montreal, QC H3A 0G4, Canada

U.K. De et al. (eds.), *Inequality, Poverty and Development in India*, India Studies in Business and Economics, DOI 10.1007/978-981-10-6274-2_1

within ACI nations is mainly driven by the availability of foreign direct investment (FDI). In addition, the paper finds other interesting elements in the relationship between growth and inequality which has profound policy implications for the ACI Economies.

Keywords Growth · Inequality · Foreign direct investment · Poverty ASEAN People's Republic of China and India

JEL Classifications H21 · O11 · O15 · O41

1.1 Introduction

During the past five decades one of the critical changes of paramount significance in the global economy is a gradual and continual transfer of the production capacity of the global economy from the West to the East Asian nations—namely Japan, Taiwan, South Korea and finally to the People's Republic of China (PRC),[1] India and Association of Southeast Asian Nations (ASEAN) nations.

Economies of ASEAN nations, PRC and India are collectively known as the ACI economies and our focus in this paper is the dynamics of growth and inequality within the ACI economies. The significant change in Asian development with the advent of the PRC and India in the 1990s is the remarkable economic growth attended by equally spectacular rising inequality in the region. All ACI economies are expected to see strong economic growth, leading to a fourfold expansion of the region's gross domestic product (GDP) by 2030. The region's share of global output is expected to rise from 15% today to nearly 30% (in 2010 constant prices) over the next two decades. By then, the size of ACI economy will be larger than those of the United States and Europe combined in terms 2010 constant prices GDP.[2] The major challenge for policymakers in the ACI economies is to create adequate wealth for around 3 billion people in an equitable fashion, which should promote income equality, thereby mitigating social heat. Achieving the goal of socially inclusive growth, however, is a formidable task for the ACI economies (Gangopadhayay and Bhattacharyay 2011).

The interrelationships between inequality and economic growth of a nation, or groups of nations, have been extensively studied in economics while an apparent

[1]This region has grown into the economic powerhouse of the global economy. In 1955 China, Japan, South Korea and Taiwan encompassed over one quarter of the global population but generated only 9% of the gross domestic product (GDP) of the globe. Within a span of five decades East Asia's population, measured against the world's total, had fallen to 23.24% while its share of the global GDP had shot up nearly threefold to 25%. During the five decades since 1955 these East Asian economies grew from among the poorest to among the richest in the world.

[2]In purchasing power parity terms, ACI's GDP is projected to be larger than the GDP of the US and Europe combined.

inconclusiveness of the literature has become one of the classic examples of the most enduring economic debates in macroeconomics (see Barro 2000; Dollar and Kraay 2002; Easterly 1999; Forbes 2000; Kraay 2005; Lopez 2004; Ravallian 1997, 2004). In an important contribution Banerjee and Duflo (2003) questioned the tenability of the assumed *linear* relationship between growth and inequality in the existing literature by establishing an inverted U curve between growth and inequality.[3]

The main goal of our paper is threefold: first, we develop a simple model of policy-induced growth in order to establish a nonlinear and wave-like relationship between growth and inequality. Second, we provide empirical support to our model to establish that the intention to use economic growth and inequality as policy instruments to shape economic development can backfire since the possibility of a wave-like function receives an empirical support from ACI data, though a more rigorous analysis is called forth. Third, we show that the nonlinear relationship between growth and inequality within ACI nations is mainly driven by the availability of foreign direct investment (FDI).

The plan of the paper is as follows: in Sect. 1.2 we provide a brief literature review. Section 1.3 also introduces the baseline model, economic data and the modelling framework. Section 1.4 provides the estimation procedure and basic results to show the nonlinear relationship between growth and inequality in ACI. Section 1.5 applies the threshold analysis to determine the role of FDI to explain the growth can bear a nonlinear relationship with inequality. Section 1.6 concludes.

1.2 Modelling Growth and Inequality: Related Literature

Several interesting and important issues are at stake in the context of growth and inequality: first and foremost, an extensive literature exists on the policy framework and institutional details that promote equitable growth (see Kanbur 2005 for a review). Second, some attempts have been made to understand the dynamics of choice of a society of those specific policies and institutions that are responsible for creating, fueling and driving equitable growth. The rational choice models of political economy provide some insights into the success, or failures, of a society in choosing appropriate institutional structures and relevant policies for promoting equitable growth.[4] There are obvious difficulties in isolating precise links between

[3]Banerjee and Duflo (2003) marshalled evidence and offered a political economy model to explain why there is little theoretical salience to the assumed linear, or even monotonic relationship between growth and inequality. From the cross-country data they established that changes in inequality and growth rate bear an inverted U-shaped relationship, which may either be caused by measurement errors or by their model. The inverse U curve can explain the divergence of estimates of the previous studies on the impact of inequality on growth.

[4]See Besley and Case (2003), Besley and Coate (2003), Case (2001), Drazen (2000), Persson and Tabellini (2000, 2003).

economic policies and their impacts on economic growth, as highlighted by Easterly (2001). Thirdly, the role of equitable growth is adequately reflected in the United Nations' strategy to reduce the incidence of global poverty by half, under the Millennium Development Goals (MDGs), by creating equitable growth by the year 2015. There is a convergence of views, or opinions, on two related themes: first, increasing economic growth holding inequality unchanged is good for a society. Admittedly, there is little discussion on the impacts of economic growth on environment. Second, inequality holding the rate of economic growth unchanged is bad for a society. However, once inequality and growth both vary, the statistical results are inconclusive about their interrelationship. Though, economists tend to still get influenced by the 'Kuznets curve', in an early work, Anand and Kanbur (1993) showed that the cross-country data cannot establish any precise relationship. Our work will try to establish the *raison-d'etra* for this finding, which was confirmed by others in subsequent work (e.g. Deininger and Squire 1998, 1999; Li et al. 1998 among others).

1.2.1 Growth, Inequality and Their Interrelationships

An extensive literature has already explored how distribution of income affects the GDP growth (see early work by Persson and Tabellini 1994; Alesina and Rodrik 1994). Note that the direction of causality is postulated to run opposite to the much-celebrated Kuznets' Hypothesis that argues that income inequality first rises and then falls during the course of economic development, or economic growth (Kuznets 1955). Alesina and Rodrik (1994) find a negative relationship between inequality and growth in a political-economy model of endogenous growth, if government spending is devoted entirely to production. Persson and Tabellini (1994) confirm the result as Alesina and Rodrik (1994) in a two-period overlapping-generations model. On the other hand, Li and Zou (1998) came to the opposite conclusion by examining the relationship between income inequality and economic growth in an endogenous growth model with distributive conflicts among agents. They find that when the household utility function is logarithmic in public consumption and exhibits a higher-than-unity degree of risk aversion in private consumption, a more equal distribution of income causes a higher rate of capital taxation in a majority voting mechanism. An increase in the rate of capital taxation lowers economic growth, which shows that income inequality can foster faster economic growth. Empirical results based on the cross-country evidence, undertaken by Li and Zou (1998), Clarke (1995), Benabou (1996), Deininger and Squire (1998, 1999), Li et al. (1998, 2000a, b), Barro (2000), Savvides and Stengos (2000), Forbes (2000), Banerjee and Duflo (2003), Chen (2003), among many others, are somewhat inconclusive.

1.2.2 The 95% Theory of Kuznets' Inverted U Hypothesis: Just a Glorified Speculation?

Growth and inequality and their mutual feedbacks on each other can hardly escape the tyranny of the oft-repeated 'iron law of empirical regularity' popularly known as the inverted U hypothesis of Kuznets. The hypothesis posits that economic growth is initially accompanied with an increasing inequality till a point, which is the hilltop of the inverted U curve, and then they bear an inverse relationship. The causality is believed to run from growth to inequality. There is no gain saying to the fact that Kuznets' inverted U hypothesis has played an important role in the continuing debate on the interrelationship between inequality and growth since his class is the work published in 1955. In his own opinion, yet, Kuznets underscored the inverted U as a 95% speculation and 5% 'empirical verification'. Moreover, his 'empirical verification' was centered on three advanced nations Germany, England and the US. The inverted U hypothesis proposes two mutually exclusive phenomena: first, at lower levels of economic development, increasing economic growth promotes rising inequality. The rising inequality is caused by economic growth since economic growth results in an important transition of an economy, at a lower level of economic development, from predominantly agrarian to an industrial society. The fundamental assumption is that the industrial sector is richer and also more 'unequal' than the agrarian sector. The rising weights and importance of the industrial sector thus cause the inequality to rise until a critical point. Secondly, economic growth beyond this critical point lowers inequality due to another important transition in the society—namely the organization of industrial workers into powerful lobbies and unions to advance their self-interests. Kuznets (1955) was cautious in labelling his own hypothesis as 'speculation' since such transitions are neither guaranteed nor sacrosanct. If there are forces within the society that thwart, or cause multiple recurrences of, these transitions the Kuznets-inverted U will never materialize.

In what follows we show the possibility of a wave function, instead of an inverted U-shape, between economic growth and inequality with significant implications.

1.2.3 The Exalted Status of the Interrelationships Between Growth and Inequality: The Immortal Triangle of Growth-Inequality-Poverty

In their important initial work Kakwani et al. (2004), Ravallion and Chen (2003), and Ravallion (2004), and subsequent finessing, they have provided the foundation for the important goal of maximizing the *reduction of poverty* via finetuning economic growth and equity. For the reduction of poverty, they have tended to agree that both faster economic growth and greater equity should be the policy priorities of national governments and international agencies.[5] The essence of the argument of the pro-poor growth (PPG) of Ravallian and Chen (2003) requires that as an inequality index; say the Gini coefficient, increases, the rate of PPG will decline relative to the actual rate of growth. Similarly, if the index falls, the rate of PPG will rise relative to the actual rate of growth. The definition of Kakwani et al. (2004) is known as the poverty equivalent growth (PEG) that is the product of the actual growth rate and the poverty elasticities with respect to income growth and income inequality. If the PEG exceeds the actual growth rate then growth is pro-poor, otherwise not.[6] Both these definitions are based on the effects of growth and inequality in reducing poverty. In simple terms, both theories seek to maximize the 'Total Poverty Elasticity' (with respect to both the growth of income and changes in inequality), by assuming a *complementarity* between economic growth and income equality in reducing poverty. However, the problem is that the cross-country regressions have not provided empirical support to the complementarity between growth and equity.

1.3 Our Modelling Framework

In our analysis X represents economic growth while x is the change in economic growth over time. In a similar vein, Y is economic inequality and y is the change in inequality over time. We posit that the policy maker receives a positive return R that is predicated on economic growth and given by[7]:

$$[R(X)/X] = a - bX,\ a > 0,\ b > 0,\ \text{and}\, X > (b/a) \tag{1.1a}$$

[5]It is well known in the literature that Kakwani et al. (2004) and Ravallian (2004) had different definitions of 'Pro-Poor Growth'. Kakwani et al. unequivocally noted the importance of identifying a *relative* improvement in the condition of the poor, which convinced them to argue that "the incomes of the poor grow faster than those of the non-poor". On the other hand, Ravallion's original position recognized that more rapid growth is 'pro-poor' if it is more poverty-reducing in terms of headcount ratios.

[6]The PEG is given by the percentage change in the poverty headcount relative to the percentage change in income per capita. The 'Total Poverty Elasticity' (TPE) combines both the 'Poverty Elasticity of Growth' and the 'Poverty Elasticity of Inequality' (PEI). The PEI is the percentage change in the poverty headcount relative to the percentage change in the Gini Coefficient. Hence, if the 'Total Poverty Elasticity' exceeds the 'Poverty Elasticity of Growth', then the reduction in inequality is reducing poverty and, by definition, the Poverty Equivalent Growth Rate exceeds the actual growth rate.

[7]One can argue governments seek economic growth since growth reduces poverty. Kraay (2005) showed that 70% short-run changes in poverty are propelled by growth in average incomes of nations.

We assume that economic inequality imposes a cost on the policy maker[8] and the policy cost, C, depends both on X and Y and given as

$$C(X, Y) = c(Y/X)^2/2, \; c > 0 \tag{1.1b}$$

Note $\partial C/\partial X < 0$ and $\partial C/\partial Y > 0$. The higher the growth the lower is the cost of inequality. The policy cost increases with increased inequality, ceteris paribus. Some of the policy costs may be purely pecuniary such as social security payment, unemployment benefits while others may be purely social like conflicts, jealousy, social deprivation, etc.

We further entertain the notion prevalent in the policy community that inequality and growth will have impacts on the time profile of the change in growth x and we express the relationship as

$$X = F(Y, X) \tag{1.1c}$$

We assume that increase in inequality induces growth and hence $\partial F/\partial y > 0$.[9] We also assume $\partial F/\partial X < 0$. The higher is the initial growth X, the lower is the change in growth rate x. We express (1.1c) as a simple linear function[10]:

$$X = hy - mX \text{ with } h > 0 \text{ and } m > 0 \tag{1.1d}$$

It is imperative that we carefully explain Eq. (1.1d) and our model of agent behaviour here before making any further progress: we postulate that the policy maker and all economic agents have 'learned to believe' the economist's model that there is a linear and positive relationship between inequality and growth. It is important to note that the so-called "threshold effects" offer a theoretical justification in terms of political economy models for higher inequality at a point in time to slower future economic growth. Banerjee and Duflo (2003) examine some of these threshold effect models and develop an overarching model to capture various

[8]There are various ways one can rationalize the cost of inequality on policy makers and one possibility is due to Ravallian (1997, 2004) who established that the effectiveness of growth in reducing poverty depends on the initial level of inequality. His 2004 estimates show that 1% increase in average income will result in a decline of 4.3% of poverty for very low inequality nations, or as little as 0.6% for high inequality nations.

[9]Following the unanimity of the empirical literature, we posit that growth does not impact on inequality (see Dollar and Kraay 2002; Easterly 1999).

[10]First, it is widely recognized and empirically verified that increases in inequality promote economic growth (see Banerjee and Duflo 2003; Li and Zou 1998; Arellano and Bond 1991). In contrast, Barro (2000) and Lopez (2004) did not find *strong* dependence of growth on inequality. Lopez (2006) and Lopez and Serven (2006) reversed their earlier findings. Secondly, impacts of X on x represent an implicit condition for convergence of growth paths.

causal links running from inequality to growth.[11] Banerjee and Duflo (2003) suggested the possibility of an inverted U curve as an empirical association between economic inequality and economic growth. The problem is that there are various causal links by which inequality impacts on growth and empirical verification of each is a serious problem (see Kanbur 2005). This problematic issue is pithily outlined by Kanbur (2005) as:

> The jury is still out, and the literature swings between combinations of papers that claim to show causality from high inequality to low growth, to those that claim to show no causality - or even that more inequality leads to higher growth (p. 226).

It is instructive to note that the choice of (1.1d) is robust, which can easily incorporate the "threshold effect" by altering the signs of the coefficients to h (<0) and m (<0), which will not change. These changes in signs will have no effect on the subsequent equilibria X_i* and their stability properties. Our model is thus capable of generating wave-like functions even when $h < 0$ and $m < 0$, which are likely to be the case for threshold effect models. What is also important is that we postulate that the linear relationship is not only the "shared mental model" but also the correct model. However, the problem starts the very moment the policy maker tries to exploit this linear relationship to achieve a desirable mix of inequality and growth. What we will show is that the attempt to influence changes in growth by changing inequality by the policy maker will create the wave-like relationship between growth and inequality. Let us now get back to the basics of the model.

The policy-induced growth model is represented by a policy maker who solves the following present value problem:

$$\text{Maximize } V(x) = \int_0^T e^{-rt}[R(X) - C(Y, X)]dt$$

Subject to

$$[R(X)/X] = a - bX,\ a > 0,\ b > 0,\ \text{and}\, X > (b/a)$$

$$C(X, Y) = c(Y/X)^2/2,\ c > 0$$

$$x = hy - mX$$

$$X(0) = a$$

[11]These models postulate that there are threshold effects in the return to human capital in the sense that substantial returns are generated only after a critical threshold of human capital is reached by decision-makers. If capital market is imperfect then these decision-makers will have to self-finance their building of human capital. In such a scenario, under a set of conditions, increase inequality will cause the accumulation of human capital to decline, which will thereby lower labour productivity and thereby reduce future economic growth.

The Hamiltonian–Jacobi–Bellman (HJB) equation is given by

$$rV(x) = \text{Max}[R(X) - C(X,\, Y) + V'(x)x] \tag{1.2a}$$

Proposition 1.3.1 *If X* represents the steady state economic growth, the Hamiltonian–Jacobi–Bellman equation is reduced to:*

$$X^*\left[h^2aX^*/(cr) - h^2bX^{*2}/(cr) - m\right] = X^*M(X^*) = 0 \tag{1.2b}$$

M is a quadratic function of X. Thus there are three possible steady state equilibria*:

$$X_1{}^* = 0 \tag{1.2c}$$

$$X_2{}^* = a + \text{SQRT}\left[\left(a^2 - 4bmcr\right)/2b\right] \tag{1.2d}$$

$$X_3{}^* = a - \text{SQRT}\left[\left(a^2 - 4bmcr\right)/2b\right] \tag{1.2e}$$

Proof By definition X^* is given by

$$x = hy - mX = 0 \tag{1.3a}$$

From the HJB equation, we have

$$V(X^*) = \left[R(X^*) - cy^2\Big/(2X^*)^2\right]\Big/r \tag{1.3b}$$

$$V(X^*) = \left[R(X^*) - cm^2/\left(2h^2\right)\right]/r \tag{1.3c}$$

Hence

$$V'(X^*) = R'(X^*)/r \tag{1.3d}$$

The Left-Hand Side (LHS) of the HJB is:

$$\text{LHS} = rV(X^*) = R(X^*) - \left(cm^2\right)/\left(2h^2\right) \tag{1.3e}$$

The Right-Hand Side (RHS) of the HJB is:

$$\text{RHS} = \max_{\{y\}}\left[R(X^*) - (cm^2)/(2h^2) + xR'(X^*)/r\right] \tag{1.3f}$$

The first-order condition requires:

$$\frac{\partial\left[(R(X^*) - cm^2/(2h^2) + (hy - mX^*)R'(X^*)/r\right]}{\partial y} = 0 \quad (1.4a)$$

Note that (1.4a) yields:

$$Y = h(a - bX^*)/(c^*r) \quad (1.4b)$$

Substituting (1.4b) into (1.3a) yields:

$$X^*\left[(h^2a)/(c^*r)X^* - (h^2b)/(c^*r)X^{*2} - m\right] = 0 \quad (1.4c)$$

Equation (1.4c) has three roots as given by Eqs. (1.2c), (1.2d) and (1.2e) that are the three steady states.

The above equilibria can be depicted in Fig. 1.1.

1.3.1 Discussion of the Theoretical Findings

In Fig. 1.1, we plot economic growth along the horizontal axis and the change in growth along the vertical axis and Eq. (1.2b) is drawn as $M(X)$ that intersects the horizontal axis at X_1*, X_2* and X_3* that are the three equilibrium growth rates, or steady states, and their stability is described arrows: X_3* is the unstable equilibrium that separates the other two stable equilibrium. We note that X_1*, X_2* and X_3* can be Pareto-ranked from the standpoint of growth. X_1* is the Pareto-worst, X_2* is the Pareto-best and are the extremal equilibria (see Milgrom and Roberts 1990 and Vives 2005) and X_3* acts as a separatrix between the extremal equilibria. If the

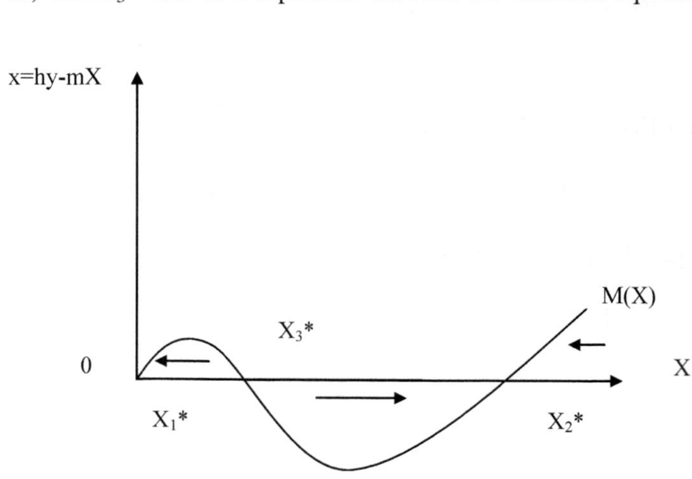

Fig. 1.1 Multiple growth equilibria

initial rate of growth $X < X_3{*}$, the system monotonically converges to the Pareto-worst equilibrium $X_1{*}$. If the initial economic growth exceeds $X_3{*}$, $X > X_3{*}$, then the system monotonically converges to the Pareto-dominant equilibrium $X_2{*}$. It is also important to note that the dynamics of growth will bring the growth rates $X{*}$ within ($X_1{*} < X{*} < X_2{*}$) as the mixed strategy outcomes, correlated equilibria and rationalization equilibria will lie in the zone ($X_1{*} < X{*} < X_2{*}$). Any kind of adaptive dynamics will take the system monotonically to either of the extremal equilibria (see Vives 1990). One can also impose an explicit dynamics to generate cyclical fluctuations within the extremal equilibria (see Vives 2005: pp. 430). Furthermore, properly mixed equilibria can also be shown to be unstable with respect to a general adaptive dynamics (see Echenique and Edlin 2004).

1.3.2 Empirical Foundation to the Nonlinear Relationship Between Growth and Inequality

We will estimate Eq. (1.4c) by using a set of panel data including observations for six ACI nations covering the period 1991–2012. Our panel consists of data for China, India and eight ASEAN nations, except Singapore, for which relevant data is available, namely, Cambodia, Laos, Indonesia, Malaysia, Myanmar, Thailand, the Philippines, Vietnam. The intuition is to use inequality as a dependent policy variable, which depends on economic growth and a set of other regressors. We consider the following variables for each country:

INQ_{it}: A measure of inequality in country i at date t,

$GROWTH_{it}$: Annual growth rate of real GDP of country i at date t,

Ω_{it}: Set of control variables including (ignoring the time and country subscripts):

1. Country EXPORT measures the internalization of the economy and is captured through annual value of exported goods and services (not scaled by GDP).
2. Country FOODP is a proxy for the cost of living with significant impacts on inequality and is captured by the index of food prices.
3. Proxy for country's available productive capacity is ENERGYO and is captured by the value of energy output.
4. Annual country PCGDP is the per capita GDP at constant prices and used as a proxy for economic development of the country.
5. Annual foreign direct investment (FDI) is a proxy for internationalization of the economy as well as a measure of the productive capacity of the country.
6. Annual value of private capital formation (KFORM) at constant prices is a proxy for the additional capital goods available for production purposes in the country.
7. The ratio of debt to GDP, DEBTGDP, is a proxy for financial deepening and the financial vulnerability of the country.
8. POPG is the annual increase in the size of the population of a country, which is used as a proxy for the expansion of the labour input as well as an indicator of budgetary needs of government to keep inequality low.

1.3.3 Inequality and Growth Data: A Small Note

The real income growth data are from the GDP figures reported in the Penn World Table 6.1. The inequality data is drawn from the Estimated Household Income Inequality Data Set (EHII)—a global dataset derived from the econometric relationship between UTIP-UNIDO, other conditioning variables, and the World Bank's Deininger and Squire data set (see http://utip.gov.utexas.edu/about.html). The UTIP-UNIDO data set source computes inequality measures for nearly 3200 country/year observations, covering over 150 countries during the period 1963–1999. Inequality is linked to a number of mathematical concepts such as skewness, variance, and dispersion. Consequently, there are several methods to compute inequality, for example the McLoone Index, the coefficient of variation, range, range ratios, the Gini Coefficient and Theil's T statistic. The main justification for choosing Theil's T statistic is that it offers a more flexible structure that often makes it more suitable than other measures.[12] If we had permanent access to all necessary individual-level data for the population of interest, measures like the Gini coefficient or the coefficient of variation would be generally satisfactory for describing inequality. Yet, in the real world, individual data is hardly ever reachable, and researchers make do with aggregated data. The rest of the dataset came from the Asian Development Bank.

1.4 Empirical Results: Panel Analysis of Determinants of Inequality

To model potential nonlinear effects of economic on inequality, we use a cubic polynomial of INQ as a function GROWTH in our econometric model. Our benchmark regression model is a model of panel estimation based on GMM estimates. In this section determinants of inequality are analyzed through panel estimations based on GMM regressions. This approach addresses the problem of potential endogeneity of all the regressors and also incorporates fixed effects. The two variants of this approach that are used are (1) the difference—GMM estimation arising from Arellano and Bond (1991) and (2) the system—GMM estimation arising from Blundell and Bond (1998). Both approaches rely on first-differencing and usage of lagged values of endogenous variables as instruments, for identification. In the Arellano–Bond estimator, lagged levels are used to instrument for the differenced right-hand side variables. In the Blundell-Bond estimator, the estimation system comprises the difference equation instrumented with lagged levels as in the Arellano-Bond estimator as well as the level equation which is estimated using

[12]Pedro Conceição and Pedro Ferreira provide a much more detailed analysis of these issues in their UTIP working paper 'The Young Person's Guide to the Theil Index: Suggesting Intuitive Interpretations and Exploring Analytical Applications'.

lagged differences as instruments. As neither estimator is perfect and has idiosyncratic limitations, results utilizing both procedures are reported.

1.4.1 The Panel Estimation Equation

Following the approach of Baele et al. (2007), the regression (analytical) model is constructed to examine the determinants of inequality in a panel set of 10 countries over 22 years (1990–2012). It is specified as:

$$\mathrm{INQ}_{it} = \beta_1\,\mathrm{INQ}_{it} + \beta_2\,\mathrm{GROWTH}_{it} + \beta_3\,\mathrm{GROWTH}_{it}^2 + \beta_4\,\mathrm{GROWTH}_{it}^3 + \beta_5\,\Omega_{it} + \varepsilon_{it}\cdots \tag{1.5a}$$

where,

INQ_{it}	A measure of inequality in country i at date t,
GROWTH_{it}	Annual growth rate of real GDP of country i at date t,
Ω_{it}	Set of control variables (ignoring the time and country subscripts) as explained in Sect. 1.4.2, pp. 10.

1.4.2 GMM Estimation Results

Table 1.1 outlines the panel summary statistics. Table 1.2 presents the panel estimation results corresponding to the estimation specification of the previous section. The results in Table 1.2 are obtained from the Arellano–Bond procedure, the Blundell-Bond procedure. Both procedures report the results obtained from using

Table 1.1 Descriptive statistics

	Mean	STD	Min	Max
GROWTH	5.58	3.81	−13.2	14.2
Ln FDI	6.74	2.45	1	11.87
Ln PCGDP	5.48	1.09	2.83	8.33
Ln IMPORT	9.31	2.09	5.09	13.88
Ln ENERGYO	9.66	2.15	4.85	13.4
Ln INQ	3.7	0.14	3.29	4.05
Ln EXPORT	9.49	1.99	4.37	13.8
Ln KFORM	9.25	2.48	3.27	160.3
DEBTGDP	66.4	74.1	9.83	578.17
Ln FOODP	5.07	0.68	3.45	6.83
POPG	1.81	0.9	−1.11	5.49
Observations	220	220	220	220

Table 1.2 GMM regression results

Variable	Model 1 (Arenallo-Bond)	Model 2 (system GMM)	Model 3 (fixed effect estimate)	Model 4 (FGLS estimate)
Lagged INQ	−0.074 (−0.41)	0.62 (6.05)*		
EXPORT	−0.0001 (−1.71)**	−6.59 e07 (−0.18)	−2.71e06 (−0.51)	−0.000014 (1.53)***
ENERGYO	0.0005 (2.56)*	2.28e−06 (0.61)	4.84e−06 (1.07)	0.000007 (4.90)*
PCGDP	0.013 (2.66)*	0.002 (1.57)***	0.0003 (0.16)	0.013 (2.66)*
GROWTH	−0.4 (1.66)**	0.11 (−0.57)	−0.24 (−0.80)	−0.55 (−2.86)*
GROWTH^2	0.002 (1.41)	−0.011 (−1.16)	−0.024 (−1.66)**	0.011 (0.90)
GROWTH^3	0.02 (1.49)***	0.0004 (0.37)	0.0016 (0.87)	0.003 (1.89)**
FDI	−0.0003 (−0.07)	−0.0006 (−1.07))	−0.0016 (−1.86)**	−0.006 (−1.10)
KFORM	−0.01 (−1.30)	−0.013 (1.92)**	0.01 (1.08)	−0.005 (−0.70)
DEBTGDP	−0.04 (1.91)**	0.015 (1.36)	0.031 (1.86)**	−0.044 (−2.43)*
POPG	0.11 (0.05)	1.23 (0.99)	−1.63 (−1.15)	2.35 (1.53)***
FOODP	0.06 (1.66)***	0.007 (0.62)	0.031 (2.81)*	−0.0021 (−0.18)
CONSTANT	29,2 (4.35)*	14.66 (2.99)*	42.85 (13.44)*	31.96 (9.75)*
			R^2 within = 0.18 between = 0.92 overall = 0.43 Wald chi2 = 38.1	Sigma u = 11.91, Sigma e = 2.57, Rho = 0.96, $F(5, 44)$ = 12.75, Prob > F = 0.0
Observations	220			
Number of groups Sargan test	10	Prob > Chi^2 = 0.048		
GMM estimation method	Difference	Difference	Difference	Difference

Dependent variable is a measure of inequality (INQ) within a country
*Significant, for double-sided critical value, at the 0.05 level, **Significant, for one-sided critical value, at the 0.05 level, ***Marginally (one-sided) significant

the "xtabond2" Stata utility6. There are four different specifications of the basic model: Model 1 captures the Arellano-Bond estimation, Model 2 captures the GMM estimate, Model 3 is the fixed effect and the Model 4 is the model of FGLS.

1.4.3 Panel Estimation Results and Findings

In Table 1.2, we summarize the panel regressions.

Panel estimation through the GMM procedure gives mixed results. The system GMM's over-identified restrictions are valid as the Sargan test result confirms. All the variables seem to play important roles in determining INQ in at least one specification of the panel regression. First and foremost, we can dichotomize determinants of INQ in ACI nations into 3 groups: first and foremost, in all specifications in which these variables are statistically significant, ENERGYO, PCGDP, FOODP & POPG are found to increase inequality, INQ. Second, EXPORT, GROWTH, and FDI are found to lower inequality for ACI nations. This is true only for those specifications in which these 3 variables are statistically significant. It is also important to note that the lagged value of INQ also lowers INQ. Third; the variable DEBTGDP has an ambiguous effect, though statistically significant, on INQ.

It is important to note that for the cubic specification, GROWTH and $GROWTH^3$ are statistically significant for two of the four specifications. $GROWTH^2$ is one-sided significant. GROWTH and $GROWTH^2$ bear an inverse relationship with INQ and are also found to be statistically significant determinants of INQ. However, $GROWTH^3$ bears a positive relationship with INQ. The non-linear relationship between GROWTH and INEQUALITY is plotted on Fig. 1.2.

Figure 1.2 illustrates the interrelationships changes in real growth rates and inequality in the ACI economies. On the basis of the available data, we are able to isolate three stages: in Stage 1, an increase in the real growth rate (GROWTH) increases inequality (INQ). We note that in Stage 1 is feasible if the real growth rate is negative, or in a contracting economy. In other words, there is a positive relationship between GROWTH and INQ in Stage 1.

As the real growth rate (GROWTH) reaches a critical value of −5.5% Stage 1 is replaced by Stage 2. In Stage 2 economic growth (GROWTH) has a dampening effect on inequality (INQ), which gives rise to an inverse relationship between growth and inequality. When the real growth rate exceeds the critical value of 10.11%, once again, the real growth rate (GROWTH) bears a positive relationship with inequality (INQ), which we call Stage 3. In Stage 3, economic growth seems to promote inequality.

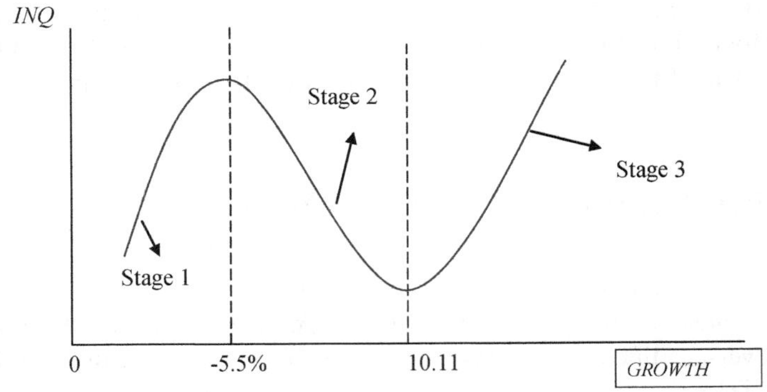

Fig. 1.2 Growth and inequality: a wave-like interrelationship

1.5 Sources of Nonlinear Relationship Between Growth and Equity: Methodology and Findings

Our point of departure from the standard models of economic growth and inequality has straightforward and testable implications: if policy makers attempt to influence one variable by choosing another, the relationship between INQ and GROWTH can turn out to be nonlinear. From the panel estimates, we found some support for our theoretical model of a wave-like relationship between INQ and GROWTH. We also explained the economic determinants of INQ in ACI nations in terms of various specifications of the panel analysis. In simple terms, we found three stages in the relationship between INQ and GROWTH, our three stages as explained in Fig. 1.2, if the policy makers seek to determine one of them by controlling the other. In this section, our focus is to explain the causes of these apparent thresholds in the relationship between INQ and GROWTH. In order to undertake the analysis of endogenous thresholds, we choose GROWTH as the dependent variable and INQ as the independent variable along with a set of regressors. The intuition is to understand how external factors like FDI impact on the growth experience of a country. As in most specifications of the previous analysis, FDI has no significant relationship with INQ. In Model 3, the specification shows some significance once we exclude the lagged variable of INQ.

1.5.1 Methodology: Reversal of Roles and Threshold Model in Terms of FDI

In this section, we attempt to understand how economic growth is impacted on by the choice of INQ and use FDI as the threshold variable. If optimally chosen, inequality can promote economic growth. At the same time, the possibility exists for the INQ to have little effects, or even ill-effects, unless they are chosen appropriately. Which of these outcomes correctly describes the relationship between INQ and GROWTH will possibly depend on other economic variables. We can describe these relationships more formally as follows:

$$\text{GROWTH}_i = \theta_{10} + \theta_{11}{}^*\text{INQ}_i + \theta_{1j}{}^*Z_j + \varepsilon_i \text{ for FDI}_i < \tau \quad (1.6a)$$

$$\text{GROWTH}_i = \theta_{20} + \theta_{21}{}^*\text{INQ}_i + \theta_{3j}{}^*Z_j + \varepsilon_i \text{ for FDI}_i > \tau \quad (1.6b)$$

Where FDI_i is a threshold variable and Z_j, chosen from the set of explanatory variables Ω_{it} as explained on pp. 13. In other words, Z_j is a set of controls, as explained before, except INQ and FDI.[13] While a continuous spline specification may be too restrictive, ideally we would want to allow the coefficients on FDI and INQ as well as the constant term to change.[14] From the explanatory variables, we chose Z_i as PCGDP_i, IMPORT_i, ENERGYO_i for these are the largest number of explanatory variables that allowed us endogenous sample splitting as per the Hansen (2000) process. We drop PCGDP_i in an alternative model of sample splitting due to its potential correlation with INQ. Note that for any given value of τ, (1.6a) is linear in its parameters, thus the simplest way to estimate τ is through conditional least squares (Hansen 2000).[15] In order to test the statistical significance of a threshold effect typically it is customary to test the null hypothesis of "no threshold effect", i.e. H_0: $\theta_{10} = \theta_{20}$, $\theta_{11} = \theta_{21}$, $\theta_{1j} = \theta_{3j}$ *for* all *j*. The alternative hypothesis assumes inequality of these coefficients.

However, since τ is only identified under the alternative, the distributions of classical test statistics, such as the Wald and likelihood ratio tests, are not asymptotically chi-squared. In essence this is because the likelihood surface is flat with respect to τ, consequently, the information matrix becomes singular and standard asymptotic arguments no longer apply. There are methods for handling hypothesis testing within these contexts. In some instances, we are able to bound the asymptotic distribution of likelihood ratio statistics (Davies 1977, 1987),

[13]This specification is quite general in that it imposes no cross-regime restrictions on our parameters. However since our focus is on how the effect of INQ on GROWTH changes, it will be useful to restrict some, or all, other model parameters.

[14]Such a specification assumes a discontinuity at the threshold, as such it is more general than a continuous spline function which is continuous at FDI $= \tau$. While methods exist for estimating τ and for approximating the asymptotic distribution of these estimators in either case, the results for discontinuous threshold models do not specialize to the case of continuous linear spline functions (Hansen 1996, 1999, 2000, 2007; Chan and Tsay 1998). In fact, the asymptotic distribution of $\hat{\tau}$ is highly non-standard in the discrete case. Here we model threshold behaviour by allowing for discrete jumps between regimes because this case imposes less structure on the model.

[15]This involves choosing $\widehat{\tau}$ so as to minimize $S(\tau)$, where $S(\tau)$ is the sum of squared residuals for any given value of τ.

alternatively, their asymptotic distribution must be derived by bootstrap methods. Hansen (2000) proposes the later. The appropriate test statistic is:

$$\mathrm{LR}_0 = \frac{S_0 - S_1}{\hat{\sigma}^2} \tag{1.7a}$$

where S_0 and S_1 are, respectively, the residual sum of squares under the null hypothesis and the alternative, and $\hat{\sigma}^2$ is the residual variance under the alternative H_1 of threshold effects. In the presence of heteroscedasticity a "wild bootstrap" is preferable to standard residual bootstrapping (Wu 1986; Davidson and Flachaire 2001). This is done in a number of stages. First, by transforming the residuals, $\hat{\varepsilon}$, from our regression analysis using the following transformation: $f(\hat{\varepsilon}_i) = \frac{\hat{\varepsilon}_i}{(1-h_i)^{1/2}}$, where h_i is the ith diagonal of the projection matrix $X(X'X)^{-1}X$ and X is simply our matrix of regressors in (1.2a). Next, we generate 999 replications of the random error, u_i, where

$$u_i = \begin{cases} 1 & \text{with Probability } 1/2 \\ 0 & \text{with Probability } 0 \end{cases} \tag{1.7b}$$

Finally, we can use the transformed residuals, $f(\hat{\varepsilon}_i)$, and the bootstrap errors, u_i, to create a bootstrap sample under the null as follows:

$$\begin{aligned} \mathrm{GROWTH}_i &= \theta_0 + \theta_{11}{}^*\mathrm{INQ}_i + \theta_2{}^*Z_i + \theta_3{}^*\mathrm{FDI}_i(\mathrm{FDI}_i < \tau) \\ &\quad + \theta_4{}^*\mathrm{FDI}_i(\mathrm{FDI}_i > \tau) + f(\hat{\varepsilon}_i)\mathrm{u}_i \end{aligned} \tag{1.7c}$$[17]

In what follows (1.7c) will be decomposed into (1.8a) and (1.8b) for our empirical results. When threshold effects are present, $\hat{\tau}$ is consistent (Hansen 2000). However, in discontinuous threshold regression models, the asymptotic distribution of $\hat{\tau}$ is non-standard. Hansen (2000) proposes calculating confidence intervals by forming a "no-rejection region" based on likelihood ratio tests on τ. Specifically, we would want to test the null: $H_0 : \tau = \tau_0$, rejecting for large values of $\mathrm{LR}_1(\tau_0)$, where

$$\mathrm{LR}_1(\tau) = \frac{S_1(\tau) - S_1(\hat{\tau})}{\hat{\sigma}^2} \tag{1.7d}$$

Hansen (2000) has derived the asymptotic distribution of $\mathrm{LR}_1(\tau_0)$, which while non-standard, requires little additional computation. Below we apply these methods to estimate the effect of corruption on measures of the quality of public infrastructure in a cross-section of countries. Following the rationale for the sequential estimation strategy provided by Hansen (1999), the method for a single-threshold model is first used to estimate, and then the grid search method is applied to find out the threshold value in order to minimize $S^2(h^2)$. One can obtain a second threshold value and more in a sequential fashion. The hypothesis tests for a multi-threshold model are similar to those for a single-threshold model, and are not described here.

Table 1.3 Threshold estimate

Threshold estimate	SSE	TP	Confidence interval	
			UV	LV
8.07 (=ln FDI)	2967	0.050	7.02	6.98

SSE Sum of squared errors, *TP* Trimming percentages, *UV* Upper value, *LV* Lower value, SSE (without threshold): 1973

Hansen (1996) suggested the use of a bootstrap technique to simulate its gradual distribution in order to establish the corresponding *p*-values. This paper uses Hansen's (2007, pp. 155) grid search method to deal with issues of squared residuals and their minimization. Once the threshold value is determined, the slope can then be obtained (Table 1.3).

1.5.2 Findings

The single-threshold model equation, which is found meaningful, is written as:

$$\begin{aligned}\mathrm{GROWTH}_i = {} & \theta_{01} + \theta_{11}{}^*\mathrm{Ln\,INQ}_i + \theta_{21}{}^*\mathrm{Ln\,PCGDP}_i + \theta_{22}{}^*\mathrm{Ln\,IMPORT}_i \\ & + \theta_{23}{}^*\mathrm{Ln\,ENERGYO}_i + \varepsilon_i \text{ for } \mathrm{FDI}_i < \tau\end{aligned} \tag{1.8a}$$

$$\begin{aligned}\mathrm{GROWTH}_i = {} & \theta_{02} + \theta_{12}{}^*\mathrm{Ln\,INQ}_i + \theta_{31}{}^*\mathrm{Ln\,PCGDP}_i + \theta_{32}{}^*\mathrm{Ln\,IMPORT}_i \\ & + \theta_{33}{}^*\mathrm{Ln\,ENERGYO}_i + \varepsilon_i \text{ for } \mathrm{FDI}_i > \tau\end{aligned} \tag{1.8b}$$

Where τ is the threshold of FDI being estimated by applying the Hansen Procedure and ε_i is the error term. To determine the possibility of a threshold, the threshold effect is analyzed under the null hypothesis there is no threshold in the natural log of trimming percentage and the confidence interval. The threshold estimate is noted to be 8.07 (Ln FDI) and the SSE for the single-threshold value is 37333 as opposed to the SSE of 43983 without a threshold. This shows the possibility of thresholds in investment in IT as a relevant variable for determining profits. The results are summarized in Tables 1.4 and 1.5.

Table 1.4 reports the F-statistic and *p*-values following the bootstrap simulations for a single threshold. It is found that the threshold effect is statistically significant at

Table 1.4 Threshold effect test

Test	LM test	*p*-value	Critical value		
			10%	5%	1%
Single threshold	32.09*	0.00*	51.1	67.4	137

*Statistically significant at the 95%, *p*-values and critical values are the results of bootstrap simulation for 5000 times

Table 1.5 Single-threshold effect of FDI on the interrelationship between growth and inequality

	Growth	Dependent	Variable
Panel A			
	Regime 1	Regime 2	Regime 3
	OLS	Ln FDI < 8.07	Ln FDI > 8.07
	(1)	(2)	(3)
Constant	14.5 (7.35)	7.8 (8.29)	6. 27 (12.85)
Ln PCGDP	0.53 (0.2)	−0.7 (0.26)	1.28 (0.45)
Ln INQ	−4.46 (0.2)	0.16 (2.54)	−3.48 (2.32)
Ln IMPORT	0.41 (0.13)	−0.35 (0.19)	0.68 (0.28)
Ln ENERGYO	0.081 (0.11)	0.35 (0.16)	−0.10 (0.26)
Threshold	No threshold	Ln FDI < 8.07	Ln FDI > 8.07
95% CI			
Bootstrap *p*-value	(0.00)		
Observations	215	215	215
Joint R^2	0.075	0.22	0.38
SSE	2967	1973	511.7
Residual variance	13.8	13.24	8.38
Bootstrap *p*-value	(0.00)	(0.05)	(0.02)
H—*p* value	0.21	0.21	

the 10% level for a single threshold whose value is reported in Table 1.4. After the threshold effect tests, the value of the single-threshold model is (Eq. 1.5a). According to Hansen's (1999) method for calculating the critical value of the likelihood ratio, at the 10% level of significance, the likelihood ratio test statistic is 51.48.

1.5.3 Discussion of Findings

- From Table 1.5, first and foremost, the threshold effect tests show that there is a threshold in FDI that plays a statistically significant role in determining the interrelationship between inequality and growth in the ACI economies.
- Second, for countries with Ln FDI < 8.07, inequality bears a *positive* relationship with growth and the effect is both economically meaningful and statistically significant. However, for those nations with Ln FDI > 8.07, inequality and growth bear an *inverse* relationship, which is economically and statistically significant.

- Third, we find that the volume of imports (IMORT) exert a negative influence on economic growth for countries with Ln FDI < 8.07 with a reversal of sign for those nations with Ln FDI > 8.07.
- Fourth, we notice similar reversals of signs for Ln PCGDP and Ln ENERGYO, however the effects are not statistically significant.
- Finally, we note that INQ plays a significant role in explaining variations in growth once we consider the endogenous threshold effects and other variables become less important.

1.5.4 Growth and Inequality: A Simplistic Exposition

In what follows in Figs. 1.3 and 1.4 we highlight our findings by plotting Regime 1, Regime 2 and Regime 3. As explained in Fig. 1.3, we represent Ln INQ along the horizontal axis and real growth rates (GROWTH) along the vertical axis and three (3) other regressors, namely, Ln PCGDP, Ln IMPORT, Ln ENERGYO, are pegged at their mean values across countries over 1991–2012.

- The blue-line G1 plots the OLS estimate of GROWTH with respect to Ln INQ for other three regressors fixed at their respective mean values, which is our Regime 1 in Table 1.5. The red-line G2 plots the same relationship between GROWTH and INQ for the countries for which Ln FDI < 8.07 (Regime 2). For those nations for which Ln FDI > 8.07, the green-line G3 plots the predicted relationship between GROWTH and INQ (Regime 3).
- From Fig. 1.3, one can see that the overall estimate (G1) and the estimate for countries with FDI above the threshold (G3), the relationship between GROWTH and INQ are negative, though the slopes are slightly different. From G1 and G3 we know that the growth is identical for Ln INQ = 3.2.

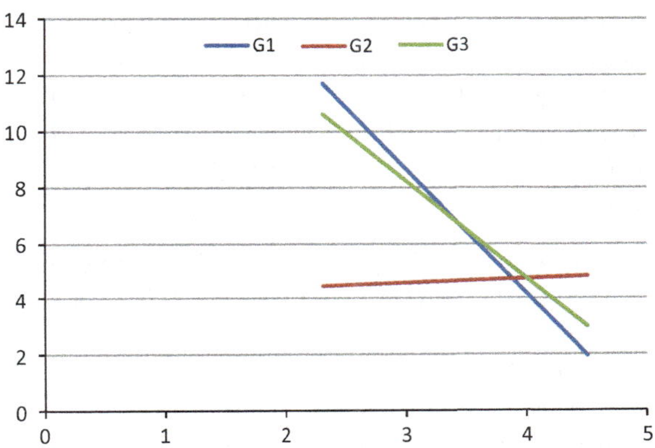

Fig. 1.3 Interrelationship between growth and equity. Note: *Vertical axis* Growth, *Horizontal axis* Ln INQ. *G1* OLS, *G2* FDI < 8.07, *G3* FDI > 8.07. Ln PCGDP, Ln IMPORT, Ln ENERGYO measured at their mean values across countries over time, based on the estimates given in Table 1.5

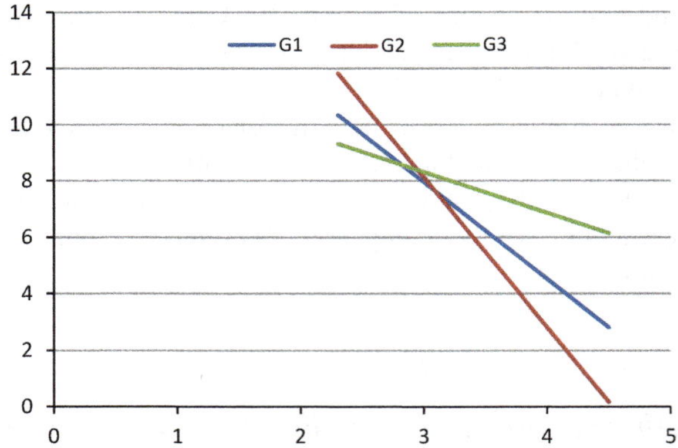

Fig. 1.4 Interrelationship between growth and equity. Note: *Vertical axis* Growth, *Horizontal axis* Ln INQ. *G1* OLS (Regime1), *G2* FDI < 8.07 (Regime 2), *G3* FDI > 8.07 (Regime 3). Ln IMPORT, Ln ENERGYO measured at their mean values across countries over time, based on the estimates given in Table 1.6. The difference between Figs. 1.2 and 1.3 is the absence Ln PCGDP in Fig. 1.4

- The relationship between GROWTH and INQ (G2) undergoes a significant change for nations for which the FDI is below the threshold (Ln FDI < 8.07). For G2, GROWTH and INQ bear an inverse relation. At the critical value of Ln INQ = 4, the growth rates converge on 4.5% for G1, G2 and G3.

1.5.5 Growth and Inequality: An Alternative Specification

In Table 1.6 we repeat the endogenous splitting of the sample, as per Hansen (1999), after dropping the PCGD variable. Everything else is unaltered. We now find a lower value of the threshold, Ln FDI = 6.76 as reported in Table 1.6. What is important is that the INQ and GROWTH bear a negative relationship for all regimes though the slope is different across regimes.

As explained in Fig. 1.4, we represent Ln INQ along the horizontal axis and real growth rates (GROWTH) along the vertical axis and two (2) other regressors, namely, Ln IMPORT, Ln ENERGYO, are pegged at their mean values across countries over 1991–2012.

- Roughly at Ln INQ = 2.8, there is a convergence of growth rates predicted by Regime 1, Regime 2 and Regime 3. The predicted real growth rate is roughly 8.2%.
- As the INQ increases beyond the critical value of Ln INQ = 2.8, ceteris paribus, this increase has a sharp impact on the real growth in countries with the FDI below the endogenous threshold (Ln FDI < 6.76). This is Regime 2 and depicted as G2 in Fig. 1.3.

Table 1.6 A test of single threshold in FDI with an alternative model (without PCGDP)

	Growth	Dependent	Variable
Panel A			
	Regime 1	Regime 2	Regime 3
	OLS	Ln FDI < 6.76	Ln FDI > 6.76
	(1)	(2)	(3)
Constant	14.57 (7.35)	20.65 (13.8)	21 (8.34)
Ln INQ	−3.46 (2.14)	−5.31 (14.24)	−1.44 (1.9)
Ln IMPORT	0.4 (0.13)	0.34 (0.34)	−0.08 (0.18)
Ln ENERGYO	−0.019 (0.12)	0.024 (0.28)	−0.71 (0.16)
Threshold	No threshold	Ln FDI < 6.76	Ln FDI > 6.76
95% CI			
Bootstrap *p*-value	(0.00)		
Observations	215	215	215
Joint R^2	0.05	0.029	0.16
SSE	3031	1359	1189.93
Residual variance	14	14.94	9.38
Bootstrap *p*-value	(0.00)	(0.05)	(0.02)
H—*p* Value	0.39		

- As the INQ increases beyond the critical value of Ln INQ = 2.8, ceteris paribus, this increase has a very moderate impact on the real growth in countries with the FDI above the endogenous threshold (Ln FDI > 6.76). This is Regime 3 and depicted as G3 in Fig. 1.3.
- As INQ declines below the critical value of Ln INQ = 2.8, ceteris paribus, this decrease in INQ has a sharp increase in real growth rates for economies with the FDI below the threshold (Regime 3). On the other hand, for Regime 3, such decrease in INQ has much moderate (positive) impacts on growth.

1.5.6 Discussion

In the existing literature, limited attempts have been made to generate a dynamic theory of income and wealth distribution integrating microeconomic models of accumulation and macroeconomic theories of factors' remuneration (see Stiglitz 1969). In this framework, it is established that the distribution of income and wealth tends asymptotically toward equality if and only if saving functions are either linear or concave. It is Stiglitz who clearly indicated that the distribution of income and wealth can have two attractors, or long-term equilibria, if the saving functions are convex. In Stiglitz's words, the convexity of saving function will generate a "two-class equilibrium". Our paper shows the possibility of multiple equilibria in a dynamic setting for the first time, to our best understanding, without exploiting the non-concavity of saving functions. It is also important to note that the cross-sectional studies point to the possibility that the marginal propensity to save increases with income and/or wealth and this empirical fact is behind the commonly held view that income equality might conflict with growth and aggregate welfare. Our findings are independent of whether saving functions are convex or concave.

In an immensely interesting work, Bourguignon (1981) showed that locally stable inegalitarian equilibria, or "stationary distributions" will exist along with the egalitarian one if the saving function is convex. Bourguignon (1981) also observed important welfare implications of the multiplicity of equilibrium as he showed that the non-egalitarian equilibria are Pareto-superior to the egalitarian equilibrium. Economic inequality in the dynamic neoclassical framework causes not only the generation of higher aggregate income and consumption per capita as could have been expected, but also higher income and consumption for all individuals. This result holds only to equilibria where all individuals have a positive wealth.

Our results confirm the main finding of Bourguignon (1981) that higher inequality (inegalitarian equilibrium) can sustain a Pareto efficient growth equilibrium (X_2*) characterized by higher inequality. Our result also confirms that the egalitarian equilibrium (X_1* = 0) is inefficient and characterized by zero inequality. These two equilibria are separated by an unstable equilibrium (X_3*) that creates a threshold effect. In contrast to the earlier papers, our model establishes that there is no monotonic relationship between inequality and growth if policy makers seek to influence economic growth and inequality. From the empirical study, we confirm the theoretical findings. Since growth and inequality have U-shaped and inverted U-shaped relationships, policy makers cannot utilize the interrelationship between growth and equity to achieve a desirable mix of growth and inequality.

1.6 Conclusion

Even though ACI has given high importance in achieving pro-poor or inclusive growth, however, income and non-income inequality have witnessed an increasing trend in recent years. In view of this, it is of utmost importance to study the relationship between economic growth and inequality.

The main goal of this paper is to establish that the desire of a policy maker to *choose* an optimal mix of inequality and growth, given a correctly expected *linear* model of growth and inequality, can lift the lid off the Pandora's box: the linear relationship between growth and inequality will break down to give way to a wave-like relationship, multiple equilibria and resultant complexities will emerge and the pertinence of the linear model to investigate the relationship between growth and inequality will disappear. From the empirical work, we find a statistical support for the wave like the relationship between growth and inequality, which casts a vexing doubt on the possibility of using appropriate policies to achieve a desirable mix of growth and equity.

In other words, the feasibility of using appropriate institutional structures to stimulate equitable growth via suitable economic policies can become untenable. As a result, the millennium goals of eradicating poverty through equitable growth can never be achieved, even if all the underlying growth models are correct and correctly predicted by policy makers. As our theoretical model shows, which is supported by the empirical study, that growth and inequality can have an inverted S-shaped relationship if policy makers try to achieve a desirable mix of growth and equity. In other words, the attempt to influence growth and inequality can give rise to a non-uniform association between growth and equity: there is a critical value of inequality below which the Kuznets curve relationship will hold. We also find another critical value of inequality beyond which the inverse Kuznets curve relationship becomes operational. Our empirical finding is that these critical values of inequality are reasonable values, which can, therefore, create enormous problems for policy makers to use growth and inequality in an instrumental fashion to reduce poverty.

We then examine the relationship between inequality and growth using Hansen's sample splitting methodology for threshold estimation for ten ACI nations over 22 years. The empirical results strongly suggest that FDI plays a crucial role to determine the relationship between growth and equality. Based on the aforementioned data set for ACI nations, we have estimated a threshold model to examine the relationship between growth and inequality. There is clear evidence of a single-threshold effect in terms of FDI for ACI nations. The impact of FDI on the relationship between growth and inequality establishes the following: the threshold analysis enables us to empirically derive a critical level of FDI below which growth and inequality can bear a positive relationship. Once FDI exceeds this critical level, or threshold, growth and inequality bear a negative relationship. From an alternative specification, we are able to observe that the relationship between growth and inequality is predicated on FDI.

ACI Growth has been accompanied by increased income and non-income inequalities. In order to achieving a socially inclusive growth, the ACI economies will not only require high economic growth, but also several major transformations in various domains—such as educational revolution; gender development; land and asset re-distribution; and increased financial inclusion or easy financial access to low-income citizens—will be necessary.

Our theoretical finding is that policy makers cannot successfully exploit the relationship between economic growth and inequality if the level of inequality is high. Thus, from the data on growth and inequality in the ACI economies, we marshal evidence that there exists an impossibility theorem that suggests that policymakers cannot optimally choose economic growth and inequality when inequality crosses a threshold. In other words, simple growth-inducing policies and measures of reducing inequality will not be able to create socially inclusive growth in the ACI economies.

References

Alesina, A., & Rodrik, D. (1994). Distributive politics and economic growth. *Quarterly Journal of Economics, 109,* 465–490.

Anand, S., & Kanbur, R. (1993). Inequality and development: A critique. *Journal of Development Economics, 41,* 19–43.

Arellano, M., & Bond, S. (1991). Some tests of specification for panel data: Monte carlo evidence and an application to employment equations. *Review of Economic Studies, 58,* 277–297.

Baele, L., Pungulescu, C., & Horst, J. T. (2007). Model uncertainty, financial market integration and the home bias puzzle. *Journal of International Money and Finance, 26,* 606–630.

Banerjee, A., & Duflo, E. (2003). Inequality and growth: What can the data say? *Journal of Economic Growth, 8,* 267–299.

Barro, R. (2000). Inequality and growth in a panel of countries. *Journal of Economic Growth, 5,* 5–32.

Benabou, R. (1996). Inequality and growth. In B.S. Bernanke & J.J. Rotemberg (eds), *NBER macroeconomics annual, Chapter 11* (pp. 11–73). Cambridge: MIT Press.

Besley, T., & Case, A. (2003). Political institutions and policy choices: Evidence from the United States. *Journal of Economic Literature, 41*(1), 171–189.

Besley, T., & Coate, S. (2003). On the public choice critique of welfare economics. *Public Choice, 114*(3), 253–273.

Blundell, R., & Bond, S. (1998). Initial conditions and moment restrictions in dynamic panel data models. *Journal of Econometrics, 87,* 11–143.

Bourguignon, F. (1981). Pareto superiority of unegalitarian equilibria in Stiglitz' model of wealth distribution with convex saving function. *Econometrica, 49*(6), 1469–1475.

Bourguignon, F. (2004). *The poverty-growth-inequality triangle.* Paper presented at the Indian Council for Research on International Economic Relations, New Delhi, February 4.

Bourguignon, F., & Da Silva, L. A. (Eds.). (2003). *The impact of economic policies on poverty and income distribution: Evaluation techniques and tools.* Washington DC: World Bank.

Case, A. C. (2001). Election goals and income redistribution: Recent evidence from Albania. *European Economic Review, 45,* 405–423.

Chan, K. S., & Tsay, R. S. (1998). Limiting properties of the least squares estimator of a continuous threshold autoregressive model. *Biometrika, 85,* 413–426.

Chen, B. L. (2003). An inverted relationship between inequality and long-run growth. *Economics Letters, 78*(2), 205–212 (February).

Clarke, G. R. G. (1995). More evidence on income distribution and growth. *Journal of Development Economics, 47,* 403–427.

Davidson, R., & Flachaire, E. (2001). The wild bootstrap, tamed at last. GREQAM Document de Travail 99A32.

Davies, R. B. (1977). Hypothesis testing when a nuisance parameter is present only under the alternative. *Biometrika, 64*(2), 246–254.

Davies, R. B. (1987). Hypothesis testing when a nuisance parameter is present only under the alternative. *Biometrika, 74*(1), 33–43.

Deininger, K., & Squire, L. (1998). New ways of looking at old issues: Inequality and growth. *Journal of Development Economics, 57,* 259–287.

Deininger, K., & Squire, L. (1999). A new data set measuring income inequality. *World Bank Economic Review, 10,* 565–591.

Dollar, D., & Kraay, A. (2002). Growth is good for the poor. *Journal of Economic Growth, 7,* 195–225.

Easterly, W. (1999). Life during growth. *Journal of Economic Growth, 4,* 239–276.

Easterly, W. (2001). *The elusive quest for growth.* Cambridge, MA: MIT Press.

Echenique, F., & Edlin, A. (2004). Mixed equilibria are unstable in games of strategic complementarities. *Journal of Economic Theory, 118,* 61–79.

Forbes, K. (2000). A reassessment of the relationship between inequality and growth. *American Economic Review, 90,* 869–897.

Galenson, W., & Leibenstein, H. (1955). Investment criteria, productivity, and economic development. *Quarterly Journal of Economics, 80,* 342–370 (August).

Gangopadhyay, P., & Bhattacharyay, B. N. (2011). *On the economics of social inclusion and protection in ASEAN economies, India and the People Republic of China.* A background paper for the Asian Development Bank Institute(ADB)/Asian Development Bank's(ADB) study on role of key emerging economies—ASEAN, the People Republic of China, and India—for a balanced, resilient and sustainable Asia, ADB/ADBI, Tokyo.

Gangopadhyay, P., & Bhattacharyay, B. N. (2015). *Is there a nonlinear relationship between economic growth and inequality? Theory and lessons from ASEAN.* CESifo Working Paper Series 5377, People Republic of China and India: CESifo Group Munich.

Hansen, B. E. (1996). Inference when a nuisance parameter is not identified under the null hypothesis. *Econometrica, 64,* 413–430.

Hansen, B. E. (1999). Threshold effects in non-dynamic panels: Estimation, testing and inference. *Journal of Econometrics, 93,* 345–368.

Hansen, B. E. (2000). Sample splitting and threshold estimation. *Econometrica, 68,* 575–603.

Hansen, B. E. (2007). Hansen B. E., Trygve Haavelmo Professor [online]. Madison, WI: Department of Econometrics, University of Wisconsin-Madison. http://www.ssc.wisc.edu/~bhansen/econometrics/Econometrics2007.pdf. Accessed on November 2001.

Kakwani, N., Khandker, S., & Son, H. H. (2004). *Pro-poor growth: Concepts and measurements with country case studies.* Working Paper of the International Poverty Centre, Brasilia, August 2004.

Kanbur, R. (2005). Growth, inequality and poverty: Some hard questions. *Journal of International Affairs, 58*(2), 223–235.

Kraay, A. (2005). *When is growth pro-poor? Evidence from a panel of countries.* World Bank Policy Research Department Working Paper No. 3225.

Kuznets, S. (1955). Economic growth and income inequality. *American Economic Review, 45,* 1–28.

Li, H., Squire, L., & Zou, H.-F. (1998). Explaining international and intertemporal variations in income inequality. *Economic Journal, 108,* 26–43.

Li, H., Xie, D., & Zou, H.-F. (2000a). Dynamics of income distribution. *Canadian Journal of Economics, 33,* 937–961.

Li, H., Xu, L. C., & Zou, H.-F. (2000b). Corruption, income distribution, and growth. *Economics and Politics, 12,* 155–182.

Li, H., & Zou, H. (1998). Income inequality is not harmful for growth: Theory and evidence. *Review of Development Economics, 2*(3), 318–334.

Li, H., & Zou, H. (2002). Inflation, growth, and income distribution: A cross-country study. *Annals of Economics and Finance, 3,* 85–101.

Lopez, H. (2004). *Pro-poor-pro-growth: is there a trade off*? The World Bank, Policy Research Working Paper No. 3378.

Lopez, H. (2006). *Did growth become less pro-poor in the 1990s*? World Bank Policy Research Working Paper, No. 3931.

Lopez, H., & Serven, L. (2006). *A normal relationship? Poverty, growth, and inequality.* World Bank Policy Research Department Working Paper, No. 3814.

Milgrom, P., & Roberts, J. (1990). Rationalizability learning, and equilibrium in games with strategic complementarities. *Econometrica, 58,* 1255–1277.

Persson, T., & Tabellini, G. (1994). Is inequality harmful for growth? *American Economic Review, 84,* 600–621.

Persson, T., & Tabellini, G. (2000). *Political economics: Explaining economic policy.* Cambridge: MIT Press.

Persson, T., & Tabellini, G. (2003). *The economic effect of constitutions.* Cambridge: MIT Press.

Ravallion, M. (1997). Can high inequality development countries escape absolute poverty? *Economics Letters, 56,* 51–57.

Ravallion, M. (2004). *Pro-poor growth: A primer*. The World Bank, Policy Research Working Paper No. 3242.

Ravallion, M., & Chen, S. (2003). Measuring pro-poor growth. *Economic Letters, 78,* 93–99.

Savvides, A., & Stengos, T. (2000). Income inequality and economic development: Evidence from the threshold regression model. *Economics Letters, 69,* 207–212.

Stiglitz, J. (1969). Distribution of income and wealth among individuals. *Econometrica, 37,* 382–397.

Vives, X. (1990). Nash Equilibrium with strategic complementarities. *Journal of Mathematical Economics, 19*(3), 305–321.

Vives, X. (2005). Complementarities and games: New developments. *Journal of Economic Literature, XLIII*, 435–479.

Wu, C. F. J. (1986). Jackknife, bootstrap and other resampling methods in regression analysis. *Annals of Statistics, 14*(4), 1261–1295.

Chapter 2
Does Institutional Quality Affect Foreign Direct Investment? A Panel Data Analysis

Girijasankar Mallik and Mamta Chowdhury

Abstract This study investigates the effects of the institutional quality along with socio-economic factors on foreign direct investment (FDI) of 156 countries using Ordinary Least Square (OLS) and Fixed Effect (FE) method. The findings of the study suggest that while corruption lowers FDI significantly, democracy, government stability, law and order, civil liberty and political rights have significant positive effects on FDI inflows. Results of the study also indicate that increased levels of educational attainment and openness in a trade regime lead to a higher level of FDI. Thus the policy prescription to attract higher FDI requires focussing on ensuring better institutional quality with a lower level of corruption along with raising the skill-base of the labour force in an outward looking external trade regime.

Keywords Corruption · Institutional quality · Foreign direct investment
Fixed effect

JEL Classification F23 · R38 · C23

2.1 Introduction

Foreign direct investment (FDI) is one of the prominent features of globalisation and a major source of capital in augmenting domestic investment and rapid economic growth. The era of financial liberalisation commencing from the early 1980s significantly increased the flow of FDI to the developing countries. However, com-

G. Mallik (✉)
School of Business, Western Sydney University, Locked Bag 1797,
Penrith South DC, NSW 1797, Australia
e-mail: g.mallik@westernsydney.edu.au

M. Chowdhury
School of Business, Western Sydney University, Penrith, Australia
e-mail: mamta.chowdhury@westernsydney.edu.au

U.K. De et al. (eds.), *Inequality, Poverty and Development in India*, India Studies
in Business and Economics, DOI 10.1007/978-981-10-6274-2_2

petition to attract FDI is observed to be strong as both advanced and developing countries are equally opting for faster economic growth. Globally, the total value of FDI increased from $80 billion in 1985 to $1.24 trillion in 2010 and expected to rise to $1.9 trillion in 2013. The flow of FDI increased to developing countries by 12% due to their stronger economic growth led by vibrant domestic demand over the last decade. South, East and Southeast Asia experienced the highest growth in FDI compared to other developing nations in recent years (UNCTAD 2011). In 2010, FDI inflow to this region accounted for $300 billion with a growth of 24% from its previous year. This growth in FDI inflow is particularly experienced by Southeast and East Asia. A strong growth of FDI is also experienced by Latin America and Caribbean countries spurred by high commodity prices, strong domestic demand and economic growth and good macroeconomic policies. Manufacturing sector shows a strong growth of FDI in recent years, which accounted for more than half of the total inflows in 2010 (UNCTAD 2011). However, FDI inflows to Africa, West-Asia, Southeast Europe and developed countries depict a downward trend in 2010.

FDI plays an important role in economic development and growth. The forces behind the movement of FDI have long been a subject of international trade and business literature. Most of the recent literature concentrates on the effect of corruption on economic growth following pioneering work by Mauro (1995, 1998). According to Shleifer and Vishny (1993), corruption is detrimental for investment and therefore reduces economic growth. However, Leff (1964) and Lui (1985) suggest that corruption may be beneficial to growth up to a certain level, because it may 'grease the wheel'.

Rampant corruption may negatively affect the perception of socio-economic stability and investment environment of a host country and thus reduce the FDI inflow. In the presence of corruption, foreign investors have to pay extra payments to get licenses or government permits. This, in turn, increases the cost of production and decreases profit margins and may be viewed as a tax on profits (Bardhan 1997). Many researchers also argued that at an initial stage corruption may increase FDI; however, in the long-run the effect of corruption on FDI should be negative. Therefore, the effect of corruption on FDI is still not clear and researchers are divided on this issue. There are also many methodological issues. For example, many researchers have used OLS to estimate the determinants of corruption, which is not appropriate. Al-Sadig (2009) argued that the negative impact of corruption disappears once the quality of institutions is considered in a cross-country model. However, there are limited studies in recent literature focussing on the influence of institutional quality, along with other economic and business factors determining the FDI inflows. Although studies on the effects of institutional quality and governance on FDI indicate mixed results, a large number of recent studies (Mathur and Singh 2013; Busse and Hefeker 2007; Wei 2000; Habib and Zurawicki 2002) find a positive relationship between institutional quality and FDI inflows. However, a few studies suggest that under specific circumstances, corruption and bribe may facilitate FDI inflows (Olson 1993; Egger and Winner 2005).

Since comprehensive empirical studies are limited, this study attempts to contribute to the gap in the literature by analysing the effects of corruption along with other institutional qualities, educational attainment and governance factors in addition to economic determinants, on FDI inflows for 156[1] countries using OLS and Fixed Effect (FE) methods for the period 1984–2009.

The remainder of the study is structured as follows: a review of the literature on the determinants of FDI inflows is discussed next. This is followed by the theoretical framework and hypothesis of the study. The empirical model and explanation of the methodology is illustrated thereafter. A discussion of the results is presented followed by a summary findings and conclusions.

2.2 Literature Review

A large volume of empirical literature centres on exploring the determinants of FDI inflow over the past decades. Diversifying risk and attain a higher return on capital is cited as principal reasons for FDI in the business and international trade literature. FDI flows from the capital abundant countries to capital scarce countries where its return is relatively higher (Hymer 1976; Barba Navaretti and Venables 2004; Markusen 2002). Kindleberger (1969) suggests domestic market imperfections in source countries motivate capital flights and FDI. Vernon's (1966) product cycle theory demonstrates that the main reason for FDI is the search for lower factor costs and to be more competitive. Resource-seeking and market-seeking motivations by multi-national corporations (MNC) have been considered as important factors for FDI movements from the early nineteenth century (Jones 1996). Product differentiation, economies of scale and imperfect competition are also added to the list of factors in determining FDI inflow using trade theory (Krugman 1980; Helpman 1981). Zhang and Marksen (1999) consider the size of an economy as an important factor for FDI while incorporating transport costs. However, according to Brainard (1997), MNCs decide to invest in a foreign country instead of exporting it products to that country if the cost of operation is less than gain from avoiding trade costs. Dunning (1988a, b, 2000) highlights ownership, location and internalisation (OLI) as the three key drivers of FDI, which comprise the basis of FDI. Favourable tax treatment is also alluded to as an important motive for FDI flowing to developing countries (Wei 2000; UNCTAD 2004).

Several empirical studies (Root and Ahmed 1979; Lee and Tan 2006; Wheeler and Mody 1992; Dunning and Narula 1996; UNCTAD 2006) have illustrated the effects of various economic factors on FDI. Locational or pull factors, such as the size of the markets, endowment of key resources and factor efficiency, are suggested as the principal determinants of FDI by the literature (Dunning 1998a, b; Stoian and Filippaios 2008). Market potential measured by growth of GDP, infrastructure facilities in the host country, openness and macroeconomic stability,

[1]Number of countries depends on the independent variables included in the model and data availability.

quality of labour are also considered as the important determining factors of FDI in the literature (Stoian and Filippaios 2008; Tarzi 2005; Jensen 2006).

Nonetheless, the socio-political factors, especially the institutional quality and good governance, bear significant influence on the FDI in the contemporary complex global business environment. The importance of institutional qualities and other relevant policies in the host countries are increasingly acknowledged by the FDI literature (Habib and Zurawicki 2002; Resnick and Li 2003; Mathur and Singh 2013). Institutional factors, such as property rights, an efficient tax system, economic freedom, transparency, corruption and bribery have both direct and indirect effects on economic growth (Rodrik 1999; Johnson and Robinson 2004). There is a growing interest in finding the relationship between institutional quality factors and FDI inflows in conjunction with economic factors. Increasing factor productivity, lowering investment cost (due to transparency and low corruption) and well-defined property rights provided by a good institutional framework, are considered to be conducive to the business environment which may facilitate domestic and foreign investment and raise GDP growth (Daniele and Marani 2006). Numerous studies (Gupta et al. 1998; Shleifer and Vishny 1993; Wei 2000) suggest a negative relationship between corruption and the investment environment which tends to have an adverse impact on economic growth. Nonetheless, a few studies argue that corruption is not necessarily having an adverse impact on GDP growth; rather it may facilitate economic activities under the egalitarian system (Braguinsky 1996; Rashid 1981). Egger and Winner (2005), thus find a positive relationship between corruption and FDI inflow.

In a cross-section study, Lee and Mansfield (1996) indicate a positive effect of intellectual property rights on FDI inflow, whereas, a negative impact of institutional uncertainty on investment is illustrated by Brunetti and Weder (1998). Various other studies (Jun and Singh 1996; Wei 2000; Busse and Hefeker 2007) conclude that democratic rights of a country as well as less internal and external conflicts can attract a higher level of FDI inflow. However, a number of studies (Egger and Winner 2005; Jaspersen et al. 2000; Wheeler and Mody 1992) find no significant effect of political stability on FDI.

Despite some evidence of the positive influence of institutional quality, there are some studies (Olson 1993; Egger and Winner 2005) indicating inconclusive or even a negative relationship between some of institutional factors and inflow of FDI. Therefore, this study investigates the effect of major institutional quality indicators along with key economic factors, determining the flow of FDI for 156 countries between 1984 and 2009 using OLS and FE methods. This study differs from previous studies in the following manner. Firstly, this study has a relatively larger sample size and incorporates more explanatory variables such as secondary education (as a proxy for skilled labour force), democracy, government stability, law and order, civil liberty, political rights as well as corruption along with other economic indicators of the host countries. The advantage of a large number of countries spread over a 26 year period is that it provides more degrees of freedom and improves the reliability of the results. Secondly, this study uses a panel fixed effect method, which is considered to be a better estimation procedure than OLS.[2] The key advantages of the panel method is that this method has more controls for unobserved heterogeneity in two dimensions and is also likely to reduce multi-collinearity in the estimations (Baltagi 2001).

2.3 Theory and Hypothesis

Macroeconomic indicators have received significant attention as determinants of FDI. Major economic factors including real GDP per capita, GDP growth, investment, government expenditure, inflation, as well as policy variables such as money supply and openness in trade regime have been recognised as important determinants in international trade and business literature (Habib and Zurawicki 2002; Mathur and Singh 2013; Asiedu 2002; Busse and Hefekers 2007). The pool of human capital is considered as an important socio-economic indicator in determining FDI as MNCs are always interested in investing in a country where skilled labour force is readily available (Egger and Winner 2005; Wheeler and Mody 1992; Mathur and Singh 2013). Zhang and Marksen (1999) and Dunning (1988a, b) also suggest human capital endowment as one of the crucial determinants of FDI. However, the quest and competition for resources by the modern multinational companies may face critical political and institutional barriers in expanding their global market share as trade and investment policies are not always conducive for capital flows. Institutional settings of a country, including the level of corruption, law and order condition, democracy, government stability, civil liberty and political rights, may facilitate or deter the FDI flows. Thus, the key hypothesis of our study is stated as follows:

Hypothesis: Institutional quality and governance influence the flow of FDI along with other socio-economic factors.

Among institutional factors, the relationship between corruption and FDI is not unanimous as corruption has been alluded to either as 'grabbing hands' or 'helping hands' in influencing the inflow of FDI (Bardhan 1997). Corruption is defined as the misuse of the public power for private gains, which is not only illegal but also improper (Tanzi 1998; Bardhan 1997; Malta Conference 1994). In general, corruption has a negative effect on FDI flow as it increases the cost of business by a

[2]OLS is optimal if the error process has some variance (heteroscedasticity).Moreover, for a multiple country panel data analysis OLS ignores the country effects (Baltagi and Griffin 1997). More seriously, if the errors are not spherical, there is no guarantee that the OLS standard errors will be correct and the estimated coefficients may be incorrect sign. FE model is a much better estimation procedure and overcome most of the problems arise from OLS. Moreover, in a panel data analysis with country FE approach allows us to distinguish more systematically between the effects of the policy changes over time as well as across countries (Busse and Hefeker 2007). For OLS to be properly applied, the errors have to be independent and homoskedastic. Those conditions are so rare that is often unrealistic to expect that OLS will suffice for such models (Davidson and McKinnon 1993).

MNC. Various other studies also found a negative relationship between corruption and FDI as it creates inefficiency raises income inequality and lowers economic growth (Wei 2000; Mauro 1995; Shleifer and Vishny 1993). Employing a large number of countries' data and both OLS and PROBIT model, Habib and Zurawicki (2002) demonstrate that the different level of corruption between host and home country discourages the FDI inflow as it is considered immoral and not conducive for the healthy business environment, at least at an operational level. Corruption deters the development of a well functioning efficient market and increases the cost-price of goods and services as bribes are not valued in the market (Boatright 2000; Habib and Zurawicki 2002). However, a number of studies suggest that by increasing allocative efficiency; bribes can create Pareto optimality and increase profits of a MNC (Rashid 1981; Lui 1985; Tanzi 1998). Using a sample of 73 countries, Egger and Winner (2005) also find a positive influence of corruption on FDI over the period between 1995 and 1999. Since the effect of corruption on FDI is found to be inconclusive, the expected sign of corruption and FDI can be either positive or negative in an empirical study.

Democratic rights are regarded as one of the important aspects of institutional quality and can influence the FDI in a country. Several studies (Busse and Hefeker 2007; Jensen 2006) suggest a positive relationship between democracy and FDI inflow. However, Resnick and Li (2003) indicate that enhanced democracy may lower FDI inflow although democracy can secure property rights and indirectly encourage FDI inflows. Mathur and Singh (2013) also find more democratic countries receive less FDI where economic freedom is not prevalent. Thus, the sign between the level of democracy and FDI is ambiguous. Other institutional and governance factors included in this model, such as government stability, enhanced civil liberty and political rights and improved law and order conditions, reduce the political risk factors and in general, positively influence the FDI inflow. Therefore, the expected sign between these factors and FDI is usually positive.

Socio-economic factors, such as GDP per capita (RGDPPCY), GDP growth (RGDPgr), government expenditure as a percentage of GDP (GRAT), domestic investment as a percentage of GDP (IRAT), openness in trade regime (OPEN), money supply as a percentage of GDP (M2RAT) and human capital (EDU) are the major features of size of a market. The larger the size of a market and the resource endowment in terms of education and skilled labour force, the higher is the FDI inflows to the country. However, a higher level of inflation (INF) in the host country may reduce FDI as it increases the cost of production and uncertainty of future investment.

Increased GDP per capita, economic growth, higher investment and government expenditure indicate higher income and expansion of an economy which attracts FDI as the market-seeking MNCs intend to invest in a larger economy to expand their business. However, the relationship between these economic indicators and FDI inflow is far from undisputed and the a priori sign could be either positive or negative since the domestic economic growth and supporting economic factors can lower FDI as much as it can attract FDI inflows since a growing economy may want to be self-sufficient and utilise their own resources to build capacity without any external support to augment domestic investment. However, the relationship between human capital and FDI inflow should be positive as MNCs require readily available skilled labour to work with imported capital and technology to ensure increased income and profit (Zhang and Marksen 1999). Greater openness in the trade regime, in general, is positively associated with FDI inflows, especially, for export-oriented MNCs as openness increases the competitiveness and exposure of a country in the global market (Edwards 1990).

2.4 Specification and Data

In an attempt to estimate the effect of institutional quality, education and other macroeconomic factors on FDI at the aggregate level, the versions of FDI model is specified as follows:

$$\begin{aligned}\ln \text{FDIRAT}_{\text{it}} = {} & \beta_0 + \beta_1 \ln \text{RGDPPCY}_{\text{it}} + \beta_2 \text{RGDPgr}_{\text{it}} + \beta_3 \text{GRAT}_{\text{it}} \\ & + \beta_4 \text{IRAT}_{\text{it}} + \beta_5 \text{INF}_{\text{it}} + \beta_6 \text{M2RAT}_{\text{it}} + \beta_7 \text{OPEN}_{\text{it}} + \beta_8 \text{EDU}_{\text{it}} \\ & + \beta_9 \text{CORRP}_{\text{it}}/\text{DEMO}_{\text{it}}/\text{GOVSTB}_{\text{it}}/\text{LAW}_{\text{it}}/\text{CIVLIB}_{\text{it}}/\text{POLRIG}_{\text{it}} + \varepsilon_{\text{it}} \cdots\end{aligned} \tag{2.1}$$

Where, lnFDIRAT is the natural logarithm of the foreign direct investment. The empirical analysis used data for 106–156[3] countries between 1984 and 2009 available from different sources. The detailed variable description and data sources are given in Table 2.3.

2.5 Estimation

First, Eq. 2.1 has been estimated using Ordinary Least Square (OLS) method in an unbalanced panel, cross-country framework. However, there are some disadvantages in using OLS estimation procedures in panel data. The coefficients obtained from the OLS method are biased and inconsistent (Egger and Merlo 2007). OLS estimation ignores country effects and suffers from omitted variable bias as the unobservable factors that are correlated with the variables are not included in the regression. Therefore, Eq. (2.1) is estimated using FE along with OLS for comparison. FE method is a better estimation procedure over OLS since it provides consistent (but not necessarily efficient) parameter estimates (Egger and Winner

[3]Number of countries depends on the independent variables included in the model and data availability.

Table 2.1 Summary statistics and correlation matrix

	lnFDIRAT	lnRGDPPCY	RGDPgr	GRAT	IRAT	INF	M2RAT	OPEN	EDU	CORRP	DEMO	GOVSTB	LAW	CIVLIB	POLRIG
lnFDIRAT	1.00														
lnRGDPPCY	0.19	1.00													
RGDPgr	0.17	0.00	1.00												
GRAT	0.06	0.23	−0.15	1.00											
IRAT	0.27	0.12	0.19	0.13	1.00										
INF	−0.03	−0.05	−0.08	−0.06	−0.06	1.00									
M2RAT	0.17	0.54	−0.04	0.21	0.20	−0.06	1.00								
OPEN	0.39	0.25	0.09	0.08	0.29	−0.03	0.35	1.00							
EDU	0.25	0.78	−0.08	0.22	0.12	−0.03	0.43	0.18	1.00						
CORRP	−0.16	−0.84	0.13	−0.44	−0.03	0.18	−0.51	−0.22	−0.63	1.00					
DEMO	0.22	0.50	−0.03	0.14	0.06	−0.04	0.28	−0.02	0.54	−0.45	1.00				
GOVSTB	0.33	0.24	0.19	0.03	0.16	−0.08	0.20	0.23	0.26	−0.11	0.18	1.00			
LAW	0.21	0.65	0.05	0.32	0.16	−0.06	0.41	0.16	0.58	−0.70	0.49	0.41	1.00		
CIVLIB	0.20	0.56	−0.03	0.10	0.04	−0.04	0.32	0.07	0.53	−0.57	0.79	0.12	0.41	1.00	
POLRIG	0.26	0.60	−0.03	0.12	0.05	−0.04	0.35	0.11	0.58	−0.63	0.77	0.16	0.46	0.93	1.00
Average	0.47	7.67	3.28	16.54	21.76	7.70	48.73	82.18	67.05	5.58	3.70	7.60	3.66	3.62	3.59
STDEV	1.77	1.60	0.05	7.04	9.01	8.86	36.74	49.44	32.51	2.53	1.66	2.25	1.50	1.91	2.22

2005). Moreover, a FE regression effectively controls for endogeneity due to time-invariant effects (Mendez and Sepulveda 2006) and if the unobservable factors are time-invariant, then fixed effects regression will eliminate omitted variable bias.

2.6 Results and Discussion

The summary statistics and correlation matrix of the variables used in the model are presented in Table 2.1. It can be seen that FDI is positively correlated with most of the variables except for corruption and inflation. The correlation between per-capita income and corruption is very high at −0.84, implying that corruption reduces per-capita income significantly. Interestingly, corruption is negatively correlated with all the institutional quality variables (e.g. democratic accountability, government stability, law and order, civil liberty and political rights) and the correlation coefficients between the institutional quality variables are highly positive. For example, the correlation between civil liberty and democracy is 0.79 and political rights and democracy is 0.77, which indicates a more democratic country has higher civil liberty and political rights, as expected.[4] The correlation coefficient between corruption and secondary education is −0.63. Since corruption reduces education (or vice versa), institutional quality, per-capita income and FDI, it may be possible that targeting corruption through improved institutional quality can enhance the performance of an economy.

Table 2.2 illustrates the OLS and FE results for different versions of the model. As discussed earlier that OLS estimates may be biased and FE provide relatively consistent parameter estimates, this study mainly analyses the estimates obtained using FE. OLS estimates are given for comparison only. The estimated coefficients (using FE) of the lnRGDPPCY mostly show a positive and significant relationship with FDI as expected by the analytical model. Habib and Zurawicki (2002) and Chakrabarti (2001) also found a positive relationship between RGDPPCY and FDI inflow as it suggests that a market-seeking MNC has better prospects in a host country with higher per-capita income. The estimated coefficients of RGDPgr and majority IRAT indicate significant positive effects on FDI as higher growth rate and domestic investment are indicators of higher return on investment which also attracts foreign investment. This result conforms to existing studies (Habib and Zurawicki 2002; Busse and Hefeker 2007). GRAT indicates a significantly negative relationship with FDI in most of the equations. This result is a contrast with that of Asiedu (2002) which finds a positive relationship between GRAT and FDI but was not significant. Although the coefficient of INF indicates a negative relationship with FDI as expected by the analytical model but coefficient values are very low and insignificant for most of the cases. Egger and Winner (2005) also find a similar result but with an insignificant coefficient value. M2RAT shows the positive and

[4]Please see the definition and variable construction in page 9.

Table 2.2 Regression results using ordinary least square and panel fixed effect methods

	OLS	Fixed effect	OLS	Fixed effect	OLS	Fixed effect	OLS	Fixed effect
Constant	1.948*** (4.01)	2.528 (1.35)	1.577*** (2.89)	2.312 (1.05)	−0.984*** (−4.33)	−5.442*** (−3.81)	−1.874*** (−7.53)	−5.344*** (−3.85)
lnRGDPPCY	−0.207*** (−4.12)	−0.571** (−2.30)	−0.259*** (−4.62)	−0.572** (1.99)	−0.180*** (−5.01)	0.223 (1.11)	−0.071** (−2.02)	0.173 (0.89)
RGDPgr	0.850 (0.81)	0.646 (0.76)	1.094 (0.97)	0.337 (0.37)	3.615*** (4.37)	2.857*** (3.89)	2.884*** (3.46)	2.590*** (3.60)
GRAT	−0.029*** (−3.78)	−0.010 (−0.74)	−0.027*** (−2.99)	−0.017 (−0.97)	−0.024*** (−3.92)	−0.050*** (−4.26)	−0.021*** (−3.42)	−0.035*** (−3.28)
IRAT	0.003 (0.41)	0.035*** (4.54)	−0.001 (−0.15)	0.046*** (5.55)	0.001 (0.20)	0.033*** (5.30)	−0.001 (−0.19)	0.035*** (5.82)
INF	−0.001 (−0.56)	0.000 (0.42)	−0.000 (−0.56)	0.000 (0.39)	−0.000 (−1.30)	−0.000 (−1.63)	−0.000 (−0.80)	−0.000 (−0.96)
M2RAT	−0.007*** (−6.15)	0.011*** (4.18)	−0.007*** (−6.19)	0.009*** (3.28)	0.006*** (6.08)	0.007*** (3.33)	−0.006*** (−6.06)	0.007*** (3.38)
OPEN	0.015*** (19.43)	0.017*** (6.93)	0.016*** (19.45)	0.015*** (5.64)	0.018*** (24.49)	0.013*** (7.31)	0.015*** (21.49)	0.014*** (7.85)
EDU	0.012*** (5.65)	0.017*** (6.93)	0.010*** (4.36)	0.012*** (2.64)	0.013*** (8.07)	0.027*** (8.84)	0.014*** (8.52)	0.021*** (7.12)
CORRP	−0.142*** (−5.46)	−0.093** (−2.22)	−0.121*** (−4.32)	−0.108** (−2.32)				
DEMO			0.173*** (5.48)	0.089* (1.84)	0.273*** (11.51)	0.183*** (5.72)		

(continued)

Table 2.2 (continued)

	OLS	Fixed effect	OLS	Fixed effect	OLS	Fixed effect	OLS	Fixed effect
GOVSTB							0.163*** (10.78)	0.153*** (10.83)
LAW								
CIVLIB								
POLRIG								
R^2	0.312	0.175	0.344	0.199	0.331	0.175	0.325	0.215
Groups/Observations	1098	122/1098	979	106/979	2026	122/2026	2036	122/2036
F-test	54.77***	17.75***	50.67***	14.55***	110.95***	72.89***	108.55***	85.62***

	OLS	Fixed effect	OLS	Fixed effect	OLS	Fixed effect
Constant	−1.874*** (−7.53)	−6.044*** (−4.29)	0.740*** (2.86)	−4.913*** (−4.31)	0.039 (0.16)	−5.781*** (−5.16)
lnRGDPPCY	−0.071** (−2.02)	0.286 (1.44)	−0.223*** (−6.62)	0.327** (2.01)	−0.189*** (−5.56)	0.396** (2.44)
RGDPgr	2.884*** (3.46)	2.762*** (3.77)	3.177*** (4.53)	2.888*** (4.80)	3.117*** (4.40)	2.880*** (4.77)
GRAT	−0.021*** (−3.42)	−0.047*** (−4.32)	−0.014*** (−2.91)	−0.017** (−2.30)	−0.013** (−2.56)	−0.016** (−2.28)
IRAT	−0.001 (−0.19)	0.035*** (5.63)	0.016*** (4.42)	0.025*** (5.51)	0.015*** (4.12)	0.025*** (5.51)
INF	−0.000 (−0.80)	−0.000 (−1.30)	−0.000* (−1.74)	−0.000** (−2.44)	−0.000** (−2.06)	−0.000** (−2.59)
M2RAT	−0.006*** (−6.06)	0.007*** (3.29)	−0.003*** (−3.42)	0.007*** (3.79)	−0.003*** (−3.31)	0.008*** (3.88)
OPEN	0.015*** (21.49)	0.014*** (8.01)	0.017*** (24.41)	0.012*** (8.32)	0.017*** (24.48)	0.012*** (8.52)

(continued)

Table 2.2 (continued)

	OLS	Fixed effect	OLS	Fixed effect	OLS	Fixed effect
EDU	0.015*** (8.52)	0.027*** (8.89)	0.014*** (9.44)	0.026*** (9.76)	0.015*** (10.23)	0.027*** (10.08)
CORRP						
DEMO						
GOVSTB						
LAW	0.163*** (10.78)	0.197*** (5.98)				
CIVLIB			0.246*** (11.49)	0.184*** (5.30)		
POLRIG					0.148*** (8.55)	0.115*** (4.22)
R^2	0.325	0.168	0.329	0.166	0.314	0.155
Groups/Observations	2036	122/2037	2526	156/2526	2526	156/2526
F-test	108.55***	73.84***	137.08***	81.72***	127.79***	80.25***

Note *t*-values are reported in parentheses and *, ** and *** indicate significant at 10, 5 and 1% levels respectively

significant effect on FDI in FE estimation as expected by the analytical model and in line with the result found by Asiedu (2002). OPEN has a highly significant positive impact on FDI as expected by the analytical framework for both OLS and FE estimations. These results are consistent with the notable literature (Asiedu 2002; Egger and Winner 2005; Busse and Hefeker 2007; Mathur and Singh 2013) as both market-seeking and export-oriented MNCs will likely incur reduced transaction costs in a more open trade regime. One of the key determinants of FDI is the human capital or skilled labour force as proxied by secondary education level (EDU) in this study. MNCs are not only interested in investing in countries with cheap labour but also with a skilled workforce which is conducive to higher return on investment. Results indicate a highly significant positive effect of EDU on FDI in all equations and consistent with the various existing studies (Zhang and Marksen 1999; Wheeler and Mody 1992; Masron and Abdullah 2010; Mathur and Singh 2013) but in contrast with Egger and Winner (2005).

Among the institutional and governance factors likely to influence FDI, corruption is considered as one of the important factors and the empirical results of the study suggest a significant negative effect of corruption on FDI inflow. Since corruption is contemplated by MNCs as a stumbling block for the expansion and cost of doing business, thus it discourages them to invest in a country with high level of corruption. In this study, the higher corruption index is assumed to be associated with higher corruption level and the result is consistent with several notable existing studies (Habib and Zurawicki 2002; Mathur and Singh 2013; Busse and Hefeker 2001; Wei 2000; Egger and Winner 2005). It is interesting to note that the coefficient of corruption has a significant negative impact on FDI even in the presence of democracy. It is also found that the absolute value of the coefficient of corruption in this study is lower than that of other institutional quality factors which are in line with the findings of Al-Sadig (2009). Other institutional qualities used in the model, such as DEMO, GOVSTB, LAW are having positive and significant effects on FDI as expected in the model and is in line with several existing studies (Masron and Abdullah 2010; Habib and Zurawicki 2002; Busse and Hefeker 2007). However, it is in contrast with Mathur and Singh (2013) which find that FDI is lower in a more democratic country. CIVLIB and POLRIG have significant positive effect on FDI indicating that in countries where citizens possess higher political rights and participation in the public decision-making process, they may choose to have lower foreign investment. Furthermore, CIVLIB and POLRIG may not necessarily ensure economic independence, which is a more attractive factor for MNCs to invest in a foreign country. Thus, a country with higher CIVLIB and POLRIG but lower economic status may not have higher FDI inflows (Mathur and Singh 2013) (Table 2.3).

Table 2.3 Description of the variables

Name of the variables	Description	Source
lnFDIRAT	Natural logarithm of the foreign direct investment, net inflows (% of GDP)	The World Bank
GRAT	Government expenditure as a percentage of GDP	The World Bank
RGDPPCY	Per-capita RGDP	The World Bank
RGDPgr	Percentage change of RGDP	The World Bank
IRAT	Gross fixed capital formation as a percentage of GDP;	The World Bank
INF	Percentage change in CPI	The World Bank
M2RAT	Money supply as a percentage of GDP	The World Bank
OPEN	Export plus Import as a percentage of GDP	The World Bank
EDU	School enrolment, secondary (% net)	The World Bank
CORRP	Corruption 1–10, where 1 is the least corrupt and 10 is the most corrupt[a]	Corruption Perception Index (Transparency International data)
DEMO	Democratic accountability (0–6) 0 = least democratic and 6 = most democratic	International Country Risk Guide (ICRG), Published by the PRS Group
GOVSTB	Government stability (0–12) 0 = least stable and 12 = most stable)	ICRG
LAW	Law and order (0–6) 0 = least law and order and 6 = highest law and order)	ICRG
CIVLIB	civil liberty (1–7) 7 = highest liberty and 1 = lowest liberty (converted from original data)	Freedom House
POLRIG	political rights (1–7) 7 = highest right and 1 = lowest right (converted from original data)	Freedom House

[a]This series constructed using corruption data ICRG using the formula: CORRP = 10 − (3/2)corrpICRG

2.7 Conclusion

Financial and economic liberalisation from the early 1980s has encouraged global flows of FDI both in developing and advanced countries. However, it is found that healthier institutional qualities are important drivers of FDI along with market factors of an economy. This study examined the effects of institutional qualities along with economic factors in attracting FDI inflow using panel FE and OLS estimates. The results of the study indicate that corruption has a negative effect on FDI even in a more democratic environment. Other institutional factors such as government stability, better law and order condition and democratic rights facilitate and encourage the inflow of FDI in a host country. Market size, openness in the trade regime and quality of workers are found to be major socio-economic determinants and positively influence FDI inflows. Thus, policy prescriptions in terms of attracting FDI should focus more on enhancing institutional quality, controlling corruption as well as raising the skill-base of the labour force in a more open external trade environment.

References

Al-Sadig, A. (2009). The effects of corruption on FDI inflows. *Cato Journal, 29*(2), 267–294.

Asiedu, E. (2002). On the determinants of foreign direct investment to developing countries: Is Africa different? *World Development, 30*(1), 107–119.

Baltagi, B. (2001). *Econometric analysis of panel data* (2nd ed.). Chichester: Wiley.

Baltagi, B., & Griffin, J. (1997). Pooled estimators vs. their heterogeneous counterparts in the context of dynamic demand for gasoline. *Journal of Econometrics, 77,* 303–327.

Barba Navaretti, G., & Venables, A. (2004). *Multinational firms in the world economy*. Princeton: Princeton University Press.

Bardhan, P. (1997). Corruption and development: A review of issues. *Journal of Economic Literature, XXXV*, 1320–1346 (September).

Boatright, J. (2000). *Ethics and the conduct of business* (3rd ed.). New Jersey: Prentice Hall.

Braguinsky, S. (1996). Corruption and schumpeterian growth in different economic environments. *Contemporary Economic Policy, XIV*, 14–25 (July).

Brainard, L. (1997). An empirical assessment of the proximity-concentration trade-off between multinational sales and trade. *American Economic Review, 87,* 520–544.

Brunetti, A., & Weder, B. (1998). Investment and institutional uncertainty: A comparative study of different uncertainty measures. *Weltwirtschaftliches Archiv, 134,* 513–533.

Busse, M., & Hefeker, C. (2007). Political risk, institutions and foreign direct investment. *European Journal of Political Economy*, 397–415.

Chakrabarti, A. (2001). The determinants of foreign direct investment: Sensitivity analyses of cross-country regressions. *Kyklos, 54,* 89–114.

Daniele, V., & Marani, U. (2006). *Do institutions matter for FDI? A comparative analysis for the MENA countries*. MPRA Paper 2426.

Davidson, R., & McKinnon, J. (1993). *Estimation and inference in econometrics*. New York: Oxford University Press.

Dunning, J. (1998a). Location and the multinational enterprise: A neglected factor? *Journal of International Business Studies, 29*(1), 45–66.

Dunning, J. (1988b). The eclectic paradigm of international production: A restatement and some possible extensions. *Journal of International Business Studies, 19*(Spring), 1–31.

Dunning, J. (2000). The eclectic paradigm as an envelope for economic and business theories of MNE activity. *International Business Review, 9,* 163–190.

Dunning, J., & Narula, R. (1996). The investment development path revisited: Some emerging issues. In J. Dunning & R. Narula (Eds.), *Foreign direct investment and governments: Catalysts for economic restructuring* (pp. 1–41). London: Routledge.

Edwards, S. (1990). *Capital flows, foreign direct investment, and debt-equity swaps in developing countries*. NBER Working Paper No. 3497. Cambridge, MA: NBER.

Egger, P., & Merlo, V. (2007). The impact of bilateral investment treaties on FDI dynamics. *The World Economy, 30*(10), 1536–1549.

Egger, P., & Winner, H. (2005). Evidence on corruption as an incentive for foreign direct investment. *European Journal of Political Economy, 21,* 932–952.

Gupta, S., Davoodi H., & Alonso-Terme, R. (1998). *Does corruption affect income inequality and poverty*? IMF Working Paper, Washington D.C.: International Monetary Fund.

Habib, M., & Zurawicki, L. (2002). Corruption and foreign direct investment. *Journal of International Business Studies, 33*(2), 291–307.

Helpman, E. (1981). International trade in the presence of product differentiation, economies of scale, and monopolistic competition: A Chamberlin-Heckscher-Ohlin approach. *Journal of International Economics, 11,* 305–340.

Hymer, S. (1976.). *The international operations of national firms: A study of direct foreign investment*. Cambridge, MA: The MIT Press.

Jaspersen, F. Aylward, A., & Knox, A. (2000). The effects of risk on private investment: Africa compared with other developing areas. In P. Collier & C. Pattillo (Eds.), *Investment and risk in Africa* (pp. 71–95). New York: St Martin's Press.

Jensen, C. (2006). Foreign direct investment and economic transition: Panacea or pain killer? *Europe-Asia Studies, 58*(6), 881–902.

Johnson, A., & Robinson, J. (2004). *Institutions as the fundamental cause of long–run growth.* NBER Working Paper Series, Working Paper 10481. Cambridge, MA: National Bureau of Economic Research.

Jones, G. (1996). *The evolution of international business: An introduction*. London: Routledge.

Jun, K., & Singh, H. (1996). The determinants of foreign direct investment in developing countries. *Transnational Corporations, 5,* 67–105.

Kindleberger, C. (1969). *American business abroad.* New Haven: Yale University Press.

Krugman, P. (1980). Scale economies, product differentiation and the pattern of trade. *American Economic Review, 70,* 950–959.

Lee, H. H., & Tan, H. B. (2006). FDI, technology transfer and economic growth in the ASEAN region. *Journal of the Asia Pacific Economy, 11*(4), 394–410.

Lee, J.-Y., & Mansfield, E. (1996). Intellectual property protection and U.S. foreign direct investment. *Review of Economics and Statistics, 78*(2), 181–186.

Leff, N. (1964). Economic development through bureaucratic corruption. *American Behavioural Scientist, 8*(3), 8–14.

Lui, F. (1985). An equilibrium queuing model of bribery. *Journal of Political Economy, 93*(4), 760–781 (August).

Malta Conference. (1994). Report of the Netherlands Ministry of Justice. In *Proceedings of the 19th Conference of the European Ministers of Justice*. La Valetta, June 14–15, 1994. Strasbourg: Council of Europe Publishing.

Markusen, J. (2002). *Multinational firms and the theory of international trade*. Cambridge, MA: The MIT Press.

Masron, T., & Abdullah, H. (2010). Institutional quality as a determinant for FDI inflows: Evidence from ASEAN. *World Journal of Management, 2*(3), 115–128.

Mathur, A., & Singh, K. (2013). Foreign direct investment, corruption and democracy. *Applied Economics, 45*(8), 991–1002.

Mauro, P. (1995). Corruption and growth. *The Quarterly Journal of Economics, 110(3),* 681–712.

Mauro, P. (1998). Corruption and the composition of government expenditure. *Journal of Public Economics, 69,* 263–279.

Mendez, F., & Sepulveda, F. (2006). Corruption, growth and political regimes: Cross country evidence. *European Journal of Political Economy, 22,* 82–98.

Olson, M. (1993). Dictatorship, democracy, and development. *American Political Science Review, 87,* 567–576.

Rashid, S. (1981). Public utilities in egalitarian LDCs: The role of bribery in achieving pareto efficiency. *Kyklos, 34,* 448–460.

Resnick, A., & Li, Q. (2003). Reversal of fortunes: Democratic institutions and foreign direct investment inflows to developing countries. *International Organisation, 57,* 175–211.

Rodrik, D. (1999). Where did all the growth go? External shocks, social conflict and growth collapses. *Journal of Economic Growth, 4,* 385–412.

Root, F., & Ahmed, A. (1979). Empirical determinants of manufacturing direct foreign investment in developing countries. *Economic Development and Cultural Change, 27*(4), 751–767.

Shleifer, A., & Vishny, R. (1993). Corruption. *Quarterly Journal of Economics, 108*(3), 599–617.

Stoian, C., & Filippaios, F. (2008). Dunning's eclectic paradigm: A holistic, yet context specific framework for analysing the determinants of outward FDI evidence from international greek investments. *International Business Review, 17,* 349–367.

Tanzi, V. (1998). *Corruption around the world: Causes, consequences, scope, and cures*. IMF Working Paper WP/98/63. Washington, D.C.: International Monetary Fund.

Tarzi, S. (2005). Foreign direct investment into developing countries: Impact of location and government policy. *The Journal of Social, Political and Economic Studies, 30*(4), 497–516.

UNCTAD. (2004). *World investment report*. New York and Geneva: United Nations.

UNCTAD. (2006). *World investment report*. New York and Geneva: United Nations.

UNCTAD. (2011). *Global investment trends*. http://www.unctad-docs.org/files/UNCTAD-WIR2011-Chapter-I-en.pdf.

Vernon, R. (1966). International investment and international trade in product cycle: The case of US firms. *Quarterly Journal of Economics, 80,* 190–207.

Wei, S.-J. (2000). How taxing is corruption on international investors? *The Review of Economics and Statistics, 82*(1), 1–11.

Wheeler, D., & Mody, A. (1992). International investment location decisions: The case of U.S. *Firms. Journal of International Economics, 33,* 57–76.

Zhang, K. H., & Marksen, J. R. (1999). Vertical multinationals and host-country characteristics. *Journal of Development Economics, 59*, 233–252.

Chapter 3
An Empirical Verification of Kuznets Hypothesis in India

Aadil Ahmad Ganaie, Sajad Ahmad Bhat and Bandi Kamaiah

Abstract The trajectory of output growth, more precisely economic growth and its interaction with other phenomena of an economy follows a complex path. Among many phenomena the one that has caught the world attention at large scale especially since the work of Piketty and Saez is the "Rising Inequality in Incomes". Though for some countries like India there was a reduction in the poverty level, there seems no positive bearing on economic growth in improving income distribution for past two decades. In this paper, we have used ARDL cointegration approach to analyze the relationship between income inequality (EHII, from UTIP-UNIDO) and its various determinants from 1964 to 2007. Besides using data on Estimated Household Income Inequality (EHII), we have used income share of top 1% as an alternative measure of inequality. Our results reveal no relevance of Kuznets Hypothesis, instead, the relationship is U-shaped in nature, implying that with the initial rise in GDP per capita inequality decreases, later on as GDP increases, inequality tends to increase. Among the control variables, CPI (price level) is found to be positively and Government expenditure negatively related to inequality, while trade openness showed no significant relationship.

Keywords Kuznets' hypothesis · GDP per capita · ARDL approach
EHII · Top 1%

A.A. Ganaie
School of Economics, University of Hyderabad,
Room No. 09, Men's Hostel NRS NX-E, Hyderabad 500046, India
e-mail: aadilganaie77@gmail.com

S.A. Bhat (✉)
School of Economics, University of Hyderabad,
Room no. 233, Men's Hostel NRS NX-E, Hyderabad 500046, India
e-mail: sajadeco@gmail.com

B. Kamaiah
School of Economics, University of Hyderabad, Hyderabad 500046, India
e-mail: kamaiahbandi@gmail.com

U.K. De et al. (eds.), *Inequality, Poverty and Development in India*, India Studies in Business and Economics, DOI 10.1007/978-981-10-6274-2_3

3.1 Introduction

1950s marked the beginning of the post-colonial era of development in Asia and Africa. From the start of this period, a new area took its birth in the economic sphere with a more universal appeal, "economics of growth and development"; with initial years focusing on the development of growth models and structural disequilibrium theories. A pause in the process came almost for some 30 years before a new shift was made towards endogenous growth theories that focused on the importance of human capital and multidimensional aspects of development with priorities to social welfare and equal opportunities for all. During the same period failure of the state as an organ to provide maximum welfare to the individuals of the society came under a severe attack and new consensus developed to minimize the role and functions of the state with high resolution for individual liberties. New thoughts and philosophies developed since the 50s' to look deeply toward the issues directly or indirectly, obstructing or harmonizing the living standards of people. In the initial years, great discourse arose with respect to convergence theory that made economists and policy makers put bullet emphasis on the growth of the national product especially in case of impoverished countries. This emphasis on growth of national product was backed by economic logic of narrowing down the high disparities in terms of different characteristics between the nations and regions of the world. But with the passage of time, it was realized that high growth rates and an increase in the GDP per capita provide no guarantee of trickle-down effect. So new aspects were defined and derived to look into the broad issues of development in combination with the process of growth, new dimensions got established to look towards links and lines that can help to broaden the prosperity of the deprived lot.

The trajectory of output growth, more precisely economic growth and its interaction with other phenomena of an economy follows a complex path. Eicher and Turnovsky (2003) from the paper titled "mechanics of economic development" of Robert Lucas (1988) deduced that, "The nature of growth is such that the welfare implications of small (and possibly simple) policy changes can be staggering. Even minute increase in the growth rate can compound into dramatic changes in the living standards over just one generation. However, the precise nature of such growth enhancing policies is often elusive, which highlights that the execution of such policies presupposes a clear understanding of the mechanics of economic growth."

Though every economy in the world is a composite of a number of dynamic and static phenomenon and structures, some processes are such, any extreme outlier can have a devastating effect on the lives of the people, and can give rise to political and social instability. Among many phenomena, the one which has caught the world attention at large scale especially since the work of Piketty and Saez, is the "Rising Inequality in Incomes" especially in the countries which on an international platform were identified as highly developed economies. These developed economies served as the role model and mantra to be followed with respect to policy strategy and economic thinking for decades. Piketty and Saez with the help of tax data available for different countries created a dataset showing the income shares of the top tail of distribution for a very long period. The dataset on incomes of the top percentage of the population shows clearly a rising trend in inequality from almost past 30-year period. One can easily identify the severity of inequalities by looking towards the Gini Coefficients as calculated by the OECD for some of the highly developed countries of the world. For the USA, the Gini index stands at 38 followed by UK, Australia, Canada and France with coefficients 35, 33, 32, and 30, respectively, coming very close to some of the least developed countries of the world. Recently the much talked, discussed, debated, and reviewed, taken as the master class in the twenty-first century namely "Capital in the Twenty First Century" book by Piketty (2014), is wholly concerned with the evolution and level of the incomes of the top income groups especially top 1%. Piketty has shown that the rate of the growth of capital being more than the income growth over time is mainly responsible for the growth of large disparities in incomes.

Even the recent trends for some developing economies are now taking a shift, showing tendencies for an increase in the level of the inequalities with the process of development especially with respect to the third largest economy in the world, India. Many studies show that there is a clear indication that income inequalities have once again started to move in an upward direction. Thus, different questions have been raised about the ongoing development strategy and the forces that are working in the economic sphere to accentuate this dynamism. This study will mainly focus on the dynamics of income distribution, more correctly tries to investigate the movements in the degree of income inequality with respect to various economic forces that have their share in influencing the noisy process of income inequality as revealed by the past research findings.

3.2 Why Care About Inequality?

Here various big questions can be raised why to think of inequalities? What a common man has to do with this phenomenon? Why will a country prioritize inequality as a policy issue in its objectives? Why at international level slogan is raised to look towards growing inequalities within countries and regions? Why not put more emphasis to have high GDP per capita growth rates such that it will take care of other dimensions of the economy? DeSa, U.N. (2013: 25) mentions that, the domination of the debate on inequalities in income, wealth, and consumption is not only because they directly affect the well-being of individuals and society, they also obstruct the opportunities that people can enjoy in their future. There are many studies that talk about the merits of economic inequalities. One among them is that it provides an incentive to work hard and thereby help in pushing the growth rates upward. To look into the matter clearly regarding this shift in the concern with respect to the economic forces involved, one must be familiar with the negative consequences of the rising disparities. Better is to mention some important negative consequences that researchers have found out and which affect the social welfare from one side or the other. Inequality can generate socio-political instability (Alesina and Perroti 1996). It gives rise to economic distortions and disincentives (Alesina et al. 1994; Persson and Tabellini 1994). It can give an evolution to Rent Seeking and Corruption and can increase macroeconomic volatility (Stiglitz 2012). Reduces overall average investment especially in human capital (Galor and Tsiddon 1996). At the world level according to Ranciere and Kumhof (2010), one of the main cause behind the Great Depression of 1930s and Recession of 2007 was the uneven distribution of income. With the increase in the incomes of the top income group before crisis, for poor and middle-income group there was an increase in debt–income ratio.

The above-mentioned consequences in all decrease the living standard of the bottom section of the society and which can directly hamper the growth of income over the long period of time especially in the case of developing countries which contain a heavy chunk of the poor population. So the need of the hour is to find the cause or more specifically factors that affect the distribution of income positively or negatively to a great extent. The foundation for seeing that cause was almost laid by Kuznets (1955).

3.3 Kuznets Hypothesis

In his path-breaking work Simon Kuznets started with some basic and fundamental questions, "*Does inequality in income distribution increase or decrease in the process of a country's economic growth? What factors determine the secular level and trends of income inequalities?*" (Kuznets 1955). In his seminal paper, which Kuznets presented while addressing American economic association, with the help of time series data for the United States, England and Germany and of cross-sectional data involving these three countries as well as Ceylon, India, and Puerto Rico, Simon Kuznets speculated that in the process of economic development, the income inequality usually upsurges during the initial phase, followed by levels off, and finally falloffs during the advanced stage. This relationship later came to be known as Kuznets inverted-U hypothesis. Though there were constraints in terms of availability of a sufficient and reliable data set which Kuznets himself admits, using his intellect he was successful to a great extent to be admired for carrying this great task. He used the ratio of the income of top 20% to that of the bottom 60% of the population (later on came to be known as Kuznets Ratio) as a measure of inequality. He found that this ratio (Kuznets Ratio) for India, Sri Lanka, and Puerto Rica were higher in comparison to the US and UK.

Also in his other study, Kuznets (1963) got further support for his inverted-U hypothesis, which involved finding wide inter-sectoral differences in per capita incomes in the less developed countries caused mainly by the disparities in income per worker between the agricultural sector and the nonagricultural one. A study carried out by Oshima (1962) predicted the same relationship.

Kuznets himself gave the explanation for this phenomenon, by suggesting the presence of a dualistic model which to a large extent is related to the traditional model put forward by Lewis as a model of dualism, "Unlimited supply of labor" (1954). The basic logic behind the whole process provided by Kuznets is that of urbanization and industrialization; as in most underdeveloped economies large proportion of population is involved with the traditional agricultural sector, in the beginning of the economic development, due to higher growth and high level of incomes in the modern industrial sector, the labor force shifts or migrates from the depressed sector to the modern sector, which leads to increase in income inequality as large difference occurs in the mean income levels between the two sectors (Wolff 2009). There are several causes in operation that bring down the level of income inequality. "One of them is the heavy absorption of the labor force by the modern sector. Also because of the migration of people from agriculture to industry, there will be a decrease in the pressure on land, which will lead to increase in incomes of people associated with agriculture. Moreover, within modern sector expansion of education will also result in equal distribution of skills which can help in improving the distribution of income" (Wolff 2009).

Taking per capita income as a gauge of development, though suffers from different limitations of its own, as a good indicator of development, and plot it on the *X*-axis and some measure of income inequality (e.g., *m*) on the *Y*-axis, the plot formed on basis of Kuznets hypothesis looks like an inverted "U" called as Kuznets curve (Fig. 3.1) and accordingly the hypothesis named as Kuznets Inverted-U Hypothesis.

The bond among economic development and inequality is complex. Studies have confirmed that the fruits of economic growth did not operate in such a way to have a trickle-down effect. Though for some countries like India there was a reduction in the poverty level, there seems no positive effect of rising output growth on improving the distribution of income in the past two decades. As pointed by Chakravarty (1987) while speaking about the development policy and planning strategy followed in India after independence noticed that "there was a tolerance

Fig. 3.1 Kuznets curve

towards income inequality, provided it was not excessive and could be seen to result in a higher rate of growth than would be possible otherwise."

There was a gradual shift in the policy strategy from socialist to a market-oriented one in case of India from mid 1980s. From the 1990s, a new turn developed with an accelerated speed of reforms concerning the whole structure of the economy by which the focal point hauled away from state intervention towards liberalization, privatization, and globalization. From academic point of view the change in the policy and planning strategy gave rise to different schools of thought categorically comprising the one who praised reforms with their own judgment of the benefits accrued from the adjustment based on analysis of the better performance of the macro indicators of the economy especially the rise in the GDP and the decrease in the level of poverty. On the other side of the game a broad group of intelligentsia came to the forefront that raised their voice against the vices of the reforms, it gave rise to the "Great Indian Debate on Poverty" which challenged the estimates that were showing a great decline in the poverty levels. The debate does not remain concentrated with the poverty issue; great attention was paid to the next big menace of "Inequality" as both shares a positive link and a kind of interdependence. The estimation of both rural and urban inequality, as well as national inequality in the case of India, rests on the household consumption expenditure surveys of NSSO. A large body of literature is available which have tried to explain regional disparities, rural–urban gap, and inequality in the case of states and also at the national level. This study will add the existing literature by using cointegration approach to analyze the relationship between inequality and its various determinants with the help of time series data.

Very few studies are in existence in the case of India, which has studied the phenomenon of income inequality and its various determinants on a longitudinal base. The reason is mainly that of the unavailability of time series data. This study will make use of the time series data estimated by Galbraith et al. (2014) under UTIP-UNIDO project and also will focus on how the income of top 1% is related to determinants of inequality

Mainly we will focus on;

- To investigate the relevance of Kuznets U hypothesis in case of India.
- To assess the direction and degree by which government expenditure, price level, and trade openness affect the income distribution.
- To investigate the relationship between the income of top 1% of population and government expenditure, real GDP per capita, trade openness and price level.

3.4 Review of Literature

The empirical work carried out by Kuznets (1955), though controversial, became the base and the reference work for further research on the subject. Thereafter, research was carried out to analyze how the level of development affects the personal distribution of income and what other factors work in the economy that have their influence on the rising or falling of income inequality. Ahluwalia (1976) used multivariate regression to estimate cross-country relationship for a sample of 60 countries including 40 developing, 14 develop and six socialist countries. Modeling two separate equations one for full sample of 60 countries controlling for socialism by introducing dummy variable in order to capture higher degree of equality observed in socialist countries and another restricted to 40 developing countries by regressing inequality measured as income share of the lowest 40 and 60%, and top 20% of population on per capita GNP and other related variables he found a strong support for Kuznets hypothesis. Using internationally comparable data set for 32 countries both developed as well developing on the household income distribution, Ram (1988) with the help quadratic regression model where real per capita income was put in log form, found some empirical support for the inverted-U hypothesis. Anand and Kanbur (1993a, b) studied Kuznets hypothesis and the underlying pattern followed by Kuznets process when different indices are used to measure inequality. Using Ahluwalia's data set they (Anand and Kanbur) did not find such type of relationship as was visualized by him, so from their results they inferred that the Kuznets relationship is missing. A lasting contribution in the area of studying development and inequality nexus came from Deininger and Squire (1996, 1998) in the form of compilation of a panel dataset for a vast majority of countries of the world which provided a new enthusiasm for the future research in this field by making use of panel and time series models to analyze the stylized hypothesis for individual countries based on almost a reliable dataset. Making use of their data set they failed to establish the very link in the vast majority of countries. They found little support for Kuznets hypothesis as either it was too flat to be noticeable or irrelevant for developing countries.

To overcome the limitation of parametric regressions, there are some studies which by using different econometric techniques have come with mixed support for Kuznets hypothesis. Among many studies, Ogwang (1994), Mushinski (2001), Frazer (2006), Zhou and Li (2011) used nonparametric and semiparametric regression and Lin et al. (2007) using parametric quantile regression model found mixed support for Kuznets hypothesis. Besides that many researchers used different models and made use of different macro variables which can influence the distribution of income. Daudey and Gracia-Penalosa (2007) taking a diversion from the previous studies, analyzed how the factor shares or rewards affect the personal distribution of income, showed that a higher labor share is associated with a lesser inequality. Angeles (2010) taking a new direction, used employment outside agriculture as the main regressor to test the Kuznets hypothesis using panel data, he does not find any support for Kuznets hypothesis. There are studies which are mainly country specific which also show variance in results. Based on surveys from 1975 to 1998 analyzing increasing inequality in Thailand, Motonishi (2006) in case of South Korea between 1975 and 1995 Sato et al. (2009) found limited support. Ho-chuan et al. (2012) reassessed the rationality of the Kuznets hypothesis with the help of alternative test strategy of Lind and Mehlum (2010). The empirical results overwhelmingly reject the inverted U relationship. To analyze the influence of urbanization on expenditure inequality in Indonesia, Sagala et al. (2013) performed panel data regression analysis in case of 33 provinces of Indonesia from 2000 to 2009. They found an inverted U relationship exists whether Gini coefficient or Thiel's index is used.

Bahmani-Oskoee and Gelan (2008) by data from 1957 to 2002 for US with the help of Cointegration and Error Correction Modeling techniques found that in short-run economic growth worsens income inequality and in long run it leads to reduction in income inequality. Shahbaz (2010) explored the relationship considering other factors also for Pakistan with the help autoregressive distributed lag model (ARDL) and error correction model (ECM). The results revealed that there exist support for Kuznets curve, and when the cubic term was used for lnGDP per capita, the results confirmed the occurrence of inverted S-shaped curve. For other variables related to inequality measured in terms of Gini coefficient, he found that HDI and unemployment seem to increase inequality and urbanization decrease inequality in the long run. Similarly, literacy rate, life expectancy, and FDI showed a worsening impact on the distribution of income. Investigating Chinese economy from 1978 to 2011 Cheng and Wu (2014) employed ARDL technique of Pesaran and Shin (1998) and identified an inverted relationship in terms of both Theils index as well as Gini coefficient. They found urbanization as the main driving force behind the relation which was captured by way of including a square term for urbanization in the model. In a panel of 31 countries divided into lower middle, upper middle and higher income countries covering period from 1990 to 2011, employing General Method of Moments (GMM) Lim and Kun Sek (2014) found only a one-way relationship between inequality and growth. It is growth that affects inequality positively and significantly with respect to high-income countries, no effect from the results was seen of inequality for all the groups. Regarding India, to examine the validity of Kuznets hypothesis for Indian Economy, Sinha (2004) investigated the relationship between inequality and per capita income during the period 1980–81 through 1997–98. Based on the data from Ahluwalia (2000) for interstate inequality and Rao et al. (1999) for national inequality measured in terms of Gini coefficients, found that there exists an augmented Kuznets curve in the form of S-shaped relationship between inequality and growth rather than U or inverted U. In a working paper, Pal and Ghosh (2007) surveyed comprehensively about the recent trends in the inequality in India. Though different studies carried out on basis of NSSO data revealed a mixed evidence about the aggregate and regional trends in inequality, but after careful analysis they came to the conclusion that after economic liberalization in the 1990s, there seems evidence regarding the increase in inequality (horizontal as well a vertical) as well as persistent poverty.

In order to investigate how financial development and financial reforms affects inequality measured in terms of Gini coefficient, Ang (2010) using time series data for India estimated that underdevelopment of the financial system results in higher income inequality. Taking the same stand like Ang (2010), from a different perspective Tiwari et al. (2013) investigated, how financial development and its square term capture the inverted relationship in India and its effects on rural–urban inequality. They used ARDL approach for the annual data from 1965 to 2008. The study revealed that financial development, economic growth, and inflation have a negative and highly significant bearing on rural–urban inequality, meaning that these factors aggravate rural–urban income inequality. In the short-run output growth and inflation lower rural–urban income inequality and trade openness increases it. A brief and careful review of relevant literature and analysis of empirical studies shows that there does not exist any clear evidence; one can put forward to get a perfect support for the inverted-U hypothesis. What we have seen is that empirical findings vary a lot from study to study. As our study will mainly focus India, we have seen a dearth in terms of time series analysis of the relationship between inequality and its various determinants.

3.5 Methodology and Model Specification

3.5.1 Variables Description

3.5.1.1 Trade Openness (TO)

It is simply computed as the ratio of the sum of total exports and imports, to the gross domestic product of a country. There is a straight positive connection between trade liberalization and trade openness. The reforms of the 1990s in India laid down also different procedures to increase the domestic economy's integration with the rest of the world and make a roadway towards competition instead of protection. Though from the beginning, the process of liberalization came under criticism from different thinkers and researchers, according to whom it was not the right time for the country to adopt such a regime in the backdrop of the low living standard of more than half of population. Before focusing on local studies, it is better to understand the framework that the economic theory builds in order to analyze how trade affects the country's income distribution. From the very basic theory, an increase in international trade increases the relative share of abundant factor (Stolper and Samuelson 1941). From this perspective, one can hope that India being a labor-abundant country, trade liberalization must have led to increase in the wages especially of unskilled labor, so a decrease in wage inequality might have happened in the context of the theory. Bensidoun et al. (2005) found that trade has a negative effect on poor because most exporting firms use educated labor. In case of India Kumar and Mishra (2008) while analyzing the impact of 1991s trade liberalization on the industry wage structure found that it has a positive bearing on the relative incomes of the unskilled labor. On the basis of their findings, they came to the conclusion that trade liberalization has led to a decline in wage inequality.

The interest in analyzing the effects of trade liberalization got further momentum when some studies found that income inequality in 90s has increased especially during 1994 and 2000. Krishna and Sethupathy (2011) using Thiel's index with respect to different states of India found that both tariff and nontariff measures of protection were uncorrelated with income inequality. According to them, though trade can have a positive impact on income distribution and abundant factor can receive an increasing share but certain factors may come in the way that can disturb this process. As different regions vary in terms of development levels, so there can exist differences in terms of access to trade, which can give way to increase in regional inequalities. Also as in the case of developing economies, there exists a restricted mobility in factors of production, that in turn can create allocative inefficiency. Thus the benefit of trade, in that case, cannot be harmonized. There may also exist economies of scale which can lead to the problem of agglomeration and fruits of economic progress in such case can get concentrated within some narrow area and other regions may fall back to keep track with developing regions in such instance. Such type of examples can be clearly noticed in the context of India where some states enjoy a kind of hegemony in terms of the industrial base and all other states with differences are lagging behind. To comment further on the issue of trade liberalization and its influence, better is to keep in mind what Baghwati and Srinivasan (2002, p. 7) have said about the issue;

> While freer trade, or "openness" in trade, is now widely regarded as economically benign, in the sense that it increases the size of the pie, the recent anti-globalization critics have suggested that it is socially malign on several dimensions, among them the question of poverty. Their contention is that trade accentuates not ameliorates, deepens not diminishes, poverty in both the rich and the poor countries the theoretical and empirical analysis of the impact of the freer trade on poverty in the rich and in the poor countries is not symmetric, of course.

So to serve the purpose we will also include it as a control variable in order to analyze its impact with respect to the national inequality level. As an explanatory variable, it is first better to look how its dimension has changed over the period of time and at what pace it has moved. For that, it is better to look it in Fig. 3.2, as can be visualized almost up to 1990 the process was almost static, with the reforms a dynamic change occurred which over the period of time has moved at an accelerated speed supported by the policies of ease followed by the government from time to time.

3.5.1.2 Consumer Price Index (CPI)

Prices play a vibrant role in shaping the structure and process of the dynamism of the economy. One of the important objectives of the monetary policy of any country is the stability of prices and accordingly, policies from time to time are designed to check their diversion from the viable path. Prices act as a conditioning variable to transform nominal incomes into a particular utility or welfare level. So any movement in them can affect the welfare of households positively or negatively given the income level of households. In another way, they show the real value of the money income of a person theoretically defined as purchasing power. One limitation in case of prices as a better indicator of the welfare level of the

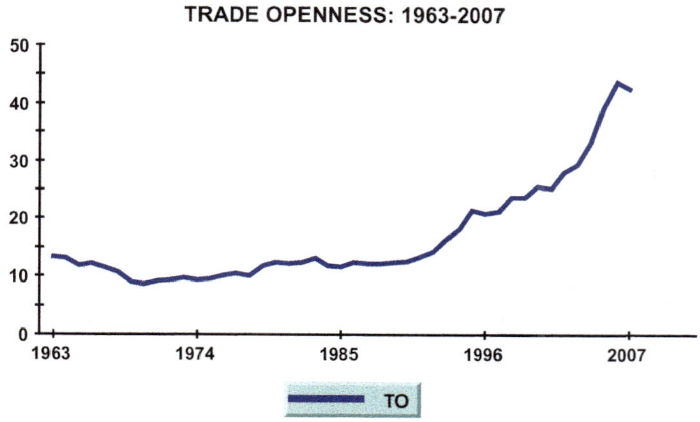

Fig. 3.2 Trend of trade openness 1963–2007

individuals is because of the differences that exist in terms of the differing pattern of expenditure of households (Oosthuizen 2007). In what way prices exert their influence on the income inequality, there are both positive as well as negative findings revealed by the past research. Studies by Datt and Ravallion (1998), Ferreira et al. (2007), Litchfield (2001), Blejer and Guearero (1990) showed that higher inflation worsens the income distribution by lowering the relative share of income held by the poor. Walsh and Yu (2012) analyzing the impact of inflation both food and nonfood, found that higher nonfood inflation is associated with worsening of income inequality at world level and individually for China and India also. According to him the logic behind this result is that individual household's income can benefit from higher prices only for goods and services they produce, and there is no individual likely to be producer of a sufficiently big share of nonfood items. Looking towards Fig. 3.3, one can easily derive the conclusion that from the start there exists rising trend in prices, though the speed of trend increases clearly after the reforms as preference shifted from government restricted model to the open market one. Ravallion (2000) while analyzing the relationship between food prices, poverty, and wages in India found that food prices do not appear to have an independent effect on rural wages. From his findings, he concluded that initially food prices can hit rural households, but in long run, due to increase in rural productivity the negative effect can be mitigated and also the effect of higher prices will be neutral in situations where a perfect adjustment in wages takes place with respect to the price increase. But there are studies that suggest that wages may not fully adjust to higher food prices. Thus poor will suffer more as food has a greater share in their consumption basket (Walsh and Yu 2012).

The conventional economic theory exposes several links through which increasing prices can have an adverse effect on the income or welfare of the people. Among one of them is the reducing ability to borrow of the poor households, so due to inflation they will fail to continue the consumption at previous levels which can

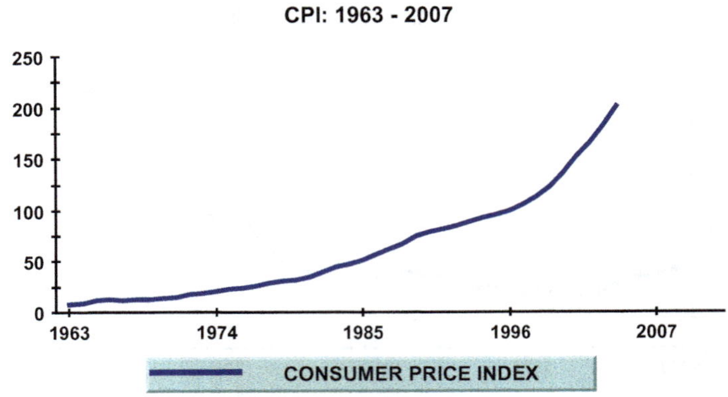

Fig. 3.3 Trend of consumer price index

in broad terms accentuate the problem of inequality. Another is the saving link; with inflation the savings of individuals with low incomes may see a decline. Thus, they in no way can make productive investments, broadening the disparity between them and those at the top level of income. With respect to India, this study will try to investigate whether any such relationship between inflation and income distribution exists or not.

3.5.1.3 Government Expenditure (GEXP)

Throughout history, the effective working of the economy has mostly rested on the well-functioning of the institutions present within the national territorial boundaries. Almost all the economies which are viewed as market economies, one can easily visualize that in no way the design of the policies catering to the needs and the welfare of the society rests perfectly on the public institutions working side by side with the private Diasporas. However, with respect to the importance of public body, there developed a lot of differences among the scholars from time to time. Looking from the mainstream economics dimension, one can expect a less relevance to a government institution to be involved in the economic activity, and it looks great to restrict its influence within some narrow matters mostly peace and security. It was within this context Washington Consensus of 1989 came to the forefront though the emphasis on it does not come from thin air. There exist some shortcomings or cons within the government sector one can easily spot. But a clear analysis, taking the ills of free market into consideration, there exists a large empty space with respect to those dimensions which has a direct bearing on the living standards of people, giving ample room for the government sector to interfere in the economic policy designing for a country. Not pulling the stretches more, better is to look deep within the existing economic research which broadly has investigated the impact and influences that government spending or more exactly the fiscal policy can exert within the space of income distribution.

Chu et al. (2000) found that income distribution before tax is less unequal in developing countries than developed ones, but they have failed to use the revenue generated from taxes to reduce the inequality levels properly. In a cross-country study Mello and Tlongson (2003) came to the conclusion that more unequal societies do spend less on redistribution; and also the results showed that periods of sustained growth are associated with reductions in poverty but no guarantee that this will make improvements in income distribution. Fiscal policies have been significant in bringing down income inequality in advanced countries, but a decline was visualized since the reforms of mid-1990s (Bastagli et al. 2012). To see the influence of communist regime Bandelj and Mahutga (2010) while analyzing Central and Eastern Europe came with the findings that income inequality has increased after the fall of communist regime in these countries. According to them the main forces which shaped the unequal distribution include expansion of the private sector, shrinkage in redistribution, and most importantly the injection of foreign investment in the domestic market.

As the main aim of social programs is to shift the national pie towards the bottom sections of the population, Salloti and Trecroci (2013) found that government spending improves the income distribution and in the reverse fiscal consolidation deteriorates it. There exist different links through which government expenditure can affect the distribution. Among them, the important ones are health expenditure and spending on education which have much to do with the welfare of the poor sections. Without the presence of public sector in those areas, a significant disturbance will occur because private sector in no way is going to do well in providing these necessary goods at an affordable price. Much of the research shows that health expenditure and spending on education improves the distribution of income in the long run. Almost much of the differences in the wage incomes are because of the differences in the skills that to a great degree depends on the level and quality of education. Indeed due to large disparities in the income levels, much of the poor strata will fail to achieve good skills as demanded by the labor market. It is in such situation there exists a dire need for the government intervention to have a large proportion of the revenue to spend on the basic services which otherwise can distort the social structure if market intervenes. It in no way means that government expenditure in all would guarantee the increase in the welfare levels, there are models which from time to time have come on the screen and have put a red mark on the work of public authority. One among them is the breeding corruption, which overall has a negative impact on the distribution of income. The biggest fault in such case is that on welfare basis more disparity will be created by creating unearned riches for the bureaucratic class.

In this study, due to methodological concerns, total government expenditure variable (GEXP) instead of government final consumption expenditure was used. The difference between them is that the total government expenditure variable

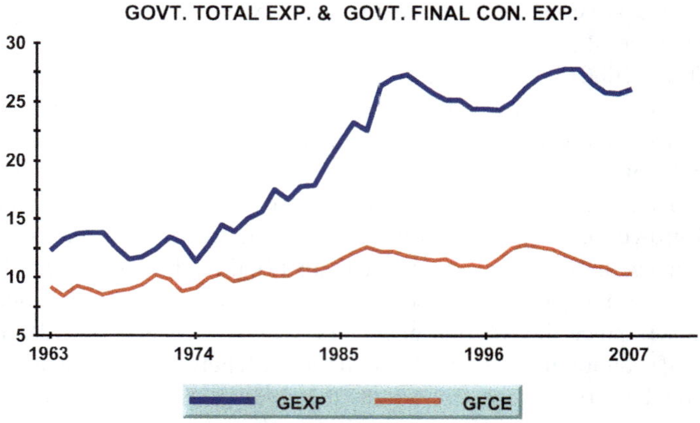

Fig. 3.4 Govt. total and final consumption expenditure in India

involves the later (government final consumption expenditure) and also it includes the expenditure that increases the assets of the state. So total government spending is the mixture of social spending as well as investment expenditure. From Fig. 3.4, one can easily identify the effect of the reforms of the 1990s in the form of the decline in the total expenditure though for a short time. But it can be seen that the growth before the reforms became stagnant after the reform period. After the great recession of the 2007 new thinking has developed which has once again provided the room for the government intervention. But because of the rising deficits more emphasis are put on the fiscal consolidation in case of India. Assuming government spending as a positive factor to improve the distribution of income, this paper tries to explore the dynamics of this relationship.

3.6 Model Specification

This work aims to investigate the Kuznets Hypothesis in the case of India empirically. There are many techniques in econometric literature to analyze the long-run relationship among various macroeconomic factors of interest empirically. For bivariate analysis, Engle-Granger (1987), and Fully Modified Ordinary Least Square (FOMLS) (Hansen and Phillips 1990) methods are noticeable. While for multivariate cointegration, Johansen (1988); Johansen and Juselius (1990); and Johansen's (1995) are common. All of the above techniques require that all e same order of integration. If the order of integration among variables is different, it will create inefficiency and hence affecting the predictive powers (Kim et al. 2011; Perron 1989, 1997). Autoregressive Distributive Lag Model (ARDL) or ARDL bounds test developed by Pesaran et al. (2001) approach to cointegration overcomes major limitation of the above procedures along with some additional improvements (see for the details Nain and Kamaiah 2012; Ahmad et al. 2014; Nain et al. 2017; among others) that has been used in this study. As time series data is used in this study, it is important to check for stationarity of variables before running the causality tests. The ARDL bounds test assumes that the variables should be $I(0)$ or $I(1)$. So, before applying this test, we determine the order of integration of all variables so as to ensure none of them is $I(2)$ by using the unit root tests. In this study we have used conventional Augmented Dickey–Fuller (ADF) tests, the Phillips-Perron test following Phillips and Perron (1988) and KPSS, The ARDL model used in this study is expressed as follows:

$$\begin{aligned}\Delta \mathrm{LGINI}_t = {} & C_0 + \delta_1 \mathrm{LGINI}_{t-1} + \delta_2 \mathrm{LRGDPC}_{t-1} + \delta_3 \mathrm{LCPI}_{t-1} + \delta_4 \mathrm{LGEXP}_{t-1} \\ & + \delta_5 \mathrm{LTO}_{t-1} + \sum_{i-1}^{p} \phi_i \Delta \mathrm{LGINI}_{t-i} + \sum_{j-1}^{q} \omega_j \Delta \mathrm{LRGDPC}_{t-j} + \sum_{l-1}^{q} \varphi_i \Delta \mathrm{LCPI}_{t-l} \\ & + \sum_{m-1}^{q} \gamma_m \Delta \mathrm{LGEXP}_{t-m} + \sum_{p-1}^{q} \eta_p \Delta \mathrm{LTO}_{t-p} + \varepsilon_t \end{aligned} \tag{3.1}$$

where δ_i are the long-run multipliers, c_0 is the drift and ε_t are the white noise errors. The first step in the ARDL bounds testing approach is to estimate Eq. (3.1) by ordinary least squares (OLS) to test for the existence of a long-run relationship among the variables. To examine the presence of long-run association among variables, the below hypothesis is tested based upon F-test given by Pesaran et al. (2001). This test is simply a hypothesis of no cointegration against the existence of cointegration among the variables.

$$H_N : \delta_1 = \delta_2 = \delta_3 = \delta_4 = \delta_5 = 0$$

i.e., there is no cointegration among the variables, against the alternative,

$$H_A : \delta_1 \neq \delta_2 \neq \delta_3 \neq \delta_4 \neq \delta_5 \neq 0$$

i.e., there is cointegration among the variables.

In the second step, once cointegration is established the conditional ARDL $(p, q_1, q_2, q_3, q_4, \ldots q_k)$ long-run model for GINI_t can be estimated as:

$$\begin{aligned}\mathrm{LGINI}_t = {} & c_0 + \sum_{i-1}^{p} \delta_1 \mathrm{LGINI}_{t-i} \sum_{i-0}^{q_1} \delta_2 \mathrm{LRGDPC}_{t-1} + \sum_{i-0}^{q_2} \delta_2 \mathrm{LCPI}_{t-i} \\ & + \sum_{i-0}^{q_2} \delta_4 \mathrm{LGEXP}_{t-i} + \sum_{i-0}^{q_4} \delta_5 \mathrm{LTO}_{t-i} + \varepsilon_t \end{aligned} \tag{3.2}$$

The above specification is also based on the assumption that the error terms are serially uncorrelated for given specification. Therefore, it is imperative that the lag order (p) of the underlying process is selected appropriately. The orders of variables in the ARDL $(p, q_1, q_2, q_3, q_4, \ldots q_k)$ model are selected using different information criteria widely used in the literature like Akaike Information Criteria (AIC), Schwarz Bayesian Criterion (SBC), etc.

In the final step, short-run dynamic parameters are estimated by an error correction model associated with the long-run estimates. The specification runs as:

$$\begin{aligned}\Delta \text{LGINI}_t = \mu + \sum_{t-1}^{l} \phi_1 \Delta \text{LGINI}_{t-i} \sum_{t-1}^{M} \omega_2 \Delta \text{LRGDPC}_{t-1} + \sum_{l-1}^{M} \varphi_1 \text{LCPI}_{t-1} \\ + \sum_{m-1}^{q} \gamma_m \text{LGEXP}_{t-m} + \sum_{\sigma-1}^{q} \eta_\sigma \text{LTO}_{t-\sigma} + \zeta \text{ecm}_{t-1} + \varepsilon_t\end{aligned} \tag{3.3}$$

Here $\phi, \omega, \varphi, \gamma,$ and η are the short-run dynamic coefficients of the model's convergence to equilibrium and ζ is the speed of adjustment. Besides, various diagnostic tests are used to ascertain the efficiency, unbiasedness, and stability of the estimates.

In the present study, for the inequality index we will wholly rely on the dataset from UTIP-UNIDO, which contains a time series account of the augmented Gini coefficient created by the Galbraith and Kum (2005) for a number of countries. The inequality measure available exists under the name of Estimated Household Income Inequality (EHII) for a time period from 1963 to 2007. Revealing the merits of the index Galbraith et al. (2014) notes that the measure is a useful alternative to other available inequality measures from different studies; it is more steady than the collations of the World Bank and WIDER. They concluded that EHII works fine in analyzing the trend of inequality and is near to the "survey based measures as an estimate of the gross income inequality". The only demerit according to them is that it does not capture fluctuations in capital mainly a problem in the US case. In our study, we will take EHII as Gini coefficient.

Besides that, to measure the robustness of the results to be derived from using EHII, we will use income share of top 1% as an alternate index for inequality, data for it is taken from the data set compiled by Piketty et al. available at the World Top Income Database for a period from 1973 to 1999. The list of independent variables include real per capita GDP and its Square term to capture the inverted U relationship, consumer price index to capture the effect of increase in prices as witnessed in case of India, General Government Total Expenditure to see the influence of government interference in the economy and Trade openness to measure the effect of globalization which received heavy criticism from different corners. The data for real GDP per capita with \$ as a unit of measurement (RGDPC) and Trade openness as a share of GDP has been taken from Heston et al. Pen World Table Version 7.1 (2012). The data from that is accepted as a reliable source throughout the world. It gives due consideration to the difference existing between countries with respect to purchasing power parity (PPP) to measure the real GDP per capita (RGDPC). For consumer price index (CPI), annual series data with the base year 2005 has been taken from World Bank. With respect to Total Government expenditure as a share of GDP, we have totally relied upon International Monetary Fund which collects statistics on the total expenditure of the general government available within country-specific data collecting bodies. The study utilizes annual time series data from 1963 to 2007 for the variables Gini Coefficients, real GDP Per Capita, consumer price index, trade openness and general government total expenditure. But for the variable share of gross domestic product by top 1% of population data is taken from 1973 to 1998. Notations of the variables used in the study hereafter are as follows:

- LGINI and LTOP are the measures of inequality in the model A and B respectively.
- LRGDPC is the natural log of real gross domestic product per capita.
- LRGDPSQ is the natural log of the square of the real gross domestic product.
- LCPI is the natural log of the combined consumer price index.
- LGEXP is the natural log of total government expenditure.
- LTO is the natural log of the ratio of exports and imports as the share of gross domestic product and taken as a measure of trade openness.

3.7 Empirical Analysis

To assess the stationarity of the variables, we have used three alternative unit root tests viz, ADF (Augmented Dickey–Fuller), PP (Phillips–Perron), and KPSS (Kwiatkowski–Phillips–Schmidt–Shin). The results of the unit root tests are shown in Table 3.1. This is to confirm that no variable is integrated of order $I(2)$. In case some variable is $I(2)$, ARDL is inappropriate due to invalid calculated F-statistics (Ouattara 2004).

3.7.1 Model A

The testing procedure of the ARDL involves three stages. The first step involves the selection of lag order on the basis of different criteria for the selection of lag order because the value of F-statistic is very much sensitive to lag order. So lag order 4 is chosen considering lowest value of the AIC and SBC as shown in Table 3.2.

First, we took LGINI as dependent variable with LRGDPC, LGEXP as independent variables and imposed 3, 2, 2 lags, respectively, and found evidence of cointegration on the basis of calculated F-statistic of 4.959, greater than the critical level of the upper bound [see Pesaran et al. 2001 (Table CI (iii), case (III), with 3.79 $I(0)$ and 4.85 $I(1)$ at 0.05 level of sig.)]. The next step is to estimate parameters of the model and check for various diagnostic tests needed for a good model. Looking at Table 3.3 for diagnostic tests shows that the results are free from the problem of

Table 3.1 Unit root tests result

Variables	ADF		PP		KPSS	
	Level	First difference	Level	First difference	Level	First difference
LGINI	-1.972	−5.722*	−1.975	−5.733*	0.525	0.162
	(0.297)	(0.000)	(0.296)	(0.000)	(0.463)	(0.463)
LRGDPC	3.132	−5.573*	5.989	−5.584*	0.848	0.688
	(1.000)	(0.000)	(1.000)	(0.000)	(0.463)	(0.463)
LTO	2.161	−4.762*	1.770	−4.740*	0.711	0.605
	(0.999)	(−0.000)	(0.999)	(0.000)	(0.463)	(0.463)
LGEXP	−1.002	−5.891*	−1.015	−5.885*	0.763	0.146
	(0.744)	(0.000)	(0.739)	(0.000)	(0.463)	(0.463)
LCPI	−0.718	−5.289*	−1.000	−4.565*	0.839	0.160
	(0.830)	(−0.000)	(0.744)	(0.000)	(0.463)	(0.463)
LTOP	−1.713	−6.451*	−1.763	−6.415*	0.179	0.174
	(0.416)	(0.000)	(0.391)	(0.000)	(0.463)	(0.463)

Notes (i) The values in the parenthesis are *P*-values for ADF and PP, while for KPSS they are critical values at 5% level of significance
(ii) *indicates significant at 1% level of significance

Table 3.2 Lag order selection criteria for model A

Order of lags	AIC	SBC
1	136.6	131.32
2	130.12	120.56
3	123.6	109.9
4	121.08*	103.2*

*indicates optimal lag selection

Table 3.3 Diagnostic tests for ARDL model with variables LGINI, LGDP, LEXP

Test statistics	LM version	*F* version
A:Serial correlation	CHSQ(1) = 0.6050E−5[0.998]	*F*(1, 30) = 0.4537E−5[0.998]
B:Functional form	CHSQ(1) = 0.079178[0.778]	*F*(1, 30) = 0.059501[0.809]
C:Normality	CHSQ(2) = 0.10692[0.948]	Not applicable
D:Heteroscedasticity	CHSQ(1) = 0.033951[0.854]	*F*(1, 38) = 0.032281[0.858]

Note A:Lagrange multiplier test of residual serial correlation
B:Ramsey's RESET test using the square of the fitted values
C:Based on a test of skewness and kurtosis of residuals
D:Based on the regression of squared residuals on squared fitted values

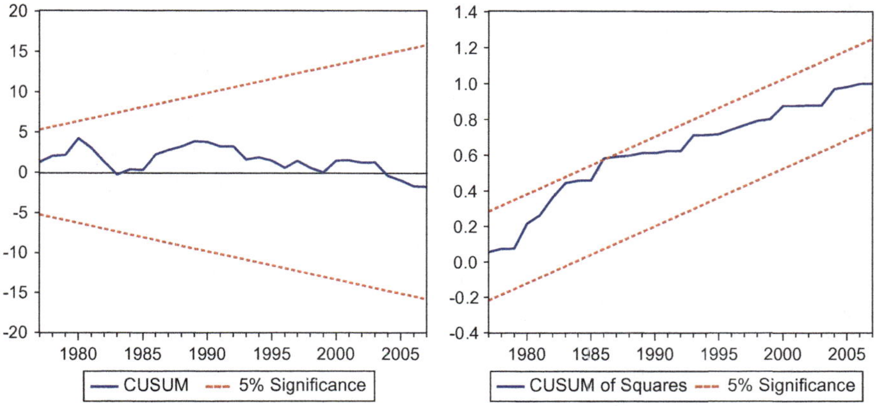

Fig. 3.5 Plot of cumulative sum and square of recursive residuals for model A

heteroscedasticity and serial correlation. The functional form is correct and the assumption of normality also gets satisfied.

Moreover the cumulative sum (CUSUM) and cumulative sum of squares (CUSUMsq) tests are also done (Fig. 3.5). These figures show that CUSUM and CUSUM square statistics are within 5% confidence interval bands which indicate the stability of estimates.

3.7.2 Long-Run and Short-Run Coefficients for Model A

The estimated long-run coefficients using the ARDL approach are reported in Table 3.4. The results indicate that RGDPC is associated positively and is statistically highly significant with income inequality. The coefficient of government expenditure is statistically significant at 5% level with a negative sign indicating that the increase in government expenditure results in the reduction of income inequality. Thus, we can say that with the increase in the level of development in terms of GDP Per Capita there is an increase in the inequality in the long run.

With respect to short run, the estimates show a change in sign and significance at levels. At lag 1 and 2 the coefficient of LRGDP per capita shows a significant negative relationship, means that in a short run increase in lagged GDP per capita is followed by decrease in inequality. So based on short run and long-run estimates following Bahmani-Oskoee and Gelan (2008), we may conclude that in the beginning with the increase in the level of development there is a decrease in inequality, but over the period of time inequality starts to increase with the increase in the level of development. So that means there is a U-shaped relationship instead of Kuznets inverted U. In case of Govt. expenditure, the results show a significant lagged positive effect on inequality, opposite to the long-run estimates. The sign of

Table 3.4 Long- and short-run estimates for model with variables LGINI, LEXP, LGDP

Regressor	Coefficient	Standard error	*T*-ratio[prob]
Long run estimates			
LRGDPC	0.137	0.043	3.202[0.003]*
LGEXP	−0.092	0.040	−2.313[0.028]**
C	3.240	0.201	16.183[0.000]*
Short-run estimates (ECM model)			
dLRGDPC	−0.023	0.048	−0.489[0.628]
dLRGDPC1	−0.127	0.051	−2.465[0.019]**
dLRGDPC2	−0.101	0.051	−2.015[0.052]***
dLGEXP	−0.015	0.021	−0.691[0.494]
dLGEXP1	0.061	0.023	2.677[0.011]**
ecm(−1)	−0.261	0.075	3.168[0.003]*

Note *, **, *** used for 1%, 5% and 10% level of significance respectively

ECM term being negative with a high level of significance provides the additional proof of stable long-run relationship (Banerjee et al. 1998; Shahbaz 2010). From Table 3.4 it is clear that the coefficient of ECMt-1 is equal to −0.261 and statistically significant at 1% level of significance. There by implying that the deviance from short run is corrected by 26.05% over each year in long run.

To fully capture Kuznets inverted U we will make use of Square of GDP per capita like previous researches (Table 3.5). Accordingly, we found that for both GDP per capita and its square estimates are insignificant. However, for govt. expenditure coefficient is once again negative and significant. The insertion of Sq. term for GDP per capita affects its significance, but the sign remains same.

Besides that, we tried to use variables like price level and trade openness as control variables as revealed from the literature to analyze how they affect income inequality in case of India. First using only price level with the GDP per capita and govt. expenditure, we find that there exists cointegration among these three variables having lag order (3 2 2 1) respectively with F-statistic equal to 4.42 $F(4, 27)$ which is greater than the upper bound as given in Pesaran et al. (2001) at 5% level of significance [Table CI (iii), case (III), with 3.23 $I(0)$ and 4.35 $I(1)$, for $K = 4$ at 0.05 level of sig. Pesaran et al. (2001)]. Also, diagnostic tests were found satisfactory. The long-run estimates as in Table 3.6 show that price level is positively related to inequality and accordingly expenditure has a same negative effect on it as

Table 3.5 Long run estimate for model with square of GDP per capita

Regressor	Coefficient	Standard error	*T*-ratio[prob]
LRGDPC	1.177	1.695	0.694[0.493]
LRGDPSQ	−0.068	0.116	−0.590[0.560]
LGEXP	−0.143	0.067	−2.129[0.042]**
C	−0.537	6.042	−0.089[0.930]

Note *, **, *** used for 1%, 5% and 10% level of significance respectively

Table 3.6 Long- and short-run estimates for model including variable CPI

Regressor	Coefficient	Standard error	*T*-ratio[prob]
Long run estimates			
LRGDPC	−0.062	0.054	−1.149[0.259]
LCPI	0.079	0.029	2.712[0.011]**
LGEXP	−0.142	0.046	−3.058[0.004]*
C	4.522	0.366	12.339[0.000]*
Short-run estimates (ECM model)			
dLRGDPC	−0.018	0.016	−1.173[0.249]
dLCPI	0.024	0.009	2.590[0.014]**
dLGEXP	−0.029	0.022	−1.350[0.186
dLGEXP1	0.072	0.023	3.074[0.004]*
ecm(−1)	−0.300	0.080	−3.728[0.001]*

Note *, **, *** used for 1%, 5% and 10% level of significance respectively

was noticed earlier. But in this case, both sign, as well as the significance of GDP per capita, has changed may be due to high multicollinearity with the CPI.

Taking trade openness (TO) also as the independent variable, we got *F*-statistic 4.16 with the lag order of 3,2,1,2,1 for LGini, LRGDPC, LCPI, LGEXP, and TO, respectively, which is greater than upper bound value of Pesaran et al. (2001), (Table CI(iii), case (III), with 2.86 *I*(0) and 4.01 *I*(1) at 0.05 level of sig.), thus confirms presence of cointegration. The results in Table 3.7 show the diagnostic tests for the model, all tests are satisfactory.

The estimated long-run coefficients using the ARDL approach are reported in Table 3.8. The results indicate that RGDPC is associated negatively but statistically insignificant with income inequality. The results also reveal that the consumer price index (CPI) is associated positively and significantly at 2% level of significance with income inequality. In other words, we can say that a rise in CPI leads to higher income inequality. The coefficient of government expenditure is statistically significant with a negative sign indicating that the increase in government expenditure results in the reduction of income inequality. The coefficient of trade openness is negative thereby implying that as the country approach more and more toward free

Table 3.7 Diagnostic tests for ARDL model including CPI and TO besides other variables

Test statistics	LM version	*F* version
A:Serial correlation	CHSQ(1) = 0.037[0.847]	*F*(1, 31) = 0.029[0.866]
B:Functional form	CHSQ(1) = 0.059[0.807]	*F*(1, 31) = 0.046[0.831]
C:Normality	CHSQ(2) = 0.352[0.838]	Not applicable
D:Heteroscedasticity	CHSQ(1) = 0.702[0.402]	*F*(1, 38) = 0.679[0.415]

A:Lagrange multiplier test of residual serial correlation
B:Ramsey's RESET test using the square of the fitted values
C:Based on a test of skewness and kurtosis of residuals
D:Based on the regression of squared residuals on squared fitted values

Table 3.8 Long- and short-run Est. ARDL model including CPI and TO besides other variables

Regressor	Coefficient	Standard error	*T*-ratio[prob]
Long run estimates			
LRGDPC	0.033	0.085	0.385[0.703]
LCPI	0.084	0.032	2.625[0.013]**
LGEXP	−0.157	0.06	2.618[0.013]**
LTO	−0.023	0.053	−0.42942[0.670]
CON	4.404	0.452	9.750[0.00]*
Short-run estimates (ECM model)			
dLRGDPC	−0.009	0.026	−0.387[0.701]
dLCPI	0.025	0.01	2.514[0.017]**
dLGEXP	−0.034	0.025	−1.380[0.177]
dLGEXP1	0.074	0.024	3.057[0.004]*
dLTO	−0.007	0.016	−0.429[0.671]
ecm(−1)	−0.302	0.081	−3.702[0.001]*

Note *, **, *** used for 1%, 5% and 10% level of significance respectively

trade, income inequality tends to decline. Looking at the coefficients, the impact of government expenditure on income inequality is highest followed by real GDP per capita and trade openness with Consumer price index having an adverse impact.

After the investigation of long-run relationship among the variables, the subsequent stage is to obtain the short-run dynamics of these variables. The results are presented in Table 3.8. An ECM (Error Correction Model) has two important parts. First, estimated short-run coefficients and the second one, error correction term (ECT) which provides the feedback or the speed of adjustment from short-run to long-run equilibrium. From Table 3.8, it is clear that the coefficient of ECMt-1 is equal to −0.301 and statistically significant at 1% level of significance. It thus implies that the aberration from short run is corrected by 30.181% over each year in the long run.

The short-run results also point that inequality decreases with increase in real GDP per capita, but the coefficient is statistically insignificant. The coefficient of CPI is positive and statistically significant, there by implying that increase in CPI inflation leads to worsening of income distribution. Similarly, the coefficient of government expenditure is negatively associated but statistically insignificant with income inequality there by indicating that increase in government expenditure leads to better and fair distribution of income. But its lag has a worsening impact. Finally, Trade openness shows the income inequality declining impact with statistically significant at 1% level.

Figure 3.6 shows the CUSUM and CUSUMsq figures indicating the stability of parameters.

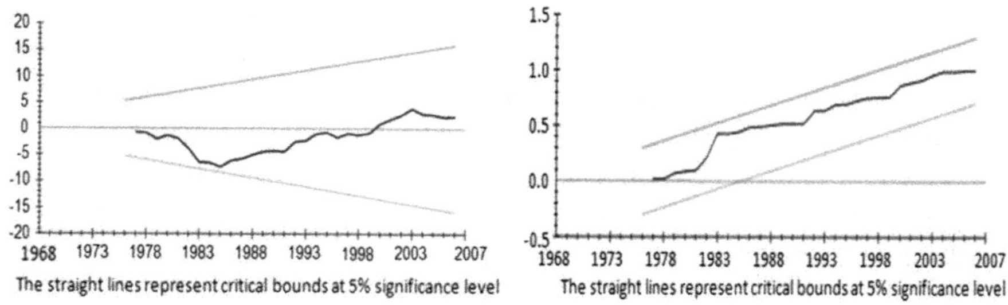

Fig. 3.6 Plot of cumulative sum and cumulative sum of square of recursive residuals

3.7.3 Model B

The study uses an alternative approach to assess whether growth is pro-poor or anti-poor in the similar fashion. That is incorporated by using another model with different specification than the model used above. In this model the share of income of top 1% of population is taken as an index of inequality with the same set of independent and control variables as in model A. The reason behind this is that, if the increase in GDP results in decrease of the above share then, we can infer that the growth is pro-poor in nature. In other words, we can say that society moves towards the fair and equitable distribution of income. The econometric methodology used for the estimation of model B is same as model A, i.e., ARDL approach of cointegration. First, we checked the order of integration of logarithmic share of top 1% (hereafter LTOP) by using three alternative unit root tests with results stated in Table 3.1. The results reveal that the variable is stationary at first difference.

Lag order 2 is selected on the basis of the lowest value of the AIC and SBC as shown in Table 3.9. When 2 lags are involved, there is a solid indication for cointegration as the *F*-statistic is 4.197 larger than the critical value of bound [see, Pesaran et al. 2001, at 5% level of significance (Table 4(A))]. The estimates for the ARDL model pass all the diagnostic checks as shown in Table 3.10. The CUSUM and CUSUMsq tests are also showed in Fig. 3.7.

The estimated long-run coefficients using the ARDL approach are stated in Table 3.11. The results specify that RGDPC is associated negatively but statistically insignificant with the share of GDP of top one percent of the population which is taken as a measure of inequality. That implies growth in GDP increases the share of rest of the population in a society more than the share of the top one percent of the population. In other words, we can say that there is a reduction in the income inequality. The coefficient consumer price index (CPI) is positive but insignificant,

Table 3.9 Lag length selection criteria for model with top 1% as inequality measure

Order of lags	AIC	SBC
1	10.76	4.67
2	9.03*	2.5*

*indicates optimal lag selection

Table 3.10 Diagnostic tests for model with top 1% as inequality measure

Test statistics	LM version	*F* version
A:Serial correlation	CHSQ(1) = 2.296[0.130]	*F*(1,18) = 1.820[0.194]
B:Functional form	CHSQ(1) = 3.578[0.059]	*F*(1,18) = 3.007[0.100]
C:Normality	CHSQ(2) = 2.086[0.352]	Not applicable
D:Heteroscedasticity	CHSQ(1) = 1.338[0.247]	*F*(1,23) = 1.300[0.266]

A:Lagrange multiplier test of residual serial correlation
B:Ramsey's RESET test using the square of the fitted values
C:Based on a test of skewness and kurtosis of residuals
D:Based on the regression of squared residuals on squared fitted values

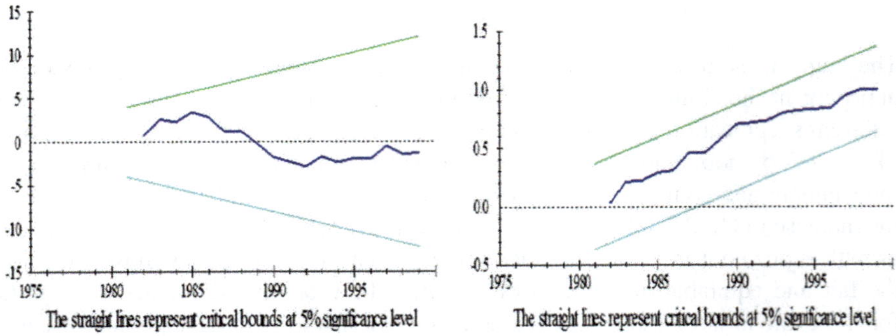

Fig. 3.7 Plot of cumulative sum and square of recursive residuals for model B

Table 3.11 Long- and short-run estimates for model with top 1% as an inequality measure

Regressor	Coefficient	Standard error	*T*-ratio[prob]
Long run estimates			
LRGDPC	−2.924	2.508	−1.166[0.258]
LCPI	1.048	0.614	1.705[0.104]
LTO	0.166	1.061	0.156[0.878]
LGEXP	0.203	0.980	0.207[0.838]
CON	18.549	15.876	1.168[0.257]
Short run estimates (ECM model)			
dLRGDPC	−1.186	0.910	−1.303[0.208]
dLCPI	0.425	0.204	0.086[0.051]***
dLTO	0.067	0.436	0.1540[0.879]
dLGEXP	0.082	0.399	0.206[0.839]
ecm(−1)	−0.405	0.168	−2.40[0.026]**

Note *, **, *** used for 1%, 5% and 10% level of significance respectively

thereby, implying that increase in CPI gives rise to income inequality. The coefficient of trade openness is positive but insignificant thereby implying that as the country approaches more and more toward free trade, income inequality tends to worsen. In other words, we can say that trade openness is pro- rich in nature. The estimate of government expenditure is also positive and statistically insignificant, thereby, implying that the increase in government expenditure gives rise to an in-egalitarian society or increase in government expenditure increase the share of GDP by top one percent more than that of the rest of the population which in turn ends with the worsening of inequality.

From Table 3.11, it is clear that the coefficient of ECMt-1 is equal to -0.406 and statistically significant, thereby implying that any aberration from the equilibrium is corrected by 40.55% over each year. The short-run dynamics results show that the share of top one percent of population decreases with increase in real GDP per capita, but the coefficient is insignificant. The coefficient of CPI shows that increase in inflation leads to increase in the share of top one percent and reduction in the share of the rest. Thus, we can say that increase in the CPI leads to the deterioration of income distribution. The coefficient of trade openness is positive but insignificant, implying that the liberalization of trade reduces the share of rest of the population in GDP whereas; it increases the share of top one percent of population. Thus openness of the trade is somewhat pro-rich in nature. Finally, the coefficient of government expenditure is also positive and insignificant thereby affecting the income inequality in the same way as CPI and trade openness.

3.8 Conclusion

Remaining as the most inconclusive relationship, Kuznets Inverted-U Hypothesis has been an important topic in development economics, especially the economics of income distribution since its inception. Though the hypothesis faced both criticism and acceptance as deduced from the past research, there were researchers who, with their empirical finding totally designated this relationship as a mess. However, a deep look at the literature reveals its importance; it served as the guide for future research. Kuznets was almost the first academician who showed a deep concern to study the change in pattern and process that will happen because of change in the national product. The angle he used to analyze the sectoral transformation of the economy is all alive debated and discussed to date. Admitting the importance of Kuznets' hypothesis, Piketty says that, it was the first theory of this sort to rely on a formidable statistical apparatus. According to him, Kuznets' work was the first high-powered effort to capture inequality in concrete terms to give a forceful push to the subject of income distribution.

To push Kuznets hypothesis forward a remarkable contribution came from Ahluwalia (1976), who not only studied the effect of GDP per capita on income distribution, but also made deep analysis to investigate the influence of other forces like share of agriculture, education levels, etc., and after that study a cluster of research flowed mostly based on the cross section data. After the compilation of Deininger–Squire data set focus was shifted toward time series and panel analysis using different tools of econometrics to gather deep understanding on the subject. Besides that different types of models were developed A new wave has started after the work of Thomas Piketty and Emmanuel Saez who, with the help of Tax data available within the country succeeded in creating a database for many countries which shows the income share of the top 1% of the population for a long time period. The data on top 1% draw high attention from the world community as it showed clear evidence regarding the rising income disparities between the top and the bottom income group over the period of time. Studies have revealed that a higher degree of disparity can give rise to political and social instability besides inefficiency and decrease in standard of living.

The debate on rising inequalities has evolved in India since planning era, but rising income inequalities gained much attention after reforms. Various studies have shown that with high growth rates though poverty levels came down same was not visualized in case of income inequality. There is clear evidence from the consumption expenditure data and data on wage levels supporting the view that in recent times inequalities have once again started to rise. This situation has put a red mark on the development process, witnessed in India since the 1990s. Because of that process of globalization has come under severe attack for creating higher disparities. The rising inequality is a matter of deep concern especially with respect to India was a large proportion of the population has failed to come above the official poverty line. Negligence to the subject of the income distribution can prove fatal for the whole country both in terms of decreasing living standard and can hamper high growth rates witnessed after the reform period.

In order to deal with the rising inequalities, and to find solutions to stop its rising trend, there is critical need to find the causes that can have great say in determining the order of distribution of income. The subject of income distribution is not new, although it was taken seriously from recent past. This study mainly analyzed the relationship between inequality and development from the empirical point of view over the period of time in the context of India. This study mainly focused on to investigate the Kuznets inverted-U hypothesis. Besides GDP Per Capita, certain control variables are found important from the investigation of past research were also used to capture the relationship perfectly. To completely understand the relationship cointegration approach of ARDL was used and due consideration was given to the functional form, serial correlation, normality assumption, and heteroscedasticity. The main empirical findings of the study are as follows:

The results indicate that RGDPC is associated positively with income inequality. The coefficient of government with a negative sign indicated that the increase in government expenditure results in the reduction of income inequality. Thus, we can say that with the increase in the level of development in terms of GDP Per Capita there is increase in the inequality in the long run.

The estimate of LCPI showed that increase in price level leads to increase in income inequality. In the short run, the estimates show a change in sign and significance at levels. At lag 1 and 2 the coefficient of LGDP per capita shows a significant negative relationship, means that in a short run increase in lagged GDP per capita leads a decrease in the inequality. So based on short run and long-run estimates following Bahmani-Oskoee and Gelan (2008), we may conclude that in the beginning with the increase in level of development there is a decrease in inequality, but over the period of time inequality starts to increase with the increase in the level of development. So that means there is a U-shaped relationship instead of inverted U. In case of Govt. expenditure, the results show a significant lagged positive effect on inequality, opposite to the long-run estimates. To fully capture Kuznets inverted U we make use of Square of GDP per capita like previous studies. Accordingly, we found that for both GDP per capita and its square, estimates are insignificant. However for govt. expenditure coefficient is once again negative and significant. The inclusion of Sq. term for GDP per capita affects its significance, but the sign remains same.

After that, we tried another model by involving price level as an additional control variable. The long-run estimates showed that price level is positively related with inequality, and accordingly expenditure has a same positive effect on it as was noticed earlier. But in this case, both sign, as well as the significance of GDP per capita, has changed may be due to high multicollinearity with the CPI. The short-run estimates show that coefficient of price level is significant and stable. Though the sign of GDP per capita remains same, it is again insignificant. However once again we find that the lag of govt. expenditure shows a significant positive relationship as was noticed earlier. Moreover, ecm(−1) is also negative with a significant coefficient.

Moreover when we added trade openness as an additional variable in the model, following were the main findings:

1. The coefficient of LGEXP is statistically significant with a negative sign indicating that the increase in government expenditure results in the reduction of income inequality.
2. The coefficient of LTO is negative thereby implying that as the country approach more and more toward free trade, income inequality tends to decline.

The short-run dynamics results of the above variables are on the same lines as mentioned above but with slight changes in the significance level. Third, the study uses an alternative approach assessing whether growth is pro-poor or not. For this purpose another model with different specification was used. In this model, the income share of the top one percent of the population is taken as a measure of inequality with the same set of regressors as in model A. The estimated long-run coefficients using the ARDL approach indicate that LRGDPC is associated negatively but statistically insignificant with the income share of top 1% of the population. This implies that growth in GDP increases the share of the rest of the population in a society more than the share of top 1%. In other words, we can say that there is a reduction in the income inequality. The effect of control variables in the model B are as follows:

1. The coefficient of LCPI is positive but insignificant thereby implying that increase in price level leads to increase in income inequality.
2. The coefficient of LTO is positive but insignificant thereby implying that as the country approach more and more towards free trade, income inequality tends to worsen.

The short-run dynamics showed that the coefficient of LRGDPC is negative but insignificant. The coefficient of LCPI is positive and statistically significant. Thus, we can say that increase in the CPI leads to the deterioration of income distribution. The coefficient of LTO is positive but insignificant implying that the liberalization of trade reduces the share of the rest of the population in GDP whereas it increases the share of top 1%. Finally, the coefficient of LGEXP is also positive and insignificant thereby effect the income inequality in the same way as CPI and trade openness does.

Our results reveal that the relationship is U shaped in nature. That implies an initial increase in GDP per capita leads to decrease in inequality, later on as the former increases, inequality tends to increase. Among the control variables, CPI (price level) is found to be positively related to inequality in all the models used in this study. Government expenditure is negatively related to inequality when Estimated Household Income Inequality (EHII) is taken as measure of inequality, while it (Government Expenditure) is positively related to inequality when income share of top 1% of the population is taken as a measure of inequality. A clear picture can be drawn from this result is that government expenditure is biased towards the upper income group. Moreover, there remained much to explore, the true dynamics of inequality that can be taken care in the future work.

References

Ahluwalia, M. S. (1976). Income distribution and development: some stylized facts. *The American Economic Review, 66,* 128–135.

Ahluwalia, M. S. (2000). Economic performance of states in post-reforms period. *Economic and Political Weekly, 35,* 1637–1648.

Ahmad, W., Nain, M. Z., & Kamaiah, B. (2014). On the role of the trend and cyclical components in electricity consumption and India's economic growth: A cointegration and cofeature approach. *OPEC Energy Review, 38*(1), 107–126.

Alesina, A., & Perotti, R. (1996). Income distribution, political instability, and investment. *European Economic Review, 40*(6), 1203–1228.

Alesina, A., Perotti, R., Alesina, A., Rodrik, D., Barro, R., BÃnabou, R., et al. (1994). Is inequality harmful for growth? Theory and evidence. *The American Economic Review, 84*(3), 600–621.

Anand, S., & Kanbur, S. R. (1993a). Inequality and development a critique. *Journal of Development Economics, 41*(1), 19–43.

Anand, S., & Kanbur, S. R. (1993b). The Kuznets process and the inequality development relationship. *Journal of Development Economics, 40*(1), 25–52.

Ang, J. B. (2010). Finance and inequality: The case of India. *Southern Economic Journal, 76*(3), 738–761. http://journal.southerneconomic.org/doi/abs/10.4284/sej.2010.76.3.738.

Angeles, L. (2010). An alternative test of Kuznets hypothesis. *The Journal of Economic Inequality, 8*(4), 463–473. doi:10.1007/s10888-009-9117-4.

Bahmani-Oskooee, M., & Gelan, A. (2008). Kuznets inverted-U hypothesis revisited: A time-series approach using US data. *Applied Economics Letters, 15*(9), 677–681. doi:10.1080/13504850600749040.

Bandelj, N., & Mahutga, M. C. (2010). How socio-economic change shapes income inequality in post-socialist Europe. *Social Forces, 88*(5), 2133–2161.

Banerjee, A., Dolado, J., & Mestre, R. (1998). Error-correction mechanism tests for cointegration in a single-equation framework. *Journal of Time Series Analysis, 19*(3), 267–283. doi:10.1111/1467-9892.00091.

Bastagli, F., Coady, D., & Gupta, S. (2012). *Income inequality and fiscal policy*. Tech. rep., International Monetary Fund. http://ideas.repec.org/p/imf/imfsdn/12-08r.html.

Bensidoun, I., Jean, S., & Sztulman, A. (2005). *International trade and income distribution: Reconsidering the evidence*. Tech. rep. http://ideas.repec.org/p/cii/cepidt/2005-17.html.

Bhagwati, J., & Srinivasan, T. N. (2002). Trade and poverty in the poor countries. *American Economic Review, 92,* 180–183.

Blejer, M. I., & Guerrero, I. (1990). The impact of macroeconomic policies on income distribution: An empirical study of the Philippines. *The Review of Economics and Statistics,* 414–423.

Bourguignon, F., & Morrisson, C. (1998). Inequality and development: The role of dualism. *Journal of Development Economics, 57*(2), 233–257.

Chakravarty, S. (1987). *Development planning: The Indian experience*. Oxford: Clarendon Press.

Chambers, D. (2007). Trading places: Does past growth impact inequality? *Journal of Development Economics, 82*(1), 257–266.

Charles-Coll, J. A. (2011). Understanding income inequality: Concept, causes and measurement. *International Journal of Economics and Management Sciences, 1*(3), 17–28.

Chen, Z. (2007). Development and inequality: Evidence from an endogenous switching regression without regime separation. *Economics Letters, 96*(2), 269–274.

Cheng, W., et al. (2014). *Understanding the Kuznets process: An empirical investigation of income inequality in China 1978–2011*. Tech. rep., Monash University, Department of Economics. http://ideas.repec.org/p/mos/moswps/2014-12.html.

Chu, K.-Y., Davoodi, H. R., & Gupta, S. (2000). *Income distribution and tax and government social spending policies in developing countries*. International Monetary Fund.

Datt, G., & Ravallion, M. (1998). Farm productivity and rural poverty in India. *The Journal of Development Studies, 34*(4), 62–85.

Daudey, E., & GarcÃ-a-PeÃ alosa, C. (2007). The personal and the factor distributions of income in a cross-section of countries. *Journal of Development Studies*, 43(5), 812–829. doi:10.1080/00220380701384406.

Deininger, K., & Squire, L. (1996). A new data set measuring income inequality. *The World Bank Economic Review, 10*(3), 565–591.

Deininger, K., & Squire, L. (1998). New ways of looking at old issues: Inequality and growth. *Journal of Development Economics, 57*(2), 259–287.

DeSa, U. N. (2013). Inequality matters. Report on the World Social Situation 2013. New York, United Nations.

Desbordes, R., & Verardi, V. (2012). Refitting the Kuznets curve. *Economics Letters, 116*(2), 258–261.

Eicher, T. S., & Turnovsky, S. J. (2003). *Inequality and growth: Theory and policy implications* (Vol. 1). US: MIT Press.

Engle, R. F., & Granger, C. W. (1987). Co-integration and error correction: Representation, estimation, and testing. *Econometrica: Journal of the Econometric Society, 55,* 251–276.

Ferreira, F. H., Leite, P. G., & Wai-Poi, M. (2007). Trade liberalization, employment flows, and wage inequality in Brazil.

Fields, G. S. (1980). *Poverty, inequality, and development*. CUP Archive.

Foster, J. E. (1985). Inequality measurement. *Fair Allocation, 33,* 31–68.

Frazer, G. (2006). Inequality and development across and within countries. *World Development, 34*(9), 1459–1481.

Galbraith, J. K. (2007). Global inequality and global macroeconomics. *Journal of Policy Modeling, 29*(4), 587–607.

Galbraith, J. K., Halbach, B., Malinowska, A., Shams, A., & Zhang, W. (2014). *The UTIP global inequality data sets 1963–2008*. http://utip.gov.utexas.edu/papers/UTIP_68.pdf.

Galbraith, J. K., & Kum, H. (2005). Estimating the inequality of household incomes: A statistical approach to the creation of a dense and consistent global data set. *Review of Income and Wealth, 51*(1), 115–143. doi:10.1111/j.1475-4991.2005.00147.x.

Galor, O., & Tsiddon, D. (1996). Income distribution and growth: The Kuznets hypothesis revisited. *Economica, 63,* S103–S117 (2554811).

Hansen, B. E., & Phillips, P. C. (1990). Estimation and inference in models of cointegration: A simulation study. *Advances in Econometrics, 8*(1989), 225–248.

Higgins, M., & Williamson, J. G. (1999). *Explaining inequality the world round: Cohort size, Kuznets curves, and openness*. Tech. rep., National Bureau of Economic Research. http://www.nber.org/papers/w7224.

Huang, H. C., Lin, Y. C., & Yeh, C. C. (2012). An appropriate test of the Kuznets hypothesis. *Applied Economics Letters, 19*(1), 47–51. doi:10.1080/13504851.2011.566172.

Jha, S. K. (1996). The Kuznets curve: A reassessment. *World Development, 24*(4), 773–780.

Johansen, S. (1988). Statistical analysis of cointegration vectors. *Journal of Economic Dynamics and Control, 12*(2), 231–254.

Johansen, S. (1995). Identifying restrictions of linear equations with applications to simultaneous equations and cointegration. *Journal of Econometrics, 69*(1), 111–132.

Johansen, S., & Juselius, K. (1990). Maximum likelihood estimation and inference on cointegration with applications to the demand for money. *Oxford Bulletin of Economics and Statistics, 52*(2), 169–210. doi:10.1111/j.1468-0084.1990.mp52002003.x.

Kanbur, R., & Zhuang, J. (2013). Urbanization and inequality in Asia. *Asian Development Review, 30*(1), 131–147. doi:10.1162/ADEV_a_00006.

Kapoor, R. (2013). Inequality matters. *Economic Political Weekly, 48*(2), 58–65.

Kim, D. H., Huang, H. C., & Lin, S. C. (2011). Kuznets hypothesis in a panel of states. *Contemporary Economic Policy, 29*(2), 250–260. doi:10.1111/j.1465-7287.2010.00218.x/full.

Krishna, P., & Sethupathy, G. (2011). *Trade and inequality in India*. Tech. rep., National Bureau of Economic Research. http://www.nber.org/papers/w17257.

Kumar, U., & Mishra, P. (2008). Trade liberalization and wage inequality: Evidence from India. *Review of Development Economics, 12*(2), 291–311. doi:10.1111/j.1467-9361.2007.00388.x/full.

Kuznets, S. (1955). Economic growth and income inequality. *The American Economic Review, 45* (1), 1–28.

Kuznets, S. (1963). Quantitative aspects of the economic growth of nations: VIII. Distribution of income by size. *Economic development and Cultural Change, 11.2*, 1–80.

Lewis, W. A. (1954). Economic development with unlimited supplies of labour. *The Manchester School, 22*(2), 139–191. doi:10.1111/j.1467-9957.1954.tb00021.x.

Lim, C. Y., & Sek, S. K. (2014). Exploring the two-way relationship between income inequality and growth. *Journal of Advanced Management Science, 2*(1), 33.

Lin, S. C., Suen, Y.-B., Yeh, C. C., et al. (2007). A quantile inference of the Kuznets hypothesis. *Economic Modelling, 24*(4), 559–570.

Lind, J. T., & Mehlum, H. (2010). With or without U? The appropriate test for a U-shaped relationship. *Oxford Bulletin of Economics and Statistics, 72*(1), 109–118. doi:10.1111/j.1468-0084.2009.00569.x/full.

List, J. A., & Gallet, C. A. (1999). The Kuznets curve: What happens after the inverted-U? *Review of Development Economics, 3*(2), 200–206. doi:10.1111/1467-9361.00061/full.

Litchfield, J. (2001). Updated Income Distribution and Poverty Measures for Chile: 1987–1998. *Background Paper, 1,* 1987–1998.

Lorenz, M. O. (1905). Methods of measuring the concentration of wealth. *Publications of the American Statistical Association, 9*(70), 209–219. doi:10.1080/15225437.1905.10503443.

Lubrano, M. (2012). The econometrics of inequality and poverty. *Lecture 4: Lorenz curves, the Gini coefficient and parametric distributions.* http://www.vcharite.univ-mrs.fr/PP/lubrano/cours/Lecture-4.pdf.

Motonishi, T. (2006). Why has income inequality in Thailand increased?: An analysis using surveys from 1975 to 1998. *Japan and the World Economy, 18*(4), 464–487.

Mushinski, D. W. (2001). Using non-parametrics to inform parametric tests of Kuznets' hypothesis. *Applied Economics Letters, 8*(2), 77–79. doi:10.1080/13504850150204093.

Nain, M. Z., Ahmad, W., & Kamaiah, B. (2017). Economic growth, energy consumption and CO_2 emissions in India: A disaggregated causal analysis. *International Journal of Sustainable Energy, 36*(8), 807–824.

Nain, M. Z., & Kamaiah, B. (2012). On the relationship between nominal and real effective exchange rates in India: Evidence from the ARDL bounds tests. *IUP Journal of Applied Economics, 11*(4), 50.

Ogwang, T. (1994). Economic development and income inequality: A nonparametric investigation of Kuznets' U-curve hypothesis. *Journal of Quantitative Economics, 10,* 139–153.

Okun, A. M. (1975). *Equality and efficiency, the big tradeoff.* Washington, D.C.: Brookings Institution Press.

Oosthuizen, M. (2007). *Consumer Price inflation across the income distribution in South Africa.* Development Policy Research Unit, University of Cape Town. http://core.kmi.open.ac.uk/download/pdf/6261866.pdf.

Oshima, H. T. (1962). The international comparison of size distribution of family incomes with special reference to Asia. *The Review of Economics and Statistics, 44,* 439–445.

Ouattara, B. (2004). *Foreign aid and fiscal policy in Senegal.* Tech. rep., Mimeo University of Manchester Manchester.

Pal, P., & Ghosh, J. (2007). *Inequality in India: A survey of recent trends.* Economic and Social Affairs Working Paper (Vol. 45).

Paukert, F. (1973). Income distribution at different levels of development: A survey of evidence. *International Labour Review, 108,* 97.

Perron, P. (1989). The great crash, the oil price shock, and the unit root hypothesis. *Econometrica: Journal of the Econometric Society,* 1361–1401.

Perron, P. (1997). Further evidence on breaking trend functions in macroeconomic variables. *Journal of econometrics, 80*(2), 355–385.

Pesaran, M. H., & Pesaran, B. (1997). *Working with Microfit 4.0: Interactive econometric analysis.* London: Oxford University Press.

Pesaran, M. H., & Shin, Y. (1998). An autoregressive distributed-lag modelling approach to cointegration analysis. *Econometric Society Monographs, 31,* 371–413.

Persson, T., & Tabellini, G. (1994). Is inequality harmful for growth? *The American Economic Review, 84*(3), 600–621.

Pesaran, M. H., Shin, Y., & Smith, R. J. (2001). Bounds testing approaches to the analysis of level relationships. *Journal of Applied Econometrics, 16*(3), 289–326. doi:10.1002/jae.616/full.

Phillips, P. C., & Perron, P. (1988). Testing for a unit root in time series regression. *Biometrika, 75* (2), 335–346.

Piketty, T. (2014). *Capital in the twenty-first century.* Harvard (US): Harvard University Press.

Ram, R. (1988). Economic development and income inequality: Further evidence on the U-curve hypothesis. *World Development, 16*(11), 1371–1376.

Ram, R. (1991). Kuznets's inverted-U hypothesis: evidence from a highly developed country. *Southern Economic Journal, 57,* 1112–1123.

Ranciere, R., & Kumhof, M. M. (2010). *Inequality, leverage and crises* (No. 10–268). International Monetary Fund.

Rangvid, J. (2001). Increasing convergence among European stock markets?: A recursive common stochastic trends analysis. *Economics Letters, 71*(3), 383–389.

Rao, M. M., Samant, A. P., & Asher, N. L. (1999). Indian Macro-Economic Data Base in a Consistency Accounting Framework (1950–51 to 1997–98): I: Identifying Sectoral and Economywide Budget Constraints. *Economic and Political Weekly,* 2243–2262.

Ravallion, M. (2000). Prices, wages and poverty in rural India: What lessons do the time series data hold for policy? *Food Policy, 25*(3), 351–364.

Ray, D. (1998). *Development economics*. US: Princeton University Press.

Rodrik, D., & Alesina, A. (1994). *Distributive politics and economic growth*. http://dash.harvard.edu/handle/1/4551798.

Sagala, P., Akita, T., & Yusuf, A. A. (2013). Urbanization and expenditure inequality in Indonesia: Testing the Kuznets hypothesis with provincial panel data. *Letters in Spatial and Resource Sciences*, 1–15. doi:10.1007/s12076-013-0106-7.

Saith, A. (1983). Development and distribution: A critique of the cross-country U-hypothesis. *Journal of Development Economics, 13*(3), 367–382.

Salotti, S., & Trecroci, C. (2013). *Can fiscal policy mitigate income inequality and poverty?* Available at SSRN 2379441. http://www.alde.es/encuentros/trabajos/s/pdf/78.pdf.

Sato, S., & Fukushige, M. (2009). Globalization and economic inequality in the short and long run: The case of South Korea 1975–1995. *Journal of Asian Economics, 20*(1), 62–68.

Sen, A. (1973). On economic inequality. *OUP Catalogue*. http://ideas.repec.org/b/oxp/obooks/9780198281931.html.

Sen, A. K. (1997a). From income inequality to economic inequality. *Southern Economic Journal, 384–401,* 1060857.

Sen, A. K. (1997b). On Economic Inequality, expanded edition with a substantial annexe by James E. Foster and Amartya Sen. Oxford: Clarendon Press. (1979). The welfare basis of real income comparisons: A survey. *Journal of Economic Literature*, *17*(1), 1–45.

Shahbaz, M. (2010). Income inequality-economic growth and non-linearity: A case of Pakistan. *International Journal of Social Economics, 37*(8), 613–636.

Shahbaz, M., & Islam, F. (2011). *Financial development and income inequality in Pakistan: An application of ARDL approach*. http://mpra.ub.uni-muenchen.de/28222/.

Sinha, N., et al. (2004). *Growth, inequality and structural adjustment: An empirical interpretation of the S-curve for Indian economy*. https://digitalcollections.anu.edu.au/handle/1885/42134.

Stiglitz, J. (2012). *The price of inequality*. Penguin UK.

Stolper, W. F., & Samuelson, P. A. (1941). Protection and real wages. *The Review of Economic Studies, 9*(1), 58–73.

Theil, H. (1967). *Economics and information theory*. http://cds.cern.ch/record/432570.

Thornton, J. (2001). The Kuznets inverted-U hypothesis: Panel data evidence from 96 countries. *Applied Economics Letters*, *8*(1), 15–16. doi:10.1080/135048501750041213.

Tiongson, E., & de Mello, L. R. (2003). *Income inequality and redistributive government spending*. International Monetary Fund.

Tiwari, A. K., Shahbaz, M., & Islam, F. (2013). Does financial development increase rural-urban income inequality?: Cointegration analysis in the case of Indian economy. *International Journal of Social Economics, 40*(2), 151–168.

Torsten, P., & Guido, T. (1994). Is inequality harmful for growth? *The American Economic Review*, *84*(3), 600–621.

Walsh, M. J., & Yu, J. (2012). *Inflation and income inequality: Is food inflation different?*(EPub). International Monetary Fund.

Wolff, E. N. (2009). *Poverty and income distribution*. UK: Blackwell Pub.

Zhou, X., & Li, K.-W. (2011). Inequality and development: Evidence from semiparametric estimation with panel data. *Economics Letters, 113*(3), 203–207.

Chapter 4
An Inquiry into the Dynamics of Inequality from the Perspective of Caste

Anoop S. Kumar and P Yazir

Abstract This study analyses the economic inequality in India, with particular reference to Kerala in the post-reform period considering different caste groups namely, SC, ST, OBC and 'Others' as mentioned in NSS Household level Consumption Expenditure Survey Data. Two rounds of NSSO data viz. 61st and 66th were taken for the purpose of analysis. Gini coefficient and overlapping index were estimated for the whole as well as the subgroups using ANOGI methodology. From the analysis, it was found that the level of overall inequality as well as the intergroup inequality is on the rise in Kerala as well as India during the period of analysis. The study also identified the possibility of stratification among the group 'Others' for both India and Kerala. Further, it was found that SC's and ST's (in particular) bear the burden of the increasing inequality. This indicates that the various welfare measures initiated by the central as well as state governments might not have reached the majority of these downtrodden communities.

Keywords Inequality · NSSO · Kerala · Gini · Caste

4.1 Introduction

The issue of economic inequality has often been debated in view of its possible impact on social and economic development. It is generally believed that equality in income could help promote long-term economic growth. Economic equality might enable more people to participate in economic activities on an equal footing. However, wiping out economic inequalities while being highly desirable has been a formidable and challenging task to the policy makers world over.

A.S. Kumar (✉)
Department of Economics, BITS Pilani KK Birla Goa Campus, Goa 403726, India
e-mail: anoopk@goa.bits-pilani.ac.in

P. Yazir
School of Economics, University of Hyderabad, Gachibowli 500046, India
e-mail: yasinbox@gmail.com

U.K. De et al. (eds.), *Inequality, Poverty and Development in India*, India Studies in Business and Economics, DOI 10.1007/978-981-10-6274-2_4

Despite the planned efforts, economic inequalities have only grown in India. In fact, it has been reported that income inequality in India during the phase of acceleration in economic growth in the post-reform period has been worsened (Nagaraj 2000; Himanshu and Sen 2004a, b; Himanshu 2007; Subramanian and Prasad 2008; Sarkar and Mehta 2010; Zhong et al. 2010; Motiram and Sarma 2011). In the light of this observation, it would be of interest to estimate the extent of inequalities with a view to assess how the poor in India are affected by the globalization process. In the literature, the issue of economic/income inequality has been examined by considering aspects such as region, state, caste, class, gender, etc. But in the Indian context, the few studies that are available on this theme seem to focus on categories such as state, region and class, and ignored caste as a possible dimension with reference to which inequalities could be examined. Given that caste is an important factor in India, it may be more appropriate to analyse economic inequalities on the basis of 'caste'.

4.2 Caste as a Basis of Analysis

The choice of 'caste' rather than 'class' as the basis for analysing economic inequalities is justified on the ground that defining a class structure using a methodology such as Marxian in India is imbued with difficulties. To define a class structure under the Marxian schema, along with the existence of private property and wage labour, the nature of relationship between the two groups should be one of exploitative and based on the demand for and supply of labour power. A capitalist's only criterion of selecting a worker is the labour power that the worker possesses. And a worker is expected to choose occupations depending upon the required skill that he might possess.

In the Indian context, it is neither easy to divide people into classes viz. workers and capitalists, nor find the relationship between them to be exploitative, as the Marxian scheme assumes to be. In the urban informal sector in India, the exact production relations are unknown. In the rural agrarian economy, it could be seen that a large proportion of people are into their occupations due to the existing caste hierarchy, lacking social mobility due to the rigid caste structure. Here, the production relations are not solely based on labour power, but factors like caste, gender which play a dominant role. In such a scenario, it will be extremely difficult to define a Marxian class structure for the purpose of an empirical analysis.

This study is limited to the four broad social groups as identified by the *Consumer Expenditure Survey of National Sample Survey* namely, Scheduled Castes or the 'Dalits' (SC), Scheduled Tribes or the 'Adivasis' (ST), Other Backward Classes (OBC)[1] and 'Others', that includes everyone other than SC, ST and OBC.

---

[1]Prior to 2004–2005, there was no separate data on OBC. The data for OBC were provided separately from 2004 to 2005 onwards.

Scheduled castes (SC) and scheduled tribes (ST) are mentioned in the Constitution of India as socially disadvantaged groups for affirmative state action. SC group has been at the bottom of the Hindu caste hierarchy that is based on birth. In the past, people belonging to this group were forced to take up jobs that were menial in social ordering and characterized by very low productivity (Sundaram and Tendulkar 2003). As Indian caste system restricts occupational mobility, they remained at the lowest end of the economic hierarchy as well. Even with the improvement in social and economic conditions over the time, most of them have remained marginalized, practising modest occupations with little or minimum exposure to educational opportunities.

ST as a social group does not come under the umbrella of the Hindu social hierarchy. Their social and economic backwardness were mainly due to their geographical isolation that resulted in lack of exposure to education as well as isolation from the social mainstream. They were susceptible to mistreatment by the others communities. They (ST's) were uprooted from their traditional habitats and occupations on the pretext of many reasons such as development projects, without any assurance for their relocation. As a result, they were demoted to the lowest end of the economic hierarchy (ibid).

The residual social group of 'Others' consisted of castes other than SC in the Hindu social hierarchy and non-ST members of other religious communities. There was a further reclassification added into the NSSO survey data in 2004–2005, collectively named OBC (other backward castes) as notified by the state as well as central governments as being socially 'backward' for eligibility to welfare programs of affirmative action, and thereby splitting 'Others' into OBC and 'Others'. Under this new classification, 'Others' represent the caste groups that do not come under the three categories mentioned above.

4.3 The Present Study

A perusal of the available studies for India reveals that while being widened, economic inequalities have varied across the Indian states. In fact, the extent of inequalities has grown in states which are developed (say, Tamil Nadu, Maharashtra, and Kerala) compared to the backward states. In the light of this interesting observation, the present study focuses on analysing the economic inequalities in India with particular reference to Kerala state, by considering caste as a basis.

Kerala is important in many ways for this study of cast- based inequality. First, income inequality in Kerala is quite skewed. If we take the state-level measure of income inequality; along with Tamil Nadu and Maharashtra, Kerala has values of Gini coefficient over and above the national average both in rural and urban sectors during the post-reform period (Planning Commission 2011). Second, Kerala model of development has attracted the attention of many scholars and economists since last four decades. Performance of most of the development indicators in Kerala has been quite impressive and even comparable with the developed countries (Parayil 2000). Third, Kerala is a state which has witnessed several social and religious reform movements that had a strong anti-caste component (Deshpande 2000) and Kerala had the world's second democratically elected communist government that came into power in 1957, who initiated strong welfare measures like land reforms that were aimed at reducing socio-economic inequalities.

In spite of all these, Kerala is one among the states that have the highest inequality in India. A careful analysis is required to understand the underlying dynamics that have led to skewed income inequalities. Hence, the specific issue examined in this chapter is to ascertain whether Kerala could reduce the social group inequality with the development strategies of the government after formation of the state.

4.4 Literature Review

Of the few works that dealt with the issue of economic inequality in Kerala, the study carried out by Deshpande (2000) stands in the forefront. The study used NSS household consumption expenditure data for 1993–1994 in order to estimate the extent of economic inequality in Kerala, using Theil's Index. The results showed that there was inter-caste economic inequality prevailing in Kerala. For rural and urban areas, results obtained using data on food expenditure, clothing expenditure, land-holding, and education levels of heads of household, indicated significant economic inequality within the SC/ST community compared to the other social groups. The results also indicated the presence of a low to medium level of overall inequality. It also suggested the existence of an upper class, which is much more pronounced in the 'Others' category, compared to the SC or ST category.

Using National Sample Survey Organization's *Surveys on Debt and Investment* of 1961–1962, 1971–1972, 1981–1982, 1991–1992, and 2002–2003, Subrahmaniam and Jayaraj (2006) analysed the distribution of wealth in India. They identified the presence of vertical and horizontal inequality in the distribution of wealth. Horizontal inequality was estimated on the basis of caste information as well as household unit level data. It was found that mean asset-holdings per household were systematically and substantially lower for SC/ST's across India. In the urban areas, within-group wealth distribution is more equal for SC/ST's compared to others. In rural areas, the Gini for the 'Others' is greater than Gini for the SC/ST. However, the estimated Theil index shows a different picture, and thereby it was not possible to arrive at a concrete conclusion.

Patterns of wealth disparities in India were analysed by Jayadev et al. (2007) using the data obtained from the *All-India Debt and Investment Surveys* (1991 and 2002). The results indicated that there have been increases in wealth levels in the country across all social groups. However, there was a small but noticeable rise in the level of interpersonal wealth inequality, which was analysed by estimating statistics such as the Gini coefficient and centile shares of wealth. They examined differences in wealth holdings by state and income in the two surveys, as well as disparities according to socio-economic categories in 2002. The final results indicated that there has been sharp difference between the growth rates of wealth holdings in the middle and upper income states and poor states, which indicated divergence in wealth outcomes. It was observed that faster growing states have seen larger increases in wealth inequality.

A comparative analysis of wealth distribution in China and India were carried out by Zong et al. (2010), based on the *China Household Income Project (CHIP)* data collected in 1995 and 2002 and *All India Debt and Investment Surveys* of the *National Sample Survey Organization* (NSSO) carried out in 1991–1992 and 2002–2003. The study estimated level and changes observed in wealth inequality in China and India. Decomposition measures of wealth inequality along with parameters such as rural–urban divide and regional differences in both China and India, and along identity categories such as caste and religion, education, and occupational groups in the case of India were also estimated.

The study found out that substantial differences exist in asset accumulation among caste and religious groups. The level of asset holdings for SC/STs was considerably different from 'Others'. For the 2002–2003 survey, where data for OBCs and 'Others' were available apart from SC/STs, there were obvious differences in wealth holdings across these groups with 'Others' being the wealthiest, SC/STs being the poorest, and OBCs falling in the middle. Here, the wealth hierarchy reflects the existing caste hierarchy. The study further states that inter-caste inequality explains a higher proportion (8–12%) of overall inequality over the reference period.

From the above literature, it is evident that caste has been an important factor that contributes to economic inequality. But the available scanty evidences pertain to either the all-India situation or a state. A detailed analysis covering the all-India and a state level is yet to be carried out. This study aims to fill the gap considering the state of Kerala along with the all-India situation. The reasons for choosing Kerala have been given earlier in this chapter. This study is expected to throw some light on the peculiar dynamics of Kerala economy. Accordingly, the present study seeks to decompose inequality in Kerala on the basis of caste structure. The remaining part of the chapter is structured as follows. Section 5 describes data, Sect. 6 explains the methodology employed, Sect. 7 deals with the analysis of results. In the last section, some implications of caste based economic inequality are discussed as concluding remarks.

4.5 Data

The data used in this analysis is taken from National Sample Survey Organization (NSSO) Consumption Expenditure Survey Rounds 61 (2004–2005) and 66 (2009–2010). In the 61st round (Schedule Type-I), 124,643 households were taken into consideration out of which 79,297 belonged to rural area, while 45,346 were from the urban area. For the 66th round (Schedule Type-I), 59,119 rural households as well as 41,736 urban households were considered, thereby constituting a total sample size of 100,855.

In the 61st round (Schedule Type-I), 5250 households were considered out of which 3300 belonged to rural area, while 1950 were from the urban area. For the 66th round (Schedule Type-I), a total sample size of 4452 households was considered of which 2606 households' belonged to rural area while 1846 households belonged into urban area. Here we have taken the Monthly Per capita Consumption Expenditure (Uniform Reference Period) [hence forth mentioned as MPCE (URP)] for the two rounds as a proxy for Household Income. The Uniform Reference Period data was taken in order to facilitate a comparative analysis between the data collected during the two rounds mentioned above.

4.6 Methodology

The present study adopts the ANOGI (Analysis of Gini) technique that was proposed by Frick et al. (2004) to decompose the inequality into various subgroups. The explanations given below regarding the methodology are mainly taken from Fricks et al. (2004) unless otherwise cited. ANOGI could be seen as equivalent to ANOVA (Analysis of Variance) performed with the Gini coefficient. To measure inequality, the Gini index is estimated as explained by the covariance formula according to Lerman and Yitzhaki (1984).

$$G = \frac{2\mathrm{cov}(y, F(y))}{\mu}, \tag{4.1}$$

where y is income or its proxy variable, $F(y)$ the rank, and μ is the mean of y.

The Gini of the entire population, G_u, can be decomposed as

$$G_u = \sum_{i=1}^{n} s_i G_i O_i + G_b, \tag{4.2}$$

where s_i denotes the share of income on overall income for group i, O_i is the overlapping index of the entire population by sub-population i, G_i represents the Gini of sub-population i, and G_b is the between-group inequality component.

The between-group inequality G_b as defined in Yitzhaki and Lerman (1991) is

$$G_b = \frac{2\mathrm{cov}(\mu_i, F_{ui})}{\mu_u} \tag{4.3}$$

Here, μ_i is the mean income of each sub-population and F_{ui} is sub-populations' mean rank in the overall population, and μ_u, overall expected income. That is, each sub-population is represented by its mean income, and the mean rank of its members in the overall distribution. The term G_b equals zero if either the mean incomes or the mean ranks are equal for all sub-populations. In extreme cases, G_b can be negative, which occurs when the mean income is negatively correlated with mean rank.

The within-group inequality, $s_iG_iO_i$, consists of three components, of which the overlapping index is the most important for measuring stratification. The overlapping index is defined as

$$O_i = O_{ui} = \frac{\mathrm{cov}_i(y, F_u(y))}{\mathrm{cov}_i(y, F_i(y))}, \tag{4.4}$$

where cov_i gives the covariance according to distribution i.

Overlapping index is defined as the inverse of stratification. Fricks et al. (2004) follow Lasswell's (1965, pp. 10) definition which states that: '*In its general meaning, a stratum is a horizontal layer, usually thought of as between, above or below other such layers or strata. Stratification is the process of forming observable layers, or the state of being comprised of layers. Social stratification suggests a model in which the mass of society is constructed of layer upon layer of congealed population qualities.*'

If we follow this definition, perfect stratification is achieved when all observations of each population are found in a specific range of income, and the ranges of the income distribution of the various sub-populations do not overlap. Yitzhaki (1982) connects stratification to the idea of relative deprivation, arguing that more stratified societies can tolerate even greater inequalities than non-stratified ones. As the idea of a perfect stratum is rare in real life, an index that describes the degree of stratification is required. The index of overlapping is actually an index describing the extent to which the different sub-populations are stratified (Frick and Goebel 2005).

The overlap defined above could be further decomposed to identify the overlapping of sub-population, i and all sub-populations that comprise the union. In other words, total overlapping of sub-population i, that is O_i, is composed by the overlapping of all sub-populations (including group i itself) by group i. This further decomposition of O_i is:

$$\begin{aligned} O_i &= \sum_{j}^{n} p_j O_{ji} = \sum_{j \neq j}^{n} p_j O_{ji} \\ &= p_i + \sum_{j \neq j}^{n} p_j O_{ji}, \end{aligned} \tag{4.6}$$

where $O_{ji} = \frac{\text{cov}_i(y, F_j(y))}{\text{cov}_i(y, F_i(y))}$ is the overlapping of group j by group i, and p_i is the share of sub-group i in the population. From this, it could be inferred that O_{ji} is equal to zero if no member of distribution j lies within the range of distribution i, which means that group i is a perfect stratum. On the other hand, if over the range of distribution i, the shape of the distribution of group j is similar to the shape of distribution i, then O_{ji} is equal to 1, and of course by definition, O_{ii} in any case is equal to 1. O_{ij} is bounded from above by 2. This maximum value will be reached if all observations belonging to distribution j that are located in the range of i are concentrated at the mean of distribution i. O_{ji} and O_{ij} are connected, in a way that, the higher the overlapping index O_{ji}, the lower O_{ij} will be. That is, the more group j is included in the range of distribution i, the less distribution i is expected to be included in the range of j. Therefore O_{ij} is an index that measures the extent to which population j is included in the range of group i.

The minimum value of O_i is given by the share of group i in the population, p_i; and its maximum value is equal to 2. $O_i = p_i$ indicates the presence of a perfect stratum. In other words, members of such a group will be fall into to a specific range of the entire distribution. If one group has a range of income that coincides with the range of income of all other members, then O_i will be equal to 1. If the distribution of income within a particular group is much more polarized than in the overall distribution, O_i will be greater than 1. This indicates the presence of two separate sections within the group, one having higher and the other having lower income compared to the mean income of the population under study (Milanovic and Yitzhaki 2002).

Apart from estimating Gini coefficients and overlapping indices, the average MPCE for each caste group will calculated for Kerala as well as for India for the two rounds under analysis. The data will be adjusted to 1993–1994 constant prices using CPI (Agricultural Labour) and CPI (Urban Non-Manual Employee) in order to see whether there are any real changes in the purchasing power of the households during the reference period.

4.7 Empirical Analysis

The decomposition of Gini into the within and between components as well as Gini coefficients for the four caste groups for both Kerala and India, are shown in Tables 4.1, 4.2, 4.3 and 4.4. Tables 4.5 and 4.6 describes the overlapping matrices for both India and Kerala, while Table 4.7 explains the mean monthly per capita consumption expenditure (MPCE) estimated for various caste groups. All the results are based on household level MPCE (Uniform Reference Period) data as a proxy for household income.

Table 4.1 Decomposition of Gini Coefficients for Kerala

Decomposition of Gini	61th round		66th round		Overall change (%)
	Gini	Percentage	Gini	Percentage	
Total	0.393	100	0.473	100	20.31
Within	0.367	93.55	0.428	89.46	
Between	0.026	6.45	0.050	10.54	

Source National Sample Survey Organization (NSSO), consumption expenditure survey rounds 61 (2004–05) and 66 (2009–10)

Table 4.2 Detailed inequality decomposition and overlap index for caste groups in Kerala

Groups	61th round				66th round				% change
	Gini	*N*	*P*	Overlap	Gini	*N*	*P*	Overlap	
ST	0.389	64	0.015	1.107	0.298	44	0.015	1.057	−23.93
SC	0.308	476	0.105	1.008	0.266	347	0.087	0.957	−13.63
OBC	0.394	3108	0.602	1.016	0.413	2642	0.624	1.010	4.82
Others	0.376	1602	0.277	0.851	0.551	1419	0.274	0.820	46.54

Source National Sample Survey Organization (NSSO), consumption expenditure survey rounds 61 (2004–05) and 66 (2009–10)

Table 4.3 Decomposition of Gini coefficients for India

Decomposition of Gini	61st round		66th round		Overall percentage change
	Gini	Percentage	Gini	Percentage	
Total	0.363	100	0.370	100	13.73
Within	0.318	87.61	0.330	88.85	
Between	0.045	12.39	0.041	11.15	

Source National Sample Survey Organization (NSSO), consumption expenditure survey rounds 61 (2004–05) and 66 (2009–10)

Table 4.4 Detailed inequality decomposition and overlap index for caste groups in India

Groups	61st round				66th round				% change
	Gini	*N*	*P*	Overlap	Gini	*N*	*P*	Overlap	
ST	0.304	16,409	0.086	1.0408	0.319	13,150	0.088	1.047	4.93
SC	0.297	20,065	0.196	1.0005	0.294	16,388	0.203	1.000	−1.01
OBC	0.323	46,236	0.410	0.9753	0.331	37,881	0.417	0.979	2.41
Others	0.389	41,892	0.308	0.8430	0.406	33,419	0.291	0.851	4.18

Source National Sample Survey Organization (NSSO), consumption expenditure survey rounds 61 (2004–05) and 66 (2009–10)
Note The **STATA** routine named **ANOGI** (Jann and Masterson 2007) was used for the decomposition of Gini Coefficients

Table 4.5 Overlapping matrix for Kerala and India: NSSO 61st round

Groups	Kerala				India			
	ST	SC	OBC	Others	ST	SC	OBC	Others
ST	1	1.197	1.125	1.040	1	1.085	1.085	0.966
SC	0.701	1	1.010	1.026	0.881	1	1.044	0.994
OBC	0.602	0.895	1	1.120	0.788	0.921	1	1.030
Others	0.440	0.670	0.8246	1	0.590	0.720	0.837	1

Source National Sample Survey Organization (NSSO), consumption expenditure survey rounds 61 (2004–05) and 66 (2009–10)

Table 4.6 Overlapping matrix for Kerala and India: NSSO 66th Round

Groups	Kerala				IIndia			
	ST	SC	OBC	Others	ST	SC	OBC	Others
ST	1	1.062	1.0859	0.925	1	1.051	1.081	1.012
SC	0.948	1	0.9919	0.862	0.944	1	1.036	0.966
OBC	0.727	0.818	1	1.110	0.854	0.923	1	1.027
Others	0.499	0.562	0.7840	1	0.662	0.732	0.844	1

Source National Sample Survey Organization (NSSO), consumption expenditure survey rounds 61 (2004–05) and 66 (2009–10)

Table 4.7 Mean MPCE (Rs) for Caste Groups—Kerala and India

Social groups/rounds	Kerala		India	
	61st round	66th round	61st round	66th round
ST	320.66	385.50	252.65	302.31
SC	410.24	396.67	287.44	313.01
OBC	563.68	625.88	337.67	374.68
OTHERS	704.95	1078.36	487.45	551.38

Source National Sample Survey Organization (NSSO), consumption expenditure survey rounds 61 (2004–05) and 66 (2009–10)
Note: Mean MPCE values adjusted to 1993–94 constant prices using CPI-AL and CPI-UNME

Tables 4.1 and 4.3 show the decomposition of Gini into within and between-group components for Kerala and India respectively. Similarly, Tables 4.2 and 4.4 give detailed inequality decompositions and overlapping indices for caste groups in Kerala and India respectively. From the estimated results, we can infer the following:

(i) Moving from 61st to 66th round, Gini values for SC and ST groups decreased in Kerala. Considering the all-India scenario, it is observed that Gini value for the ST group registered a marginal increase while Gini value for the SC group registered a marginal decrease.
(ii) Taking the overall picture from 2004–2005 to 2009–2010 for Kerala, it could be observed that there is a sharp increase in the overall inequality levels

(20.31%). The between-group component of inequality is also found to be rising over the years. In the 61st round, the between component of Gini could explain 6.45% of the total inequality. When it comes to the 66th round, there is a sharp increase, as the between component accounted for 10.53% of the total inequality in Kerala (see Table 4.1).

While considering the all-India scenario, a similar trend could be observed. The overall inequality increased by 13.73%. This increase is not sharp as compared to Kerala which stands at 20.31%. In the 61st round, the between component Gini could explain about 12% of the total inequality. In the 66th round, the between component of Gini accounted for 11.15% of the total inequality in India. Thus both in case of Kerala and India, the overall inequalities have gone up during 2004–2005 to 2009–2010.

(iii) After observing Gini coefficients for the different caste groups in Kerala (see Table 4.2), it is seen that for the ST group, inequality decreased by −23.13% while moving from the 61st to 66th round. For the SC group, there is a decrease of −13.13% over the entire period. An increase of 4.60% in inequality for the OBC group and 34.77% increase in inequality in the 'Others' category is observed. While considering the all-India case (see Table 4.4), inequality among the ST group increased by 4.93%, while that of the SC group decreased by around 1% during 2004–2005 to 2009–2010. For the OBC group, inequality increased by 2.41%, and for the 'Others', inequality increased by 4.18%.

In the foregoing analysis of the decomposed Gini coefficients, an overview of the persisting issue of economic inequality among various caste groups in Kerala and India has been presented. It will be interesting to see whether economic inequality has any effects on these particular groups. To answer this question, values of the overlapping index are analysed for Kerala as well as India for the reference period. Overlapping index O_i is a measure to find out the extent of stratification a particular group has undergone compared to others. O_i is bounded from below by the share of population (p_i) of the group under consideration, and bounded above by 2. For a group i, if the condition $O_{i\,=}\, p_i$ is satisfied, then that group forms a perfect stratum. If $O_i = 1$, then consumption expenditure of that group falls into the distribution of the entire population. If $1 < O_i \leq 2$, then it could be inferred that there is evidence of polarization within the said group.

Considering overlapping index values for Kerala (Table 4.2), it is seen that the ST group shows a value greater than 1 for all the two rounds. It indicates the presence of polarization within the ST group. For the SC group, the overlapping index registered a decrease of 0.05 in the 66th round. For the OBC group, overlapping index registered a value greater than 1 for the 61st and 66th round, thereby indicating polarization. The 'Others' category shows the minimum value of overlapping index among the four groups.

At the all-India level (Table 4.4); the ST group has overlapping index value greater than 1 for all the two rounds, indicating that polarization among them. For the SC group, the overlapping index registers value close to 1 for the two rounds. Here, it could be said that the range of consumption expenditure of the SC group falls into the range of the entire distribution. For the OBC group, the overlapping index shows relatively high values (approximately 0.97) for both the 61st and 66th rounds. It implies that the consumption expenditure of the OBC group also does not form a stratum, rather falls into the range of entire distribution. The 'Others' group has the least value of overlapping index showing a decreasing trend.

From the analysis of values of overlapping index, It could be observed that the criteria for perfect stratification, i.e. $O_i = p_i$ is not satisfied for any groups while considering Kerala as well as entire India. In such situation, the overlapping matrices, which give a relative measure of stratification (group differentiation), are taken into consideration for further analysis.

The overlapping matrix is especially useful when the criterion for perfect stratification is not satisfied. It gives an idea about the extent of stratification a particular group has undergone compared to the other groups. The rows in the table represent the group whose distribution is used as the base distribution. When group '*i*' is taken as the base and if it has a low overlapping index value O_{ij} w.r.t another group '*j*', it implies that there is less probability of groups '*i*' and '*j*' sharing common characteristics related to income, or in this case consumption expenditure.

For the 61st round, taking the ST group as the base does not produce any distinct groups, indicating that there is polarization prevailing within the ST group. While taking the SC group as the base, ST form a distinct group, with a value of overlapping index around 0.7, indicating that they are separated from each other somewhat in terms of consumption expenditure. With the OBC group taken as base, two distinct groups, namely SC and ST are formed. From the value of the overlapping index, it is evident that the OBC and ST groups are separated to an extent, with a fraction of the ST group falls into the consumption range of the OBC group. With 'Others' as the base, it could be seen that they are separated from SC and ST groups. However, there exists a significant part of OBC group that share similar consumption expenditure patterns as 'Others'. In the 66th round, the situation is almost similar while considering the SC, ST and OBC groups as the base. While taking the 'Others' as the base, it is clear that the overlapping index is comparatively small and decreasing over the years. It indicates that the 'Others' category is moving towards the formation of a stratum.

In the 61st round, taking the ST group as base does not create any distinct groups, which give evidence of polarization prevailing within the ST group. Taking the SC group as base, ST group and OBC group form distinct groups. However, with relatively high values of overlapping index (approx. 0.9), it could be said that these groups share some common characteristics. With the OBC group base, two groups, namely ST and SC are formed. Here, the OBC group is somewhat separated from the ST group compared to the SC group, having a value of overlapping index around 0.8. With 'Others' as the base, three groups are formed with moderate values of overlapping index, indicating the possibility of stratification.

In the 66th round, the result is analogous to that of 61st round while taking the SC and ST groups as base. With the OBC group as base, two separate groups, namely SC and ST are formed, with lower values of overlapping index compared to the previous round. Taking ‘Others’ as the base, it could be seen that the values of the overlapping index w.r.t the other three groups are declining over time, while the ‘Others’ group is progressing towards becoming a stratum.

From the above analysis, it is evident that there is polarization present within SC and ST groups at the all-India level. In Kerala, the SC group is marginally better. In case of the OBC group, it could be said that they somewhat share the consumption expenditure characteristics of SC and ST groups. However, they are separated from the ‘Others’ category. There is also evidence of the ‘Others’ showing a trend towards becoming a stratum at the Kerala as well as all-India level.

After analysing the values of the overlapping matrices, it could be said that there is relatively high probability of the poor people belonging to the ‘Others’ category sharing the same consumption expenditure characteristics of the other three groups, rather than the comparatively well-to-do people from the other three categories sharing characteristics similar to the ‘Others’ group. After observing the values of the overlapping coefficients, it could be said that stratification is taking place in Kerala at a faster rate compared to all-India level.

From the 61st to 66th rounds, the MPCE for the ST group increased for Kerala as well as India. From the 61st to 66th round, while the national average of MPCE of SC group shows an increasing trend, the same for Kerala is has marginally come down. When the mean MPCE of the OBC group and ‘Others’ are considered, there is an increasing trend visible at both Kerala as well as at all-India level. However, the change in MPCE of ‘Others’ from the 61st to 66th round is very high in Kerala as compared to the all-India scenario. It is of interest that in the 66th round, the mean MPCE of ‘Others’ in Kerala is almost double the national average of the same category.

From the following analysis, it is evident that the extent of income inequality as well as mean purchasing power in Kerala is higher compared to the national average. This presents an interesting situation. Some possible reasons for this behaviour are discussed in the coming section.

4.8 Concluding Remarks

Putting together the empirical evidences presented above, it is clear that the overall level of inequality rose faster in Kerala than in India as a whole during the reference period, i.e. from 2004–2005 to 2009–2010. For Kerala, a major part of variation of inequality over the period of analysis could be explained by the intergroup inequality component that has been increasing over the years. It could mean that the welfare measures taken up by the state in the post-liberalization era have not produced the desired effect in reducing inequality between various caste groups.

Considering the value of overlapping index for Kerala, it is evident that the ST group had to mostly bear the burden of worsening inequality. The polarization among the scheduled tribes is persistent over time. It reinforces the fact that the welfare measures initiated by the central as well as state governments have not reached to the majority of the population. It would imply that while a minority gets benefits of the various schemes, there are others who could not reap the benefits.

For the SC group, it could be inferred that the welfare measures are more widely accessible to the people compared to the ST group as the results show absence of polarization among this group. This could be attributed to the socio-political environment of Kerala, where a lot of progressive movements had taken place in order to bring people belonging to the SC group into the mainstream.

For the OBC group of Kerala, the overlapping index shows indication of polarization in the 61st and 66th round. A detailed study may be required to understand the dynamics of this issue, although it could be assumed that migration to Gulf (GCC) countries might have a contribution.

At the all-India level, a similar trend could be observed after analysing the overlapping coefficients. The ST group remains polarized. The SC and OBC groups, along with the ST group share some similar characteristics related to the consumption expenditure. However, they are separated from the 'Others' group to an extent.

Another interesting point is the possibility of stratification among 'Others'. This behaviour is visible both at Kerala as well as all-India level. However, it is happening at a comparatively faster pace in Kerala. This claim is substantiated by the reducing overlapping coefficients as well the high mean MCPE of this group. The 'Others' group consists of the upper caste people, who might be financially better off compared to others, with relatively more purchasing power. Such a scenario indicates formation of an elite class over the time. The separation of 'Others' from the rest of the groups could be attributed to the economic disparities as well as prevailing caste hierarchy.

It should be noted that in India, caste still plays an important role determining one's economic and social status. The social hierarchy is reflected in the economic hierarchy as well, where the SC and ST groups come to the bottom of the group in both cases. Even though the marginalized sections (ST and SC) are comparatively better off in Kerala, the extent of economic inequality among them is high. Also, a majority among these groups are not able to avail the benefits of the various welfare programs aimed at them. Steps should be taken by the central as well as state governments in order to ensure that the welfare measures are properly reached and distributed evenly among the target groups.

References

Deshpande, A. (2000). Does caste still define disparity? A look at inequality in Kerala, India. *The American Economic Review, 90*(2), 322–325.

Frick, J. R., Goebel, J., Schechtman, E., Wagner, G. G., & Yitzhaki, S. (2004). *Using analysis of Gini (Anogi) for detecting whether two sub-samples represent the same universe: The SOEP experience*. Discussion Paper No. 1049, IZA, Germany.

Frick, J. R., & Goebel, J. (2005). *Regional income stratification in unified Germany using a Gini decomposition approach*. Discussion Papers—504, German Institute for Economic Research, Berlin.

Himanshu. (2007). Recent trends in poverty and inequality: Some preliminary results. *Economic and Political Weekly, 42*(6), 497–508.

Jann, B., & Masterson, T. (2007). *Anogi: Stata module to generate Analysis of Gini*. Retrieved from http://ideas.repec.org/c/boc/bocode/s456730.html. (Accessed July 05, 2015).

Jayadev, A., Motiram, S., & Vakulabharanam, V. (2007). Patterns of wealth disparities in India during the era of liberalization. *Economic and Political Weekly, 42*(39), 3853–3863.

Lasswell, T. E. (1965). *Class and stratum*. Boston, Massachusetts: Houghton Mifflin Company.

Lerman, R., & Yitzhaki, S. (1984). A note on the calculation and interpretation of the Gini index. *Economics Letters, 15,* 68–363.

Milanovic, B., & Yitzhaki, S. (2002). Decomposing world income distribution: Does the world have a middle class? *Review of Income and Wealth, 48*(2), 78–155.

Motiram, S., & Sarma, N. (2011). *Polarization, inequality and growth: The Indian experience*. Working Paper—2011–011, IGIDR, Mumbai.

Nagaraj, R. (2000). Indian economy since the 1980s: Virtuous growth or polarization? *Economic and Political Weekly, 35*(32), 2831–2839.

Parayil, G. (2000). *Kerala: The Development Experience: Reflections on Sustainability and Replicability*. London: Zed Books.

Planning Commission. (2011). *Data book for Deputy Chairman*. Retrieved from http://planningcommission.nic.in/reports/genrep/ar_eng1112.pdf (Accessed August 07, 2015).

Sarkar, S., & Mehta, B. S. (2010). Income inequality in India: Pre- and post-reform periods. *Economic and Political Weekly, 45*(37), 45–55.

Sen, A., & Himanshu. (2004a). Poverty and inequality in India-I. *Economic and Political Weekly, 39*(38), 4247–4263.

Sen, A., & Himanshu. (2004b). Poverty and inequality in India—Growing disparities in the 1990s. *Economic and Political Weekly, 39*(39), 4361–4375.

Subramanian, S., & Jayaraj, D. (2006). *The distribution of household wealth in India*. Research Paper No. 2006/116, Prepared within the UNU-WIDER project on Personal Assets from a Global Perspective.

Subramanian, S., & Prasad, S. (2008). *Rising inequality with high growth isn't this trend worrisome? Analysis of Kerala experience*. Working Paper—401, CDS, Trivandrum.

Sundaram, K., & Tendulkar, S. D. (2003). *Poverty among social and economic groups in India in the nineteen nineties*. Working paper—118, Centre for Development Economics, Delhi School of Economics.

Yitzhaki, S. (1982). Relative deprivation and economic welfare. *European Economic Review, 17,* 99–113.

Yitzhaki, S., & Lerman, R. (1991). Income Stratification and Income Inequality. *Review of Income and Wealth, 37*(3), 313–329.

Zhong, W., Vakulabharanam, V., Ruparelia, S., Ming, Y., Deshpande, A., & Banerjee, L. (2010). Wealth Inequality: China And India: India China Institute collaborative Project. *Prosperity and inequality in India and China, 2008–2010*. New York: India China Institute, The New School.

Chapter 5
Can Horizontal Inequalities Explain Ethnic Conflicts? A Case Study of Bodoland Territorial Area Districts of Assam

Rupan Boro and Rajshree Bedamatta

Abstract Inequalities play a major role in political and ethnic conflicts in different regions of the world. However economic literature has largely focused on vertical inequalities, i.e. inequalities among individuals as opposed to groups of people. In the recent times the focus has shifted to the role of horizontal inequalities, which refer to inequalities between groups of people sharing common identity such as race, ethnicity, language, religion or region (Stewart 2000). Therefore, they are multi-faceted and include various dimensions (for, e.g. socio-economic, political and cultural status). This chapter refers to the recent Bodo-Muslim conflict in the Bodoland Territorial Area Districts of Assam (BTAD) in 2012. We measure economic horizontal inequalities (EHIs) classifying population of BTAD into STs, SCs, OBC, other/general and Muslims using population weighted group Gini index (GGini). NSSO unit level data of 61st and 66th Consumer-Expenditure rounds have been used for calculations. We find that there are significant spatial and horizontal economic inequalities in the BTAD districts compared to the other districts of Assam. Among the social groups, Muslims are found to be the poorest while SCs are better off followed by the STs (mostly Bodos). In Assam as a whole, the extent of land owned by the ST households is found to be the highest while it is lowest among the Muslims. In sharp contrast, land ownership among Muslims is comparatively higher than the other groups (including the dominant Bodo group) in BTAD.

Keywords Horizontal inequality
Ethnic conflicts and Bodoland territorial area districts

R. Boro (✉) · R. Bedamatta
Department of Humanities and Social Sciences,
IIT Guwahati, Guwahati 781039, India
e-mail: bororupan71@gmail.com

R. Bedamatta
e-mail: rajshreeb@gmail.com

U.K. De et al. (eds.), *Inequality, Poverty and Development in India*, India Studies in Business and Economics, DOI 10.1007/978-981-10-6274-2_5

5.1 Introduction

People in a society with diverse ethnic or religious settings often engage in competition over resources. Bardhan (1997) argues that such competition leaves the marginalised and disadvantaged groups without access to socio-economic and political opportunities, subsequently leading to deprivation. Prolonged periods of relative deprivation may lead to ethnic conflicts causing disintegration in the society (Gurr 1968). The diverse ethno-linguistic groups in the state of Assam have strong aspirations of preserving their own distinct identity and improving socio-economic and political positions including cultural status. Such aspirations have led to intense competition over accessing economic resources and political power (Pathak 2013; Mahanta 2013; Motiram and Sarma 2014). Secessionist and ethno-political conflicts have marred the fabric of Assamese society for a long period of time (Xaxa 2008; Pathak 2013). Some such secessionist conflicts are the Bodoland movement, ethnic clashes between Bodo-Muslim, Bodo-Santhal and Rabha-Non-Rabha groups in the Western Plains region and between Hmar-Dimasa, and Karbi–non-Karbi tribes in the hills districts of Assam. Such conflicts have caused large numbers of deaths and massive internal displacement of population coupled with considerable loss of property.

Bodoland Territorial Area Districts (BTAD) and the districts surrounding them in western Assam is one of the most conflict prone regions of India. It has seen severe massacres and group-based conflicts since the 1990s, besides the secessionist Bodoland movement launched by the indigenous Bodo people since 1960s. The group-based conflicts since the 1990s represent an example of intense ethno-linguistic fractionalization (Motiram and Sarma 2014). The conflict between the Bodo and Muslim groups has been one of the largest in the recent decades, as well as a more recurrent one.[1] Motiram and Sarma (2014) based on a study of the BTAD, with data from the National Sample Survey Organisation (NSSO), have concluded that group-based inequalities in the region is likely to grow in the coming years.

Studies on the Bodoland secessionist movement by Das (1982), Goswami and Mukherjee (1982), Gohain (1989), Mishra (1989), George (1994), Xaxa (2008), and Basumatary (2012) have highlighted issues surrounding group discrimination, in-migration of non-tribals into tribal areas, alienation of land, and domination of 'alien' language and culture. However a systematic study of group-based inequalities based on socio-economic sample surveys has been lacking. In the

[1]The effects of this conflict are even worse than the widely discussed case of Gujarat in 2002 (ibid). People from northeastern origin were targeted in Pune, Bangalore, Mumbai and other parts of the countries as retaliation of this conflict. It left 65 dead, hundreds of wounded and loss of properties by affecting 5780 villages (Chirang and Kokrajhar District Administrations 2015). Besides, the Bodoland secessionist movement claimed 1607 lives in Assam out of which more than 80% were inhabitant of original districts of BTAD over a period of 16 years from 1987 to 2003 (BTC 2013).

economic literature, group-based inequalities have been referred as horizontal inequalities as against vertical inequalities that highlight inequalities within groups.

This chapter argues that the presence and perpetuation of horizontal inequalities among different ethnic groups can be used to explain ethno-political conflicts in BTAD and its neighbouring districts. In order to develop this argument, the chapter has used the framework of measuring horizontal inequalities developed by Mancini, Stewart and Brown (2010) to explain civil conflicts. The National Sample Survey Organisation (NSSO) unit level data pertaining to 61st and 66th rounds of Consumption Expenditure and Employment Unemployment for the BTAD districts and Assam have been analysed. NSSO unit level data for Assam as a whole, Western Assam and the BTAD districts have been analysed for three different dimensions. They are (i) average monthly per capita consumption expenditure (MPCE), (ii) operational and ownership holdings of land and (iii) administrative positions.

5.2 Measurement of Inequalities

The civil conflict literature has been rising since the 1990s. Quantitative and econometric approaches to understanding the nexus between ethnicity, inequality and violent conflicts have also been attempted (for example, Fearon and Laitin 2003; Collier and Hoeffler 2004; Dixon 2009; and Lindquist 2012). Many studies have concluded that although theoretically the link between economic inequality and civil (and ethnic) conflicts can be established, empirical evidences do not support a significant cause and effect relationship. For example, the works of Fearon and Laitin (2003) and Collier and Hoeffler (2004) calculated Gini coefficient for income inequality and conducted a regression analysis on ethnic conflicts as the independent variable. They hypothesised a positive relationship between levels of ethnic diversity and propensity to civil conflicts, but empirical investigation did not provide significant results between 'ethnic fractionalization' and 'ethnic civil conflict' (see Lindquist 2012 for a detailed discussion).

One of the reasons for no conclusive evidence on an empirical relationship between inequalities and ethnic conflicts, it is claimed, could be due to the measure of inequality that is chosen. There is now a sizeable economic literature that focuses on the differences between horizontal inequalities (His) and vertical inequalities (Vis). Vertical inequalities are measured based on extensive use of the techniques of Lorenz ratio and Gini coefficient confined to economic variables such as income, consumption expenditure, or other wealth indicators. They capture the differences between individuals in a society where people are grouped based on a geographical area or on conventional variable(s), such as income, for which inequality can be numerically measured. For example, to measure income inequality people are classified into groups based on geographical location or certain level of income irrespective of their social and ethnic identities. Therefore such measurements fail to capture inequality between the groups sharing common identity; and as such been largely neglected in the development discourse (Stewart 2000; Ostby 2007; Mancini et al. 2010; Lindquist 2012).

Horizontal inequalities are measured grouping the individuals based on non-economic variables like ethnicity, religion and language and thus it can capture the differences in socio-economic conditions between the groups (Stewart 2000 and Ostby 2007). Based on this difference in measure of inequality, economists have sought to inquire the motives behind group mobilisation leading to violence. Many scholars have empirically shown a positive and statistically significant relationship between HIs and risk of violent conflicts (Stewart 2000, 2010; Langer 2005; Tiwari 2008; Mancini 2010). HIs are shown as the basis for group mobilisation and political or ethnic conflicts such as these provide powerful grievances, which the leaders of deprived groups use to mobilise people for political action.

5.2.1 Concept of Horizontal Inequalities

Unlike VIs, HIs are therefore multifaceted and incl ude socio-economic, political and cultural status dimensions. Horizontal Economic Inequality (HEI) incorporates inequalities in access to and ownership of assets like financial, livestock, human, and social and also in employment opportunities and incomes. HIs in social dimension (HSI) encompasses the variation in access to a range of social services such as education, health care, sanitation, and housing and human outcomes from such services. Horizontal Political Inequality (HPI) occurs when there is inequality in distribution of political opportunities and power including control over the army, participation at the level of cabinet, parliament, bureaucracy and local government. The cultural status horizontal inequality (HCI) reflects the variations in recognition of cultural practices like language, dress, religion and way of living (ibid).

5.2.2 Role of Horizontal Inequalities in Explaining Ethnic Conflicts

Studies on violent ethnic or political conflicts have strong pointers to HIs as primary cause of conflicts. Differential treatment of people based on language, religion and religious observation, and culture results in identity formation and cleavages among the groups (Langer 2005, 2010, Tiwari 2008; Stewart 2010). Giving priority to the language or religion of one group by recognising as official one, leave others feel undermined and humiliated. This results in deep sense of alienation and frustration among the underprivileged groups which lead to mobilisation along cultural lines (Bardhan 1997; Langer 2005, 2010). For example, the enactment of the 1956 Official Languages Act to make Sinhalese the only official language of Sri Lanka and the 1972 constitutional amendment which gave Buddhism 'foremost status' in the country are policies of political and social exclusion of the Tamil minority, which in turn has provoked demands for greater autonomy and armed conflicts (Bardhan 1997). In a society with unequal distribution of political power and opportunities among the elites, the sharp socio-economic inequalities along the cultural differences are often placed in national political sphere. HIs in such a society give strong incentive to both the leaders and people for political mobilisation. Thus, the coexistence of socio-economic and political inequalities along cultural differences create extremely explosive and volatile socio-political situations, as a leader, in such a society, has not only strong incentive for political mobilisation but also can gain easy support from the group members who are also concerned about their own groups' position (Langer 2010; Brown and Langer 2010; Stewart 2010). In fact, HPI is more likely to motivate the leaders of the excluded groups for agitation. If they fail to fulfil their aspiration through agitation or protests, violence follows.

Stewart (2010) in her study of political mobilisation among the Blacks in South Africa compares the GDP per capita and educational attainment of the whites and blacks. She opines that white minority which had acquired political power through colonial rule used both political power and economic resources to entrench itself politically and enhance its socio-economic conditions. It resulted in sharp socio-economic inequalities between the groups. For instance, it was only 8% of white's GDP per capita for the Black in 1980. Moreover, relatively much higher expenditure on schooling and healthcare services on each White child compared to the Black resulted in poor education and health outcomes among the Blacks compared to the Whites. She documents that socio-economic HIs are the major cause of political mobilisation among the Blacks in South Africa. Similarly, Ostby (2007) in her study of civil conflicts in 55 developing countries during 1986–2003 measures HIs in terms of three alternative group identifiers like ethnicity, religion and region. She measures HEI based on variation in household assets while HSI on educational attainments among the groups. HIs in both dimensions are found to have positive effect on the probability of conflict.

Mancini (2010) also draws same inference for conflicts in Indonesia. He measures HIs in terms of education, land ownership, public sector employment and child mortality rates to test their link with conflicts. He finds that the HIs in all dimensions have positive association with the likelihood of deadly conflicts. Among these four dimensions, HIs in child mortality rates is found to have strongest impact on conflicts. He argues that group differences in child mortality rates reflect inequalities in other socio-economic conditions like, household wealth, levels of education, housing conditions and so on. Other studies on ethnic or separatist conflicts break-out in different countries, for instances studies on Maoist mobilisation in Nepal by Murshed and Gates (2005), Tiwari (2008), Nepal et al. (2011), and conflicts in Indonesia, Philippines and Coat d'Ivoire by Brown and Langer (2010) have also shown positive association of HIs with violent conflicts.

The perceptions of people on group identity and their impact in access to public amenities and services, and on favouritism and discriminatory attitude of the government also play significant role in escalating such ethnic or separatist conflicts (Langer and Ukiwo 2010; Stewart 2010). Langer and Ukiwo (2010) in their comparative study of Ghana and Nigeria find that perception has played a significant role in escalating severe ethno-communal and religious conflicts. While in Ghana majority of the people regard occupation and nationality as important identity of people, in Nigeria the ethnicity/language, religion and region are regarded important. Relatively larger proportions of people in Nigeria than Ghana perceive that the ethnic or religious background affects access to government amenities and services. This difference in perception of people in Nigeria and Ghana is shown as an important reason, of why Nigeria has been facing recurrent ethno-communal and religious conflicts, while Ghana is able to avoid such conflicts despite both the countries facing similar measured socio-economic inequalities including political exclusion among the groups (Langer and Ukiwo 2010). Prevalence and rising HIs therefore are shown as major factor provoking ethnic strife or secessionist movements in many countries. Both the perceived and measured HIs provide strong grievances to the deprived groups for political mobilisation, protest and agitation against the government or advanced groups.

5.3 Demographic Profile of Assam

Assam's prolonged secessionist and ethno-political conflicts also deserves attention within this paradigm of horizontal inequalities and ethnic conflicts. The state of Assam has been home to diverse ethnic, religion and cultural groups. Its population has risen to 3.12 crore in 2011 from 2.66 crore in 2001 and 2.44 crore in 1991 at an annual growth rate of 1.75 and 1.60 between 1991–2001 and 2001–2011, respectively. Following the social group classification followed in rest of the country, population of Assam may also be broadly classified into general, schedules castes and scheduled tribe households. Among them, non-tribal and non-SC population forms the majority, who speak Assamese, Bengali and a mix of other languages. Both the STs and SCs represent 12 and 7% respectively as per census, 2011. The ST population of Assam consists of 22 different ethno-linguistic groups such as Bodos, Mising, Mikir/Karbi, Rabha, Deori, Nagas, Khasis, etc. who speak their own dialect. The SCs consist of 17 groups of people like Basfors, Banyas, Dhobis, Hira and so on. Among the tribal population, Bodos constitute a numerically large

Table 5.1 Population by tribes and their share in total tribal population of Assam

Tribe	Population			Percentage of total STs		
	1991	2001	2011	1991	2001	2011
Bodo	11,84,569	13,52,771	–	41	41	–
Miri	3,81,562	5,87,310	–	13	18	–
Mikir/Karbi	3,55,032	3,53,513	–	12	11	–
Rabha	1,35,905	2,77,517	–	5	8	–
Kachari	1,14,779	2,35,881	–	4	7	–
Lalung	1,12,424	1,70,622	–	4	5	–
Dimasa	84,654	110,976	–	3	3	–
Deori	32,633	41,161	–	1	1	–
Others	4,72,863	2,89,795	–	16	6	–
Total STs	28,74,421	33,08,570	38,84,321	13	12	12
SCs	16,59,412	18,25,949	22,31,321	7	7	7
State population	2,24,14,292	2,66,55,528	3,12,05,576	–	–	–

Source Registrar general and census commissioner, Government of India, 1991, 2001 and 2011

group, representing nearly a quarter (41%) followed by Mising (18%) and Karbi (11%) as per census of India, 2001 (Table 5.1).

The people of Assam have also been classified into six major religion groups: Buddhists, Christians, Hindus, Jains, Muslims and Sikhs (Tables 5.4 and 5.5). Among them, the Hindus with 61% are majority as per census of 2011. The Muslims in BTAD represent 19% as against constituting 34% of the total population in the state. The classification of people based on socio-religious groups have shown that people belong to OBC and general categories altogether comprise 44% in western Assam (Table 5.5). Between 1991 and 2001, among the socio-religious groups, growth rate of Muslim population with 2.6% per annum has been the highest while it is the lowest among the SCs (0.01% in Western Assam and 0.9% in Assam). The growth rate among the STs on the other hand in the western Assam has been recorded at 0.6% as against 1.42% in the state as a whole.

The BTAD region is inhabited by various ethno-linguistic and religious groups. It is said that the Bodo Accords have left the non-Bodo people with fear of losing legitimate democratic rights and of being deprived from socio-economic opportunities (Mahanta 2013). Gradually it has resulted in cleavages between the Bodo and non-Bodo groups in BTAD. Formation of the Oboro Surakshya Samiti (Non-Bodos Protection Committee) and the Sanmalita Janagastia Sangram Samiti (SJSS: United Ethnic Peoples' Struggle Committee) bears evidence of this (Mahanta 2013 and Pathak 2013). These organisations have been holding protests before and after creation of the BTC. Leaders of the non-Bodo organisations have the perception that BTC government favours the Bodos only (Mahanta 2013). They also claim that all the educational institutions, hospitals, government departments are set up only in the Bodo-dominated areas apart from disproportionate representation of the Bodos in employment and administrative sector (ibid). Therefore there is a perception that socio-economic and political resources and unequally distributed among the groups.

5.4 Methodology

In this study, we use group Gini (GGini) coefficient based on Mancini et al. (2010) to measure economic inequality among the social groups. Gini coefficient, a widely used approach, measures variance in performance of each group with every other group, where observations are grouped based on the variable for which inequality is measured (Ray 2010). However, measuring HIs requires grouping the individuals based on non-economic variables such as ethnicity, religion or caste. We group the individuals based on religion and caste to measure inequalities among them. Since the number of individuals is not same for all the groups an un-weighted measurement would attach equal weight to all groups and thus the changes in position of very small group would have the same effect as the large group (Mancini et al. 2010). Therefore, weights attached are based on population share of each group. In addition to that, we test if the inequality among the groups is statistically significant using one-way Analysis of variance (ANOVA).

5.4.1 Measurement of HIs

$$\text{Population weighted GGini} = \frac{1}{2\overline{Y}} \sum_{r}^{R} \sum_{s}^{S} P_r P_s \left| \overline{Y_r} - \overline{Y_s} \right|,$$

where $\overline{Y}$ is mean of variable (say average MPCE of all groups), R = population size of Rth group (Say population size of Muslims), S = population size of Sth group (say population size of STs), $\overline{Y}_r$ is mean of variable for group R (say MPCE of Muslims), $\overline{Y}_s$ is mean of variable for group S (say MPCE of STs), P_r is share in total population of group R or Muslims, and P_s is share in total population of group S or STs.

5.4.2 Data Source

To measure HEI and establish causal connections with group-based conflicts, we have to depend on a reliable dataset. The sources of data used for this study are Census of India and National Sample Survey Organisation (NSSO). Population data by different social groups are based on 1991, 2001 and 2011 census. Census data are available on household amenities and occupations however the data cannot be disaggregated by social groups. Thus census data are not enough to fulfil our objective. Similarly the NSS, though it collects nationally representative large sample data for estimating important socio-economic parameters, it furnishes information merely at state level. Since our objective is to measure HIs in the BTAD, we have used unit level data of NSS. The NSSO 61st (2004–2005) and 66th (2009–2010) Consumption Expenditure and Employment Unemployment round data have been used to calculate the population weighted group Gini coefficients.

5.4.3 NSS Unit Level Data Used in the Study

NSS collects data from large sample surveys conducted throughout the country and provides important information on various socio-economic aspects which are relied on by policy makers, researchers and planning agencies. The NSS classify each state into numbers of sub-state or region to select first stage unit (FSU), i.e. sample villages in rural and blocks in urban sectors from which sample households are surveyed. Sample villages are selected in rural areas taking district as strata while the sample blocks are selected from a sub-region or strata which are formed based on the size class of town (Chaudhuri and Gupta 2009). Thus, the surveys allow reliable estimate at regional level but not at district level. Regional-level estimation could be made for the purpose of our study if our concerned districts were included in a region. But the districts we have considered are spread across different regions. For example, in 56th round of survey, Assam has been classified into three sub-regions: Plains eastern, Plains western and Hills. The BTAD districts of Bongaigaon, Barpeta and Nalbari were included in Plains eastern, Kokrajhar in Hills region while Darrang, Dhubri and Kamrup in Plains western. However, there have been shifts in sampling design since the 61st round (2004–2005).

The new sampling design defined district as strata where both the rural and urban sectors are taken as part of that district for selection of sample villages and blocks from both the sectors allowing estimation at district level too. Moreover, each sector or stratum has been divided into two sub-stratums to select FSUs from the districts. Villages within each district in the sample frame have been arranged in ascending order of population and then the sub-stratum has been demarcated in such a way that each sub-stratum comprises a group of villages and has more or less equal number of population. Similarly, the urban sub-stratum has been framed in such a way that each sub-stratum has more or equal number of blocks or FSUs. Thereafter, sample villages and blocks have been selected from each sub-stratum of a district.

For selecting households from the selected villages or blocks, the households are further classified into three second stage stratum (SSS). In rural sector, households are classified into relatively affluent households, households with principal earnings from other than agriculture activities and other households. Classification of the households in the urban sector on the other hand has been made on the basis of monthly per capita consumption expenditure (MPCE). Based on this classification two households had been surveyed from the first SSS while four households from each of other two SSS. Since the sampling schemes used in the surveys prior to 61st round allowed to make neither district level estimation nor regional level estimation for our study, we have used two quinquennial surveys of 61st and 66th rounds on 'consumption expenditure' and 'employment and unemployment' covering about 10 years period from 2004–05 to 2009–10.

As already discussed, the specific dimensions used to measure horizontal inequalities are average MPCE, ownership and operational holdings of land and administrative positions held by households in the sample dataset.

MPCE is defined as ratio of the aggregate household consumption expenditure referring monetary value of consumption of various goods and services during a reference period to household size. Entitlement of land ownership is measured based on extent of land owned and land possessed. The former refers to a piece of land owned by any member of household vested with the permanent heritable ownership with or without right to transfer, while the latter refers to land owned including leased-in and neither leased-in nor leased-out (i.e. encroached) excluding leased-out land. Based on National Classification of Occupation (NCO) we have taken five sub-groups of occupation like legislators and senior officer, managers, professionals and technicians, and clerks (office and customer service clerks) and renamed as administration. These are the occupations associated not just with security but also with the matter of ethnic pride and prestige. Many researchers have used these occupations to measure HPI (e.g. see Otsby 2007; Tiwari 2008).

5.4.4 Data Limitations

Small size of sample of each district that may not cover all the social groups prevent us from having district level estimates of socio-economic parameters by social groups. Therefore, we estimate the socio-economic status of the various social groups at regional level. We group the four districts of BTAD with their original districts and rename it Western Assam. It comprises eight districts of Barpeta, Bongaigaon, Darang, Dhubri, Kamrup, Kokrajhar, Nalbari and Sonitpur based on 61st round survey while 12 districts including new districts of Baksa, Chirang, Kamrup Metro and Udalguri in the 66th round survey. One more limitation of using the unit level data for us is that information are collected by classifying population broadly into four groups: scheduled tribes (STs), scheduled castes (SCs), other backward classes (OBC) and others/general but not collected ethnicity wise. Thus the surveys do not have separate information for Bodo ethnic group. However, the Bodos represent the STs in western Assam as they constitute more than 70% of total ST population in the eight districts based on census of 2001 (Table 5.2). Therefore, socio-economic status of the STs can be treated as that of the Bodos. The surveys on the other hand have extensive religion-wise information as the information is collected classifying people into eight major religion groups. The socio-religious classification of the people is mutually exclusive and thus it is

Table 5.2 Bodo population and their share in total ST population in undivided BTAD, Assam

	Population	ST	Bodo	Percentage, ST	Percentage of Bodo in total ST
Kokrajhar	905,764	304,985	287,268	34	94
Dhubri	1,637,344	32,523	22,208	2	68
Bongaigaon	904,835	110,696	102,610	12	93
Barpeta	1,647,201	123,266	117,120	7	95
Nalbari	1,148,824	202,577	176,576	18	87
Kamrup	2,522,324	250,393	140,023	10	56
Darrang	1,504,320	249,861	207,878	17	83
Sonitpur	1,681,513	195,083	140,293	12	72
Western Assam	11,952,125	1,469,384	1,193,976	12	72
Assam	26,655,528	3,308,570	1,352,771	12	41

Source Authors' calculation from the data of Registrar general and census commissioner, Government of India, 2001

possible to identify a household of any religious group and which social category that household belongs to. That makes it possible for us to separate household of a religious group from any social group. We have excluded Muslims from all social categories (STs, SC, OBC and other) and categorised them as a separate group for the sake of our study. Based on NSS's socio-religious classification we have grouped households into five categories: Muslims, STs, SCs, OBC and General.

5.5 Horizontal Inequalities for Assam Based on Group Gini

Consumption expenditure, entitlement of land ownership and occupations are important indicators of economic status of people in a society. For example in rural sector, majority of households depend on agriculture and allied activities. The land therefore serves as means of livelihood for many households in rural sector by giving employment and earning opportunities. The variations in distribution of and access to these variables among the different social groups indicate economic inequalities in a society. Hence, we have taken monthly per capita consumption expenditure (MPCE), land ownership and occupation to measure HIs. The preceding table depicts HEI measured by population weighted group Gini (GGini) which implies higher the values more the inequalities.

Table 5.3 Horizontal inequalities measured by population weighted GGini

	2004–05 (61st round)		2009–10 (66th round)		
	Assam	W. Assam	Assam	W. Assam	BTAD
MPCE	0.35*	0.36*	0.45*	0.47*	0.33*
Land owned	0.67*	0.67*	0.61*	0.39**	0.27
Land possessed	0.73*	0.64*	0.66*	0.64*	0.47**
Administration	0.87*	0.99*	0.98*	0.87*	0.99*

Source Authors' calculation from the unit level data of NSSO's 61st and 66th round surveys on "Consumption expenditure" and "Employment and unemployment"
Note Data for MPCE is based on consumer-expenditure rounds while others are based on employment and unemployment rounds
*indicates significant at 1% level, **at 5% level and ***at 10% level

5.5.1 Horizontal Inequalities in Consumption Expenditure

The GGini value measured by MPCE is statistically significant across the regions in both the years (see Appendix Table 5.10 to 5.14). The inequalities in western Assam had risen from 0.36 in 2004–2005 to 0.47 in 2009–2010 while in whole Assam it had risen from 0.35 to 0.45 during that period. Thus, the HI in western Assam has not only been higher than that of whole Assam but also has risen at greater magnitude. Among the social groups, the consumption expenditure of the Muslims is the lowest across the regions in both the years (Table 5.7). Similarly, the MPCE of STs in both Assam (Rs. 571 in 2004–2005 and Rs. 890 in 2009–2010) and western Assam (Rs. 589 in 2004–2005 and Rs. 881 in 2009–2010) has been lower not only the average MPCE of whole Assam (Rs. 591 in 2004–2005 and Rs. 933 in 2009–2010) and that in western Assam (Rs. 581 in 2004–2005 and Rs. 893 in 2009–2010) but also that of all other groups.

It is worth to note that HIs in BTAD is relatively lower in comparison to that in other regions as indicated by its GGini value 0.33 compared to 0.45 and 0.47 of whole Assam and western Assam respectively during 2009–2010. However, consumption expenditure of all the groups in BTAD is relatively lower than that of their respective own groups in both Assam and western Assam in 2009–2010. For example, average MPCE of Muslims in BTAD has been recorded at just Rs. 575 compared to own group's MPCE Rs. 764 and Rs. 732 in western Assam and whole Assam respectively in 2009–2010. Similarly, MPCE of general group with Rs. 748 in BTAD was much lower than its MPCE (Rs. 1152) in whole Assam during that year.

5.5.2 Horizontal Inequalities in Operational and Ownership Holding of Land

Similar statistically significant inequalities in entitlement of land ownership have been found in both the whole Assam and western Assam (see Table 5.15 to 5.24). It is also observed from the Table 5.3 that inequalities in land ownership have reduced in 2009–2010 in both the regions. Inequality in land owned in western Assam which was significant at 1% level in 2004–2005 had become significant at 5% level in 2009–2010. The fall in inequality in land ownership may be resulted by fall in the gap between the highest and lowest extents of land ownership during 2004–2005 to 2009–2010. For example, the difference in the land owned between the Muslims and STs in whole Assam was 0.54 hectares (1.24 hectares of STs and 0.70 hectares of Muslims see Table 5.8) in 2004–05 which had fallen to 0.35 hectares (1.11 hectares of STs and 0.77 hectares of Muslims) in 2009–2010. Similarly in western Assam, the land owned (1.32 hectares) and possessed (1.31hectares) of STs in 2004–2005 fallen to 0.70 and 0.76 hectares of owned and possessed respectively in 2009–2010 causing fall in gaps between the highest and lowest extents. The GGini values measured by land owned (0.27) and land possessed (0.36) in BTAD have been lower than the respective values for both the state as a whole and western Assam in 2009–2010. Moreover, inequality in land owned is not statistically significant while that with respect to land possessed is significant at 5% level in BTAD during 2009–2010. Thus BTAD's HIs in land ownership entitlement is not only less compared with other regions but also statistically less significant. However, it is interesting to note that the land ownership among the Muslims is found relatively lower than the extent of ownership of the other groups in both the western Assam and whole state in 2009–2010. In sharp contrast, extent of land ownership among the Muslims is relatively higher than the other groups including the STs (dominant groups) in BTAD the group which has highest extent of ownership in other regions.

5.5.3 Horizontal Inequalities in Administrative Position

Horizontal inequalities in BTAD as measured by MPCE and land owned have been found relatively lower in comparison to that of other regions. However, its HEI (0.99) based on administrative as principal earning source or primary occupation of the household have been found statistically significant as well as relatively higher than those in both western Assam (0.87) and whole state (0.98) in 2009–2010. The proportion of the household belongs to different social groups with this occupation indicates the Muslims household is the lowest in entire regions in 2009–2010 (see Table 5.9). It is also observed that households with administrative as principal occupation of all the social groups except the SCs in BTAD are relatively lower than their respective groups in both the western Assam and the state of Assam as a whole in 2009–2010.

5.6 Conclusion

Analysis of NSSO unit level data shows that horizontal or group-based inequalities do exist in Assam. The level of inequality based on group Gini estimate is found to be highest in the dimension of administrative positions, followed by land possessed, land owned and by average monthly per capita consumption expenditure. The GGini estimates for both the 61st and 66th rounds are found to be statistically significant in all the dimensions. As far as the dimension of administrative positions is concerned, horizontal inequalities seem to have consistently risen between the period 2004–2005 and 2009–2010. In fact, group-based inequalities based on administrative positions are found to be close to 1 in Western Assam in 2004–2005 and in BTAD in 2009–10.

The average MPCE estimates show that the levels of consumption expenditure in BTAD are the lowest compared to Western Assam and Assam. Similarly, the proportion of population holding administrative positions is also lowest in BTAD, and this is true across all social groups (including the Bodo and Muslim groups). While proportion of population holding administrative positions are very low in BTAD when compared to Western Assam and Assam, Gini close to 1 shows that inequality within groups in BTAD is extremely high.

Appendix 5.1

See Tables 5.4, 5.5, 5.6, 5.7, 5.8 and 5.9.

Appendix 5.2

List of ANOVA tables.

Table 5.4 Classification of the population by religion in Assam, 2011

District	Hindu	Muslim	Christian	Sikh	Buddhist	Jain	Others/not stated
Dhubri	19.92	79.67	0.21	0.01	0.01	0.09	0.08
Goalpara	34.51	57.52	7.72	0.08	0.02	0.05	0.11
Barpeta	29.11	70.74	0.06	0.01	0	0.02	0.06
Morigaon	47.2	52.56	0.09	0.01	0.01	0.03	0.11
Nagaon	43.39	55.36	0.95	0.11	0.04	0.04	0.11
Sonitpur	73.95	18.22	7.18	0.07	0.26	0.05	0.27
Lakhimpur	76.49	18.57	4.43	0.04	0.1	0.02	0.34
Dhemaji	95.47	1.96	1.27	0.04	0.13	0.02	1.1
Tinsukia	88.96	3.64	5.79	0.15	1.22	0.06	0.17
Dibrugarh	90.35	4.86	3.99	0.17	0.35	0.08	0.18
Sivasagar	87.51	8.3	2.88	0.08	0.34	0.02	0.86
Jorhat	92.31	5.01	1.93	0.14	0.22	0.07	0.34
Golaghat	85.99	8.46	4.74	0.11	0.36	0.05	0.29
Karbi Anglong	80.1	2.12	16.5	0.04	0.65	0.04	0.54
Dima Hasao	67.07	2.04	29.57	0.1	0.32	0.03	0.88
Cachar	59.83	37.71	2.17	0.02	0.02	0.1	0.17
Karimganj	42.48	56.36	0.98	0.01	0.04	0.04	0.09
Hailakandi	38.1	60.31	1.29	0.01	0.07	0.04	0.17
Bongaigaon	48.61	50.22	0.8	0.05	0.03	0.12	0.16
Kamrup	57.82	39.66	2.19	0.02	0.01	0.09	0.21
Kamrup Metro	84.89	12.05	1.5	0.29	0.13	0.74	0.41
Nalbari	63.71	35.96	0.06	0.01	0	0.13	0.14
Darrang	35.25	64.34	0.18	0.05	0.01	0.08	0.1
Kokrajhar	59.64	28.44	11.4	0.01	0.19	0.04	0.28
Chirang	66.5	22.66	10.32	0.02	0.08	0.03	0.39
Baksa	82.4	14.29	2.85	0.02	0.13	0.03	0.29
Udalguri	73.64	12.66	13.25	0.03	0.2	0.01	0.2
BTAD	71.25	19.12	9.14	0.02	0.16	0.03	0.28
Assam	61.47	34.22	3.74	0.07	0.18	0.08	0.25

Source Registrar general and census commissioner, Govt. of India, 2011

Table 5.5 Social group composition of population in Assam in 2001

District	Muslims	ST	SC	Others
Goalpara	54	16	5	25
Marigaon	48	16	13	24
Nagaon	51	4	9	36
Lakhimpur	16	23	8	52
Dhemaji	2	47	5	46
Tinsukia	3	6	3	88
Dibrugarh	4	7	4	84
Sibsagar	8	4	3	84
Jorhat	5	12	8	75
Golaghat	8	10	5	77
Karbi-Anglong	2	56	4	38
North Cachar Hills	2	68	2	27
Cachar	36	1	14	48
Karimganj	52	0.4	13	34
Hailakandi	58	0.3	11	31
Kokrajhar	20	34	3	43
Dhubri	74	2	4	20
Bongaigaon	39	12	10	39
Barpeta	59	7	6	27
Kamrup	25	10	7	59
Nalbari	22	18	8	53
Darrang	36	17	5	43
Sonitpur	16	12	5	67
Western Assam	38	12	6	44
Assam	31	12	7	50

Source Authors' Calculation from Census of India, 2001

Table 5.6 Compound annual growth rate of the population by social groups in Assam

District	1991–2001				2001–2011		
	Muslims	ST	SC	Others	ST	SCs	Others
Goalpara	2.79	1.36	−0.15	1.5	5.80	1.08	1.2
Lakhimpur	2.79	1.66	−4.49	1.4	1.79	7.87	1.5
Dhemaji	4.00	2.55	1.53	1.2	1.87	1.57	1.6
Morigaon	2.46	2.06	0.62	1.3	1.26	−5.17	2.4
Nagaon	2.82	2.50	27.50	1.1	2.56	−19.26	2.0
Golaghat	2.43	1.01	1.72	1.3	1.75	1.20	1.1
Jorhat	2.38	1.58	1.02	1.3	1.29	1.71	0.8
Sibsagar	2.16	1.87	1.37	1.4	1.68	2.06	0.8
Dibrugarh	1.31	0.63	2.22	1.3	1.53	1.87	1.1
Tinsukia	2.89	2.70	0.00	1.7	2.01	3.80	1.4
Karbi−Anglong	5.68	2.86	1.01	1.0	1.75	1.99	1.2
N. C. Hills	3.39	2.65	0.53	1.4	1.69	4.30	0.3
Karimganj	2.63	7.33	1.55	1.5	−3.94	2.44	2.0
Hailakandi	2.43	1.39	0.83	1.4	−1.71	1.89	2.0
Cachar	2.22	1.18	0.91	1.5	−0.59	1.78	1.8
Dhubri	2.62	0.08	0.34	1.2	−15.09	−0.52	2.0
Kokrajhar	1.77	−0.77	0.05	2.7	−0.90	0.05	0.2
Bongaigaon	2.80	−2.43	0.72	1.1	−16.23	1.34	−1.0
Barpeta	2.33	1.10	0.67	1.0	−13.98	−1.13	0.9
Nalbari	2.28	1.21	−0.34	1.1	−19.43	−3.53	−2.2
Kamrup	2.95	1.57	0.34	2.4	−3.14	0.15	−5.2
Darrang	2.56	1.06	−0.34	0.9	−28.75	−3.53	−2.9
Sonitpur	3.51	2.49	1.27	1.5	1.76	2.15	1.0
Western Assam	2.60	0.6	0.01	1.6	1.0	2.5	1.5
Assam	2.60	1.42	0.96	1.5	1.62	2.03	2.2

Source Authors' calculation from census of 2001 and 2011

Table 5.7 Average monthly per capita consumption expenditure (in Rs.) among the social groups in Assam

	2004–05			2009–10		
	Rural	Urban	Total	Rural	Urban	Total
Assam						
Muslims	481	1038	508	705	1298	732
ST	561	834	571	880	1160	890
SC	510	811	547	850	1275	917
OBC	576	1105	627	1056	1412	1080
Others	617	1157	715	888	1814	1152
All	543	1058	591	863	1540	933
Western Assam						
Muslims	463	1170	497	724	1438	764
ST	575	847	589	868	1354	881
SC	567	890	604	823	1143	881
OBC	552	777	585	855	1592	896
Others	613	1198	714	875	2223	1248
All	532	1051	582	798	1738	894
BTAD						
Muslims	–	–	–	574	845	575
ST	–	–	–	793	1492	816
SC	–	–	–	836	925	845
OBC	–	–	–	711	1110	722
Others	–	–	–	712	1059	748
All	–	–	–	722	1154	738

Source Authors' calculation from NSSO's consumption expenditure 61st and 66th Rounds

Table 5.8 Average extent of land ownership in hectare among the social groups in Assam

	2004–05			2009–10		
	Household share	Land owned	Land possessed	Household share	Land owned	Land possessed
Assam						
Muslims	33	0.70	0.70	32	0.77	0.82
ST	19	1.24	1.29	15	1.11	1.16
SC	10	0.61	0.61	11	0.62	0.58
OBC	16	0.84	0.73	25	1.00	0.93
Others	22	0.97	0.87	17	0.66	0.62
All	100	0.87	0.83	100	0.84	0.83
Western Assam						
Muslims	40	0.72	0.72	40	0.67	0.69
ST	17	1.32	1.31	12	0.70	0.76
SC	8	0.71	0.75	12	0.51	0.43
OBC	13	0.83	0.70	21	0.72	0.65
Others	22	1.04	0.92	15	0.49	0.38
All	100	0.91	0.84	100	0.64	0.61
BTAD						
Muslims	–	–	–	22	0.82	0.84
ST	–	–	–	35	0.72	0.84
SC	–	–	–	13	0.64	0.63
OBC	–	–	–	19	0.66	0.54
Others	–	–	–	10	0.82	0.66
All	–	–	–	100	0.73	0.73

Source Authors' calculation from NSSO's 61st and 66th rounds surveys on employment and unemployment

Table 5.9 Classification of the households by principal occupations among the social groups in Assam

	2004–05				2009–10			
	Administrative	Service and sale workers	Farmers and fishing	Others	Administrative	Service and sale workers	Farmers and fishing	Others
Assam								
Muslims	8	18	55	19	10	9	48	34
STs	7	8	74	11	10	9	60	21
SC	7	22	53	17	20	12	34	34
OBC	10	12	68	10	14	9	44	33
Others	16	17	54	12	25	16	30	28
All	10	16	60	15	15	11	43	31
Western Assam								
Muslims	8	14	62	15	9	11	43	28
STs	7	8	77	8	18	8	51	22
SC	7	22	62	10	20	13	22	44
OBC	10	12	71	8	16	8	35	40
Others	20	18	53	9	19	24	33	23
All	12	15	62	11	15	12	38	35
BTAD								
Muslims	–	–	–	–	6	10	62	22
STs	–	–	–	–	12	9	58	20
SC	–	–	–	–	20	11	41	27
OBC	–	–	–	–	10	8	46	35
Others	–	–	–	–	16	6	38	40
All	–	–	–		13	9	52	26

Source Authors' calculation from the unit level data of NSSO 61st and 66th rounds surveys on employment and unemployment

Table 5.10 One-way anova in consumption expenditure by social groups in Assam during 2004–2005

Social group	Mean	Std. dev.	Freq.	Obs.
ST	570.55976	191.51336	44738.18	780
SCs	547.15856	271.90227	24934.59	405
OBC	627.4104	675.63112	43744.19	799
Muslims	507.92281	275.38918	81171.93	1191
General	715.07834	378.23599	57279.1	1066
Total	590.79623	395.18486	251867.99	4241

Analysis of variance

Source	SS	Df	MS	F	Prob > F
Between groups	26,379,889	4	6,594,972.2	43.9	0.0000
Within groups	635,785,461	4236	150,091		
Total	662,165,349	4240	156,171.07		

Source Unit level data of NSSO's 61st round of consumption expenditure

Table 5.11 One-way ANOVA in consumption expenditure by social groups in W. Assam during 2004–2005

Social group	Mean	Std. dev.	Freq.	Obs.
STs	588.80932	188.62912	18932.33	309
SCs	604.44783	261.5188	9923.18	144
OBC	585.44737	201.14696	13384.51	238
Muslims	496.73769	296.54312	45620.31	589
General	714.49059	388.89052	25975.47	430
Total	581.55747	305.27563	113835.8	1710

Analysis of variance

Source	SS	Df	MS	F	Prob > F
Between groups	11,921,565	4	2,980,391.21	34.49	0.0000
Within groups	147,345,627	1705	86,419.7226		
Total	159,267,192	1709	93,193.2076		

Source Unit level data of NSSO's 61st round of consumption expenditure

See Tables 5.10, 5.11, 5.12, 5.13, 5.14, 5.15, 5.16, 5.17, 5.18, 5.19, 5.20, 5.21, 5.22, 5.23 and 5.24.

Table 5.12 One-way ANOVA in consumption expenditure by social groups in Assam during 2009–2010

Social group	Mean	Std. dev.	Freq.	Obs.
STs	890.33388	404.41317	4,307,388.7	566
SCs	916.86339	542.47405	3,282,141.5	449
OBC	1080.0081	1279.4606	6,984,810.7	869
Muslims	732.40396	350.51031	8,989,451.2	876
General	1151.8848	834.01823	4,581,745.9	684
Total	932.63433	802.36263	28,145,538	3444

Analysis of variance

Source	SS	Df	MS	F	Prob > F
Between groups	90657264	4	22664315.9	36.66	0.0000
Within groups	2.13E+09	3439	618173.073		
Total	2.22E+09	3443	643785.787		

Source Unit level data of NSSO's 66th round of consumption expenditure

Table 5.13 One-way ANOVA in consumption expenditure by social groups in W. Assam during 2009–2010

Social group	Mean	Std. dev.	Freq.	Obs.
STs	881.28272	416.38964	1387866.4	220
SCs	881.09865	436.27238	1334834.6	204
OBC	895.96244	506.39999	2578564.2	325
Muslims	764.05786	411.6324	5218876.9	482
General	1248.2772	867.32452	1972870	295
Total	893.278	555.26278	12493012	1526

Analysis of variance

Source	SS	df	MS	F	Prob > F
Between groups	41065035	4	10266258.7	36.39	0
Within groups	429118015	1521	282128.873		
Total	470183050	1525	308316.754		

Source Unit level data of NSSO's 66th round of consumption expenditure

Table 5.14 One-way ANOVA in consumption expenditure by social groups in BTAD during 2009–2010

Social Group	Mean	Std. dev.	Freq.	Obs.
STs	816.03252	318.80141	895043.11	150
SCs	844.58958	299.19943	280219.74	61
OBC	721.74166	228.62375	492281.1	76
Muslims	575.16464	142.90405	570145.7	61
General	748.1483	335.49911	215703.59	60
Total	738.43061	285.62236	2453393.2	408

Analysis of variance

Source	SS	*df*	MS	*F*	Prob > *F*
Between groups	3975101.9	4	993775.477	13.7	0.0000
Within groups	29228013	403	72526.0864		
Total	33203115	407	81580.1345		

Source Unit level data of NSSO's 66th round of consumption expenditure

Table 5.15 One-way ANOVA of land owned (Hect.) by social groups in Assam during 2004–2005

Social group	Mean	Std. dev.	Freq.	Obs.
STs	1.2450146	1.1395874	875942.5	763
SCs	0.60961658	0.85985673	457730.79	380
OBC	0.8369611	0.95493909	751038.55	677
Muslims	0.69874328	0.78853124	1508476.6	1129
General	0.96950207	1.1981494	1005965.3	868
Total	0.87570782	1.015986	4599153.7	3817

Analysis of variance

Source	SS	*df*	MS	*F*	Prob > *F*
Between groups	1735.34947	4	433.837369	43.92	0.0000
Within groups	3765.445666	3812	0.987787424		
Total	3938.98059792	3816	1.03222762		

Source Unit level data of NSSO's 61st round of employment and unemployment

Table 5.16 One-way ANOVA of land owned (Hect.) by social groups in W. Assam during 2004–2005

Social group	Mean	Std. dev.	Freq.	Obs.
STs	1.3197704	1.0952924	376992.4	292
SCs	0.70928202	0.87355021	178830.17	134
OBC	0.8303384	1.0317085	243758.35	214
Muslims	0.72051164	0.79741769	875055.88	560
General	1.0464946	1.1349641	427731.98	335
Total	0.90607009	990.33605	2102368.8	1535

Analysis of variance

Source	SS	*df*	MS	*F*	Prob > *F*
Between groups	81.343002	4	20.3357504	21.86	0.0000
Within groups	1.42E+09	1530	0.930164226		
Total	1.50E+09	1534	0.980765493		

Source Unit level data of NSSO's 61st round of employment and unemployment

Table 5.17 One-way ANOVA of land owned (Hect.) by social groups in Assam during 2009–2010

Social group	Mean	Std. dev.	Freq.	Obs.
STs	1.1085337	1.3451117	763967.8	529
SCs	0.62453496	0.81821536	593355.07	376
OBC	1.0095601	0.9721318	1283758.4	756
Muslims	0.7668845	0.83254149	1629938.8	830
General	0.65754056	1.0934305	872233.6	627
Total	0.84323862	1.0166492	5143253.7000	3118

Analysis of variance

Source	SS	*df*	MS	*F*	Prob > *F*
Between groups	95.325528	4	23.831382	23.73	0.0000
Within groups	3.13E+09	3113	1.00428201		
Total	3.22E+09	3117	1.03357569		

Source Unit level data of NSSO's 66th round of employment and unemployment

Table 5.18 One-way ANOVA of land owned (Hect.) by social groups in W. Assam during 2009–2010

Social group	Mean std.	Dev.	Freq.	Obs.
STs	0.69854698	0.96602275	266600.12	195
SCs	0.50628412	0.6322644	251756.08	167
OBC	0.72160697	0.74814871	488589.62	297
Muslims	0.67117497	0.72650323	905905.43	445
General	0.48977006	0.6324147	330706.28	250
Total	0.64016793	745.48404	2243557.5	1354

Analysis of variance

Source	SS	*df*	MS	*F*	Prob > *F*
Between groups	10.267546	4	2.56688639	4.67	0.0010
Within groups	741.657408	1349	0.549783104		
Total	751.924953	1353	0.555746455		

Source Unit level data of NSSO's 66th round of employment and unemployment

Table 5.19 One-way ANOVA of land owned (in hectares) by social groups in BTAD during 2009–2010

Social group	Mean	Std. dev.	Freq.	Obs.
STs	0.71919023	0.64757668	160542.04	129
SCs	0.64211361	0.59648175	61967.16	50
OBC	0.66102405	0.76454013	86236.92	66
Muslims	0.82554873	0.77281767	98553.75	60
General	0.82211214	0.97047998	44430.89	54
Total	0.7308402	0.72867752	451730.76	359

Analysis of variance

Source	SS	*df*	MS	*F*	Prob > *F*
Between groups	1.7357478	4	0.43393696	0.82	0.5159
Within groups	188.351846	354	0.532067361		
Total	1.90E+08	358	0.530970932		

Source Unit level data of NSSO's 66th round of employment and unemployment

Table 5.20 One-way ANOVA of land possessed (in hectares) by social groups in Assam during 2004–2005

Social group	Mean	Std. dev.	Freq.	Obs.
STs	1.2917632	1.1002839	878997.81	777
SCs	0.60988484	0.84936609	497235	423
OBC	0.73006262	0.93092715	877234.88	784
Muslims	0.69677895	0.8104331	1563313.3	1177
General	0.87353781	1.1805928	1121329.9	990
Total	0.83998871	1.0080575	4938110.9	4151

Analysis of variance

Source	SS	*df*	MS	*F*	Prob > *F*
Between groups	209.861683	4	52.4654209	54.28	0.0000
Within groups	4.01E+09	4146	0.966542428		
Total	4.22E+09	4150	10.161799		

Source Unit level data of NSSO's 61st round of employment and unemployment

Table 5.21 One-way ANOVA of land possessed (in hectares) by social groups in W. Assam during 2004–2005

Social group	Mean	Std. dev.	Freq.	Obs.
STs	1.3083271	1.0644361	379443.6	300
SCs	0.74968602	0.91766487	182054.08	145
OBC	0.69622901	0.99332497	289674.74	247
Muslims	0.7229533	0.81108318	901083.11	578
General	0.92506881	1.1420985	463132.22	372
Total	0.86416922	0.98880352	2215387.7	1642

Analysis of variance

Source	SS	*df*	MS	*F*	Prob > *F*
Between groups	77.896662	4	19.4741656	20.88	0.0000
Within groups	1.53E+09	1637	0.932536469		
Total	1.60E+09	1641	0.977732.396		

Source Unit level data of NSSO's 61st round of employment and unemployment

Table 5.22 One-way ANOVA of land possessed (in hectares) by social groups in Assam during 2009–2010

Social group	Mean	Std. dev.	Freq.	Obs.
STs	1.1578748	1.3830119	680905.12	476
SCs	0.58174086	0.81185647	585133.89	384
OBC	931.46644	0.99887883	1396675.3	827
Muslims	0.8199732	917.57056	1650450.8	853
General	0.61627138	1.1247826	858039.93	642
Total	0.83382232	1.0510519	5171205	3182

Analysis of variance

Source	SS	*df*	MS	*F*	Prob > *F*
Between groups	100.253856	4	25.063464	23.32	0.0000
Within groups	3.41E+09	3177	1.07454492		
Total	3.51E+09	3181	1.10471018		

Source Unit level data of NSSO's 66th round of employment and unemployment

Table 5.23 One-way ANOVA of land possessed (in hectares) by social groups in W. Assam during 2009–2010

Social group	Mean	Std. dev.	Freq.	Obs.
STs	0.75927996	1.0285426	272822.03	198
SCs	0.431671	0.61826295	274229.45	188
OBC	0.64941308	0.77607613	553363.36	334
Muslims	0.69351967	0.7997166	940484.94	470
General	0.38257126	0.60804215	361846.84	283
Total	0.61411536	0.78989148	2402746.6	1473

Analysis of variance

Source	SS	*df*	MS	*F*	Prob > *F*
Between groups	25.071182	4	6.2677956	10.3	0.0000
Within groups	893.351642	1468	0.608550165		
Total	918.422825	1472	0.623928.549		

Source Unit level data of NSSO's 66th round of employment and unemployment

Table 5.24 One-way ANOVA of land possessed (in hectares) by social groups in BTAD during 2009–2010

Social group	Mean	Std. dev.	Freq.	Obs.
STs	0.84843938	0.7761701	161903.76	135
SCs	0.63427137	0.6172958	62989.42	54
OBC	0.54375062	0.76688134	102096.68	77
Muslims	0.83772071	0.76413476	99195.65	64
General	0.66336318	0.89793599	57833.29	73
Total	0.73198762	0.77559748	484018.8	403

Analysis of variance

Source	SS	*df*	MS	*F*	Prob > *F*
Between groups	6.4910051	4	1.62275127	2.74	0.0282
Within groups	235.33268	398	0.59128814		
Total	2.42E+08	402	0.601551455		

Source Unit level data of NSSO's 66th round of employment and unemployment

References

Bardhan, P. (1997). Method in the madness? A political-economy analysis of the ethnic conflicts in less developed countries. *World Development, 25*(9), 1381–1398.

Basumatary, K. (2012). *Political economy of bodoland movement*. New Delhi: Akash Publishing House.

Brown, G. K., & Langer, A. (2010). Cultural status inequalities: An important dimension of group mobilization. In Frances Stewart (Ed.), *Horizontal inequalities and conflict: understanding group violence in multiethnic society*. UK: Palgrave Macmillan.

Chaudhuri, S., & Gupta, N. (2009). Levels of living and poverty patterns: A district-wise analysis for India. *Economic and Political Weekly, XLIV, 9,* 99–110.

Collier, P., & Hoeffler, A. (2004). Greed versus grievance in civil war. *Oxford Economic Paper, 56,* 563–595.

Das, N. (1982). The Naga movement. In K. S. Singh (Ed.), *The tribal movement in India* (Vol. 1). Pathna: Manohar Book Service.

Dixon, J. (2009). What causes civil war? Integrating quantitative research findings. *International Study Review, 11*(4), 707–735.

Fearon, J. D., & Laitin, D. D. (2003). Ethnicity, insurgency, and civil war. *American Political Science Review, 57*(1), 75–90.

George, J. S. (1994). The Bodo movement in Assam: Unrest to accord. *Asian Survey, 34*(10), 878–892.

Gohain, H. (1989). Bodo Stir in perspective. *Economic and Political Weekly, 24*(25), 377–1379.

Goswami, B. B., & Mukharjee, D. B. (1982). The Mizo political movement. In K. S. Singh (Ed.), *The tribal movement in India* (Vol. 1). Pathna: Manohar Book Service.

Government of Bodoland Territorial Council. (2013). Kokrajhar: The Bodoland Guardian.

Gurr, T. (1968). A causal model of civil strife: A comparative analysis using new indices. *The American Political Science Review, 62*(4), 1104–1124.

Langer, A. (2005). *Horizontal inequalities and violent conflicts: Cote d'Ivoire. Human Development Report Office, Occasional Paper 2005/32*. New York: UNDP.

Langer, A. (2010). When do horizontal inequalities lead to conflicts? Lessons from a comparative study of Ghana and Cote d'Ivoire. In Frances Stewart (Ed.), *Horizontal inequalities and conflict: Understanding group violence in multiethnic Society*. UK: Palgrave Macmillan.

Langer, A., & Ukiwo, U. (2010). Ethnicity, religious and state in Ghana and Nigeria: Perceptions from the street. In Frances Stewart (Ed.), *Horizontal inequalities and conflict: Understanding group violence in multiethnic society*. UK: Palgrave Macmillan.

Lindquist, M. K. (2012). Horizontal education inequalities and civil conflict: The nexus of ethnicity, inequality, and violent conflict. *Undergraduate Economic Review, 8*(1), 1–21.

Mahanta, N. G. (2013). Politics of space and violence in Bodoland. *Economic and Political Weekly, 48*(23), 49–58.

Mancini, L. (2010). Horizontal inequalities and communal violence: Evidence from Indonesia districts. In F. Stewart (Ed.), *Horizontal inequalities and conflict: understanding group violence in multiethnic societies*. UK: Palgrave Macmillan.

Mancini, L., Stewart, F., & Brown, G. K. (2010). Approaches to the measurement of horizontal inequalities. In F. Stewart (Ed.), *Horizontal Inequalities and Conflict: Understanding Group Violence in Multi ethnic Societies* (pp. 85-105). UK: Palgrave Macmillan.

Mishra, U. (1989). Bodo stir: Complex issues. *Unattainable Demands. Economy and Political Weekly, 24*(21), 1146–1149.

Motiram, S., & Sarma, N. (2014). The tragedy of identity: Reflection on violent social conflict in Western Assam. *Economic and Political Weekly, 49*(11), 45–53.

Murshed, S. M., & Gates, S. (2005). Spatial-horizontal inequalities and the maoist insurgency in Nepal. *Review of Development Economics, 9*(1), 121–134.

Nepal, M. A., Bohara, K., & Gawande, K. (2011). More inequality, more killings: The maoist insurgency in Nepal. *American Journal of Political Science, 55*(4), 886–906.

Ostby, G. (2007). Horizontal inequalities, political environment and civil conflict evidence from 55 developing countries 1986–2003. *World Bank Policy Research Paper* 4193.

Pathak, S. (2013). Ethnic violence in Bodoland. *Economic and Political Weekly, 47*(34), 19–23.

Ray, D. (2010). *Development economics*. New Delhi: Oxford University Press.

Stewart, F. (2000). Crisis prevention: Tackling horizontal inequalities. *Oxford Development Studies, 28,* 245–262.

Stewart, F. (2010). *Horizontal inequalities and conflict: Understanding group violence in multiethnic society*. UK: Palgrave Macmillan.

Tiwari, B. N. (2008). Horizontal inequalities and violent conflict in Nepal. *Himalaya, the Journal of the Association for Nepal and Himalayan Studies, 28*(1), 33–48.

Xaxa, V. (2008). *State, society, and tribes: Issues in post Colonial India*. India: Pearson Education.

Chapter 6
Selection and Performance of Self-Help Groups in West Bengal: A Case Study

Archita Ghosh and Tithi Bose

Abstract Our country is experimenting with Self-Help Groups for over 20 years. After the NABARD, panchayats started experimentation with self-help groups in their own way since 1999. Swarojgar Yojana, world's greatest credit-based poverty alleviation scheme relying on self-help was first announced in 1997 to glorify 50 years of independence. Swarnajayanti Gram Swarojgar Yojana (SGSY), microcredit-based scheme, came into effect from April, 1999. This scheme was planned to promote group loans, encourage small-scale savings and group enterprises to develop agency in some predetermined stages. The District cells and the panchayats worked in cooperation with the local level banks to organize the groups and implement the programme at the local level. Many studies have tried to investigate the progress of the self-help groups and their impact on rural livelihood and female empowerment during the last decade. In our micro-level study, we shall try to probe into the factors which play key role in involving the rural households with the self-help groups. The chapter tried to find out the determinants of association with these groups in two different districts at the village panchayat level on the basis of primary survey. Our findings suggest that not only economic factors but social and political factors play an important role in determining association of rural households to the SGSY programme.

Keywords SGSY · SHGs · Beneficiary · Panchayats · Political Social

A. Ghosh (✉)
Department of Economics, University of Kalyani, Kalyani, West Bengal, India
e-mail: archig2002@yahoo.co.in

T. Bose
Department of Economics, Haldia Government College, Haldia, India
e-mail: tupur4u@gmail.com

U.K. De et al. (eds.), *Inequality, Poverty and Development in India*, India Studies in Business and Economics, DOI 10.1007/978-981-10-6274-2_6

6.1 Introduction

Developing countries since 1990s have started to follow development strategies based on participatory mode. A new concept of microcredit encouraging capacity building and mobilizing agency among the commoners came into practice in the developing world around 1970s. Need for greater role of women in the development process started to be acknowledged from the 1990s and policies were organized to involve women more intensively. In India, Swarnajayanti Gram Swarojgar Yojana (SGSY), which was transformed into National Rural Livelihood Mission (NRLM) in June 2011, can be sited as an initial attempt of the state in alleviating poverty through capability enhancement and agency development with special emphasis on participation of women.

SGSY (NRLM), basically a microcredit programme that works through self-help groups, is formed especially with women members at the village panchayat level. The Swarojgar scheme was planned to promote group loans, encourage small-scale savings and group enterprises to develop agency in some predetermined stages. The District Rural Development Cell (DRDC) is the prime implementing agency in the district and the local level self-government institutions (Panchayats) are the associating organizations at the local level. The District cells and the panchayats work in cooperation with the local level banks to execute the whole process. However, after nearly two and a half decades since its inception, studies found that this programme has not been able to attain all its goals. The problem is found to exist even at the level of its execution through panchayats. In this chapter, in an attempt to assess the workings of the programme, we first bring out the performance of the programme at different levels and then try to investigate the factors that determine association of the rural households with the programme. Performance of the programme is evaluated on the basis of available secondary data. Association of people with the programme has been looked into on the basis of primary data. Thus the study will examine at the micro-level how group membership is decided. The chapter will try to judge whether the prescribed factors like poverty level, caste, etc. decide the beneficiaries or some other socio-political, economic and the cultural factors decide group involvement. Here we have the scope of assessing elite capture and political control of the programme. In this respect, involvement of the panchayats is also evaluated. We have used an econometric model to evaluate the factors that determine flow of benefits of SGSY.

The residual part of the chapter is organized as follows. The first section gives a brief account of the programme and the required criteria for selection of beneficiaries under SGSY. In the next section, we give a brief review of the literature on the progress of SGSY in our country and the role of panchayats in executing poverty alleviation programmes. The next section discusses about the physical and financial progress of the programme at the national as well as state level since inception. In the fourth section, survey results and analysis are demonstrated. The final section concludes.

6.2 About SGSY

SGSY (NRLM) is a self-employment scheme that follows a process-oriented approach[1] based on demand. The Swarojgar Yojona, world's greatest credit-based poverty alleviation scheme and a well-organized successor of IRDP (Integrated Rural Development Programme), came into effect on 1 April, under the Ministry of Rural Development. Six different self-employment and training schemes and sub-schemes under IRDP were merged to form this scheme. This programme was later in 2011 transformed into NRLM.

Social mobilization of the poor through SGSY was a major shift from previous supply-driven approach. The prime ideology behind formation of self-help groups through SGSY was to raise consciousness, participation among the marginalized, especially women and evoke their voices for their rights. SGSY can be cited as an initial attempt of the state in alleviating poverty through capability approach and agency development. A feeling of solidarity, increased awareness of group members, self-reliance and transparency are the influencing factors in forming groups.

The principal aim of this scheme was to bring the downtrodden families above the below poverty line within 3 years by providing them small loans for self-employment. In the previous credit-based schemes like IRDP, loans used to be given on individual mobilization. This newly innovated Swarojgar scheme (SGSY) was planned to promote group loans, encourage small-scale savings and group enterprise to develop agency at some predetermined stages. Funding for the project is shared by the Centre and States in 75:25 ratio. DRDC is the prime implementing agency in the district and the panchayats are the associating organizations at the local level. The district cells and the panchayats worked in cooperation with the local level banks. Groups are formed initially with 10 or 15 persons from the BPL families of the area. These groups are called Self-Help Groups (SHG) and the individual members of the group are known as Swarojgaris. Group members are trained so that they can prepare livelihood plans, negotiate about their rights and entitlements, and manage the group themselves. They can also help the poorest members and are expected to function in democratic ways.

Under the scheme DRDC may involve local NGOs for forming the self-help groups. Funds received by the DRDC for helping the groups are kept in savings bank accounts opened in branches of the principal participating banks in the scheme and earn interest at the prevailing rates till the amount is given as loans to the Swarojgaris.

The process of fund disbursement under this self-employment scheme is segmented in some centrally prescribed steps. The primary stage is comprised of raising thrift habit among the members of the newly formed groups. Therefore in

[1]A process-oriented approach is characterized by partnership, sharing lived experiences, people's understanding and ability to act. It can be stated as a collective development of effective responses, which cannot be pre-determined but are relevant to the lives of the people who extend them and are, therefore more likely to be sustainable.

the first 6 months after group formation, the group members are trained to save money. Initially they have to build up a corpus fund by saving a certain amount every week or month. These savings are kept in a local or field bank. After 6 months, the group is evaluated by a team comprising of the Project Director, a member of the Block Development Office and a representative of the bank. If it passes the evaluation test, it is given Grade I status and is paid an amount as a revolving fund. They also receive another amount as loan from the bank, which is called cash credit or matching corpus fund. Individual members can borrow from these two funds.

After completion of one year, groups have to go through another evaluation process. Getting passed this test they get Grade II status and become liable to get credit cum subsidy facilities. This stage is called bank credit linkage.

SGSY has a special focus on women self-help groups. It affirmed that 50% of the beneficiaries will be Scheduled Castes and Schedule Tribes and at least 40% will be women. The participatory process was encouraged through intensive community action. Gram Sabhas were especially emphasized in this connection to promote participation.

The current version of SGSY, i.e. NRLM lays emphasis on universal mobilization of BPL families[2] and skill development of rural youth. It is different from SGSY through its '(a) shift from the present allocation based strategy to a demand driven strategy, enabling the States to formulate their own livelihoods-based poverty reduction action plans, (b) focus on targets, outcomes and time bound delivery, (c) continuous capacity building, imparting requisite skills and creating linkages with livelihoods opportunities for the poor, including those emerging in the organized sector, and (d) monitoring against targets of poverty outcomes' (http://www.rural.nic.in). Panchayats now play only a role of assisting the institutions of the poor. There will be mutual exchange of ideas and experiences between such institutions and the panchayats in regard to running the groups.

Aajeevika (The name NRLM got later) is based on an Intensive Block Strategy. Intensive Block is a block (sub-district) identified by the State Rural Livelihoods Mission (SRLM) in the first phase of implementation of Aajeevika to demonstrate the best practices and processes in several spheres like ensuring Participatory Identification of Poor (PIP), targeting the poorest of poor, facilitating financial and economic inclusion of the poor by creating strong institutional platforms for them in the next 3 years, etc. In the process, it makes self-sufficient Community Resource Persons (CRP). Once the intensive work is completed in these selected blocks, these provide social capital for the poor and serve as training sites for the project staff and the SHG members. Later Aajeevika is implemented to other blocks also in a systematic manner.

[2]Ajeevika attempts universal mobilization by putting a target of including 11% BPL families of rural India. 50% of the beneficiaries would be SCs/STs, 15% will be minorities and 3% disabled. At least one woman member from each identified family will be included in the SHGs.

6.3 Progress of SGSY (NRLM)

The progress of SGSY at the national level can be assessed by maturity level of the groups. As revealed from the available secondary information, progress of SGSY is impressive in case of number of group formation but not at all satisfactory as far as economic performance of the groups is concerned. From April, 1999 up to 2012, 43 lakhs self-help groups were formed under the scheme. Out of them, 30 lakh SHGs obtained the status of Grade I and 14.63 lakhs Grade II. But only about 13.71 lakh SHGs could obtain credit for undertaking economic activities. Thus only 22% of the SHGs was matured enough to take up economic activities financed by bank credit and supported by subsidy (Annual Report, Ministry of Rural Development, 2011–2012). Groups have been formed by external catalysts like NGOs or panchayats but they have not tried to integrate the stages. Therefore, there exists a huge difference between the number of groups that passed Grade I and that passed Grade II. Groups have been formed but their sustainability can be questioned. However, the figure improved to 35% if we extend the period up to November 2012 (Annual Report, Ministry of Rural Development, 2012–2013). This hints at better performance of NRLM.

The programme since inception assisted 1.06 crore swarojgaris. And according to the rule the programme in practice tried to work in favour of the most vulnerable groups, such as scheduled tribes and scheduled castes and women. The scheduled caste and schedule tribe swarojgaris accounted for about 47.46% of the total swarojgaris. Women accounted for 60.6% of the total swarojgaris assisted since inception. Minorities accounted for 10.6% of total swarojgaris. During 2010–2011, a total of 21.09 lakh Swarojgaries were assisted, out of which 14.24 lakh (67.49%) were women. In 2011–2012, 16.77 lakh Swarojgaries were involved in with SGSY, out of which 11.03 lakh (65.80%) were women. During the period April 2012–November 2012, out of 4.38 lakhs swarojgaris assisted, 79.74% were women (Annual Report, Ministry of Rural Development, 2012–2013).

Regarding the performance of the individual states we see that none of the states has succeeded to fully utilize the available fund. Investment for infrastructural support and capability enhancement is not channelized in the desired manner. The absence of proper capacity enhancement, infrastructural support, administrative encouragement, awareness and democratic participation has hindered the process of meaningful, economically productive group activities (Annual Reports, Ministry of Rural Development, 2008–2009, 2010–2011, and 2011–2012).

Annual Report, 2009–2010, Ministry of Rural Development reveals a wide gap between fund utilization and credit mobilization in most of the states. West Bengal is not an exception. The state manages to utilize only 60% of the total fund which is higher than the national average of 58%. But West Bengal lags far behind the national average in credit mobilization. Only 26% of available credit is disbursed. Credit subsidy ratio in the state is also poor which is far below the national target of 3:1 showing the inefficiency of the groups and the credit linkage process.

The renamed programme NRLM performs very well in terms of universal mobilization. The target of including 300 districts and 2100 blocks in 3 years has been fulfilled as we see that up to December 2014, 316 districts and 2125 blocks have come under NRLM. So far 20 lakhs SHGs have been formed and 2.4 crores households have been mobilized (Annual Report, Ministry of Rural Development, 2014–2015).

However, in case of bank and credit linkage it was seen that up to December 2014, only 31% of total targeted SHGs have been linked with bank and only 39% of total targeted loan amount has been released. All the north eastern states exhibited very poor performance in this aspect. In case of training and settlement also, all the states except Goa lag far behind the target up to December 2014. Performance of northeastern states is even worse in this respect also.

If we consider the aspect of physical performance, West Bengal performs a little better than the national average in terms of coverage of beneficiaries and involvement of Scheduled Castes. The state manages to involve SC swarojgaris up to 38%, which is marginally above the national average (35%). Women participation is also encouraging. About 90% of the swarojgaris are women. However, as far as the ST coverage is concerned, the picture is appalling.

A special emphasis is attributed to West Bengal, whenever we discuss about the implementation and progress of the rural development programmes through the panchayats. There was a prolonged success story of West Bengal panchayats in implementing the welfare schemes at the grass root level and in mobilizing the poor through political participation at the panchayat level. Panchayats in the state served as the local agents of the government sincerely till 1980s and were able to arouse reliability among the mass. But the initiative started to fade in the 1990s. And the state began to lag behind in implementing the welfare schemes than the other states. The 73rd constitutional amendment in 1993 announced panchayats as the obligatory third tier of the federal structure and gave them sole authority over the responsibilities bestowed upon them. But the panchayats were loosing their popularity and position in the state. Several factors resulted in loss of participation of the commoners.

Empirical studies demonstrate that the programme is once again a play of numbers to fulfil the targets at the grass root levels just like the previous credit-oriented programmes. According to the 11th Five-Year Plan Report (published by the West Bengal Government), three and a half lakh SHGs have been organized in the state out of which more than one and a half lakh SHGs have been formed only by people living below the poverty line. Field studies also reveal that the primary objective of SGSY to bring the assisted poor families above the poverty line could not be achieved because of lack of social mobilization, inadequacies in external facilitation, inadequate access to credit and the absence of extension service, linkages, co-ordination and convergence. Like other programmes, SGSY is also suffering from lack of initiative, innovation, collaboration and understanding (Roy 2007).

In the years of NRLM, West Bengal like other states of India lag behind the target in respect of SHGs' bank and credit linkages and in training and settlement. This particular scenario of less-than-target achievement raises question behind selection and or performance of SHGs. In this chapter, we try to look into the matter of selection of beneficiary SHGs based on a primary survey.

Assessment of any programme may be done from two perspectives; the first one is a macro-level analysis that involves aggregate data on financial and physical achievements. For that we have collected secondary data for the focused village panchayats from Block Development Offices in the respective districts. The gram panchayat level scenario of the physical progress of SGSY in 2009–2010 can be seen from Table 6.1. Purulia and North 24 Parganas are the two districts selected for the primary survey. Hingalganj Block is one of the less advanced remote blocks in North 24 Parganas completely dependent on agriculture. On the other hand, Purulia itself is a backward district. All the blocks in the district are more or less homogeneous in terms of climatic condition, soil pattern and cultural and anthropological background. Discrepancy between the two districts can be seen in terms of group formation, gradation of the groups and credit linkage.

The second perspective, which is the major focus of our study, involves a primary survey to find out how the vulnerable section (for whom the programme is targeted) is benefitted from the programme. We have made a sample survey of four gram panchayats in two blocks of Purulia and North 24 Parganas. Choice of the districts is completely purposive to reveal a contrast scenario. Hingalganj is the block in North 24 Parganas and Hura is the block in Purulia selected for the study. The study tried to capture effects of different factors like political awareness, association with the party, democratic participation at the gram sansads, involvement with the panchayat activities, social bonding, dependence on common property resources, whether benefited by other government schemes and the perception of the local dwellers. The probable determinants have been identified by a review of the existing literature. The review has been presented in the next section.

Table 6.1 Physical Progress of SGSY at the Village Panchayat Level in 2009-10

District/block	Gram panchayat	No of SHGs formed	No of women SHG formed	No of SHG passed grade 1	No of SHG pending for Grade 1	No of SHG passed grade II	No of SHG pending for Grade 2	No of SHG under Bank Linkage
Purulia/Hura	Daldali	2	2	0	12	0	0	0
	Jabarrah	2	2	0	6	0	0	0
24 Parganas (N)/ Hingalganj	Hingalganj	69	66	52	…	3	12	2
	Sandelbil	185	176	153	…	24	40	24

Source Secondary data available at the Block Office

6.4 Review of Literature

The term microfinance or microcredit has obtained spectacular importance in development literature for the last one and half decades mostly because of its achievements in combating poverty by reaching poorer families in a more effective way (Kaladhar 1997). The idea of supplementary credit distribution to the vulnerable section of society was primarily initiated by nationalizing some commercial banks in 1969. Although IRDP in the 1980s was initiated to alleviate poverty by disbursing credit to the vulnerable section, still a major portion of the rural population is deprived of institutional credit delivery. According to an estimate, money lenders still cover more than 56% of rural people's credit needs (Khandelwal 2007). The Rural Finance Access Survey (RFAS), 2003 reports that 41% of rural households have a deposit account while 21% of the same have access to credit from a formal source. Microfinance (or microcredit) appears to be the only policy instrument in recent years to fill the gap of formal credit sector in rural India by extending credit especially to the socially backward community.

The major criticism against microcredit process in India lies in its failure to address the poorest section of the society. In India, implementation and execution of the poverty alleviation programmes is mostly hampered by the socio-political factors. Most of the literature has identified the power relations, class difference, economic status, gender issues, age and political adherence as the local factors inhibiting the process of mass participation and democratic practice at the panchayat level in selecting the beneficiaries, formulating plans, and implementing the welfare programmes (Alsop et al. 2000; Nambiar 2001; Ghatak and Ghatak 2002; Behar 2003; Bardhan and Mookherjee 2004). The reasons which can intensify the chances of a targeted social programme to be regressive (i.e. benefiting the non-poor proportionately more than the poor) include weak and incomplete identification processes of the poor, caste and class interests that influence the distribution of resources, wrong geographical distribution of targeted services and the non-poor's interest in the programmes (Dutrey 2007). In India, specific studies on performance of the welfare programmes and selection of the beneficiaries have discussed on different aspects of under-coverage, leakage and elite capture. These errors can be categorized as exclusion of eligible beneficiaries and inclusion of ineligible beneficiaries (Rath 1985; Bagchee 1987; Kurian 1987). According to a study all the poverty alleviation programmes including the self and wage employment programmes till 1990s functioned relatively better regarding targeting through panchayats in villages where landlessness, proportion of low caste people and illiteracy rates are low. The study also revealed that increased landlessness in the villages increases the proportion of non-development expenditure at the village panchayat level. Thus, the study hinted towards distortions in the accountability of the panchayats and concluded that political control leads to massive leakages of the poverty alleviation programmes towards the medium and big landowners between the villages at the cost of the intended beneficiaries (Bardhan and Mookherjee 2004).

6.5 Data and Methodology

For our purpose we have chosen two districts. The choice of districts is purposive to expose the contrast scenario. Purulia is a backward district and North 24 Parganas is an advanced one. Villages under four village panchayats in two blocks of Purulia and North 24 Parganas are selected to make a contrast study. We have made a sample survey of the beneficiaries of the programme, that is who have got an opportunity to be in the self-help groups as well as of non-beneficiaries who are actually poor. Villagers were interviewed to collect information about ethnicity, gender, family size, type of house, assets, milch animals, education, income, consumption pattern, savings and lending habit.

We are trying to factor out the determinants of being a beneficiary of SGSY programme, which is a qualitative variable. The dependent variable is a binary one which takes the value of 1 and 0. When the respondent is a group member, VSHG = 1 and when she is not, VSHG = 0. Here we are computing the Logit of being a beneficiary of SGSY, i.e. getting associated with the Self-Help Groups under SGSY. Logit is the log of the odds ratio $[P_i/(1 - P_i)]$, where P_i is the expected probability of being a group member or P_i is the probability of VSHG = 1 and $(1 - P_i)$ is the probability of VSHG = 0.

6.6 Findings from the Primary Survey

Based on the factors found from a review of the existing literature in the previous section, we have tried to find out empirically the factors that might have determined who would be a beneficiary of SGSY. To assess the determinants of the scheme, we treat a target group comprising of the beneficiaries and the control group comprising of the non-beneficiaries. This micro-level study is based on primary data collected from each block in each district.

Here the explanatory variables are qualitative and quantitative. The explanatory variables or the predictors are economic and socio-political. In Table 6.4 in the appendix, we present a list of the probable explanatory variables along with their expected relationship with the dependent variable.

Age (VA), Marital Status (VM), caste (VC), Education status(VES), Per Capita Consumption at the household level (VCOM), Arable Land at the Household Level (VAL), Non Land Asset Value comprising of tangible assets and live stocks (VNLV), Information flow through Mass Media (VIM), Gram Panchayat Visit (VGP), Gram Sansad Presence (VGS), Block Development Office Visit (VBD), Political Adherence (VP), Informant about schemes (VIMN), People meet at GPO (VMG), Information from Neighbours (VIN), People in Need (VPN), Poverty status (VBP), Dependence on Common Property (VCP), Community Support (VCS) are considered as the predictors of being a beneficiary at the panchayat level.

We have also considered some interactive dummies like interactive dummy between BPL status and caste (VBPC), between marital status and caste (VMC).

VNLV is valued by second-hand value of the tangible assets and average market price of live stocks. VC = 1 for the backward castes and 0 otherwise. When the respondent is illiterate, VES = 0 and 1 otherwise. Whenever beneficiary visits GP or BDO, VGP = 1 and VBD = 1, otherwise 0. VM = 1 for widow, separated and unmarried. VP = 1 for apolitical views and opposition and 0 for supporters of party controlling the village panchayat. For VPN, VIMN, VMG, the value equals 1 if informants are Panchayat-related Personnels (elected or recruited), otherwise 0.

We have selected one block from each of our chosen districts and run separate regressions for each of the blocks. The block level data is an aggregate of data collected from the villages under two gram panchayats in each block. It is to be noted here, we have ignored some variables which are supposed to influence the dependent variable. However, as shown by the data collected, they have significant correlations with one or more of some other variables. To avoid the problem of multicolinearity and to get better results, we have run different regression equations on a trial-and-error method by excluding those variables. The set of explanatory variables for different regressions may be different based on the nature of data obtained.

Each slope coefficient is a partial slope coefficient and measures the change in the estimated logit for a unit change in the value of the regressor, holding other regressors constant or unchanged. Actually, a better interpretation can be given in terms of log of odds ratio. That is if β_i is the coefficient of VC, then β_i measures the change in the log of odds in favour of being included in SGSY group if one belongs to a backward class, other things being the same.

If the slope coefficient of VGP is 2.214902, this means that if a person visits gram panchayats frequently, the estimated logit increases by 2.21 units signifying a positive relationship. This implies that other variables being constant; a visit to GP increases the log of odds by 2.21 in favour of being selected as beneficiary.

In Tables 6.2 and 6.3, we present the results obtained for our selected four gram panchayats.

As the data in Table 6.2 show, all the coefficients except VA, VBD, VBPMC and VP have their expected signs. However, except VP, other three coefficients are not significant. VP, i.e. political adherence along association with NGOs (VNGO), being informant about schemes (VIMN) and visit to gram panchayats (VGP) meetings make significant impact on inclusion of the villagers in self-help groups. Holding a good relationship with gram panchayat personnel, frequently visiting gram panchayats, a strong political base, and NGOs leave a positive impact on determining the beneficiaries of SGSY. The positive sign of political adherence is quite surprising hinting towards a strong organization among the group members against the ruling party. As many NGOs are functioning in the district to empower the villagers and spread awareness among them, it can be concluded that NGOs are playing quite a significant role in forming the groups. Significance of the constant term implies that external factors, which are not considered in the regression, significantly influence the selection process.

Table 6.2 Results of regression of VSHG on various explanatory variables block: Hura, District: Purulia

Variable	Coefficient (*p*-value)
C	−5.112*** (0.0003)
VA	−0.047** (0.015)
VBPMC	−3.644***(0.015)
VIM	1.558* (0.063)
VIMN	2.096*** (0.003)
VMC	2.686** (0.0433)
VNGO	2.608*** (0.0008)
VNLV	−2.31E−05 (0.606)
VP	1.991*** (0.001)
VM	1.483*(0.079)
VCP	1.229** (0.015)
VGP	2.215*** (0.002)
VIN	−0.551 (0.385)
VBD	−0.683 (0.236)
S.E. of regression	0.344
Sum squared residual	20.384
Log likelihood	−67.725
LR statistic (14 df)	68.603
Probability (LR stat)	3.45E−09
Akaike info criterion	0.885
McFadden R-squared	0.336
Total observations	150

Source Primary survey conducted during 2011–2012

In Hingalganj Block, contact with Block Development Offices, BPL status, political adherence, contact with the gram panchayats significantly determine the beneficiaries of SGSY. Most strikingly BPL status leaves a significant negative impact on selection of beneficiaries, which implies the households above the poverty line are having opportunity to be included in the groups. Political adherence has a negative sign signifying supporters of the ruling party are mainly preferred to be the group members. Per capita consumption also has an influence at 10% level which can be ignored.

Table 6.3 Results of regression of VSHG on various explanatory variables block: Hingalganj, District: North 24 Parganas

Variable	Coefficient (p-value)
C	−1.562 (0.286)
VBEN	0.698 (0.329)
VA	−0.026 (0.298)
VBP	−1.886*** (0.007)
VC	0.479 (0.394)
VCOM	0.0002** (0.010)
VIMN	0.842 (0.153)
VIN	−0.320 (0.719)
VBD	−1.699*** (0.008)
VNGO	0.238 (0.795)
VCS	−1.092* (0.076)
VGP	2.631*** (0.0008)
VP	−1.668*** (0.005)
Mean dependent var	0.297
S.E. of regression	0.3794
Sum squared resid	19.434
Log likelihood	−60.889
Restr. log likelihood	−90.066
LR statistic (12 df)	58.355
Probability(LR stat)	4.49E−08
Akaike info criterion	0.998
McFadden R-squared	0.324
Total observations	150

Source Primary survey conducted during 2011–12

6.7 Conclusion

In this chapter, our primary objective was to find out the factors that might have caused biased selection of beneficiaries in SGSY. Our micro-level study suggests that association with the village panchayats is one of the key determinants in beneficiary selection under SGSY. Though gram panchayats are the key agents in determining the beneficiaries, biased selection of villagers as group members still remains a matter of worry. People who are more related with panchayat personnel enjoy the opportunity to get informed about the schemes and have greater chances to be included in the self-help groups under SGSY. Selection of beneficiaries in most of the cases is not based on economic factors. Poverty level in terms of asset possession and consumption should be considered to include the vulnerable section within the groups. While selecting beneficiaries, backward castes are also not given due weightage. This finding also goes against what is desirable. Our study also suggests that decision process centres around gram panchayats in villages. In most cases people with a political influence frequently visit gram panchayats and acquaintance with the panchayats play a major role in selecting the group members instead of the neediest one. Therefore, panchayats should function efficiently in an unbiased manner to select the group members. In this respect gram panchayats should conduct gram sansads and use these democratic platforms in a well preferred, unbiased manner to organize the villagers under self-help groups and power in formulating the local level plans of the schemes, monitoring the execution process and inspecting fund utilization pattern. As the gram sansads are not organized regularly and participation in gram sansads is very low at the village level, rural community cannot reap the benefits of democratic participation. The institutional discouragement and the socio-political structure of the society hinder the active participation of all poor people irrespective of any other criteria. Therefore, the society is not able to assess the quality and the adequacy of the welfare programmes. Deficiency of the public evaluation and intervention has resulted in distortion of the whole delivery mechanism. Proper and unbiased functioning of the self-government institutions can show the right direction in this respect. Our empirical analysis discloses that political patronage practice is very much relevant in the distribution process. Comparatively, the economically well-off class manages to reap the political support and the benefit of the welfare programmes. The efficacy of SGSY could be improved and it can be restructured as a glorious attempt in the coming years if its experiences are reviewed and lessons are drawn from the past. The renamed and restructured NRLM has the target of universalizing the SHG coverage of all poor households by 2021. Although the target of universal mobilization may solve the problem of non-involving people in NRLM, steps should be taken to encourage the groups for uplifting themselves to the higher stages and avail bank credit. Proper monitoring must be there to deter any elite capture in getting credit, training and placement.

Appendix

See Table 6.4.

Table 6.4 Explanatory variables and the expected signs of their coefficients

Serial no.	Name of the variable	Explanation	Expected sign of the coefficient
1	Age (VA)	Age of the respondent. Aged should be more preferred as group members as they are the weaker section	+
2	Arable Land at the Household Level (VAL)	Arable land signifies asset possession at the household level. Land poor people should be preferred as group members. Therefore, the coefficient of Arable land should have a negative sign	−
3	Block Development Office Visit (VBD)	Block Development Offices should have a positive role in group formation	+
4	Poverty status (VBP)	BPL households should be more preferred while forming groups	+
5.	Beneficiary of Indira Awas Yojona (Vben)	As the flow of benefit under different schemes is directed on the basis of acquaintance, political patronage, it is expected that IAY beneficiaries will be more preferred while forming SGSY groups. Thus Vben is expected to have a positive sign	+
6.	Caste (VC)	VC is 1 when it stands for backward castes. It is mandated to prioritize SC/ST as group members	+
6	Per Capita Consumption at the household level (VCOM)	Consumption signifies economic status of the family. As SGSY is targeted for the poor, households with low level consumption should be preferred first	−
7	Dependence on Common Property (VCP)	Literature reveals poor are more dependent on common property resources as they serve as last resort for earning. Therefore, people more dependent on common property resources can be signified as more poor and should be more preferred while forming groups	+
8	Community Support (VCS)	Community support hints position of the respondent in the community. His or her bonding with the neighbours and reputation is judged by community support. Therefore, positive coefficient of VCS implies people who can find economic support from the community are	±

(continued)

Table 6.4 (continued)

Serial no.	Name of the variable	Explanation	Expected sign of the coefficient
		eligible as group members. On the other hand negative sign implies who do not find any sort of economic support within the community due to lack of recognition are more vulnerable and preferred as group members	
9	Education status (VES)	Education status signifies awareness. Therefore more educated people may have a greater chance to be included as group members	+
10	Gram Panchayat Visit (VGP)	Visit to Gram Panchayats implies better contact with the Gram Panchayat offices which should have a positive role on group members	+
11	Gram Sansad Presence (VGS)	Presence at Gram Sansads should have a positive impact on group formation because Gram Sansads should serve as platforms for beneficiary selection of different poverty alleviation schemes	+
12	Information flow through Mass Media (VIM)	Information from mass media should leave a positive impact on beneficiary selection by making the villagers aware of Government schemes	+
13	Informant about schemes (VIMN)	VIMN is 1 when informant is a GPO functionary. Therefore, Panchayat functionary should have a positive role in forming groups	+
14	Information from Neighbours (VIN)	Information from neighbours should have a positive role in beneficiary selection as it reveals contact of the respondent with her community	+
15	Marital Status (VM)	VM is one for Separated, divorced, widow or unmarried. They are the most vulnerable section in the village community and should be preferred in selecting group members	+
16	People meet at GPO (VMG)	If panchayats work efficiently people related with Gram Panchayats will meet with the people and know their requirements and demands	+

(continued)

Table 6.4 (continued)

Serial no.	Name of the variable	Explanation	Expected sign of the coefficient
17	Non Land Asset Value comprising of tangible assets and live stocks (VNLV)	High value of Non land assets implies a better economic position. Therefore resource poor people should be preferred as group members and VNLV should have a negative relation with selection of beneficiaries of SGSY	−
18	Political Adherence (VP)	VP is 1 for opposition and apolitical attitude. A sort of political patronage plays a key role in selection of beneficiaries of different development and poverty alleviation schemes at the village level. Therefore, supporters of ruling party are mostly selected as beneficiaries of different government schemes and the relation between political adherence and selection of beneficiaries is expected to be negative in our study	−
19	People in Need (VPN)	As the Gram Panchayat serves as self-government institutions at the village level, panchayats function in an expected manner if the GPO functionaries stand by the poor in their hard times	+
20	Interactive Dummy between BPL status, marital status and caste (VBPMC)	As the BPL households and the people belonging to the backward castes should be preferred while selecting the group members of the self-help groups. Widows and separated women who are more exposed to vulnerability should be more preferred as group members. Therefore, interactive dummy between BPL status, marital status and caste is expected to have a positive sign	+
21	Interactive dummy between marital status and caste (VMC)	Widows, separated women and backward castes being the marginalized section should be preferred as group members while forming self-help groups under SGSY	+

References

Alsop, R., Krishna, A., & Sjoblom, D. (2000). *Are gram panchayats inclusive? Report of a study conducted in Rajasthan and Madhya Pradesh.* Background Paper No. 3 of the World Bank's unpublished *Overview of Rural Decentralization in India. 3,* World Bank.

Bagchee, S. (1987). Poverty alleviation programmes in seventh plan: an appraisal. *Economic and Political Weekly, 22*(4), 139–148.

Bardhan, P., & Mookherjee, D. (2004). Poverty alleviation efforts of West Bengal panchayats. *Economic and Political Weekly, 39*(9), 965–974.

Behar, A. (2003). Madhya Pradesh: Experiment with direct democracy, time for reappraisal. *Economic and Political Weekly, 38*(20), 1927–1929.

Dutrey, A. P. (2007). *Successful targeting? Reporting efficiency and costs in targeted poverty alleviation programmes.* Social Policy and Development Programme Paper Number 35, United Nations Research Institute for Social Development, November 2007.

Ghatak, M., & Ghatak, M. (2002). Recent reforms in the panchayat system in West Bengal towards greater participatory governanace? *Economic and Political Weekly, 37*(1), 45–57.

Kaladhar, K. (1997). Microfinance in India: Design, structure and governance. *Economic and Political weekly, 32*(42), 2687–2706.

Khandelwal, A. K. (2007). Microfinance development strategy for India. *Economic and Political Weekly, 42*(13), 1127–1135.

Kurian, N. J. (1987). Anti-poverty programme: A reappraisal. *Economic and Political Weekly, 24* (12), A13–A20.

Nambiar, M. (2001). Making the gram sabha work. *Economic and Political Weekly, 36*(33), 3114–3117.

Rath, N. (1985). Garibi hatao: Can IRDP do it? *Economic and Political Weekly, 20*(6), 238–246.

Roy, D. (2007). *Mid-term evaluation of the composition and working of Swarnajayanti Gram Swarozgar Yojana in 24 Parganas South District (West Bengal), study supported by Planning Commission*, Government of India.

Chapter 7
Financial Inclusion Through Kisan Credit Cards in Arunachal Pradesh—The Truth Behind Aggregating Numbers

Samir R. Samantara

Abstract Arunachal Pradesh, though strategically very imperative, is one of the utmost backward states in India in the traditional wisdom of economic constraints. The extensive inaccessibility and separation from the main stream of the country postured daunting problems to the efforts of socioeconomic improvement of the state. This chapter studies the question of convergence in Arunachal Pradesh agriculture since the last decade. It focuses on the problems of (a) whether there has been a catching-up propensity (β-convergence) of slow-growing districts with fast-growing ones; and (b) whether there has been a propensity towards convergence (σ-convergence) in agricultural productivity during 2000–2010 over a representative cross section of Arunachal Pradesh districts. The chapter also examines the process of Galton's fallacy through growth-terminal level regressions for robustness of the results. The propensity of low-KCC concentration districts to catch up with high-KCC concentration districts is examined through the unconditional β-convergence approach, and the operation of Galton's fallacy through growth-terminal agricultural productivity-level regressions. The shrinking of variance in productivity levels is tested by using the σ-convergence approach and the robustness of the results is tested by using alternative test statistics. The results suggest that comparatively agriculturally poor districts, if not all, have been able to catch up with the agriculturally rich districts, demonstrating β-convergence. Although the growth of KCC loans varied across the districts, the average speed of

---

A portion of this chapter has been reproduced from Samantara (2015) Financial Inclusion through Kisan credit Cards in Disadvantages region Like Arunachal Pradesh—Is there district-level convergence? Indian Journal of Agricultural Economics 70(3):217–230. Requisite permissions (electronically) has been obtained from the publisher of the above journal. All the citation analysis are also available in http://ageconsearch.umn.edu/bitstream/230039/2/07-Samir%20Samantara.pdf.

The views expressed are those of the author and not of the organization he belongs to. Usual disclaimer applies.

S.R. Samantara (✉)
National Bank for Agriculture and Rural Development (NABARD),
Assam Regional Office, Guwahati 781006, India
e-mail: samir.samantara@gmail.com

U.K. De et al. (eds.), *Inequality, Poverty and Development in India*, India Studies in Business and Economics, DOI 10.1007/978-981-10-6274-2_7

convergence remained more or less equal during both the periods. However, inter-district differences in growths of KCC loans have significantly declined in the state indicating σ-convergence. Neither did the low (agriculture) productivity districts grow faster, nor did the high (agriculture) productivity districts grow slower to demonstrate the catching-up or β-convergence process. These tendencies are likely to continue in Arunachal Pradesh agriculture unless adequate investments or technological interventions are made to enhance agriculture productivity. This would furthermore help in credit deepening and credit widening (both horizontal and vertical financial inclusion) through KCC loans, leading to a further convergence. State governments and banks should create enabling environment that can improve credit absorption capacity of farmers and geographical areas, accelerate flow of credit and loan recovery simultaneously.

Keywords Convergence · Agricultural productivity · Kisan credit card
Financial inclusion and technological innovation

7.1 Introduction

Arunachal Pradesh, though strategically very important, is one of the most backward States in India in the traditional sense of economic parameters. The long isolation and separation from the main stream of the country, posed formidable problems to the efforts of socioeconomic development of the State. Further, the State's inhospitable topography, challenging climatic conditions and communication bottle-necks make the cost of creation and maintenance of infrastructure extremely high (Samantara 2006a, b). Arunachal Pradesh is situated in the Northeastern part of India with 83,743 km^2 area and has a long international border with Bhutan to the west (160 km), China to the north and northeast (1080 km) and Myanmar to the east (440 km). It stretches from snow-capped mountains in the north to the plains of Brahmaputra valley in the south. The state has 18 districts, 27 census towns and 3863 inhabited villages. Arunachal Pradesh has a bank network of 88 branches of commercial banks, 27 branches of Arunachal Pradesh Rural Bank (APRB) and 32 Branches of Arunachal Pradesh State Cooperative Apex Bank (APSCAB) Ltd.

7.2 Data and Methodology

This paper examines the question of convergence in Arunachal Pradesh agriculture since the last decade. It focuses on the questions of (a) whether there has been a catching-up tendency (β-convergence) of slow-growing districts with fast-growing ones; and (b) whether there has been a tendency towards convergence (σ-convergence) in agricultural productivity during 2000–2010 over a representative cross section of Arunachal Pradesh districts. The paper also tests the operation of Galton's fallacy through growth-terminal level regressions for robustness of the results. The tendency of low-KCC concentration districts to catch up with high-KCC concentration districts is studied through the unconditional β-convergence approach (Samantara 2012a, b), and the operation of Galton's fallacy through growth-terminal agricultural productivity-level regressions. The diminution of variance in productivity levels is tested using the σ-convergence approach and the robustness of the results is tested using alternative test statistics. Concentration of short-term credit in the form of KCC in agriculture is the total short-term credit in agriculture per hectare of net sown area, and agriculture productivity is the agriculture production per hectare of net sown area (Samantara and Badatya 2000). Details on the district-wise short-term KCC loans and agricultural productivity were collected from the district-wise Potential Credit Plans published from NABARD. Details on net sown area were obtained from the Directorate of Statistics and Evaluation (*Government of Arunachal Pradesh*).

On the empirical front, modeling and testing the convergence hypothesis is far from settled. As Islam (2003) observed that either conditional or unconditional, the informal and formal cross section approaches, the panel approach, and the time series approach (in part) had all studied β-convergence. The formal cross section approach and panel approach have been used to study club-convergence and total factor productivity (TFP) convergence (Samantara and Kulkarni 2002). The time series approach has been used to investigate convergence both within an economy and across economies. But the cross section and panel approaches suffer from endogeneity bias, since variables such as investment growth rate in agriculture and agriculture productivity growth rate used as explanatory variables in growth-convergence equations are likely to be jointly determined. Despite the observations of Hotelling (1933), Friedman (1992), Lichtenberg (1994), and Sala-i-Martin (1996) and the criticisms of Quah (1993), researchers have continued to be interested in β-convergence for the reason that σ-convergence requires β-convergence. The other reason is that β-convergence could provide information on the structural parameters of growth models. The present study investigated both (unconditional) β-convergence and σ-convergence in short-term KCC loan and agriculture productivity across the districts in Arunachal Pradesh. Along with the growth-initial productivity regressions to study β-convergence, the paper attempted to fit growth-terminal productivity regressions for testing Galton's fallacy (Samantara 2008).

7.3 The Model

(a) β-Convergence and Galton's Fallacy

Following Sala-i-Martin's (1996) exposition, the paper used the following equation to investigate unconditional β-convergence across the districts. Assuming that β-convergence holds for districts $i = 1, 2, \ldots, N$. Natural log-income of ith district at time t could be approximated by

$$\ln y_{i,t} = \alpha + (1-\beta)\ln(y_{i,t-1}) + u_{i,t}, \tag{7.1}$$

where, $y_{i,t} =$ credit (or agriculture) productivity in district i at time t, $0 < \beta < 1$ and $u_{i,t}$ has zero mean, finite variance, σ_u^2, and independent over t and i. Since α is assumed to be constant across districts, balanced growth paths were identical (allowing different $\alpha_i s$ for $0 < \beta < 1$ could imply conditional β-convergence).

Manipulating Eq. (7.1) resulted

$$\ln(y_{i,t}/y_{i,t-1}) = \alpha - \beta\ln(y_{i,t-1}) + u_{i,t} \tag{7.2}$$

Thus, $\beta > 0$ implied a negative correlation between growth and initial log productivity. Between any period t and $t + T$, Eq. (7.2) could be written as

$$(1/T)\ln(y_{i,t+T}/y_{i,t}) = \alpha - \beta\ln(y_{i,t}) + u_{i,t} \tag{7.3}$$

Replacing $y_{i,t}$ on the right-hand side of Eq. (7.3) with $y_{i,t+T}$

$$(1/T)\ln\left(y_{i,t+T}/y_{i,t}\right) = \alpha - \beta\ln\left(y_{i,t+T}\right) + u_{i,t} \tag{7.4}$$

Equation (7.4) referred to the relation between growth and the terminal year. $\beta > 0$ in Eq. (7.3) and a consequent $\beta < 0$ in Eq. (7.4) represented Galton's fallacy observed in Friedman (1992). The growth rates obtained in Eqs. (7.3) and (7.4) consider only the initial and terminal year productivity levels and ignore values in the rest of the period. To avoid this limitation, the paper used trend growth rate in Eqs. (7.3) and (7.4) given by

$$ri = \alpha - \beta\ln\left(y_{i,t}\right) + u_{i,t} \tag{7.3a}$$

$$ri = \alpha - \beta\ln\left(y_{i,t+T}\right) + u_{i,t}, \tag{7.4a}$$

where, $r_i =$ trend growth rate between any two time period t and $t + T$, which could be obtained from the ordinary least squares (OLS) estimate β in the following regression.

$$\ln y_t = \alpha - \beta_t \tag{7.5}$$

$$r = \exp(\beta) - 1 \tag{7.6}$$

where $Y_t =$ credit or agriculture productivity at time 't'.

(b) ***σ*-Convergence**

Existence of β-convergence might not necessarily imply σ-convergence among districts. The (σ) convergence hypothesis could be expressed as

$$\frac{\mathrm{d}[\mathrm{Var}(\ln(y_{i,t})] < 0}{\mathrm{d}_t}, \tag{7.7}$$

where, $Y_{i,t}$ = credit (or agriculture) productivity in district i at time t and var($y_{i,t}$) denoted variance across districts. Equation (7.5) could be formally tested (McCunn and Huffman 2000) using var

$$[\ln(y_{i,t})]\,\varphi_1 + \varphi_2 t + \varepsilon_t, \tag{7.8}$$

where, ε_t = zero mean random disturbance term. Sufficient condition for productivity (credit or agriculture) convergence across districts was negative φ_2 and significantly different from zero. When φ_2 was not significantly negative, unconditional convergence did not occur, or growth rates across districts might diverge over time. To test the robustness of the results (σ-convergence), the paper followed the tests suggested by Lichtenberg (1994) and Caree and Klomp (1997). Lichtenberg (1994) showed that the test of mean-reversion hypothesis $\beta < 0$ (based on the t distribution with $n - 2$ degrees of freedom) was equivalent to a test of

$$T_1 = \{\mathrm{var}(\ln y_{i,t})\}/\{\mathrm{var}(\ln y_{i,t+T})\} = R_2/(1+\beta)^2 > 1, \tag{7.9}$$

where, $y_{i,t}$ and $y_{i,t+T}$ = productivity levels in initial and terminal years of any given time period t and $t + T$ respectively. Caree and Klomp (1997) observed that the test statistic proposed by Lichtenberg (1994) discounted the dependency between the two Caree and Klomp (1997) proposed two alternative test statistics (robust to shorter time periods)

$$T_2 = (N - 2.5)\ln\left[1 + \left\{1\left(\sigma_1^2 - \sigma_T^2\right)^2\right\}/\left\{4\left(\sigma_1^2\sigma_T^2 - \sigma_{1T}^2\right)\right\}\right] \tag{7.10}$$

$$T_3 = [\sqrt{N}(\{\sigma_1^2/\sigma_T^2\} - 1)/\{2\sqrt{1} - \Pi^2 N\} \tag{7.11}$$

Test statistic $T_2 = \chi 2$ (1) distribution and T_3 = Normal distribution with $N - 1$ degrees of freedom. The paper computed all T_1, T_2 and T_3 statistics in examining the convergence hypothesis.

7.4 Findings and Discussion

Trends in KCC loans and agricultural productivity in Arunachal Pradesh during 2000–2010 are presented in Fig. 7.1. Agricultural productivity was calculated as the ratio of agriculture production per hectare of net area sown and KCC loans growth was calculated as the ratio of KCC loans disbursed per hectare of net area sown in agriculture. To account for year-to-year fluctuations, growth rates were estimated from 2-year moving averages of the data series. Average agricultural productivity increased consistently through the period with an average growth of 2.34% per annum. The 2000–2005 period registered an annual growth of 2.21% and it increased slightly to 2.47% during 2005–2010. Average KCC loans also increased but not as much average agricultural productivity. Average KCC loans growth attained during 2000–2010 (1.14%) was less than the growth realized in agricultural productivity. But unlike KCC loans, where growth was almost equal in both the periods, agriculture productivity increased significantly for the same period. Such an upward shift in agriculture productivity growth could be attributed to a significant increase in agriculture production (Samantara 2009).

Though the magnitudes differed, KCC loans increased in all the districts between 2000 and 2010. The growth was highest in East Siang (3.58%), followed by East Kameng (2.90%) and Upper Siang (2.82%), while districts such as Lower Dibang Valley (2.14%), Tawang (1.46%), Anjaw (1.16%) and Tirap (1.14%) increased at a moderate rate (Table 7.1). Contrary to KCC loans, large number of districts achieved significant growth in agricultural productivity. They included East Kameng (3.92%), Lower Dibang Valley (3.34%) and Dibang Valley (3.13%). Rest of the districts recorded growth rates (1–3%) during 2000–2010.

7.4.1 Convergence in Productivity: β-Convergence

As mentioned earlier, the convergence phenomenon was studied for different periods. First, convergence in KCC loans and agriculture productivity was examined for the entire period (2000–2010). Subsequently, this period was divided into

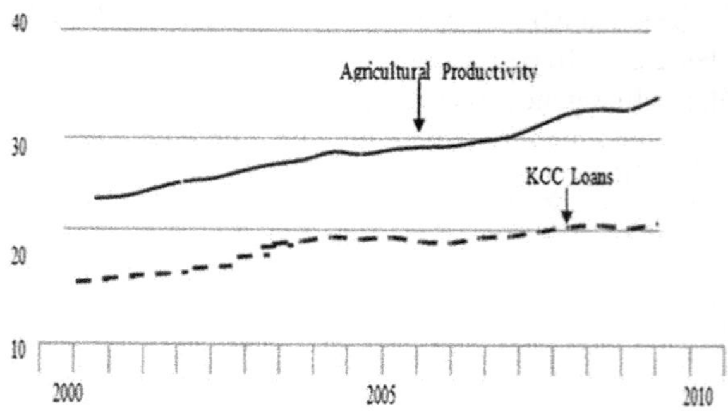

Fig. 7.1 KCC loan and agricultural productivity in Arunachal Pradesh (2000–2010). *Source* Author's calculation

Table 7.1 KCC loans and agriculture productivity growth in Arunachal Pradesh (2000–2010)

Districts	Avg. KCC loan (Rs.)	Avg. agri. productivity[a] (kg/ha)	Annual growth	
			KCC loans	Agri. productivity
Tawang	40,562	1543	1.46	2.60
West Kameng	44,263	1521	−0.52	0.91
East Kameng	46,897	1523	2.90	3.92
Papum Pare	51,452	1625	1.22	2.25
Lower Subansiri	58,452	1765	0.61	2.59
Upper Subansiri	59,325	1423	0.32	2.82
East Siang	45,623	1670	3.58	2.28
West Siang	58,429	1546	0.50	2.16
Upper Siang	44,369	1495	2.82	1.54
Dibang Valley	45,442	1356	0.21	3.13
Lower Dibang Valley	44,289	1564	2.14	3.34
Lohit	51,235	1452	0.12	2.57
Changlang	49,648	1523	0.76	1.32
Tirap	52,369	1654	1.14	2.11
Kurung Kumey	58,796	1578	0.73	2.16
Anjaw	54,278	1469	1.16	1.89
Longding	59,985	1546	0.21	2.32

Source Author's calculation
Note [a]Productivity of major crop (Rice) has been taken proxy for agricultural productivity (Though the author acknowledges this as limitation of the present research, but it may not affect the overall results and interpretations)

two sub-periods 2000–2005 and 2005–2010 to study the convergence phenomenon in two different periods. To test whether the speed of convergence had been higher after 2005, attempt has been made to study the convergence during 2000–2005 and 2005–2010. The growth-initial productivity regression for 2000–2010 reinforced existence of β-convergence in KCC loans growth across the districts (Table 7.2). The coefficient of KCC loans in the initial year (2000) against growth was negative (−1.172) and it was highly significant (P-value = 0.031), indicating that the districts with lower KCC loans grew faster than the districts with high-KCC loans (Fig. 7.2). KCC Loans growth was highest in East Siang (3.58%), followed by East Kameng (2.90%) and Upper Siang (2.82%), But, in absolute terms, it was low in these districts, that is, Rs. 45,623 per hectare (ha) in East Siang, Rs. 46,897/ha in East Kameng, and Rs. 44,369/ha in Upper Siang against the State average of Rs. 50,906/ha in 2010. Other districts that grew fast despite low initial KCC loans were Tawang, and Lower Dibang Valley. Annual average KCC loans growth in these districts for the year 2000 and 2010 was 1.46 and 2.14%, respectively. On the other hand, districts such as Lower Subansiri, Upper Subansiri, Kurung Kumey and Longding, where the initial KCC loans level was relatively high, grew by less than

Table 7.2 β-convergence and Galton's Fallacy in KCC loans (2000–2010)

Explanatory variable	Dependent variable				
	Coef	$P > \|t\|$	R^2	Shapiro-Wilk $P > \|z\|$	White-$P > \chi^2$
Period: 2000–2010	KCC loans growth (2000–2010)				
ln (KCC loans)—2000	−1.172	0.031	0.273	0.568	0.458
ln (KCC loans)—2010	−0.578	0.422	0.043	0.326	0.814
Period: 2000–2005	KCC loans growth (2000–2005)				
ln (KCC loans)—2000	−1.533	0.037	0.260	0.846	0.465
ln (KCC loans)—2005	−0.794	0.366	0.055	0.554	0.286
Period: 2000–2010	KCC loans growth (2005–2010)				
ln (KCC loans)—2005	−1.520	0.108	0.163	0.764	0.654
ln (KCC loans)—2010	−0.32	0.764	0.006	0.729	0.936

Source Author's estimates

1.0%. Thus, while districts with low-KCC loans grew faster, by more than 2.00%, high-KCC loans districts grew by less than 1.00%, indicating a strong (β) convergence across them.

As one could see from Table 7.2, the speed of convergence (coefficients of the initial years in growth-initial productivity regressions) decreased over time, while the speed of convergence remained more or less unaltered in both the periods (1.53%), with a significant drop in *P*-values, from 1.46% during 2000–2005 to 1.20% during 2005–2010. Moreover, for 2005–2010, the convergence hypothesis could not be established strongly, indicated by low significance of the coefficient corresponding to the initial productivity variable (*P*-value = 0.270). This evidence was against the general belief that low-productivity districts performed better during 2005–2010. For example, between 2000 and 2010, low-productivity districts such as Lower Subansiri (2.59%), Upper Subansiri (2.82%), Kurung Kumey (2.16%) and Longding (2.32%) performed relatively better than West Kameng (0.91%), Upper Siang (1.54%), and Changlang (1.32%), the districts with relatively high initial KCC loans levels (Fig. 7.3). But the speed of convergence across districts between 2000 and 2010 was camouflaged by the underperformance of west Kameng, which registered a negative growth rate (−0.52%) during this period. Having the lowest initial KCC loans level (Rs. 44,263/ha), a negative growth rate in the district concealed the efforts of better-performing districts.

Contrary to KCC loans growth, the analysis failed to reject the null hypothesis of no (β) convergence in agricultural productivity in different periods through negative but insignificant coefficients and much lower coefficients of determination in the growth-initial year agricultural productivity regression (Table 7.3). No tendency to grow faster was observed in the low-agriculture productivity districts, or to slow growth in the high-agriculture productivity districts. Average agriculture productivity was the highest in East Siang (1670 kg/ha.), followed by Tirap (1654 kg/ha) and Papum Pare (1625 kg/ha). During 2000–2010, agriculture productivity grew by 2.16, 2.11 and 2.25% in East Siang, Tirap and Papum Pare, respectively. In

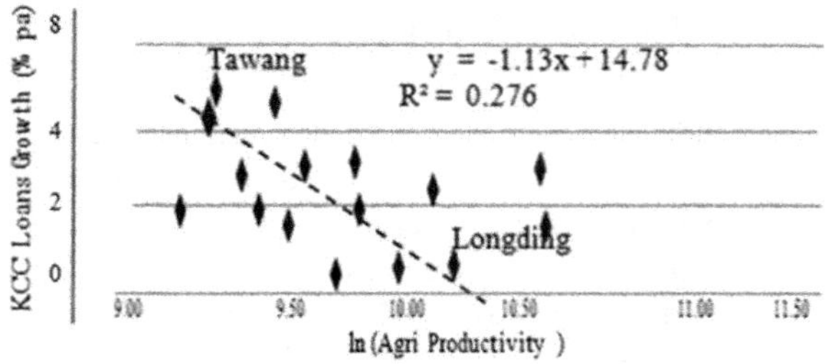

Fig. 7.2 Beta convergence in KCC loans (2000–2010). *Source* Author's calculation

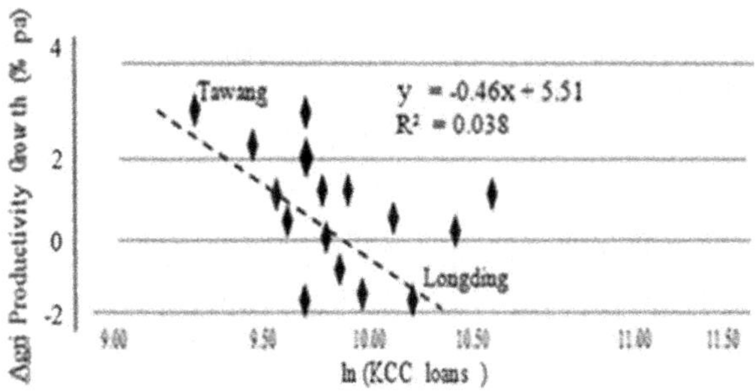

Fig. 7.3 Beta convergence in agricultural productivity (2000–2010)

Table 7.3 β-convergence and Galton's Fallacy in agricultural productivity (2000–2010)

Explanatory variable	Explained variable				
	Coef	$P > \|t\|$	R^2	Shapiro-Wilk $P > \|z\|$	White-$P > \chi 2$
Period: 2000–2010	Agricultural productivity (2000–2010)				
ln (agri. prod^y)—2000	−0.473	0.447	0.039	0.662	0.923
ln (agri. prod^y)—2010	0.348	0.574	0.022	0.215	0.208
Period: 2000–2005	Agricultural productivity growth (2000–2005)				
ln (agri. prod^y)—2000	−0.953	0.376	0.053	0.293	0.785
ln (agri. prod^y)—2005	0.697	0.532	0.027	0.176	0.019
Period: 2000–2010	Agricultural productivity growth (2005–2010)				
ln (agri. prod^y)—2005	−0.224	0.819	0.004	0.645	0.701
ln (agri. prod^y)—2010	0.909	0.329	0.064	0.833	0.533

Source Author's estimates

contrast, Dibang Valley, which had the lowest agriculture productivity (1356 kg/ha), grew by 3.13%, compared to Papum Pare (3.34%) and East Kameng (3.92%), the districts with the higher agriculture productivity growth. Thus, the outcomes did not establish β-convergence in agriculture productivity.

7.4.2 Galton's Fallacy

The tendency to converge (β-convergence) disappeared when the growth was plotted against the terminal year rather than the initial year, the factors inclined to diverge rather than converge. This phenomenon could be referred as Galton's fallacy or statistical (regression) fallacy (Friedman 1992). Hotelling (1933) observed this singularity and mentioned it as a statistical fallacy resulting from the method of grouping and suggested σ-convergence was superior to β-convergence. This paper, in addition to investigating β-convergence through productivity regressions, also examined the operation of so-called Galton's fallacy through growth-terminal productivity regressions in KCC loans and agriculture productivity (Tables 7.2 and 7.3). The paper failed to establish such statistical fallacy both in KCC loans and agriculture productivity in all the periods. The β-convergence observed in the growth-initial productivity regressions did not continue when growth rates were regressed against terminal years rather than the initial years, shown by the negative and highly insignificant terminal year KCC loans coefficients and the lowest coefficients of determination in different periods. Thus, the seemingly converging tendency in the growth-initial level regressions turned up to have no relation in the growth-terminal productivity regressions. The results of agriculture productivity regressions proved the same, except the difference of the positive terminal productivity coefficients. The results invalidated the assumption of superiority of σ-convergence over β-convergence as argued by Hotelling (1933) and Friedman (1992). Since β-convergence was a necessary but not a sufficient condition for convergence, the σ-convergence approach was adopted.

7.4.3 σ-Convergence

The trend in cross-sectional dispersion of KCC loans and agriculture productivity in all the districts was studied using standard deviation in a natural logarithm as a measure of dispersion. The results obtained by regressing standard deviation of (natural logarithm) KCC loans and agriculture productivity against the time variable were shown in Table 7.4. To test the robustness of the results, the test statistics suggested by Lichtenberg (1994) and Caree and Klomp (1997) were calculated (Table 7.5).

Plotting the coefficient of variation against time showed that except in few years, dispersion in KCC loans across districts declined gradually (Fig. 7.4). The coefficients of the time variable were negative and highly significant in all the periods, except 2005–2010. During 2005–2010, though the coefficient was negative, it was significant only at higher level of significance. These results were inconsistent with those obtained in the β-convergence approach. Hence, the paper rejected the null of no convergence in KCC loans. The test statistic T_1 failed to establish convergence in KCC loans in different periods, thereby supporting the view of Caree and Klomp

Table 7.4 σ-Convergence in KCC loans growth and agriculture productivity (2000–2010)

Explained variable	Coef	$P > \|t\|$	R^2	Shapiro-Wilk $P > \|z\|$	Breusche-Godfrey $P > \chi2$
Period: 2000–2010					
SD[ln(KCC loans)]	−0.005	0.000	0.802	0.994	0.355
SD[ln(Agri. prod^y)]	−0.001	0.824	0.003	0.932	0.069
Period: 2000–2005					
SD[ln(KCC loans)]	−0.006	0.044	0.416	0.998	0.413
SD[ln(Agri. prod^y)]	−0.002	0.625	0.031	0.608	0.164
Period: 2005–2010					
SD[ln(KCC loans)]	−0.005	0.000	0.776	0.868	0.913
SD[ln(Agri. prod^y)]	0.002	0.093	0.281	0.060	0.972

Source Author's estimates

Table 7.5 Results of alternative test statistics of σ-convergence

Variable	Lichtenberg (1994)		Caree and Klomp (1997)			
	T_1	Critical F	T_2	Critical $\chi2$	T_3	Critical t
Period: 2000–2010						
ln(KCC loans)	1.530	2.400	4.003	3.841	1.645	1.746
ln(Agri. Productivity)	0.981	2.400	0.009	3.841	−0.109	1.746
Period: 2000–2005						
ln(KCC loans)	1.271	2.400	1.792	3.841	1.021	1.746
ln(Agri. Productivity)	1.059	2.400	0.070	3.841	0.262	1.746
Period: 2005–2010						
ln(KCC loans)	1.203	2.400	0.990	3.841	0.807	1.746
ln(Agri. Productivity)	0.927	2.400	0.198	3.841	−0.811	1.746

Source Authors' estimates
Note Critical values are significant at 5% level and at 10% level; critical values for T_1, T_2 and T_3 will be 1.970, 2.705, and 1.337, respectively

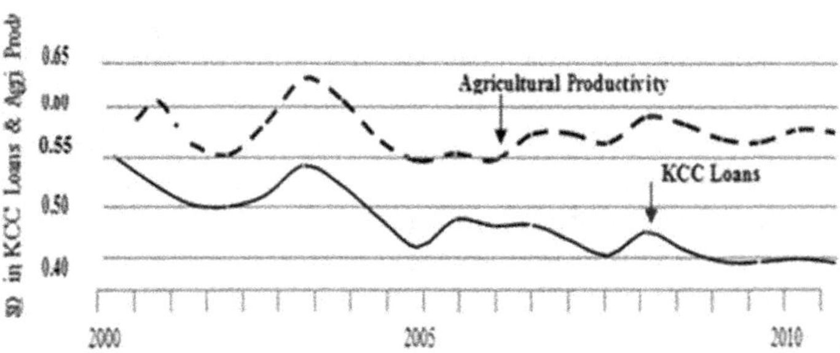

Fig. 7.4 Sigma convergence in KCC loan and agricultural productivity (2000–2010). *Source* Author's calculation

(1997) that the T_1 statistic is biased towards finding no convergence. Both T_2 and T_3 statistics established convergence during 2000–2010, but they failed to do so for the other periods, as observed in earlier approaches of convergence analysis.

Unlike KCC loans, no trend was observed in the standard deviation of agriculture productivity. The coefficients were negative and insignificant most of the regressions (except during 2000–2010, where the coefficient was significant at the 10% level). Hence, the study could not reject the no convergence null hypothesis in the case of agriculture productivity. Similar results were obtained in the alternative tests. A consistent increase in KCC loans was found in all the districts since 2000. The growth in KCC loans was higher in districts that had low initial (KCC loans) levels than in districts with high levels of initial (KCC loans) levels. The results suggest that comparatively agriculturally poor districts, if not all, have been able to catch up with the agriculturally rich districts, demonstrating β-convergence. Although the growth of KCC loans varied across the districts, the average speed of convergence remained more or less equal during both the periods. However, inter-district differences in growths of KCC loans have significantly declined in the state indicating σ-convergence. Neither did the low (agriculture) productivity districts grow faster, nor did the high (agriculture) productivity districts grow slower to demonstrate the catching-up or β-convergence process. These tendencies are likely to continue in Arunachal Pradesh agriculture unless adequate investments or technological interventions are made to enhance agriculture productivity. This would furthermore help in credit deepening and credit widening (both horizontal and vertical financial inclusion) through KCC loans, leading to a further convergence.

7.5 Summary and Conclusions

Strategic planning and implementation is necessary to develop agriculture and make North East Region (NER) in general, Arunachal Pradesh in particular, marginally, if not significantly, surplus in food production by integrating research, extension and education duly supported by a time-bound reforms in land tenure system in the state. Agricultural development strategy has to be evolved depending on resources, environment, and people's requirements and primacies. Private sector participation could provide additional resources and create necessary environment to generate employment opportunities, better utilization of resources and enhance credit flow impacting directly on farm-sector development. With appropriately defined targets, clear outcomes, strategies and coordinated planning, Arunachal Pradesh could become increasingly self-reliant in food production. Effective computer-based monitoring/management information system could facilitate timely implementation of programmes with improved quality, service delivery without cost-cum-time over runs and produce intended outcomes. Since banks have a significant role as a catalyst to accelerate the process of agricultural development in Arunachal Pradesh they should be pro-active and make financial services available to farmers by establishing branches at strategic locations and through technology applications. In a time-bound programme, they should provide Kisan Credit Cards along with suitable insurance products to all eligible farmers. Banks should design simple borrower-friendly lending policy, procedure, documentation, customized and flexible financial products that match requirements of farmers in Arunachal Pradesh rather than one-fits-all for the country as a whole. The factors responsible for low performance as compared to targeted included inter alia, difficult topography, sparse population settlements, inadequate infrastructure, discouraging land tenure system, lack of agricultural entrepreneurship, massive amount of grants/subsidies under Government programmes, law and order conditions in some parts of the state. State Governments, banks and print/electronic media should create enabling environment that can improve credit absorption capacity of farmers and geographical areas, accelerate flow of credit, and loan recovery simultaneously.

References

Caree, M., & Klomp, L. (1997). Testing the convergence hypothesis—A comment. *Review of Economics and Statistics, 79*(4), 683–686.

Friedman, M. (1992). Do old fallacies ever die? *Journal of Economic Literature, 30*(4), 2129–2132.

Hotelling, H. (1933). Review of the triumph of mediocrity in business. *Journal of American Statistical Association, 28*(184), 463–465.

Islam, N. (2003). What have we learned from the convergence debate? *Journal of Economic Surveys, 17*(3), 309–362.

Lichtenberg, F. R. (1994). Testing the convergence hypothesis. *Review of Economics and Statistics, 76*(3), 576–579.

McCunn, A., & Huffman, W. (2000). Convergence in US productivity growth for agriculture, implications of inter-state research spill-overs for funding agricultural research. *American Journal of Agricultural Economics, 82*(2), 370–388.

Quah, D. (1993). Galton's fallacy and tests of the convergence hypothesis. *Scandinavian Journal of Economics, 95*(4), 427–443.

Sala-i-Martin, X. (1996). Regional cohesion, evidence and theories of regional growth and convergence. *European Economic Review, 40*(6), 1325–1352.

Samantara, S. R. (2006a). Infrastructure–agriculture linkages. *Indian Journal of Agriculture Economics, 61*(3), 254–256.

Samantara, S.R. (2006b). Infrastructure–agriculture linkages in Chhattisgarh. *Chhattisgarh Journal of Economics* (2nd Annual Conference), pp. 45–51.

Samantara, S. R. (2008). Economic growth and deforestation—A study in Odisha. *Indian Journal of Agriculture Economics, 63*(3), 436–437.

Samantara, S. R. (2009). Revisiting the non-farm employment debate—Review of issues and evidence. *APRACA, Journal of Rural Finance (A Quarterly Journal of Asia-Pacific Rural and Agricultural Credit Association* (APRACA), International Edition), *7*(2), 34–39.

Samantara, S. R., & Badatya, K. C. (2000). Agriculture growth and instability. *Agriculture Economics Research Association* (Conference Issue), pp. 42–46.

Samantara, S. R., & Kulkarni, B. N. (2002). Employment generation through credit linked non-arm activities. *Indian Journal of Labour Economics, 45*(4), 783–792.

Samantara, S. R. (2012a). Diversification of economic activities under rural non-farm sector. In B. Sen & M. Chinara (Eds.), *Economic development and poverty in India* (pp. 78–94). New Delhi: New Century Publications.

Samantara, S. R. (2012b). Developmental role of institutional incentives for agricultural marketing in India. *Indian Journal of Agricultural Marketing, 23*(3), 63–71.

Samantara, S. R. (2015). Financial Inclusion through kisan credit cards in disadvantages region like Arunachal Pradesh—Is there district-level convergence? *Indian Journal of Agricultural Economics, 70*(3), 217–230.

Chapter 8
Insurance and Banking Habits Regulating Economic Stability of the People of Char Areas (Riverine) in Lower Assam

Kishore K. Das

Abstract Riverine (Char area) of the Brahmaputra flowing through Assam are most backward and neglected areas. There about 2251 Chars covering about 10% population of Assam. This chapter tries to examine the Insurance and Banking habits regulating economic stability of the people of char areas in Lower Assam. This study is based on the survey '*Dynamics of socio-economic development of Char areas of Lower Assam*' was conducted during the year 2003–2005 under the financial support of University Grants Commission, New Delhi on randomly selected char areas. Insurance and banking habits have been considered in the survey to study the economic stability of the people. A log-linear model and contingency table have been considered in this study. It is observed that the proportion of insured households in the low income group is nil; it rises to a small in the lower middle group and then goes up in the upper middle group and after that steadily increases to the high income group. The economic status reveals that only the upper middle income and high income group households have been able to avail the facility of banking and insurance. The households in the low income group and lower middle income group went unrepresented.

Keywords Insurance · Banking · Log-linear model

8.1 Introduction

A char is nothing but a landmass surrounded by flowing river water inhabited by people and animals. There are 2251 char areas in 14 districts out of 23 districts of Assam (Socio-economic Survey Report 2002–2003). Among these char areas, a large numbers are densely populated. These areas constitute those lands, which go under water, except a very few chars, during monsoon flow of the Brahmaputra River and remain dry thereafter. The majority inhabitants of the Chars are Muslim

K.K. Das (✉)
Department of Statistics, Gauhati University, 781 014 Guwahati, Assam, India
e-mail: daskkishore@gmail.com

U.K. De et al. (eds.), *Inequality, Poverty and Development in India*, India Studies in Business and Economics, DOI 10.1007/978-981-10-6274-2_8

(98.4%). The people living in these areas are very poor and they have to brave floods and erosion of their lands every year. The risks of health hazard are also high. The socio-economic conditions of the Chars are appalling.

Keeping in view these basic backgrounds of the people in char areas, the project was completed with the title Economic Development of Char Areas in Assam: Phase-I., which is a humble endeavour in a process to measure the level of development and study the socioeconomic status of the char areas and put forward necessary recommendations. The project was initiated under the banner of the Department of Statistics, Gauhati University, Guwahati, undertook a survey in the Char areas of Assam precisely, in the districts of Barpeta, Dhubri and Goalpara. This survey was sponsored by the University Grants Commission, New Delhi. These chars although not big in size, their socio-economic development plays a major role in the overall development of the state.

8.2 Data and Methodology

8.2.1 Sample Design

The sample design adopted for the survey is a multi-stage stratified sampling and systematic sampling. The main fieldwork for the survey in the three districts was carried out by the investigators. It was carried out in the year 2003–2004. There are 2251 char areas in 14 districts out of 23 districts of Assam. We have considered only three districts, which have been chosen using random number generated from Casio calculator by the Rnd function. The districts Barpeta, Dhubri and Goalpara were found for the study as first stage. In the second stage, the Chars of these districts were selected adopting the probability proportional to size (PPS) procedure. Households of the char areas were chosen by systematic sampling as third stage.

Here we investigated the economic planning of the households, like whether they are members of cooperative societies, have any bank account, insurance policy, etc. We have also asked the households if any member of that household has/had ever taken a loan from cooperative society or bank or against insurance policy.

From the survey, we have come to know that none of the sampled households is a member of any cooperative society. This speaks volumes of the fact that the culture of cooperative societies has not yet touched upon these backward areas of Assam. The authorities seriously need to do something about this.

As far as savings in private depository institutions are concerned, only negligible (0.3%) households have invested in these institutions.

A log-linear model and contingency table have been considered to find the study. It is observed that the proportion of insured households in the low income group is nil; it rises to a small in the lower middle group and then goes up in the upper middle group and after that steadily increases to the high income group. The economic status reveals that only the upper middle income and high income group households have been able to avail the facility of banking and insurance. The households in the low income group and lower middle income group went unrepresented.

8.3 Banking in the Char Areas of Lower Assam

The information on whether a household has any bank account throws some light on the economic condition of that particular household. Obviously those households, which earn their livelihood on a day-to-day basis, cannot imagine of having an account in bank. This is why we put a question on this aspect of economic planning. And what we have found matches with our expectation. Just 8.2% of the sampled households have any bank account. In other words, 91.8% of the sampled households cannot think of savings in a bank. So it can be said that, in general, the people residing in the char areas of lower Assam earn their livelihood on a day-to-day basis Fig. 8.1.

The picture is even dimmer in case of Barpeta district where only 5.3% of the households have bank account. The proportion of households having bank account in the other two districts of Dhubri and Goalpara are nearly equal (10.2 and 10.3% respectively) Fig. 8.2.

Almost half (47.3%) of the households that have any bank account, deposit their money in Pragjyotish Gaonlia Bank, a regional rural bank (RRB). The other two big

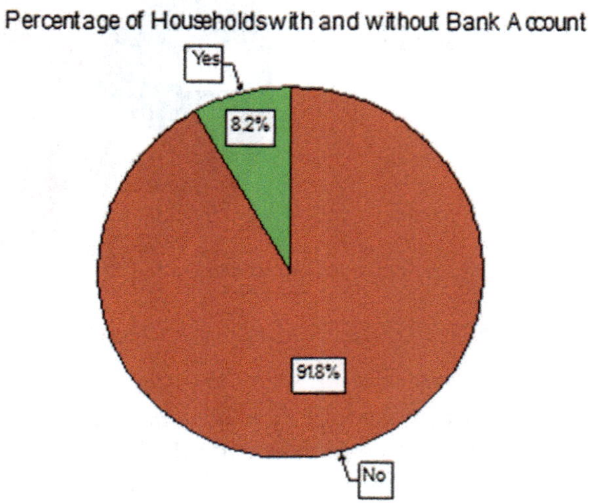

Fig. 8.1 Pie chart of percentage of households with and without bank accounts

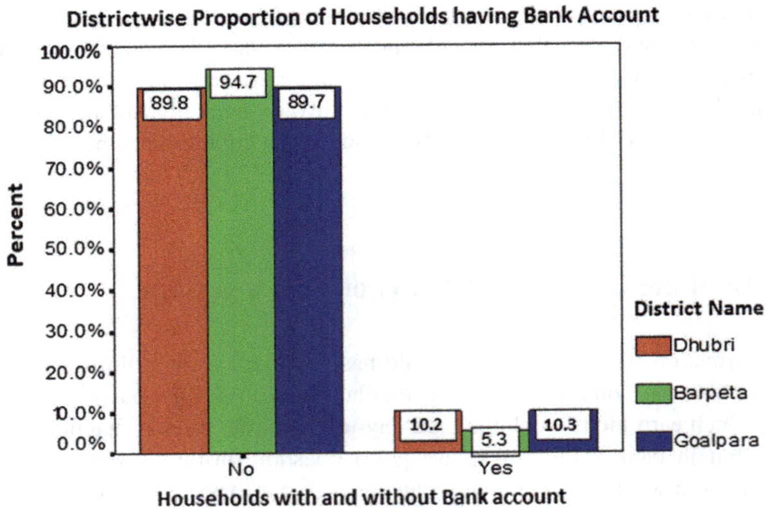

Fig. 8.2 Clustered bar chart showing district wise proportion of households having bank account

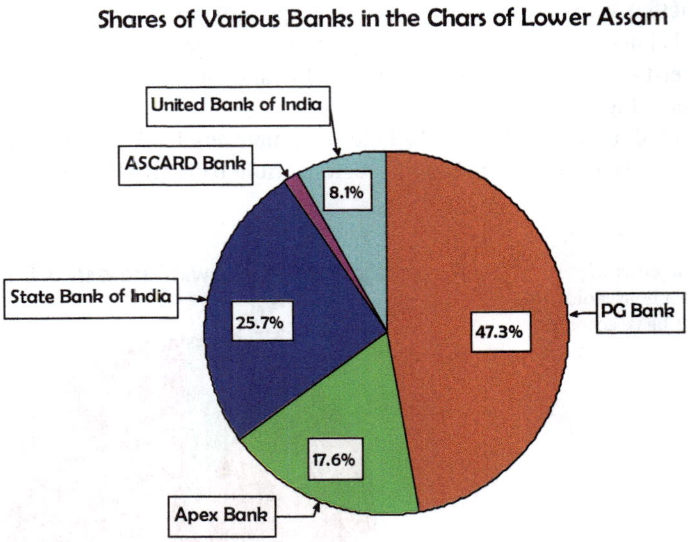

Fig. 8.3 Pie chart of various banks' shares in the char households

catchers of the money of these households are State Bank of India (SBI) (25.7%) and The Assam Co-operative Apex Bank Limited (17.6%). The remaining 9.5% of the households are shared by United Bank of India (UBI) (8.1%) and ASCARD Bank (1.4%) Fig. 8.3.

8.4 Insurance Sector in the Char Areas of Lower Assam

In case of insurance policy vis-à-vis the char households, almost a similar picture emerges. To be precise, only 5% of the sampled households have any insurance cover. The remaining 95% households do not have any security for the future. Dhubri district takes the lead with 9.1% insured households, followed by Barpeta (4%) and Goalpara (2.6%) Figs. 8.4 and 8.5.

Of all the households that are insured, 93.3% have got life insurance policies. One positive sign that have surfaced from this enquiry is that the people residing in the char areas have started insuring their crops, though in a very small proportion (only 2.2%). Crop insurance with respect to the char areas is very important when we take into account the fact that their crops are extremely vulnerable to natural calamities like flood.

8.5 Relation Between Banking and Insurance with Respect to Char Households

We have here made an attempt to examine if there exists a significant relationship between a char household having a bank account and it having an insurance policy. We construct a two-way contingency table on the nominal categorical variables—households with bank account and households with insurance policy; each with two categories—yes and no.

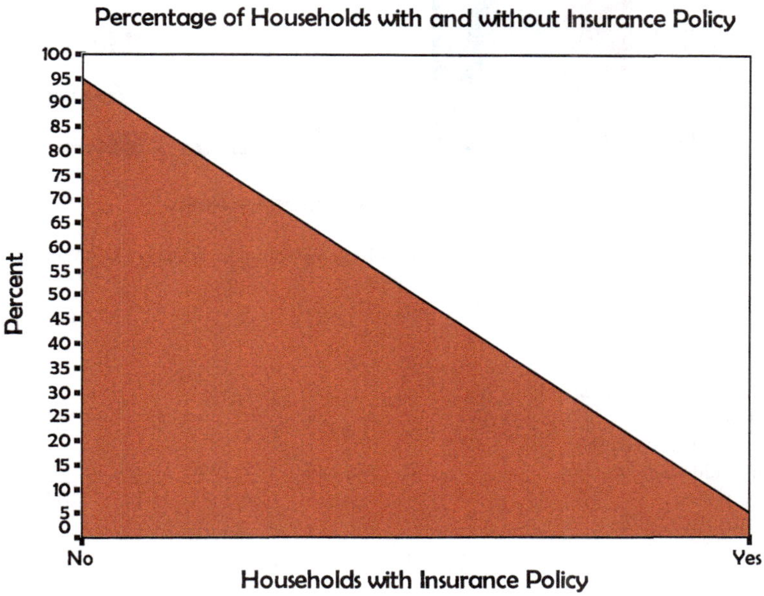

Fig. 8.4 Area diagram showing distribution of households with regard to insurance policy

We now proceed to perform the chi-quare Test of independence of attributes. The chi-square test compares the number of cases falling into each cell of the table with the frequency that would be expected if there were no association between the two variables that form the Table 8.2.

The contingency Table 8.1 demonstrates that 90.2% of the sampled households have neither a bank account nor an insurance policy and another 3.4% households have both a bank account and an insurance policy. Only a small 6.4% households have either a bank account or an insurance policy.

The exact p-value (<0.0005) under Fisher's Exact Test is significant at 5% level of significance, as it is less than our chosen significance level 0.05. So we reject the null hypothesis of independence between banking and insurance vis-à-vis char households in the population and conclude that there is a significant association between the two categorical variables.

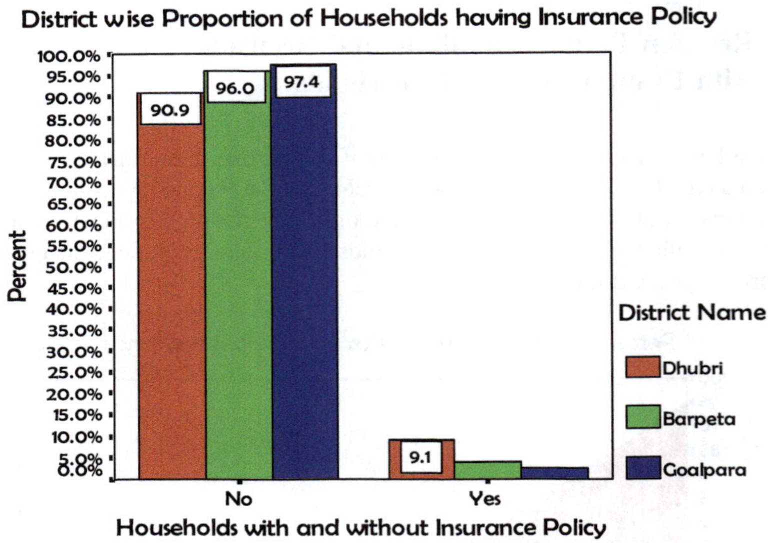

Fig. 8.5 Clustered bar chart showing district wise proportion of households having insurance policy

Table 8.1 Contingency table showing households with/without bank account and households with/without insurance policy

Banking * insured cross-tabulation					
Bank account	Yes	Count	31	43	74
		% to total	3.4	4.8	8.2
	No	Count	14	812	826
		% to total	1.6	90.2	91.8
Over all		Count	45	855	900
		% to total	5.0	95	100

Source Primary survey conducted during 2003–2004

Table 8.2 Chi-square test of independence between banking and insurance

Chi-square tests	Value	df	Exact sig. (2-sided)	Exact sig. (1-sided)
Pearson chi-square	231.027[b]	1	0.000	0.000
Continuity correction[a]	222.642	1		
Likelihood ratio	114.764	1	0.000	0.000
Fisher's exact test			0.000	0.000

Note [a]Computed only for a 2 × 2 table
[b]1 cells (25.0%) have expected count less than 5. The minimum expected count is 3.70
Source Primary survey conducted during 2003–2004

Table 8.3 Contingency table of economic class of households and bank account

Economic class of a household * bank account cross-tabulation			Bank account		Total
			No	Yes	
Economic class of a household	Low economic class	Count	179		179
		% within bank account	22.2		20.3
	Lower middle economic class	Count	258	14	272
		% within bank account	31.9	19.2	30.9
	Upper middle economic class	Count	249	17	266
		% within bank account	30.8	23.3	30.2
	High economic class	Count	122	42	164
		% within bank account	15.1	57.5	18.6
Total		Count	808	73	881
		% within bank account	100.0	100.0	100.0

Source Primary survey conducted during 2003–2004

8.5.1 Odds Ratio and Relative Risk for the "Insurance" × "Banking" Cross-tabulation

The sample odds ratio is defined as in Eq. (8.4.1).

$$\hat{\theta} = \frac{n_{11}n_{22}}{n_{12}n_{21}} \tag{8.4.1}$$

where $\hat{\theta}$ represents the maximum likelihood estimate (MLE) of the true odds ratio, and n is the count obtained in each cell.

For our data, $\hat{\theta} = \frac{31 \times 812}{14 \times 43} = 41.81395$

Risk estimate

	Value	95% confidence interval	
		Lower	Upper
Odds ratio for insured (Yes/No)	41.814	20.729	84.346
For cohort banking = Yes	13.698	9.640	19.463
For cohort banking = No	0.328	0.212	0.506

Source Primary survey conducted during 2003–2004

The relative risk estimate is a measure of association between the presence or absence of a factor and the occurrence of an event. Here we take the factor to be 'Banking', i.e. whether a household has a bank account or not, and having or not having an insurance policy as the event. For the contingency Table 8.1, the relative risk of being insured is nearly 42 (13.698/0.328 = 41.814) times among households which have a bank account than among the households which do not have a bank account. And the 95% confidence interval for the relative risk (which is equal to the *odds ratio* in this case as the probability of the outcome of interest is very small) does not include 1, indicating that there is a significant difference in the occurrence of insured households between households which have a bank account and households which do not have a bank account.

8.5.2 *Measures of Association Between Banking and Insurance*

Since the two nominal categorical variables-households with/without bank account and households with/without insurance policy, are not independent in the population, they are associated. We now give below some indices that measure the degree of association between these two variables.

Symmetric measures

		Value	Approx. sig.	Exact sig.
Nominal by nominal	Phi	0.507	0.000	0.000
	Cramer's V	0.507	0.000	0.000
	Contingency coefficient	0.452	0.000	0.000

Source Primary survey conducted during 2003–2004

The nominal symmetric measures under the above-referred chi-square test suggest that though the relationship between a household having a bank account and its having an insurance policy is significant, the strength of this relationship is not so strong. The relationship is moderate because value of each of the coefficients revolves around 0.5.

Directional measures

			Value	Exact sig.
Nominal by nominal	Goodman and Kruskal tau	Bank account dependent	0.257	0.000
		Insurance policy dependent	0.257	0.000
	Uncertainty coefficient	Symmetric	0.264	0.000
		Bank account dependent	0.224	0.000
		Insurance policy dependent	0.321	0.000

Source Primary survey conducted during 2003–2004

The nominal directional measures are appropriate when both variables are nominal, categorical variables. The nominal directional measures indicate both the strength and significance of the relationship between the row and column variables of a contingency table. These coefficients are measures of association between categorical variables based on the idea of using one variable to predict the other. The value of each statistic can range from 0 to 1 and indicates the proportional reduction in error in predicting the value of one variable based on the value of the other variable.

In this case, the low significance values for both *Goodman and Kruskal tau* and the *uncertainty coefficient* indicate that there is a relationship between the two categorical variables. But the temperate values for both the test statistics indicate that the relationship between the two variables is a moderate one. Nevertheless, the test statistic value of 0.321 of *uncertainty coefficient* indicates that by trying to predict whether a char household will have an insurance policy when the household having or not having a bank account is known, one can reduce the error rate by 32.1% over what he/she could expect by random chance.

After all these analyses, we come to the conclusion that the households having a bank account are more likely to have an insurance policy than the households which do not have a bank account.

8.6 Relation Between Economic Class of a Household and its Having Bank Accounts

Common experience tells us that the more affluent a household is the more is the chance of its having a bank account. We would like to see whether this perception applies in case of char areas of lower Assam too. So we did a chi-square test of independence on these two categorical variables (Agresti 1984, 1990) Table 8.4.

The result was as one would expect. The test on the null hypothesis that there is no relationship between the two variables tabulated, produced a significant *p*-value at 5% level of significance. So we reject the null hypothesis of no association at 5% alpha-level and conclude that these two factors-economic statuses and having a bank account are associated in the population of char areas of lower Assam.

The 4 × 2 contingency Table 8.3, having four categories of economic class of a household (low, lower middle, upper middle and high) and two categories of bank account (yes or no), also illustrates this. From the table, we can see that in the households having a bank account, the proportion of low economic class is nil. The proportions of lower middle economic class and upper middle economic class in the households having a bank account are 19.2 and 23.3% respectively; the remaining 57.5% households fall in the high economic class.

Thus we are now in a position to infer that the households falling in the upper economic class are more likely to have a bank account than their counterparts in the lower economic class.

8.7 Relation Between Income Level of a Household and its Having an Insurance Policy

Let us now test the null hypothesis that income level of a household does not influence whether it will have an insurance policy in the chars of lower Assam. For testing this hypothesis, we have constructed the following 4 × 2 contingency table and then performed a chi-square test of independence of attributes on the table, as shown in Table 8.6.

Table 8.4 Chi-square test of independence of economic class and having bank account for the households in the chars of lower Assam

Chi-square tests				
	Value	df	Asymp. sig. (2-sided)	Exact sig. (2-sided)
Pearson chi-square	85.721[a]	3	0.000	0.000
Likelihood ratio	80.059	3	0.000	0.000
Fisher's exact test	75.872			0.000

Note [a]0 cells (0.0%) have expected count less than 5. The minimum expected count is 13.59
Source Primary survey conducted during 2003–2004

Table 8.5 Contingency table of income level of households and insurance policy

Income level of a household * insurance policy cross-tabulation

			Insurance policy		Total
			No	Yes	
Income level of a household	Low income group	Count	246		246
		% within insurance policy	29.4		27.9
	Lower middle income group	Count	204	1	205
		% within insurance policy	24.4	2.2	23.3
	Upper middle income group	Count	206	4	210
		% within insurance policy	24.6	8.9	23.8
	High income group	Count	180	40	220
		% within insurance policy	21.5	88.9	25.0
Total		Count	836	45	881
		% within Insurance policy	100.0	100.0	100.0

Source Primary survey conducted during 2003–2004

Table 8.6 Chi-square test of independence between income level of households and their having an insurance policy

Chi-square tests

	Value	df	Asymp. sig. (2-sided)	Exact sig. (2-sided)
Pearson chi-square	104.298[a]	3	0.000	0.000
Likelihood ratio	94.485	3	0.000	0.000
Fisher's exact test	88.240			0.000

Note [a]0 cells (.0%) have expected count less than 5. The minimum expected count is 10.47
Source Primary survey conducted during 2003–2004

The chi-square test statistic with $(4-1) \times (2-1) = 3$ degrees of freedom is significant at 5% alpha-level; p-value (<0.0005) being less than the chosen level of significance (0.05). So the two categorical variables under consideration are not independent in the population of char areas of lower Assam. That is to say, these two variables are associated at 5% risk level. An inspection of the 4 × 2 contingency in Table 8.5 shows that the proportion of insured households in the low income group is nil; it rises to a small 2.2% in the lower middle group and then goes up to 8.9% in the upper middle group and after that steadily increases to 88.9% in the high income group. To summarise, the chance of possessing an insurance policy for a household falling in the upper income group is more than that of a household falling in the middle or lower income group.

8.8 Contingency Table of Economic Level, Banking and Insurance

We will consider here examining the associations between the three factors-economic class of a household, its having bank account and its having an insurance policy, simultaneously. For this, the contingency table is presented below Table 8.7.

8.9 A Log-linear Model to Describe the Three-way Contingency Table 8.7

Generalised linear models (GLM) with a log link are known as *log-linear* models (Christensen 1997). Log-linear analysis involves the generation of tables containing the possible combinations of the factors and a model of the expected frequencies of each combination, followed by the generation of statistical values that allow one to examine the significance of each factor and the goodness-of-fit of the model. The analysis typically begins with all the associations and interactions possible between the factors and then proceeds to eliminate those which can be, while retaining a reasonable fit between the expected cell frequencies generated by the model and the observed frequencies.

Data collected for categorical variables can be described in terms of a count of the number of instances which occurred for each combination of variables. Generalised linear models for count data (Log-linear Models) assume that the random component will follow a *Poisson* distribution. This distribution provides us with an estimate of the probability of the response variable—the frequency count of each cell of a contingency table and can therefore be used to make predictions about the likelihood of obtaining a value in each cell of the contingency table.

Table 8.7 Way contingency table of economic level, banking and insurance

			Insurance policy	
Economic class of a household			No	Yes
Low economic class	Bank account	No	179	0
		Yes	0	0
Lower middle economic class	Bank account	No	257	1
		Yes	14	0
Upper middle economic class	Bank account	No	246	3
		Yes	14	3
High economic class	Bank account	No	112	10
		Yes	14	28

Source Primary survey conducted during 2003–2004

Here we are interested to build a parsimonious model for prediction purposes, i.e. to predict the frequency count of each cell of the contingency table.

When all possible combinations of factors, i.e. all possible effects, are included in a log-linear analysis, then the model is said to be *saturated*. The saturated model in our case will be

$$\text{Log}\,\mu_{ijk} = \lambda + \lambda_i^E + \lambda_j^B + \lambda_k^I + \lambda_{ij}^{E,B} + \lambda_{ik}^{E,I} + \lambda_{jk}^{B,I} + \lambda_{ijk}^{E,B,I} \quad (8.4.2)$$

(i = 1, 2, 3, 4; j = 1, 2; k = 1, 2)

where μ_{ijk} are the cell frequencies; the letters **E, B** and **I** are simply variable labels and stand for 'Economic Class', 'Banking' and 'Insurance' respectively and do not raise λ to the *power* of E or B or I and i (= 1, 2, 3, 4), j (= 1, 2) & k (= 1, 2) are the levels of these three categorical variables in that order.

A saturated model provides a perfect fit for the data, i.e. the expected frequencies equal the observed frequencies. Saturated models do not offer any simplification or smoothing of the data and since the observed values are the same as the expected ones, we cannot obtain any goodness-of-fit statistics. In model building, one aims to build a simpler description of the data through the inclusion of only some of the factors and their combinations. To put it another way, the rationale behind generating a model is to obtain an *unsaturated* model with the fewest effects, but which still approximates the observed frequencies sufficiently well.

We had tried to fit many unsaturated models to our data and found that the following model is a good fit of the observed frequencies.

$$\text{Log}\,\mu_{ijk} = \lambda + \lambda_i^E + \lambda_j^B + \lambda_k^I + \lambda_{ij}^{E,B} + \lambda_{ik}^{E,I} \quad (8.4.3)$$

(i = 1, 2, 3, 4; j = 1, 2; k = 1, 2)

The Model 4.3 [hereinafter we shall refer to it as **Model (EB, EI, BI)**] is nested within Model 4.2 [Model (EBI)] as all the terms which appear in this model also appear in Model 4.2. Simply speaking, Model (EB, EI, BI) is a subset of the Model (EBI). Both the models are *hierarchical*, which means that each term includes all lower order terms.

The *likelihood ratio statistic* (G^2), which has a chi-square distribution for large samples, for the Model (EB, EI, BI) is 1.5335 with 3 degrees of freedom and the *p*-value is equal to 0.6746. So the Model (EB, EI, BI) is a good approximation of the data since the G^2 is *non-significant*, because we are looking for models in which the expected frequencies generated by the model are not significantly different from the observed cell frequencies. This is an important point, which is in contrast to the common practice of looking for *p*-values of 0.05 or less, and significant differences. In a log-linear model, we are testing the difference between the expected counts from the model and the actual data, rather than comparing a model of independence with the observed counts as one would do in a traditional chi-square test.

Table 8.8 Three-way contingency table of economic level, banking and insurance with the *predicted counts*

			Insurance policy	
Economic class of a household			No	Yes
Low economic class	Bank account	No	179	0
		Yes	0	0
Lower middle economic class	Bank account	No	257.51	0.49
		Yes	13.49	0.51
Upper middle economic class	Bank account	No	246.14	2.86
		Yes	13.86	3.14
High economic class	Bank account	No	111.35	10.65
		Yes	14.65	27.35

Source Primary survey conducted during 2003–2004

There are in total 29 parameters, including the constant λ, in the Model (EB, EI, BI). Of these 29 parameters, 16 are aliased (or redundant) parameters and they are set to zero. Most of the statistical software packages give the estimates of the parameters along with their 95% confidence intervals. In this way, the log μ_{ijk} s (i = 1, 2, 3, 4; j = 1, 2; k = 1, 2) can be obtained. By taking exponentiation of the log μ_{ijk} s (i = 1, 2, 3, 4; j = 1, 2; k = 1, 2), we would get the required 16 expected (predicted/fitted) frequencies μ_{111}, μ_{112}, μ_{121}, μ_{122}, μ_{211}, μ_{212}, μ_{221}, μ_{222}, μ_{311}, μ_{312}, μ_{321}, μ_{322}, μ_{411}, μ_{412}, μ_{421} and μ_{422}.

In log-linear analysis, adjusted residuals larger than 1.96 in absoluter magnitudes indicate a poor model fit for that cell of the table, while the sign indicates the direction of the discrepancy. Negative values indicate expected values lower than observed, and positive values indicate expected values that are larger than the observed count for that cell. In our case, there is no such adjusted residual which is greater than 1.96 in absolute magnitude Table 8.8.

8.10 Institutional Loan in the Char Areas of Lower Assam

Next we investigated whether the char households have availed the facility of taking loan either from cooperative societies or from banks or against their insurance policies (if any) during the last 5 years from the reference date of the survey (i.e. in between 01-01-1998 and 31-12-2002). What we have found out is only a meagre 1.6% sampled households have been able to avail this facility. On making further enquiry on this issue, we came to know that 42.9% of these households have taken loan for buying cow. Another 28.6% households told that the loan taken was an agricultural credit. This is another indicator of the agrarian economy of the char areas of lower Assam Fig. 8.6.

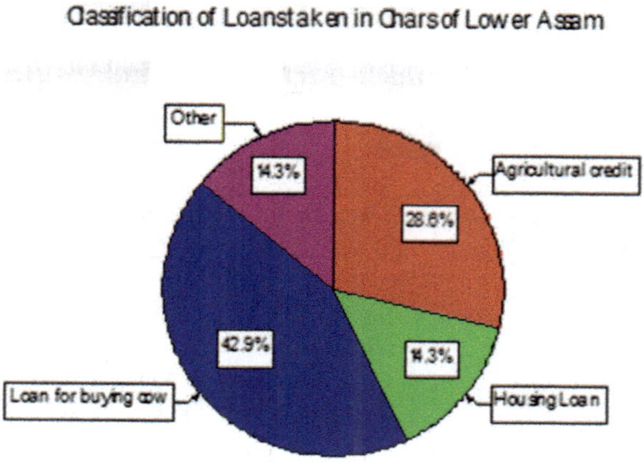

Fig. 8.6 Pie chart showing classification of loans taken in chars of lower Assam

We feel that there is an urgent need to provide cheap loan to the people of char areas who depend mainly on agriculture for their livelihood. The banks can provide loans for buying seeds, manures, pesticides, chemicals and other vital inputs like thresher, tractor, etc. which are needed in agricultural activities. This way the agricultural output would increase and the farmers will also be able to repay the loan within the stipulated period. Hence the nationalised banks should devise some special schemes for the char areas.

8.11 Economic Status of Households that Have Taken Institutional Loan

The cross-tabulation between the households that have taken loan from a cooperative society or bank or against insurance policy during the last 5 years (from the reference date of the survey) and its economic status reveals that only the upper middle income group and high income group households have been able to avail this facility. The households in the low income group and lower middle income group went unrepresented as far as taking loan is concerned. The proportions of upper middle income group and high income group households among the households that have taken loan are 28.6 and 71.4% respectively Table 8.9.

Table 8.9 Cross-tabulation of income level and institutional loan for households

Cross-tabulation of income level and institutional loan							
		Loan from co-op/Bank/Insurer				Total	
		No		Yes		Count	Col %
		Count	Col %	Count	Col %		
Income level of a household	Low income group	246	28.4	0	0.0	246	27.9
	Lower middle income group	205	23.6	0	0.0	205	23.3
	Upper middle income group	206	23.8	4	28.6	210	23.8
	High income group	210	24.2	10	71.4	220	25.0
Total		867	100	14	100	881	100

Source Primary survey conducted during 2003–2004

References

Agresti, Alan. (1984). *Analysis of ordinal categorical data*. New York: John Wiley and Sons.

Agresti, Alan. (1990). *Categorical data analysis*. New York: John Wiley and Sons.

Christensen, Ronald. (1997). *Log-linear models and logistic regression* (2nd ed.). New York: Springer.

Socio-economic Survey Report (2002–2003) of char areas of Assam (2004). Directorate of char areas development Assam.

Chapter 9
Institutional Barriers to Development in the State of Nagaland

Chothazo Nienu

Abstract Assessing Nagaland's economy from the usual economic denominators like Gross State Domestic Product (GSDP), Per Capita Income, Human Development Index (HDI), economic growth rate, etc., gives the misleading picture that the state is doing well. There are other indicators which show the weak side of the state's economy: there is a preponderance of the service sector, the public administration contributes nearly a fifth of the state's GSDP, the industrial sector is small, the infrastructure is poor and the state is dependent on the central government. The state's economy has these ills because of the political problem that it is stuck in, resulting in the existence of many nationalist groups and a consequent weak government. Unless this is solved, Nagaland will continue to have the same economic problems it is having.

Keywords Gross state domestic product (GSDP) · Service sector
Administration · Political problem

9.1 Introduction

On 1st July 2015, a businessman was assaulted in Dimapur, the commercial capital of the state (Businessman Assaulted in Dimapur Market 2015). A month later, another businessman was murdered by unknown persons in the same city (One Shot Dead in Dimapur 2015). Prominent news going around during that time was the killing of two school children in the conflict between the Assam Rifles security forces and the Naga nationalist group, the Nationalist Socialist Council of Nagaland —Khaplang (NSCN-K). This had occurred while the Assam Rifles were returning after a successful raid on the Naga nationalist group, the NSCN-K, where two cadres of the nationalist group were killed. The villagers stopped the convoy of the security forces and demanded the bodies of the slain cadres and in the confusion

C. Nienu (✉)
School of Economics, University of Hyderabad, Hyderabad, India
e-mail: chothanienu@gmail.com

U.K. De et al. (eds.), *Inequality, Poverty and Development in India*, India Studies in Business and Economics, DOI 10.1007/978-981-10-6274-2_9

that ensued the two innocent children were killed (Assam Rifles Puts Burden of 16 July Shooting on People 2015). This was a few days after the NSCN-K ambushed the Indian Army in Manipur killing 18 of them and injuring 11 (Manipur Ambush 2015). The security forces after that had, out of suspicion, arrested five youth in the capital city of Kohima and subjected them to interrogation inflicting on them physical and mental scars. After they were abused, it was learnt that the five youth were arrested by mistake and they were law-abiding citizens (AFSPA Unleashes Its Brutality 2015).

The rule of law, the security of life and property, are pre-requisites for economic progress to take place. All these requisites can exist only where there is a strong government committed to providing security of life and property to all the individuals. The presence of forces which compete with the government to pull it down or which makes its functioning difficult brings instability and thus stifles development. The latter seems to be the feature of Nagaland's economy and the chapter argues that unless a strong well-functioning government exists, the state will not be able to solve its economic problems.

9.2 Economic Scenario in Nagaland

The economic scenario in the state is analyzed before embarking to understand the features inhibiting its development. Nagaland has a population of 19.78 lakhs according to the 2011 census. The state has an area of 16,579 km^2 with a population density of 119 persons per square km. Literacy rate according to the 2011 census stands at 79.55%. The sex ratio according to the 2011 census is 931 females per 1000 males (as compared to 940 for the country). The Infant Mortality Rate is 23. The unemployment rate is 16 persons per 100 persons. The state comes in the category of Medium in the Human Development Index (Statistical Handbook of Nagaland 2013).

9.2.1 Structure of the Economy

There is a preponderance of the service sector in Nagaland's economy. As of 2012–13, 66% of its Gross State Domestic Product (GSDP) came from the service sector, 16.5% from the industrial sector and nearly 18% from the agriculture and allied sector (see Table 9.1). In terms of employment, as of 2014–15, 61% of the state's population is engaged in agriculture and allied activities while 32% are engaged in the service sector. Only 7.6% of the work force is engaged in industry (The Employment Scenario in Nagaland 2015).

Table 9.1 Percentage share to total state GSDP (at constant 2004–05 prices)

Years	2004–05	2005–06	2006–07	2007–08	2008–09	2009–10	2010–11	2011–12	2012–13
Agriculture and allied	23.50	22.33	21.37	21.96	21.74	21.12	20.98	19.34	17.72
Industry	16.60	19.94	19.24	19.58	20.18	18.55	16.44	16.46	16.49
Services	59.90	57.75	59.39	58.46	58.09	60.33	62.58	64.26	65.80

Source Planning commission

Table 9.2 State's GSDP growth rate at current prices (per cent)

Year	Nagaland	North East Region	India
2004–05	–	–	–
2005–06	12.83	11.12	14.10
2006–07	10.15	9.93	16.60
2007–08	11.27	10.65	15.90
2008–09	16.85	15.17	15.75
2009–10	11.56	18.41	15.18
2010–11	11.70	16.77	18.66
2011–12	17.86	13.63	15.77
2012–13	13.11	11.45	11.88
2013–14	13.22	15.61	11.54
2014–15	13.24	–	–

Source Table constructed from NER Databank

Table 9.3 GSDP growth rate at constant (2004–05) prices (per cent)

Year	Nagaland	North East Region	India
2005–06	10.22	4.82	9.48
2006–07	7.80	5.38	9.57
2007–08	7.31	5.87	9.32
2008–09	6.34	7.37	6.72
2009–10	6.90	10.33	8.59
2010–11	9.35	6.26	8.91
2011–12	8.32	6.07	6.69
2012–13	6.45	5.80	4.47
2013–14	6.52	7.83	4.74
2014–15	6.80	NA	NA

Source Table constructed from NER Databank

The overall growth rate of the state's economy is good. This is more so when the GSDP is calculated at current prices showing an average growth rate of more than 10% per annum. This means that the income of state doubles in less than 10 years. The growth rate of the state compared with the average growth rates of the other northeastern states and the whole country shows that there is not much difference in the growth rates and the state does equally well (Table 9.2).

There is a high growth rate even when the growth rate of the economy is measured at constant prices or the per capita income is measured at both current prices and constant prices (Tables 9.3, 9.4 and 9.5).

The general picture that then emerges from studying the GSDP is that the state's economy is doing well. Contrary to popular beliefs, the industrial sector in the state has shown good growth rates over the years. This can be seen in Table 9.6.

However, the smallness of the industrial sector means that the high growth in this sector does not reflect much in the overall state's GSDP. Looking at the economic indicators like HDI, income level and growth rate of the economy, and

Table 9.4 Per capita net state domestic product at current prices (in per cent)

Year	Nagaland	India
2004–05	–	–
2005–06	11.01	12.38
2006–07	8.21	15.02
2007–08	9.35	14.80
2008–09	15.56	13.82
2009–10	8.78	13.42
2010–11	10.58	16.80
2011–12	14.75	14.50
2012–13	10.18	9.67
2013–14	10.32	9.64
2014–15	10.34	NA

Source Table constructed from NER Databank

Table 9.5 Per capita GSDP at constant (2004–05) prices (per cent)

Year	Nagaland	India
2005–06	8.65	7.75
2006–07	6.05	7.89
2007–08	6.40	8.07
2008–09	4.62	4.69
2009–10	3.97	6.76
2010–11	8.38	6.79
2011–12	5.34	5.10
2012–13	3.82	2.12
2013–14	3.85	2.70
2014–15	3.85	NA

Source Table constructed from NER Databank

sectoral contribution to the GSDP may give the wrong impression that the economy is doing well. A closer scrutiny/analysis of the economy will give a different picture.

9.2.2 Dependence and Stagnation of Nagaland's Economy

The state's administration contributes 16% to the state's GSDP. Table 9.1 has shown that the industrial sector also contributes the same amount to the states' GSDP. This comparison shows that a lot is spent for running the government's administration. The problem with this is that while government administration facilitates production, it does not lead to direct production of goods and services which could be exchanged in the market. Spending too much on administration thus becomes a wastage as beyond a certain level, spending on administration only

Table 9.6 Growth rate of GSDP in industry (2000–01 to 2013–14) (in per cent)

Year	2000–01	2001–02	2002–03	2003–04	2004–05	2005–06	2006–07
Growth rate	7.11	11.11	14.09	9.82	−1.14	16.97	14.87
Year	2007–08	2008–09	2009–10	2010–11	2011–12	2012–13	2013–14
Growth rate	10.00	15.54	7.51	−14.97	6.55	6.57	–

Source Planning commission

reveals diversion of resources which could be better used for productive investment. Among the northeastern states, only Manipur and Mizoram spend more than Nagaland on public administration when measured as a proportion of state's GSDP (Table 9.7).

The state government is dependent on the central government for its revenue as its internal revenue mobilization is weak. In fact, over-dependence on the central government for its revenue is a feature all the northeastern states excepting Assam. Table 9.8 shows that the state received 80% of its total revenue from the centre.

Not only does the state generate a miniscule amount of revenue as a proportion of its total revenue, its absolute value has also been low. It could raise only Rs. 333.39 crores as tax revenues in 2013–14.

Tax rates and tax base has remained the same, growth in the economy leads to higher tax collection. In fact, the growth in tax revenue due to growth in the economy is how governments around the world are able to finance its social security programmes. That the state government is not able to raise proper revenue of its own when the economy is growing reflects poorly on the quality of governance.

There are 140,000 government employees in the state (1.40 Lakh Government Employees in Nagaland 2015). A huge proportion of the government expenditure goes to its employees. Since the employees do not engage in services which brings monetary returns to the state (as seen in the Table 9.9 on non-tax revenue), the government is left with less resources to invest in the state.

This has been one reason why the infrastructure position of the state is very poor. The state has been hampered by the lack of proper infrastructure. Data have shown that from 2003 to 2008, the Compound Annual Growth Rate (CAGR) of road was 4.06% for the whole country while it was 1.68% for Nagaland making the road growth to be low (Brahmachary 2007). The state has only one railway station with the rail tracks distance been 12.84 km. The only airport is in Dimapur leaving Kohima, the state capital, the only capital city in the country without an airport. Apart from transport, communication facilities also leave much to be desired. Mobile phones services were introduced only in 2003 (Vajpayee Launches Mobile Service in Nagaland, Calls for Peace 2003. Even with this, the insecurity in the state always threatens to take pre-paid mobile services away. Facilities which are enjoyed in other parts of the country are introduced only with time.

The state imports electricity from outside the state to the tune of 457.47 million kWh (Statistical Handbook of Nagaland 2013).

Table 9.7 Proportion of public administration contribution to states' GSDP among Northeastern states, 2012–2013 (rupees in lakhs)

Categories	States							
	Nagaland	Arunachal Pradesh	Assam	Manipur	Meghalaya	Mizoram	Sikkim	Tripura
Public administration	252,944	113,259	134,988	253,951	223,849	155,176	52,247	212,044
GSDP	1,567,638	1,094,145	1,181,714	1,248,423	1,829,639	836,292	570,284	1,699,667
Proportion of public administration to state's GSDP (in percentage)	16.13	10.35	11.423	20.34	12.23	18.55	9.16	12.47

Source Table constructed from NER Databank

Table 9.8 Centre's total grants to northeastern states (2010–11) (as a percentage of total revenue)

	State						
	Nagaland	Arunachal Pradesh	Assam	Manipur	Meghalaya	Mizoram	Tripura
Total revenue	80	79.4	41.3	71.2	64.1	75.9	66

Source RBI data

Table 9.9 Nagaland's own revenue (rupees, in crores)

	2012–13	2013–14
Own tax revenue	339.95	333.39
Own non-tax revenue	207.17	216.57
Total	547.12	549.96

Source Audit report on state finances

Table 9.10 Micro, small and medium enterprises (MSME) in Nagaland

Year	Particulars	Numbers
2008–2009	Regd. MSME	717
	Employment generated	4302
2009–2010	Regd. MSME	704
	Employment generated	4224
2010–2011	Regd. MSME	2062
	Employment generated	12,192
2011–2012	Regd. MSME	1092
	Employment generated	6444
2012–2013	Regd. MSME	560
	Employment generated	3360

Source Table constructed from NER databank

Social infrastructures like schools and hospitals provided by the government have been found to be unsatisfactory. These lacunae have been filled by the private sector, with its resultant exclusionary and profiteering principle.

Apart from the infrastructure bottlenecks which the state suffers, the most daunting problem facing the state is the lack of employment opportunities. Lacking any big industries, as of 2012–13, registered Micro, Small and Medium Enterprises (MSME) could employ only 3360 workers. This has fallen steeply from the 12,192 it employed in 2010–2011 (Table 9.10).

9.2.3 Why Nagaland Is Dependent and Poor?

Different explanations have been given while explaining the lack of economic progress in the state. These include the geography, the lack of proper infrastructure, and the lack of proper institutions to facilitate development. While geography could explain partly why development has not taken place, considering the increase in the cost of transportation due to the difficult terrains and the lack of durability of works, to say that all the ills of the economy is due to the geography entirely misses the point. This is also true of lack of proper infrastructure. In fact, the lack of proper infrastructure has been mostly due to the institutional failures.

Institutions have been defined as the rules of the game. For Douglass Cecil North, institutions are the 'formal and informal rules [or norms] governing human behaviour'. Similarly, Lin and Nugget defined institutions as 'A set of humanly devised behavioural rules that govern and shape the interaction of human beings, in part by helping them to form expectations of what other people do'. On the whole, institutions have been understood to include (a) the extent of property rights' protection; (b) the degree to which laws and regulations are fairly enforced; (c) the ability of the government to protect the individual against economic shocks/macroeconomic stability (d) to provide social protection/providing insurance, and (e) the extent of political corruption ('The role of institutions in economic development'). Needless to say, these features of what constitute proper institutions can be provided only where the government is strong and is committed to provide security of life and property to its citizens with affirmation for rule of law. It is the lack of these that has been the undoing for economic development in the state.

The reason a strong government has failed to come about is because of the many nationalist political groups in the state demanding cessation from the Indian union. These political groups have been given the name 'Insurgent Groups' in mainstream media. The chapter is not an attempt to understand whether their demands are legitimate or not or understand why these groups have emerged. It is to understand how the presences of many political groups have hampered qualitative economic growth and development in the state.

The foremost effect which one sees due to the presence of many political groups is the weakening of the authority of the legitimate government set up through democratic process as enshrined in the Indian Constitution. Not only a parallel government but parallel governments exist in many parts of the state which weaken the security of properties and lives of the people. Where there is insecurity in these aspects, investments cannot flow in from other parts of the country. Existing production units also function with less efficiency and finds difficulty expanding as a huge share of the profits are taken away by the nationalist groups.

The unsolved Naga Political issue has breed corruption in governance. Cases of nationalist groups interfering in the election process and getting involved in threats are not unknown. These are done at the behest of the politicians who then works closely with insurgent groups once they come to power. Needless to say, proper governance cannot be expected from such a government.

Unsolved political problem and all its entailment have changed the mindset of the people. Thus, people are satisfied with the low quality of works with the allusion that the quality of works must have been affected because of demands of the political groups.

The perpetuations of poverty in parts have also been due to the existence of parallel governments. People are not able to save from their income because of the high price of goods due to extortion demands by the political groups from the populace and business community. With no saving and social security, people go to the money lenders in times of unforeseen needs thus incurring debts.

The state possesses rich natural resources in the form of oil, natural gas, minerals, coal, forest resources, water, and so on. These are not put to any good use because various conditions put forth by the insurgent groups.

There are also frequent bandhs bringing a halt to the whole economy. These may be in the form of the political groups calling for bandhs to assert their authority in the state or bandhs by the people and civil society groups against the activities of the political groups because of the wrong activities like extortion, murder, threats or robbery committed by the political groups. These bandhs may be in the form of closure of business establishments, shops, government offices, schools, and so on. Needless to say, all these lead not only to immediate loss of economic activities but also to instability and unpredictability in the state's economy. Instability leads to speculation and hoarding on the side of the business community and panic buying on the part of the consumers. The result is price rise and black marketing.

A result of the political problem in the state is also what may be called 'Intellectual slack'—the inability to think and reason beyond political conflict. The best minds are occupied with efforts to solve the conflict. Problems of conflict, views and counter views fill the newspapers and magazines so that there is limited room for other social and cultural interactions. This is a hindrance to the development of human capital.

9.3 Conclusion

A study found that more than Rs. 937 crores were spent by the candidates contesting elections for the sixty seats to the 2012 Nagaland Legislative (Nagaland Pol. Parties Spend Over Rs. 937 Crores in Assembly Polls 2013). The huge amount of money spent by the candidates show that what is lacking in Nagaland is not capital but the proper environment for investments to be made. Unless a viable environment exists, where proper institutions could come up, Nagaland will continue to reel under the present syndrome of economic stagnancy and dependence.

References

AFSPA Unleashes Its Brutality. (2015, June 9). *The Morung express*. Retrieved from http://morungexpress.com.

Assam Rifles Puts Burden of July 16 Shooting on People. (2015, July 17). *The Morung express*. Retrieved from http://morungexpress.com.

Brahmachary, P. (2007). *Development of infrastructure in the districts of Nagaland: Trends and disparities*. A thesis submitted to Assam University in Partail Fulfilment of the Requirement for the Degree of Doctor of Philosophy in the Department of Economics (p. 112). Retrieved from http://shodhganga.inflibnet.ac.in/handle/10603/20472.

Businessman Assaulted in Dimapur Market. (2015, July 3). *The Morung express*. Retrieved from http://www.nagalandpost.com.

Government of India. *Data-book compiled for use of planning commission* (p. 81). Retrieved from http://planningcommission.gov.in.

Government of India. (2015). *Finances of the state Government* (p. 1). Retrieved from http://www.saiindia.gov.in/english/home/our_products/Audit_Report/Government_Wise/state_audit/recent_reports/Nagaland/2015/SF/Chap_1.pdf.

Government of Nagaland. (2013). *Statistical handbook of Nagaland* (p. 21, 78–81).

Manipur Ambush. (2015, June 5). *The Indian express*. Retrieved from http://indianexpress.com.

Nagaland Pol. Parties Spend Over Rs. 937 Crores in Assembly Polls. (2013, November 8). *WebIndia123* Retrieved from http://news.webindia123.com/news/articles/india/20131108/2280298.html.

North East Resources Databank. Retrieved from http://databank.nedfi.com/.

One Shot Dead in Dimapur. (2015, August 3). *Nagaland Post*. Retrieved from http://www.nagalandpost.com.

The role of institutions in economic development. Retrieved from http://www.palgrave.com/resources/sample-chapters/9780230222298_sample.pdf.

Vajpayee Launches Mobile Service in Nagaland, Calls for Peace. (2003, October 2008). *Silicon India news*. Retrieved from http://www.siliconindia.com.

Vyasan, R. (2015, August 17). The employment scenario in India. *The Morung express*. http://morungexpress.com.

Part II
Poverty at State Level with Focus North-East

Chapter 10
A Study of Multidimensional Poverty in Northeast India

Supravat Bagli

Abstract The primary objective of this chapter is to compute a multidimensional poverty index (MPI) for each state and for each district in northeast India. This index covers three dimensions—Knowledge, Health and Living condition. We have taken illiteracy rate and financial illiteracy rate as deprivation indicators under knowledge dimension. Health dimension includes the use of unsafe drinking water and no access to improved sanitation as indicator of deprivation. The dimension of living condition is comprised of four indicators viz. households having dilapidated residence, no census assets, no access to electricity or solar energy for lighting and no access to improved fuel for cooking. The MPI has been calculated gauging the normalised inverse 'Euclidian distance' of the observed vector of the indicators of deprivation from the vector indicating worst state of multidimensional poverty. This study distributes weight equally across the selected dimensions and equal weight has been consigned with each indicator within a dimension. The study has mainly used the data published by Directorate of Population Census of India 2011. We have observed that Meghalaya is the most deprived state in northeast India while Mizoram, Tripura are in relatively better-off position among the northeastern states. This study has explored that the Kurung Kumey district belonging to Arunachal Pradesh is the poorest district among the 86 districts. However, among the ten most deprived districts eight are not located in Meghalaya. None of the districts in Mizoram, Tripura and Sikkim come in the ten most multidimensionally poor districts. On the other hand, Aizawl district of Mizoram is the least deprived among the districts in North-East India. No one of the ten least multi dimensionally poor districts belong to the state of Meghalaya. The disparities among the states and among the districts in terms of the indicators under consideration have also been revealed. However, there is no straightforward relation between MPI of the states and percentage of population live below poverty line income.

S. Bagli (✉)
Presidency University, Kolkata, West Bengal, India
e-mail: supravat.bagli@gmail.com

U.K. De et al. (eds.), *Inequality, Poverty and Development in India*, India Studies in Business and Economics, DOI 10.1007/978-981-10-6274-2_10

Keywords Normalised inverse Euclidian distance
Multidimensional poverty index · Population census · States in northeast India

10.1 Background

The state of poverty of a household/person is the manifestation of inadequate socio-economic well-being. Although, poverty is a multidimensional issue we usually calculate it taking per head income or consumption as yardstick. However, income or consumption centric measures of poverty have already been castigated as real measure to reveal multidimensional poverty of a country. Health, education and living standard are identified as major non income dimensions of poverty. In order to quantify multiple dimensions of poverty Mahbub ul Haq proposed the concept of Human Development Index (HDI). Since 1990 Human Development Reports at different levels have been reporting HDI as achievement index of the nations, states and districts. This measure takes into account of the arithmetic average of the standardised indicators. It fails to put more emphasis on more deprived indicators. In order to overcome this problem we have found Human Poverty Index. Recently the concept of Multidimensional Poverty Index (MPI) has been developed. The multidimensional poverty Index emphasised on non income aspects of poverty. Moreover, the methodology of MPI is applicable at the community level as well as individual/household level. However, all measures of poverty by UNDP assume indicators as substitute to each other. So far, the multidimensional poverty indices for the countries have been appearing in UNDP human development reports since 2010. In India as a whole more than half of the population are multidimensionally poor. But we have no idea regarding the multidimensional poverty of the states, particularly northeastern states, in India. Perhaps no district level human development report in India has reported the multidimensional poverty index of the district or of its block. With this end in view, the present study has tried to bring the close picture of multidimensional poverty of each state and for each district in northeast India.

Apart from the introductory section this chapter has four sections. A brief review of relevant literature and the objectives of this study have been presented in Sect. 10.2. In Sect. 10.3, research methodology applied in this study has been specified. We have discussed the empirical findings of this study in Sect. 10.4. Section 10.5 concludes this chapter indicating some policy prescription for further development of the people in northeast India combating the imbalances in development.

10.2 Literature Survey and Objectives

The issue of multidimensional poverty is as old as the idea of capability approach for development. Under the auspices of UNDP during the last quarter century we have got different poverty measures like HDI, HPI, GDI and MPI which cover multiple dimensions of poverty. In addition to the measures of UNDP, several studies have tried to report the multidimensional poverty of different regions. Mehta and Shah (2003) have measured multidimensional poverty indices for the districts of 15 states in India including Assam from northeast India. The study has used published data reported in India Rural Development Report (NIRD), 1999 and Planning Commission Report 2000. They have considered infrastructure and agricultural productivity in addition to income, education and health, as dimension of multidimensional poverty. They have revealed that six of the seven most multidimensionally poor districts are located in four of the seven most income poor states. However, none of the district in Assam is included in the seven districts with highest multidimensional poverty. Applying household level data Alkire and Santos (2010) have first computed Multidimensional Poverty Index (MPI) for hundred and four developing countries. In order to cover multidimensional aspects of poverty they have considered three dimensions, viz. education, health and living standard, comprising ten indicators. The MPI combines a set of existing deprivations of the persons/households. UNDP Human Development Report (2010) has revealed that south Asia and Sub-Saharan Africa are the home of the majority of the multidimensional poor in the world. It is reported that in India 55.4% of the population is multidimensionally poor. Among the states in Indian the extent of multidimensional poverty is lowest in the state of Kerala and highest in Bihar. It is reported that for the northeastern states as a whole the value of MPI was 0.30 and 57.6% population are multidimensionally poor in 2008–9. Alkire et al. (2014) have proposed more advanced methodology for measuring MPI and thereby inequality among the multidimensionally poor households or subgroups. It is pertinent to note that MPI is a non-income measure of poverty and thereby the fundamental flaws concentrating upon income or consumption data for estimating poverty have been eradicated in the measure of MPI. The Indices of Housing Deprivation (IHD) for the Indian states have been reported by Bagli (2013). Percentage of households residing dilapidated residence; percentage of households not having access to safe drinking water; percentage of households without electricity and percentage of households without scientific sanitation facility are the indicators of housing deprivation. For measuring IHD the study has used the normalised inverse Euclidian distance of the observed deprivation index vector from the vector of acute deprivation. He has reported that housing deprivation is lowest in Delhi and highest in Orissa among the states in India. Among northeastern states housing deprivation is least in Sikkim and highest in Assam. The study has explored a negative and significant correlation of IHD with HDI of the states in India. The relation between backward population index and IHD is statistically insignificant. Bhattacharya and Halder (2014) have computed a weighted deprivation index and inequality of Reproductive and Child Health (RCH) status for the districts in West Bengal applying PCA and standard methodologies of measuring inequality. They have used data of Household and Facility survey under Reproductive and Child Health project at three time points. They have found that the districts are clearly uneven with respect to the health care services and its utilisation. They have found female literacy as an important determinant of RCH status. Based on a set of primary data Bagli (2015b) has also reported the MPI of two CD blocks of the district of Bankura in West Bengal. It is reported that MPI of Chhatna block is almost three fold higher than that in Kotulpur block. In another paper Bagli (2015a) reveals that per capita household income, landholding, major occupations and castes as significant determinants of multidimensional poverty for SC and ST households in Bankura district. The probability to be an extreme multidimensional poor is lower for a tribal household compared to a scheduled castes household. However, in contrast to scheduled castes, scheduled tribes are more likely to be marginal poor and vulnerable. In order to become familiar with the Multidimensional poverty in northeast India and to locate the most multidimensionally poor district in this region we set the objectives of this study.

First, we seek to investigate the incidence and concentration of multidimensional poverty of the states in northeast India. Second, this study explores which states are found to be closed to each other based on the observed indicators of multidimensional poverty. Third, we determine the relative position of the districts of northeast India based on the computed multidimensional poverty Index for the districts in this zone.

10.3 Research Methodology

Keeping in mind the objectives this chapter computes a multidimensional poverty index (MPI) for each state and for each district of north east region of India. This index covers three dimensions—Knowledge, Health and Living condition. We have taken illiteracy rate and financial illiteracy rate as deprivation indicators under knowledge dimension. Illiteracy rate is measured by the percentage of population aged above six years, who are unable to read and write. Very recently, the financial literacy has been considered as an important indicator of inclusive development. By financial literacy, we mean the knowledge of how to avail formal financial services like savings, credit, payment, insurance, remittance, etc. Due to financial illiteracy people may fail to make their money plan in a proper way. Sometimes, people lose their money owing to financial illiteracy. 'Sarada Scam' in West Bengal is a burning example of how the financial loss arises due to financial illiteracy. To this end, we have taken financial illiteracy as an indicator of knowledge deprivation. It has been measured by the percentage of households having no access to any banking services. No point to deny that access to safe drinking water and scientific sanitation facility are the basement of health and hygiene in life. Health dimension of multidimensional poverty in this study covers the percentage of households using unsafe source of drinking water and households having no access to improved sanitation as indicator. In this study, tap water but untreated, water from uncovered well, water from spring, river, pond, lake, etc., as source of drinking water have been considered as unsafe drinking water. The households where members used to defecate in the open space have been taken as household having no access to improved sanitation.

The dimension of living condition is comprised of four indicators viz. households having dilapidated residence, no census assets, no access to electricity or solar energy for lighting and no access to improved fuel for cooking. In accordance with the population census, 2011 dilapidated residence refers to the residences which are in the verge of breaking down and require immediate repairs or those houses broke and are that cannot be repaired easily. If the household own no one of the assets like Bicycle, Transistor, Television, Computer, Mobile Phone, Motorcycle, etc. we refer it as a household with no census assets. The households who use fuel like crop residue, cow dung cake, firewood, coal lignite and charcoal, etc., which causes indoor pollution have been considered as the households using dirty fuel for cooking. The percentage of households, who use kerosene or other oil for lighting or have no lighting arrangement in residence are considered as deprived of electricity or solar energy for lighting in residence. In our index, each selected dimension has got equal weight and weight of a dimension equally distributed among the indicators under the dimension. The details of the dimensions, indicators and corresponding weights for measuring MPI have been specified in Table 10.1.

The conventional measures of multidimensional poverty except MPI ignores to present the number instances the people suffer from multidimensional poverty. In this study the incidence of multidimensional poverty, that is, a head count ratio of multidimensional poverty for each state and for each district has been computed following the simple formula

$$\mathrm{MHCR} = \frac{\sum_{i=1}^{8} N_i}{8N} \times 100,$$

where $i = 1, 2, 3, \ldots, 8$, indicator, N_i number of persons/household deprived from ith indicator, and N stands for total households in the state/district.

Table 10.1 Multidimensional poverty: its dimensions and indicators with weight

Dimension	Indicators	Weight (W_i)
Knowledge	(1) Percentage of illiterate population (2) Percentage of financially literacy households	1/6 1/6
Health	(1) Percentage of households using unsafe source of drinking water (2) Percentage of households having no access to improved sanitation	1/6 1/6
Living standard	(1) Percentage of households having dilapidated residence (2) Percentage of households having no census assets (3) Percentage of households using dirty cooking fuel (4) Percentage of households having no access to electricity	1/12 1/12 1/12 1/12

Source Author's own justification

In order to gauge the intensity of multidimensional poverty first of all we have placed the indicator in scale 0 to W_i which indicates the deprivation index for the particular indicator. We have computed the weighted deprivation index (D_i) for ith indicator following the formula

$$D_i = W_i \frac{A_i - m_i}{M_i - m_i},$$

where i = 1, 2, 3,..., 8, W_i = weight attached to the dimension i, $0 \leq w_i \leq 1$, D_i = weighted deprivation index of ith indicator, A_i = actual value of ith indicator, M_i = maximum value of ith indicator and m_i minimum value of ith indicator.

The minimum and maximum values of the indicators are observed among the districts as applicable, in northeast India. Now based on the indicator deprivation indices the position of *j*th state/district in the eight dimensional 'Cartesian Space' can be plotted by the vector (D_{1j}, D_{2j}, D_{3j}, D_{4j}, D_{5j}, D_{6j}, D_{7j}, D_{8j},). In this Cartesian Space vector (0, 0, 0, 0, 0, 0, 0, 0) capture the best situation where multifaceted deprivation is absent. The acute multidimensional poverty is represented by the vector $(W_1, W_2, W_3, W_4, W_5, W_6, W_7, W_8)$. Finally, we have calculated the Multidimensional Poverty Index (MPI) measuring the normalised inverse 'Euclidian distance' of the vector of observed situation from the vector of acute multidimensional poverty. The formula for computation of MPI is as follows:

$$\text{MPI} = 1 - \sqrt{\frac{\sum_{i=1}^{8} (W_i - D_i)^2}{\sum W_i^2}}.$$

The normalisation of Euclidian distance is done in order to ensure the range of MPI from '0' to '1'. As the inverse distance has been taken, higher value of MPI represents higher level of poverty. Thus, the value '0' indicates no multidimensional poverty and '1' indicates extreme multidimensional poverty. This distance-based approach has an advantage over the UNDP methodology of measuring achievement or deprivation Index. In UNDP methodology, the index presents the arithmetic or geometric average of the standardized indicators. It assumes perfect substitutability across the dimensions or indicators. Under this assumption, a decrease in value of one indicator can be compensated by an increase of equal magnitude in another indicator. Thus, if all dimensions or indicators are equally important for the all over index value the perfect substitutability among the indicators is not appropriate. The distance-based approach does not suffer from this limitation. Our MPI formula does satisfy the properties of normalisation, symmetry, monotonicity, proximity, uniformity and signalling. But methodology of HDI follows only the properties viz. normalisation, symmetry, monotonicity. Thus, our distance-based measure of multidimensional poverty is superior to the measures based on UNDP methodology. In order to categorise the states or districts in accordance with its MPI value this study has set three sub-ranges. The high level of multidimensional poverty has been denoted by the range $0.5 < \text{MPI} \leq 1$. The range

$0.2 < \text{MPI} \leq 0.5$ indicates moderate level of poverty. The relatively low level of multidimensional poverty has been specified by the range $0 \leq \text{MPI} < 0.2$.

In order to investigate which states are similar with respect to the selected indicators of multidimensional deprivation we have employed the tool of cluster analysis following squared Euclidian distance method. Finally, to show the possible clusters of the states we have drawn a Dendrogram adopting average linkage method.

Secondary sources of data have been used for empirical analysis of this study. The data for the indicators of multidimensional poverty, and aggregate workforce participation for the states and districts in northeast India have been collected from Population Census Report (2011), Government of India. Data for income poverty has been collected from the report of the Planning Commission, Government of India (2014). We have considered all the states and districts in northeast India and census data for studying the nature and ranges of multidimensional poverty. Thus there is no sampling error problem in the findings and accordingly the findings are more reliable compared to the findings of any study based on sample.

10.4 Findings and Discussion

Table 10.2 presents the description of the indicators of multidimensional poverty across the states in northeast India. In Fig. 10.1 it is reported that illiteracy is highest in the state of Arunachal Pradesh while financial illiteracy is moderate in this state. Illiteracy rate is least in the state of Mizoram. The variation of illiteracy

Table 10.2 Descriptions of the indicators of MPI for the states in northeast India

Indicators	Mean	Median	SD	CV	Max	Min
Illiterate population	21.44	21.75	8.29	38.68	34.62	8.66
Households having no access to banking facility	50.04	51.45	17.19	34.36	71.40	20.80
Households use unsafe source of drinking water	58.18	59.45	15.96	27.43	80.80	29.80
Households have no improved sanitation facility	22.70	18.75	12.40	54.64	38.00	8.10
Households live in dilapidated residence	4.88	4.60	2.73	55.99	10.70	1.80
Households do not have census asset	25.93	25.70	6.68	25.78	35.80	18.20
Households have no access to electricity or solar power for lighting	28.80	29.30	16.88	58.61	62.20	7.30
Households use dirty fuel for cooking	72.20	75.95	13.41	18.57	86.40	47.20
MHCR	35.52	38.35	6.96	19.59	43.92	25.27

Source Author's computation based on census data, 2011

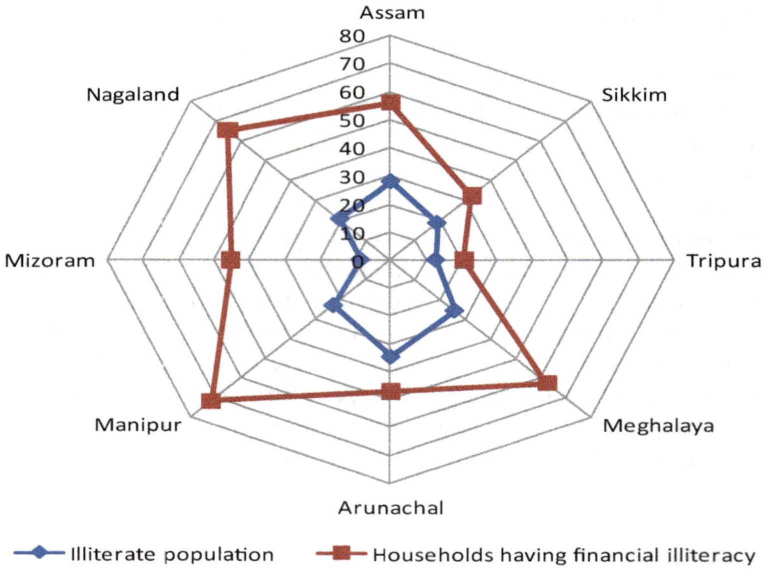

Fig. 10.1 Distribution of knowledge among the states in northeast India. *Source* drawn based on census data, 2011

rate across the states is not so prominent. The financial illiteracy is highest in Manipur followed by Nagaland and Meghalaya among the states in northeast India. In average half of the households in northeast India are financially excluded. The mean and variability of financial illiteracy are relatively high compared to normal illiteracy. Thus financial exclusion is a serious problem in North eastern states Fig. 10.2.

We observe that in average 58% households in northeast India collect drinking water from unsafe source. Percentage of households having access to unsafe source of drinking water is highest in Nagaland followed by Sikkim and Manipur. Problem of the use of unsafe drinking water is lowest in Assam, but in this state one third of the households have no improved sanitation facility. 38% of households in Arunachal Pradesh, which is highest among the states in northeast India, do not have improved sanitation facility. Average access to scientific sanitation facility is highest in the state of Mizoram. Moderate level disparity prevail among the states regarding the access to safe drinking water while a high level disparity is present among the states in respect of access to improved sanitation Fig. 10.3.

The problems of dilapidated residential house and non access to electricity or solar power for lighting are severe in Assam among the states under consideration. In terms of asset holding Meghalaya is poorest state in northeast India followed by Nagaland and Arunachal Pradesh. Poverty in terms asset is lowest in the state of Sikkim. Inequality of having dilapidated house across the states is very high. On the other hand, poverty in terms of asset holding has low mean and low variance.

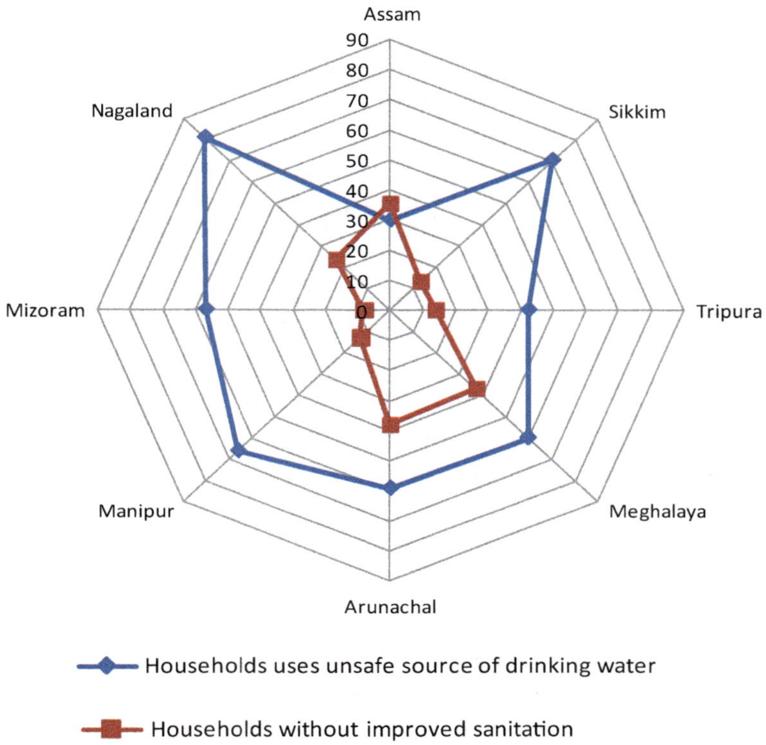

Fig. 10.2 Distribution of health indicators among the states in northeast India. *Source* drawn based on census data, 2011

Fig. 10.3 Distribution of asset and housing poverty among the states in northeast India. *Source* drawn based on census data, 2011

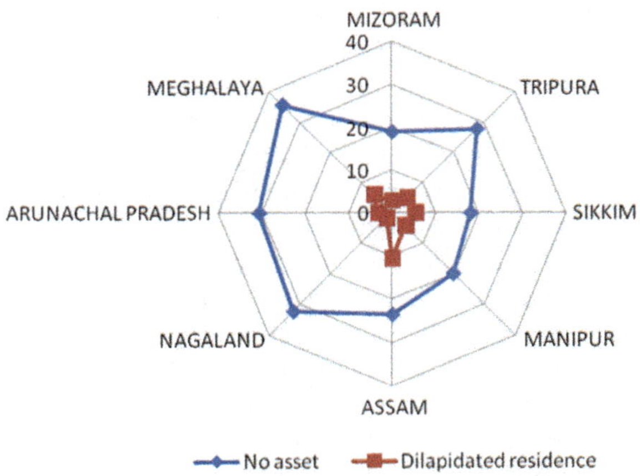

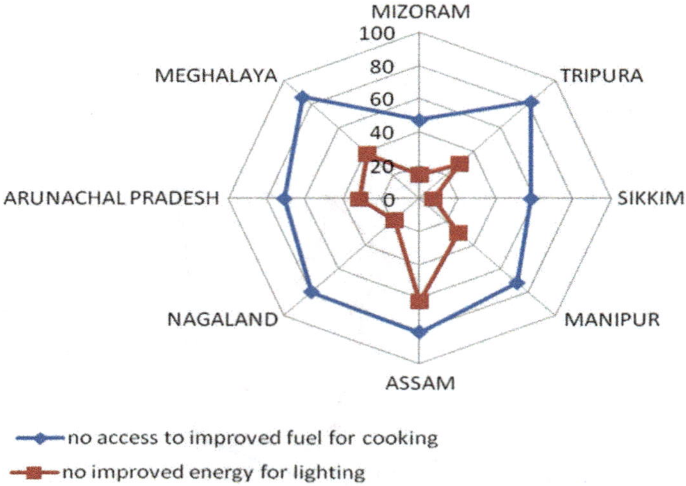

Fig. 10.4 Distribution of energy poverty across the states in northeast India. *Source* drawn based on census data, 2011

Meghalaya is also poorest among the north eastern states in terms of access to improved fuel for cooking. In average 72% households in the states in northeast India use dirty fuel for cooking. In North-Eastern states 28% of households cannot use electricity or solar power for lighting. It varies from 7 to 62% across the states. The state of Sikkim is best among the states in northeast India in terms of having access to improved power for lighting Fig. 10.4.

All these indicators provide important and useful information regarding the multidimensional poverty of an economy. However, individual indicator provides only partial information on the deprivation. Actually from the individual indicators we find head count ratio for the respective indicator. Using single indicator may also lead to a misinterpretation of the extent of multiple dimensions of poverty. Further, individual indicator fails to compare the state of multidimensional poverty among the states/districts. To this end, we have measured incidence of the multidimensional poverty computing multidimensional poverty head count ratio and gauged extent of multidimensional poverty computing MPI.

The measure of multidimensional poverty head count ratio reveals that 35% of the households across the states of northeast India are multidimensionally poor. The incidence of multidimensional poverty is highest in the state of Meghalaya where 43% households are multidimensionally poor. It is however, pertinent to note that only 12% households in Meghalaya are income poor. We have found that value of MPI ranges from 0.180 to 0.702 across the states. In accordance with computed MPI the state of Meghalaya is the most deprived followed by Arunachal Pradesh and Nagaland while Mizoram, Tripura are relatively better in position among the north-eastern states. Table 10.3 shows that multidimensional poverty level is high in the states of Meghalaya, Arunachal Pradesh and Nagaland. The states of Sikkim,

Table 10.3 Population below poverty line (Tendulkar methodology) and MPI of the states

States	BPL population (%)	Rank of poverty line	MHCR	MPI	Rank of MPI
Mizoram	20.4	4	25.27	0.1808	8
Tripura	14.0	6	29.35	0.2044	7
Sikkim	8.2	8	27.93	0.3010	6
Manipur	36.9	1	37.37	0.4641	5
Assam	32.0	3	40.75	0.4906	4
Nagaland	18.9	5	40.23	0.5578	3
Arunachal Pradesh	34.7	2	39.33	0.6175	2
Meghalaya	11.9	7	34.92	0.7023	1

Source Government of India planning commission June, 2014 and author's computation based on Census data 2011

Manipur and Assam suffer from moderate level of multidimensional poverty. The multidimensional poverty is relatively low in Mizoram and Tripura. In Mizoram, one fifth of the population live below poverty line and one fourth are multidimensionally poor. In Manipur 37% of population are income poor as well as multidimensionally poor while rank of this state in accordance with the value of MPI is five among the eight states. Comparison of the ranks of the states in terms of income poverty head count ratio and ranks in term of MPI infers hardly an association between income poverty and multidimensional poverty of the states in northeast India.

The closeness of the values of indices does not ensure the similarity of the states in respect of the multiple dimensions/indicators of poverty. To study the similarity of the states in respect of the indicators of multidimensional poverty we have done cluster analysis. The result has been presented in Fig. 10.5. It explores that in respect of the indicators of multidimensional poverty Assam is distinct from the other states in northeast India. It is different from Sikkim and Manipur which are moderate in respect of MPI. Further, Sikkim is similar to Mizoram which is least suffering from multidimensional poverty. However, Meghalaya, Nagaland and Arunachal Pradesh come under same cluster with Manipur. In accordance with the figure of MPI Tripura and Mizoram are relatively better but they fall in different clusters.

Least multidimensional poverty of the state of Mizoram as a whole does not imply that all the districts in Mizoram have least multidimensional poverty. Further, severe multidimensional poverty of Meghalaya does not indicate extreme multidimensional poverty of its all districts. We have extended our study at the district level to realize the incidence and extent of multidimensional poverty across the districts in northeast India. Table 10.4 has depicted the descriptive statistics of the indicators of MPI for the districts. In respect of the district level data one fourth population are illiterate which varies from 2 to 51%. More than half of the households in the districts have no access to banking facility. It ranges from 9 to 90%. We find that in some districts more than 80% households have no access to

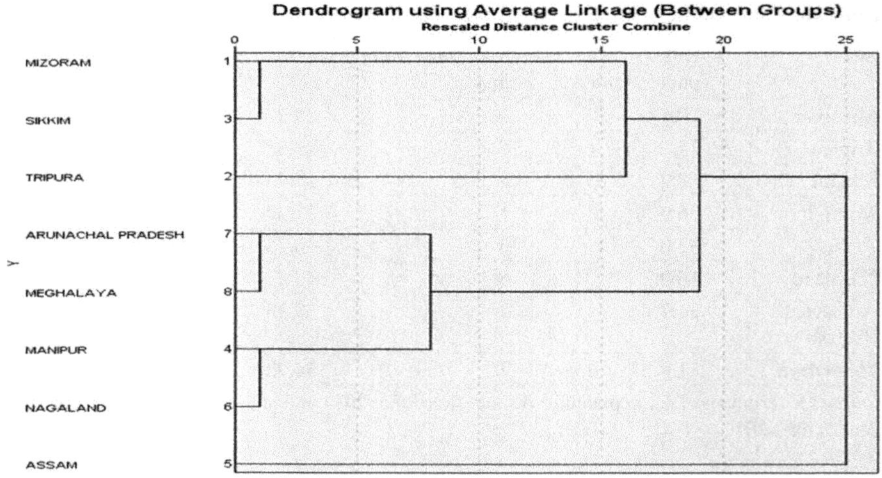

Fig. 10.5 Results of cluster analysis with respect to the Indicators of MDI. *Source* Author's computation

Table 10.4 Description of MPI and its indicators for the districts in northeast India

Indicator	Mean	Median	SD	CV	Skew	Max	Min
Illiterate population	25.39	25.59	10.56	41.61	−0.02	51.25	2.09
Households having no access to banking facility	55.40	58.65	18.83	33.99	−0.30	89.50	9.40
Households use unsafe source of drinking water	57.72	60.30	25.77	44.65	−0.45	94.10	3.80
Households have no improved sanitation facility	29.94	28.80	18.12	60.54	0.56	74.50	1.10
Households live in dilapidated residence	5.94	4.90	4.25	71.52	0.97	17.60	0.50
Households have no access to electricity or solar power for lighting	38.66	37.50	23.75	61.43	0.06	81.60	2.10
Households use dirty fuel for cooking	78.27	81.70	17.35	22.16	−1.31	99.20	20.70
Households do not have census asset	28.89	28.20	14.03	48.55	0.42	60.80	5.00
MHCR	40.30	40.96	10.56	26.38	−0.31	66.61	13.18
MDI	0.46	0.45	0.14	31.01	0.02	0.90	0.12

Source Author's computation

electricity. It not only makes deprivation of lighting, it accumulates the deprivation of the access to the facilities of modern IT. The descriptive statistics are shown in Table 10.4 focus a wide disparity across the districts in respect of the indicators of multidimensional poverty. In average, 40% of the households in the districts of North East are multidimensionally poor which varies from 13 to 67%.

Average value of MPI of the districts is 0.46 which ranges from 0.12 to 0.90 across the districts. Tables 10.5a and 10.5b presents the multidimensional poverty head count ratios and values of MPI for the districts in northeast states. This study has explored the district of Kurung Kumey belonging to Arunachal Pradesh as the poorest district among the 86 districts of eight northeastern states. In this district two third of the population are multidimensionally poor. More than half of the population in this district are illiterate; 80% households do not have access to banking facility. It is saddening that three fourth of the households have no access to improved sanitation and 88.2% households use unsafe source of drinking water. In this district, 12.3% households reside at dilapidated house, 70.1% households have no electricity or solar power for lighting at night and only 3.7% households have access to LPG or improved fuel for cooking. It is relevant to note that among the ten most deprived districts eight are not located in Meghalaya. None of the districts in Mizoram, Tripura and Sikkim come in the ten most multidimensionally poor districts. On the other hand, Aizawl district of Mizoram is the least deprived among the districts. No one of the ten least multi dimensionally poor districts belongs to Meghalaya.

The distribution of multidimensional poverty has also been annotated across the states. In accordance with the value of MDI, 31 districts (36%) in northeast India suffer from high level of multidimensional poverty. The level of multidimensional poverty of 51 districts (59%) is at moderate level. Only 4.6% of the districts in northeast India have low level of multidimensional poverty. The distribution of the districts with different level of multidimensional poverty has been presented in Table 10.6.

The state of Mizoram has least multidimensional poverty among the states in northeast India. But only two out of eight districts in Mizoram have low level multidimensional poverty. One district in Mizoram, namely Lawngtlai, has high level of multidimensional poverty. Other five districts are moderate poor in accordance with our measure. The state of Tripura has low level of multidimensional poverty but 75% of the districts in this state are under the group of moderate multidimensionally poor districts. However, in Meghalaya, which is poorest among the states, multidimensional poverty levels of six of the seven districts are high. Although the state of Arunachal Pradesh is very poor, one half of the districts in Arunachal Pradesh are not very poor.

Table 10.5a MPI and worker population ratios of the states in northeast India

State	District	MHCR	MPI	Rank	TWPR
Districts with high level of multidimensional poverty					
Arunachal Pradesh	Kurung Kumey	66.61	0.900	1	50.666
Arunachal Pradesh	Anjaw	51.81	0.679	2	59.344
Arunachal Pradesh	East Kameng	53.16	0.671	3	49.497
Nagaland	Mon	59.30	0.662	4	70.339
Assam	Chirang	52.59	0.657	5	47.413
Arunachal Pradesh	Upper Subansiri	51.84	0.649	6	47.018
Meghalaya	West Khasi Hills	53.60	0.639	7	55.138
Assam	Kokrajhar	52.20	0.635	8	45.471
Meghalaya	Jaintia Hills	47.45	0.634	9	50.682
Nagaland	Kiphire	54.62	0.627	10	53.900
Mizoram	Lawngtlai	51.73	0.626	11	47.758
Nagaland	Tuensang	53.80	0.626	12	61.039
Manipur	Tamenglong	54.19	0.624	13	58.244
Meghalaya	West Garo Hills	49.30	0.613	14	48.173
Meghalaya	South Garo Hills	52.41	0.605	15	46.379
Nagaland	Longleng	54.88	0.590	16	73.882
Manipur	Senapati	48.49	0.575	17	56.184
Assam	Sonitpur	45.16	0.573	18	46.810
Assam	Udalguri	46.89	0.571	19	48.028
Assam	Dhubri	53.32	0.568	20	42.367
Assam	Karbi Anglong	46.42	0.567	21	47.654
Assam	Baksa	48.04	0.551	22	49.172
Arunachal Pradesh	Changlang	44.44	0.551	23	51.461
Arunachal Pradesh	Dibang Valley	41.90	0.543	24	51.373
Meghalaya	Ribhoi	44.34	0.539	25	51.691
Manipur	Chandel	46.66	0.533	26	60.032
Assam	Goalpara	43.94	0.524	27	43.343
Arunachal Pradesh	Lower Dibang Valley	49.91	0.523	28	48.460
Meghalaya	East Garo Hills	39.60	0.523	29	48.518
Arunachal Pradesh	Lohit	39.77	0.506	30	50.027
Assam	Karimganj	48.69	0.504	31	39.260
Districts with moderate level of multidimensional poverty					
Assam	Darrang	46.35	0.500	32	42.073
Manipur	Ukhrul	50.24	0.499	33	55.099
Assam	Dima Hasao	43.45	0.498	34	46.799
Assam	Lakhimpur	42.93	0.498	35	48.565
Assam	Dhemaji	44.69	0.490	36	54.444
Nagaland	Peren	46.07	0.487	37	76.926
Assam	Bongaigaon	40.92	0.482	38	41.099

(continued)

Table 10.5a (continued)

State	District	MHCR	MPI	Rank	TWPR
Arunachal Pradesh	Upper Siang	37.25	0.477	39	58.170
Assam	Cachar	43.52	0.476	40	41.090
Nagaland	Phek	42.66	0.469	41	59.173
Arunachal Pradesh	West Kameng	34.23	0.469	42	58.770

Source Government of India planning commission June, 2014 and author's computation based on Census data 2011

10.5 Conclusion with Policy Prescriptions

This study reveals that multidimensional poverty is unevenly distributed across the districts in northeast India. Most of the districts in Meghalaya which is poorest among the states are multidimensionally extreme poor. Moreover, we have observed that the districts situated at the international border are extreme poor. The least poor districts have hardly border with foreign country. The problems of illiteracy, sanitation, water facility and housing condition are prominent and there is wide variation across the states and districts.

In order to extend education and to drive illiteracy of the common people, the Government should plan to establish primary school at each habitation which has no access to primary and upper primary, schools. In implementation part the Government has to put attention regarding language, number of teachers in the existing and coming primary schools. The proper authority has to advice the banking institutions and NGOs to serve the people of unbanked regions putting emphasis on the most financially excluded zones like Tamenglong in Manipur Kiphire in Nagaland. In this connection, we can utilise the financial inclusion policy of the Government of India in an effective manner and financial exclusion rank wise. As a section of households are already shocked by the fraud chit funds like SARADA, a continuous advertisement and campaign from the part of the Government is necessary for making successful financial literacy and financial inclusion of the unbanked people in this district.

The state Governments have already prepared a plan to supply potable drinking water through piped water supply scheme to all rural areas. In this plan, the districts have planned to supply safe drinking water by tapping water from rivers, check dams and impounding reservoirs. The government has another plan to extend safe drinking water and toilet facility for each school in the districts. However, there is no any priority list. Thus, the plans and programmes may be implemented in an indiscriminate way which may increase the inequality across the districts/blocks. Therefore, consultation with the existing district-wise distribution of the access to unsafe drinking water is needed to make a priority list for implementing the project. The decentralised plan is suitable for development on priority basis.

Northeast India needs some active plan for universal sanitation programme. We draw attention of the authority to take necessary steps for ensuring access to

Table 10.5b MPI and Worker Population ratios of the States in northeast India

State	District	MHCR	MPI	Rank	TWPR
Nagaland	Wokha	43.16	0.456	43	53.632
Assam	Morigaon	42.17	0.452	44	44.247
Assam	Hailakandi	46.55	0.451	45	39.094
Arunachal Pradesh	West Siang	37.39	0.450	46	50.480
Assam	Barpeta	42.97	0.443	47	39.965
Manipur	Thoubal	40.99	0.440	48	54.013
Nagaland	Zunheboto	41.17	0.435	49	65.857
Arunachal Pradesh	East Siang	34.15	0.428	50	46.629
Arunachal Pradesh	Tirap	40.04	0.424	51	54.573
Assam	Kamrup	37.62	0.423	52	47.739
Mizoram	Mamit	39.78	0.422	53	55.509
Assam	Nagaon	39.30	0.415	54	41.458
Manipur	Bishnupur	36.56	0.413	55	53.343
Manipur	Churachandpur	37.05	0.411	56	51.819
Arunachal Pradesh	Lower Subansiri	34.24	0.405	57	41.538
Sikkim	North district	35.47	0.397	58	59.846
Arunachal Pradesh	Tawang	31.06	0.387	59	64.634
Sikkim	West district	35.23	0.380	60	58.269
Tripura	Dhalai	39.00	0.372	61	48.362
Nagaland	Kohima	31.03	0.368	62	49.557
Assam	Golaghat	31.03	0.367	63	51.489
Meghalaya	East Khasi Hills	35.75	0.367	64	47.576
Assam	Jorhat	32.41	0.367	65	51.528
Assam	Sivasagar	32.85	0.351	66	48.011
Sikkim	South district	30.07	0.342	67	57.017
Mizoram	Saiha	34.54	0.341	68	41.476
Tripura	North Tripura	36.76	0.338	69	41.811
Assam	Tinsukia	30.09	0.328	70	48.617
Mizoram	Lunglei	30.72	0.328	71	57.436
Manipur	Imphal East	27.47	0.325	72	49.182
Assam	Nalbari	32.27	0.325	73	39.571
Nagaland	Mokokchung	35.16	0.309	74	57.481
Assam	Dibrugarh	30.48	0.308	75	48.194
Tripura	South Tripura	31.76	0.281	76	48.013
Manipur	Imphal West	24.53	0.280	77	46.783
Sikkim	East district	22.39	0.270	78	54.647
Nagaland	Dimapur	22.25	0.261	79	46.156
Arunachal Pradesh	Papum Pare	19.21	0.253	80	43.442
Mizoram	Kolasib	24.94	0.236	81	52.037
Mizoram	Champhai	23.74	0.236	82	57.414

(continued)

Table 10.5b (continued)

State	District	MHCR	MPI	Rank	TWPR
Districts with low level of multidimensional poverty					
Tripura	West Tripura	23.35	0.200	83	45.487
Assam	Kamrup Metropolitan	14.52	0.159	84	43.501
Mizoram	Serchhip	18.52	0.135	85	58.228
Mizoram	Aizawl	13.18	0.123	86	50.190

Source Government of India planning commission June, 2014 and author's computation based on Census data 2011

Table 10.6 State-wise distribution of district level multidimensional poverty in northeast India

States	Total number districts	Number of districts with high level of multidimensional poverty (%)	Number of districts with moderate level of multidimensional poverty (%)	Number of districts with low level of multidimensional poverty (%)
Mizoram	8	1 (12.5)	5 (62.5)	2 (25)
Tripura	4	0	3 (75)	1 (25)
Sikkim	4	0	4 (100)	0
Manipur	9	3 (33.33)	6 (66.67)	0
Assam	27	9 (33.33)	17 (6.96)	1 (3.7)
Nagaland	11	4 (36.36)	7 (63.64)	0
Arunachal Pradesh	16	8 (50)	8 (50)	0
Meghalaya	7	6 (85.71)	1 (14.29)	0
Northeast India	86	31 (36.04)	51 (59.3)	4 (4.65)

Source Author's computation

improved sanitation facility for the all households in northeast India. For this purpose, the continuous campaign focusing the importance of sanitation for healthy life is more necessary than releasing fund for constructing sanitation at the household level. In this respect, we can use the audio visual media more extensively which have high popularity.

In order to reduce energy poverty, northeast states have to improve the infrastructure of electricity and LPG supply for the districts which are most deprived in this regard. After all, as there is wide disparity across the districts in northeast India in terms of deprivation, the fund for reducing multidimensional poverty should be allocated on equitable basis not on equality basis across the districts.

References

Alkire, S., & Santos, M. E. (2010). *Acute multidimensional poverty: A new index for developing countries*. United Nations Development Programme Human Development. Reports Research Paper, July, 2010, Working paper no. 38.

Alkire, S., Santos, M. E., & Seth, S. (2014). Multidimensional poverty index 2014: Brief methodological note and results. The Oxford Poverty and Human Development Initiative (OPHI). Oxford Department of International Development, University of Oxford. Contact details: ophi@qeh.ox.ac.uk.

Bagli, S. (2013). A study on measuring housing deprivation in India. *International Journal of Development Studies, 5*(1), 173–177.

Bagli, S. (2015a). Multidimensional poverty of SC and ST households: An empirical study in Bankura district. A paper presented in a National Seminar at NIRD. Available at www.nird.org.in.

Bagli, S. (2015b). Multidimensional poverty: An empirical study in Bankura District, West Bengal. *Journal of Rural Development, 34*(3), 242–327.

Bhattacharya, G., & Halder, S. (2014). Trend, differential and determinants of deprivation of reproductive and child health in the districts of West Bengal, India. *Journal of Health Management, 16*(1), 93–112.

Government of India. (2011). Population census report, 2011. Registrar General of India.

Mehta, K. A., & Shah, A. (2003). Chronic poverty in India: Incidence, causes and policies. *World Development, 31*(3), 491–511.

Planning Commission. (2014). Government of India, report of the expert group to review the methodology for measurement of poverty. Available at www.planningcommission.in.

United Nations Development Programme. (2010). *Human development report, 2010*. New York: Palgrave Macmillan.

Chapter 11
Poverty, Inequality and Relative Deprivation Among Northeastern States of India: Evidence from NSS

Mohammad Kashif Khan and Balakrushna Padhi

Abstract One of the foremost objectives of post-independence Indian planning has been to eradicate poverty, reduce inequality, thus improving the lives of those battered by deprivation and suffering. With some of the initiatives by government, presently Indian economy is experiencing higher growth since last two decades of new economic policy regime. So it is an appropriate time to review and examine the precise impact of reform process on poverty, inequality and deprivation. The objective of this present study is to examine poverty, inequality and relative deprivation among northeastern states of India during 2004–05 (61st Round) and 2011–12 (68th Round) of NSSO's Consumer Expenditure Survey Rounds data. This chapter used headcount ratio to measure poverty, relative deprivation index to understand the level of deprivation among the northeastern states of India. In addition, we have used Gini Coefficient for inequality prevalence. Our analysis depicts that the headcount poverty ratio of Tripura has highest in rural northeastern states, which has worse than national averages in 2004–05. Results also divulge that states like Sikkim, Mizoram, Tripura and Meghalaya have less than 10% poverty level in 2011–12 in urban area. The highest reduction in poverty has shown in rural Tripura during 2004–05 to 2011–12. The urban poverty is lower for all the states than rural area. Further results of relative deprivation show that, only Tripura is relative deprived state in rural whereas Sikkim and Manipur in Urban during 2004–05. The number of relative disadvantages states has increased in 2011–12 for both rural and urban. The highest relative disadvantages are in Arunachal Pradesh for rural, and in Manipur for the urban area during 2011–12. The highest relatively advantages are Nagaland in 2004–05 and Sikkim 2011–12 for both place in rural and urban among all the northeastern states. Relative disadvantages have increased or relative advantages have decreased during 2011–12 from 2004–05 in all

M.K. Khan (✉)
School of Economics, University of Hyderabad, Hyderabad, Telangana 500046, India
e-mail: kashifiips@gmail.com

B. Padhi
Centre for Study of Regional Development (CSRD), Jawaharlal Nehru University, New Delhi 110067, India
e-mail: padhi.balakrushna5@gmail.com

U.K. De et al. (eds.), *Inequality, Poverty and Development in India*, India Studies in Business and Economics, DOI 10.1007/978-981-10-6274-2_11

northeastern states except for Tripura and Sikkim in rural. Inequality is lower in rural area as compare to urban area both periods except Sikkim in 2004–05 and Arunachal Pradesh both periods. Within rural area, the inequality has increased in 2011–12 for Sikkim and Nagaland whereas urban area two more states joined in this category, i.e. Tripura and Meghalaya. Oaxaca Blinder results show that sector, state and education play key role in differences of mean expenditure of poor and non-poor for endowment as well as return to endowment impact.

Keywords Poverty · Inequality · Decomposition · Relative deprivation Northeast India

JEL Classification D63 · I30

11.1 Introduction

Indian economy has witnessed a vivid transformation in its economic erection with the structural transformation since 1990s. From a 'lumbering elephant' to a 'running tiger'[1] (Nayyar 2006), it has made hasty and noteworthy progress over the last two decades. Although still a relatively poor country, its rapid expansion in economic sphere in terms of growth potential since 1990s makes it an important player in the world economy. As the Indian economy has experienced almost two decades of new economic policy regime, it is an appropriate time to review and examine the precise impact of the reform process on various segments of our economy (Sahu 2012). We can find that the growth process is uneven in various parts in terms of its distribution. So it has come under stark criticism for the nature of growth itself. Albeit paradoxical, such criticisms are more often than not justified given the assessment of the strictures which typify inclusion. In this context if we look at the changing nature of inequality and poverty it gives a gloomy picture. In Indian economy, it has shown that while the money metric poverty declined but the disparity or inequality in the level of income has widened substantially. When we talk about equity, it relates to a degree of equality in the living conditions of people regarding income and wealth, that society consider desirable. The observed phenomenon in India defeats this purpose. As the recent approach of the government talks about inclusive growth which entails equality in opportunity, the observed phenomenon raises questions in that regard. So while talking about welfare orientation approach it is essential to measure the dividends of growth in terms of income distribution. The more crucial issues to discuss here is about an examination of poverty and inequality.

While there is a good deal of studies dealing with the national level poverty and inequality scenario, sub-national specific studies are not many to come by Abraham

[1]For details kindly see Nayyar (2006).

(2009), Rangarajan et al. (2007). Even studies evaluating the state level poverty, inequality and employment scenario have limited their analysis to seventeen major states only, Assam being the only northeastern state featured in this list (Rangarajan and Kaul 2009; Bhaumik 2007; Chadha and Sahu 2004; Chauhan et al. 2015; Padhi et al. 2015). Thus, the north-eastern region has not received due consideration in poverty and inequality studies, partly due to the problem of inadequacy or non-availability of statistically authentic data. Notwithstanding, the thin sample coverage of the north-eastern region due to geographic limitations and consequently the statistical reliability of the data, few researchers have attempted for a detailed and incisive assessment of various facets of employment based on different rounds of NSS data (Srivastav and Dubey 2003; Sahu 2012). In this present study, we have attempted to examine the trends and patterns of poverty and inequality from consumer expenditure surveys of 2004–05 and 2011–12.

This chapter contributes to poverty and inequality at the regional level and sub sector level. It also addresses in many ways the poverty and inequality in the northeast states of India Firstly, this chapter uses the group of poverty and inequality indices for robustness of results. Secondly, the relative deprivation index for advantage/disadvantages of state. This study is organized into seven sections. Section 11.2 presents the need of the study. Section 11.3 describes the data setting. The data sets used for this analysis has explained in Sect. 11.4. Section 11.5 presents the method of poverty, inequality and Relative Deprivation Index, Sect. 11.6 presents the result of the poverty and inequality in rural–urban place of residence and the result of the relative deprivation index; section. Section 11.7 presents conclusion along with final takeaway from these results.

11.2 Need of the Study

There is a dearth of study which has extensively analyzed the poverty, inequality and deprivation in northeastern states of India. This study will add to the literature of poverty, inequality and deprivation in development literature. Although this crucial topic has been debated since independence but, few papers have extensively analyzed poverty, inequality and deprivation in northeast India any research paper. Relative deprivation is important to study, as World Bank (2000) define poverty as ‘deprivation in well-being’. This particular topic has found a place in government reports like for the north eastern state (NIRD and NERC 2008; MDoNER and NEC 2008) but not in research papers in the recent time period. To the best of our knowledge, there are only few studies which deal with this area in northeastern states of India (Sahu 2012; Srivastav and Dubey 2003; Niti 2015).

11.3 Settings

The North East region of India comprises of eight states, conventionally referred as 'seven sister states' and one brother state, namely Arunachal Pradesh, Assam, Manipur, Meghalaya, Mizoram, Nagaland, Tripura and Sikkim. Although mostly hilly, potentially arable land rich in natural resources is found in vast tracts on both sides of the Brahmaputra river valley. In spite of fertile land and relatively educated people (68.5% literacy rate, compared to 64.8% nation-wide) the North-East remains one of the most underdeveloped regions in India (Nair et al. 2013). But, all the development process in north east regions is not rosy, economy of the region marked with pervasiveness of unskilled labour force and two-third of the work force of this region engage in the agriculture sector. This region also lack of fecund investment, basic infrastructure facilities and pervasiveness of unskilled labour force, these states remain economically backward (Mahajan 2009). The eight states of North-East endowed with a large amount of forest and natural resources account for almost 4% of the total population and 8% of India's geographical area of the country (Niti 2015). Still these regions are not completely self-sufficient in agricultural production. In terms of Industrial development, the region is manifest by lack of proper or nearly absence of proper industries or manufacturing unit. Most of the industries are found only in Assam, Meghalaya and Arunachal Pradesh, which are medium scale and few large scale industries. As it is stated by study of Mahajan (2009) that 'The traditional industries in which production is carried out at substance level are handicrafts and weaving industries. The swelling tertiary sector is the result of an arbitrary arrangement in which a lion's shares of states. Outlays are used in paying salaries and maintaining the huge army of unproductive government employees (Mahajan 2009)'.

Given this context, *the primary objective of this present study is to examine the prevalence of poverty and inequality among North Eastern States of India. Second objective is to examine the relative deprivation in the north eastern region.*

11.4 Data Source

This chapter makes use of two rounds of National Sample Survey Organization (NSSO) 61st (July 2004–June 2005) and 68th (July 2011–June 2012) rounds of the India's nationally representative survey on 'Household Consumption Expenditure' of unit level data provided by the NSSO. The data were collected through the multi-stage stratified sampling design was used for the 61st and 68th round survey, with a total of 12,629 in rural household and 5069 urban households selected randomly from 516 number of villages survey and 514 Urban Survey Frame blocks, respectively, for 61st round, with a total of 9144 in rural household and 4979 urban households selected randomly from 1145 number of villages survey and 624 Urban Survey Frame blocks for 68th round, respectively. The data collected on the household characteristics, food and non-food consumption expenditure, etc. (NSSO 2006, 2013). The 61st and 68th NSSO round has been used for the temporal comparison of poverty, inequality of household consumption expenditure in the rural and the urban area northeast India. This chapter uses the poverty line based on the Tendulkar poverty line given in expert committee to review methodology for measurement of poverty by headed by Rangarajan (Planning Commission 2014).

11.5 Methodology

In the present study we used FGT measure, Gini coefficient and Relative deprivation index methodology to understand the pattern of inequality and poverty in North-Eastern regions of India.

11.5.1 FGT Index

This study uses the popular FGT measures of poverty index for a better understanding of the extent of poverty. The Foster-Greer-Thorbecke (FGT) poverty measure for a given population can be defined as,[2]

$$P_a = \frac{1}{N}\sum_{i=1}^{q}\left(\frac{z - y_i}{z}\right)^a, \tag{11.1}$$

where

N Size of the sample
Z Poverty line
y_i Variable of interest[3]
a Parameter[4].

In this FGT estimates of poverty, the three measures of poverty (head count measure of poverty, poverty gap and poverty square index) are calculated based on the three values of α.

[2]Some of the analysis and equations of FGT poverty measure has taken from Jha and Sharma (2003). For details kindly check Jha and Sharma (2003).

[3](Monthly Per Capita Consumption Expenditure (MPCE) based on Mixed Reference Period (MRP) in this analysis).

[4]"when α is larger the index puts more weight on the position of the poorest", Chapter 4, Measures of Poverty accessed on http://siteresources.worldbank.org/PGLP/Resources/povertymanual_ch4.pdf.

11.5.1.1 Head Count Index of Poverty (PG0) α = 0

$$\mathrm{PG0} = \frac{q}{N} \tag{11.2}$$

This Index gives us the head count estimates of poverty. In other words, it estimates the proportion of the population that is poor. But one of the problems of this estimate is that this Index does not indicate how the poor the poor are. In other words, it fails to estimate or capture the extent to which individual income falls below the poverty line (Jha and Sharma 2003). So, there is a second measure of poverty, i.e. Poverty Gap Index (PG1). This Index measures 'the extents to which individuals fall below the poverty line (the poverty gaps) as a proportion of the poverty line' (Haughton and Khandker 2009).

11.5.1.2 Poverty Gap (PG0) α = 1

$$\mathrm{PG1} = \frac{1}{N}\sum_{i=1}^{q}\frac{(z - y_i)}{z}. \tag{11.3}$$

In the above equation, the PG1 captures the acuteness of poverty, as it measures the total shortfall of poor from the poverty line. The sum of these poverty gaps gives the minimum cost of eliminating poverty if transfers were perfectly targeted. But this measure does not reflect changes in inequality among the poor. In other words, this measure does not consider the importance of the number of poor who are below the poverty line. Here it is essential to use both measures of poverty jointly for evaluating the extent of poverty (Jha and Sharma 2003).

11.5.1.3 Square Poverty Index (PG2) α = 2

$$\mathrm{PG2} = \frac{1}{N}\sum_{i=1}^{q}\left(\frac{z - y_i}{z}\right)^2. \tag{11.4}$$

The square poverty index measures the severity of poverty more accurately. The squared poverty gap ('poverty severity') index (PG2) averages the squares of the poverty gaps relative to the poverty line.

So, while discussing poverty all these measures are important to discuss basically, Head Count Ratio (PG0), Poverty Gap index (PG1) and Square Poverty Index (PG2).

11.5.2 Gini Coefficient

In this study, the Gini Index basically measures inequality in the distribution of Monthly per capita consumption expenditure. The Gini coefficient[5] (Dutta 2005) varies between 0 and 1 and it is defined as follows:

$$\text{Gini} = \frac{1}{2n^2\overline{w}}\sum_{i=1}^{n}\sum_{j=1}^{n}\left|w_i - w_j\right|, \tag{11.5}$$

where

n Number of individuals in the sample
w Arithmetic mean per capita consumer expenditure
w_i Income of individual i, and
w_j Income of individual j.

11.5.3 Measuring Relative Deprivation Index

There are various methods to measure deprivation which first used by the Jayaraj and Subramanian (2002) for the ailment deprivation (U_i) and later Joe (2010) for relative deprivation of the undernourishment in India. It is defined by Joe (2010) and Joe and Mishra (2009) as 'For a given population it is defined as the ratio of the number of ailing persons to the total population and is analogous to the poverty head count ratio'. The formula for the relative disadvantage index (RDI)[6] is following which gives the value of this index is:

$$\text{RDI}(\delta i^*) = \left(\frac{\varnothing_i}{1-\varnothing_i}\right)\left(\frac{U_i}{U} - 1\right)\ldots\forall\,\varnothing_i \geq U \tag{11.6}$$

$$\text{RDI}(\delta i^*) = \left(\frac{U_i - U}{1-U}\right)\ldots\forall\,\varnothing_i < U \tag{11.7}$$

where, i presents the number of states (ranges from i = 1, 2, 3, …, k); $\varnothing_i$ is the share of the state i in the total country's population; U is the aggregate level poverty head count ratio (here India's poverty); U_i is the poverty head count ratio of state i. Here poverty is negative outcome, i.e. more the value of head count worse is the situation in the state, lower the value better the situation in the state. In this case of

[5]For detail understanding of the methodology kindly follow Dutta (2005), Chauhan et al. (2015) and Haughton and Khndker (2009).

[6]For a better understanding of this methodology kindly see, Joe (2010) and Jayaraj and Subramanian (2002).

poverty, state is relatively disadvantages whenever RDI (δi^*) value is positive and relatively advantages whenever RDI (δi^*) is negative (Joe 2010).

11.6 Results and Discussion

11.6.1 Pattern of Poverty in Rural–Urban Northeast India

This chapter uses the three methods of poverty measure, i.e. headcount ratio which very popular measure instead of having measurement limitation, second is refined version of headcount ratio is poverty gap and third is square poverty Index, the three measures of poverty popularly known as the Foster-Greer-Thorbecke (FGT) measure of Poverty Index. Table 11.1 presents the value of all these measures for all northeastern states and all India in the rural and urban area. Our analysis of headcount ratio found that Tripura has highest poverty level in rural North East worse than national averages, i.e. 41.9, second worse is Manipur with 39.24% poverty level and so on. The states like Nagaland, Meghalaya are far better than national average of poverty. The other better performing states are Mizoram which has far better than the national level average.

States like Sikkim and Arunachal Pradesh and have 10 and 8 and% point lower head count ratio than national average, respectively. Indicator poverty gap varies 1.014–9.5 in Nagaland and Tripura, respectively; ranking is similar to the headcount. The ranking of all measure for rural northeastern states are similar with any measures (Table 11.1). The other important sector is urban. There are plenty of literature which shown the significant of the urban area in reducing poverty. In India urban centers are the engine of growth, 70% of GDP contribution comes from the urban area. Migration happens in urban area with the hope of the better economic activity than the rural area. In this context, we are taking the queue from the aforesaid literature and analyzing poverty, poverty gap and FGT among urban northeastern states and all India. We found that Manipur (i.e. 34.3%) has highest poverty level among northeastern states of India, much above the national level (i.e. 25.8%). The states like Nagaland, Mizoram have less than 10% poverty level whereas all other northeastern states have highest than 20% of poverty level. In other words, in the urban area only two states have higher than the national average. Similar trend found for the two other measure poverty gap. The poverty gap varies from 5.1 in Manipur to 0.54 in Nagaland. But interesting pattern found for FGT measure. The highest value found in Arunachal Pradesh (1.3) and lowest found in Nagaland (0.099) (Table 11.1).

The highest poverty exists in Arunachal Pradesh and lowest in Sikkim where the ranges vary from 38.9 to 9.85, respectively. There are four states Sikkim, Meghalaya, Tripura and Nagaland lower than national poverty level in the rural area during 2011–12. The poverty level has been drastically declining among all the since 2004–05. But one state, Meghalaya's poverty has been increased more than

Table 11.1 FGT and RDI measures of northeast India

States	Rural					Urban				
	HCR	Ranking of HCR	PG	FGT	RDI	HCR	Ranking of HCR	PG	FGT	RDI
61st round-2004–05										
India	41.9	8	9.66	3.17	–	25.8	9	6.1	2.05	–
Sikkim	31.9	4	5.65	1.44	−0.17	25.9	7	3.4	0.89	0.002
Arunachal Pradesh	33.6	5	7.4	2.45	−0.14	23.5	5	4.6	1.25	−0.03
Nagaland	9.71	1	1.01	0.19	−0.55	4.26	1	0.5	0.1	−0.29
Manipur	39.2	7	5.7	1.25	−0.05	34.3	8	5.1	1.03	0.11
Mizoram	23	3	3.48	0.89	−0.32	7.95	2	1	0.22	−0.24
Tripura	44.4	9	9.54	2.88	0.04	22.5	4	3.8	0.96	−0.04
Meghalaya	14	2	1.39	0.23	−0.48	24.7	6	2.8	0.54	−0.01
Assam	36.4	6	7.03	2.01	−0.09	21.8	3	4.2	1.14	−0.05
68th round-2011–12										
India	25.7	5	5.05	1.5	–	13.7	5	2.7	0.8	–
Sikkim	9.85	1	0.96	0.15	−0.21	3.67	1	0.5	0.1	−0.12
Arunachal Pradesh	38.9	9	9.79	3.14	0.18	20.3	7	4.9	1.92	0.08
Nagaland	19.9	4	3.75	1.02	−0.08	16.5	6	1.8	0.3	0.03
Manipur	38.8	8	6.64	1.55	0.18	32.4	9	6.1	1.71	0.22
Mizoram	35.4	7	7.51	2.39	0.13	6.36	2	0.6	0.1	−0.08
Tripura	16.2	3	2.17	0.45	−0.13	7.42	3	1.7	0.52	−0.07
Meghalaya	12.5	2	1.58	0.32	−0.18	9.26	4	1.5	0.26	−0.05
Assam	33.9	6	5.79	1.44	0.11	20.6	8	3.8	1.0	0.08

Source Authors own estimation based on 61st and 68th consumption expenditure rounds. *Note HCR* Head Count Ration, *PG* Poverty Gap, *FGT* Foster-Greer-Thorbecke, *RDI* Relative Deprivation Index

10% point. Major reduction in poverty has happened in Tripura which was the highest poverty in 2004–05 but it reduces 21.9% points in 2011–12. In other words, reduction in poverty was higher than the national reduction of poverty in percentages points Tripura all other states is lower than the national reduction in poverty during these two NSSO rounds (Table 11.1).

When we tried to analyze their ranking in two periods, we found that Meghalaya and Manipur ranking remains same, whereas Arunachal Pradesh, Nagaland, Mizoram's ranking falls. The states like Tripura, Sikkim and Assam have in their raking of head count ratio. The biggest gainer of ranking is Tripura it gains 5 ranks, last raking in 2004–05 to third in 2011–12 (Table 11.1). The other like poverty gap and FGT also shows very interesting pattern to be discussed here in 2011–12. Lowest poverty gap is in Sikkim and higher in Arunachal Pradesh. But if we see FGT, we found similar pattern in 2011–12 (Table 11.1).

The chapter found that urban area poverty is lower for all the states than the rural area. The highest was found in Manipur and lowest in Sikkim during the period 2011–12. The states like Sikkim, Mizoram, Tripura and Meghalaya have less than 10% poverty level in 2011–12 in urban areas. States like Manipur, Assam, Arunachal Pradesh and Nagaland have higher than national level poverty, the other remaining state have lower than national averages of poverty level (Table 11.1). Further we also found that head count ratio ranking of the Mizoram and Manipur remained same or showed no change in their rankings. The biggest gainer in ranking is Sikkim with 6 point ranks. Meghalaya and Tripura are also the gainer with 2 and 1 rank, respectively. The biggest fall was in case of Nagaland, Assam and Arunachal Pradesh in their rankings (4, 4 and 1 raking falls) (Table 11.1).

11.6.2 Relative Deprivation Among Northeastern States

This study also tries to understand the relative deprivation index among the North Eastern State of India. This index provides the information on the relatively disadvantages/advantages of states level poverty among the North Eastern State of India. This index adjusts outcome with two counts, first with the prevalence of an outcome with respect national level outcome and second with the outcome with respect to its share of population. With help of temporal RDI, we assess the poverty reduction in term of inclusiveness as Shukla and Mishra (2014) have used RDI for same purpose. This chapter also examines the relative deprivation in the rural and urban sector during 2004–05 and 2011–12 separately. The negative value of RDI value means states have relative advantages for the incidence of poverty. The positive value of RDI is showing the relatively disadvantages of the states with the incidence of the poverty. The study of relatively deprivation index for the place is residence, i.e. rural and urban is very significant because both have a different structure of the economy as well as living condition as Ravallion has described the poverty as 'urbanization of poverty' (Ravallion 2002).

The highest negative value is reflected by Nagaland and highest positive value is by Tripura. In other words, Nagaland is having highest relatively advantages of poverty and Tripura is the most disadvantaged state of rural northeast India during 2004–05. In the rural area, Tripura is the only state which relatively disadvantages position of poverty with respect to National level poverty and its share of the population in rural north east population. Further, we analyzed the relative deprivation in rural areas during the period 2011–12. The magnitude of RDI is lower in 2011–12 than 2004–05 except for Sikkim and Tripura. The big changes of RDI value have been in Tripura being relatively disadvantages in 2004–05 to relatively advantages position in 2011–12 whereas conversely true for states like Arunachal Pradesh, Manipur, Mizoram and Assam (Table 11.1). The poverty reduction is more inclusive in Tripura between these two time periods than any other North East State of India.

The highest relatively advantages states are Nagaland and relatively disadvantages states are Manipur in Urban area during 2004–05. The relatively disadvantages states are higher number in urban than rural in 2004–05. The magnitude of relatively disadvantages is higher in urban as compared to their counterpart in 2004–05 and the contrary result found for relatively advantages position states. In 2011–12 urban, states like Sikkim, Mizoram, Tripura and Meghalaya have relatively advantages of poverty and other states have relatively disadvantages position. When, we compare urban 2004–05 to 2011–12. Then we find that RDI value magnitude is lower in 2011–12 than 2004–05 for both advantages and disadvantages sates except for Sikkim and marginal improvement for Tripura.

The overall pattern of poverty and inequality is different in rural and urban northeastern states. For a better understanding of the changing poverty and inequality among northeastern states of India both in the rural and urban setting, first we have taken both the periods poverty and inequality figures. After that we have subtracted the 2011–12 poverty and inequality figures with the 2004–05 figures to check the increase or decrease in it. While most of the states shows a decline in the level of poverty and inequality in rural India, Arunachal Pradesh showing an increase in the level of Inequality. The picture is same for the urban area as well for Arunachal Pradesh. In the urban area while most of the north eastern showing decline in the level of poverty with a simultaneous increase in the level of inequality level. In the urban area Nagaland is showing an increase in the level of poverty. Both in the rural and urban area Sikkim has shown highest decline in the level of poverty and inequality (Figs. 11.1 and 11.2).

11.6.3 Inequality in Northeastern States of India

Table 11.2 presents the value of a very popular measure of inequality is Gini coefficient in rural, urban and total in 2004–05 and 2011–12 in northeastern states of India. The very popular measure of inequality in literature is Gini coefficient. We founds that the value of Gini coefficient is highest in Sikkim and lowest in Manipur.

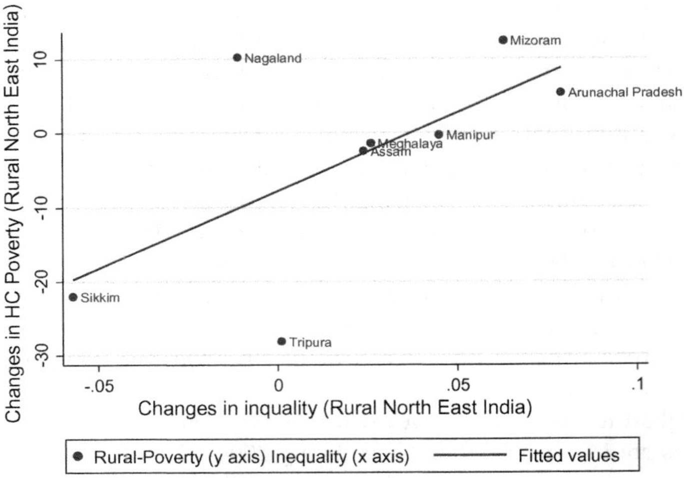

Fig. 11.1 Changing poverty and inequality in the rural northeast India (2004–05 to 2011–12). *Source* Authors own calculation based on 61st and 68th NSSO consumption round

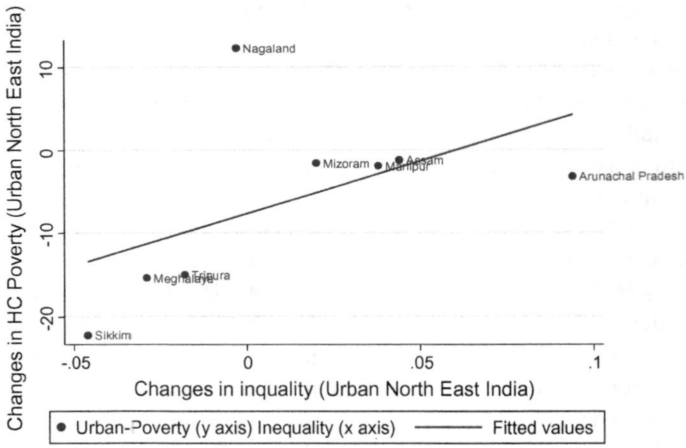

Fig. 11.2 Changing poverty and inequality in the urban northeast India (2004–05 to 2011–12). *Source* Authors own calculation based on 61st and 68th NSSO consumption round

These results alter when we look in the rural and urban area. The highest Gini value is in Arunachal Pradesh and Tripura in rural and urban area, respectively. The lowest Gini value is in Meghalaya for the rural and Manipur in Urban area.

Table 11.2 also presents Gini coefficient during 2011–12 for both the rural and urban place of residence in northeast India. The state Arunachal Pradesh has the highest value of Gini coefficient and Manipur has lowest level of Gini value. When we look the Gini value by rural–urban classification, we found that Arunachal

Table 11.2 Gini coefficient inequality in northeast India, 2004–05 and 2011–12

State	2004–05			2011–12		
	Person	Rural	Urban	Person	Rural	Urban
Sikkim	0.268	0.254	0.246	0.237	0.197	0.2
Arunachal Pradesh	0.262	0.262	0.235	0.353	0.341	0.329
Nagaland	0.243	0.206	0.234	0.222	0.195	0.231
Manipur	0.161	0.152	0.165	0.2	0.197	0.203
Mizoram	0.235	0.186	0.229	0.294	0.249	0.249
Tripura	0.265	0.211	0.314	0.252	0.212	0.296
Meghalaya	0.204	0.15	0.261	0.234	0.176	0.232
Assam	0.235	0.192	0.309	0.263	0.216	0.353

Source Authors own estimation based on 61st and 68th consumption expenditure rounds

Pradesh has the highest amount of Gini value and Meghalaya has lowest in the rural whereas Assam has highest Gini value and Sikkim is lowest in the urban area. We can see that State differ with highest lowest value of Gini coefficient rural–urban classification. This reflects different levels of inequality in the rural and urban areas of north east regions.

We have used 61st and 68th round of NSSO for the comparative analysis of the inequality between these two periods. Within rural area, the inequality has increased in 2011–12 for Sikkim and Nagaland whereas urban area two more states joined in this category, i.e. Tripura and Meghalaya.

What are changes happen in Gini coefficient among the North Eastern State. We found that there are three categories of state first state whose Gini value has decline to rural- urban and all. In this category states are Sikkim and Nagaland. Second, another extreme case is state whose Gini value has increased during 2004–05 to 2011–12. This category states are Arunachal Pradesh, Manipur, Mizoram and Assam. The other two states come in between, i.e. Tripura's overall and urban inequality has declined whereas Meghalaya's only in urban inequality declined (Table 11.2).

11.7 Conclusion

This chapter tries to understand the poverty, inequality, relative deprivation among the North Eastern region of India during 2004–05 and 2011–12 by using 61st and 68th round of NSSO data.

Our analysis depicts that the headcount poverty ratio of Tripura has highest in the rural northeastern states, which has worse than the national averages in 2004–05. Results also divulge that states like Sikkim, Mizoram, Tripura and Meghalaya have less than 10% poverty level in 2011–12 in the urban area. The highest reduction in poverty has shown in the rural Tripura during 2004–05 to 2011–12.

The urban poverty is lower for all the states than rural area. Further results of relative deprivation show that, only Tripura is relative deprived state in rural whereas Sikkim and Manipur in Urban during 2004–05. The number of relative disadvantages states have increased in 2011–12 for both rural and urban. The highest relative disadvantages are in Arunachal Pradesh for the rural area and Manipur for the urban area during 2011–12. The highest relatively advantages are Nagaland in 2004–05 and Sikkim 2011–12 for both place in rural and urban among all the northeastern states. Relative disadvantages have increased or relative advantages have decrease during 2011–12 form 2004–05 in all northeastern states except for Tripura and Sikkim in rural. It means that there more inclusive nature poverty decline in both these two states during this study period. Inequality is lower in the rural area as compare to urban area both periods except Sikkim in 2004–05 and Arunachal Pradesh both periods. Within rural the inequality has increase in 2011–12 for Sikkim and Nagaland whereas urban area two more states joined in this category, i.e. Tripura and Meghalaya. These results clearly reflect the need for a proper policy for the north eastern states of India.

References

Abraham, V. (2009). Employment growth in rural India: Distress-driven? *Economic and Political Weekly, 54*(16), 97–104.

Bhaumik, S. K. (2007). Growth and composition of rural non-farm employment in India in the era of economic reforms. *The Indian Economic Journal, 53*(3), 40–65.

Chadha, G. K., & Sahu, P. K. (2004). Recent changes in agricultural employment in rural India: A state-level analysis. *Agricultural Situation in India, 61*(5), 249–272.

Chauhan, R. K., Mohanty, S. K., Subramanian, S. V., Parida, J. K., & Padhi, B. (2015). Regional estimates of poverty and inequality in India, 1993–2012. *Social Indicators Research* (pp. 1–48). Springer.

Commission, Planning. (2014). *Report of the expert group to review the methodology for measurement of poverty*. New Delhi: Government of India.

Dutta, P. V. (2005). *Accounting for wage inequality in India. Indian Journal of Labour Economics*, *48*(2), 273–295.

Haughton, J., & Khandker, S. R. (2009) *Handbook on poverty + inequality*. World Bank Publications.

Jayaraj, D., & Subramanian, S. (2002). Child labour in Tamil Nadu in the 1980s: A preliminary account of its nature, extent and distribution. *Economic and Political Weekly, XXXVIII*(10), 941–954.

Jha, R., & Sharma, A. (2003). Spatial distribution of rural poverty: Last three quinquennial rounds of NSS. *Economic and Political Weekly*, 4985–4993.

Joe, W. (2010). *On measurement and interpretation of health inequalities: An application in Indian context* (Unpublished Ph.D. theses). New Delhi: Centre for Development Studies, Trivandrum, Jawaharlal Nehru University.

Joe, W, & Mishra, U. S. (2009). *On examining health inequalities in Arab countries: Some policy considerations*. Paper presented at XXVI IUSSP International Population Conference, Marrakech, September 27–October 2, 2009.

Mahajan, S. K. (2009). Attainment of human development: A study of North-East India. *Delhi Business Review, 10*(2), 63–71.

Ministry of Development of North Eastern Region and National Eastern Council. (2008). *North Eastern Region vision 2020*. New Delhi: Government of India.

Nair, M., Ravindranath, N. H., Sharma, N., Kattumuri, R., & Munshi, M. (2013). Poverty index as a tool for adaptation intervention to climate change in Northeast India. *Climate and Development, 5*(1), 14–32.

National Institute of Rural Development (NIRD) and North Eastern Regional Center (NERC). (2008). Poverty eradication/alleviation in North East India: An approach–summary report. *The North Eastern Council, Shillong*. http://www.indiaenvironmentportal.org.in/files/Cover_Page9550048814.pdf.

Nayyar, D. (2006). Economic growth in independent India: Lumbering elephant or running tiger? *Economic and Political Weekly, 41*(15), 1451–1458.

Niti, A. (2015). *Comprehensive roadmap for development of Northeastern states and similarly positioned eastern states of Bihar, Jharkhand, Chhatishgarh, Odisha and West Bengal*. New Delhi: Government of India.

NSSO. (2006). *Level and pattern of consumer expenditure*, 2004–05. Report No. 508(61/1.0/1). New Delhi: Ministry of Statistics and Programme Implementation, Government of India.

NSSO. (2013). *Key indicators of household consumer expenditure in India*. (NSS KI 68/1.0). New Delhi: Ministry of Statistics and Programme Implementation, Government of India.

Padhi, B., Mishra, U. S., & Khan, M. K. (2015). Is poverty comparable across varying size of population among Indian states? In A. Heshmati, E. Maasoumi, & G. Wan (Eds.), *Poverty reduction policies and practices in developing Asia*, (pp. 205–215). Asian Development Bank (ADB), Springer.

Rangarajan, C., & Kaul, P. I. (2009). Employment performance of the states. *Money & Finance, 4*(1), 1–16.

Rangarajan, C., Kaul, I., & Seema, S. (2007). Revisiting employment and growth. *ICRA Bulletin-Money & Finance, 3*(2), 57–68.

Ravallion, M. (2002). On the urbanization of poverty. *Journal of Development Economics, 68*(2), 435–442.

Sahu, P. P. (2012). Employment situation in North Eastern Region of India: Recent trends and emerging challenges. In *V. V. Giri National Labour Institue, NLI research studies series, No.* 096/2012.

Shukla, V., & Mishra, U. S. (2014). Is the recent reduction in India's poverty inclusive? *Economic and Political Weekly, XLIX*(47), 70–75.

Srivastav, N., & Dubey, A. (2003). Unemployment in North East India: Some issues. In A. C. Mohapatra & C. R. Pathak (Eds.), *Economic liberalization and regional disparities in India: Special focus on the North-Eastern Region* (pp. 208–220). Shillong: Star Publishing House.

World Bank. (2000). *World Development Report 2000/2001: Attacking Poverty*. Washington, DC: World Bank.

Chapter 12
Deprivation of Women in Northeast India: An Exploratory Study

Papita Dutta

Abstract Deprivation of women is an obstacle in effective human capital formation as well as in determination of future demographic dividend of an economy. Deprivation of women is a multidimensional and context specific issue. This study has attempted to investigate the extent and inequality of some indicators of deprivation of women across the states of northeast India. Female illiteracy rate, Incidence of child marriage, proportional gap of female headed households, workforce non-participation rate for female, rate of crime committed against women are the indicators considered in this study. This study is based on secondary data published by directorates of population census, 2011, and National Crime Records Bureau, 2012. In order to determine the positions of the states in northeast India and to compare them with West Bengal in respect of deprivation of women a weighted deprivation index for women (WDIW) of each state has been developed. We basically follow the Anand and Sen (Concept of human development and poverty: A multidimensional perspectives, UNDP: Background Paper for Human Development Report 1997) methodology for computing indices. Only the relevant principal components of the indicators have been replaced in place of the indicators and weights are generated from Principal Component Analysis (PCA). Atkinson measures of inequality have been applied to gauge the inequality of deprivation of women. This study explores that among the states in northeast India deprivation of women in Meghalaya is least, followed by Nagaland, Mizoram. Assam is the worst in position among the states of northeast India. In contrast to the state of West Bengal all the states of northeast India are better in position in terms of deprivation of Women. However, the states of northeast India are less diverse in terms of multifaceted deprivation of women.

Keywords Child marriage · Crime against women · Female illiteracy
Northeast india · Deprivation of women

P. Dutta (✉)
Gushkara Mahavidyalaya, Burdwan, West Bengal, India
e-mail: pdutta.economics@gmail.com

U.K. De et al. (eds.), *Inequality, Poverty and Development in India*, India Studies in Business and Economics, DOI 10.1007/978-981-10-6274-2_12

12.1 Introduction

Women in India are no doubt a deprived section of total population. Deprivation of women has multiple dimensions in our society. The major dimensions are economic, social and familial. Deprivation of women is an obstacle in effective human capital formation as well as in determination of future demographic dividend of an economy. In recent times, the agendum of reducing deprivation of women has received a deep attention of public policy makers. Thus, the study of intensity and inequality of the deprivation of women is pertinent. The North Eastern part of India covers seven sister states, Arunachal Pradesh, Assam, Manipur, Meghalaya, Mizoram, Nagaland and Tripura, along with the state of Sikkim. There are different communities and each have their own distinct culture and historical context. Majority of the people come under tribal community but no two tribes have the same culture and history. In northeast India, patriarchal system is strong in some states while matrilineal system is also operating in some communities. The feminists claim that socio-economic deprivation of women is a product of patriarchal culture. In this study we want to examine this claim. In the socio-economic spheres, a large section of tribal women work in agriculture. Very few women are employed in non agricultural activities. Here few female have participated in direct politics. Besides, Christianity has contribution to improve education and empowerment of women in northeast India. This chapter examines the nature of deprivation of women across the states in northeast India where socio-cultural environment are heterogeneous.

Remaining part of this study has four sections. Section 2 presents a brief review of relevant literature and the objectives of this study. In Sect. 3 we have defined the indicators of multifaceted deprivation of women. The research methodology of this study has been specified in Sect. 4. We have discussed the empirical findings in Sect. 5. Section 6 concludes this chapter indicating some policy prescription for further development of the women in northeast India.

12.2 Motivation and Objectives

The literature on empowerment or deprivation of women is very old. Feminist advocates of this literature viewed empowerment or deprivation of women as an instinct of development (Rowlands 1995; Prabhu et al. 1996; Kabeer 2001; Tripathi 2011). The economists, who advocate capability approach for development, consider empowerment of women as an instrument of development (Sen 1999; Malhotra et al. 2002; Alsop and Heinsohn 2005). In order to accelerate inclusive development, the economists and governmental authorities in India have recommended the reduction of deprivation, particularly, deprivations of women. In literature we find several gender sensitive indices to gauge impact of gender inequality on human development. For example, Gender-related Development Index (GDI) adjusts the Human Development Index (HDI) for gender inequalities in the three dimensions namely life expectancy, education and income. The Gender Empowerment Measure (GEM) seeks to measure relative women representation in economic and political power. It considers gender gaps in political representation, in professional and management positions in the economy, as well as gender gaps in incomes. These measures show the deprivation of women compared to men. But there is no standard measure that reports the nature of deprivations/achievements of women exclusively. No doubt deprivation of women has multidimensional spheres. Many studies theoretically and empirically developed empowerment index of women. The extent of deprivation of women and its quantification at the state level has been less discussed in literature. Very few studies have tried to examine the deprivation of women in their family, and how far they are given the opportunity to access health facilities and education compared to their male counterparts. With this research gap, we have been motivated to study the intensity and inequality of deprivation of women of the states in northeast India.

The specific objectives of this study are as follows.

First, this study explores the extent of multifaceted deprivation of women of the states in northeast India. In this step a comprehensive index of deprivation of women for each state including West Bengal has been computed.

Second, we have compared the extent of multifaceted deprivation of the states of northeast India with that of the state of West Bengal.

Third, we have examined the nature of inequality across the states in terms of the selected indicators and index of multifaceted deprivation of women.

12.3 Indicators of Multifaceted Deprivation of Women and Data Sources

Deprivation is a multidimensional issue. Deprivation of women may have several dimensions and indicators. The selection of the indicators and weight of the indicators are to some extent context specific. With this end in view, to investigate the intensity and inequality of multifaceted deprivation of women across the states in northeast India we consider the following indicators of multifaceted deprivation of women.

Female illiteracy rate: Illiteracy not only deprives a person from reading and writing, it also has some cumulative and dynamic consequences upon the society. Illiteracy of women reduces employability, social consciousness and empowerment of the women. In long run it may induce child marriage and child labour and even reduce child education. Illiteracy is thus definitely an important indicator of deprivation of women. Illiteracy rate is measured by the percentage of female aged above 6 years, who are unable to read and write.

Incidence of child marriage: Female children are often viewed as burden to the guardian particularly to the poor and unconscious guardians. In most of the cases child marriages take place by the will of the guardian. The unconscious guardians actually deprive their girl children from social and economic points of view. The child marriage is thus a social curse in our society. It has a long term adverse effect on education, health and longevity of the women. Not only that, child marriage stunts growth of personality and self dignity of the women. The incidence of child marriage is measured by the percentage of women aged below 18 years of age who are ever married.

Gap of female headed households: In an ideal society proportion of male and female headed households should be equal. But in our society a low proportion of households are headed by female persons. In patriarchal society men act as the head of the households. Consequently females do not get chance to participate in most of the familial decision making issues. However, in hard times when men are absent or are dead, women take up the role as the households head and they have to take several familial and economic decisions. Moreover, among some communities like Khasi in northeast India matrilineal system is sustaining where female headed households are common till now. We examine whether the status of the women under the matrilineal customs are higher than that of the women living in patriarchal society. So the difference of actual percentage of households headed by females from the fifty is the gap of female headed households. It is an important indicator of deprivation of women in family.

Workforce non-participation rate for female: Nobody would deny that females in our society work hard for their family. It is unfortunate that in Economics this hard work is not treated as economic activity. In accordance with the customs of the society a large number of women take part in household work, sacrificing their own dreams. As a result, active workforce participation of women is low compared to that of men. Therefore, the percentage of women failing to participate in workforce is a real indicator of the multifaceted deprivation of women.

Crime committed against women: Crime committed against women is a crude dimension of deprivation of women. The frequency of domestic violence and outdoor violence against women are hindrances to female emancipation and healthy living. The deaths of women due to violence are not rare in our country. This indicator is used to capture deprivation of freedom of women to live a healthy life. It is shocking to note the report of National Crime Records Bureau 2012, that in the state of Assam 9% of women faced crime while in India as a whole 4.1% of women faced crime in 2012. In this study, number of cognizable crimes committed per thousand female populations has been considered as a measure of crime committed against women.

The indicators individually focus on the deprivation of women from the angle of the particular dimension. One state may be better in position in terms of one indicator and at the same time the state is worse in terms of other indicators. Thus assessment of the deprivation of women taking a single indicator may be misleading. To this end, this study has been designed to compute a comprehensive index for multifaceted deprivation of women. This study is based on secondary data published by directorates of population census, 2011, and National Crime Records Bureau, 2012.

12.4 Methodology

There are different methodologies to compute the index of deprivation at aggregate level. The formula of Human poverty index, developed by Anand and Sen (1997), is suitable to compute the index of multidimensional deprivation for women. The formula for deprivation index for five deprivation indicators under consideration is as follows.

$$\mathrm{SDIW}(\alpha) = \left[\frac{1}{5}\sum_{i=1}^{5} D_i^{\alpha}\right]^{1/\alpha} \tag{12.1}$$

It follows some good properties of an index. This index assumes that all the indicators are equally important. Thereby the weights of the indicators have been considered as equal. However, it is not a realistic assumption. The selection of indicators and their corresponding weight is a vital problem in the construction of an index. In this study we have applied principal component analysis which reduces the number of indicators and guide us to attach the weight to each Principal component (PC) in accordance with their contribution in total variability in the data set. This study has used the eigenvalues as the weight of the PCs. Then the formula for weighted index can be written as follows.

$$\mathrm{WDIW}(\alpha) = \left[\frac{1}{\sum w_i}\sum_{i=1} w_i(\mathrm{PC})_i^{\alpha}\right]^{1/\alpha} \tag{12.2}$$

In formula (12.2) w_i is eigenvalue of ith PC and i is running from 1 to that number of PC for which eigenvalues are greater than one. In this chapter we have applied PCA after taking standardisation of the original indicators and extracted PCs based on Kaiser Normalisation criteria. Thus we estimate two indices for deprivation of women of northeastern states of India. One index has been estimated following formula (12.1), called simple deprivation index of women (SDIW) and other index has been estimated using formula (12.2) which is referred to as weighted deprivation index of women (WDIW). In our analysis we have reported the results after normalisation of the index and assuming $\alpha = 5$.

In order to categorize the states in accordance with its SDIW/WDIW value this study has set three sub-ranges. The high intensity of deprivation of women has been denoted by the range, $\bar{I} + 0.5S < \mathrm{WDIW} \leq 1$. The range $\bar{I} - 0.5S < \mathrm{WDIW} \leq \bar{I} + 0.5S$ indicates moderate intensity of deprivation. The relatively low intensity of deprivation has been specified by the range $0 \leq \mathrm{WDIW} \leq \bar{I} - 0.5S$. Here $\bar{I}$ and S denote mean and standard deviation of deprivation index, respectively.

An attempt has also been taken to gauge the inequality for indicators of deprivation as well as for the indices of deprivation of women. The Gini measure of inequality is not suitable for non-monetary values of the deprivation, because in the case of non-monetary deprivation the value of deprivation indicators are greater for poor and lower for rich. So, we apply Atkinson measures of inequality (Atkinson 1970). The family of Atkinson measure is originated from welfare point of view. It considers normative judgement about social welfare. Considering the additivity and homotheticity assumption in welfare function Atkinson family of inequality measure can be written as follows (Sen 1973).

$$A_{\varepsilon}(x) = 1 - \left[\frac{1}{n}\sum_{i=1}^{n}\left(\frac{x_i}{\mu}\right)^{\varepsilon}\right]^{1/\varepsilon} \quad \text{for } \varepsilon \leq 1 \text{ and } \varepsilon \neq 0$$

$$= 1 - \prod_{i=1}^{n}\left(\frac{x_i}{\mu}\right)^{1/n} \quad \text{for } \varepsilon = 0$$

where ε denotes the inequality aversion parameter, n stands for number of states (9), x_i stands for the ith indicator/index of deprivation. The value of ε ranges from 1 indicating no preference for equality to minus infinite indicating extreme preference for equality. In this study the values of $\varepsilon = 0.5$, 0 and -1 have been considered for measuring inequality of the indicators and indices under consideration.

12.5 Empirical Results and Discussion

Sex ratio is the primary indicator of women status in a specific zone. The Fig. 12.1 shows the sex ratio across the states in northeast India. In terms of overall sex ratio, women are most deprived in the state of Sikkim and least deprived in Meghalaya.

The sex ratio of the old age people is higher than 1000 in India as well as in the state of West Bengal, Meghalaya, Tripura and Manipur. It indicates that the longevity of women is greater than that of men or 60 years back there were very little problem of 'missing girls' among the people in these states. In respect of child sex ratios, northeastern states are in better position compared to India as a whole. The states of northeast India, except Manipur and Nagaland, are better than West Bengal. In the index of deprivation we did not include sex ratio as it is not an indicator of direct deprivation of existing women. Besides, regarding sex ratio there is a little variation across the states under consideration.

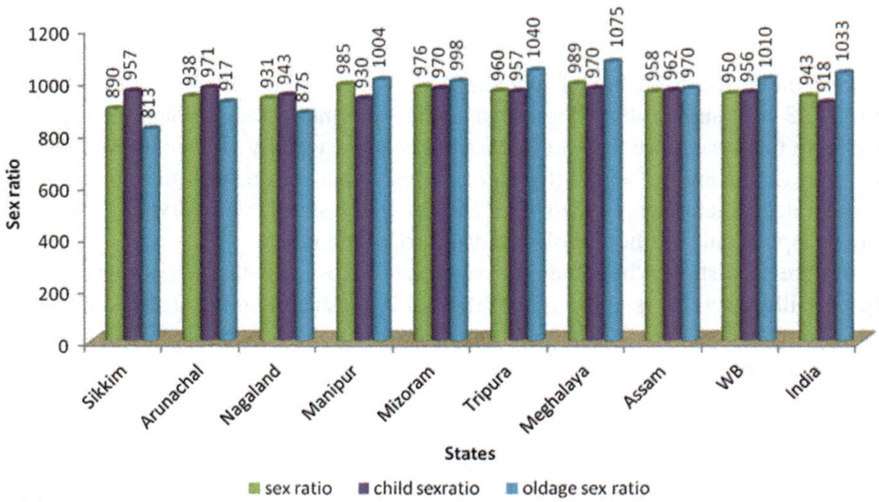

Fig. 12.1 Sex ratio of the states in northeast India. (*Source* Drawn based on census data 2011)

Fig. 12.2 Incidence of child marriage across the states in northeast India. (*Source* Drawn based on census data 2011)

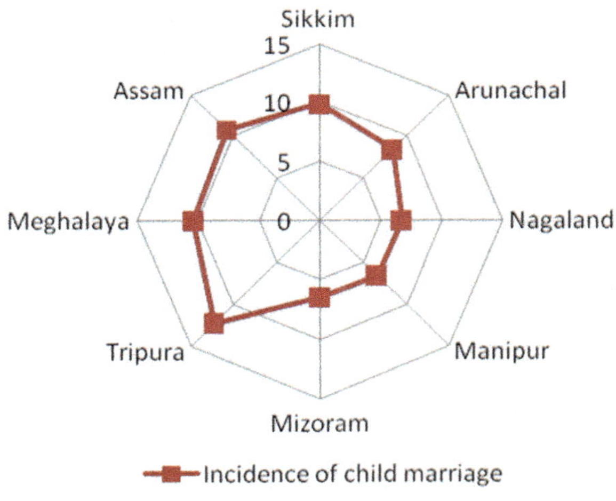

Figure 12.2 presents the incidence of child marriage across the states in northeast India. The incidence of child marriage is highest in the state of Tripura followed by Assam, Meghalaya and Sikkim which are in second last radar. The curse of child marriage is relatively low in the state of Mizoram. In spite of the existence of the matrilineal system, child marriage in Meghalaya is not below 10%. However, in contrast to West Bengal, where incidence child marriage is 13%, all the states in northeast states are better off in this respect.

Unlike many Indian states, Meghalaya, particularly Khasi-Jaintia and Garo societies, have historically followed a matrilineal system. In this customs the ancestry and inheritance are traced through women. The youngest daughter inherits all wealth and she also takes care of her parents. Therefore, households are controlled under the headship of women. This is transmitted in the census data. In Fig. 12.3 it is shown that Meghalaya is distinct among the northeastern states in India. In this state more than 30% households are headed by women. Other states of northeast India are far behind the state of Meghalaya with respect to female headed households. Again compared to West Bengal all the states come forward in terms of giving opportunity of household headship to women.

Figure 12.4 shows the female illiteracy rate across the states in northeast India. Female illiteracy rate is highest in Arunachal Pradesh among the states followed by Assam, Manipur. Female illiteracy rate is lowest in Mizoram, where 90% women are literate, preceded by Tripura. However, there is wide variation across the states regarding female literacy rate. It is pertinent to note that female literacy rate of all the states in northeast India is higher than that of West Bengal.

Figure 12.5 shows the non-participation rate of women in workforce. In Assam the non-participation is highest followed by Tripura. Among the states in northeast India and India as a whole workforce participation rate for women (52.3%) is highest in the state of Nagaland. The gap between women and men workforce participation rates is lowest in Nagaland among the states in India (Census 2011). Thus women of Nagaland are least deprived of getting enter into workforce. It is again found that the workforce participation for women in West Bengal is lower than any state in northeast India. Moreover, women participation in workforce of the states except Assam and Tripura in North East India are higher than that of Indian average. As per Census 2011, women workforce participation rate in India is 25.51% against 53.26% for males. Women participation in work force is lower than male participation because most of the women are engaged either in unpaid work or in informal sector. They also face significant wage differentials in comparison with their male counterparts.

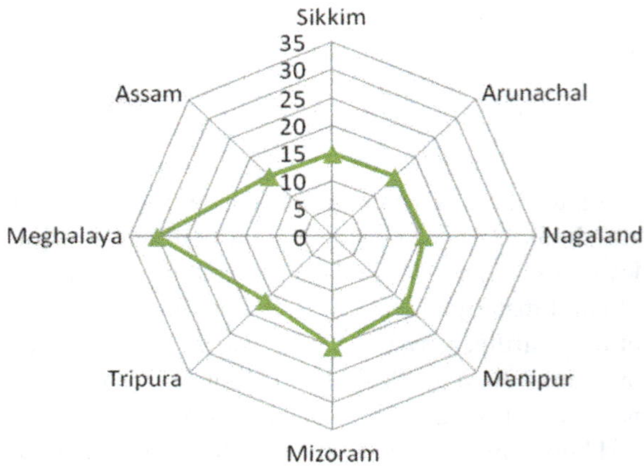

Fig. 12.3 Female headed households across the states in northeast India. (*Source* Drawn based on census data 2011)

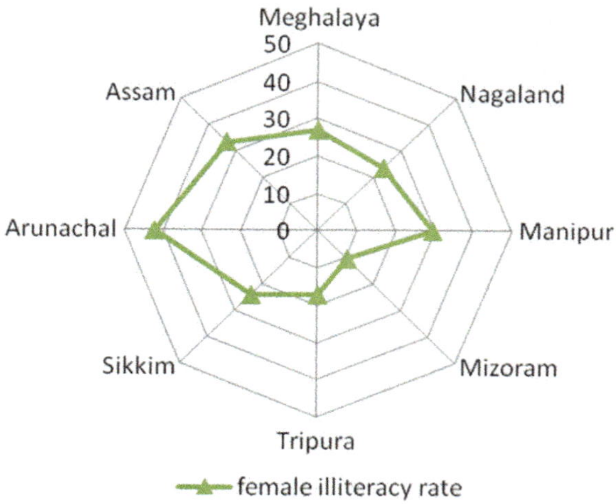

Fig. 12.4 Female illiteracy rate across the states in northeast India. (*Source* Drawn based on census data 2011)

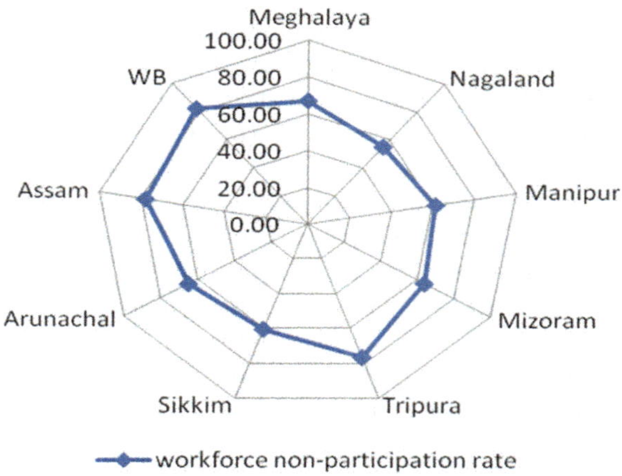

Fig. 12.5 Workforce non-participation of women across the States in northeast India. (*Source* Drawn based on census data 2011)

In Fig. 12.6 it is observed that regarding the phenomenon of crime against women there is wide variation across the states in North–East India. The total of cognizable crimes during 2012 varies from 89 women per thousand in Assam to 5 per thousand women in Nagaland. The incidence of total cognizable crimes includes reported indoor and outdoor violence against women. However, the figures include only the reported cases. Thus actual incidence of crime would be higher than the figures reported. The statistics of crime against women focus that a large number of women in the states of Assam and Tripura are not physically and mentally safe.

Uni-dimensional discussion of deprivation of women demonstrates that in respect of longevity reflected in sex ratio and in respect of the access to ancestor's physical asset and control over the household decision captured by female headed households women in the state of Meghalaya are least deprived among the states

Fig. 12.6 Incidences of crimes against women across the states in northeast India. (*Source* Drawn based on census data 2011)

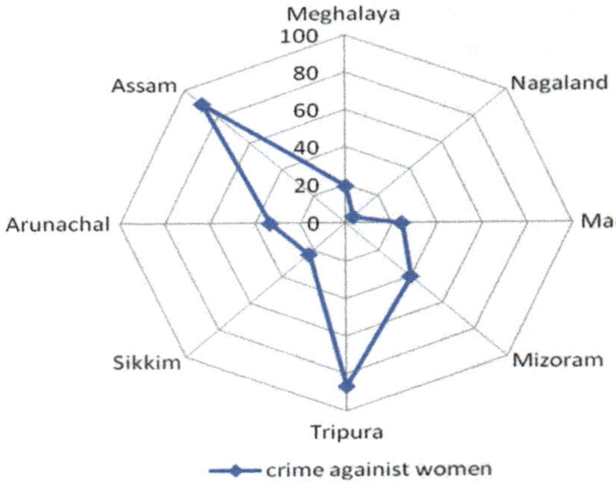

under study. The women in the state of Mizoram compared to other states are come forward in respect of the access to education and getting marriage at a higher age. The deprivations of women in workforce participation and in terms of violence are lowest in Nagaland among the all states and UTs in India. Therefore, from the uni-dimensional analysis we cannot determine the position of the states in accordance with the deprivation of women.

With this end in view we have computed a comprehensive index of deprivation for women considering the above mentioned indicators. In this index weights are determined by Principal Component Analysis (PCA). Table 12.1 shows the appropriateness of the PCA for the data set. The KMO measure of sample adequacy and Sphericity test support the application of PCA in our data set.

Table 12.2 presents the result of PCA of the data set. It shows that two components are much important to present the variation of the data ser of the indicators of deprivation of women. The first component explains 59% of total variation while the second component explains 21% of total variation in the data set.

Before going to compute weighted deprivation index for women of the states in northeast India we have presented the descriptive statistics of the indicators and Indices in Table 12.3.

Table 12.4 demonstrates the position of the states in northeast India along with the state of West Bengal. In accordance with the value of simple deprivation index

Table 12.1 Appropriateness test of principal component analysis

KMO and Bartlett's Test		
Kaiser-Meyer-Olkin Measure (KMO) of Sampling Adequacy. (sample will be adequate if the value is greater than 0.5)		0.543
Bartlett's test of sphericity	Approx. Chi-square	24.495
	df	10
	Sig.	0.006

Source Author's computation

Table 12.2 Results of PCA of the indicators of deprivation of women

Total variance explained						
Component	Initial eigenvalues			Extraction sums of squared loadings		
	Total	% of variance	Cumulative (%)	Total	% of variance	Cumulative (%)
1	2.930	58.607	58.607	2.930	58.607	58.607
2	1.031	20.613	79.220	1.031	20.613	79.220
3	0.880	17.603	96.823			
4	0.123	2.467	99.290			
5	0.035	0.710	100.000			

Extraction method Principal component analysis.

Source Author's computation

Table 12.3 Descriptions of the indicators of deprivation of women in northeast India

Indicator (%)	Mean	Median	SD	CV	Max	Min
Incidence of child marriage	9.43	9.86	2.52	26.72	13.32	6.50
Lack of female headed families	32.19	34.29	4.95	15.37	35.25	19.77
Female Illiteracy rate	27.98	27.11	10.60	37.88	42.62	10.73
Non-worker force participation	67.64	64.56	8.99	13.29	81.92	55.26
Incidence of crime against women	4.36	3.36	3.09	71.01	8.95	0.47
SDIW	53.23	48.57	11.34	21.30	70.41	40.87
WDIW	0.573	0.595	0.284	49.65	0.950	0.110

Source Author's computation

measured following Anand and Sen (1997) we see that deprivation of women is highest in Assam among the states in northeast India including West Bengal followed by Tirupur West Bengal and Meghalaya. The composite deprivation is least in the state of Nagaland. However, in this methodology we have attached equal weight with the indicators. However, all indicators are not equally important in overall deprivation of women. For example, deprivation of ancestor's wealth is definitely more important compared to education and child marriage. Again, access to inherited property may reduce the incidence of domestic violence, deprivation to participation in household's decision and illiteracy. So the indicators are highly correlated. It makes difficulty to determine the relative importance of the indicators. Here we determined the relative importance with the help of PCA as specified in methodology section.

Now we discuss the position of the states under study in accordance with the weighted deprivation indices. This study explores that among the states in northeast India women's deprivation in Meghalaya is least, preceded by Nagaland, Mizoram. In respect of women's deprivation, Assam is the worst in position among the states

Table 12.4 Weighted deprivation index for the women in northeast India

State	SDIW	Rank	WDIW	Rank
West Bengal	64.55	3	0.950	1
Assam	70.41	1	0.770	2
Sikkim	44.52	8	0.732	4
Arunachal Pradesh	48.57	5	0.714	3
Tripura	68.65	2	0.595	5
Manipur	45.2	7	0.583	6
Mizoram	47.35	6	0.583	7
Nagaland	40.87	9	0.119	8
Meghalaya	48.94	4	0.110	9

Source Author's computation

in northeast India. However, in contrast to the state of West Bengal all the states in northeast India are better in position in terms of women's deprivation. Only two states namely Meghalaya and Nagaland have low level intensity of deprivation of women. However, these two states are most deprived in accordance with the multidimensional poverty (Bagli 2015). The women of Tripura, Manipur and Mizoram have almost same level of deprivation and they are belonging to moderate range of deprivation. The average deprivation of the women is at high level in the states of Assam, Sikkim and Arunachal Pradesh (Table 12.5).

We see that as the preference for equality becomes stronger the value inequality measure (Atkinson measure) becomes stronger. In accordance with the all measures under consideration the inequality across the states for the WDIW is higher than that for the SDIW of the states. Among the indicators of deprivation, the inequality in crime against women across the districts is the highest for all measures. The inequality for non-participation in workforce is least across the states for each measure of inequality. Moreover, extents of inequalities are low but different across the indicators under consideration. Almost all the values of inequality measure are less than 0.3. Thus the states of northeast India are less diverse in terms of multifaceted deprivation of women.

Table 12.5 Inequality of the deprivation indices and its indicators across the states in northeast India

Indicators/Indices	A (0.5)	A (0)	A (−1)
Incidence of child marriage	0.016	0.032	0.064
Lack of female headed families	0.006	0.013	0.030
Female illiteracy rate	0.035	0.073	0.156
Non-worker force participation	0.004	0.008	0.015
Incidence of crime against women	0.123	0.259	0.530
SDIW	0.010	0.019	0.036
WDIW	0.077	0.184	0.430

Source Author's computation

12.6 Concluding Remarks

This study, therefore, reveals that women of the state of Meghalaya and Nagaland are more empowered compared to the women of other states. On the other hand, women of the states of Assam, Sikkim and Arunachal Pradesh are most deprived relative to the other states. So far the inequality across the states is not very strong in respect of deprivation of women. However, the women of all the states of northeast India are less deprived compared to the women in West Bengal. It may be true that matrilineal system within Khasi-Jaintia and Garo societies is helpful for preventing women from deprivation. As in this system women enjoy inheritance of family assets and wealth, they are empowered persons in the family and in the community. However, in other states like Assam where in most of the cases sons of the family inherit family assets and wealth; consequently, women are suffering from more deprivation. Therefore, equal right of male and female in family wealth should be implemented more strongly. This not only empowers the women within household, it also improves their status outside the family. It is a good instrument to reduce the violence against women, because, a large number of domestic violence occurs due to dowry or wealth. Besides, we have to emphasise on the accessibility of education for women across the states in an equitable basis. It is reported that NABARD and local governments have already taken several initiatives for skill development of women. The government should extend more and more skill development programmes for women across the states in northeast India. It will increase the employability of the women and prevent the women from the curse of child marriage.

So far, the deprivation of women may vary according to ones religion, caste and financial condition or may be different from district to district. This study did not encompass the range of all these matters in the study of inequality and intensity of deprivation of the women in northeast India. Therefore, for formulating appropriate decentralised planning for alleviating deprivation of women, area specific micro level study is needed.

References

Alsop, R., & Heinsohn, N. (2005). Measuring empowerment in practice: Structuring analysis and framing indicators. *World Bank Policy Research Working Paper 3510*, February 2005.

Anand, S., & Sen, A. K. (1997). *Concept of human development and poverty: A multidimensional perspectives*. UNDP: Background Paper for Human Development Report.

Atkinson, A. B. (1970). On measurement of inequality. *Journal of Economic Theory, 2*(3), 244–263.

Bagli, S. (2015). *A study of multidimensional poverty in North–East India*. Paper prepared for National Seminar on Poverty and Inequality with special Emphasis on North East India to be held at NEHU, India during October 8–11, 2015.

Government of India. (2011). *Population Census Report*, 2011. Registrar General of India.

Government of India. (2012). *Crime in India 2012 statistics*. National Crime Records Bureau Ministry of Home Affairs. Retrieved from http://ncrb.gov.in.

Kabeer, N. (2001). Resource, agency, achievement: Reflections on the measurement of women's empowerment, in 'discussing women's empowerment–Theory and practice. In A. Sisask (ed) *SIDA Studies* (No. 3, pp. 17–57). Stockholm: Novum Grafiska, AB.

Molhotra, A., Sidney, R. S., & Boender, C. B. (2002). Measuring women's empowerment as a variable in international development. *The Gender and Development Group of the World Bank and the World Bank's Social Development Group*, pp. 1–47. Retrieved From: www.aed.org/LeadershipandDemocracy/upload/MeasuringWomen.pdf.

Prabhu S. K., Sarker, P. C., & Radha, A. (1996). Gender-related development index for Indian states: Methodological issues. *Economic and Political Weekly*, 31(43), ws72–ws79.

Rowlands, J. (1995). Empowerment examined. *Development in Practice, 5*(2), 101–107.

Sen, A. (1973). *On economic inequality*. Oxford: Oxford University Press.

Sen, A. (1999). *Development as freedom*. Oxford: Oxford University Press.

Tripathi, T. (2011). *Women's empowerment: Concept and empirical evidence from India*. Paper presented in a National Seminar, Delhi School of Economics, Retrieved from: www.ededse.org/ws2011/papers/Tulika%20Tripathti.pdf.

Chapter 13
Levels of Living in the North Eastern States of India

Anika M.W. Kshiar Shadap

Abstract This chapter attempts to examine the levels of living and assess the disparities across the states in the North Eastern Region (NER) of India. It also discusses the changes in the levels of living over the years. Data from varied sources like the National Sample Surveys on consumer expenditure and employment and unemployment, the Census of India and the National Family Health Surveys have been used. The level of living has been measured by a wide range of indicators like employment, per capita consumption expenditure, nutritional intake, educational attainment, demographic structure, literacy rates, household amenities, consumer durables and summary health indicators. In this chapter, each of these indicators have been presented, discussed and have also been combined into a composite index called the standard-of-living index. For comparative purposes, the analysis in the chapter is carried out for each of the eight states in NER and also for the all India average. The study covers a period of about 20 years from 1991 to 2012. Results for rural and urban areas have been presented separately. The chapter highlights the disparities in the NER and underscores the fact that development has mostly bypassed the rural areas.

Keywords Levels of living · North–East india · Standard of living index

13.1 Introduction

The North Eastern Region (NER) of India comprises eight states of Arunachal Pradesh, Assam, Meghalaya, Manipur, Mizoram, Nagaland, Tripura and Sikkim. This region is isolated from the rest of India and is connected only through the very narrow Siliguri Corridor which is just about 20 km wide. It is surrounded by International borders with China in the north and north–east, Bhutan and Nepal in the north–west, Myanmar in the south and south–east and Bangladesh in the south–

A.M.W. Kshiar Shadap (✉)
St. Edmund's College, Shillong, India
e-mail: anika_kshiar@yahoo.com

U.K. De et al. (eds.), *Inequality, Poverty and Development in India*, India Studies in Business and Economics, DOI 10.1007/978-981-10-6274-2_13

west. The north eastern region is rich and varied in its topography, flora and fauna, cultures, languages etc.

In spite of the fact that there is abundance and a variety of natural resources, yet the region experiences a lot of challenges 'in terms of delivery of services and access to growth opportunities' (GOI 2011b). The region has been doing well in the various indicators of Human Development Index as has been mentioned in the Human Development Report of the North Eastern States that the Ministry of DONER has brought out in 2011. However the report continues to say that when we delve deeper and beyond the HDI, we see the reality of the region. For example, even though the region has high production of fruits and vegetables yet states like Assam, Tripura and Sikkim have very high incidence of anaemia among women. There is also high Maternal Mortality Rate in Assam and high dropout rates in six of the North Eastern states. In a way all these statistics show that the NER still has miles to go in its quest for development. We also see that a lot of efforts are made by the centre through various schemes for the development of the region. Some of the problems faced by the NER which may be mentioned are unemployment, inadequate infrastructure especially with regard to transport and communication, unfavourable location in the sense making it inaccessible, insurgency (Sengupta 2007), immigration (Sen 2008; Dutta 2010), etc. We can say that the problems of growth and development here are different from what the rest of the country is facing. We also find that there is heavy dependence on agriculture as we note that around 60% of workers in the NER are employed in the agricultural sector (Sahu 2012) and so it means that the secondary and tertiary sectors have not developed that much. Development seems to be concentrated only in the main town areas and going just a few kilometres away from them, we see the reality of underdevelopment.

We also find that the North–East is better than the all-India average, in terms of some human development indicators yet majority of the population are marginalized and they find themselves excluded from the benefits of development. It was found that the urban sector has greater access to various facilities than the rural sector, be it the health facilities, educational facilities, transport facilities or even the basic amenities like supply of drinking water, supply of electricity, etc. (GOI 2011a, b). There are a lot of regional disparities when it comes to socio-economic development of the North-Eastern states even though the government tries to bring about balanced regional development (Dutta 2010) as can be seen in the development goals of the government.

This chapter attempts to examine the levels of living and assess the disparities across the states in the NER of India. We would like to examine and see if the levels of living have remained the same or has changed over a period of about 20 years. This chapter also tries to rank the North Eastern states according to their level of performance in the various indicators taken in this study using a composite index called the Standard of Living Index. We have tried to formulate our own index because it gives us the freedom to include more indicators of level of living than what the HDI or the PQLI would.

13.2 Data and Methodology

Data

The data are drawn basically from two rounds of the National Sample Survey on consumer expenditure and employment and unemployment, i.e. 50th round (1993–94) and 68th round (2011–12).

We have also used the census data of 2001 and 2011.

Apart from these, data from National Family Health Surveys are also used.

Methodology

In this analysis we consider the eight states of the North Eastern Region of India namely Arunachal Pradesh, Assam, Meghalaya, Manipur, Mizoram, Nagaland, Tripura and Sikkim.

In this chapter we have compared the level of living of the people of the north eastern states. Since there are many indicators of level of living and it would be impossible to study each and every indicator, this study will focus only on a few indicators of levels of living like the conditions of the houses that people occupy, the kinds of occupations that they are engaged in, the educational attainment, the head count ratio, the per capita total expenditure per day and the per capita calorie intake per day. We have compared these indicators across states and sectors (i.e. rural and urban) and also with the all India scenario to see where each state stands. In order to make the comparison more simple and understandable we have constructed a simple index for each of the indicators. This way, we will be able to rank each state according to their performance in each of the indicators. We will also be taking the average of all the indices which will be called the 'Standard of Living Index'. Using this composite index, we will rank the states in order of their level of living.

Concepts

Level of Living: Level of living is a measure of the consumption of goods and services by an individual or group or it is the level of wealth, comfort, material goods and necessities available to a certain socio-economic class of society.

Standard of Living Index: The Standard of Living Index is found out by first calculating the dimension index which was done for each indicator considered in this chapter. For the construction of the index, the methodology used is that followed by the UNDP while calculating the Human Development Index (UNDP 1990). This may be mentioned as follows:

$$\text{Dimension index} = \frac{\text{actual value} - \text{minimum value}}{\text{maximum value} - \text{minimum value}}$$

The maximum and minimum values used for each indicator while constructing the index are given in Table 13.1.

Table 13.1 Maximum and minimum values of indicators of levels of living

Indicators	Maximum	Minimum
Proportion of good houses	100	0
Proportion of graduates	100	0
Proportion of non-poor	100	0
Calorie intake	2503	1703
Workers in non-elementary occupation	100	0
Per capita total expenditure	1768	542

After the dimension index has been found for each of the indicators mentioned above, we have found the average of all these indices to get the 'Standard of Living Index'.

13.2.1 Poverty

The Head Count Ratio (HCR) is the simplest measure of poverty. It measures the proportion of a population living below the poverty line. If Q is the number of people that live below the poverty line and N is the population then:

$$\mathrm{HCR} = Q/N * 100$$

The poverty line used in this chapter is based on, the Report of the Expert Group headed by S. Tendulkar, which reviewed the methodology for estimation of poverty (GOI 2009). This poverty estimate is based on the Mixed Reference period (MRP) where the recall period is over 365 days for lower frequency consumption goods (like clothing, footwear, etc.) and 30 days for higher frequency consumption goods (like food). This is unlike the old method where the Uniform Reference Period (URP) of 30 days was used.

13.2.2 Calorie Intake

The Planning Commission has taken 2400 (rural) and 2100 kcal (urban) as the minimum daily calorie consumption requirement. However, recently the Planning Commission (2012), has reduced the daily calorie requirement per person per day to only 1770 kcal based on the recommendation of Food and Agriculture Organisation (FAO 2004).

The normative calorie consumption for Indians as given by the ICMR differentiates between men and women. The recommended calorie requirement for a man (weighing 60 kg) doing sedentary work is 2425 kcal, for one doing moderate work, it is 2875 kcal and for one doing heavy work, it is 3800 kcal. On the other hand the calorie requirement for a woman (weighing 50 kg) is 1875, 2225 and 2925 kcal for those doing sedentary, moderate and heavy work respectively.

13.2.3 Per Capita Total Expenditure

The consumer expenditure of a household is the sum total of monetary values of all the goods and services, consumed by the household on domestic account during the reference period. Per Capita Total Expenditure (PCTE) is the household consumer expenditure over a period of 30 days divided by household size i.e. it is the monthly per capita expenditure per person per day (GOI 1993, 2011a). In this chapter, we have deflated the current values of the PCTE at 2004–05 constant prices by the following process. The deflator was found by using the formula,

$$\text{deflator} = \frac{\text{OPL}_{\text{current year}}}{\text{OPL}_{\text{base year}}}$$

where, base year considered here is 2004–05 and OPL, is the official poverty line.

After the deflator has been generated, the deflated PCTE was found by using the following formula,

$$\text{PCTE}_{\text{at 2004–05 prices}} = \frac{\text{PCTE}_{\text{current year}}}{\text{deflator}}$$

13.2.4 Condition of Houses

We consider three types of conditions that the houses according to the Census, may be classified under—good, liveable and dilapidated. 'Good' is considered to be the house in a better condition while 'dilapidated' is when the house is in a worse condition.

13.2.5 Main Source of Income

The NSSO classifies the households by their main source of income (GOI 1993, 2011a). It finds out where 50% or more of the income of a particular household come from. When there are multiple sources of income available and none of these sources account for 50% or more of the income of a particular household, then the source of income is classified as 'mixed'.

The main sources of income of the population in the rural sector are classified as self-employed in non-agricultural activities, agricultural labour, other kinds of labour, self-employed in agriculture and mixed sources of income. The main sources of income of the population in the urban sector are classified as self-employed, regular wage or salaried employee, casual labour, and mixed source of income.

13.2.6 Educational Attainment

In this section, we have not gone into the details of the levels of education attained by the population aged 15 years and above. We have only considered two groups, those who are illiterate and those who have received higher education i.e. graduates and above.

13.2.7 Occupation

We have divided the population into two groups, those engaged in elementary occupation and those engaged in non-elementary occupation. Elementary occupation would refer to those occupations where no skill is required by the workers or labourers employed. On the other hand non-elementary occupation refers to those occupations where some skill is required by the workers employed. When people are engaged in non-elementary occupation, they would be paid higher wages than those engaged in elementary occupation. In the tables describing 'occupation', we have only found out the percentage of people engaged in non-elementary occupation since those that do not fall in this category would fall in the category of elementary occupation.

13.3 Analysis

In this section, we will discuss and analyse the results on the various variables discussed in Sect. 13.2.

13.3.1 Head Count Ratio

In Table 13.2, we have presented the proportion of the population that is poor in the 50th NSS (1993–94) round and the 68th NSS (2011–12) round.

We see that poverty, as measured by the head count ratio, has decreased over the time period 1993–94 to 2011–12 from 45.30 to 21.92% respectively, at the All

Table 13.2 Head count ratio by state and sector in 1993–94 and 2011–12

State	1993–94			2011–12		
	Rural	Urban	Total	Rural	Urban	Total
Arunachal Pradesh	60.00	22.60	54.50	38.93	20.33	34.67
Assam	54.90	27.70	51.80	33.89	20.49	31.98
Manipur	64.40	67.20	65.10	38.80	32.59	36.89
Meghalaya	38.00	23.00	35.20	12.53	9.26	11.87
Mizoram	16.60	6.30	11.80	35.43	6.36	20.40
Nagaland	20.10	21.80	20.40	19.93	16.48	18.88
Sikkim	33.00	20.40	31.80	9.85	3.66	8.19
Tripura	34.30	25.40	32.90	16.53	7.42	14.05
All India	50.10	31.80	45.30	25.70	13.70	21.92

Source GOI (2009 p. 18 and 2013 p. 6)

India level. Among the states we see that poverty has decreased in seven states but has increased only in the case of Mizoram.

In 1993–94, poverty among the north eastern states was highest in Manipur with 65.10% which was higher than the all-India average of 45.30% and lowest in Mizoram with 11.80%. On the other hand, in 2011–12, Manipur still had the highest poverty ratio at 36.89% which was once again higher than the all India average of 21.92% and it was lowest in Sikkim with 8.19%.

It is also seen that in the state of Mizoram the poverty ratio has almost doubled to 20.40% in 2011–12 from 11.80% in 1993–94. On the other hand the state of Manipur which had the highest poverty ratio in 1993–94 at 65.10% has declined by almost half in 2011–12 to 36.89% but is still the state with the highest poverty ratio in the north east. Except for the states of Manipur, Meghalaya and Sikkim, we do not see drastic changes in the poverty ratio in the other states.

When we look at the rural-urban break up we see that there is greater percentage of the population living below the poverty line in the rural sector than the urban sector in the NER in both the rounds of the survey.

Over the two decades, disparities in the urban and rural sectors, was seen to be high in some states and very low in some other states. In 1993–94, the highest disparity in the poverty ratios was seen in Arunachal Pradesh (around 37 percentage points) and Assam (around 27 percentage points). It was found to be lower in the other states. However we see that two states, Manipur and Nagaland exhibit higher poverty ratios in the urban sector compared to all the other states that show poverty ratios to be higher in the rural sector.

In 2011–12, on the other hand, we see that disparities have decreased in most of the states, as well as at the all-India level. However, we see an increase in disparity in case of Manipur, Nagaland and Mizoram. It is also seen that Mizoram has shown a huge increase in disparity from around 10 percentage points in 1993–94 to around 30 percentage points in 2011–12.

13.3.2 Nutritional Intake in Terms of Calories

When we study the calorie intake, we will be looking at the per capita calorie intake per day. Let us consider Table 13.3 that show us the calorie intake per day in each of the states of the North East.

In 1993–94, Nagaland has the highest per capita calorie consumption of 2191 kcal which is higher than the national average of 2134 kcal while Sikkim has the lowest per capita consumption of only 1909 kcal which is much lower than the national average. However in the 68th round we see that the state having highest per capita calorie consumption is no longer Nagaland but is Tripura with 2259 kcal per day. This is higher than the national average of 2089 kcal. The lowest calorie consumption among all the states in the country is Meghalaya (which happens to be one of the north eastern states) with only 1703 kcal. The calorie consumption in case of Meghalaya has been declining. This is not only lower than the national average but also lesser than the normative calorie requirement as recommended by the ICMR and the minimum calorie requirement of 1770 calories as recommended by the Planning Commission in 2012.

On the other hand, if we consider the trend of calorie consumption over the time period considered i.e. 1993–94 to 2011–12, we notice that there has been a decline in nutritional intake in terms of calorie consumption in the states of Arunachal Pradesh, Manipur, Meghalaya, Mizoram and Nagaland. An increase in nutritional intake was seen only in the case of Assam, Sikkim, Tripura, as well as at the All India level.

When we consider the rural-urban break up, we notice that in most of the states in the NER, there is higher calorie consumption in the urban sector than in the rural sector both in 1993–94 and 2011–12. Considering the occupation of majority of the people is in agriculture, it would be expected that calorie consumption should be

Table 13.3 Per capita calorie intake per day by state and sector in 1993–94 and 2011–12

State	1993–94			2011–12		
	Rural	Urban	Total	Rural	Urban	Total
Arunachal Pradesh	2132	2509	2176	1880	2088	1921
Assam	1983	2108	1996	2011	2040	2014
Manipur	2157	2071	2133	1978	1919	1962
Meghalaya	1977	2066	1990	1688	1757	1703
Mizoram	2111	2201	2139	2041	2172	2101
Nagaland	2199	2169	2191	1909	1982	1935
Sikkim	1892	2110	1909	2018	1964	2009
Tripura	1925	2040	1941	2259	2259	2259
All India	2153	2077	2134	2101	2060	2089

Source Special tabulation by the author using unit record data collected by the NSSO on Consumer Expenditure during the 50th round (1993–94) and the 68th round (2011–12)

higher in the rural sector. Of course there are a few exceptions in the case of Manipur and Nagaland in 1993–94 and Manipur and Sikkim in 2011–12. At the all India level, both the rounds have shown that there is higher calorie intake in the rural sector and not in the urban sector.

13.3.3 Per Capita Total Expenditure

Let us consider the following table where we consider the PCTE of each of the states in the NER and the all India average.

With regard to the per capita total expenditure we notice that there are some states in the NER, like Meghalaya, Mizoram, Nagaland and Tripura, have higher PCTE values than the National Average as seen in 1993–94. However in 2011–12 it was seen that only Arunachal Pradesh, Mizoram and Nagaland have higher PCTE than the national average (Table 13.4). In 1993–94, we see that the state with the highest PCTE was Nagaland with Rs. 779/- which was higher than the national average of Rs. 585/- and the lowest PCTE was that of Assam which was only Rs. 471/-. In 2011–12, once again we see that the state with the highest PCTE was Nagaland with Rs. 1108/- which was higher than the national average of Rs. 900/- and the state with the lowest PCTE was Assam with only Rs. 665/-.

When we consider the PCTE by the rural-urban break up we see that there was higher expenditure in the urban sector than the rural sector among more or less all states over the last two decades. We see that over the two decades there has been an improvement in the PCTE both at the state level and the national level. This comparison is possible because the values are at constant prices of 2004–05.

Table 13.4 Per capita total expenditure by state and sector in 1993–94 and 2011–12 (at 2004–05 prices)

State	1993–94			2011–12		
	Rural	Urban	Total	Rural	Urban	Total
Arunachal Pradesh	528.46	879.67	570.08	947.95	1114.38	980.64
Assam	431.14	817.83	470.56	624.27	1017.56	665.35
Manipur	501.22	570.12	520.05	702.04	699.90	701.47
Meghalaya	596.00	946.06	644.11	774.60	1084.05	839.75
Mizoram	650.70	980.25	754.84	804.06	1164.08	970.34
Nagaland	732.76	907.10	779.30	1051.80	1210.73	1107.99
Sikkim	497.69	924.79	531.74	845.37	1073.69	885.04
Tripura	572.74	873.68	612.81	674.22	943.35	715.76
All India	489.41	874.24	585.14	716.63	1361.80	900.97

Source As in Table 13.3

13.3.4 Condition of Residential Houses

This category of data has been taken for the census of 2001 and 2011. It was not possible to use the census of 1991 because the data available is not comparable with the data in census 2011. The condition of houses is another indicator of level of living. In the following tables we see the proportion of people living in good, liveable and dilapidated houses. The better the housing conditions the better will be the level of living.

As far as the Census of 2001 (Table 13.5) is concerned, we notice that majority of the houses can be categorised as 'good' or 'liveable' houses, with a very small percentage of the houses in 'dilapidated' condition. When we distinguish between rural and urban sector, we see that there are differences in the condition of the houses that people live in. Majority of the houses in the rural sector are 'liveable' houses with a slightly lesser percentage in 'good' condition. In the urban sector, however we find that majority of the houses are in 'good' condition while a lower percentage are in 'liveable' condition. Therefore it can be said that in terms of condition of residential houses, the urban sector has better houses compared to rural sector.

However it may be mentioned that while all the states in NER and the all India average show that about the same percentage of houses can be classified as either 'good' or 'liveable' houses and only a relatively smaller percentage i.e. less than 7.5% of the houses are in 'dilapidated' condition. In case of Assam, on the other hand, we notice that the majority of the houses are classified as 'liveable', a smaller percentage classified as 'good' while around 10% of the houses are in 'dilapidated' condition. Mizoram seems to be having a better level of living in terms of this indicator as we see that just less than 2% of houses are in 'dilapidated' conditions while the rest of the houses are in 'good' or 'liveable' condition.

It may be concluded from Table 13.5, that people in the NER are not suffering from chronic poverty in terms of the condition of the houses they live in.

When we consider the census of 2011 (Table 13.6), we see that the percentage of good houses has increased across states and at the all India level over the census of 2001. The majority of houses in both the rural and the urban sectors are classified as 'good'. We also notice that in this census, Mizoram has the highest percentage of 'good' houses at 62.32% while Assam has the lowest with only 32.81%. In all the other states, more than 48% of houses are in 'good' condition. However, we still see that there is an exception only in the case of Assam where the majority of the houses, i.e. 56.63%, can be classified as 'liveable' while in all other states, majority of the houses are in 'good' condition. Again while at the national average 5.39% of houses can still be classified as 'dilapidated', in Assam, the figure is double at around 10.90%. We also see that the state with the lowest percentage of 'dilapidated' houses is Nagaland and not Mizoram as was the case in 2001.

Table 13.5 Percentage distribution of houses by their condition in 2001

State	Rural			Urban			Total		
	Good	Liveable	Dilapidated	Good	Liveable	Dilapidated	Good	Liveable	Dilapidated
Arunachal Pradesh	43.03	54.29	2.68	55.39	39.82	4.79	45.83	51.00	3.16
Assam	24.42	64.68	10.90	51.96	41.47	6.57	28.36	61.36	10.28
Manipur	41.38	53.86	4.77	62.14	34.12	3.74	46.58	48.91	4.51
Meghalaya	35.95	58.12	5.93	60.96	34.57	4.46	41.28	53.10	5.62
Mizoram	43.28	54.12	2.60	59.23	39.72	1.05	51.31	46.87	1.82
Nagaland	40.98	56.25	2.77	49.88	45.52	4.60	42.72	54.16	3.13
Sikkim	45.94	45.87	8.19	86.18	12.23	1.59	50.70	41.89	7.41
Tripura	39.86	52.23	7.91	61.53	34.25	4.22	43.89	48.89	7.22
All India	45.02	48.67	6.31	64.10	32.25	3.65	50.37	44.07	5.56

Source Census 2001

Table 13.6 Percentage distribution of houses by their condition in 2011

State	Rural			Urban			Total		
	Good	Liveable	Dilapidated	Good	Liveable	Dilapidated	Good	Liveable	Dilapidated
Arunachal Pradesh	49.44	47.07	3.49	58.34	38.79	2.87	51.65	45.01	3.33
Assam	27.98	60.16	11.85	59.07	35.24	5.69	32.81	56.30	10.90
Manipur	49.41	45.87	4.72	63.60	31.96	4.44	54.16	41.21	4.63
Meghalaya	42.17	50.92	6.91	69.70	27.58	2.72	48.08	45.91	6.01
Mizoram	49.67	46.00	4.32	73.75	24.75	1.50	62.32	34.83	2.84
Nagaland	48.51	49.71	1.78	62.07	36.04	1.89	52.38	45.81	1.81
Sikkim	46.70	46.33	6.97	80.30	17.91	1.79	55.96	38.50	5.54
Tripura	50.90	43.76	5.33	63.83	31.95	4.22	54.51	40.47	5.02
All India	46.08	47.34	6.58	68.68	28.43	2.89	53.34	41.26	5.39

Source Census 2011

13.3.5 *Classification of Households by Main Source of Income*

Let us consider the main sources of income of the population of each of the states of NER as follows in Table 13.7:

When we look at the rural sector we find that the major source of income of the people in different states of the NER is from agriculture (where people are self employed). It can be seen that over 40% of the population derive their income from this source with the exception of Tripura (26%). About 65% of the population of Mizoram derive their income from agriculture. This is much higher than the national average of about 38%. Unlike the rest of the states in NER, it can be seen that the majority (about 43%) of the population in Sikkim derive their income from mixed sources. It may also be noted that Tripura is the only state in the north east where almost an equal percentage of people derive their income from the various sources listed in the Table 13.7.

In the urban sector (Table 13.8) it is also seen that the majority of the population in all the states of the NER derive their income through regular wage or salary. This is also true at the all-India level. Meghalaya has the highest percentage of population deriving their income from this source (55%) which is higher than the national average. The next most important source of income for the people of the NER is through self-employment. Except for Arunachal Pradesh, about 25% or more of the total population of different states derive their income from this source. About 41% of the population of Mizoram derive their income from this source which is again higher than the national average.

When we consider the 68th round (2011–12), we see that there are a few developments in the classification of major source of income in the rural sector (Table 13.9). The new classifications added are regular wage or salaried

Table 13.7 Percentage distribution of households by main source of income in 1993–94: rural

State	Self-emp non-agri	Agri lab	Other lab	Self-emp agri	Mixed	Total
Arunachal Pradesh	4.98	3.52	1.35	63.49	26.65	100.00
Assam	11.57	22.97	11.74	41.93	11.79	100.00
Manipur	15.86	5.64	3.33	54.59	20.59	100.00
Meghalaya	7.71	12.31	5.68	63.18	11.12	100.00
Mizoram	8.09	8.61	0.97	64.57	17.76	100.00
Nagaland	8.68	2.57	1.48	56.30	30.97	100.00
Sikkim	9.06	7.13	2.25	38.85	42.72	100.00
Tripura	19.82	15.15	19.43	26.38	19.23	100.00
All India	12.71	30.34	7.97	37.82	11.17	100.00

Source Special tabulation by the author using unit record data collected by the NSSO on Employment and Unemployment during the 50th round (1993–94)

Table 13.8 Percentage distribution of households by main source of income in 1993–94: urban

State	Self-emp	RWSE	Casual labour	Mixed	Total
Arunachal Pradesh	14.03	52.05	7.63	26.29	100.00
Assam	35.00	46.27	6.91	11.82	100.00
Manipur	36.98	44.39	3.97	14.66	100.00
Meghalaya	25.29	55.19	7.41	12.11	100.00
Mizoram	40.91	45.32	7.65	6.11	100.00
Nagaland	30.10	52.08	4.54	13.28	100.00
Sikkim	36.82	43.24	2.36	17.58	100.00
Tripura	30.49	39.05	12.51	17.95	100.00
All India	33.72	43.34	13.24	9.70	100.00

Source As in Table 13.7

employee, casual labour in agriculture and in non-agricultural activities. This classification still allows comparisons to be made with the 50th round (1993–94) since the categories of the main sources of income are still present.

When we look at the rural scenario, we see that the people derive their main source of income from agriculture (where people are self-employed). In this round too we see that majority of the people of Mizoram (about 71%) derive their income from this source which is double the national average which stands only at 34.32%. In all the other states of the NER we see that 43% (or more) of the population derive their income from this source with the exception of Tripura. The next main source of income for the people of the NER is from the category of self-employed in non-agricultural activities and regular wage or salaried employee. We notice a shift towards regular wage or salaried employment and self employment in non-agricultural activities in the rural sector which was not there in the 50th round.

Table 13.9 Percentage distribution of households by main source of income in 2011–12: rural

State	Self-emp agri	Self-emp non-agri	RWSE	Casual lab agri	Cas-lab non-agri	Mixed	Total
Arunachal Pradesh	61.61	10.85	16.28	1.92	2.44	6.90	100.00
Assam	43.65	24.49	11.78	7.56	9.36	3.15	100.00
Manipur	46.71	24.32	19.60	2.06	2.85	4.47	100.00
Meghalaya	43.34	21.10	15.10	11.15	5.28	4.03	100.00
Mizoram	70.68	10.51	14.97	0.01	2.50	1.32	100.00
Nagaland	57.57	12.66	21.73	0.00	0.36	7.68	100.00
Sikkim	55.53	10.81	25.35	0.02	6.12	2.16	100.00
Tripura	23.95	18.09	9.23	6.97	33.67	8.08	100.00
All India	34.32	15.51	9.62	20.97	13.52	6.06	100.00

Source Special tabulation by the author using unit record data collected by the NSSO on Employment and Unemployment during the 68th round (2011–12)

Table 13.10 Percentage distribution of households by main source of income in 2011–12: urban

State	Self-emp	RWSE	Casual labour	Mixed	Total
Arunachal Pradesh	23.96	56.75	9.85	9.44	100.00
Assam	45.43	33.39	7.72	13.46	100.00
Manipur	58.23	25.80	2.95	13.01	100.00
Meghalaya	26.51	46.22	14.02	13.25	100.00
Mizoram	34.93	52.05	7.20	5.82	100.00
Nagaland	26.96	59.00	3.58	10.47	100.00
Sikkim	36.25	54.29	3.26	6.20	100.00
Tripura	33.54	36.89	12.06	17.51	100.00
All India	35.26	41.69	11.80	11.25	100.00

Source As in Table 13.9

This indicates that the non-agricultural activities are developing in the rural sector of the NER.

In the urban sector (Table 13.10) we see that the main source of income is regular wage or salaried employment. About 59% of the population of Nagaland derive their income from this source which is higher than the national average of about 42%. Manipur on the other has a very small percentage of its population dependent on this source of income which is just about 26%. The next most important source of income is from the category of self-employment. Majority of the population of Manipur (i.e. about 58%) derive their income from this source which is again much higher than the national average of about 35%.

13.3.6 Educational Attainment

In this section we will look at the percentage of the population who are illiterate and the percentage of the population who have graduated or have attained post graduation degree. We will compare and see if the population who are illiterate have decreased over the period of 20 years or so.

In Table 13.11, we see that Arunachal Pradesh has the highest percentage of people who are illiterate, i.e. 65%. This is higher than the all India average of about 48%. All the other states have a lower percentage of people who are illiterate than the all India average with Mizoram having the lowest with only about 10% being classified as illiterate. When we consider the rural urban break up, we notice that there is a higher percentage of people who are illiterate in the rural sector while only a small percentage of illiterates in the urban sector.

When we consider the percentage of graduates and post-graduates, the highest percentage is attained by Manipur followed by Nagaland which is higher than the national average of 4%. All the other states have a lower percentage of graduates and post-graduates than the national average. When we consider the rural sector, we

Table 13.11 Percentage distribution of population aged 15 years and above who are illiterate and who have graduated in 1993–94

State	Rural		Urban		Total	
	Illiterate	Graduate and PG	Illiterate	Graduate and PG	Illiterate	Graduate and PG
Arunachal Pradesh	70.20	1.08	27.77	7.01	65.03	1.80
Assam	36.33	1.43	13.20	10.83	33.72	2.49
Manipur	33.80	4.86	21.05	12.07	30.17	6.91
Meghalaya	42.74	0.64	8.97	12.39	38.24	2.21
Mizoram	13.47	0.88	1.95	4.25	9.78	1.96
Nagaland	22.84	2.62	8.91	11.98	19.21	5.05
Sikkim	38.60	1.79	12.16	7.91	36.46	2.28
Tripura	30.00	2.43	12.17	11.27	27.53	3.66
All India	55.78	1.61	25.77	10.77	47.97	3.99

Source As in Table 13.7

see that Manipur has the highest percentage of graduates and post graduates, followed by Nagaland, Tripura and Sikkim. All the other states have a lower percentage than the national average of 1.61%. The Urban sector shows that Meghalaya has the highest percentage of graduates and post graduates, followed by Manipur, Nagaland, Tripura and Assam. All the other states in the NER have lower percentages than the national average.

When we take the rural urban break-up we see that Arunachal Pradesh is still the state with the highest percentage of illiterates which is higher than the national average. When we look at the percentage of graduates and post graduates, we see that in the rural sector, Manipur has the highest percentage with about 5%. In the urban sector however, the highest percentage is attained by Meghalaya with 12.39% and Manipur with 12.07% is not so far away in next place. In both the sectors it can be seen that most of the states have lower percentages in illiterates than the national average and higher percentages in graduates and post graduates than the national average. In total however, we see that the percentage of graduates and post graduates are lower than the national average except for Manipur and Nagaland.

In the 2011–12, we see that the literacy rate as well as the percentage of graduates and post graduates has increased throughout the NER and at the national level (Table 13.12). Although Arunachal Pradesh is still the state with the highest illiteracy rate yet it is lower than the national average of about 30%. This same scenario is also found in the rural and urban sectors too. It may be noted that the lowest illiteracy rate is found in Mizoram followed by Meghalaya and then by Nagaland not so far off. In the rural sector Meghalaya has the lowest illiteracy rate followed by Mizoram and Nagaland. In the urban sector on the other hand we see that Mizoram has the lowest illiteracy rate followed by Meghalaya and Nagaland.

Table 13.12 Percentage distribution of population aged 15 years and above who are illiterate and who have graduated in 2011–12

State	Rural		Urban		Total	
	Illiterate	Graduate and PG	Illiterate	Graduate and PG	Illiterate	Graduate and PG
Arunachal Pradesh	31.34	4.59	11.30	15.88	27.55	6.72
Assam	18.84	2.60	7.64	15.25	17.54	4.07
Manipur	17.10	8.50	10.72	19.89	15.45	11.46
Meghalaya	5.43	2.15	1.08	20.46	4.46	6.22
Mizoram	6.32	3.54	0.55	11.06	3.46	7.27
Nagaland	9.83	10.96	2.29	22.81	7.19	15.11
Sikkim	16.84	3.44	6.81	11.51	15.00	4.92
Tripura	19.63	1.86	8.17	17.22	17.66	4.51
All India	36.34	3.76	16.09	18.10	30.17	8.13

Source As in Table 13.9

When we consider the percentage of graduates and post graduates we see a difference in 2011–12 where Nagaland now has the highest percentage instead of Manipur which had the highest percentage in 1993–94. However both Manipur and Nagaland have a higher percentage than the national average. All the other states have lower percentages than the national average. When we consider the rural sector we see that the same situation prevails where Nagaland has the highest percentage of graduates and post graduates followed by Manipur and Arunachal Pradesh. All the other states have percentages lower than the national average. The scenario in the urban sector is no different where Nagaland has the highest percentage followed by Meghalaya and Manipur. All the other states fall below the national average.

In both the years, we see that the illiteracy rate is highest in Arunachal Pradesh and lowest in Mizoram. However, we see that illiteracy rate has come down in all the states as well as at the all India level over the period 1993–94 to 2011–12. We also notice that the percentage of the population that has received higher education i.e. graduation and above has also gone up in all the states of the NER as well as at the national level over the same time period. The state with the highest percentage of the population that has received higher education (graduate and above) in 1993–94 is Manipur and the state with the lowest percentage is Arunachal Pradesh among the states in the NER. In the 2011–12, the scenario is somewhat different with Nagaland now having the highest percentage and Assam having the lowest. We also notice huge disparity in the level of illiteracy between the rural and urban sectors with illiteracy being more pronounced in the rural sector than in the urban sector.

13.3.7 Occupation

We will consider the following table that describes the population engaged in non-elementary occupation.

In 1993–94, we see in Table 13.13 that in all the states of the NER there is a higher proportion of the population engaged in non-elementary occupation. It is only in the case of Assam that the percentage of people working in non-elementary occupation is the same as the national average i.e. 66.44%, while all the other states have much higher percentages. Hence there seems to be a higher percentage of people engaged in elementary occupation in Assam and Tripura which is 30% and above compared to all the other North Eastern states which are well below 20%.

When we look at the rural sector we see that Assam has the highest percentage of the population engaged in elementary occupation with about 35% followed by Tripura. However, all the states of the NER have percentages below the national average of about 36%. Mizoram has the lowest percentage with only 2.34%. We also see that a higher percentage of people are engaged in non-elementary occupation compared to the national average in the rural sector. When we consider the urban sector we notice that there seems to be a slightly higher percentage of the population engaged in elementary occupation in the four states of Arunachal Pradesh, Meghalaya, Mizoram and Nagaland, compared to the rural sector.

In 2011–12, we see that at the all India level there has been an increase in population engaged in non elementary occupation in most of the states of NER. Except for the state of Tripura, we see that in all the other states, there seems to be a higher percentage of people engaged in non elementary occupation than the national average. We also see that three states, viz. Manipur, Mizoram and Tripura on the other hand have experienced an even lower percentage of people engaged in non elementary occupation 2011–12 compared to 1993–94.

Table 13.13 Percentage of population engaged in non-elementary occupations in 1993–94 and 2011–12

State	50th round			68th round		
	Rural	Urban	Total	Rural	Urban	Total
Arunachal Pradesh	91.55	81.39	90.68	92.09	87.78	91.45
Assam	64.67	84.03	66.44	78.50	87.10	79.39
Manipur	92.00	94.84	92.69	77.07	90.54	80.16
Meghalaya	86.21	83.78	85.99	84.61	88.08	85.16
Mizoram	97.66	93.28	96.38	91.52	90.27	91.00
Nagaland	95.21	87.86	93.60	99.29	97.49	98.80
Sikkim	81.02	87.46	81.51	95.02	92.55	94.63
Tripura	67.73	81.46	69.47	47.95	79.97	52.02
All India	63.67	77.13	66.44	67.94	83.89	72.16

Source Special tabulation by the author using unit record data collected by the NSSO on Employment and Unemployment during the 50th round (1993–94) and 68th round (2011–12)

When we compare the rural and urban sector in 2011–12, we see that four of the states of NER i.e. Assam, Manipur, Tripura and Meghalaya and at the all India level, there is a much higher percentage of people engaged in elementary occupation in the rural sector than in the urban sector. However when we look at the overall trend, we see that it has remained the same as in 1993–94.

13.4 The Standard of Living Index

In order to compose the Standard of Living Index we have taken only some of the indicators of level of living. In our index we have taken the following indicators and have calculated the dimension index for each indicator as explained in the section, 'Data and Methodology'. After that we have taken the average of all the dimension indices which will give us the composite index. The higher the index value, the higher is the level of living of the people. We have used the data of census 2011 and the NSS data of the 68th round (2011–12) for the various indices. The dimension index has been calculated for rural and urban sector separately as well as for each state as a whole and for the all India average. The various dimension indices are given below:

13.4.1 Proportion of Good Houses

In this section we are taking only the proportion of good houses in order to see what proportion of the houses in the North Eastern states are in good condition. In a way, the higher the proportion of good houses will indicate that people are better off. We calculate the dimension index for the proportion of good houses in each state using Table 13.6, as follows:

According to this index, Mizoram has the highest percentage of 'good' houses, followed by Sikkim and Tripura while Assam has the lowest percentage. The index also reveals that there are more 'good' houses in the urban sector than in the rural sector (Table 13.14).

13.4.2 Proportion of Graduates

In this section we have used Table 13.12 to find the proportion of the population whose educational qualification is graduation and above. The higher the proportion of the population having higher qualification indicates that the people are better off (Table 13.15).

Nagaland has the highest index value of graduates followed by Manipur. All the other states have index values lower than the all India average. This shows that

Table 13.14 Index of houses in good condition in 2011

State	Index (R)	Index (U)	Index (All)
Arunachal Pradesh	0.49	0.58	0.52
Assam	0.28	0.59	0.33
Manipur	0.49	0.64	0.54
Meghalaya	0.42	0.70	0.48
Mizoram	0.50	0.74	0.62
Nagaland	0.49	0.62	0.52
Sikkim	0.47	0.80	0.56
Tripura	0.51	0.64	0.55
All India	0.46	0.69	0.53

Source As in Table 13.6

Table 13.15 Index of graduates in 2011–12

State	Index (R)	Index (U)	Index (All)
Arunachal Pradesh	0.05	0.16	0.07
Assam	0.03	0.15	0.04
Manipur	0.09	0.20	0.11
Meghalaya	0.02	0.20	0.06
Mizoram	0.04	0.11	0.07
Nagaland	0.11	0.23	0.15
Sikkim	0.03	0.12	0.05
Tripura	0.02	0.17	0.05
All India	0.04	0.18	0.08

Source As in Table 13.9

there is a very small percentage of the population who have received higher education. It is seen that the index values are higher in the urban sector than the rural sector and also that the disparity between them is also large.

13.4.3 Proportion of Non-poor

In this section we are using Table 13.2 to find the proportion of non-poor and not the poor because the index that we are constructing will measure the level of living of the people. As such, each of the components will measure the proportion of the population who are better off. The higher the index value, the higher is the proportion of people who are non-poor and the lower the proportion of the population who live in poverty (Table 13.16).

The index shows that there are five states with higher values than the national average showing that at least in these states fewer people are poor than at the national level. The highest values are obtained by Sikkim followed by Meghalaya

Table 13.16 Index of non-poor in 2011–12

State	Rural	Urban	Total	Index (R)	Index (U)	Index (All)
Arunachal Pradesh	61.07	79.67	65.33	0.61	0.80	0.65
Assam	66.11	79.51	68.02	0.66	0.80	0.68
Manipur	61.20	67.41	63.11	0.61	0.67	0.63
Meghalaya	87.47	90.74	88.13	0.87	0.91	0.88
Mizoram	64.57	93.64	79.60	0.65	0.94	0.80
Nagaland	80.07	83.52	81.12	0.80	0.84	0.81
Sikkim	90.15	96.34	91.81	0.90	0.96	0.92
Tripura	83.47	92.58	85.95	0.83	0.93	0.86
All India	74.30	86.30	78.08	0.74	0.86	0.78

Source As in Table 13.2

and then Tripura. The lowest value was obtained by Manipur. It is also seen that the index values are higher in the urban sector than the rural sector in all the states and the all India level.

13.4.4 Index of Calorie Intake

A dimension index has also been calculated for this indicator using the values generated in Table 13.3, in order to determine which states have better nutritional intake. When we look at all the states of the country, we find that Himachal Pradesh has the highest calorie intake of 2503 kcal per day and Meghalaya has the lowest intake of 1703 kcal per day in 2011–12. We notice that it is one of the states in the NER that has the lowest calorie intake in the whole country. In our calculation of the dimension index we use these two values for the maximum and minimum value (Table 13.17).

Table 13.17 Index of per capita calorie intake in 2011–12

State	Index (R)	Index (U)	Index (All)
Arunachal Pradesh	0.22	0.48	0.27
Assam	0.38	0.42	0.39
Manipur	0.34	0.27	0.32
Meghalaya	−0.02	0.07	0.00
Mizoram	0.42	0.59	0.50
Nagaland	0.26	0.35	0.29
Sikkim	0.39	0.33	0.38
Tripura	0.69	0.69	0.69
All India	0.50	0.45	0.48

Max Himachal Pradesh with 2503 cal per day and Min Meghalaya with 1703 cal per day

Source As in Table 13.3

The index reveals that Tripura has the highest calorie intake followed by Mizoram. All the other states have values below the national average. In fact Meghalaya has the lowest calorie intake. This shows that the calorie intake on the whole is very poor in the NER. It was also seen that except for Manipur, Sikkim and Tripura, there is higher calorie intake in the urban sector than in the rural sector.

13.4.5 Proportion of Workers in Non-Elementary Occupation

In this section we calculate the index for the proportion of people who are engaged in non-elementary occupation using Table 13.13. Those engaged in non-elementary occupation must have acquired some skill in order to do the work assigned to them. It is expected that the wages will also be higher in such occupations and so they will be better off than those who are engaged in elementary occupation (Table 13.18).

This index reveals that the highest value was obtained by Nagaland followed by Sikkim, Mizoram and Arunachal Pradesh. There are very high percentages of people engaged in non elementary occupation. With the exception of Tripura all the other states have obtained values greater than the national level. Taking the rural and urban sector we find that the index values are higher than the national level and the index is more or less the same in both the sectors.

13.4.6 Index of Per Capita Total Expenditure

In this section, we find the dimension index for the per capita total expenditure using Table 13.4. Among all the states in the country we found that Kerala had the maximum PCTE at Rs. 1768/- and Chhattisgarh had the minimum with Rs. 542/- in 2011–12. These values have been used in the calculation of this dimension index (Table 13.19).

The index of PCTE reveals that the values in the NER are lower than the national level except in the case of three states of Nagaland, Mizoram and Arunachal Pradesh. When we look at the rural and urban sector, we see that the index is higher in the urban sector than the rural sector among all states and all-India level with the exception of Manipur which obtained the same value. A certain level of disparity is there although it is not very large.

Table 13.18 Index of workers in non-elementary occupation in 2011–12

State/Occupation	Rural			Urban			Total		
	Elementary	Non-elementary	Index	Elementary	Non-elementary	Index	Elementary	Non-elementary	Index
Arunachal Pradesh	7.91	92.09	0.92	12.22	87.78	0.88	8.55	91.45	0.91
Assam	21.50	78.50	0.79	12.90	87.10	0.87	20.61	79.39	0.79
Manipur	22.93	77.07	0.77	9.46	90.54	0.91	19.84	80.16	0.80
Meghalaya	15.39	84.61	0.85	11.92	88.08	0.88	14.84	85.16	0.85
Mizoram	8.48	91.52	0.92	9.73	90.27	0.90	9.00	91.00	0.91
Nagaland	0.71	99.29	0.99	2.51	97.49	0.97	1.20	98.80	0.99
Sikkim	4.98	95.02	0.95	7.45	92.55	0.93	5.37	94.63	0.95
Tripura	52.05	47.95	0.48	20.03	79.97	0.80	47.98	52.02	0.52
All India	32.06	67.94	0.68	16.11	83.89	0.84	27.84	72.16	0.72

Source As in Table 13.13

Table 13.19 Index of PCTE in 2011–12

State	Index (R)	Index (U)	Index (All)
Arunachal Pradesh	0.33	0.47	0.36
Assam	0.07	0.39	0.10
Manipur	0.13	0.13	0.13
Meghalaya	0.19	0.44	0.24
Mizoram	0.21	0.51	0.35
Nagaland	0.42	0.55	0.46
Sikkim	0.25	0.43	0.28
Tripura	0.11	0.33	0.14
All India	0.14	0.67	0.29

Max PCTE Kerala-Rs. 1768 and Min Chhattisgarh with Rs. 542 among the states
Source As in Table 13.3

13.4.7 The Standard of Living Index (Composite Index)

The Standard of Living Index is a composite index of the above six indicators that have been calculated. Here we take the index calculated for each indicator and for each state as a whole. We have simply taken the average of all these indicators and arrived at a value in the column 'composite index' in the following table:

In the column of the composite index we have compared the values attained by each state with the all India value which is 0.48. We notice that five of the states in the NER are below the all-India average. This implies that their level of living is below the national average. These states are Arunachal Pradesh, Assam, Manipur, Meghalaya and Tripura. Three states, i.e. Mizoram, Nagaland and Sikkim have levels of living which are higher than the national average of 0.48. When we rank the states we find that there are two states at the top most position which are Mizoram and Nagaland at 0.54. Sikkim is at the second position with the index at 0.52. Tripura is the at the third position with the index value at 0.47, Arunachal is in the fourth position at 0.46, Manipur and Meghalaya share the fifth position at 0.42 and Assam is in the sixth position at 0.39. According to the index we have computed using the six indicators of level of living Mizoram, Nagaland and Sikkim enjoy the highest levels of living whereas Assam has the lowest levels of living in the NER. The other states have slightly lower levels of living than the national average (Table 13.20).

13.5 NFHS-3

In this section we look at the NFHS-3 report of the GOI (IIPS & Macro International 2007) and take a few excerpts from it which relate to the NER in the various indicators of level of living. The report mentions that the National

Table 13.20 Standard of living index

State	Good houses	Graduates	Non-poor	Non-elementary occupation	PCTE	Calories	Standard of living index	Rank
Arunachal Pradesh	0.52	0.07	0.65	0.91	0.36	0.27	0.46	4
Assam	0.33	0.04	0.68	0.79	0.10	0.39	0.39	6
Manipur	0.54	0.11	0.63	0.80	0.13	0.32	0.42	5
Meghalaya	0.48	0.06	0.88	0.85	0.24	0.00	0.42	5
Mizoram	0.62	0.07	0.80	0.91	0.35	0.50	0.54	1
Nagaland	0.52	0.15	0.81	0.99	0.46	0.29	0.54	1
Sikkim	0.56	0.05	0.92	0.95	0.28	0.38	0.52	2
Tripura	0.55	0.05	0.86	0.52	0.14	0.69	0.47	3
All India	0.53	0.08	0.78	0.72	0.29	0.48	0.48	

Source Special tabulation by the author using NSSO Socio Economic Survey (unit record data), 68th round (2011–12) and Census 2011

Development Council (NDC) emphasised that the economic growth is linked to key human development in areas such as education, health and poverty reduction. Therefore, attaining these will bring about the realisation of economic growth in a country. The report highlights that many of the facilities that improve the living standards of people is seen to be more accessible for people living in the urban areas than those living in the rural areas. In the following section we will mention the north eastern states that figure in the NFHS-3 report, either for poor or excellent amenities that affect the level of living of the people.

When we look at the condition of the houses that people live in we find that the only two states in India with less than 15% of households living in pucca houses are the north eastern states of Tripura (12%) and Manipur (11%).

One of the two states with the fewest people having access to electricity is Assam with only 38% and the state with the least population having access to electricity is Bihar (28%).

In another important amenity i.e. access to safe drinking water, we find that more than one-third of the population of three North Eastern states obtain drinking water from an unimproved source. These states are Manipur, Meghalaya and Nagaland.

However in case of access to toilet facility, we find that the north eastern states are in a better position with three states having over 95% of the households with access to this facility viz. Manipur, Tripura and Mizoram.

We now consider some of the health indicators of the report. Infant and child mortality is rather high in the states of Assam and Arunachal Pradesh in the north east. There are three states in the north east viz. Arunachal Pradesh, Meghalaya and Nagaland that have lower than average reported neonatal mortality but have higher than average post-neonatal and child mortality. The report also shows that Assam has high levels of perinatal mortality while Sikkim, which is another state in north east, has very low levels of perinatal mortality.

Considering the nutritional status of children, it is found that it is related very strongly to nutrition of mothers. Again, children of households with lower standard of living are more likely to be under nourished. It was found that nutritional problems are much higher than average in Meghalaya and less evident in the three states of north east, i.e. Mizoram, Sikkim and Manipur. It may be noted that in the above analysis it was found that Meghalaya has the lowest calorie intake in the country hence the problems in nutrition.

Anaemia is high all over the country. However there are only a few states where less than half of the children are anaemic. Two of these states belong to north east viz. Manipur (41%) and Mizoram (44%).

Considering the nutritional status of men and women, it is found that the percentage of women who are short is highest in Meghalaya (22%) followed by Tripura (19%). However the percentage of women who are too thin is lowest in several of the states of north east. Among men on the other hand, it is found that over 40% of men are too thin in Tripura. It was also found that there are high levels of anaemia for both men and women in Tripura and Assam, for men in Sikkim and for women in Meghalaya. The situation is even worse in case of Assam for both men and women.

13.6 Conclusion

The dimension indices show some important points worth mentioning. There is a very small percentage of the population who have received higher education in various states of the NER. There are very high percentages of people engaged in non elementary occupation in most of the states with the exception of Tripura. Fewer people are poor than at the national level in five of the north eastern states. Most of the states have lower calorie consumption than the national average. It was also seen that the per capita total expenditure (PCTE) were lower than the national level except in the case of three states. On the whole the indices together indicate that the level of living in five of the north eastern states is lower than the national average. It was also seen that all the dimension indices as well as the standard of living index indicate that the population in the urban sector are better off than the population in the rural sector among all states and at the all India level. This is supported by the NFHS-3 report which says that many of the facilities that improve the living standards of people is more accessible for people living in the urban areas than those living in the rural areas. We can conclude that development has been higher in the urban sector than the rural sector.

According to the standard of living index we have computed Mizoram, Nagaland and Sikkim enjoy the highest levels of living whereas Assam has the lowest levels of living in the NER. The other states have slightly lower levels of living than the national average.

In conclusion we can say that there is a lot of disparity among the north eastern states in the different level of living indicators discussed above. Different states are better off in some indicators but worse off in others. Moreover our analysis has shown that in each of the indicators discussed above, urban sector performed better than the rural sector. Yet we also notice that there are always some states that perform better than the national average in each of the indicators. We may say that untapped potential for further development is definitely present in the north east.

References

Dutta, P. C. (2010). Population growth and development in the north-eastern region of India. In B. J. Deb (Ed.), *Population and development in north east India*. New Delhi: Concept Publishing Company Pvt. Ltd.

FAO. (2004). *Human energy requirements. Report of a joint FAO/WHO/UNU expert consultation.* WHO United Nations. Retrieved August 20, 2015 from http://www.fao.org/docrep/007/y5686e/y5686e00.htm.

Government of India. (1993). *NSS 50th round (July 1993–June 1994), Instructions to field staff vol-1*. New Delhi: National Sample Survey Organisation, Ministry of Statistics and Programme Implementation.

Government of India. (2009). *Report of the expert group to review the methodology for estimation of poverty*. New Delhi: Planning Commission.

Government of India. (2011a). *NSS 68th round (July 2011–June 2012), Instructions to field staff vol-1.* New Delhi: National Sample Survey Organisation, Ministry of Statistics and Programme Implementation.

Government of India. (2011b). *Human development report of north eastern states.* New Delhi: Ministry of Development of North Eastern Region.

Government of India. (2013). *Press note on poverty estimates, 2011–12.* New Delhi: Planning Commission.

Indira Gandhi National Centre for the Arts. (n.d). *North east India: An introduction.* Retrieved August 6, 2015 from www.ignca.nic.in/craft002.htm.

International Institute for Population Sciences (IIPS) and Macro International. (2007). *National Family Health Survey (NFHS-3), 2005–06: India: Volume I.* IIPS Mumbai.

Sahu, P. P. (2012). *Employment situation in the north eastern region of India: Recent trends and emerging challenges.* New Delhi: V.V. Giri National Labour Institute.

Sen, R.K. (2008). Poverty, economic development and population dynamics in north east India. In A.K. Ray & S. Sengupta (Eds.), *Population dynamics in north east India.* New Delhi: O. M. Publications.

Sengupta, K. (2007). Disparity in human development in the states of north-east India: A threat to development. In A.K. Ray & S.K. Agnihotri (Eds.), *Terrorism and peace initiatives in north east India.* New Delhi: O. M. Publications.

UNDP. (1990). *Human development report 1990.* New York: Oxford University Press.

Wikipedia. (n.d.). *Human development index.* Retrieved August 21, 2015 from https://en.wikipedia.org/wiki/Human_Development_Index.

Chapter 14
Urban Poverty Reduction Through Local Governance in Nepal

Dil Nath Fuel

Abstract Urban poverty and increasing urban (municipal) population are the major concern in the development arena in Nepal. In 1954, the urban population in Nepal was 3% of the total population. However in 2011, the urban population residing in the country constitutes 17% of its total population. As such scenario, the formulation of policy strategy for the better life of such rapidly increasing urban population is to be done as early as possible. Fiscal decentralization has been taken as the policy strategy for reducing poverty in most of the countries. In this backdrop, this article intends to examine the association between fiscal decentralization and poverty reduction in the municipalities of Nepal. This study is based on the poverty head count ratio and fiscal decentralization variables adopted from the data of all (58) municipalities in Nepal for the period 1983–2010. The poverty measures and fiscal decentralization variables are used for the study from 1983 through 2010. The comparison in the state of poverty and fiscal decentralization before and after the enactment of Local Self Governance Act, 1999 (LSGA) in Nepal is to be analyzed. Descriptive as well as analytical method is adopted.

Keywords Nepal · Municipality · Poverty · Fiscal decentralization

JEL Classification O53 · H70 · I32

14.1 Introduction

Nepal has been adopting unitary and centralized system in the governance since the long time. Nowadays, the country is in transitional stage and is moving to state reconstruction and would be converted from unitary structure to the federal state. The building process for the forthcoming constitution is under way. The Interim

D.N. Fuel (✉)
Economics Education, Tribhuvan University, Kirtipur, Nepal
e-mail: dnfuel@gmail.com

U.K. De et al. (eds.), *Inequality, Poverty and Development in India*, India Studies in Business and Economics, DOI 10.1007/978-981-10-6274-2_14

Constitution of Nepal, 2007 (MoLJ 2007) has stated "There shall be made progressive restructuring of the State with inclusive, democratic federal system of governance, by doing away with the centralized and unitary structure of the State so as to end discriminations based on class, caste, language, gender, culture, religion and region." The periodic plan, Three Year Plan Approach Paper (2010–11 to 2012–13) has spelled out the policies on fiscal decentralization (NPC 2010) more clearly. It is evident that the foundation of democratic federal system of governance is fiscal decentralization. However, the practice of fiscal decentralization is still in preliminary stage in Nepal. The municipalities in Nepal are relatively more autonomous and advanced local bodies than the Village Development Committees and the District Development Committees in Nepal (Silwal 2012). As such, the fiscal decentralization to the municipalities in Nepal shall be the interesting area of studies to make guiding principle of the state. Although, the empirical study on the impact of fiscal decentralization in the municipalities of the country has not been conducted. This study tries to fulfill the gap on the aforesaid subject matter by means of empirical analysis on the change in incidence of poverty in the course of fiscal decentralization in Nepal.

We know that there has been the large variation in the status of the municipalities in Nepal. The geographical location, age of formation as a municipality, resource mobilization, size of population, infrastructural facilities, and the overall institutional performance of the municipalities are the basis of differentiation (MuAN 2003). Therefore, "One size fits all policy" is not suitable for the urban governance system in Nepal. I have found that poverty has been smoothly decreasing in the urban area of the country since three decades. But the fiscal decentralization policy has not been found significant to decline poverty in Nepal. The municipalities in the plain region are relatively richer in resources but they are relatively unsuccessful to reduce poverty in their region. The reason behind this interesting result might be the lack of good governance in the local level in plain region of the country. Nowadays, Nepal has been on the path of state restructuring process through the forthcoming constitution. Nepal has been adopting the policy of fiscal decentralization after the enactment of Local Self Governance Act, 1999 (LSGA) for the betterment of the people (MoLJ 1999). So, this is the proper time to review the impact of LSGA and its amendment in Nepal.

Municipal (urban) level poverty and its mounting population is one of the major concerns in the development arena in Nepal. In the year 1954, the urban population in Nepal was only 3% of the total population. However in 2011, the total urban population residing in the country constitutes 17% of its total population. It means, 17% of the total population resides in 2.23% of the total land area of the country. As such rapidly increasing urban population, the formulation of policy strategy for the betterment of the life of people is to be adopted as early as possible.

As we know that poverty is a multidimensional concept. Therefore, poverty could not be reduced through a single remedial measure like fiscal decentralization. The cause of poverty might be the lack of good governance in the local bodies (municipalities) of the developing countries like Nepal. For the poverty reduction, the fiscal autonomy power should be given to the municipalities or to the local level governments. The fiscal autonomy is the major component of fiscal decentralization. As such, fiscal decentralization has been accepted as the effective policy strategy for reducing poverty in most of the countries for more than two decades (Besley and Coate 2003; Faguet 2004; Sepulveda and Martinez-Vazquez 2010).

The objective of this chapter is to analyze the trend on poverty incidence in the municipalities of Nepal for the period 1983–2010. Moreover, it tries to assess the municipal level fiscal decentralization indicators; namely, Relative Size, Tax Autonomy, Own Source of Revenue, Vertical Imbalance, Social Programmes Indicator, Municipal Expenditure, and Service Provide Indicator for the entire period as well as the prior and posterior period of fiscal decentralization in Nepal.

The chapter is structured in five orderly sections. Present section presents the introduction. The methodology of the study is in second section. Third section is devoted to the empirical estimation of the results. Finally, fourth section concludes with summary of findings.

14.2 Methodology of the Study

This empirical study is mainly exploratory and descriptive in nature based on secondary data collected from the 58 municipalities in Nepal for the period 1983–2010. Some basic statistical tools for the analysis are mentioned below.

14.2.1 Descriptive Statistics

The summary or descriptive statistics is used to describe the main feature of information quantitatively. It summarizes the key characteristics of dataset often with descriptive figures and is presented in the tabular form. It has been used for summarizing a number of statistical features of the sample in the research. We shall use summary statistics to measure central tendency (arithmetic mean and median), maximum value, minimum value, measures of variability (standard deviation and coefficient of variation-CV), skewness, kurtosis, and the number of observations of time series data. The summary measures help us to summarize the information on the basis of initial description of the data as part of more extensive statistical analysis or they may be sufficient in and of themselves for a particular investigation.

The measures of central tendency are numerical values that tend to locate in some sense the average of a set of data. The arithmetic mean (mean) is the most common measure of central tendency and it shows the average value of data. The median is the middle value of the set of data when the data are ranked in order according to magnitude. The maximum and the minimum values refer to the highest and lowest magnitude of data. Standard deviation is the average distance of observation to the arithmetic mean. Coefficient of variation shows the deviation as a percentage of arithmetic mean. The kurtosis indicates the characteristics of the extremes of a frequency distribution of data. The benchmark of standard of distribution is the perfect normal distribution which has zero kurtosis by definition. The skewness is the degree of asymmetry in a frequency distribution of data. A perfect symmetrical frequency distribution has no (zero) skewness. If the distribution of the variable is strongly skewed, it may be more appropriate to use nonparametric test of statistical significance (Pindyck and Rubinfeld 1998). The number of observations in this study refers to the time span of corresponding data expressed in number of years.

14.2.2 Graphical Exposition and Trend Line

The statistical information or data may be presented in some graphic or diagrammatic form. The graphical method of presentation of data is better for visualization. In this method, the observation shall be presented in graphical diagram. It provides a better understanding on the overall tendencies of data points within the time series. We display the time series data of poverty in the Nepalese municipality through exponential trend line is specified as stated below.

$$\text{POVIN} = A\mathrm{e}^{bt},$$

where A is the shift parameter and b is the growth rate parameter of the incidence of poverty (POVIN) over the time period t. The negative value of b indicates decreasing trend in incidence of poverty and vice versa.

14.2.3 Variables for the Study

We have specified the poverty variable and fiscal decentralization variables for the municipal level study as outlined below.

(1) Poverty Incidence (POVIN): Poverty incidence (incidence of poverty or head count index or poverty head count ratio) is simply the share of population that is defined as poor. It is the share of total population whose consumption is below than the specified amount of expenditure on food and nonfood items by the country. It measures the percentage of population living below the defined poverty line.

We have eight measures of fiscal decentralization variables and each carries different aspect of fiscal decentralization. The most frequently used measures of fiscal decentralization in cross country analysis are subnational shares of total government expenditures or revenues. These two indicators show the authority of local governments over expenditures and revenues. We apply these popular concepts to measure fiscal decentralization. We also follow the autonomy, accountability and service delivery measures of fiscal decentralization for the construction of variables. The specified fiscal decentralization variables are stated below.

(2) Relative Size (SIZE): It is the ratio of total municipal expenditure to the total expenditure on local development expressed in percentage of the country in a year. It shows the comparison of municipal expenditure to the expenditure via central government to the local government in Nepal. It means, higher the relative size higher is the independent absorption (expenditure) capacity of municipality.

(3) Tax Autonomy (AUTO): It is the share of tax revenue of municipality to the total municipal revenue of the municipality in percentage. It depicts the sovereignty of revenue collection then for the autonomy in expenditure. It is the measure of revenue decentralization. It means, higher the tax autonomy higher is the autonomy in expenditure.

(4) Own Source of Revenue Per Capita (OSR): It is the ratio of own source of revenue of the municipality to the total population of the municipality. It reveals the contribution done by each local resident to the revenue source of municipality. The greater the share of own source of revenue, the greater accountability of the local governments to the local residents who pay taxes.

(5) Vertical Imbalance (VIMB): It is the share of central grants to the total municipal revenue in percentage. It indicates the dependency (fiscal independence) of central grant in the municipal expenditure. The notion is, the greater the share of central grant in total municipal expenditure, the greater responsibility to the central government rather than the answerability to the local people. It too reveals the intergovernmental fiscal relation in the governance system.

(6) Social Programme Indicator (SOC): It is the share of social programme (education, health, forestry, cultural and sports, disaster relief, financial assistance and miscellaneous) expenditure of the municipality to the total expenditure of the municipality in percentage. In other words, it is the amount of expenditure done for the social welfare especially to the deprived groups of the municipal population. Therefore, it refers to the social responsibility of the local government.

(7) Expenditure Per Capita (EXPC): It is the ratio of total municipal expenditure to the total municipal population of the respective year. This indicator measures the aggregate expenditure (current, social and capital investment) done to each local resident through municipal budget. The higher the expenditure per capita indicates the higher investment is done for the better life of local residents. It is the part of expenditure decentralization.

(8) Service Provider Indicator (SERV): It is the number of municipal employee in per 1,000 municipal populations. The larger the number of municipal employ the better is the level of services to the local people. The higher the value of SERV the better the level of municipal service delivery.

14.2.4 Nature and Sources of Data

For this study, we entirely based on secondary data. The empirical study on all 58 municipalities of Nepal is based on the following data sources. The first is the Financial Database by German Technical Cooperation (GIZ or GTZ)/ Urban Development through Local Efforts (UDLE) Programme, Nepal. GIZ/UDLE has maintained annual time series data of 28 years on municipal revenue, expenditure, population, area, and the number of employees of the each and every municipalities of Nepal since the fiscal year 1982–83 to 2009–10. For the sake of simplicity in computation, the dual value of the fiscal year like 1982–1983 has been changed to 1983 only. Therefore, for the municipal level and country level estimation, only a single later half figure will be used to denote fiscal year in place of dual numeral.

The poverty data of the municipalities of Nepal were compiled from the publications of National Planning Commission (NPC) Secretariat, Central Bureau of Statistics (CBS), Nepal and Ministry of Health Nepal. These are: Population Census Report 1981, Population Monograph of Nepal, Population Census Report 1991, Nepal Living Standard Survey 1995–96, Nepal Labour Force Survey 1998–99, Household Consumption Survey of Rural Nepal 2000–2001, Population Monograph of Nepal (Vol. 1 and 2), Population Census Report 2001, Nepal Demographic Health Survey 2001, Nepal Living Standard Survey 2003–04 (Statistical Report Vol. 1 and 2), Nepal Demographic and Health Survey 2006, Small Area Estimation of Poverty, Calorie Intake and Malnutrition in Nepal 2006, Nepal Population Report 2007, Passage to India: Migration as a Coping Strategy in Times of Crisis in Nepal 2008, Nepal Living Standards Survey 2010–11 (Highlights), Nepal Living Standards Survey 2010–11 (Statistical Report Vol. 1 and 2), Nepal Population and Housing Census 2011 (Vol. 1 and 2), and Population Census 2011, (Brief Results). The monetary data for our study has been obtained from the Quarterly Economic Bulletin, (Vol. 46 No. 4) of Nepal Rastra Bank (the central bank of Nepal). The available data might be inadequate; however, it offers some suggestive evidence on the extent of fiscal decentralization and poverty at the national and municipal level in Nepal. Moreover, World Population Data Sheet, Government Finance Statistics (GFS), PovCalNet (http://iresearch.worldbank.org/PovCalNet/jsp/index.jsp) of the World Bank and Meta Data of World has been used from internet sources.

14.3 Empirical Estimation of the Results

The empirical estimation has been done by using the econometric software package EViews 3.1 of the computer. This econometric package is user friendly and easily available. The summary statistics of poverty incidence and fiscal indicators with the trend of the same variables shall be presented diagrammatically for all the categories of municipalities. The impact of fiscal decentralization on poverty reduction in total, hilly, terain (tarain), eastern, western, old and new municipalities in Nepal is successively analyzed in the analysis section of the study. At first, the information of these municipalities is compiled separately in 58 tables. Then the aggregate value of all municipalities is in separate table. Again, for the task of data management in our study, we classify municipalities on the ground of their topographic feature, geographical location where they are in and their age of formation in the form of municipality. This classification facilitates the comparison for the study. We consider the aggregate data of each category for the estimation. The classification is listed in Appendix.

14.3.1 Incidence of Poverty and Fiscal Indicators in All 58 Municipalities of Nepal

We know that the urban area of Nepal indicates the total area occupied by 58 municipalities of the country. In this section, we shall present summary statistics of urban poverty of Nepal for the period 1983–2010. Then we shall present the summary statistics of fiscal indicators for the total municipalities in the same period. Moreover, we shall analyze the trend of poverty of all municipalities in Nepal with the help of bar diagram and trend line.

14.3.1.1 Descriptive Statistics on Incidence of Poverty and Fiscal Indicators in All 58 Municipalities of Nepal

It could be observed from Table 14.1 that the average value of incidence of poverty at the total urban area of Nepal in the period 1983–2010 is 18.57%. The relative size is defined as the proportion of total expenditure of all municipalities in the given year and the total expenditure through ministry of local government of the same year multiplied by 100 is 41.2% in an average. The tax autonomy measured as the proportion of total local tax of municipalities to the total revenue, expressed in percentage, is in an average 55%. The average value of own source of revenue per capita is NPR 391.2. The vertical imbalance which is measured in the total grants to the total revenue of the same year expressed in percentage is 16.5% (in an average) indicates that the municipalities of Nepal are highly dependent on central grants. The municipality expenses are around 7.7% of its total expenditure only to the social programmes like education, health, and culture. The average expenditure per head of the municipal population is NPR 498.41. As a final point, the service indicator expressed as the number of municipal employee per 1000 municipal population is about 2.65.

Now, we compare the average value of the indicators of the all 58 municipalities before (1983–1999) and after (1999–2010) the fiscal decentralization in Nepal. If we see the incidence of poverty in the all 58 municipalities in Nepal, it was found

Table 14.1 Descriptive statistics on incidence of poverty and fiscal indicators in all 58 municipalities of Nepal

	Poverty incidence in all 58 municipalities (%)	Relative size (%)	Tax autonomy (%)	Own source of revenue (Nepali currency per capita)	Vertical imbalance (%)	Social programmes indicator (%)	Municipal expenditure (Nepali currency per capita)	Service provide indicator (per 1000 population)
Period: 1983–2010								
Mean	18.57	41.22	55.04	391.17	16.47	7.71	498.41	2.65
Median	21.42	37.57	57.60	415.96	16.00	7.25	534.63	2.61
Maximum	28.00	92.10	72.94	523.34	37.15	18.42	765.18	3.23
Minimum	7.63	18.60	25.43	215.62	4.47	1.71	282.50	1.90
Std. Dev.	6.96	18.99	11.29	95.61	8.74	4.35	142.39	0.34
CV	37.47	46.07	20.51	24.44	53.07	56.36	28.57	12.99
Skewness	−0.33	1.30	−0.73	−0.67	0.64	0.79	−0.07	−0.35
Kurtosis	1.70	4.00	3.26	2.19	2.80	3.05	1.93	2.61
Observations	28	28	28	28	28	28	28	28
Period: 1983–1999								
Mean	23.47	43.88	61.05	365.64	12.46	5.21	429.13	2.84
Median	23.3	37.47	60.3	384.95	14.49	4.89	386.86	2.85
Maximum	28	92.1	72.94	497.22	23.19	8.52	671.42	3.23
Minimum	17.23	18.6	48.59	215.62	4.47	1.71	282.5	2.53
Std. Dev.	3.13	23.61	6.76	109.20	5.92	2.31	128.37	0.23
CV	13.36	53.79	11.06	29.86	47.50	44.30	29.91	8.04
Skewness	−0.27	0.84	0.16	−0.23	0.06	0.06	0.41	0.11
Kurtosis	2.29	2.40	2.28	1.46	1.67	1.66	1.69	1.69
Observations	17	17	17	17	17	17	17	17

(continued)

Table 14.1 (continued)

	Poverty incidence in all 58 municipalities (%)	Relative size (%)	Tax autonomy (%)	Own source of revenue (Nepali currency per capita)	Vertical imbalance (%)	Social programmes indicator (%)	Municipal expenditure (Nepali currency per capita)	Service provide indicator (per 1000 population)
Period: 2000–2010								
Mean	11.00	37.11	45.74	430.63	22.65	11.58	605.47	2.34
Median	9.55	38.64	46.72	443.41	22.72	11.3	594.61	2.42
Maximum	16.06	48.47	57.65	523.34	37.15	18.42	765.18	2.67
Minimum	7.63	25.67	25.43	358.12	10.77	6.42	490.42	1.90
Std. Dev.	3.33	7.17	10.69	52.72	8.99	3.92	87.24	0.27
CV	30.32	19.32	23.38	12.24	39.67	33.83	14.41	11.35
Skewness	0.50	−0.15	−0.41	0.02	0.20	0.34	0.59	−0.40
Kurtosis	1.55	2.14	2.13	2.02	1.75	2.12	2.39	1.82
Observations	11	11	11	11	11	11	11	11

Source Author's own calculation based on secondary data

that more than 50% of the same has been decreased after fiscal decentralization. The relative size, tax autonomy and service provide indicator have been decreased. On the contrary; own source of revenue per capita, vertical imbalance, social programme indicator, and expenditure per capita have increased after fiscal decentralization in Nepal.

14.3.1.2 Incidence of Poverty in All 58 Municipalities of Nepal

To examine the changing trend in incidence of poverty, we use exponential tendency of yearly data on incidence of poverty or poverty head count ratio of the period 1983–2010 in the municipalities of Nepal. This is a well-accepted methodology to examine the changing trend of the indicator in time series analysis. The same method shall be applied to analyze the changing trend of incidence of poverty in the all categories of the municipalities in the following subsections as well.

Figure 14.1 depicts the incidence of poverty of all 58 municipalities in Nepal. This shows the scenario of the total urban poverty in Nepal for the time period 1983–2010. The poor population from the defined poverty line in the urban area of Nepal has been declined smoothly. In 1983, the poverty head count ratio was 27.57% and it reaches to 7.63% in the year 2008. It seems that urban head count poverty ratio has been increased in all categories (hilly, terain, eastern, western, old and new) of the municipalities in the year 2010. Here, it has reached to 15.5% in the year 2010. Because in the year 2010–11 Central Bureau of Statistics, Nepal has adjusted the national poverty line as 2,220 kilocalorie per capita per day (NPR 19,261.00 per person per year). However, the regionally adjusted national poverty line was defined as 2,124 kilocalorie per capita per day (that is, NPR 5,089.00 per person per year) in 1995–96; 2,144 kilocalorie per capita per day (NPR 7,696.00 per person per year) in 2003–04 (up to 2008–09). As such, the value of incidence of poverty was shifted up due to the upward shifting of national poverty line in the year 2010. In the real sense, the incidence of poverty has been declining onwards 2010. Poverty in 2010 has been calculated as per the new food basket. Therefore, we cannot compare it to the same of the previous years. The more interesting matter is that the poverty has been declined rapidly after 1999 than that of prior time period. The year 1999 is the promulgation of Local Self Governance Act, 1999 in Nepal and it has been taken as the turning point towards fiscal decentralization in Nepal.

14.3.2 Incidence of Poverty and Fiscal Indicators in 28 Municipalities in the Hill Areas of Nepal

The municipalities located to the hill, mountain, and valley in Nepal are termed as hilly municipalities. In this section, the poverty and fiscal indicators of the hilly municipalities of Nepal and summary statistics of the same for the period 1983–2010 shall be discussed.

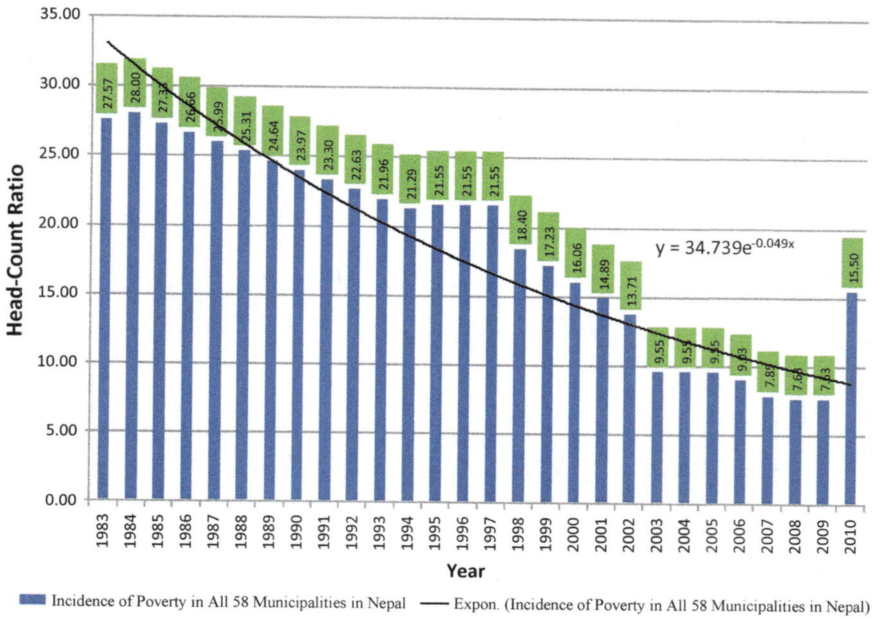

Fig. 14.1 Incidence of poverty in all 58 municipalities in Nepal

14.3.2.1 Descriptive Statistics on Incidence of Poverty and Fiscal Indicators in All 28 Municipalities in the Hill Areas of Nepal

Table 14.2 reveals the summary statistics of the variables of the hilly 28 municipalities in Nepal. The average of poverty incidence and the average value of relative size are 18.2 and 21%, correspondingly. The average tax autonomy and vertical imbalance are 51.3 and 17.3%, respectively. The mean value of own source of revenue per capita is NPR 403.9 and the expenditure per capita is NPR 509.6. The average social programmes indicator is 8.3%. About three municipal employees provide the municipal service to per 1,000 populations.

We are going to compare the mean value of the indicators of hilly municipalities at the time of prior and posterior of fiscal decentralization in Nepal. It seems that incidence of poverty, tax autonomy, and service provide indicator have been decreased after fiscal decentralization. But the relative size, own source of revenue per capita, vertical imbalance, social programme indicator, and expenditure per capita by the municipalities have been considerably higher after fiscal decentralization in the municipalities of hills.

Table 14.2 Descriptive statistics on incidence of poverty and fiscal indicators in all 28 municipalities in the hill areas of Nepal

	Poverty incidence in 28 hilly municipalities (%)	Relative size (%)	Tax autonomy (%)	Own source of revenue (Nepali currency per capita)	Vertical imbalance (%)	Social programmes indicator (%)	Municipal expenditure (Nepali currency per capita)	Service provide indicator (per 1000 population)
Period: 1983–2010								
Mean	18.23	21.00	51.26	403.92	17.26	8.33	509.58	2.82
Median	20.25	19.44	52.17	435.10	18.32	7.84	556.27	2.76
Maximum	26.46	49.68	72.15	568.50	37.38	20.94	805.43	3.51
Minimum	2.56	6.34	27.27	141.17	3.44	1.84	232.64	1.96
Std. Dev.	6.32	10.31	11.28	125.73	9.46	5.29	177.71	0.42
CV	34.66	49.11	22.01	31.13	54.79	63.54	34.87	14.82
Skewness	−0.89	1.10	−0.20	−0.91	0.23	0.63	−0.24	−0.18
Kurtosis	3.48	4.08	2.47	2.55	2.18	2.62	1.89	2.38
Observations	28	28	28	28	28	28	28	28
Period: 1983–1999								
Mean	22.26	20.84	57.44	363.23	13.22	6.02	420.82	3.05
Median	22.16	16.33	55.92	403.84	14.69	4.24	427.42	3.07
Maximum	26.46	49.68	72.15	511.09	24.50	13.24	734.73	3.51
Minimum	16.72	6.34	43.65	141.17	3.44	1.84	232.64	2.60
Std. Dev.	2.92	12.86	7.97	141.35	7.47	4.18	160.58	0.30
CV	13.12	61.73	13.87	38.92	56.53	69.47	38.16	9.81
Skewness	−0.26	1.00	0.17	−0.40	0.08	0.77	0.28	−0.10
Kurtosis	2.15	2.94	2.00	1.53	1.44	1.94	1.80	1.88
Observations	17	17	17	17	17	17	17	17

(continued)

Table 14.2 (continued)

	Poverty incidence in 28 hilly municipalities (%)	Relative size (%)	Tax autonomy (%)	Own source of revenue (Nepali currency per capita)	Vertical imbalance (%)	Social programmes indicator (%)	Municipal expenditure (Nepali currency per capita)	Service provide indicator (per 1000 population)
Period: 2000–2010								
Mean	12.00	21.25	41.70	466.81	23.51	11.90	646.76	2.45
Median	14.68	21.23	42.12	461.03	23.69	10.56	657.03	2.52
Maximum	16.04	29.03	54.01	568.50	37.38	20.94	805.43	2.77
Minimum	2.56	14.01	27.27	379.17	9.39	4.67	480.06	1.96
Std. Dev.	4.89	4.72	8.74	59.58	9.02	4.95	99.59	0.29
CV	40.71	22.22	20.97	12.76	38.38	41.60	15.40	11.73
Skewness	−1.34	0.11	−0.07	0.14	−0.18	0.53	−0.03	−0.49
Kurtosis	3.19	2.21	1.86	1.82	2.13	2.53	1.97	1.92
Observations	11	11	11	11	11	11	11	11

Source Author's own calculation based on secondary data

14.3.2.2 Incidence of Poverty in 28 Hilly Municipalities of Nepal

As can be seen from Fig. 14.2, the poverty incidence of the 28 hilly municipalities in Nepal has been declining over the time period 1983–2010. In the hill urban area, the decline of poverty is much more rapid than the urban terai. However, urban terai is well connected by road network, well equipped and these are the centers for foreign trade, especially to India. It concludes that terain municipalities are relatively weaker to reduce poverty.

14.3.3 Incidence of Poverty and Fiscal Indicators in 30 Terain Municipalities of Nepal

The municipalities located in the terai or plain region of Nepal are called terain municipalities. This section is devoted to the analysis on poverty and fiscal indicators of the terain municipalities of Nepal spanning over the period 1983–2010.

14.3.3.1 Descriptive Statistics on Incidence of Poverty and Fiscal Indicators in 30 Terain Municipalities of Nepal

The data of variables in Table 14.3 imply that the average value of poverty incidence and relative size of terain municipalities are 31.6 and 14.5%, respectively. In terain

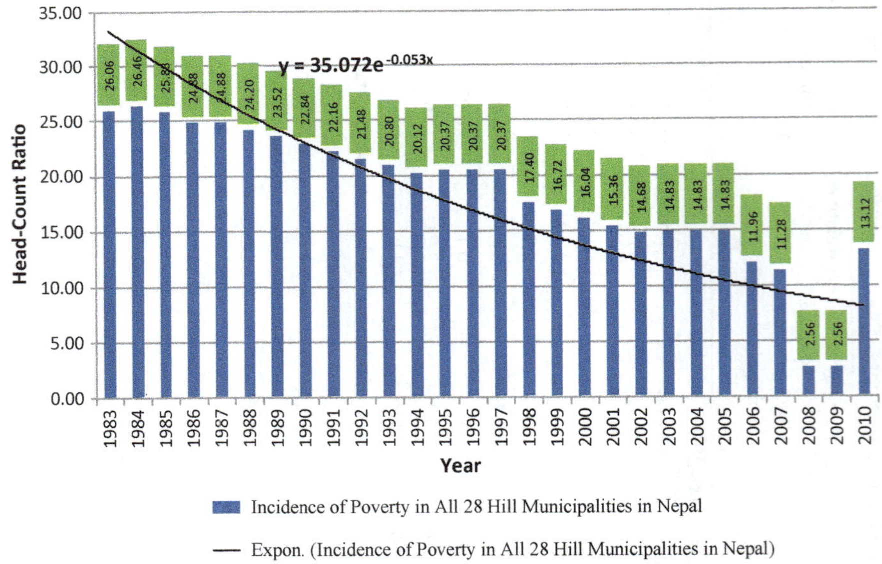

Fig. 14.2 Incidence of poverty in 28 Hilly municipalities in Nepal

Table 14.3 Descriptive statistics on incidence of poverty and fiscal indicators in 30 terain municipalities of Nepal

	Poverty incidence in 30 tarain municipalities (%)	Relative size (%)	Tax autonomy (%)	Own source of revenue (Nepali currency per capita)	Vertical imbalance (%)	Social programmes indicator (%)	Municipal expenditure (Nepali currency per capita)	Service provide indicator (per 1000 population)
Period: 1983–2010								
Mean	31.63	14.51	59.50	376.54	15.83	10.38	423.97	2.49
Median	34.89	16.50	61.96	393.09	14.09	8.78	400.23	2.50
Maximum	45.63	24.49	80.51	506.49	42.30	35.81	1339.53	3.16
Minimum	12.20	2.46	23.57	260.97	3.97	2.80	75.91	1.84
Std. Dev.	9.96	6.95	11.89	78.33	8.68	7.52	321.69	0.35
CV	31.49	47.92	19.98	20.80	54.82	72.38	75.88	13.89
Skewness	−0.34	−0.38	−1.12	−0.11	1.31	1.80	1.16	−0.03
Kurtosis	2.06	1.86	4.48	1.65	4.56	6.34	4.30	2.24
Observations	28	28	28	28	28	28	28	28
Period: 1983–1999								
Mean	38.41	11.37	64.59	368.43	12.10	11.35	231.31	2.67
Median	38.13	9.82	66.24	388.01	13.75	5.68	146.07	2.66
Maximum	45.63	24.49	80.51	506.49	22.85	35.81	479.76	3.16
Minimum	28.84	2.46	51.16	260.97	3.97	2.80	75.91	2.17
Std. Dev.	5.09	7.28	7.37	91.94	4.88	9.54	151.61	0.29
CV	13.26	64.01	11.41	24.96	40.29	84.07	65.54	10.84
Skewness	−0.23	0.57	0.07	0.08	0.21	1.20	0.44	−0.22
Kurtosis	2.11	2.22	2.77	1.35	2.60	3.65	1.55	2.21
Observations	17	17	17	17	17	17	17	17

(continued)

Table 14.3 (continued)

	Poverty incidence in 30 tarain municipalities (%)	Relative size (%)	Tax autonomy (%)	Own source of revenue (Nepali currency per capita)	Vertical imbalance (%)	Social programmes indicator (%)	Municipal expenditure (Nepali currency per capita)	Service provide indicator (per 1000 population)
Period: 2000–2010								
Mean	21.15	19.35	51.64	389.08	21.59	8.89	721.70	2.23
Median	23.4	19.66	53.32	398.16	21.21	8.84	580.11	2.29
Maximum	27.68	21.72	65.80	471.87	42.30	11.35	1339.53	2.56
Minimum	12.20	16.33	23.57	309.91	11.72	5.96	490.77	1.84
Std. Dev.	5.25	1.77	13.51	52.48	10.26	1.67	286.39	0.25
CV	24.83	9.17	26.17	13.49	47.53	18.81	39.68	11.06
Skewness	−0.67	−0.37	−0.74	−0.13	0.69	−0.35	1.38	−0.24
Kurtosis	2.31	1.85	2.58	1.79	2.35	2.33	3.37	1.69
Observations	11	11	11	11	11	11	11	11

Source Author's own calculation based on secondary data

municipalities, the tax autonomy indicator in an average and vertical imbalance indicator are 59.5 and 15.8% roughly. The average own source of revenue and expenditure per capita are NPR 376.5 and NPR 424 approximately. Around 10.4% of the total budget of the terain municipalities is expenses on the social programmes. The average service provider indicator is 2.5 employees each 1,000 municipal populace in terai. The interesting fact is that the hilly municipalities are better performer in fiscal decentralization than the terain municipalities in Nepal.

Let us consider the average indicators of the terain municipalities in the prior (1983–1999) and posterior (2000–2010) in Nepal. We clearly find that incidence of poverty, tax autonomy, social programme indicator and service provide indicators have been lowered after fiscal decentralization. On the other hand, relative size, own source of revenue per capita, vertical imbalance and expenditure per capita by the municipalities have been remarkably bigger after fiscal decentralization.

14.3.3.2 Incidence of Poverty in 30 Terain Municipalities of Nepal

Referring to Fig. 14.3 it is clear that the incidence of poverty in the terain municipalities in Nepal has been declined over the period 1983–2010 in Nepal. In Sect. 14.3.2, we discussed that the municipalities in the hill are relatively weaker in physical infrastructure facilities and road connectivity than the municipalities in terai. Though the poverty has been declining in terain municipalities slower than the hilly municipalities of the country. One cause of this slow decline in poverty is the poor governance in terain municipalities. The next cause might be the unmanageable trend of migration from rural hill and or terai to the urban terai region. It is a well-known fact that there was huge flow of population to terai from the hills. However, since about the decade the urban terai has been more unsecure than the remaining part of the country. It made the population flow slow down to the urban terai.

14.3.4 Incidence of Poverty and Fiscal Indicators in 34 Municipalities in the Eastern Region of Nepal

The municipalities located in the eastern and central development region of Nepal are termed as eastern municipalities. The total number of eastern municipalities is 34. The purpose of this section is to assess the poverty and fiscal indicators of the eastern municipalities of Nepal for the period 1983–2010.

14.3.4.1 Descriptive Statistics on Incidence of Poverty and Fiscal Indicators in 34 Municipalities in the Eastern Region of Nepal

The incidence of poverty and fiscal decentralization variables of the 34 municipalities in Nepal are presented in Table 14.4. The average value of poverty

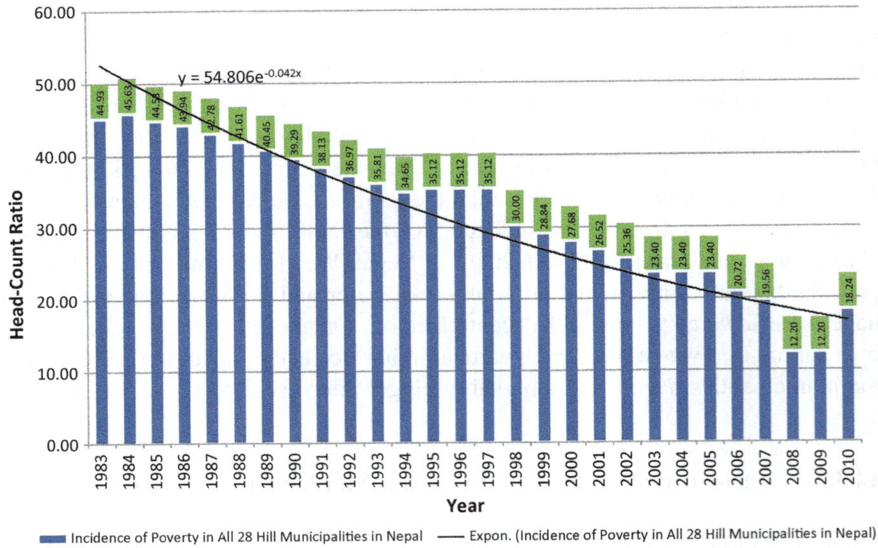

Fig. 14.3 Incidence of poverty in 30 Tarain municipalities in Nepal

incidence is 22.2% and the average value of relative size is 31.5%. The own tax covers the 56.7% of the total revenue in eastern municipalities. The average dependency on grants to the total revenue of eastern municipalities is 13.4%. The mean value of own source of revenue per capita and the average expenditure per capita are NPR 434.9 and NPR 526.8, correspondingly. The average expense is 7.8% of its total budget annually in the social programmes at the eastern municipalities. The average value of service provider indicator is 2.8 municipal employees per thousand eastern municipal populations in Nepal.

Let us look at the average figure of the indicators of eastern municipalities comparing earlier than (1983–1999) fiscal decentralization and later than (2000–2010) the same in Nepal. It appears the higher value of own source of revenue per capita, vertical imbalance, social programme indicator, and expenditure per capita have been amplified after fiscal decentralization. Next side, the remaining indicators, namely, incidence of poverty, relative size, tax autonomy, and service provide indicators are reduced after fiscal decentralization in Nepal.

14.3.4.2 Incidence of Poverty in 34 Municipalities in the Eastern Region of Nepal

The incidence of poverty in 34 municipalities in eastern Nepal is presented in Fig. 14.4 which shows that the poverty head count ratio in this region has been declining rapidly in the period 1983–2010. The eastern part of Nepal is relatively more developed than the western part of the country. This is the main cause for the

Table 14.4 Descriptive statistics on the incidence of poverty and fiscal indicators of 34 eastern municipalities in Nepal

	Poverty incidence in 34 eastern municipalities (%)	Relative size (%)	Tax autonomy (%)	Own source of revenue (Nepali currency per capita)	Vertical imbalance (%)	Social programmes indicator (%)	Municipal expenditure (Nepali currency per capita)	Service provide indicator (per 1000 population)
Period: 1983–2010								
Mean	22.21	31.45	56.67	434.90	13.35	7.81	526.83	2.77
Median	24.28	27.68	58.10	467.02	11.83	6.90	556.44	2.80
Maximum	31.56	72.81	74.54	614.44	32.47	19.66	778.57	3.39
Minimum	6.36	13.70	32.28	223.98	3.62	1.23	289.13	2.07
Std. Dev.	6.98	15.34	10.58	117.06	8.14	4.79	157.93	0.32
CV	31.42	48.80	18.67	26.92	60.96	61.33	29.98	11.51
Skewness	−0.64	1.38	−0.55	−0.65	0.90	0.83	−0.20	−0.30
Kurtosis	2.80	4.16	2.72	2.18	2.99	3.14	1.71	2.71
Observations	28	28	28	28	28	28	28	28
Period: 1983–1999								
Mean	26.74	33.99	61.54	395.32	10.41	5.14	451.34	2.90
Median	26.64	28.07	58.96	423.86	10.23	4.38	389.94	2.91
Maximum	31.56	72.81	74.54	550.12	18.49	9.67	744.92	3.39
Minimum	20.33	13.70	51.35	223.98	3.62	1.23	289.13	2.54
Std. Dev.	3.45	18.95	6.78	127.44	5.14	2.69	149.96	0.26
CV	12.91	55.75	11.01	32.24	49.39	52.35	33.22	8.97
Skewness	−0.23	0.88	0.43	−0.20	0.10	0.39	0.49	0.06
Kurtosis	2.03	2.45	2.07	1.41	1.56	1.90	1.81	1.78
Observations	17	17	17	17	17	17	17	17

(continued)

Table 14.4 (continued)

	Poverty incidence in 34 eastern municipalities (%)	Relative size (%)	Tax autonomy (%)	Own source of revenue (Nepali currency per capita)	Vertical imbalance (%)	Social programmes indicator (%)	Municipal expenditure (Nepali currency per capita)	Service provide indicator (per 1000 population)
Period: 2000–2010								
Mean	15.20	27.51	49.15	496.07	17.89	11.94	643.49	2.56
Median	17.97	27.28	47.84	511.87	18.68	11.87	643.36	2.64
Maximum	19.55	35.74	64.58	614.44	32.47	19.66	778.57	2.87
Minimum	6.36	18.07	32.28	399.52	7.15	6.01	547.15	2.07
Std. Dev.	4.84	5.76	11.23	65.05	9.95	4.42	81.91	0.29
CV	31.82	20.95	22.85	13.11	55.63	36.98	12.73	11.43
Skewness	−1.04	−0.21	0.08	0.09	0.25	0.44	0.28	−0.49
Kurtosis	2.65	2.22	1.63	2.20	1.51	2.30	1.78	1.85
Observations	11	11	11	11	11	11	11	11

Source Author's own calculation based on secondary data

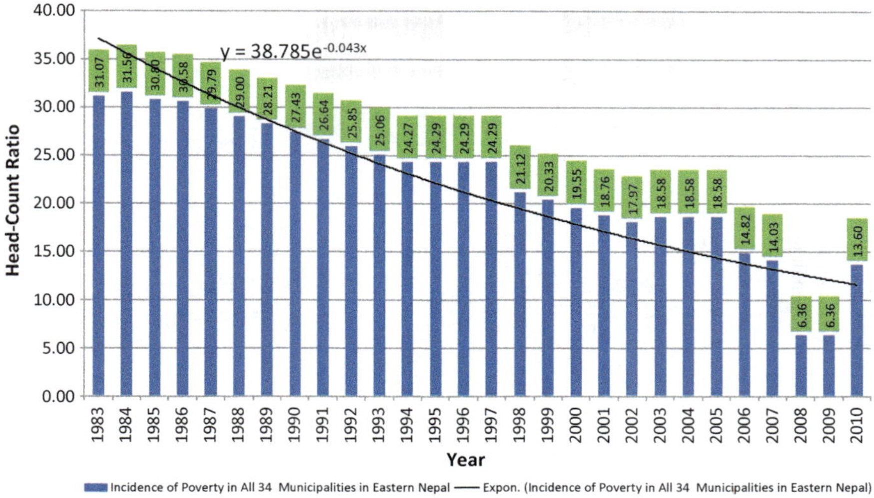

Fig. 14.4 Incidence of poverty in 34 municipalities in Eastern Nepal

better performance of municipality in poverty reduction. The capital city Kathmandu and Lalitpur, other big cities like Biratnagar and Birgunj are lying in the eastern region might be the other causes of better result in poverty reduction.

14.3.5 Incidence of Poverty and Fiscal Indicators in 24 Municipalities in the Western Regions of Nepal

The municipalities situated in the western, mid-western and far-western development regions are western municipalities of the country. This section deals with the summary statistics of poverty and fiscal indicators of the western municipalities of Nepal for the period 1983–2010. We shall also analyze poverty and fiscal decentralization indicators of the western municipalities for the same period.

14.3.5.1 Descriptive Statistics on Incidence of Poverty and Fiscal Indicators in 24 Municipalities in the Western Region of Nepal

On the basis of Table 14.5 it can be concluded that the incidence of poverty is higher in western part of Nepal than the eastern one. The average poverty incidence in 24 western municipalities is 31.1%. The average relative size and tax autonomy are more or less 8 and 50.8% respectively. The average own source of revenue per capita and average value of expenditure per capita are also lower in western

Table 14.5 Descriptive statistics on incidence of poverty and fiscal indicators in 24 municipalities in the western regions of Nepal

	Poverty incidence in 24 western municipalities (%)	Relative size (%)	Tax autonomy (%)	Own source of revenue (Nepali currency per capita)	Vertical imbalance (%)	Social programmes indicator (%)	Municipal expenditure (Nepali currency per capita)	Service provide indicator (per 1000 population)
Period: 1983–2010								
Mean	31.08	9.78	50.77	283.82	26.03	7.38	428.83	2.36
Median	35.08	9.13	51.65	291.78	24.61	7.15	422.66	2.47
Maximum	46.38	19.30	76.37	383.27	50.27	14.73	735.01	3.16
Minimum	8.91	4.77	14.60	183.96	6.61	1.54	261.05	1.54
Std. Dev.	11.08	3.84	14.35	55.33	12.12	4.06	120.99	0.47
CV	35.65	39.31	28.28	19.49	46.57	55.08	28.21	19.74
Skewness	−0.38	0.91	−0.49	−0.15	0.23	0.35	0.79	−0.13
Kurtosis	2.09	3.33	2.74	2.27	2.12	1.92	3.40	1.94
Observations	28	28	28	28	28	28	28	28
Period: 1983–1999								
Mean	38.67	9.89	59.77	284.76	19.27	5.32	370.00	2.68
Median	38.23	9.15	61.99	295.02	17.50	4.28	341.86	2.69
Maximum	46.38	19.30	76.37	383.27	37.18	14.00	503.85	3.16
Minimum	28.14	4.77	40.90	183.96	6.61	1.54	261.05	2.29
Std. Dev.	5.46	4.77	8.32	65.55	8.65	3.27	79.52	0.25
CV	14.12	48.22	13.92	23.02	44.89	61.60	21.49	9.38
Skewness	−0.28	0.73	−0.36	−0.31	0.41	1.21	0.16	0.37
Kurtosis	2.24	2.32	3.24	1.79	2.30	3.90	1.69	2.52
Observations	17	17	17	17	17	17	17	17

(continued)

Table 14.5 (continued)

	Poverty incidence in 24 western municipalities (%)	Relative size (%)	Tax autonomy (%)	Own source of revenue (Nepali currency per capita)	Vertical imbalance (%)	Social programmes indicator (%)	Municipal expenditure (Nepali currency per capita)	Service provide indicator (per 1000 population)
Period: 2000–2010								
Mean	19.35	9.60	36.85	282.38	36.48	10.56	519.75	1.87
Median	20.59	9.10	39.05	273.57	37.47	10.92	514.79	1.88
Maximum	26.88	12.73	50.58	369.27	50.27	14.73	735.01	2.20
Minimum	8.91	7.59	14.60	237.74	22.57	5.15	362.65	1.54
Std. Dev.	5.88	1.85	9.73	37.25	8.90	3.01	120.12	0.21
CV	30.37	19.26	26.42	13.19	24.39	28.47	23.11	11.18
Skewness	−0.76	0.51	−0.92	1.08	−0.13	−0.18	0.57	0.02
Kurtosis	2.69	1.84	3.60	3.73	2.33	2.12	2.44	1.84
Observations	11	11	11	11	11	11	11	11

Source Author's own calculation based on secondary data

municipality than the eastern municipalities, having merely NPR 283.8 and NPR 428.83. The average vertical imbalance indicator is 26%; the mean value of social programme indicator is 7.4% roughly. The dependency on central grants of western municipalities is nearly twice than that of the eastern municipalities. The average service provider indicator is 2.4 municipal employees per thousand western municipal population of the country.

Consider the mean value of the indicators of the incidence of poverty and fiscal decentralization in the period before fiscal decentralization and after the period of fiscal decentralization in the western municipalities in Nepal. As we note that incidence of poverty, relative size, tax autonomy, own source of revenue per capita and service provide indicator are found lowering after fiscal decentralization, the remaining three indicators, that is, vertical imbalance, social programme indicator and expenditure per capita by the western municipalities are approximately doubled after fiscal decentralization.

14.3.5.2 Incidence of Poverty in 24 Municipalities in the Western Region of Nepal

The western sector of Nepal is relatively less developed than the eastern sector of the country. Thus, the performances of municipalities are evidently weaker in service delivery and poverty reduction in their jurisdictions. However, Fig. 14.5 shows that the incidence of poverty in the western municipal area has been decreasing smoothly in the study period 1983–2010.

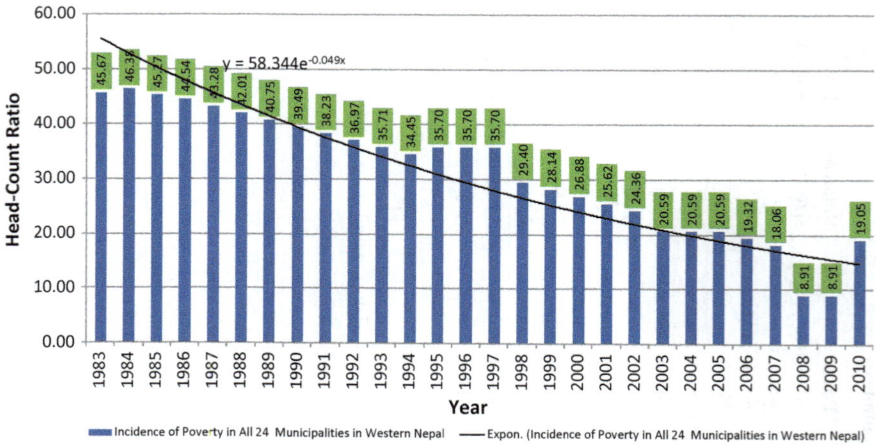

Fig. 14.5 Incidence of poverty in 24 municipalities in Western Nepal

14.3.6 Incidence of Poverty and Fiscal Indicators in 29 Old Municipalities in Nepal

The municipalities which were declared as the municipal status before 1982 are the old municipalities in Nepal. We analyze the state of poverty and fiscal indicators of the 29 old municipalities of Nepal for the period 1983–2010 under this section.

14.3.6.1 Descriptive Statistics on Incidence of Poverty and Fiscal Indicators in 29 Old Municipalities in Nepal

Table 14.6 discloses the summary statistics of the variables of old municipalities in Nepal. Poverty incidence which is an independent variable for our study having an average value 21.3% in the old municipalities in Nepal. The average value of relative size, tax autonomy, vertical imbalance and social programme indicator are 36.6, 57.1, 13.8 and 8% respectively. The proportion of own source of revenue to the total revenue is much better in old municipalities than the newly formed municipalities. The average value of own source of revenue indicator is 423 Nepalese rupees. However, the expenditure per capita in both categories of municipalities is nearly equal by average value of NPR 512 for old municipalities. The average service provider indicator in old municipalities is 2.8 and is higher in quantity than the new municipalities in Nepal.

The differences between the regimes of before and after the fiscal decentralization on the basis of indicators of the old municipalities in Nepal have been computed. Incidence of poverty, relative size, tax autonomy and service provide indicators have been decreased after fiscal decentralization regime. Nevertheless, own source of revenue per capita, vertical imbalance, social programme indicator and expenditure per capita have been augmented after fiscal decentralization regime.

14.3.6.2 Incidence of Poverty in 29 Old Municipalities in Nepal

The old municipalities are comparatively well equipped, resourceful and developed in Nepal. Their quality in service delivery is better. The incidence of poverty in old municipalities is relatively lower than the new municipalities in Nepal. Figure 14.6 reveals the incidence of poverty in the 29 old municipalities in Nepal. The poverty head count ratio in the old municipalities has been declining in the period 1983–2010. It reaches the lowest in 2008.

Table 14.6 Descriptive statistics on incidence of poverty and fiscal indicators in 29 old municipalities in Nepal

	Poverty incidence in 29 Old Municipalities (%)	Relative size (%)	Tax autonomy (%)	Own source of revenue (Nepali currency per capita)	Vertical imbalance (%)	Social programmes indicator (%)	Municipal expenditure (Nepali currency per capita)	Service provide indicator (per 1000 population)
Period: 1983–2010								
Mean	21.25	36.64	57.14	423.05	13.82	8.02	511.97	2.81
Median	23.44	30.27	58.30	449.23	13.37	6.84	552.61	2.83
Maximum	30.62	86.42	73.26	618.29	32.14	20.96	719.27	3.28
Minimum	6.15	18.25	32.32	215.62	3.50	1.67	282.47	2.11
Std. Dev.	6.81	18.77	9.98	115.32	7.62	5.06	148.55	0.31
CV	32.07	51.22	17.47	27.26	55.10	63.03	29.02	10.89
Skewness	−0.55	1.43	−0.52	−0.60	0.51	1.02	−0.28	−0.44
Kurtosis	2.60	4.02	2.93	2.26	2.58	3.47	1.64	2.61
Observations	28	28	28	28	28	28	28	28
Period: 1983–1999								
Mean	25.78	41.44	62.00	377.01	11.22	5.22	434.72	2.91
Median	25.58	30.34	61.46	404.98	11.42	4.46	389.85	2.89
Maximum	30.62	86.42	73.26	531.55	23.19	8.75	679.80	3.28
Minimum	19.51	18.60	48.59	215.62	3.50	1.67	282.47	2.58
Std. Dev.	3.36	22.43	7.06	117.75	6.08	2.46	135.21	0.25
CV	13.05	54.12	11.39	31.23	54.18	47.14	31.10	8.69
Skewness	−0.20	0.85	−0.05	−0.23	0.30	0.12	0.42	0.01
Kurtosis	2.09	2.30	2.15	1.47	1.89	1.61	1.65	1.44
Observations	17	17	17	17	17	17	17	17

(continued)

Table 14.6 (continued)

	Poverty incidence in 29 Old Municipalities (%)	Relative size (%)	Tax autonomy (%)	Own source of revenue (Nepali currency per capita)	Vertical imbalance (%)	Social programmes indicator (%)	Municipal expenditure (Nepali currency per capita)	Service provide indicator (per 1000 population)
Period: 2000–2010								
Mean	14.24	29.23	49.64	494.21	17.84	12.34	631.36	2.64
Median	15.99	30.19	51.35	503.73	17.57	11.91	617.06	2.75
Maximum	18.75	39.95	60.81	618.29	32.14	20.96	719.27	2.99
Minimum	6.15	18.25	32.32	386.20	5.78	5.95	534.59	2.11
Std. Dev.	4.29	6.85	9.34	67.43	8.26	5.05	67.14	0.32
CV	30.15	23.45	18.82	13.64	46.28	40.88	10.64	12.00
Skewness	−1.16	−0.25	−0.36	0.09	0.18	0.38	−0.01	−0.45
Kurtosis	3.01	2.14	2.08	2.34	2.11	2.10	1.78	1.82
Observations	11	11	11	11	11	11	11	11

Source Author's own calculation based on secondary data

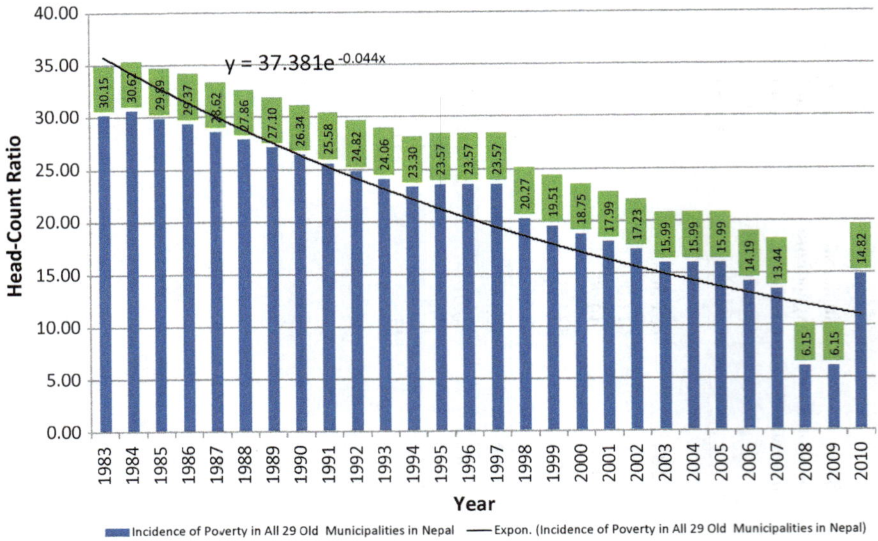

Fig. 14.6 Incidence of poverty in 29 old municipalities in Nepal

14.3.7 Incidence of Poverty and Fiscal Indicators in 29 New Municipalities in Nepal

The municipalities, declared after the year 1982 are new ones. This section presents the summary statistics of poverty and fiscal indicators of the new municipalities of Nepal for the time period 1988–2010. After that we shall examine the same indicators for the same time period in the different subsections.

14.3.7.1 Descriptive Statistics on Incidence of Poverty and Fiscal Indicators in 29 New Municipalities in Nepal

As can be seen from Table 14.7, the matter of our interest of the study, for example, poverty head count ratio and fiscal decentralization variables of 29 new municipalities in Nepal. The average value of poverty head count ratio or poverty incidence is 28.7% and is higher than the old municipalities in Nepal. The reason is that the rural sub-urban areas were declared as a new municipality indicates higher poverty. The cause is the incidence of poverty is higher in rural areas of the country than the poverty incidence in urban ones. The average value of relative size is also more than 6 times lesser in new municipalities having vale of 5.6% only. The average tax autonomy, vertical imbalance and social indicator are 40.6, 35.3 and 6.6% respectively. The average own source of revenue is NPR 262. 2 and average expenditure per capita is NPR 486.2 correspondingly. The service provider

Table 14.7 Descriptive statistics on incidence of poverty and fiscal indicators in 29 new municipalities in Nepal

	Poverty incidence in 29 new municipalities (%)	Relative size (%)	Tax autonomy (%)	Own source of revenue (Nepali currency per capita)	Vertical imbalance (%)	Social programmes indicator (%)	Municipal expenditure (Nepali currency per capita)	Service provide indicator (per 1000 population)
Period: 1988–2010								
Mean	28.72	5.58	40.64	261.21	35.30	6.61	486.21	1.69
Median	28.67	6.92	43.39	260.57	33.19	7.96	438.19	1.55
Maximum	42.66	9.35	62.61	394.28	60.90	11.04	904.11	2.56
Minimum	10.09	1.54	14.04	145.72	13.03	0.00	283.28	1.25
Std. Dev.	9.70	2.76	11.92	60.40	10.92	3.42	156.58	0.37
CV	33.77	49.40	29.32	23.12	30.94	51.73	32.20	22.19
Skewness	−0.37	−0.39	−0.53	0.18	0.64	−0.58	1.23	0.84
Kurtosis	2.11	1.52	2.74	2.61	3.47	2.07	4.26	2.59
Observations	23	23	23	23	23	23	23	23
Period: 1988–1999								
Mean	36.54	3.47	47.32	275.26	31.81	4.13	444.94	1.88
Median	36.14	2.21	47.25	284.23	32.96	4.25	467.97	1.95
Maximum	42.66	7.14	62.61	394.28	56.14	9.09	675.76	2.56
Minimum	28.67	1.54	35.08	145.72	13.03	0.00	283.28	1.25
Std. Dev.	4.14	2.12	7.39	75.73	10.31	2.88	120.25	0.42
CV	11.34	61.14	15.62	27.51	32.40	69.80	27.03	22.49
Skewness	−0.50	0.73	0.51	−0.30	0.58	0.22	0.21	−0.10
Kurtosis	2.65	1.95	2.99	2.08	4.27	2.23	2.18	1.89
Observations	12	12	12	12	12	12	12	12

(continued)

Table 14.7 (continued)

	Poverty incidence in 29 new municipalities (%)	Relative size (%)	Tax autonomy (%)	Own source of revenue (Nepali currency per capita)	Vertical imbalance (%)	Social programmes indicator (%)	Municipal expenditure (Nepali currency per capita)	Service provide indicator (per 1000 population)
Period: 2000–2010								
Mean	20.19	7.88	33.35	245.88	39.11	9.32	531.24	1.48
Median	22.82	7.84	30.51	249.36	35.57	9.14	432.62	1.46
Maximum	27.39	9.35	47.82	314.67	60.90	11.04	904.11	1.73
Minimum	10.09	6.58	14.04	198.15	27.95	7.84	366.95	1.30
Std. Dev.	5.89	0.77	11.85	34.97	10.73	1.06	183.73	0.14
CV	29.19	9.75	35.53	14.22	27.43	11.40	34.59	9.19
Skewness	−0.70	0.22	−0.13	0.34	0.86	0.13	1.21	0.64
Kurtosis	2.32	2.61	1.62	2.49	2.51	1.84	3.02	2.43
Observations	11	11	11	11	11	11	11	11

Source Author's own calculation based on secondary data

indicator is 1.7 employees per thousand show the weaker service delivery in new municipalities of Nepal. The summary statistics supports the findings of previous studies regarding the new municipalities in Nepal.

We examine the state of indicators in the pre fiscal decentralization era (1988–1999) and post fiscal decentralization era (2000–2010) in the new municipalities in Nepal. After fiscal decentralization era the incidence of poverty, tax autonomy, own source of revenue per capita and service provide indicator have been lowered. Thus the other indicators, notably, the relative size, vertical imbalance, social programme indicator and expenditure per capita through the new municipalities have been increased during fiscal decentralization.

14.3.7.2 Incidence of Poverty in 29 New Municipalities in Nepal

The new municipalities are relatively weaker in resources, service delivery, physical infrastructure and organizational capabilities. Except few cases, new municipalities are not developed. From Fig. 14.7 we understand that the incidence of poverty in new municipalities has been decreasing rapidly over the time period 1988–2010 in Nepal. The head count poverty ratio is the highest in the year 1988 and lowest in the year 2008 in the new municipalities.

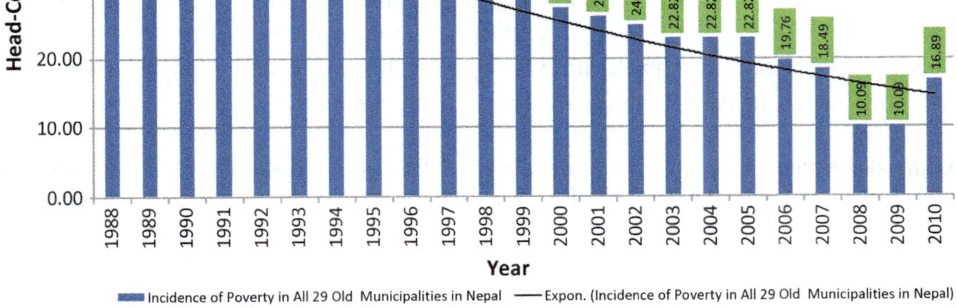

Fig. 14.7 Incidence of poverty in 29 new municipalities in Nepal

14.4 Summary and Conclusion

From the estimation of result we categorized the total 58 municipalities of Nepal in seven categories, namely, total, hilly, terain, eastern, western, old and new. We considered the descriptive statistics of the indicators of each and every category of municipalities in the preliminary part of each section. The descriptive statistics helped us get the average value of the indicators over the time period. It also facilitated comparison of the state of indicators between prior and posterior of the promulgation of Local Self Governance Act, 1999 in Nepal. In all the cases it is found distinct and comparable result of the indicators in prior and posterior to the enactment of Local Self Governance Act, 1999 in Nepal.

We have considered the trend of incidence of poverty for each categories of the municipality with bar diagram and trend line across the year 1983 to year 2010 in Nepal. In all the cases, we found the incidence of poverty has been smoothly declining over the time period. It means the poverty in the urban area of the country has been decreasing in Nepal over the last three decades. The decreasing trend of poverty before the enactment of Local Self Governance Act, 1999 is slower, however, after the enactment of Local Self Governance Act, 1999 the decreasing rate in the incidence of poverty is rapid one. It was found that the incidence of poverty is higher in the terain municipalities whereas the same is lesser in the hilly municipalities in Nepal. On the basis of this result, we can conclude that there might be positive impact of fiscal decentralization on poverty in Nepal.

The fiscal indicators of the municipalities in Nepal have been discussed in each of the seven categories over the time period 1983–2010. The indicators which we have considered are relative size, tax autonomy, own source of revenue per capita, vertical imbalance, social programme indicator, expenditure per capita, and service provider indicator of the municipalities. These indicators represent different dimensions of the fiscal decentralization at the municipal level in Nepal. A clear discrepancy between the municipalities is evident. Despite the geographical location and age of formation of the municipalities in all indicators eastern regional, old generation, hilly municipalities are the best performer of fiscal decentralization. That is western regional, new generation and terain municipalities are relatively weaker in the fiscal decentralization in Nepal. This is the interesting fact for fiscal decentralization in Nepal which we found from the analysis.

Acknowledgements The author is grateful to Dr. Maniklal Adhikary, Professor of Economics, the University of Burdwan, W B-713104, India, for his support and suggestions. However, the author takes responsibility for any remaining errors.

Appendix: Classification of Municipalities in Nepal

S.N.	Municipalities	Topography	Location	Generation	District	Zone	Region
1	Ilam	Hilly	Eastern	Old	Illam	Mechi	EDR
2	Bhadrapur	Terain	Eastern	Old	Jhapa.	Mechi	EDR
3	Damak	Terain	Eastern	Old	Jhapa	Mechi	EDR
4	Mechinagar	Terain	Eastern	New	Jhapa	Mechi	EDR
5	Biratnagar	Terain	Eastern	Old	Morang	Koshi	EDR
6	Dharan	Terain	Eastern	Old	Sunsari	Koshi	EDR
7	Inaruwa	Terain	Eastern	Old	Sunsari	Koshi	EDR
8	Itahari	Terain	Eastern	New	Sunsari	Koshi	EDR
9	Dhankuta	Hilly	Eastern	New	Dhankuta	Koshi	EDR
10	Khandbari	Hilly	Eastern	New	Sankhuwasabha	Koshi	EDR
11	Rajbiraj	Terain	Eastern	Old	Saptari	Sagarmatha	EDR
12	Lahan	Terain	Eastern	Old	Siraha	Sagarmatha	EDR
13	Siraha	Terain	Eastern	New	Siraha	Sagarmatha	EDR
14	Triyuga	Hilly	Eastern	New	Udaypur	Sagarmatha	EDR
15	Janakpur	Terain	Eastern	Old	Dhanusha	Janakpur	CDR
16	Jaleswor	Terain	Eastern	Old	Mahottari	Janakpur	CDR
17	Malangawa	Terain	Eastern	New	Sarlahi	Janakpur	CDR
18	Bhimeswar	Hilly	Eastern	New	Dolakha	Janakpur	CDR
19	Kamala Mai	Hilly	Eastern	New	Sindhuli	Janakpur	CDR
20	Kathmandu	Hilly	Eastern	Old	Kathmandu	Bagmati	CDR
21	Kirtipur	Hilly	Eastern	Old	Kathmandu	Bagmati	CDR
22	Lalitpur	Hilly	Eastern	Old	Lalitpur	Bagmati	CDR
23	Bhaktapur	Hilly	Eastern	New	Bhaktapur	Bagmati	CDR
24	Madhyapurthimi	Hilly	Eastern	New	Bhaktapur	Bagmati	CDR
25	Banepa	Hilly	Eastern	Old	Kavre Palanchok	Bagmati	CDR
26	Dhulikhel	Hilly	Eastern	New	Kavre Palanchok	Bagmati	CDR
27	Panauti	Hilly	Eastern	New	Kavre Palanchok	Bagmati	CDR
28	Bidur	Hilly	Eastern	New	Nuwakot	Bagmati	CDR
29	Birgunj	Terain	Eastern	Old	Parsa	Narayani	CDR
30	Hetaunda	Hilly	Eastern	Old	Makwanpur	Narayani	CDR
31	Kalaiya	Terain	Eastern	Old	Bara	Narayani	CDR
32	Bharatpur	Terain	Eastern	Old	Chitwan	Narayani	CDR
33	Ratnanagar	Terain	Eastern	New	Chitwan	Narayani	CDR
34	Gaur	Terain	Eastern	New	Rautahat	Narayani	CDR
35	Pokhara	Hilly	Western	Old	Kaski	Gandaki	WDR
36	Lekhnath	Hilly	Western	New	Kaski	Gandaki	WDR
37	Byas	Hilly	Western	New	Tanahun	Gandaki	WDR
38	Gorkha	Hilly	Western	New	Gorkha	Gandaki	WDR
39	Waling	Hilly	Western	New	Syangja	Gandaki	WDR

(continued)

(continued)

S.N.	Municipalities	Topography	Location	Generation	District	Zone	Region
40	Putali Bazar	Hilly	Western	New	Syangja	Gandaki	WDR
41	Baglung	Hilly	Western	New	Baglung	Dhaulagiri	WDR
42	Siddharthanagar	Terain	Western	Old	Rupendehi	Lumbini	WDR
43	Butwal	Terain	Western	Old	Rupendehi	Lumbini	WDR
44	Tansen	Hilly	Western	Old	Palpa	Lumbini	WDR
45	Kapilvastu	Terain	Western	Old	Kapilvastu	Lumbini	WDR
46	Ramgram	Terain	Western	New	Nawalparasi	Lumbini	WDR
47	Ghorahi	Terain	Western	Old	Dang	Rapti	MWDR
48	Tulsipur	Terain	Western	New	Dang	Rapti	MWDR
49	Nepalgunj	Terain	Western	Old	Banke	Bheri	MWDR
50	Birendranagar	Terain	Western	Old	Surkhet	Bheri	MWDR
51	Guleria	Terain	Western	New	Bardiya	Bheri	MWDR
52	Narayan	Hilly	Western	New	Dailekh	Bheri	MWDR
53	Dhangadi	Terain	Western	Old	Kailali	Seti	FWDR
54	Tikapur	Terain	Western	New	Kailali	Seti	FWDR
55	Dipayal	Hilly	Western	Old	Doti	Seti	FWDR
56	Bhimdutta	Terain	Western	Old	Kanchanpur	Mahakali	FWDR
57	Amargadhi	Hilly	Western	New	Dadeldhura	Mahakali	FWDR
58	Dasarathchand	Hilly	Western	New	Baitadi	Mahakali	FWDR

Note

(1) Kathmandu is Municipal Corporation; Biratnagr, Birgunj, Lalitpur and Pokhara are Sub-municipal Corporation and remaining 53 cities are Municipalities

(2) Gorkha, Ghorahi and Bhimdutta were previously called Prithvi Narayan, Tribhuwan Nagar and Mahendra Nagar respectively

(3) EDR, CDR, WDR, MWDR and FWDR are the abbreviation form of Eastern Development Region, Central Development Region, Western Development Region, Mid-Western Development Region and Far-Western Development Region respectively

(4) Recently declared municipalities are not considered for the study because of the unavailability of data

References

Besley, T., & Coate, S. (2003). Centralized versus decentralized provision of local public goods: A political economy approach. *Journal of Public Economics, 87*(12), 2611–2637.

Faguet, J. (2004). Does decentralization increase responsiveness to local needs? Evidence from Bolivia. *Journal of Public Economics, 88,* 867–894.

MoLJ. (1999). *Local self governance act, 1999.* Kathmandu: Ministry of Law and Justice (MoLJ).

MoLJ. (2007). *The interim constitution of Nepal, 2007* (Eighth Amendment, May 28, 2010). Kathmandu: MoLJ.

MuAN. (2003). *Resource mobilization strategy for new municipalities based on Gulariya Municipality.* Lalitpur, Nepal: Municipal Association of Nepal (MuAN).

NPC. (2010). *Three year plan approach paper (2010/11–2012/13).* Kathmandu: National Planning Commission (NPC).

Pindyck, R. S., & Rubinfeld, D. L. (1998). *Econometric models and economic forecasts* (International Edition). Singapore: Irwin/McGraw-Hill.

Sepulveda, C. F., & Martinez-Vazquez, J. (2010). *The consequences of fiscal decentralization on poverty and income inequality.* Working Paper No. 10-2, February, 2010. Georgia: Andrew Young School of Policy Studies, Georgia State University.

Silwal, S. (2012). Municipal resource generation system and its mobilization trends in Nepal: The experience of western development region. *Journal of University Grants Commission, 1*(1), 216–234.

Chapter 15
Rural Poverty and Employment Guarantee Scheme: Reflections from West Bengal

Manjima Mandal and Amal Mandal

Abstract Public works programme or workfare programme has emerged as the strategic intervention in addressing unemployment, poverty as well as infrastructure building. The central plank of the programme is that income transfer particularly during distress times enables consumption soothing for the poor households and the resultant sustainable assets generate another bout of livelihood avenues. MGNREGA in India is the largest employment guarantee programme in the world in terms of statutory ordination as well as coverage. It has evoked positive expectations as it is poised to reduce poverty, reverse inequality and out-migration and to resuscitate rural economy by improving infrastructure and agricultural productivity. Notwithstanding the prodigious potentialities and few survey evidences on the affirmative impacts on rural poverty, it is equally emphatic that the success of MGNREGA would hinge on many pre-requisites like rolling out of at least the stipulated days of work to the poor especially during the time of joblessness (as in lean agricultural session) and the undertaken works having clear focus on agricultural productivity and rural livelihood. With the general objective of peeking at whether and how MGNREGA is reaching out to areas/ regions with larger concentration of rural poor, this chapter singles out the poorest district of West Bengal (i.e. Cooch Behar) and its poorest administrative Block (i.e. Dinhata-I) and explores the association between the progress of MGNREGA and participation of the poor in the sample district and Block. The analysis of the aggregate official data evinces that MGNREGA has fallen short of offering the envisaged number of person-days, thus it has not catered to the subsistence demands of the poor. In other words, a clear relationship between the outreach of MGNREGA and the proportion of the poor households seems to be missing and this is likely to have little impact on the poverty eradication efforts and outcome. Together with such disconnect, the

M. Mandal (✉)
Central Bank of India, Cooch Behar, India
e-mail: manjimacob9@rediffmail.com

A. Mandal
Political Science, Tufanganj College, Cooch Behar, WB, India
e-mail: amalcob@rediffmail.com

U.K. De et al. (eds.), *Inequality, Poverty and Development in India*, India Studies in Business and Economics, DOI 10.1007/978-981-10-6274-2_15

chapter also highlights few other procedural dimensions which hold up the general fruition of MGNREGA.

Keywords Employment guarantee scheme · BPL · Person-days generated Poverty eradication · Migration · West Bengal · Cooch Behar

15.1 The Promise of Breakthrough

Public works programme—otherwise known as workfare programme—has emerged as the strategic intervention in addressing unemployment, poverty, distress migration as well as buttressing basic infrastructure. Such programme is favoured in developed countries as a means to reduce disincentives provoked by social security systems and in the developing countries, it is being embraced not only for better target benefits to the poor but also to use the growing labour force to build up infrastructure (Ravi and Engler 2015). The rationales of the programme rest on some critical planks. By affording income transfer particularly during distress times, such programme enables consumption soothing of the poor households. The substantial and sustainable assets like infrastructure coming out of the programme works generate another bout of employment/livelihood potentialities.

Such programmes, as in India and elsewhere, have few common and crucial characteristics. (i) The central/federal government funds the activities related to the works which are open to anybody willing and able to avail the opportunity. (ii) Such works offer a living wage notified by the government and decent working conditions and facilities. (iii) By its basic nature, the programme is not targeted social protection programme or welfare programme for the poor. Rather it is universal in nature where anybody can work under the envisaged design and provisions. (iv) The programme is demand driven and not definitely supply oriented and its design favours self-selection. The potential beneficiaries decide whether and when to seek and actually work. (v) From administrative standpoint, the programme is highly rewarding. In many other erstwhile welfare programmes the government sought to select the beneficiaries where the administrative cost was quite high and the possibility of wrong selection was unavoidable. But in case of self-selection, the administrative cost is minimal and aberration is least. (vi) The primary purpose of such programme is to palliate poverty of those who face joblessness and income deprivation. Yet, the programme is not anti-poverty per se. The design is such where non-poor will find least incentive to participate in manual, strenuous and occasional works with fixed wage rate. It does have positive impacts on various dimensions of poverty when and where only the really poor people are incentivized to embrace the programme. The incremental income from works would certainly impact the livelihood of the poor households (hereafter HHs).

Compared to employment guarantee programme in many other countries, MGNREGA (Mahatma Gandhi National Rural Employment Guarantee Act) in India is the most comprehensive in terms of statutory ordination and coverage.

Covering the entire length and breadth of India, MGNREGA—hereafter *the programme*—has reportedly opened up enormous number of person-days, certainly much more than the previous welfare and anti-poverty programmes. And serious headways into the food insecurity, migration and rural poverty are supposed to be unequivocal. The programme has evoked positive expectations and euphoria, arguably bordering on bravura. This robust 'social protection' and employment programme is all set to reduce poverty, reverse inequality and to regenerate rural economy by improving infrastructure and enhancing agricultural productivity (UNDP 2010).

Few survey reports reveal its significant impacts on extreme poverty, measured in terms of increase in monthly per capita expenditure on food and non-foods among HHs, per capita consumption expenditure and reduction on the number of meals foregone by the participating HHs (Liu and Deininger 2010; Ravi and Engler 2015; Coffey et al. 2011; IDYWC 2010; Kareemulla et al. 2009). It has provided basic income assurance to a large number of beneficiaries (NREGA Sameekha 2012), and because of such works only a minuscule proportion of rural HHs opt for alternative employment options (NSSO 2012).

Notwithstanding the potentialities and survey assertions, it is also imperative to emphasise that the impact of the programme would hinge on many preconditions such as the outreach of the programme, participation of the poor, the extent and seasonality of the employment, timely wage payment, rise in market wage in agriculture as well as non-agriculture works and enhancement of agricultural productivity. More legislation and consequent programme are likely to mean little, given the awful Indian experience of poverty alleviation efforts.

One absorbing debate is whether the finding of NSSO (2010–11) that poverty has declined considerably was anyway related to the successful implementation of the programme. However, in the poverty debate one has to tread cautiously and the role of the programme should not be over-stated. Even if one accepts the official poverty line of Rs. 816 per capita per month for the rural areas (a la Tendulkar Committee 2009), a typical five member HH will have to earn at least Rs. 48,960 per annum to come out of poverty clutches. If three members of the HH participate, say, in 100 days of work—as is the stipulation—it can on average earn Rs. 45,000 (@150/- per day). One moderately poor HH can move out of poverty for the year, if it is provided with 100 days of work. For the ultra poor (<75% of poverty line income), 100 days of work will certainly reduce the intensity but not the incidence of poverty.

Arguably the most important prerequisite for denting in rural poverty will be the availability of at least 100 days of work and that too during the times of joblessness as in the agricultural lean season (August–November in West Bengal) and the nature of programme works having a particular focus on enhancing agricultural productivity. In other words, the focus and consequent efficacy must be on poverty ridden geographical regions and pockets. Otherwise, the spectre of poverty will continue to haunt or hobble, notwithstanding some improvement or breakthrough here and there.

15.2 Objective and Methodology

Is the programme reaching particularly to the poverty concentrated areas or is it serving the rural landless, agricultural labourers or the rural poor who hail necessarily from lower social stratum and who need the programme most?

Admittedly, one authentic way to ascertain the efficacy of the programme relating to poverty is the survey-based investigation in a specific locale. However, the focus of this chapter is not on survey-based exploration but on analysis of official data concerning mainly the person-days created in poverty-ridden areas. Such aggregate level analysis seems important for the reason that if and when there are not enough work opportunities, justification for primary-level investigation will be least. After all, the very objective of the programme can come into fruition only when sufficient work opportunities are made available to the rural poor. And the person-day per HH is one objective and an important indicator for such estimation.

Confining investigative attention exclusively to the state of West Bengal, the chapter explores the aggregate performance of the programme in one district that has the highest proportion of BPL (below poverty line) households, agricultural labourer and incidence of migration in the state. Moreover, the administrative Block having the most BPL HHs, labourers and migration in the district has also been attended to for the purpose of gaining some insights into the progress and impact of this flagship as well as touted programme.

In West Bengal, the sample district is Cooch Behar and the administrative block is Dinhata-I. Such selection is not based on subjective choice but on the official figures of BPL HHs, agricultural labourer and extent of migration for causal labouring. Based on the BPL Survey, 2002 (subsequent survey is yet to be published) and Rural Household Survey, 2005 (undertaken by the Department of Panchayats and Rural Development), the district and block have been singled out as they have the highest proportion of BPL HHs and labourers in the state and district respectively.

West Bengal is a state that is hobbled by inordinately higher rates of population density, unemployment, migration, sagging agriculture and of course poverty, more so in rural Bengal. All these features, both individually and collectively, make a strong case for successful and sustained MGNREGA.

According to Census Report, 2001 the work participation rate in West Bengal has increased in percentage term. But this is singularly because of increase in marginal workforce. The significant decrease in the main workforce and a consequent jump in marginal workers essentially imply that new jobs have been opened mostly outside of the organised or formal sector of state economy. Such trends entrench uncertainty and vulnerability of the workforce.

As per NSSO Report (61st Round, 2004–05), West Bengal holds the dubious distinction of having the highest (10.6%) number of HHs not having enough food every day for some months of a year. Moreover, the state holds the inauspicious third rank in respect of percentage of rural HHs not getting enough food every day in all months of a year. Such persistent hunger coupled with starvation deaths bodes ill for the poor of the state.

Regarding the incidence of poverty, there is the claim that the reduction of poverty in West Bengal has been phenomenal and this is because of successful land reforms impacting positive changes in economic relations and agricultural upsurge. Establishment of panchayats has also reinforced the momentum and reach of land reforms. The panchayats have led to the effective implementation of development policy without target failure, leakage or hijacking by elites. Undoubtedly, during 1981–91 the annual exponential agricultural growth was as high as 6.4% and during this decade the decrease of poverty was unequivocal (28%). However, in subsequent decades there has been stagnation and decline in agriculture, sharp fall in agricultural productivity and because of such reversals, the rural poverty reduction could not be sustained, as in 1993–2005.

In the state, more than 60% of rural and 40% of state population depend on agriculture which contributes about 30% of state's GDP. However, agriculture has not undergone structural overhauling in strict and dispassionate terms. The touted land reform remains parochial in general and unfinished in particular. Out of total 10 lakh acre of acquired land, only 2.5 lakh acres have actually been distributed. And, out of 3 million bargadars, only 1/2 has been registered. When 40% rural HHs are landless, 13% Pattadars lost possession of land and 14% bargadars get evicted from land (HDRWB 2004), the situation is amply worrisome.

At the same time, the reverse trend in real wage has set in. The real wage for both casual agricultural and non-agricultural workers has slumped in between 1993–2000. Both in percentage and absolute number, the extent of agricultural labourers has increased significantly. Thus, many rural HHs remain engaged in those works that offer trifling little prospect of sufficient income necessary for getting out of poverty trap. To cut a long story short, agriculture in West Bengal is rapidly becoming non-remunerative for the small and marginal farmers, a sizable portion of the rural workforce is being pushed out of agriculture and the growing number of marginal works with lesser and exploitative wage rates are stark starring at the rural HHs.

Regarding the incidence and frequency of poverty in West Bengal, there are several estimates with contrasting methodologies and these divulge disparate results. In the poverty discourse, there is a virtual duel between central and state governments. While central government tends to deflate poverty, state governments try to peg it at the maximum level so much so that it does not discredit them. The underlying reason is that the resource allocation from central government is based on the proportion of poor in the states.

Without entering into the debate as to the representative and comprehensive methodologies etc., let us focus on poverty estimates by the West Bengal government itself. Two specific recent sources are BPL Survey, 2002 and Rural Household Survey (RHS), 2005. The RHS, in particular, is fundamentally different from others estimates. It was based on 12 parameters (housing, clothing, education, migration, etc.), each with 5-point scale. In the survey, each HH could score maximum 60 and minimum 12 points. Less than 33 was the cut off score for designating HH as BPL. Moreover, the survey was undertaken by the state government employees (i.e. primary school teachers). And more importantly, the survey results are being used for offering targeted benefits to rural people (houses under IAY for instance).

What the BPL and RHS reports reveal are not very cheering or emboldening. The state's own surveys substantiate that rural poverty is no less enormous. BPL Survey, 2002 found total 34% HHs as BPL, 49% as agricultural labourer and 16% HHs resorting to migration for causal labouring (Table 15.1). Both in absolute and percentage terms, the figures do not validate the assertion that rural poverty in the state is manageable or palatable. Among districts, while Purulia and Uttar Dinajpur had more than 40% BPL HHs, the highest position was apportioned by Cooch Behar (52%). Contrary to popular expectation, Purulia, one least developed and tribal inhabited district, did not have ominous extent of poverty.

Table 15.1 Rural poverty in West Bengal

District	Total families (No)	BPL HH (%)		Agricultural labour HH (%)	HH migrating for casual labour (%)
		BPL survey[a]	RHS		
Bankura	775,826	28.9	42.5	42.3	14.2
Birbhum	722,169	42.3	44	54.6	23.2
Burdwan	1,180,811	33.5	26.4	50.6	16.7
Cooch Behar	689,316	51.8	46	59.2	23
Dakshin Dinajpur	432,476	31.7	43.5	48.9	11.9
Darjeeling	276,911	24.4	44.9	39.6	11.5
Hooghly	878,164	21.8	29.1	41.7	13.3
Howrah	686,328	14.9	32.2	38.1	10.2
Jalpaiguri	781,701	35.54	35.8	50.6	8.9
Malda	792,311	39.2	38.8	53.4	17.2
Murshidabad	1,407,378	39.9	43.3	54.6	20.2
Nadia	962,299	37.2	34.2	54	16.5
North 24 Parganas	1,214,718	29.3	37.7	51.3	14.3
Paschim Medinipur	1,163,394	36.4	32.9	42.2	21.8
Purba Medinipur	865,847	32	26.9	47.2	21.8
Purulia	639,246	32.9	43.7	41	13.8
South 24 Parganas	1,488,874	34.2	37.2	50.5	20.9
Uttar Dinajpur	567,560	40	41	52.4	14.5
Total	15,525,329	34.1	43.8	51	21

Source Rural Household Survey (2005), Department of Panchayats and Rural Development, Government of West Bengal

[a]*Source* of column three: BPL Survey (2002), Government of West Bengal

If BPL Survey Report was not damning, RHS, 2005 really is. RHS corroborates not only the massive extent of poverty but also the worsening situation over the years. RHS discloses that out of total 1.5 crore rural HHs, 43.8% was BPL, 51% agricultural labourer, 57% landless, 31% marginal farmers and 21% HHs opting to migration. Compared to BPL Survey, 2002, the situation had thus aggravated, not a credible report card for the state. Malda district accounted for the highest BPL HHs (58.7%), closely followed by Cooch Behar and Murshidabad. However, computing the average ranking of the districts, Cooch Behar is found to be the most poverty infested district. Out of total 689,316 HHs, 55.6% was BPL, 59% was agricultural labourer, 53% landless and 25% inclined to migration in Cooch Behar. Despite having 2nd rank in BPL, Cooch Behar stood first in two other parameters (Agricultural labourer and migration). Cooch Behar has thus been regarded as the poorest district in the state.

In the poorest district of Cooch Behar, Dinhata-I Block has the highest rate of poverty in overall rankings. Though Dinhata-I has less than 3.5% of BPL HHs than the first ranked Block, it accounted for highest extent of agricultural labourer and migration. Like Cooch Behar district, Dinhata-I is thus found to be the most poverty stricken block. Based on such rankings, Cooch Behar and Dinhata-I Block have been taken as the sample unit for the exposition of progress of the programme in West Bengal.

The rest of the chapter is organised as follows. In the next section, an overview of the progress and performance of the programme in West Bengal has been furnished—mainly as the background information on which the reflections should be posited. Then relatively detailed dissection of performance of the programme is made in the district Cooch Behar and Dinhata-I Block. And together with overall trends perceptible in the district Cooch Behar, few general remarks are appended at the last part.

15.3 Poverty of Progress!

West Bengal tends to be one intriguing state where the outreach and effectiveness of the programme could have been much more substantial than what it is till date. Some specific reasons for positive expectations being that: the then ruling Left Front, CPI(M) in particular, passionately supported the employment guarantee Bill and proclaimed strong political commitment to it (unlike many other ruling parties). The panchayat system—having pivotal role to play relating to this programme—is supposed to be vibrant, dynamic and representative in the state. Moreover, about 27% of total HHs is BPL and the state has the highest unemployment rates. However, since inception of the programme, the state has fumbled and its performance is comparatively and considerably dismal. To use the prognosis of Drèze and Oldiges (2009), the lurching in West Bengal is perhaps due to the ambivalent attitude of the state government towards MGNREGA right from the beginning.

The performance of the programme in West Bengal has been no less poor right from the commencement. Since inception of the programme, West Bengal fared poorly compared to other Indian states (like Andhra Pradesh, Tamil Nadu, Rajasthan) and its performance was not in any way commensurate with the number and nature of poor people in the state. Against the demand of employment, only 14 person-days of job could be provided in 2006–07 which later on increased to 25 in 2007–08 and 26 in 2008–09. And the corresponding national person-days were 43, 42 and 47. The state's average person-days have subsequently stagnated and could not come anyway near to the national average: 20 in 2009–10, 25.6 in 2010–11, 27 in 2011–12 and 31.7 in 2012–13. The average person-day per HH in the state was 20, 25, 27 and 31.7 in 2009–2011.

Among its 18 districts, North 24 Parganas could provide the highest 28 person-days and Uttar Dinajpur provided barely 11.6 and Cooch Behar 13.7 days during in 2009–10 (Table 15.2). Incidentally, North 24 Parganas fared better among the districts consistently and comparatively. The average higher person-days in Darjeeling could be because of its better performance in 2011–13. Cooch Behar stood last in 2010–2013: the 4-year average generation of person-days was just 14.5, closely followed by Uttar Dinajpur, Siliguri and Dakshin Dinajpur. Incidentally, all the major poor performers were from the Northern region of the state.

Table 15.2 Average person-days generated in districts of West Bengal (2009–13)

District/Year	2009–10	2010–11	2011–12	2012–13	Average
Bankura	22.63	37.65	30.57	34.68	31.4
Birbhum	22.38	26.38	36.09	40.99	31.5
Burdwan	23.28	32.79	25.43	28.59	27.5
Cooch Behar	13.74	13.98	14.1	16.17	14.5 [1st]
Dakshin Dinajpur	19.18	20.33	21.38	23.74	21.2 [4th]
Darjeeling Hill Council	20.85	37.52	50.15	59.25	41.9
Hooghly	17.18	28.68	30.73	36.19	28.2
Jalpaiguri	25.45	23.2	25.99	23.71	24.6
Malda	18.67	22.34	28.94	28.16	24.5
Murshidabad	18.85	24.8	21.93	24.83	22.6
Nadia	19.33	19.16	19.08	39.08	24.2
North 24 Parganas	28.31	32.22	34.6	43.9	34.8
Paschim Medinipur	26.77	29.87	24.76	26.29	26.9
Purba Medinipur	23.35	23.63	26.72	34.25	27.0
Purulia	26.75	33.47	28.69	33.49	30.6
Siliguri	12.64	17.2	18.32	18.19	16.6 [3rd]
South 24 Paragans	17.16	20.32	32.12	40.55	27.5
Uttar Dinajpur	11.56	17.04	18.4	17.82	16.2 [2nd]

Source NREGA Website
Note In parentheses ascending rank of few districts

Though West Bengal could hardly reap benefits from the programme (Rao et al. 2008), there has been debate as to its turnaround in subsequent years. In 2013–14, the state is reported to have gained some ground. Till 2011–12 the state was among the worst performing states in terms of person-days, with an average figure of around 20 days against the Indian figure of 45 days. Total person-days had never earlier crossed 10 crore in the state that has about one crore job card holder, one-half of which are active job seekers.

The state government in West Bengal claimed that the state topped in 2012–13 with implementation of projects worth Rs. 4475.80 crore, which is the highest in the country, and generated employment for 57.76 lakh families. In an advertisement published in local dailies (May 16, 2013) the Panchayat and Rural Development Department claimed that West Bengal had achieved a total man-days of about 20 crore which is 109 per cent higher than the national target. "Compared to the 2011–12 financial year, we have increased 33 per cent more man-days in 2012–13 which itself is an achievement."

In 2013–14 the state is supposed to have emerged as one of the best performing states and it generated over 11.3 crore person-days that positioned it as the 5th ranking state. This was due to the change of attitude of the state government. Earlier the programme was treated as one of many schemes. Now it was being regarded as the most important scheme (The Telegraph 2014).

However, the claim is not without contestation. The national statistics suggest that the state ranked 24th on the 2012–13 list. The former Union Minister of State for Urban Development Ms. Deepa Das Munsi retorted: "The state has ranked 24th on the list. It is all about statistical jugglery. West Bengal is on the top of the list in terms of getting sanctioned funds under MGNREGS and its disbursement. But since the numbers of total families are more in our state, statistics show a different picture as we have to divide total man-days with the number of total households."

Though only handful in-depth studies have so far been undertaken in West Bengal, their general conclusions are not unequivocally heartening. Among the positives, the additional employment had increased the rate of wage for agricultural labourers. The combined effects of such employment and higher wage rate impacted (as in Birbhum) positive changes in per capita annual income of programme workers, monthly per capita expenditure on food consumption (Sarkar 2011). Another positive contribution (again in Birbhum) was the outcome of better quality jobs—better working environment, higher daily wage compared to the prevailing market rates (Dey 2009). Consequent upon such works, the overall living standard had reportedly improved a bit. Due to incremental income, HHs could spend more on food, clothing, housing and education (Ghosh 2011). Moreover, few sample Job Card holders used the programme income to start, run or expand rural business. The programme tended to have fan rural entrepreneurship (Mangatter 2011).

However, the villagers were generally unaware about the provisions of the programme even in the areas where it had relatively been successful in creating a substantial number of person-days. In some areas people were not aware of the wage rates, and they in almost all the areas, were not aware of the fact that they are legally entitled to at least 100 days of employment and unemployment allowance in the absence of work (Das 2013). Another striking point is that villagers did not know that it is a demand-based programme where applicants should get work within 15 days of applying for the work. There were times during the lean season when they could work neither as an agricultural labourer nor in the programme works as the panchayats reported unavailability of works. As a result, they migrated to the adjacent cities to find employment (Das et al. 2012).

The situation was found to be more disquieting at the Gram Panchayat (GP) level. Survey reports in Birbhum attested that while the demand was to the extent of 204 days, the actual works could be to the tune of just 61 days—meeting about 10% of demand and 20% of entitlement. The variations of performance across GPs were equally emphatic: the better performing GPs created about three times more jobs than the laggard ones (Dey 2009).

More worrisome is the finding that during agricultural lean session when traditional agricultural activities dry up and poor households try to cope up the severe scarcity of livelihood with distress migration and selling off durable possessions, the programme works fail to emerge as the succour. The abnormally lower extent of employment during lean session essentially implies that the programme stumbles to provide income safety net to the poor HHs (Dey 2009). One probable accounting reason is that during lean session the monsoon does not permit earth works, which are the predominant component of the project works. Thus, unless the fixation with the earth works is shifted to other works, the succour is unlikely to be imminent in West Bengal.

Surely, the programme is universal and rights based. The poor people otherwise finding income-earning opportunity difficult should get the works. Yet, the works could not be availed as entitlement and as per demand. Political clientelism punctures their rights. As in Cooch Behar district, the ruling party supporters (at GP) worked in significantly higher number of days and they earned more than the non-ruling party supporters. Perceived supporters of non-ruling party were denied works even after recording demand (Das 2015). Seen overall, political clientelism may be preferable to regressive elite or caste-based domination, but such political manoeuvring or manipulation mars the universal entitlement of the rural poor.

The programme must receive due importance and must be better implemented in areas having higher concentration of poor people. But survey evidences evince otherwise: relatively successful implementation in those GPs having fewer agricultural labourer (as in Birbhum). At the same time, the availability of programme fund at GP and block levels was not associated with the number of job cards and public demand for employment (Mukherjee and Ghosh 2009).

Thus, the fundamental question survives. If the poverty concentrated GPs do not come up with commensurate works absorbing labour force demand and if the programme fund does not conform to the demand, the very efficacy of the programme will remain awry.

The programmes could not stem even the short-term migration by ‘any of the member of the households’ (Das 2015). However, it was observed that had the number of days of getting work increased the probability of migration would have deceased. This could have been possible through creation of more employment opportunities especially during lean season and overall increase in rural agricultural and non-agricultural wage rates.

What is unequivocal is the fact that almost all the survey reports contend that unpalatable is the extent of employment offered, denial of works, untimely wage payment and scanty coverage to the marginalised stratum of rural HHs. The programme benefits could be greater and comprehensive if HHs were provided with more works, especially during distress times.

15.4 Cooch Behar District

To reiterate, Cooch Behar district has the largest proportion of BPL HHs (51.8%), agricultural labourer (59%) and out-migration for causal labouring (23%) and these are in sharp contrast to the incidences and figures of West Bengal. Thus, the programme must receive foremost importance in order to arrest or alleviate all the disquieting features. However, closer look at the official figures relating to the implementation of the programme does not divulge reassuring trends. In fact, the overall situation is worse and to some extent unacceptable.

In contrast to the usual feature where the official figures tend to testify that almost all HHs demanding employment have been provided works, the position of Cooch Behar district is evidently eerie. While in the first year of implementation about 60% of total HH demanding employment could be offered works, there was sharp slump in the engagement of workers in subsequent years. Though the initial demand for work in 2007–08 was somewhat modest compared to the succeeding years, the momentum could not be sustained in the following years and this perhaps points to the petering out of the popularity of the programme. Compared to the total number of demand for employment (273,508) in 2007–08, it slumped to 228,955 in 2008–09 and 205,173 in 2009–10. The public demand rose a bit in 2010–11 but again dipped in next two years. Thus, the perceptible pattern of high demand was followed by a slip thereafter. However, the demand for employment increased by about threefold in 2013–14.

While barely 55% HHs had on average been offered employment during 2009–14 (Table 15.3), such appalling rates reveal the inability of the implementing agencies to come up with adequate, if not sufficient number of projects that could have absorbed the labour demand. Almost identical trend over the years indicates that the authorities did not redirect or re-marshal the initiative or strategy.

More ominous is the average person-day per HH. Except in 2009–10, abysmally low person-days had been created, the average of which was barely 19 days. The number of HHs completing 100 days of work was just 12 in the second year, though it increased gradually particularly during 2013–14.

Starting with a meagre number in 2007–08, the volume of works undertaken increased over the years particularly from 2009–10. But the works completion rates were certainly unenviable—only 17% each in 2011–12 and 2013–14 and the 7 year

Table 15.3 Employment status under MGNREGA in Cooch Behar

Variables	2007-08	2008-09	2009-10	2010-11	2011-12	2012-13	2013-14	Average
HH demanded works (No.)	273,508	228,955	205,173	339,573	297,134	247,271	310,117	271,675
HH received work (%)	60.3	34.8	64.9	45.3	41.3	40.1	NA	55
Average person-day per HH	22.7	15.2	31.9	13.6	14.1	16.61	36.1	19
No. of HH received 100 day work	25	12	251	263	490	527	21,773	3334
No. of work taken up	2852	2765	4572	5118	7709	6114	11,789	5845
Work completion rate	36.8	47.6	50.2	39.5	17.1	33.6	17.1	34.6
Road connectivity works (%)	57.2	55.5	64.2	58.7	60.9	68.9	67.5	61.8
Flood control works (%)	10.5	9.2	4.1	4.5	2.9	3.6	3.4	5.4
Land development works (%)	13	17.4	18.9	22.2	13.4	9.5	10.7	15

Sources MGNREGA Website

average is 34.6%. Such low completion rate might be due to selection of unviable project works, abandonment of work in subsequent stages or arguably less probable is the nature of works having longer duration or gestation period.

In a poverty-stricken district, durable assets and enhancement of agricultural productivity should get due importance. Yet, the nature of works undertaken shows odd trends. The road connectivity has all along received highest priority—well over 55% of total works and 62% on average. Such emphasis on roads etc. may have long-term implications on the economic growth, but it throws up many vexing questions (taken up later). In the first 2 years, activities relating to flood control might have received some weightage but those lost steam in later years. Compared to flood control works, land development works have received more eminence but not to the extent of having lasting impact on agricultural growth in particular.

15.5 Dinhata-I Block

Dinhata-I in Cooch Behar district has the highest incidences of poverty, more so the share of agricultural labourer and migration. How has the programme progressed in the Block? Has it catered to the economic plights of the poor or has it sought to rejuvenate the local agriculture?

Let us start with few aggregate dimensions in Dinhata-I. Till 2014, total job cards were 74,468, of which 57% are active which is somewhat higher than the state average figure of around 50%. Out of total 154,234 workers, 37% was active workers for the programme. Total person-days generated in the block were 247,920 in 2012–13, 794,081 in 2013–14 and 1,124,184 in 2014–15 and during these three years the average person-days per HH happened to be 11.9, 27.9 and 33.6 respectively. Some improvements over the years are thus noticeable—though they fall far short of the guaranteed days and the palliative effects on the poor HHs are suspect. The average per-day wage rate was Rs. 145, 150 and 168 in between 2012–15. It is also worth mentioning that the average cost per worker was Rs. 252 in 2012–13, 173 in 2013–14 and 210 in 2014–15. Thus, the cost of work is considerably high and with this expenditure tangible benefits ought to have been created; otherwise the amount could go down the drain.

At disaggregate level, 16 GPs in Dinhata-I together have 50,325 BPL HHs (Table 15.4). Among the GPs, the higher BPL HHs were concentrated in Okrabari, followed by Petla, Putimari I and Matalhat. Conversely, Putimari-II had the lowest BPL, followed by Dinhata Village I and Bara Atiabari-II.

It may be instructive to note that the number of HH completed 100 days of work in the BPL concentrated GPs was rather moderate, 60 in Petla, 16 in Matalhat, 15 in Orkabari. The performance of these three GP was however far better than four other GPs who stumbled to offer significant number of days to each HH. Much higher rates are observed for moderately poor GP—Gitaldaha I and II.

Out of the major BPL concentrated GPs and in terms of ranking according to the generation of total person-days and person-day per HH, the position of Gitaldaha I

Table 15.4 MGNREGA performance in Dinhata-I block of Cooch Behar (cumulative till 2014–15)

Gram panchayat	No. of BPL HH[a]	HH demanded employment	HH provided employment	Person-days generated	Person-day per HH	Person-day SC (%)	Person-day women (%)	HH completed 100 days
Bara Atiabari-I	2425	2477	2317	75,671	40.4	35	52.2	16
Bara Atiabari-II	1906	1218	1872	35,858	19.2	27	43.4	0
Bara Soulmari	2784	2455	2630	64,934	34.7	49.8	64	18
Bhetaguri-I	2301	1927	1392	62,108	33.2	68.3	43.8	25
Bhetaguri-II	3587	2854	1300	76,609	40.9	50.6	79.3	4
Dinhata Vill-I	1949	1446	2896	49,140	26.3	42.3	70	10
Dinhata Vill-II	3133	1322	2601	19,225	10.3	47.3	9.7	0
Gitaldaha-I	3266	2914	1278	141,051	75.3	4.4	43.8	212
Gitaldaha-II	2074	2606	440	137,227	73.3	31.7	41.9	267
Gosanimari-I	3592	1394	2359	26,758	14.3	73.7	49.9	0
Gosanimari-II	2790	966	2878	8488	4.5	71.3	57.8	0
Matalhat	4424	2387	3451	69,653	37.2	65	50	16
Okrabari	5564	2984	2848	91,025	48.6	15	56.7	15
Petla	4489	3502	1622	112,530	60.1	45	50	60
Putimari-I	4445	2931	33,420	119,811	64.0	45.6	55.5	181
Putimari-II	1596	1726	2317	34,096	18.2	39.9	70.8	2
Average	50,325	35,109	65,621	1,124,184	17.1	38.5	53	826

Sources MGNREGA Website, [a]Rural Household Survey (2005)
SC Scheduled caste

seems notable, as it occupies first rank among all GPs. For other GPs, particularly second- and third-ranked GPs, the performance was moderate. Seen from overall perspective, the progress and performance of Gitaldaha I and II are outstanding relatively and considerably. And this perhaps authenticates many other local dynamics rather than mere presence of BPL HHs.

The share of SC in the total person-day was somewhat low, 38.5 on average. And this seems lower because the district has the highest extent of SC—more than 52% of total population—in the state. However, the meagre visibility of SC may be due to the considerable presence of Muslim population in Dinhata-I and whose participation is not recorded separately in the database. As to the share of SC workers, one has to tread cautiously because the SC population in the GPs many very considerably and the ranking should better be based on absolute number of SC in each GP concerned. Tentatively, fifth ranked GP Gosanimari I employed higher number of SCs and Gitaldaha I and Okrabari offered the least.

Work completion rate is yet another indicator that amplifies the health—sound or otherwise—of the programme. Suffice it to mention, West Bengal fairs poorly and the state has received flak from Comptroller and Auditor General (CAG) on this front. In Dinhata-I, the work completion rate is more or less akin to the state. The average rate for the 16 GPs of the Block was 51 during 2009–14. Year-wise, the highest rate was in 2009–10 and lowest in 2013–14. Among GPs, worst performer was Gitaldaha I—otherwise better performing one—which could not complete even single work in 2011–14 and its average rate stood at just 3 during 2009–14. Less than average 50% completion rate was observed in Gosanimari-I, Bara Atiabari-II and Bara Soulmari. Conversely, more than 80% rate could be achieved in Putimari-II and Bhetaguri-I. Such poor, if not awful rates vindicate either the selection of non-viable projects—may be because of scarcity of fund or substandard planning or lack of concerted initiatives of the GPs concerned. Either way, clear dearth of fruition of projects is unlikely to bolster the rural economy and infrastructure and mere creation of person-days will have trifling little influence on poverty etc.

15.6 Beyond the Rhetoric of Rights-Based Programme

Pre-requisites for poverty reduction efforts are the augmentation of productivity and profitability of agriculture, generation of gainful employment opportunities and inclusion of SCs, STs and women in the programme process and development of resources in deficient areas. In the absence of diversification of agriculture and rural economy as well as occupational diversification of the labour force, the livelihoods of the poor households dependent on agriculture revolve around the productivity of agriculture. The programme has the potentiality to address the issues of rural unemployment and poverty and to revitalise agriculture. However, the programme will have to come full circle if the potentialities are to be harnessed.

Like many other states, West Bengal is, however, besieged with many problems and inconsistencies as to the successful implementation of the programme. Survey and anecdotal evidences inform that the programme suffers from few procedural and substantial imbroglios, which stultify the overall outreach and efficacy of the programme as well as its positive impact on rural poverty.

Many rural people are not adequately aware about the procedures and process of the programme. Such insufficient knowledge makes them hardly equipped in actualising the demand driven nature of the programme as well as putting pressure on the implementing agencies as to their specific needs particularly during distress time. Such inadequacy is due to the imperviousness or inability of the implementing and other public agencies.

For the ordinary rural people the programme paraphernalia are rather complex and cumbersome. Registration for job card, written application for employment for at least 14 days at a stretch, receiving the dated receipt of the application, claim of unemployment allowance if works are not given within 14 days of demand all are tall order for the semi-literate poor people who remain busy with subsistence struggle and find little time to go or parley with GP officials etc. Because of poor knowledge, cognitive incapacity and scarcity of time, most people tend to depend on the power brokers—party functionaries and panchayat officials—who virtually control the demand, availability of works and selection of workers. Such intermediation was neither anticipated nor serves the interests of the poor. Unless direct linkage between people and implementing agencies is restored, the poor are likely to suffer and for this purpose some simplicity and predictability of the programme may be imperative.

The success of the programme depends squarely on the commitment, involvement and ability of GPs. Job card registration, receipt of work demand, assortment of labour demand including its seasonality, preparation of labour budget and self of projects (often in synchronisation with Gram Sabha), engagement of workers with work-site facilities, measurement of work, maintenance of muster roll and database, etc., all are the onus of GPs. The fundamental question is whether or how far GPs are devoted, equipped and willing to undertake all the responsibilities.

Together with the almost perennial shortage of manpower and technical know-how, etc, another problem is the preparation of annual and perspective plans. GPs are to implement at least 50% of total works and they are reportedly implementing close to 83% of total MGNREGA works. The programme puts serious governance pressures on panchayats. Each GP in particular has to make a perspective plan and annual plan for implementing the scheme. The perspective plan is an extensive exercise that includes charting of the village's resources, its poverty, its demands, work situations and based on these facts prescribing a template for future development requirements. The annual plan involves identifying needy people, scooping works for them in advance and also preparing horde of accounts. GPs are to get the plans approved by block and district officials as well. While these are easily said than done, it is also important to reiterate that the works can be offered if there is factual estimation of labour demand and approved shelf of projects in the annual and perspective plans.

At the same time, delay in allocation of fund throws GPs into the ire of the workers. Otherwise overburdened GPs find themselves really stretched in all inclusive sense. The poverty ridden GPs are generally far off from the block headquarter and they are relatively understaffed and technically wanting and this is one reason accounting for the failure of GPs in the poverty concentrated areas.

Timely availability of fund is another constraint. December–March is the usual period when works are relatively and substantially made available. But for inexplicable reasons, the fund availability during this eventful period gets a beating. Unless this session is used most effectively, the performance of the programme will remain skewed.

Fund based on the labour budget from the central and state government is not always made available to the implementing authorities, particularly to GPs. Allocation from the government takes time to reach to the implementing agencies. The situation has recently reached such a pass where wage payment is delayed for at least 6 months. Murmur is heard in many GPs where payment has not been paid for a year. Such delay discourages the poor to bank on the programme and agencies to spur or sustain their interests.

While in few other states the average engagement per active job card is somewhere in between 40–50 days, in West Bengal the disaggregate data divulge that about one-fourth job card holders receive <10 days of work in a year and another quarter work in the range of 11–20 days. With such meagre (and inconsistent) income, one cannot positively change the economic fortune. It cannot substantially be income safety net for a poor family. To be effective in the fight against poverty, the intervention must provide longer period of engagement and timely payment of wage.

West Bengal faces some exclusive impediments. Here the land–man ratio and population density are quite high and at times adverse. Available land for undertaking programme works is rather paltry. High cropping intensity in many Southern districts restricts the availability of land further. At the same time, whatever free land was available has already been used up, say for social forestry.

Long spell of monsoon throws yet another spanner. During this period any type of works requiring land cannot be embarked on. Flood and flood-like situation, particularly in Northern districts, sap the possibility of earth-related works. As such, the poor HHs do not in general get works during agricultural lean session when they find alternative works really scanty. Thus, unavailability of works during the tough times dashes the popularity and positive impact of the programme on poverty etc.

Situation-specific and regenerative resource generations are not getting appropriate emphasis. In the arid areas plantation, afforestation and water conservation and flood control measures in flood-prone zones—in other words, planning of works with long-term perspective—are exception rather than the rule. Conversely, earth works seem to be the preoccupations of Bengal's panchayats. Since their rejuvenated journey from 1977, GPs in West Bengal are expending huge funds on kutcha road construction. One specific reason for such fixation is that such works do not last long and these get washed away or perish soon. Thus, the same work can be undertaken again and again, utilising the fund and creating considerable man-days.

This sort of obsession continues under MGNREGA. Fairly and squarely, unless the obsession with road connectivity and earth works is done away with, it is unlikely that the rural regeneration and poverty alleviation will descend in foreseeable future.

15.7 The Futurity

It bodes ill when MGNREGA is not as effective in poverty basket as it must. In poor states and poverty concentrated areas, the demand for employment is expected to be comparatively higher and the public agencies will have to offer larger quantum of works. But the ground realities do not testify such a trend. In fact, in poor states the demand might be higher but the richer states usually come up with more employment. Indeed 2010–11 figures present a damming story. Poorer states like Uttar Pradesh, Bihar, West Bengal and Madhya Pradesh which together account for 59% of total BPL population generated just 34% of total employment. Conversely, richer states like Andhra Pradesh and Tamil Nadu with just 8% of BPL share catered to 23% of aggregate employment. Similarly, the GPs with more poor people, agricultural labourer and incidence of migration are lagging behind in generating proportionate employment. Unless such gaps are bridged fairly and quickly, the rural poverty is unlikely to be tackled head on.

The guaranteed employment is likely to contribute to not more than one-fourth to one-third of income required for meeting basic needs of the poor HHs. To overcome the plight of poverty, the income contribution has to be more than what is presently available or made possible. The impact on poverty can be emphatic as well as sustainable if the development schemes of the state and central government converge with the programme and local governments (panchayats) function with concerted commitment. Few convergence attempts are recently being made and these are likely to enlarge the ambit. But the capacity building and devotion of panchayats are still not receiving due priority. Nonetheless, with the elapse of a decade, the steam and support to the programme tends to be fizzling out—one ironic trend discernable for most of the erstwhile public programmes. Somewhat cynical attitude and scuttling tendencies on the part of the (central) government may bode ill for this otherwise proverbial programme!

References

Coffey, D., Papp, J., & Spears, D. (2011). *Dual economies or dual livelihoods? Short-term migration from rural India and non-agricultural employment*. World Bank Policy Research Paper No. 5765. World Bank: Washington.

Das, U. (2013). Can the rural employment guarantee scheme reduce short term migration: Evidence from West Bengal, India. *Development Economics: Microeconomic Issues in Developing Economies, 72*(2), 410–416.

Das, U. (2015). Does political activism and affiliation affect allocation of benefits in the rural employment guarantee programme? Evidence from West Bengal, India. *World Development, 67,* 202–217.

Das, U., Singh, A., & Mahanto, N. (2012). Awareness about Mahatma Gandhi National Rural Employment Guarantee Act: Some evidence from the northern parts of West Bengal, India. *Economics Bulletin, 32*(1), 528–537.

Dey, S. (2009). *Evaluating India's National Rural Employment Guarantee Scheme: The case of Birbhum district, West Bengal.* The Hague: Graduate School of Development Studies, International Institute of Social Studies.

Drèze, J., & Oldiges, C. (2009). How is NREGA doing? *Frontline, 26*(4), 14–22.

Ghosh, J. K. (2011). *Impact of NREGA on wage rates, food security and rural urban migration in West Bengal.* Agro-Economic Research Centre, Study No. 169. Visva-Bharati.

Government of West Bengal. (2004). *Human development report*: *West Bengal* (HDRWB). Development and Planning Department: Kolkata.

Institute for Development of Youth, Women and Children. (2010). *Impact of MGNREGS on sustainable asset creation and livelihood.* Report submitted to Ministry of Rural Development (Govt. of India) and UNDP.

Kareemulla, K., Reddy, S. K., Rao, K., & Venkateswarlu. (2009). Soil and water conservation works through NREGS in Andhra Pradesh—An analysis of livelihood impact. *Agricultural Economics Research Review, 22,* 443–450.

Liu, Y., & Deininger, K. (2010). *Poverty impacts of India's National Rural Employment Guarantee Scheme: Evidence from Andhra Pradesh.* Paper presented at the Agricultural & Applied Economics Association, (AAEA, CAES, & WAEA Joint Annual Meeting), Denver, July 25–27.

Mangatter, S. (2011). *Does the Mahatma Gandhi National Rural Employment Guarantee Act strengthen rural self employment in Bolpur subdivision (West Bengal, India)?* Germany: Philipps University.

Ministry of Rural Development, Government of India. (2012). *MGNREGA Sameeksha: An anthology of research studies, 2012.* Orient BlackSwine: New Delhi.

Mohanty, B.K. (2014, December 7). Laggard Bengal leaps to top 5. *The Telegraph.*

Mukherjee, S., & Ghosh, S. (2009). *What determines the success and failure of '100 days work' at the panchayat level? A study of Birbhum district in West Bengal.* Institute of Development Studies: Kolkata.

NSSO (National Sample Survey Organisation). (2012). *Survey of MGNREGA*, 2011–12. Govt. of India: New Delhi.

Rao, K. H., & Durgaprasad, P. (2008). Rural poverty alleviation in India: Contribution of NREGS. *IASSI Quarterly, 27*(1&2), 15–30.

Ravi, S., & Engler, M. (2015). Workfare as an effective way to fight poverty: The Case of India's NREGS. *World Development, 67,* 57–71.

Sarkar, P. K., & Supriya. (2011). Impact of MGNREGA on reducing rural poverty and improving socio-economic status of rural poor: A study in Burdwan District of West Bengal. *Agricultural Economic Research Review, 24,* 437–448.

UNDP (United Nations Development Programme). (2010). *What will it take to achieve millennium development goals*? Washington.

Chapter 16
Poverty in Rural West Bengal: Trend Over Four Decades

Arindam Chakraborty

Abstract Poverty is generally conceptulised as the inability of an individual to attain some basic needs of life or to secure a normative minimum level of living. The basic needs consist of food and non-food requirements and those who are unable to attain so are considered to be poor. In reality, the concept of poverty is viewed from a wider angle. The basic requirements primarily include the levels of income and consumption. Apart from these, it not only covers the health and education but also takes into account the vulnerability and risks; marginalisation and exclusion of the poor from the mainstream of society. So the concept of poverty is multidimensional. In 1962 an Official Working Group defined the normative minimum for the first time and subsequently reviewed by several Expert Groups in 1979 (Alagh), 1993 (Lakdawala), 2009 (Tendulkar) and in 2014 (Rangarajan) and they tried to find out the percentage of people living below the so called poverty line both in rural and urban India. The estimates reveal that in West Bengal rural poverty showed a declining trend in the last four decades since the 1970s. This chapter deals with the nature and extent of poverty in rural West Bengal during the last four decades, taking into account the poverty estimates of the different Expert Groups. It ends up with some kind of an analytical decomposition of the changes in rural poverty into growth and inequality effects on the basis of poverty and inequality estimates done by Jha in (Economic and Political Weekly, 35(11):921–928, 2000).

Keywords Poverty line · HCR · Gini coefficient · Mean consumption
Growth effect · Inequality effect

A. Chakraborty (✉)
S.R. Lahiri Mahavidyalaya, Majdia, Nadia, WB, India
e-mail: arindamfulia@gmail.com

U.K. De et al. (eds.), *Inequality, Poverty and Development in India*, India Studies in Business and Economics, DOI 10.1007/978-981-10-6274-2_16

16.1 Introduction

In the discourse of development economics, the concept of poverty makes a considerable room. Poverty is a global phenomenon in the sense that its ubiquitous presence can be seen in almost all countries in the world either in the form of absolute or relative sense. Now the problem with taking poverty as a relative concept is that it cannot be eliminated from the face of the world as there will always be a section of people who are poor in relative terms. So poverty should be conceptualized from absolute sense which indicates the non-fulfilment of some capabilities or some basic requirements of life (Sen 1984). Now in a developing nation like ours, economic policy should not dwell only on achieving higher growth, rather overall development should get the priority. Economic policy is to be framed in such a way that people can attain the basic needs of life. It is to be ensured that the benefits of growth should reach to all sections of the society. So eradication of poverty is an important objective on the part of the policy makers. In our country, since independence the importance of poverty reduction and provisions of other basic needs have been emphasized in all five-year plans particularly since the Fifth Five-Year Plan. The government has always maintained a two-pronged approach—promoting economic growth and direct action towards poverty alleviation (Dev 2000).

Now the question is what is poverty? In simple terms, poverty can be defined as the inability of an individual to attain some basic needs of life or to secure a normative minimum level of living. The basic needs consist of food and non-food requirements and those who are unable to attain so are considered to be poor. Sometimes, the concept of poverty is viewed from a wider angle. The basic requirements primarily include the levels of income and consumption. But in broader concept, it not only covers the health and education but also takes into account the vulnerability and risks; marginalisation and exclusion of the poor from the mainstream of society (World Development Report 2000/2001). So the concept of poverty is multidimensional.

However, in this chapter, the concept of poverty has been narrowed down to the attainment of basic needs of life in terms of food and non-food requirements and the poverty measures are based on these requirements. The chapter deals with the nature and trends of rural poverty in West Bengal for last four decades since 1970s. For the purpose poverty estimates of Jha (2000) as well as of several Experts Groups constituted by the Planning Commission of India have been taken into cognizance. It also lends an analytical decomposition of the changes in rural poverty into growth and distribution effects on the basis of poverty and inequality estimates done by Raghabendra Jha for the period from 1958–97.

16.2 Defining Poverty Line—A Review

It is natural that for survival every human being requires a certain minimum consumption of food and non-food items. Those who are unable to attain these are known as poor. But what constitutes poverty is not fixed. Rather it varies over time and across the countries. Nevertheless, it is of utmost need to find a measure of poverty. This measurement enables us to assess the performance of the economy in the question of the provision of a certain minimum standard of living to all its citizens. Therefore, poverty measurement bears important policy implications. In our country, there have been several studies relating to poverty measurement. From time to time, the Planning Commission of India has formed several Groups to review the issues relating to the methodology of poverty measurement so that the poverty estimates can keep pace with the changing economic situations.

In 1962, an Official Working Group defined the normative minimum for the first time. It was an amount of Rs. 20 per capita per month consumer expenditure for rural areas (and Rs. 25/- for urban areas) at 1960–61 all India prices. It was based on an average per capita per day nutrition norm of 2400 calories in rural areas (2100 calories in urban areas). As per the Indian constitution (PPD 1962) the state should provide the minimum expenditure to be incurred on health and education. Actually, this amount has been considered enough for getting food that would ensure minimum energy needed for an active and healthy life and also the minimum amount of clothing and shelter.

Consequently, several scholars have reviewed the empirical basis of the targeted national minimum per capita expenditure. Bardhan (1970), corresponding to this all India norm, considered Rs. 15/- per capita per month at 1960–61 all India rural prices to be relevant for rural areas (Rs. 22.5 for urban areas). Dandekar and Rath (1971) estimated the same poverty line for rural India considering the calorie norm of 2250 calories per capita per day.

In 1979, Dr. Y.K. Alagh headed the Planning Commission Task force on Projections of Minimum Needs and Effective Demand which defined the poor as "those whose per capita consumption expenditure lies below the midpoint of the monthly per capita expenditure class having a daily calorie in take of 2400 in rural areas and 2100 in urban areas". Corresponding to those norms, the poverty lines were estimated with reference to the NSS data for the year 1973–74. The poverty line emerged to be Rs. 49.09 per capita per month at 1973–74 prices for rural India (Rs. 57/- for urban areas).

However, Y.K. Alagh's methodology of measuring poverty as devised in 1979 has been updated and improvised later. In 1993 an Expert Group under the headship of Lakdawala updated and improvised it and then in 2009 by another Expert Group headed by Tendulkar did so. Due to these improvisations that basically relied upon the NSSO's sample surveys on consumption expenditure by households a better method emerged that made it easy to adjust the differences in inter-state and inter-region price changes (Planning Commission 2014).

Table 16.1 Poverty lines for rural India and rural West Bengal (per capita per month)

Year	Alagh (1979) methodology (for India)	Lakdawala (1993) methodology (for West Bengal)	Tendulkar (2009) methodology (for West Bengal)	Rangarajan (2014) methodology (for West Bengal)
1973–74	Rs. 49.09	Rs. 54.49		
1977–78		Rs. 63.34		
1983–84		Rs. 105.55		
1987–88		Rs. 129.21		
1993–94		Rs. 220.74		
1999–00		Rs. 350.17		
1904–05		Rs. 382.82	Rs. 445	
1909–10			Rs. 643.2	Rs. 767.2
1911–12			Rs. 783	Rs. 934.10

Source Planning Commission (2014)

In view of the faster growth of macroeconomic variables like real income and real consumption between 2004–05 and 2011–12 as well as the inability of the poverty estimates of Tendulkar in reflecting the changing times and aspirations of people, the Planning Commission had to form a new Expert Group under the headship of Rangarajan. The new Expert Group was formed in 2012 in order to estimate poverty in India taking into cognizance the changed perceptions relating to the minimally acceptable standards of living in the country (Planning Commission 2014).

In order to derive state-level rural and urban poverty, the Expert Group (Tendulkar), made a departure from the previous practice of using two separate poverty lines for rural and urban areas and considered the all-India urban poverty line basket as the only reference. However with a view to deriving state-level rural and urban estimates the Expert Group (Rangarajan) has reverted to the practice of having two different all-India rural and urban poverty basket lines. On the basis of the 2010 ICMR norms differentiated by age, gender and activity-status, the Expert Group has re-estimated the average requirements of calories, fats and proteins. Also the rural–urban age and gender distribution of the population according to 2011 Census and the broad work-status distribution have been taken into account. The Group submitted its report in 2014.

The Poverty Lines estimated by Task Force (1979) for rural India and by different Expert Groups for rural West Bengal are detailed in Table 16.1.

16.3 Measures of Poverty and Inequality

In measuring poverty we can talk about a lot of measures for poverty such as Head Count Measure, Poverty Gap Measure, Sen's *P*-measure, etc. However, in this study Head Count Ratio (HCR) has been taken as poverty measure. Head count measure is the percentage of population living below the poverty line for the base year. This is the cumulative proportion of population with consumer expenditure less than the poverty line. In order to measure poverty for subsequent years, the poverty line is updated generally by using deflator based on market prices so that changes in prices can be taken into account since consumer expenditure data are at current prices.

Simply Head count ratio is defined as:

$$H = q/n = \text{proportion of persons below the poverty line}$$

where 'n' denotes the total number of persons in the population and 'q' the number of poor, persons among them. So the HCR measures the proportion of units in the population that are classified by the given norm.

Among the inequality measures, the Gini Index is an important one which is a statistical device that measures relative dispersion without any reference to social welfare. It measures the extent to which the distribution of income among individuals or household within an economy deviates from a perfectly equal distribution. The Gini Index measures the area between the Lorenz curve and a hypothetical line of absolute equality. As defined here, a Gini Index of zero would represent perfect equality and an index of 100 would imply perfect inequality. To measure the inequality among the rural people in West Bengal in this chapter Gini index has been taken into account.

16.4 Review of Existing Studies

In surveying the literature on poverty in West Bengal focus has been given to rural poverty as the chapter encompasses the rural poverty in West Bengal.

The Planning Advisory Board (PAB), Government of West Bengal in its unpublished report, entitled 'Measurement of poverty and Inequality in rural West Bengal' (1979) worked out the percentage of rural poor in West Bengal during the decade 1963–64 to 1973–74. The poverty lines chosen were the Dandekar-Rath norm of Rs. 15/- per capita and the Planning Commission's norm of Rs. 18.90/- at 1960–61 prices corresponding to the normative dietary requirement as recommended by nutritional experts and inflated by CPIAL. The head count ratio for 1963–64 was found to be 67% which increased to 75% in 1973–74, on the basis of weighted prices for all expenditure classes, while on the basis of a normative calorie intake of 2200 per capita per day, the head count ratio was found to increase from 73 to 81% between 1963–64 and 1973–74. The report supplemented the study on the incidence of poverty by head count measure with measure of relative inequality like Gini coefficient and Sen's measure of absolute poverty giving more weight to the inequality among poor people. Both these measures show an increase between 1963–64 and 1973–74 (the Gini coefficient rising from 0.262 to 0.297 and the Sen's measure rising from 0.329 to 0.373), although for the intervening year, there were ups and downs in the values of these two estimates of poverty.

Chatterjee et al. (1991) in their study tried to evaluate the structural causes of rural and urban poverty in West Bengal in 1970s and 1980s. They also tried to highlight the other dimensions of poverty like quality of life, malnutrition etc. To measure poverty they used head count measure, poverty gap measure and Sen's *P*-measure while for measuring inequality they used Gini coefficient and Atkinson's measure. The Planning Commission's (1979) poverty line of Rs. 49/- for rural areas and Rs. 57/- for urban areas at 1973–74 prices have been used as poverty thresholds in the study.

The major findings of their study concerning the overall changes in the extent of rural poverty may be summed as follows: (a) There have been modest declines in both poverty and inequality from 1973–74 to 1977–78 (annual average growth rate of head count ratio was −0.81 and annual average change in Gini coefficient was −0.33); (b) these have been followed by still lower rates of decline from 1977–78 to 1983 (−0.50 for HCR and −0.47 for Gini coefficient); (c) poverty and inequality have declined at faster more significant rates from 1983 to 1986–87 (−6.43 for HCR and −5.54 for Gini coefficient) and after.

They, however, suggested reasons for the observed pattern in the rate of growth (negative) of the HCR which are as follows:

(1) The low rate of fall of the HCR during 1973–74 to 1977–78 compared to that during 1983 to 1986–87 is accounted for by (a) the lower overall trend in average product in the subperiod 1970–71 to 1977–78 compared to that in the sub-period 1982–83 to 1988–89; (b) the very low trend in average food product per hectare in particular in the first sub-period and (c) the absence of any direct anti-poverty programmes.
(2) A still lower rate of fall of the HCR during 1977–78 to 1983, in spite of the presence of direct anti-poverty programmes, may be accounted for by the negative significant trend growth rates in the average product per worker and average food product per hectare.
(3) The significant rate of fall of the HCR during 1983 to 1986–87 and after, may be attributed to (a) the higher overall trends in average product in the sub-period 1982–83 to 1988–89 compared to those in other previous sub-period; (b) the significant trend in the average food product per hectare in trend sub-period and (c) the continuation of the direct anti-poverty programmes.

Ghosh (1993) in his study showed the changes in the extent of rural poverty in West Bengal during the period 1957–58 to 1986–87. His main objective was to test the existence of trickle-down hypothesis in rural West Bengal. He adopted the per capita consumer expenditure of Rs. 15/-per month at 1960–61 prices as poverty line. Using the NSS consumer expenditure data he calculated both the head count ratio and Sen's index of poverty.

The estimate of the study showed that during the period under study the rural poverty in West Bengal declined, although there was an increase in poverty during 1967–68 and 1968–69. Rural population in West Bengal below the poverty threshold declined from 62.3 to 50.8% during the period 1957–58 and 1986–87.

With a view to assessing the trickle-down hypothesis in rural West Bengal, he measured agricultural performance in terms of both state domestic product from agriculture at constant prices per head of rural population (SDPAR) and agricultural labour productivity (ALP) which is the output per hectare multiplied by land–labour ratio. The results of this study indicate significant inverse relationship between rural poverty and agricultural performance by either SDPAR or ALP, confirming thereby the existence of trickle-down process in rural West Bengal.

He also made a growth-redistribution decomposition of changes in rural poverty. His study reflected that growth effect on rural poverty was found to be stronger than distribution effect which was also demonstrated by the results derived from decomposition exercise done by Chatterjee (1998).

Chattopadhyay (2005) in his study made a modest attempt to explore the impact of spectacular agricultural growth on income distribution in rural West Bengal during the 1980s and early 1990s. For the purpose, the study used data from the NSS large surveys and compared the result derived from consumption expenditure data with that derived from the data available from different reports of Farm Management Studies (FMS).

The study observed that prior to the 1980s the estimated rate of growth of agricultural output in West Bengal was very poor. It was even less than the rates of growth of the rural and total population of the state. This resulted in sheer poverty among a significant portion of the rural population. However, the rural employment and average daily earnings of agricultural labour households in agricultural occupations increased significantly during 1983 to 1993–94, consequent to the acceleration in agricultural growth. This resulted in a fall to a significant extent in the degree of inequality in the distribution of rural consumption expenditure. However, when the growth rate of agricultural output declined substantially during the later part of the 1990s, it affected rural income distribution in a reversed way, with a deceleration in the growth rate of rural employment and average earning of the agricultural labour households.

So, during the period of impressive agricultural growth distribution of income in rural West Bengal was in favour of the poorer classes of the population or marginal and small farmers. However, in the following period neither the impressive agricultural growth nor the favourable change in rural income distribution could be sustained. So during the period of sluggishness of agricultural growth, i.e. during the later part of 1990s, inequality in farm income distribution increased.

16.5 Rural Poverty in West Bengal

This part of the chapter will focus on the nature and extent of rural poverty in West Bengal during the period 1974–2012. This part is divided into two sections. Section 16.5.1 represents the estimates of poverty in rural West Bengal. Section 16.5.2 deals with the trends in poverty estimates representing the annual growth rates of the estimates. It also represents the percentage point decline in poverty ratio per year for all the estimates.

16.5.1 Section I: Nature of Estimates of Poverty

In this section, for analysis the poverty scenario in rural West Bengal during the period 1974–2012, the poverty estimates of Jha (2000), Lakdawala (1993), Tendulkar (2009) and Rangarajan (2014) are used. Table 16.2 presents the empirical results in poverty during 1974–2012 in rural West Bengal. In case of Jha's estimate, poverty threshold adopted is Rs. 49/-per capita monthly expenditure for rural areas at 1973–74 prices.

Some key features of the nature of poverty in rural West Bengal during this period are:

(i) In case of all the estimates poverty rates show a downward trend but as the poverty lines differ we get different figures for poverty rates even in the same year.
(ii) In Jha's estimate, rural poverty in West Bengal declines from 63.24% in 1974 to 26.93% in 1997 i.e. in 1997, over a quarter of the rural population in West Bengal lived below the poverty line.
(iii) The poverty estimate shows a more or less declining trend during the period under study except for the year 1991 when the county resorted to economic reforms with the HCR pegging at 39.11%.
(iv) In Lakdawala estimate with a different set of poverty lines, we find rural poverty in West Bengal showing a falling trend. Poverty level declines from 73.16% in 1993–94 to 28.6% in 2004–05.
(v) In absolute figure also the number of poor people in rural West Bengal declined from 257.96 lakh in 1973–74 to 173.22 lakh in 2004–05. What is interesting in case of Lakdawala estimate is that in percentage figure poverty declined from 73.16 in 1973–74 to 63.05 in 1983, but in the absolute figure it increased, might be for a rise in a number of rural population in West Bengal.
(vi) As the Rangarajan methodology generates higher poverty line than that of Tendulkar, the percentage of people living below the poverty line is higher in the former case. While Tendulkar estimate indicates that in 2011–12 around 22.5% of people in rural West Bengal are poor, the figure sticks to 30.1% for

Table 16.2 Poverty estimates and number of poor people in rural West Bengal, 1974–2012

Year	Jha estimate (2000)	Lakdawala estimate (1993)		Tendulkar estimate (2009)		Rangarajan estimate (2014)	
Year	Percentage of persons	Percentage of persons	No. of persons (lakh)	Percentage of persons	No. of persons (lakh)	Percentage of persons	No. of persons (lakh)
1973–74	63.24	73.16	257.96				
1977–78	56.25	68.34	259.69				
1983–84	49.21	63.05	268.60				
1986–87	34.1						
1987–88	34.87	48.30	223.37				
1989–90	26.19						
1990–91	39.11						
1992–93	28.15						
1993–94	27.27	40.80	209.9				
1994–95	26.32						
1995–96	27.02						
1997–98	26.93						
1999–2000		31.22	180.11				
2004–05		28.6	173.22	38.2	231.2		
2009–10				28.8	177.8	37.8	233.1
2011–12				22.5	141.1	30.1	188.6

Sources (1) Jha (2000) (column-2), (2) Planning Commission (2014) (column-3 to 8)

Rangarajan estimate. If we consider the absolute figure it reveals that in 2011–12 around 188.6 lakh people are poor in rural West Bengal as per Rangarajan methodology while it is 141.1 lakh in case of Tendulkar methodology.

16.5.2 Section II: Trends of Poverty Estimates

In this section, our goal is to find out the trends of poverty estimates which will be done by considering the annual growth rates of the estimates. The methodology is as simple as follows:

If H_1 and H_2 are the head count ratios for the first and second periods, respectively, then the proportionate change in poverty will be $(H_2 - H_1)/H_1 = V$ and the annual average rate of change is V/No. of years × 100. Apart from depicting annual average, the table also represents the percentage point decline in poverty ratio per year for all the estimates. If H_1 and H_2 are the head count ratios for the first and last periods respectively, then percentage point decline in poverty ratio per year is $(H_2 - H_1)$/No. of years.

It is observed from Table 16.3 that in Jha's estimate the HCR over the period 1974–97 has fallen at the rate of 2.49%, although this falling trend is not maintained always round through the period. Particularly during the period 1974–90, it declined at an incomparably faster rate than that of 1992–97. In view of the falling trend of head count ratio, the 1990–91 is a remarkable one when it accelerated at an alarming rate of 49.33%; although the following year showed a drastic fall, yet the increase in the previous year was not satisfactorily compensated.

In case of other estimates, the annual growth rates are −1.96% for the period 1974–2012, −5.87% for the period 2005–2012 and −10.18% for the period 2010–2012 respectively for Lakdawala, Tendulkar and Rangarajan estimates. If we consider the decline in poverty ratio by percentage point per year we see that they are 1.57 for Jha's estimate, 1.43 for Lakdawala estimant, 2.24 for Tendulkar estimate and 3.85 for Rangarajan estimate. As the Lakdawala estimate covers the longest period it can be asserted that during the period from 1974 to 2005 the rural poverty in West Bengal has fallen by 1.43% point per year.

16.6 Decomposition of Changes in Poverty

This part of the chapter attempts some kind of an analytical decomposition of the changes in poverty into the growth effect and the distribution effect as it has been done by Ghosh (1993). The growth effect is the impact of growth on poverty where as the distribution effect is the impact of a change in the distribution of income poverty.

In this section for analysis, the poverty scenario in rural West Bengal during the period 1958–97, the estimates of Jha (2000) relating to poverty, inequality and real mean consumption are used. Table 16.4 presents the empirical results on the poverty and inequality measure during 1958–97 in rural West Bengal.

The poverty is measured in terms of head count ratio revealing the incidence of poverty while for measuring inequality the Gini coefficient is adopted. The head count ratio and Gini index are expressed as percentages. Table 16.4 also depicts the estimate on real mean consumption which is expressed in rupees per capita per month. Real mean consumption has been considered as a proxy for growth. Poverty threshold adopted in the estimate is Rs. 49/-per capita monthly expenditure for rural areas at 1973–74 prices.

This part of the chapter shows how changes in poverty measure can be rigorously decomposed into Growth Effect and Inequality Effect. Often an interest is shown to quantify the relative contribution of growth and redistribution on changes in poverty. In fact, in the recent years several attempts have been made to analytically decompose changes in poverty into (a) change due to overall growth when the distribution of income does not change and (b) change due to altered income distribution where overall growth is zero. Overall growth in these studies is

Table 16.3 Trends in the poverty estimates of rural West Bengal, 1974–2012

	Annual growth rates (%)								Decline in poverty ratio (percentage point per year)			
	1974–1990	1990–1991	1991–1992	1992–1997	1974–1997	1974–2005	2005–2012	2010–2012	1974–1997	1974–2005	2005–2012	2010–2012
Jha estimate	−3.66	49.33	−28.02	−0.87	−2.49				1.57			
Lakdawala estimate						−1.96				1.43		
Tendulkar estimate							−5.87				2.24	
Rangarajan estimate								−10.18				3.85

Source Computed from Table 16.2

Table 16.4 Poverty and inequality estimates of rural West Bengal, 1958–97

NSS round	Year	HCR	Gini coefficient	Real mean consumption
13	1958	52.92	26.81	53.96
14	1959	48.31	28.06	58.34
15	1960	50.41	27.08	56.15
16	1961	32.36	25.6	67.8
17	1962	50.2	27.68	58.63
18	1964	55.68	26.37	52.93
19	1965	56.54	23.88	50.31
20	1966	64.38	26.3	46.76
21	1967	67.85	25.56	45.38
22	1968	75.84	24.08	40.33
23	1969	69.63	23.13	44.25
24	1970	60.15	25.11	49.38
25	1971	62.57	26.32	48.02
27	1973	60.51	30.64	50.95
28	1974	63.24	30.13	48.78
32	1978	56.25	29.75	53.7
38	1983	49.21	28.83	56.59
42	1987	34.1	24.27	64.21
43	1988	34.87	25.57	65.32
45	1990	26.19	25.25	71.71
46	1991	39.11	27.62	65.4
48	1992	28.15	24.21	68.54
50	1994	27.27	25.41	70.45
51	1995	26.32	24.02	71.21
52	1996	27.02	21.97	70.21
53	1997	26.93	22.42	71.21

Source Jha (2000)

analytically captured by considering rising mean consumption over the years and any change in the income distribution is assumed to be reflected in Lorenz curve.

In the chapter, however, the decomposition analysis is based on the results of multiple linear regressions. The period of study has been divided into two sub-periods, viz. (i) 1958–90, that is up to the year preceding the year of adoption of the new economic policy in the country; (ii) 1991–97, that is post-reforms period. This is done just to see the strength of the impact of the factors on poverty in the pre-reforms and post-reforms. Also the analysis has been undertaken for the overall period, 1958–97. The estimated results of the Regressions showing the effect of the growth and distribution factors on rural poverty in West Bengal are presented Table 16.5.

Table 16.5 Growth-redistribution decomposition, 1958–97: results of multiple regressions dependent variable—HCR

	Intercept	Gini coefficient	Real mean consumption	R^2
Sub-period-I 1958–90	128.041	0.452* (0.154) *t* value 2.940	−1.596* (0.039) *t* value −40.520	0.990
Sub-period-II 1991–97	138.451	0.471 (0.679) *t* value 0.694	−1.737** (0.627) *t* value −2.773	0.902
Overall: 1958–97	127.389	0.425* (0.135) *t* value 3.154	−1.569* (0.279) *t* value −50.061	0.992

Notes (1) Coefficient with * and ** are significant at 1 and 10% levels, respectively. (2) Figures in the parentheses are standard errors of the coefficients

The results in Table 16.5 are to be interpreted in the following way. As expected, the coefficients of Gini index turn out to be positive and significant which indicate that this variable is directly related to the incidence of poverty while the negative coefficients of mean consumption imply the inverse relation between growth and the incidence of poverty.

In the pre-reforms period, that is during 1958–90, we get highly significant coefficients for both the factors and the result shows that both the factors have resulted in reducing poverty but the coefficient of mean consumption having larger value played more important role in reducing poverty during that period. However the result of post-reforms period, that is during 1991–97, is quite different from that of pre-reforms period. From the results given in Table 16.5, it is clear that during 1991–97, with insignificant coefficient, the Gini index has negligible effect in reducing poverty and the coefficient of mean consumption being significant at 10% level has the only impact on poverty reduction. Thus while in the pre-reforms period, both the factors have resulted in reducing poverty, in the post-reforms period, poverty reduction has been the outcome of only growth in rural West Bengal.

However for the entire period, 1958–97, both coefficients are highly significant. The result shows that during 1974–97, if distribution had remained constant and only mean consumption had risen to the extent it actually had, the head count ratio would have fallen on the average at the rate of 1.5%. Likewise, if growth had been zero and only inequality had declined the way it did, the head count ratio would have fallen on the average at the rate of 0.4%. Thus growth effect on rural poverty in West Bengal during 1958–97 is found to be stronger than inequality effect.

16.7 Conclusion

This chapter with the help of different poverty estimates of the Expert Groups has tried to focus on the nature and extent of rural poverty in West Bengal during the period 1974–2012. All of the poverty estimates show more or less declining trend during the period under study except for the year 1991 when the county resorted to economic reforms. In the absolute figure the number of poor people in rural West Bengal declined from 257.96 lakh in 1973–74 to 188.6 lakh in 2011–12 as per Rangarajan methodology. As the Lakdawala estimate covers the longest period it can be asserted that during the period from 1974 to 2005 the rural poverty in West Bengal has fallen by 1.43% point per year.

In growth-distribution decomposition analysis of the changes in rural poverty in West Bengal we have got the same results the previous studies arrived at. Our results show that during 1958–97 both coefficients of growth and distribution are highly significant and growth effect on rural poverty in West Bengal is found to be stronger than inequality effect. This implies that rapid economic growth can be the best measure for eradicating poverty in India (Jha 2000). However, we should not ignore the distribution of income as it has some impact on reducing poverty. So Government should design its policies regarding tax, public expenditure, social sector in such a way that an even distribution of income can be ensured.

Appendices

Appendix 1: Results of Multiple Regressions: 1958–90

Dependent variable—HCR, $R^2 = 0.99$, adjusted $R^2 = 0.989$

	Coefficients	Std. Error	*t* stat	*P*-value
Intercept	128.041	4.543	28.183	0.000
Gini coefficient	0.452	0.154	2.940	0.009
Real mean consumption	−1.596	0.039	−40.520	0.000

Appendix 2: Results of Multiple Regressions: 1991–97

Dependent variable—HCR, $R^2 = 0.902$, adjusted $R^2 = 0.837$

	Coefficients	Std. Error	*t* stat	*P*-value
Intercept	138.451	57.242	2.419	0.094
Gini coefficient	0.471	0.679	0.694	0.537
Real mean consumption	−1.737	0.627	−2.773	0.069

Appendix 3: Results of Multiple Regressions: 1958–97

Dependent variable—HCR, $R^2 = 0.992$, adjusted $R^2 = 0.991$

	Coefficients	Std. Error	*t* stat	*P*-value
Intercept	127.389	4.402	28.940	0.000
Gini coefficient	0.425	0.135	3.154	0.004
Real mean consumption	−1.569	0.031	−50.061	0.000

References

Bardhan, P. K. (1970). On the minimum level of living and the rural poor. *Indian Economic Review, 5*(1), 129–136.

Chatterjee, B. (1998). Poverty in West Bengal: What have we learnt? *Economic and Political Weekly, 33*(47–48), 3003–3014.

Chatterjee, B., Roy, S., & Bhattacharya, B. (1991). Incidence of poverty and its change over time and the evaluation of poverty alleviation measures in West Bengal. Report prepared for the World Bank.

Chattopadhyaya, A. K. (2005). Distributive impact of agricultural growth in rural West Bengal. *Economic and Political Weekly, 40*(53), 5601–5610.

Dandekar, V. M., & Rath, N. (1971). Poverty in India-II: Policies and programmes. *Economic and Political Weekly, 6*(2), 106–146.

Dev, S. M. (2000). Economic reforms, poverty, income distribution and employment. *Economic and Political Weekly, 35*(10), 823–835.

Ghosh, M. (1993). Test of trickle-down hypothesis in rural West Bengal. *Indian Journal of Agricultural Economics, 48*(2), 216–225.

Jha, R. (2000). Growth, inequality and poverty in India: Spatial and temporal characteristics. *Economic and Political Weekly, 35*(11), 921–928.

Planning Advisory Board. (1979). *Measurement of poverty and inequality in rural West Bengal*. West Bengal: Government of West Bengal.

Planning Commission. (2014). *Report of the expert group to review the methodology for measurement of poverty*. New Delhi: Government of India.

Sen, A. (1984). Poor, relatively speaking. *Resources, Values and Development* (pp. 325–345). Delhi: Oxford University Press.

World Bank. (2000/2001). *World development report (2000/2001): Attacking poverty*. New York: Oxford University Press.

Chapter 17
A Study on Spatial Statistical Method of Poverty and Sustainable Development of North-Eastern States of India

Manoshi Phukon and Rajeshwar Singh

Abstract The interrelationship between 'population and economic development' and 'poverty and human development' is direct but negative. Both are two faces of a coin and they are mutually exclusive. Rising population affects the economic growth of a region and hence this exacerbates starvation and brings poverty in the population. Poverty magnifies the problem of hunger, poor health forms, malnutrition. Educating women, children and adults in the population would help to control the growth rate of population, work for spouse, better health care and livelihood. Several concepts are available in the literature to measure poverty. The goal of this chapter is to analyse the spatial distribution of poverty levels from the viewpoint of several poverty indicators and looks into mitigation of poverty and sustainable development in North-Eastern states of India through three important pillars of development, namely economic, social and education.

Keywords Anti-poverty programmes and policies · Environmental sustainability Human development · Population growth · Spatial distribution

17.1 Introduction

The concept of poverty is related to socially perceived deficiency with respect to vital human needs. Income dimension is the central part of most poverty-related problems to understand the poverty. Increasing per capita income affects the act of the economy and marginalizes even more the lower percentile of population without redistributing part of the wealth giving a negative impact in reducing the poverty (Molini 2005). The relation between poverty and human development (HD) is direct but negative. Both are two faces of a coin and they are mutually

M. Phukon (✉) · R. Singh
Department of Statistics, North Eastern Hill University, Shillong, India
e-mail: phukonmanoshi@gmail.com

R. Singh
e-mail: rsingh4906@yahoo.com

U.K. De et al. (eds.), *Inequality, Poverty and Development in India*, India Studies in Business and Economics, DOI 10.1007/978-981-10-6274-2_17

exclusive. Speedy growth of population, inequality in income, degradation of environment and corruption are the biggest challenge in NE India. This chapter considers for the mitigation of poverty by controlling the rapid growth of population through three essential pillars of development like economic, social and education. Economic growth is a pre-requisite in reducing the poverty due to increasing mean income and narrowing the income distribution (Ajakaiye and Adeyeye 2001). Another work of this chapter will be based on the selected poverty indicators are spatially autocorrelated with each other or not. Generally, poverty level based on different indicators. We will consider here four poverty indicators, namely per capita income, level of education, long-term unemployment and person living in without earned income. Mainly look out all the states of North-East which will specifically show the weight matrix, i.e. $W_{ij} = 1$. Spatial statistical methods are very helpful tools for study of poverty dimension through poverty indicators. Basically, measures of spatial autocorrelation quantify the existence of clusters in the spatial arrangement of a specified variable, while global and local versions of almost all measures can be estimated.

Goodchild (1987) discussed spatial autocorrelation in general that objects or activities at different places located nearby on the surface of earth are associated with some degrees and it reflects the first law of Tobler in human geography.

Most published measures of spatial autocorrelation can recast as a (normalized) cross-product statistic that indexes the degree of relation between corresponding entries from two matrices—one specifying the spatial connections among a set of n locations and the other reflecting a very explicit definition of similarity between the set of values on some variable x realized over n locations (Hubert and Arabie 1991).

17.2 Data and Methods

Data under the study are collected from NSSO of India, Directorate of economics and statistics, Report on employment and unemployment survey, 2011 Census and web pages available in the Internet through google. We will consider two data sets, viz., NSS 66th round during 2009–2010 and 68th round during 2011–12 reports in India for eight states of North-East of India to carry out the analysis.

Moran in 1950 proposed a measure of spatial autocorrelation and this is called Moran Index (I), which is related to the conventional correlation coefficient. The value of this index takes as 1 (having strong positive spatial autocorrelation) and −1 (having strong negative spatial autocorrelation). This index has been applied to compute the spatial autocorrelation and defined as

$$I = \frac{1}{P}\frac{\sum_i \sum_j W_{ij}(Z_i - \overline{Z})(Z_j - \overline{Z})}{\sum_i (Z_i - \overline{Z})^2}, \tag{17.1}$$

where $P = \frac{1}{n}\sum_{ij} W_{ij}$, Z_i denotes the observed value of population at location 'i', $\overline{Z}$ is the average of the Z_i over the n locations and W_{ij} is the spatial weight measure of contiguity and it takes value as 1 for location nearer to each other and 0 otherwise.

Choices of W_{ij} are the most important measure in the analysis. Prior information on range and intensity of spatial covariance between regions are needed to specify weights in the neibourhood. Ordinary techniques are required for row standardization, length of common boundary and distance functions. The matrix W_{ij} is used for weighing procedure as resist to a binary connection matrix allowing weights to be chosen, which are considered appropriate from previous deliberation. W_{ij} presents immense elasticity in defining the structure of the county system and it allows objects to be taken into account. Usually, W_{ij} depends on the geographical arrangement of the observations or contiguity. W_{ij} takes non-zero values when two locations share a common boundary or within a given distance of each other (Anselin 1992).

17.3 Various Poverty Indicators

Various poverty indicators used in analyses are listed below:

(a) **Per capita income**: Communicating average income by using per capita income is also used as a measure of wealth for a nation. To measure of standard of living for a country is judged by per capita income in earlier years expressing in terms of a common used international currency into PPP (purchasing power parity). Above points help in knowing the per capita income is often used to measure a country's standard of living. It is usually expressed in terms of a commonly used international currency under PPP such as US dollar or now the euro.

(b) **Level of Education**: Formal learning is typically divided into a number of educational stages covering early childhood education, primary education, secondary education, tertiary and higher education. Seven levels of education recognized by UNESCO following International Standard Classification of Education system from Level 0 (pre-primary education) to Level 6 (second stage of tertiary education). The database of country-specific education systems and their stages are sustained by UNESCO's International Bureau of Education.

(c) **Long-Term Unemployment**: If people are not working but actively seeking work then unemployment is occurred and its rate measures the prevalence of unemployment. This rate is obtained by dividing a number of unemployed persons to all persons currently put into labour force. During abnormal time period like depression, the country usually experiences relatively a higher unemployment rate.

(d) **Population living in a Household with no Earned Income or Low Work Intensity**: The activity related to capacity to do work is called work intensity and it affects differently to both, developed and developing country with different intensity. Multitask; time poverty, health implications and policy considerations are different characteristics for work intensity in which multitasking overlaps many activities that negatively impact the livelihood of people, especially women in the developing world. While time poverty relates to the lack of time for leisure and rest activities after time spent on working. A negative correlation is expected between multitasking and time poverty. An attempt will be made to include more women in workforce for the development and also for women empowerment.

17.4 Methodology

A null hypothesis and an alternative hypothesis are to be set up before computation of various Moran's I values. To make easier the calculation and understanding, re-evaluation of the method will be done part by part at first. Therefore, it is considered that values $\{Z_i\}$ and weights $\{W_{ij}\}$, which is merged by techniques with a function, which fulfil the following standard:

(i) If (Z_i, Z_j) are both positive or both negative, $f(Z_i, Z_j) > 0$.
(ii) If (Z_i, Z_j) are a mix of positive and negative, $f(Z_i, Z_j) < 0$.
(iii) If (Z_i, Z_j) are both have large values, $f(Z_i, Z_j)$ is also large.
(iv) Reflection of pattern adjacency in W must be explained to compute.

Multiplying the state values together with optionally adjusted overall mean value for all states including the adjacency information provides $\sum_i Z_i$ and $\sum_j Z_j$ or with mean adjustment and weights included in $\sum\sum W_{ij}(Z_i - \overline{Z})(Z_j - \overline{Z})$ produces a covariance values. This value is divided by the sum of the weights, which gives, $\frac{\sum_i\sum_j W_{ij}(Z_i-\overline{Z})(Z_j-\overline{Z})}{\sum_i\sum_j W_{ij}}$. Moran's I is defined as

$$I = \frac{1}{P}\frac{\sum_i\sum_j W_{ij}(Z_i - \overline{Z})(Z_i - \overline{Z})}{\sum_i (Z_i - \overline{Z})^2} \tag{17.2}$$

where $P = \frac{1}{n}\sum_{ij} W_{ij}$.

The technique to compute Moran's I could be referred to de Smith, Goodchild and Longley (2015).

17.4.1 Statistical Significance of Moran's I

Under the normality assumption the variance of Moran's I is computed as:

$$Var_N\,(I) = \left(\frac{1}{S_0^2(n^2-1)}\,(n^2S_1 - nS_2 + 3S_0^2) - E_N(I)^2\right), \tag{17.3}$$

where n = number of observations $E_N\,(I) = -\frac{1}{n-1}$ $S_0 = \sum_{ij} W_{ij}$.

If W_{ij} is symmetric, then $S_1 = \frac{1}{2}\sum_i^n (W_{ij} + W_{ji})^2 = 2\sum_{ij} W_{ij}$.

Again if W_{ij} is symmetric, then $S_2 = \sum_j^n (W_i + W_j)^2 = 4\sum_i W_i^2$.

The standard deviation Moran's I are given by $\mathrm{SD}_N(I) = \sqrt{\mathrm{Var}_N\,(I)}$, while standard Z-scores of Moran I is obtained from $Z = \frac{(I - E_N(I))}{\sqrt{\mathrm{Var}_N\,(I)}}$.

Figure 17.1 given below indicates the placement of North-East states through the map and this figure indicates that Sikkim has no neighbourhood state comparing to the remaining states. Generally, the weight matrix takes value from 0 to 1 and defined as

$$W_{ij} = \begin{cases} 1 & 'i'\text{ neighbour }'j' \\ 0 & \text{otherwise} \end{cases}.$$

Spatial autocorrelation for a single variable cross-sectional data set is tested using the magnitude of an indicator and combining the value observed at each

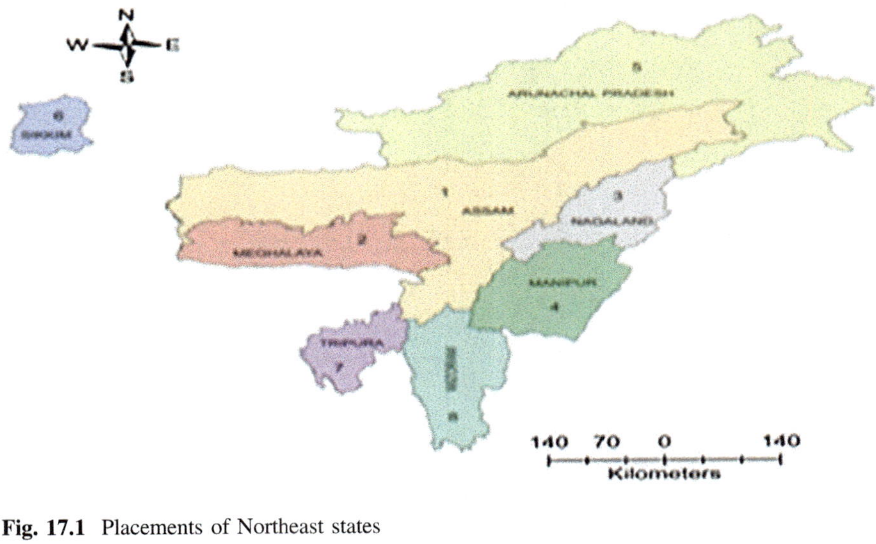

Fig. 17.1 Placements of Northeast states

Table 17.1 Weight matrix

States	Codes	States and codes							
		Assam (1)	Meghalaya (2)	Nagaland (3)	Manipur (4)	Arunachal Pradesh(5)	Sikkim (6)	Tripura (7)	Mizoram (8)
Assam	1	0	1	1	1	1	0	1	1
Meghalaya	2	1	0	0	0	0	0	0	0
Nagaland	3	1	0	0	1	1	0	0	0
Manipur	4	1	0	1	0	0	0	0	1
AP	5	1	0	1	0	0	0	0	1
Sikkim	6	0	0	0	0	0	0	0	0
Tripura	7	1	0	0	0	0	0	0	1
Mizoram	8	1	0	0	1	0	0	1	0

Source Author's calculation

location with the average value at neighbouring locations. Spatial autocorrelation statistic takes an extreme value as compared to no spatial autocorrelation under the null hypothesis (Anselin 1992).

Table 17.1 given above illustrates distribution of weights along with their codes. Unadjusted variance and covariance matrix are computed excluding Sikkim and only seven states comprising seven cells are considered for computation. Deviations from the overall mean value in the column and row bounding by 7×7 matrix with value C has been placed in each cell. The variance is obtained from the diagonal elements of matrix and the off diagonal elements give the covariance. Off diagonal elements of the matrix are required the adjustment in their weights. The total of these adjusted values is the row sum. The sum of diagonal values of the matrix is SSD. Moran's I is computed by (17.1).

17.5 Result and Discussion

Tables 17.2 and 17.3 demonstrate values in Moran's I with their p-values in four poverty indicators for the first data set and the second data set, respectively. Null and alternative hypotheses for both data sets are as: H_0: There is no spatial autocorrelation among four poverty indicators. H_1: There is spatial autocorrelation among four poverty indicators.

According to the Moran's I, the spatial autocorrelation coefficient with p-values are less than the Moran's I value in the both data sets, first and second. The null hypothesis is rejected. Thus, the variables are behaving significantly positively spatially autocorreleted and similarly values are clustered together. Hence, all the

Table 17.2 Moran's I value for first data set

Poverty indicators	Moran's index	p-value
Per capita income	0.4080	0.0536
Average level of education	0.3724	0.2020
Long term unemployment	0.4306	0.1916
Population living without earned income	0.5521	0.1710

Source Directorate of economics and statistics, Government of India

Table 17.3 Moran's I value for second data set

Poverty indicators	Moran's index	p-value
Per capita income	0.6273	0.0160
Average level of education	0.3526	0.2057
Long term unemployment	0.2466	0.2260
Population living without earned income	0.9186	0.6126

Source Directorate of economics and statistics, Government of India

selected poverty indicators have a high degree of positive autocorrelation among the states of North-East except Sikkim.

As we know, poverty is the creation of social, political and others factors and its occurrence depends upon place, time and society. A person, who fails to obtain the minimum level of calories, falls below the poverty line. Chakravarty and Majumder (2007) discussed that poverty is a multidimensional phenomenon and its analysis needs more dimensions than income. Rowntree (1901) defined families in poverty if their total earning is insufficient to meet the ‘minimum necessities of merely physical efficiency’ under income approach. The concept of poverty reflects failure in human life with many dimensions—unemployment, hunger, illness and health care, homelessness, powerlessness and victimization and social injustice. All of them are adding up to an assault of human dignity. Rapid growth of population in NE India is worrisome and great challenge. It is one such region that exhibits accelerated population growth—both natural (in terms of exponential growth) and artificial (illegal migrants from neighbouring countries) increases—after independence. An urge is required to have at most one girl child (with low fecundity) in each family and use of contraception for controlling the rapid growth of population. Practice of contraceptives should be encouraged through awareness. There is a need to enhance the amount of incentive for the family planning sterilization of male and female to control the rapid growth of population. Good impact of this is visible in rural areas. The sex ratio in 2011 is very good (above 900) in all NE states except Sikkim and in each state, an increasing trend is expected in future years, which is good sign of improvement in sex ratio within NE. Population projection based on migration, fertility, mortality and sex-age composition gives better approximation.

State-wise poverty from 2000 to 2014 is demonstrated in Table 17.4, in which poverty rates associated with five states like Arunachal Pradesh, Assam, Manipur, Meghalaya and Mizoram exhibit peculiar behaviour from 2011 onward but poverty rates in Nagaland, Sikkim and Tripura are reducing year by year. This indicates that programmes and policies for poverty reduction were implemented nicely in these three states. More attention is required to implement those policies in remaining five states. Poverty is multidimensional and a much broader concept than, what is generally thought of. The term human deprivation can only be identified through elasticities of various poverty indices. Alleviation of poverty is a great challenge before the governments and societies on the globe including NE India.

As we know jhum (or shifting) cultivation is popular for agricultural practice in North-East India. People cut valuable and pre-matured trees and burn them with other smaller plants in the forest under shifting cultivation, which affects the environment. There is a need to stop this practice for the environmental sustainability. Time came to protect the trees and other plants in forests and all other places for better livelihood because trees are the best friends of us and they (trees) keep the environment healthier and balanced by observing harmful substances present in the air. They (trees) also keep away from natural calamity such as flood, draught, cloudbursts, etc. Continued deforestation in North-East brings people in deprivation from valuable forest resources like wood products, food and medicines. That is why it is needed to plant more trees in North-East India using the principle ‘my earth my

Table 17.4 State-wise changes in poverty rate since 2000 in North-Eastern region of India

Year	Arunachal Pradesh	Assam	Manipur	Meghalaya	Mizoram	Nagaland	Sikkim	Tripura
2000	39.4	40.9	33.8	37.9	25.7	37.9	41.4	39.0
2001	37.35	39.16	30.77	35.32	25.06	36.32	38.21	39.01
2002	33.47	36.06	28.54	33.87	19.47	32.67	36.55	34.44
2003	32.67	35.09	27.54	30.87	18.25	30.98	33.68	23.44
2004	29.47	32.29	26.64	30.67	16.82	32.67	36.55	34.44
2005	33.47	36.09	28.54	33.87	19.47	29.30	31.69	28.35
2006	31.5	36.1	25.8	32.9	21.3	30.8	34.6	31.4
2007	17.6	19.7	17.3	18.5	12.6	19.0	20.1	18.9
2008	15.6	18.4	15.1	16.41	10.6	15.07	20.5	18.4
2009	15.3	17.2	16.4	11.2	16.9	46.4	22.5	32.8
2010	16.8	17.1	16.1	18.5	12.1	15.2	20.1	22.5
2011	28.20	31.10	34.40	38.00	16.10	15.30	9.00	31.10
2012	22.8	25.9	37.9	47.1	17.7	21.1	20.9	13.0
2013	34.67	31.98	36.89	11.87	20.40	18.88	5.19	14.05
2014	24.67	27.98	30.98	10.29	18.32	16.56	8.19	12.02

Source Directorate of economics and statistics, Government of India

duty'. Land reforms are requiring to achieve redistributive justice and to attain higher levels of agricultural production and income in rural areas. The successful implementation of land reforms is responsibility rests with concerned state government. Flood and erosion are related to some other major problems faced in North-East India and during the last 50 years, erosion taken by the mighty river Brahmaputra has eaten away half of the river island Majuli, which is believed to be the home of Assamese culture. Improvement of access to clean and safe water and sanitation is the most significant environment priority for the poor in the region. Inadequate protection and conservation of environment bring substantial direct and indirect impacts on health and livelihoods by increasing the vulnerability of poor people throughout the region. The most sufferers from environment health problems among poor are especially the women and children. Urban population suffers from faecal contamination of water and food due to poor or non-existence of excreta disposal systems. Most of the major rivers' water near cities and industrial areas became faecal contaminated and this brings various types of diseases in NE. Increasing demand of fresh water will be short due to high growth in population in this region.

Singh (2012) discussed that scholars, policy makers, academicians, educationists and religious leaders have been discussing the relationship between population and development. This is true that the relationship between population and development is negative. If population will increase rapidly, the economic growth is affected and hence the development is also affected.

Human rights perspective may be applied as strategy for poverty reduction. A view has been emerged that the denial or non-fulfilment of human rights (HR) also constitutes the poverty. There may be few certain kinds of human right matters, which exacerbate severity of the poverty. The HR can be relevant to poverty in three different ways—constitutive relevance, instrumental relevance and constraint-based relevance. Instrumental relevance characterizes in two different types such as evaluative and causative. Amartya Sen in his pioneering work on families demonstrated the causative relevance of some human rights. The causative relevance also exacerbates less extreme but persistent poverty. A wide range of civil and political rights should be protected. HR and poverty are complementary to each other. HR approach reduces the poverty by empowering the poor as the powerlessness weakens them but empowerment enhances the capabilities of poor persons and their freedom of choice is expanded. HR equalizes the distribution and exercise of power between and within societies. The poor get frequent experience of social exclusion, alienation, discrimination, isolation and inequality in gender, income and socio-cultural factors like the religion, colour, ethnicity, social hierarchy, etc. That is why it is needed to promote and protect non-discrimination, equality and empowerment.

Development thus can be achieved by shifting ill being to well being with good quality of life under equality. Poverty line should not be determined using the selection of low level of income only but also selection of lack of or little wealth and lack of low quality of other assets like education, health, shelter, clothing, furniture, personal means of transport, etc. Only scientific criterion can justify drawing the poverty line. Self-employment programme and allied programmes under rural development programme place prominence on focused approach to poverty alleviation, capitalizing advantages of group lending and overcoming the problems associated with multiplicity of programmes. Acceleration of economic growth together with focusing on sectors, which are employment intensive, facilitates the removal of poverty in the long run. Strategies like economic growth and redistribution are not only required to eradicate the poverty but also direct intervention in many areas—reducing population growth, empowerment, expanding education, eliminating discrimination and corruption, securing human rights and social justice; different types of deprivations related to human lives are interrelated and reinforce one another. Empowering poor persons will remove formal and informal institutional barriers that prevent them from taking action to improve their well being. Main industries are available on tea based, crude oil and natural gas, silk, bamboo and handicrafts in this region. The states are heavily forested and have plentiful rainfall.

The measure of social development is based on the UNDP Human Development Index (HDI). Whereas per capita GDP is correlated with (though does not directly measure) longevity and education, the HDI measures per capita income, longevity and education directly. GDP measures productivity in the aggregate. Contrasting per capita GDP, the HDI is able to distinguish between standard of living and income. In addition to it, indicators like Gini coefficient of income distribution and percentage of population below poverty line are used. The important dimensions of social development like literacy, infant mortality rate, expectation of life and composite indices such as physical quality of life (PQLI), Human development index (HDI) and gender-related development index (GDI) are used. NFHS 1992–93 report shows that total fertility rate is reduced as the level of education increased in different religions and also for total population.

To educate women has many advantages in the societies. The educated mothers are able to take better care of themselves and their families and children. Education or formal schooling plays a greater role in affecting reproductive behaviour and increased knowledge of health, hygiene, cleanliness, sanitation and demand for fewer children in the families. Education also promotes better antenatal lifestyles and educated parents place greater emphasis on child quality than the child quantity. They prefer, in general, fewer but better educated, healthier and well-nourished children. The education reduces the number of children a couple has by encouraging contraception. It also minimizes the fear of adopting such new technologies and also makes individuals think and realize. Planning is a systematic attempt by the government to analyze the existing situation, sort out the requirements and choose the measures needed to accomplish the selected goals to transform the society deliberately. Education is the key to development and the most powerful weapon available in the fight against inequality to reduce poverty.

The aim of anti-poverty policies and programmes for North-East India should be based on reduction of population growth, expanding education, eliminating discrimination and corruption, securing human rights and social justice. Anti-poverty programmes are designed specifically in such a way that they generate both the self and wage employments in rural areas in order to improve their effectiveness and impact on the decant and get better their sustainability. Emphasis will be given to cover entire area and all poor. Funds of all programmes and policies are directly released to village councils through village punchayats. Singh (2011) provided an example that Bihar government has been implementing the programmes and policies available in nice way assuming prime duty and as a result Bihar achieved annual growth rate of development above 11% in financial year 2008–09. One may say that ‘Where there is will, there is a way’. Most of the anti-poverty policies and programmes in North-East India suffer from human diseases like discriminations, corruptions and selfishness. Good governance guarantees the transparent use of public funds, encourages growth of public and private sectors, promotes effective of public services and helps to establish the rule of law. Regular monitoring of anti-poverty and anti-corruption programmes and policies in North-East India are required with full will-power and honesty.

17.6 Concluding Remark

Moran’s I spatial autocorrelation coefficient with p-values on four poverty indicators such as per capita income, average level of education, long term unemployment and population living without earned income is computed for the first data set and the second data set, respectively, and found behaving significantly positively spatially autocorreleted. Hence, all the selected poverty indicators have a high degree of positive autocorrelation among the states of North-East except Sikkim.

To improve quality of lives of all the people in the region is possible only by lowering the rate of population growth and the infant mortality rate; increasing the per capita income, level of education, expectancy of life and healthcare and eliminating discriminations, all sorts of corruptions and environmental pollutions from North-East India. Government should make programmes and policies and then implement those policies seriously and nicely with full willpower to combat the poverty from North-East India. The anti-poverty programmes and policies should continue. There is a need to develop a good technology so that maximum share of fund of the programmes and policies should reach to the beneficiaries who need badly as the relief to come out from poverty in the region.

Attempts should be made for compulsory education to all children, women and adults for lowering the rate of population growth and the rate of pollution, better health facilities to all, implementation of birth control and healthcare programmes and free from all sorts of corruptions in the societies.

The Brahmaputra and all other rivers in North-East India should be interconnected with pucca banks on both the sides of the rivers, if possible but gradually. Special emphasis on tapping the tourism potential in North-East India is required and to be given under Tourism Policy to promote better livelihood.

Better lives are possible in North-East India by increasing per capita income, level of education, expectancy of life, women empowerment, ensuring equality in each section of population, providing better health care and lowering the infant mortality rate. Encouragement to work for both the spouse in each household is required for the betterment of income and their lives in North-East India.

References

Ajakaiye, D. O., & Adeyeye V. A. (2001). The nature of poverty in Nigeria, *NISER Monograph Series No.* 13. Nigerian Institute of Social and Economic Research, Ibadan, Nigeria.

Anselin, L. (1992). *Spatial econometrics: Method and models*. Boston: USA, Kluwer Academic Publishers.

Chakravarty, S. R., & Majumder, A. (2007). Measuring human poverty by population and factor decomposable indices. *The Indian Economic Journal, 55*(1), 67–77.

Goodchild, M. F. (1987). A spatial analytical perspective on geographical information system. *International Journal of Geographical Information Systems, 1*(4), 327–334.

Hubert, L. & Arabie, P. (1991). The assessment of spatial autocorrelation through constrained multiple regression, *Geographical Analysis*, *23*(2), 95–111.

Molini, V. (2005). The transformation of the Vietnamese earnings distribution during the transition: A micro-simulation using shapley's value, *SOW-VU Working Paper, Amsterdam.*

Rowntree, B. S. (1901). *Poverty: A study of town life*. London: Macmillan.

Singh, R. (2012). Sustainable development of Northeast India. *International Journal of Research in Commerce, Economics and Management, 2*(8), 116–123.
Singh, R. (2011). Alleviation of poverty in India. *Journal of Social and Economic Policy, 8*(1), 43–53.
Smith, De M., Longley, L., & Goodchild, M. (2015). *Geospatial Analysis*, Fifth Edition, The Winchelsea Press.

Chapter 18
Hunger, Governance Failure and Its Outcome: An Analysis of the Historical Experience of the Mizo Hills District of Undivided Assam

Malabika Das Gupta

Abstract Eradication of extreme poverty and hunger is foremost among the Millennium Development Goals (MDGs) that were adopted in the Millennium Summit of the United Nations in 2000. Eradication of hunger figures among the MDGs because freedom from hunger is a human right. It is also treated as a MDG because hunger related malnutrition results in ill health leading to loss of productivity of the working age population and the productive potential of a country by affecting the health of its children. Loss of lives due to hunger and malnutrition can also lower the productive capacity of countries both in the short and the long run. Eradication of hunger is also important because persistent hunger leads to political and social crisis. Using Census data and secondary data sources, it will be shown in the chapter that famine and hunger caused by rodents and the Assam government's failure of governance in providing relief to the starving Mizos were proximate causes of the 20-year long insurgency and social unrest in the Mizo Hills from 1966 to 1986. The chapter will focus on a historical analysis of the failure of the Assam government in dealing with hunger and famine in the Mizo Hills District, the political economy operating behind its failure of governance and the outcome of this failure.

Keywords MDG · Hunger · Mizo hills district · Insurgency

M. Das Gupta (✉)
Tripura University, Agartala, India
e-mail: dasgupta.dg@rediffmail.com

M. Das Gupta
Institute of Development Studies Kolkata, Kolkata, India

Present Address:
M. Das Gupta
Department of Economics, Centre for Urban Economic Studies,
Calcutta University, Kolkata, India

U.K. De et al. (eds.), *Inequality, Poverty and Development in India*, India Studies in Business and Economics, DOI 10.1007/978-981-10-6274-2_18

18.1 Introduction

Persistent hunger in a population can result from an extreme and protracted shortfall in the supply of food due to natural and/or man-made causes. It can also occur due to the inability of people to have access to food even when there is an adequate supply of it mainly because of their low purchasing power and the government's failure to ensure that their nutritional needs are met. Alternatively, it can result from a combination of both these supply and demand-related factors.

Persistent hunger leads to starvation, debility and starvation-related diseases among the affected population and can also cause a large number of deaths due to causes associated with hunger.

Eradication of hunger is important because freedom from hunger is a human right. Eradication of hunger assumes importance because hunger results in ill health leading to a loss of productivity of the working age population. It also results in a lowering of the productive potential of a country in the years to come by adversely affecting the health of its children who constitute its future work force. Loss of lives due to hunger and malnutrition can also lower the productive capacity of countries both in the short and the long run by reducing their number of workers. The eradication of hunger is also important because persistent hunger can lead to social and political crisis.

18.2 Objective of the Chapter

In North east India also, as in the rest of the world, persistent hunger has led to social unrest.[1] The focus of the chapter is on a historical analysis of the failure of the Assam government in dealing with hunger and famine in the Mizo Hills

[1]Historically, there are other examples from the northeast region of India which show that persistent hunger fomented anti-Indian feelings culminating in the separatist movement. During 1946–47, Nagaland reeled under a severe food shortage due to drought conditions and consequent under production of food. Neither the colonial rulers nor the Indian government tried to tackle the problem of hunger among the Nagas. This gave rise to a strong anti-Indian feeling among them and was one of the causes that spawned secessionist feelings among the Nagas. During the Second World War, the Marwari and Sikh merchants who had entered the princely state along with the British bought up all the rice produced in the valley to satisfy the wartime needs of the Allied forces. This created an artificial food scarcity in Manipur. The severity of the famine-like situation which developed prompted the womenfolk of Manipur to organize an all-women movement known as the *Nupilan* movement of 1939–40 protesting against the export of local rice by outside traders (Nag 2008; Yambem 1978). Nag (2008) stated that "the breaking out of the *Nupilan* on the eve of Indian Independence had far-reaching implications as far as the shaping of anti-India attitude of the Meities was concerned. The artificial famine resulting from the hoarding of essential commodities by the Marwari and Sikh traders created the image of Indian traders as 'unscrupulous people'. The continuation of such practice by these merchants despite protest movements and social ostracization only promoted the negative image of … Indians in the Meitei mind". (p. 21)

District, the political economy operating behind its failure of governance and the outcome of this failure. On the basis of Census data, and data collected from primary and secondary sources on the Mizo Hills District it is shown in this chapter that (a) the indifference of the Assam government to repeated warnings by different organizations in the Mizo Hills District about an impending famine and widespread hunger due to the flowering of bamboos and the consequent increase in the rat population of the District and (b) the failure of the government to provide timely and adequate assistance to the starving Mizos during the Mautam famine of 1959 to 1961 were the proximate causes of the 20- year long insurgency and social unrest that prevailed in the Mizo Hills from 1966 to 1986.

The approaches of the Mizos themselves and the British in dealing with the periodic famines in the past set the background of the chapter. The next part of the chapter analyses the Government of Assam's approach to hunger and famine in the Mizo Hills District in the post-independence period, the political economy behind it and the outcome of the failure of governance of the Assam government.

18.3 Background

Dense bamboo groves cover the slopes of the Lushai Hills (as the Mizo Hills were earlier called) and the Lushais (the present-day Mizos) practised slash and burn or shifting cultivation by clearing the hill slopes of the bamboo forests. The output produced on their jhums was barely enough to sustain them.

Hunger and famine have systematically stalked the Lushai Hills at periodic intervals. They have been preceded by a gregarious flowering of bamboos throughout the hills, the 'thing' bamboos flowering once every thirty years and the 'mau' variety once every fifty years. Historically, the flowering of the bamboo has ushered in a period of famine and hunger for the Mizos because when the bamboos bear fruits after flowering, the rat menace starts in the hills. Rats are very fond of eating the bamboo fruits and the nutrients in the bamboo seeds make them breed prolifically. The huge rat population eats up all the bamboo fruits and then devour the standing crops in the jhum fields as well as the stock of food grains of the Mizos, leaving them with very little food so that the flowering of bamboos is associated with famine and hunger in the Lushai Hills. The bamboos die after flowering and bearing fruits and after some years, the rat population also goes down because there is not enough food to sustain their huge numbers as the supply of rice and bamboo seeds is exhausted. So, gradually, the famine gets over and the harvest and food supply in the Mizo Hills goes back to normal till the bamboos start flowering again after a predictable interval.

Though the context in which the famines occurred in the Mizo Hills in post-independence India was totally different from that of the pre-independence period, an analysis of the response of the state and of the people to the famines in the past is required to see where the Assam government failed. The material for this section is derived mainly from Nag (2008).

According to Nag (2008: 58–92), before the advent of the British in the Lushai Hills, the Lushais had their own coping mechanisms when the periodic Mautam and Thingtam famines struck. They were familiar with the association between the flowering of bamboos and famines caused by rodents and took a number of steps to mitigate hunger and starvation. In a bid to control the rodent population, they killed the rats and ate them and cultivated crops like tapioca and colocasia in their jhums instead of rice to supplement their diet because the rats do not eat these crops. The Lushai chiefs who were the only people in villages who could stockpile rice by virtue of cultivating large jhums with the help of slaves and the forced labour that their subjects were obliged to provide to them gave food and shelter to distressed families that offered themselves as their lifelong slaves. During times of famine, entire villages turned into traders exchanging forest products they collected for rice and other staple food items with people living in the plains. When all these coping mechanisms failed, they migrated en masse to the plains of Cachar and Sylhet temporarily and lived on the charity of the plainsmen and returned to their villages in the hills only when the severity of the famine lessened.

The British colonialists made their first contact with the Lushais in the Cachar frontier in 1765 when they acquired the Diwani of Bengal. They had to confront the Lushais when they annexed Cachar in 1832 as the Lushais raided the British subjects in Cachar from time to time. In the 1870s, the British government was troubled by repeated raids by the Lushais both in the Cachar and Chittagong frontiers which it was unable to check through a series of military expeditions to subjugate the recalcitrant Lushais.[2]

A famine broke out in the Lushai Hills in 1881 following the flowering of bamboos and a consequent increase in the rat population which led to a massive destruction of the rice crops standing in the fields and stored in the granaries of the Mizos and their chiefs. Widespread hunger stalked the hills as a result and the starving Mizos entered the British territories in large numbers in search of food and livelihood till the famine subsided. The British government felt that an opportunity had come their way to end the hostility of the Lushais during the famine and realized that what several years of warfare against the Lushais had failed to accomplish could be achieved by coming to the aid of the starving Lushais. The British authorities took care of the immigrant Lushais as well as their brethren who had not migrated to the plains. Relief was provided to the starving Lushai migrants

[2]The Lushais regularly raided the region for headhunting and kidnapping. After the discovery of tea in Assam, there was a rush by planters to acquire foothill lands for establishing tea gardens in Cachar. This threatened the Lushais who feared that the British would invade the hills, depriving them of their homeland. They were also aggrieved because the tea gardens encroached on their hunting grounds and therefore they conducted raids on the British territories.

who were employed by the government and the tea planters to build roads and clear forests in exchange for food. The starving Mizos brought forest products like bamboo, wild rubber and honey to the plains with them to exchange for rice. Trade marts were set up in the foothills where the Lushais could exchange these forest products for rice sold by private traders from the plains. The British administration facilitated trading by the Lushais by abolishing the duty charged on forest products at the forest toll stations temporarily. The relief measures of the British government also extended to the Lushai Hills which were not a part of the Empire at that time. Government depots were set up in the Lushai Hills to store paddy to be given out as loans to people who were certified by the chiefs or headmen as individuals who could not buy paddy. Roads and paths were constructed deep inside the Lushai Hills by the British with labour provided by the starving Lushais in exchange for food as wages for moving food grains to starving villagers. Private traders from the plains were encouraged by the British government to send rice up to the main markets of Tipaimukh and Changsil in the Lushai Hills. Nag (2001) reported

> about 18,000 maunds of rice and 2000 maunds of paddy was (sic) exported to the interiors of Mizo hills in 1881–82 alone. During that crisis the total expenditure in famine relief stood at Rs. 2240 (p. 1032).

The relief measures provided by the British bore fruit. They changed the image of the British from foes to friends in times of need in the minds of most of the Lushais. The British earned the gratitude and loyalty of the chiefs who had benefited from the relief measures provided by their erstwhile enemy. It is not merely a coincidence that by 1898, only a few years after the famine ended; the conquest of the Lushai Hills by the British was completed. When the famine was over, the British could defeat the hostile Lushai chiefs and gain control over the entire Lushai Hills with the help of friendly chiefs, thanks to their relief work among the Lushais during the famine years.[3]

The next rat famines following the flowering of bamboos occurred in the Lushai Hills in 1911–12 and in 1929–30 when the Lushai Hills had become a part of the British Empire. Scarce commodities were procured and supplied to the hills by the British administration through traders from the plains to alleviate hunger among the Lushais during the famine. Food godowns were set up all over the Lushai Hills. The

[3]It was easy for the British to subjugate the Lushais because the famine had ruined their economy. About 15,000 people including chiefs and warriors perished in the famine due to starvation. Many of the fighting men had migrated permanently to Manipur, Tripura and the Chittagong Hill Tracts. The famine was followed by pestilence, plague and other epidemics that debilitated the population. The fighting power of the Lushais was gone because their guns and ammunition of the Lushais had been sold or exchanged for food and could not be recovered as they had nothing to exchange with the plainsmen. Rubber trees died of over-tapping, bamboos had been over-harvested and the Lushais were in a state of destitution and could not afford to put up a resistance against the British (Nag 2008). The British could establish their supremacy in the Lushai Hills not only because the Mautam famine had devastated the Lushais but also because their relief operations had boosted their strategic strength inside the hills by allowing them to build roads and paths deep in the hills that were inaccessible to them before the famine.

government entered into a contract with a few Marwari food grain traders from Cachar who procured rice and paddy locally and transported them to the godowns in the Lushai Hills. The food grains were sold to the Lushais from the godowns and those who were not in a position to buy food grains were given loans of food grains to be repaid in cash or kind. If the loans could not be repaid by the Lushais, they had to repay them in terms of forced labour for construction works. To encourage the Lushais to kill rats that created the food shortage, the government started giving monetary incentives for rats killed. The benevolence of the colonial administration in providing famine mitigated to a large extent the hunger and starvation of the famine-affected Lushais and made the British rulers popular among them.

Christian Missionaries had not made much headway in converting the Lushais till the famines of 1911–12 and 1929. The famines provided them a great opportunity to spread Christianity as the Missionaries helped the government and the famine-stricken people by superintending the distribution of food, ministered to the sick and provided employment to them in Church-related activities. Their humanitarian activities not only reduced hunger in the hills during the famine but also helped the Church to win over the Lushais and spread Christianity among them Nag (2008).

18.4 The Mautam Famine of 1959 to 1961

After India's independence, the Lushai Hills District of Assam was renamed as the Mizo Hills District. It had an Autonomous District Council which was essentially a legislative body. It could hardly take any action on its own and had to depend on the Government of Assam for almost everything as it did not have money of its own.

As predicted by the Mizos, the bamboos started flowering all over the Mizo Hills District of Assam in the 1950s. This led to a sizeable increase in the rodent population in the hills, setting off alarm signals of an impending famine in the district.

18.5 Failure of Governance with Regard to Hunger

The Assam Government's failure of governance in dealing with the situation manifested itself in several ways. *Its neglect of advance warning about an impending famine by the Mizos was the chief among them.* The Mizos knew the periodicity of the occurrence of famines and they could also predict the famine correctly. According to their prediction the next Mautam was to take place in 1959 and they issued advance warnings to the Assam government about it. However, the Assam government's attitude was marked by a total disregard of the danger signals of a massive famine predicted by the Mizos. When the bamboos started flowering in the 1950s and the rat population of the District started increasing, a non-governmental organization, the Anti-famine Campaign Organization (AFO) was formed to encourage the people to kill the rats, produce alternative food products like bananas and teach the people how to survive in the famine situation following the traditional anti-famine practices of the pre-British days. When the Minister of Supplies of Assam visited Aizawl in 1954, the AFO apprised him of the grim situation and requested him to set up food stores and strengthen the food supply network all over the district as the British had done earlier to mitigate the impending shortage of food. The Minister, however, dismissed the whole idea of rats causing a famine as tribal superstition and did not act on the advice of the AFO (Nag 2008).

As the famine became imminent, Mizo Union, the political party that controlled the District Council began taking steps to mitigate the food crisis that was about to engulf the District though it was cash strapped. It warned the Assam Government about the impending Mautam famine and in 1958, it passed a unanimous resolution asking the Assam government for a grant of Rs. 15 lakhs to tackle the imminent famine. But the government turned a deaf ear to the District Council's request for funds as it was not convinced that there was a link between the flowering of bamboos and a rat famine. It sent an entomologist in response to the District Council's SOS for expert advice to deal with the situation. The expert camped for a couple of nights at Aizawl and reported that there was no evidence whatsoever to connect the increase in the rat population to that of the flowering of the bamboo, providing the Assam government with an excuse for following a policy of inaction, neglecting the Mizo wisdom based on their long experience of rat famines in the past.

As a result of the neglect of advance warnings, matters came to a head in 1959 when the destruction of crops by rats resulted in an acute shortage of food in the Mizo Hills district.

Some idea of the degree of destruction due to the rat famine can be had by referring to the crop cutting survey data for the District. The yield in pounds per acre as per the Crop Cutting Survey for the District reported in the District Census Handbook of the Mizo Hills District of Assam for 1961 (1965, Table 3.5, p. 216) are reproduced in Table 18.1. The figures show that there was a drastic reduction in the yield per acre in the district as a whole in 1959–60. The low yield reported in 1959–60 was due to the loss of crops because of the widespread damage caused by rats.

When the famine actually started, the Assam government did not take prompt action which is another evidence of its failure of governance. Though the famine had begun in 1958, even in 1959 the Mizo Hills District was not declared as a famine-hit zone by the Assam Government. In 1959, when the Finance Commissioner of the Central Government visited the District, he saw the havoc created by the famine and recommended an immediate supply of food to the District to feed the hungry Mizos and trucks and jeeps to carry the food grains to the famine-affected areas. However, the Government of Assam's reaction to his recommendations was slow and it started releasing the relief material for the Mizo Hills only from August 1959. Nag (2008) reported,

Table 18.1 Yield Rates of Principal Crops of the Mizo Hills District (pounds/acre as per Crop Cutting Survey)

Crop	1956–57	1957–58	1959–60
Boro paddy (spring)	1200	1200	–
Sali paddy (winter)	896	–	300[a]
Maize	500	500	200
Total cereals[$]	400	400	300

Notes (1) [$]average of the items for which data are available, (2) [a]low yield due to 70% of the crop lost because of widespread damage by rats
Source Census of India 1961, Assam. District Census Handbook, Mizo Hills, Table 3.5, p. 216

> it was only when, on the desperate appeal of the district administration, the Tribal Welfare Minister of Assam, Williamson Sangma visited Aizawl and a (sic) angry public demonstration confronted him that he recommended the declarations (sic) of the Mizo Hills as a famine affected area. As a result of this declaration relief was (finally) sanctioned to the famine affected people (p. 249).

The failure of the Assam government to take appropriate action even when famine relief work was started at long last was another evidence of governance failure in dealing with the famine. When relief operations were carried out by the District Commissioner's office, relief materials did not always reach the needy as the office did not have the necessary infrastructure and manpower to handle the massive relief operation. There were complaints about bias in the distribution of relief material. The Buddhist Chakmas and the Hindu Riangs who lived in the border areas felt that they were discriminated against in the distribution of relief materials while the Christians were favoured. Relief work was seriously hampered as there were no proper roads in the Mizo Hills at that time to facilitate the rapid movement of relief material. In the absence of motorable roads in the villages, rice had to be carried as head loads by people to remote villages that made the movement of relief material extremely slow. Due to bad weather, food was sometimes airdropped to affected villages but bad packaging led to the wastage of this relief material. Bad weather and hilly terrain sometimes meant that relief meant for one village was airdropped in another village where relief was not needed. The despatch of relief material was also often held up at Silchar, the only gateway in the plains to the Mizo Hills, because of logistic reasons.

18.6 The Political Economy Behind the Failure of Governance

What explains the failure of the Assam government to deal with the famine situation? An apologist for the Assam government will blame the difficult terrain, the lack of connectivity, the settlement pattern in the Mizo Hills for its shortcomings in dealing with the famine situation. But this is not the entire story. There is a good deal of truth in the belief of the Mizos that the Assam government's insensitivity to their advance warnings about an impending famine and its indifference to their plight reflected a lack of concern for the tribal Mizos who were socially, culturally and economically different from the majority of the population of the state.

It will not be wrong to say that the Assam government also played politics with famine relief and 'the Chaliha government was more concerned with district level politics than the organization of relief work to the distressed people' (Chaube 1999, p. 179). Initially, the Assam Government decided to distribute the relief material to the famine-affected people directly through the Deputy Commissioner's office, bypassing the District Council in order to improve its image and counter the growing perception among the Mizos that the state government was insensitive to their sufferings and had deliberately delayed the sanctioning of relief. Its decision was also prompted by its desire to marginalize the Mizo Union which controlled the District Council that had repeatedly pointed out to the government the need for action to tackle the rat famine which it had ignored. There was a strong plea by the Mizo Union for relief work to be conducted through the District Council which had the infrastructure and the necessary manpower to reach the relief material to the remotest of villages but its plea fell on deaf ears. The Chief Minister of undivided Assam, B. P. Chaliha was unwilling to hand over the relief work to either the Mizo Union which he distrusted and disliked or to AFO. Instead, the Assam government decided to put the Mizo National Famine Front (MNFF), a voluntary organization started for famine relief in charge of famine relief, totally bypassing the District Council in a bid to marginalize the political party at the helm of affairs in the District Council.

The failure of the Assam Government to learn from the British also contributed to its failure of governance. During the British period and even before the Lushai Hills had come under the control of the British, the British government and the Church had helped in famine relief for the Mizos and had won over the Mizo people. Though famine relief was prompted by the imperialist agenda of the government and the proselytizing zeal of the Church, it helped in bringing the Lushai Hills under the control of the British and winning the loyalty of the Lushai people. In the Mizo Hills District of Assam in independent India, the role of the Indian and Assam governments in addressing starvation and hunger among the Mizos was totally different from that of the British.

18.7 Insurgency—The Fallout of Assam's Failure of Governance in the Lushai Hills

From the District Census Handbook of 1961 it appears that the total number of deaths in the District spiked to 2068 in 1958 from 1873 in 1957 (1965, Table 2.1, p. 210) although the entire increase in the number of deaths in the district between 1957 and 1958 cannot be attributed to starvation due to the rat famine. The number of starvation deaths in the District due to the Mautam famine is widely believed to have been 15,000 although the source of this information is not quoted. The famine probably had such disastrous consequences because famine relief provided by the government and the Church in the British period had made the Lushais totally dependent on relief provided by outside agencies instead of depending on their own age-old coping strategies. The British government had stopped the migration of Lushais to the plains at times of famine by confining them within the hills. The British had also stopped the exchange of forest products by the tribals with food grains by the plainsmen in the markets in the foothills. The spread of Christianity had also changed the traditional food habits of the Lushais who were discouraged from eating rats so a monetary incentive had to be provided by the government to the people during the famines to promote the killing of rats to control the rodent population.

However, hunger and starvation did not prevail uniformly all over the District. In Aizawl town, there was enough rice, some of it have come to the town all the way from the United States of America. Consequently, the price of rice was Rs. 21.60 per *maund* and paddy was sold in the town at Rs. 13 per *maund*. The town dwellers had the purchasing power to buy rice but in the rural areas people had neither the purchasing power nor did the supply of rice and paddy reach them (Nag 2008). People from villages therefore in their desperation migrated to Aizawl in search of food. With regard to the impact of the Mautam famine of 1959–61 on population growth in Aizawl, Kumar (Kumar 1993) said:

> The great famine (*Mautam*) of 1960 which brought havoc to (an) already poor agricultural economy of the Lushai Hills forced people from rural areas to migrate to the only urban centre (Aizawl) in search of (a) livelihood. (p. 130)[4]

Field work done in Aizawl by other researchers confirms Kumar's statement. One migrant to the town at the time of the famine reported that the rats ate up not only the kernels of the rice in his fields but the whole stalks. He tried poisoning the rats and though this produced some result, there were still so many of them that he felt helpless against the rat menace and left his farm and went to Aizawl to avoid starvation (Shoumatoff 2007). This migrant stayed on in Aizawl even after the famine was over. Others, unlike him, took refuge in Aizawl temporarily to avoid hunger and possible death from starvation. A respondent who was from Ailawng village migrated to Aizawl in 1958 because he and his family had nothing to eat in the village as all their crops were destroyed by rats and the family had no choice but to migrate. They lived with their relatives in Aizawl and when the famine was over, they moved back to their village in 1961 because they had been unable to build a house in Aizawl or find a secure means of livelihood there.

However, insurgency seems to have been the most important fallout of the Mautam famine. The MNFF had done exemplary famine relief work even in the

---

[4]In an ongoing 'outside' project funded by The Asiatic Society, the author is examining whether this is the historical reason for the high concentration of population in the primate urban centre of Aizawl as evidenced in the growth of population of the town between 1951 and 1961.

remotest corners of the Mizo Hills District through its volunteers which won the voluntary organization immense popularity among the Mizos but besides famine relief, the MNFF had another agenda. The indifference of the Assam Government to the plight of the starving Mizos when the predicted rat famine broke out in the hills despite being forewarned and the inefficient way in which famine relief was provided by it to the affected population when the government finally woke up to the reality of the famine had given a boost to the anti-Indian feeling that already existed among the Mizos and helped in alienating them still further from both the Assam and the Central governments. The MNFF cashed in on its popularity with the Mizos, fomented the anti-Indian feelings generated by the government's indifference towards the starving Mizos and its handling of famine relief work after it had become long overdue and carried on a vigorous anti-government and anti-Mizo Union propaganda along with its famine relief work all over the Mizo Hills District.

When the famine subsided in 1961, this ultimately culminated in the formation of the MNF party which morphed from the MNFF. Right from its inception, the MNF had a secessionist agenda of independence from India and in 1966, the MNF under the leadership of Laldenga started an armed uprising against the Government of India for establishing an independent Mizoram. One of the main planks in their anti-Indian propaganda to gain popular support for its secessionist cause against the Indian government and struggle for independence was the apathy of the mainland to the danger signals of the famine and the shortcomings of famine relief provided to the starving Mizos. Although there were other deep-seated causes for the bitter and long freedom movement in the Mizo Hills District of Assam, the indifference of the Assam government to the warnings of the Mizo people when the bamboos flowered and its inefficiency in dealing with hunger, pestilence and death caused by the rat famine were the proximate cause of the two decade long insurgency that broke out in the Mizo Hills District in 1966 under the leadership of the MNF.

18.8 Conclusion

The British, by providing famine relief and reducing hunger among the Mizos earned their gratitude and loyalty even when they did not control the Lushai Hills. They could even annex their land with the help of the loyal Chiefs whose approbation they had won when they embarked on their paternalistic attempts at famine relief to win over the Lushais and had made them loyal subjects of the British. In sharp contrast, the indifference of the Assamese government to the plight of the Mizos during the Mautam famine which stalked the Mizo Hills from 1959 to 1961, its indifference to the warnings of the impending famine by the Mizos and its inefficiency in managing the relief operations when it finally woke up to the reality of the situation alienated the Mizos, turned them into bitter enemies of the Indian government and led to the outbreak of a 20-year long insurgency in the Mizo Hills. The chapter shows on the basis of the experience of one of the constituent states of the North eastern region of India that the eradication of hunger is extremely important because failure to eradicate hunger can be a proximate cause of widespread social unrest and can spawn insurgency.

References

Chaube, S. K. (1999). *Hill politics in North-East India*. Delhi: Orient Longman.

Government of Assam. (1965). *Census of India 1961 Assam*. District Census Handbook. Mizo Hills. Gauhati: Tribune Press.

Kumar, G. (1993). Urban growth of Aizawl. In A. C. Sinha, Pariyaram M. Chacko and I. L. Aier (Eds.), *Hill cities of eastern Himalayas: ethnicity, land relations and urbanisation* (pp. 119–142). New Delhi: Indus Publishing Company.

Nag, S. (2001). Tribals, rats, famine, state and the nation. *Economic and Political Weekly, 34*(5), 1025–1033.

Nag, S. (2008). *Pied pipers in north-east India: bamboo flowers, rat-famine and the politics of philanthropy (1881–2007)*. New Delhi: Manohar.

Shoumatoff, A. (2007). Waiting for the plague. Vanity Fair. December 2007.

Yambem, S. (1978). NupiLan: Manipur women's agitation, 1939. *Economic and Political Weekly, 11*(8), 325–331.

Chapter 19
Conflicts Leave a Trail of Poverty and Malnutrition: Evidences from Assam

Kalyan Das

Abstract It is immensely important to read and review the processes and conditions those govern the courses of human development in the environment human being live (Bronfenbrenner in The ecology of human development: experiments by nature and design. Harvard University Press, Cambridge, 1979). Along with the family, society and school environment, instability and unpredictability caused to the family by catastrophes in livelihood avenues are the most destructive force to children's development. This chapter tries to capture the environment of children in three relatively backward and conflict prone districts of Assam—Darrang, Udalguri and Baska. Children in a country like India are affected by certain indirect factors such as poor governance, corruption and poor implementation of rule of law (prime determinants of conflicts!). On the other hand, there are direct impacts from—ethnic conflicts, violent crimes and sexual assault on women and children—all cause unpredictability and uncertainties at home and in the local economy even leading to loss of livelihood. The final outcomes are dehumanisation of people trapped in unemployment and poverty, lack of schools (reasons for dropouts are mostly economic) and lack of access to health care services (poor public provisioning). All are significant determinants, which affect well-being in the families. Assessments reveal that in the study areas more than 50% of the children are chronically malnourished (height for age SD score), much higher than state (21%) and country average (24%, NFHS-3 data). In this context, in addition to assessment of the social and economic environment, need is also to construct indicators of insecurities. Considering that conflicts induce setback to the day to day life and development initiatives, it is important to read, assess, rectify and replace the inherent or existing regulatory factors by the society and polity (Aglietta in Economy and Society 19(2): 153–216, 1975). The issue is that to what extent these are possible to break the vicious cycle.

Keywords Poverty · Malnutrition · Livelihood · Regulation

K. Das (✉)
OKD Institute of Social Change and Development, VIP Road, Guwahati 781036, India
e-mail: kalyanaugust@yahoo.com

U.K. De et al. (eds.), *Inequality, Poverty and Development in India*, India Studies in Business and Economics, DOI 10.1007/978-981-10-6274-2_19

19.1 Conditions Governing the Process of Development

A large section of people in our society live in a web of insecurities, conditions very often not created by them. Exploring deeper into the causes, one could ascertain that insecurities in fact are due to the failure of the State to impose effective regulations or poor governance factor on the existing structure of government and regulations.[1] The most apparent and important indicators of insecurities for human being are poverty and unemployment, the fallouts of which are huge.[2] The process of escalation of poverty and unemployment emerges from multiple sets of factors following their independent as well as interlinked path.[3] Recent Human Developments Reports (HDRs)[4] have indicated that the main threat to maintaining the progress in human development comes from the increasingly evident unsustainable production and consumption patterns. In this context, along with the issue of use of exhaustible resources and clean energy,[5] degradation of our land and forest resources[6] caused by excessive and unplanned development also come to the forefront of discussion. The issue of trade-off between economic well-being and environmental sustainability is now apparent, but the changing environment resultant on natural as well as anthropogenic factors, also creates constraints in the resource based livelihood sectors and impede well-being of people—leading to generation of crisis in the economy in the long run. Exhaustion, degradation or deterioration of resources creates multiple forms of negative externalities,[7] which limit or adversely implicate

[1]Prime responsibilities of the State are to adopt effective regulations and ensure good governance. Moreover, provisioning of resources in certain economic and social sectors is an important obligation of the State. It is also right that State needs not to initiate and take responsibility in all development sectors– unless the issue of inclusion and distributive justice come. These however, can be also addressed by adopting appropriate regulation and control. The citizens are basically put into insecurities by host of factors - direct as well as indirect ways. Details can be found in Bajpai (2000).

[2]Some of the details on these are explained in Acharya et al. (2011) and Das (2011).

[3]For example inappropriate regulations in a livelihood sector and a conflict in a society produce the same impact- loss of income in a household. For example, the ban on timber felling in December 1996 in North East India had a negative impact on livelihood. During 1995–96 to 2001–02 number of timber units in the region declined from 461 to 136 and employment from 17126 to 1146 (ASI, various years). This could have been avoided had the resource utilisation was made to the working plans to ensure sustainability.

[4]For instance, the Human Development Report 2010 (UNDP, p. 81).

[5]A large number of environmental problems are associated with the production and combustion of coal. The same is the case for petroleum. Numerous studies across the world have assessed the negative externalities caused by these two resources.

[6]Land and forest are non-exhaustible and renewable resources; need effective working plans and regulations to sustain the returns. Conflict of interest is obvious with overcrowding and unsustainable uses.

[7]These are in the forms of increase in air temperature, pollution, high water runoff at surface and subsequent impacts of flood and erosion, crisis is water supply, health outcomes and the fallouts would never end. Some of these indirect threats appear in a households or society, but are difficult to measure compared to the direct threats of physical abuses and killings.

the capabilities of the people to ensure their well-being. The need for effective policy and regulations comes in such context.

Can we root all from of crisis and conflicts to the indications made in the HDR—exhaustible and unsustainable production and consumption pattern in a society.[8] The process however takes multiple routes (direct or indirect!) to generate anxiety and subsequently crisis and conflict (indicated in Footnote 3), and negative externalities are enormous in the process (poverty, malnutrition, diseases and deaths!).[9]

Natural resources at possession of the people, though have limited carrying capacity, but effective state provisioning, planning and governance help to raise the inclusion level through such resources (make the resource sustainable in the long run). It is also right that the incapability of the State to make effective plan and regulate, corruption, misappropriation of resources—limit the inclusion level to a significant extent.[10] Some of the clear outcomes we observe are—incapability of a section of people to ensure decent livelihood and health and education security for their offspring as we are trying to indicate. We observe ample evidences how access to sustainable resources get limited or even ceased, and capability to explore and earn a livelihood are affected by ineffectiveness on the governance factor and emergent conflicts (they are of many forms—conflicts over resources, crisis over social issues or evils, etc.) affect the path of sustainability or destroy the entire system of a livelihood sector.

In the development ladder of human being childhood occupy the most critical stage upon which depend much of the later developments. Child development literature is replete with writings on how children grow and develop into mature human beings; the role of parents and care givers; the role of the environment and society at large; importance of nutrition and overall well-being of the family, and so on. We however observe that due to several reasons like injury, illness, abuse, non-fulfilment of basic needs like food and medical care make it hard for a child to get the required stimulations for healthy growth and development and to acquire certain abilities in certain times in life. Some of the other elements in the environment which affect child development are child's home, school and the larger cultural contexts like the national economy and the political culture. It is thus immensely important to read and review the processes and conditions those govern the courses of human development in the environment human being live.[11]

The UN Convention on Rights of the Childs specially recognises that the child, for the full and harmonious development of her personality, should grow up in a family environment, in an atmosphere of happiness, love and understanding. Still even after 25 years from adoption of UNCRC, an alarmingly large number of

[8]These are resultant of either high population growth or high personal consumptions and both factors move together. There are also inequalities in command over resources and consumption; induce resource use to maximum possible extent.

[9]Issue is how we can relate these to our study context?

[10]Backwardness of our study villages would to a large extent explained by these factors and emerging conflicts rub the salt.

[11]Bronfenbrenner (1979).

children continue to be deprived of basic rights and amenities. It is now recognised world over that there is a clear link between poverty, social exclusion and children at risk of losing their rights. Children in such situation are more vulnerable to malnutrition and long-term poverty, less likely to attend school and more likely to suffer from diseases and die young.

In view of the above, this chapter tries to capture the social environment of the children in three relatively backward[12] and conflict prone districts[13] of Assam, namely Darrang, Udalguri and Baska by exploring the grassroots situation of children and the environment they live, along with the responses of the State and civil society.

In this context, in addition to assessment of the social and economic environment, need is also to construct indicators of insecurities or areas of crisis. Considering that conflicts induce setback to the day to day life and development initiatives, it is important to read, assess, rectify and replace the inherent or existing regulatory factors of by the society and polity (Aglietta 1975). The issue is that to what extent these are possible to break the vicious cycle.

19.2 Possibility of Identifying the Areas of Risks and Insecurities

As indicated in the section I crisis in livelihood, and insecurities faced by people arise from a web of interrelated factors of regulations and governance. The determinants in the regulatory and governance domain to a good extent are all-encompassing to address a situation, but challenges are—how can we capture and have the measures? For example, uncertainties and unpredictability in the local economy to a large extent is prompted by either nonexistence, or implementation of ineffective plans, regulations and governance.

As indicated, children in country like India are affected by certain indirect factors such as poor governance, corruption and poor implementation of rule of law (prime creators of negative externalities or determinants of conflicts!). For example, unregulated wages in backward areas have serious consequences in the families to ensure child education and health needs. On the other hand, there are direct impacts from—ethnic conflicts, violent crimes and sexual assault on women and children—all cause unpredictability and uncertainties at home front and in the local economy even leading to loss of livelihood. The final outcomes are dehumanisation of people trapped in unemployment and poverty, lack of schools (reasons for dropouts are

[12]Udalguri district was formed in 2004, carving it out from the Darrang district. Darrang is ranked 22nd among the 23 district in Human Development Index of Assam (Government of Assam 2003). Baska was carved out largely from Nalbari (ranked 16th) and Barpeta district (ranked 9th in HDI).

[13]These backward districts show inter-community conflicts for quite sometimes and tensions still persists.

mostly economic) and lack of access to health care services (we observe poor public provisioning in the social sector of the country). All are significant determinants, which affect well-being in the families.

Setting aside the natural and environmental factors that we have indicated in section I, rest of the factors are related to the failure to ensure the rule of law in a poorly governed state. We here argue that the outcomes culminated in violation of child rights. The determining factors of insecurities brought to a household are may be difficult to assess and explain in a home environment, but identification would help in effective interventions.

The chapter derives data from a study[14] designed basically to capture information on certain indicators of home and social (and political) environment; presumed to reflect the status of well-being and security of the children.

19.3 Study Area and Sampling

The study covered six revenue circles, in the three districts of Darrang, Baska and Udalguri. The relative remoteness of locations of the villages and absence of basic infrastructure and services could imply higher level of social exclusion in the villages.

The study acquired information from 30 villages in the three districts and covered 1962 households at first stage of inquiry. The villages are located in the interior and underdeveloped areas; some of the villages in recent times have experienced ethnic and communal violence leading to displacements and death of people. The villages of Dalgaon (Darrang district) and Udalguri circles (Udalguri district) covered in this study are affected by the violence and conflicts of 2008.[15] These villages and selected based on the information acquired on severity of prevailing insecurity (and anxiety). The rest of the villages in four revenue circles of Harisinga, Khorabari, Goreswar and Majbat are selected drawing the numbers from the random number table, using the entire list of villages of respective revenue circles. This is assumed that underdevelopment and conflicts[16] in the study area are putting the children into risks of poverty and their upward progress.

---

[14]The study was conducted for the SOS Children's Villages of India during 2009–10 to capture the social environment of the children in three districts of Assam- Darrang, Udalguri and Baska and understand the situation of children without parental care or at risk of losing parental care.

[15]The clashes that broke out on October 3, 2008 between Bodos and immigrant Muslim settlers in Udalguri and Darrang districts led to the displacement of over two lakh people. The cause of the violence is the aftermath of the clashes broke out between the two communities in August 2008 following the killing of a Bodo youth by supporters of a bandh called by the Muslim Students Association, Assam. The bandh had been called in protest against the harassment of Indian citizens in the name of identification of illegal Bangladeshi migrants. Details can be extracted from newspaper reportages of that period.

[16]Here a question may be which factor explains larger part of insecurity and anxiety—underdevelopment or violence.

Table 19.1 Households covered for the study

District	Revenue circles	No. of villages	No. of HH covered at stage I	No. of HH covered for detailed survey
Udalguri	Harisinga	6	368	40
	Majbat	5	285	35
	Udalguri	2	143	11
Darrang	Khoirabari	4	280	31
	Dalgaon	8	568	55
Baska	Goreswar	5	318	40
Total		30	1962	212

Presence of parents at home, their good health and sources of a decent livelihood, a liveable home, a decent home environment free from alcoholism and domestic violence, devotion of time on children and a societal environment- free from perceived threat and repression; all could indicate that the children, in general are not exposed to any kind of risks. Considering that violence and conflicts induce setback to the day to day life and development initiatives, it is important to read and assess, rectify and replace the inherent or existing regulatory factors by the society and polity.

Based on the perception of the interviewers on prevailed insecurity in the households, altogether 212 households were selected from the list of 1962 households for a detailed survey. The detailed survey covered the aspects on livelihood sources and income, place of work, availability of land-agriculture as well as homestead, return from agriculture, availability of livestock, presence of parents at home, educational dropouts and reasons, ailments and disabilities, nutritional level of the children below the age of 6 years, awareness on health and hygiene, parenting status, behavioural issues of the parents and children, overall environment and infrastructure of the family and the society, supports received from the state in the home front for overall well-being (Table 19.1).

Apart from acquiring information from listing of household and the detailed survey, FGDs were conducted in two villages affected by the conflict and violence. Moreover, some interviews were conducted with civil society members, village headman, teachers, ASHA workers, anganawadi worker, farmer, trader, etc. The FGDs and personal interviews provide wide perspectives on the need of strengthening the home and societal environment for overall security and well-being of the children in the villages.

19.4 The Findings

19.4.1 Overview of the Economic Situation

Occupations in most of the sample villages reflect rising casualisation of the workforce. Agriculture remains the main occupation in about 28% of the

Table 19.2 Main livelihood sources in the households sampled in second stage

Agriculture	Casual labour	Trade	Too old	Begging	Pension and remittance	Craft	Others	Total
19	162	14	2	3	2	2	7	212

Source Field work 2009–10

households, which has become un-remunerative to support a household as the survey reveals. Because of this many farmers' households now have taken recourse to casual work (about 8% households) and petty trade (about 2%) to supplement household income. Overall casual work (about 34%), trade and business (about 7%), transport sector jobs (4%) are becoming important sources of livelihood in the villages. There are some households in the sample villages with jobs in teaching and services sectors (104 households or about 7%). It is also found that some households derive income from certain skilled jobs in carpentry, tailoring and goldsmith (Table 19.2).

The key interviews reveal that the economic condition of most of the villages is poor. Agriculture, though is the major source of livelihood, this is not remunerative enough to lead a decent life and ensure all the needs of the children (reported by ASHA worker at village Kalitapara). In the villages, there is a large section of casual workers and lack capital for self-employment initiatives (told by the village headman, Balabari, the teacher at village Ajagar, the Anganawadi worker at village Sidhakhowa). Flood is also forcing people in some villages to adopt casual works (ASHA worker at village Gorbasti). The poor not having access to land resources too depend on casual work (Village Council Development Committee—VCDC president at village Tengajhar) and the income from casual work is meagre to fulfill the basic needs (ASHA worker at village Rajapukhuri, the teacher at village Bihapara). People struggle to ensure their livelihood and this leaves no time for most of the people to think of other matters (the farmer at village Chaparabari). The casual jobs are not available in required numbers in the villages. Joblessness led frustration often lead to domestic violence (the village headman at village Singimari). Joblessness in some villages also forces the poor to take recourse to sell country liquor (the teacher at village Polashbasti) and in diverse petty jobs in trade and non-motorised transports of rickshaw pulling and pushcarts. Economic condition in some villages is however reportedly good (VCDC member at Nagrasara village).

The reported monthly income from the main occupation reflected that in most of the households (143 households or 67%) earning was less than Rs. 1900/a month (the poverty line figure in a rural household) during the time of the survey. Un-remunerative income forces the people to look for subsidiary income, mostly in casual works. This helps substantially to improve the household income; the derived result is that after incorporation of income of subsidiary sources, 43 sample households out of the 143 had able to raise their monthly income level beyond Rs. 1900/.

19.4.2 Situation of the Children in the Study Area

The survey found 1593 households (81% of the total listed) with children below 18 years of age. In 44% households there were children below 6 years of age. Presence of single parents was captured in 6% of the total households with children below 18 years (about 5% only with the presence of mother). There were seven households where children had no parents.

This, however, reflects only one part of risks the unfortunate children face because of not having parents. There are several factors those put children at risk of losing care.

19.4.2.1 Status of Health

General ailments were reported in 132 households (8.3%) out of the 1593 households listed with children below 18 years. Physically and mentally challenged children are captured in 60 households (3.8%) among the 1593 households. This number of 60 is significant in the sample, Indicate magnitude of the problem in the study areas.

General ailments reported in the households are fever, cough, pneumonia, malaria, diarrhoea, asthma, malnutrition, abdomen pain, jaundice, pharyngitis, tonsillitis, measles, dermatological diseases (scabies!), etc.

The ASHA worker at Rajapukhuri village reported that prevalence of diarrhoea and anaemia is very common in the village. The village headman at No. 2 Jhargaon, also reported that malaria, diarrhoea, fever and cough are common in the village. The anaganaadi worker at Sidhakhowa reported that diarrhoea and fever are the common ailment in the village and there is no concern for health and hygiene in most of the households. Immunisation coverage of the children in the sampled households is poor; only 35% households reporting full immunisation coverage of their children.

Physical challenges faced by the unprivileged children are in the form of epilepsy, polio, impairedness in hearing, speech and sights. There are also presences of spastic children in the sampled households. It is found that disabilities of the children in most of the cases remain unattended.

19.4.2.2 Malnourishment

An effort was made to measure the status of malnourishment of the children below 6 years of age. Accordingly, weights and heights are measured of 109 children in the sample households. Three nutritional status indicators height for age (stunting), weight for height (wasting), weight for age (underweight) are expressed in standard deviation units from the median of reference population. The height for age index is an indicator of linear growth retardation and cumulative growth deficits. Children whose height for age SD score is below minus two standard deviations from the median of the reference population are considered short of their age and are chronically malnourished and children below minus three SD are severely malnourished and stunted. This reflects failure to receive adequate nutrition over a long period of time.

The deviations of scores of weight for height index reflect thinness of children for their height and their current nutritional status. This may be the result of inadequate food intake or recent episode of illness causing loss of weight. On the other hand, weight for age is a composite index of height for age and weight for height; the standard deviations reflecting underweight of the children.

The results showed that more than 50% children in the sample villages are chronically malnourished (the NFHS-3 figures for Assam were 21% and country as a whole was 24%); the proportion of male being more at 59% compared to the female children (about 42%). It is found that malnourishment level is more in the conflict prone villages of Dalgaon circle area (growth of 69% children below the age of six are stunted), compared to the villages of Harisinga (33.3%), Majbat (50%) and Goreswar circles (42.4%). Male–female variations are found to be significant in all the circles, except in Majbat circle (Table 19.3d).[17]

Wasted growth, however, is observed more in Harisinga circle (33.3% below minus 2 SD); compared to average of all the villages (15.6%) and Dalgaon circle villages (24.1%). This figure is much lower in Majbat (8.1%) and Goreswar circle villages (6.1%). The reported ailment in the villages of Majbat and Goreswar circle was relatively less and this could be the result of better index in wasting in these two circles (Table 19.3).

19.4.2.3 Access to Quality Education

The survey revealed that access to quality education in most of the villages is poor. The ICDS centres aimed at taking care of child nutrition and health problems and to ensure pre-school education and has an important role to play in creating a base for proper mental, physical and social development of the underprivileged children. Regrettably, it was reported in most of the villages that the ICDS centres remain closed for the most part of the year and functions whenever there are supplies of food items for the children. Visit to ICDS centres revealed that although these supplement the nutritional requirements of children to an extent, if supplies are in place, but other expected services like health checkup, referral services, nutritional and health checkup were found missing.

[17]The survey for the study was conducted one year after the conflict. It is difficult to assess to what extent conflict has contributed to malnutrition (stunting—inadequacy of nutrition over a long period of time) and the effect of backwardness. On the other hand, wasting is reflection of recent episode of crisis. To this argument—backwardness has the larger influence in malnutrition of the children; and conflict in the backward villages aggravated the situation.

Table 19.3 (a) Malnourishment in all study villages; (b) malnourishment in villages of Dalgaon circle; (c) malnourishment in villages of Harisinga circle; (d) Malnourishment in villages of Majbat circle; (e) Malnourishment in villages of Goreswar circle

a

	All children	Male children	Female children
Height for age (stunting)			
% below—3 SD	33.0	37.5	28.3
% below—2 SD	50.5	58.9	41.5
Weight for height (wasting)			
% below—3 SD	5.5	5.4	5.7
% below—2 SD	15.6	19.6	11.3
Weight for age (underweight)			
% below—3 SD	14.7	21.4	7.5
% below—2 SD	24.8	32.1	17.0
N	109	56	53

b

	All children	Male children	Female children
Height for age (stunting)			
% below—3 SD	44.8	40.0	7.1
% below—2 SD	69.0	73.3	28.6
Weight for height (wasting)			
% below—3 SD	10.3	13.3	7.1
% below—2 SD	24.1	20.0	28.6
Weight for age (underweight)			
% below—3 SD	20.7	26.7	14.3
% below—2 SD	44.8	53.3	35.7
N	29	15	14

c

	All children	Male children	Female children
Height for age (stunting)			
% below—3 SD	26.7	28.6	25.0
% below—2 SD	33.3	42.9	25.0
Weight for height (wasting)			
% below—3 SD	13.3	0	25.0
% below—2 SD	33.9	42.9	25.0

(continued)

Table 19.3 (continued)

c			
	All children	Male children	Female children
Weight for age (underweight)			
% below—3 SD	33.3	42.9	25.0
% below—2 SD	46.7	42.9	50.0
N	15	7	8
d			
	All children	Male children	Female children
Height for age (stunting)			
% below—3 SD	37.5	45.5	30.8
% below—3 SD	50.0	54.5	46.2
Weight for height (wasting)			
% below—3 SD	0	0	0
% below—3 SD	8.3	18.2	0
Weight for age (underweight)			
% below—3 SD	4.2	9.1	0
% below—3 SD	8.3	18.2	0
N	24		13
e			
	All children	Male children	Female children
Height for age (stunting)			
% below—3 SD	24.2	35.3	12.2
% below—3 SD	42.4	58.8	25.0
Weight for height (wasting)			
% below—3 SD	3.0	5.9	0
% below—3 SD	6.1	11.8	0
Weight for age (underweight)			
% below—3 SD	9.1	17.6	0
% below—3 SD	12.1	23.5	0
N	33	17	16

Source Calculation based on data generated from field work 2009–10

School dropouts are captured in 204 sample households (12.8%) out of the total 1593 households listed with children below 18 years. The respondent houses cited numerous reasons for school dropout; poor economic condition being the prime reason for dropout, indifferent in studies and household responsibilities the children need to bear (Table 19.4).

Interaction at household level reflected that teachers' attendance and classes at local primary school are irregular; parents are unable to take up the matter seriously. Some parents cannot afford to provide school dresses and books, leading to school

Table 19.4 Reasons for school dropouts

District	Revenue circles	Total dropouts	Economic reason	Not interested in study	Fear for school	Physical problem	Mentally challenged	Domestic response (Ibilities/lost of parents)	Effect conflict
Udalguri	Harisinga	34	16	4	1	2	–	5	–
	Majbat	30	17	5	1	–	–	5	–
	Udalguri	25	11	5	2	–	–		6
Darrang	Khoirabari	24	16	1	–	–	2		–
	Dalgaon	74	46	8	–	2	4	1	–
Baska	Goreswar	17	9	2	5	2	–		–
		204	115 (56.4)	25 (12.3)	9 (4.4)	6 (2.9)	6	11 (5.4)	6

Source Field work 2009–10

dropouts. The key interviews reflect serious gap between the presence of physical infrastructure, delivery of quality education and subsequent role of the teachers.

19.4.3 The Social Environment Reflected by the Survey and Key Interviews

As is the case with all poverty ridden areas are disposed towards conflict and violence, the study locale too project a negative environment, detrimental towards children's overall growth and well-being. The conflict prone locality in Dalgaon circle area has lagged behind in economic, educational and overall development process. The communal conflict of 2008 has retarded development process of the Bhakatapara locality to a significant extent. Apart from economic and societal depression that engulfs the entire life system, the children's health, both physical and mental are hugely affected. The conflict induced fear psychosis among the children and made them directionless. Although the situation has improved, it will require time to bring back the normal situation (as reported by Mr. B.B., Teacher, Bhakatpara village).

Moreover, alcoholism and nuisance crated by the alcoholics and general conflicts among villagers are common in some villages. The behaviour of people lack social responsibility (as reported by Ms. D. D. teacher at village Polashbasti; Mr. K farmer at village Pathakpur; Mr. N.M., President, VCDC at village Tengajhar and many others). Significant presence of domestic violence is reported in some villages.

The survey found alcoholism in about 37% of the total households. Domestic violence is parents in more than 10% households. As indicated in earlier section joblessness and poor economic conditions led frustration is one of the major causes of domestic violence.

Moreover, there is poor reflection of opportunities and infrastructure for the children for games and extra-curricular activities in the villages. Among the 212 households only in 17 households this was reported that children get opportunity play in an organised way in the villages. Apart from this access to newspapers, community support to sustain motivation of the children are virtually absent in the households. It was also found that perceived threat of violence and repression loom large more particularly in the villages of Udalguri, Dalgaon and Goreswar circles.

One, however, finds some encouraging environment in few villages. As reported in the key interview the poor village of Balabari in Dalgaon area has some strong social bonding and the village is free from any internal conflict. In some villages, the society stands by on the importance of education, but the illiterate parents in most cases are not responsive (reported by the ASHA worker). In past few years, there is improvement in education with rising level of educational attainment (the village headman at No. 2 Jhargaon) (Table 19.5).

Table 19.5 Overall home environment in the listed households

District	Revenue Circles	Total HH with Children	Alcoholism	Domestic violence	Time devoted to play	Time devoted to teach	Perceived threat of violence	Perceived threat of repression
Udalguri	Harisinga	289	148 (51.2)	7 (2.4)	5 (1.7)	68 (23.5)	0	1
	Majbat	214	123 (57.5)	19 (8.9)	82 (38.3)	73 (34.1)	15 (7.7)	0
	Udalguri	119	49 (41.2)	26 (21.8)	3 (2.5)	16 (13.4)	116 (97.5)	0
Darrang	Khoirabari	238	80 (33.6)	27 (11.3)	157 (66.0)	100 (42.0)	23 (9.7)	2
	Dalgaon	479	72 (15.0)	69 (14.4)	70 (14.6)	143 (29.9)	370 (77.2)	21
Baska	Goreswar	254	109 (42.9)	19 (7.5)	156 (61.4)	134 (52.8)	83 (32.7)	4
Total		1593	581 (36.5)	167 (10.5)	473 (29.7)	534 (33.5)	607 (38.1)	28 (1.8)

Source Field work 2009–10

19.4.3.1 Parenting Skills and Status of Parenting

Weak attachment of parents to their children and lack of involvement is reflected by the figures of devotion of time in teaching and playing. However, this is not always by their choice. It rather reflects overall quality of life, which is devoid of many things, but most importantly the resources, the lack of which hamper any enrichment, whether physical, mental or overall well-being of the family. It is found that 82% parents of the total 212 households surveyed at stage II unable to devote their time or help their children in teaching, 33% cannot ensure food and 14% cannot give health care. In addition to these 46%, households have presence of alcoholism and family violence. It may be relevant to say that heads of the households in 65% sample households are illiterate and in 11% households they are just literate not even completed their primary schooling.

19.4.3.2 Constraints to Earn a Decent Livelihood for Well-being of the Children

Loss of sources of income and property was reported in the villages affected by the ethnic conflict of 2008. The peasants of the Sherpur village (Dalgaon circle) used to lease land from the neighbouring villages inhabited by different communities. The aftermath of the conflicts now makes it unfeasible. Moreover, now it is not possible for the traders of the Sherpur village to enter the neighbouring villages, with whom they had business transactions for long. This virtually has affected the income sources and forcing many of them to migrate out for jobs even to the places outside the state.[18]

The ethnic conflict shattered the entire economic base of this village. Limited land resources left little space to ensure livelihood from village based activities. It is found that only 71 households (33.5%) of the total 212 households in all sampled villages could ensure their livelihood working within the village. Members of 121 households (57%) have move out of their village, but mostly confines to the boundary of the revenue circle for jobs. Absence of the earning members during the entire day obviously has effect on the care received by their children.

Agriculture land is not available in 153 households (72.2% of the sample of 212 households) and another 31 households (14.6%) just have less than an acre of agriculture land, not sufficient enough to grow food required for the entire family. Overall, there is no return from home grown paddy in 146 households (68.9%). Food security from home production is found to be ensured only in 19 households of the total 212 sample households.

---

[18]Conflicts, unsustainable agriculture caused by environmental factors of flood, erosion and land degradation are the major reasons of huge outflow of workers to the Metros and industries and lower end services of south India (Das and Chutia 2011).

Homesteads to a great extent could supplement household income from the productions of fruits and vegetables along with supplementing nutritional requirements of the children. In the sample, there were 18 households without homestead and 103 households with a homestead of less than one bigha (0.33 acre) land.

Milch cow was found in 77 households, goat in 59 households, poultry in 110 households (one for commercial purpose) and pigs in 23 households. These resources supplement family income and nutritional requirements of the children.

19.4.3.3 Support of the State in Consolidation of the Impoverished Households

State supports under the flagships programmes of IAY (32% households received support), NREGA (43%), ICDS (32%) and TSC (9%) fail to support majority of the impoverished households. Moreover, those who have able to avail benefits under the programmes, majority of them expressed dissatisfaction with the support received.

It was found that 83% households in the listed households are Katchha houses and about 11% houses are in non-liveable conditions.

19.4.3.4 Civil Society Interventions for Supportive Care for Children

For a thorough understanding of the child related issues in the study areas, two FGDs were held among the villagers. The FGDs at Bhakatapara village on 14 November 2009 and in Sherpur village, 3 December 2009 revealed certain crucial aspects of child development that need crucial attention.

The major problem in the Bhakatpara village (Dalgaon circle) started with the conflict that bounced during October 2008. The basic issue since then has been a sense of insecurity among the children. Killings and burning down of villages, which the children witnessed, have left them utterly shaken with fear and constant feeling of insecurity. It has left a deep psychological scar in the minds of the people and especially the children.[19] The misunderstandings among different groups of people have to be removed and peace is to be established (discussant, retired head master).

Earlier there used to be schools for art and culture, songs, dance, debates, etc., where children used to get opportunity to develop their talents and also get engaged. But now after the disturbances all such organisations have closed leading to deprivation from these extra-curricular activities (Female, member of a local NGO).

One of the reasons for backwardness of this society is the habit of taking alcohols. People are in the habit of preparing and drinking homemade alcohols.

---

[19]This indicates that psychological distress comes to the fore than the miseries of poverty and malnutrition in the violence and conflict infected villages.

There have been attempts in the past to stop the families engaged in preparing and selling drinks from this business, but they ask for alternative livelihood. Most of the poor day labourers spend whatever they earn by way of daily wage on alcohol and mete out violence upon their wives and children.

The social and political bodies though discuss several matters of the society issues of education and children never figure in their discussions. Moreover, the knowledge base of social organisations is inadequate to accomplish the actions they think or plan (Discussant male, teacher). The discussion also questioned the aptitude of the teachers of the schools in the locality. The result is that many conscious parents have shifted their students to the nearby towns.

The impoverished and conflict prone village of Sherpur (in the same Dalgaon circle) is not covered by drinking water supply of PHED. The FGD indicated that lack of supply of safe drinking water is the cause that children are suffering from diarrhoea, liver problem, etc. Malaria is also rampant in the village. There is also the problem of electricity and health facilities. Moreover, among the poor working community of the village there is no appreciation for the education system, no timetable for eating or doing other daily activities. As parents are busy doing hard labour to earn they have hardly any time left to take care of the children. People feel some interventions model is required to generate demonstrative impacts, apart from making provisions of certain additional support facilities in the village and usher the progress of the village (Male discussant, age 35). People clearly raised voices on the need of civil society and institutional interventions. Institutional model could create a good environment. They cited example that a student from the SOS village (note) has become engineer and another has passed hotel management (male discussant, age 50).

Ensuring restoration of jobs and business activities is the main issue in Sherpur village (Male discussant, age 55). There were 195 traders in the villages with their shops at Bhakatpara market. But since the day of the conflict last year none of them could go back. All their goods have been looted. Many of them have left the village to look for job. There is a sense of fear all the time and children suffer because of that. There is effort for peace initiatives. Only few people from the conflicting village came forward. Very few open up to address the issues. The prime need at present is to open the daily and weekly markets, which will facilitate free movements of all the villagers. There will be interactions and it will slowly eradicate feeling of distrust and fear (Male, discussant 45 year).

19.5 Discussion

The study derived enough indications on insecurities (Table 19.6) faced by the people in the backward and conflict ridden villages. Casualisation of the workforce and livelihood crisis is now apparent in the backward as well as in the conflict prone villages. We find that figures of malnourishment of children are very distinct in the villages affected by violence and conflict. We can state that violence and conflicts

Table 19.6 Indicators and areas of risk factors for policy interventions

Indicator derived from the study	Areas of risk factors
Domestic violence, alcoholism, non-liveable home	Socio-cultural
Casualisation of workforce	Economic
Ailments, mentally and physically challenged children, malnutrition	Health
Threat of violence	Political–environmental
Threat of violence, school dropouts	Psycho-social

leave a trail of malnourishment in the affected villages—which are severe compared to general backwardness of the study area.

Moreover, a composite score of such indicators of insecurities (quantified) would put the conflict ridden villages on the top ladder of insecurities.[20] The negatives indicators generated can be clubbed into certain areas or components of risk factors- as indicated in Table 19.6. The grouping could help to focus on adopting appropriate policy and specific interventions. Overall, risks and insecurities loom large over the children from all components—making it difficult to comment which factor is most inclusive.

The indications tell us that on all fronts—socio-cultural, political, economic and social sectors; the existing regulatory mechanisms and provisioning at the village level are inappropriate, which have generated the crisis situations. In notional term the mode of regulations,[21] which consist of the behaviours, social norms and customs and state enforceable laws in the local spaces, is appeared to be unsuitable to carry forward smooth functioning and building up the society and economy. Any problem at the grassroots, at the first stage ideally needs to be solved by the local level social regulations or institutions at the first stage. The State supported regulations come to act if the local level institutions and regulations fail. Overall, the social institutions and regulations of the government must have the capability to read, address and solve the crisis situation that strikes at the social and economic spaces. Otherwise, it will call for a new mode of regulation. In our country context, there may be one national mode of regulation, imposed through rigid government policies at regional and local scale. However, there may be many local modes with their link to the national mode of regulations. In certain occasions, we cannot expect a particular mode to suit to all local conditions; and this calls for coupling of multiple modes (Tickell and Peck 1992). The whole contribution of regulation theory (Aglietta 1979; Lipietz 1987) is about sustaining a social and economic space. The issue is how the regulatory bodies—society and the State read or capable to read the critical situations.

[20]Das and Dutta (2012) prepared a composite index of insecurities of the indicators presented in Table 19.6. Ranking of the villages showed that the villages affected by violence are on top ladder.

[21]A mode of regulation involves a complex assemble of productive institutions, social and political relations and regulate the society-wide process of accumulation toward long term sustainability (Schoenberger 1989).

References

Acharya, A., Singdeo, S. K., & Rajaretnam, M. (2011). *Human Security: From Concept to Practice – Case studies from Northeast India and Orissa*. Singapore: World Scientific.

Aglietta, M. (1975). Regulation theories in retrospect and prospect. *Economy and Society, 19*(2), 153–216.

Aglietta, M. (1979). *A theory of capitalist regulations*. London: New Left Books.

Bajpai, K. (2000). *Human security: Concept and measurement*, Kroc Institute Occasional Paper #19: OP1, August. http://www.hegoa.ehu.es/dossierra/seguridad/Human_security_concept_and_measurement.pdf.

Bronfenbrenner, U. (1979). *The ecology of human development: Experiments by nature and design*. Cambridge: Harvard University Press.

Das, K. (2011). Constructing a human security governance index for northeast India. In A. Acharya, S. K. Singdeo & M. Rajaretnam (Eds.), *Human security: From concept to practice*. Case studies from Northeast India and Orissa. Singapore: World Scientific.

Das, K., & Chutia, D. (2011). Outward Bound, *The Assam Tribune*, February 6.

Das K., & Dutta, I. (2012). *Children in conflict prone and underdeveloped districts of Assam: How congenial is the environ to ensure wellbeing*. Research Paper Series 03/2012, OKD Institute of Social Change and Development, Guwahati.

Lipietz, A. (1987). *Mirages and miracle: The crisis of global fordism*. London: Verso.

Schoenberger, Erica. (1989). Thinking about flexibility: A response to gertler. *Transactions of the Institute of British Geographers, 14*(1), 98–108.

Tickell, A., & Peck, J. A. (1992). Accumulation, regulation and geographies of post-Fordism: Missing links in regulationist research. *Progress in Human Geography, 16*(2), 190–218.

Part III
Agricultural and Environmental Perspectives

Chapter 20
Integrating Management for Land–Water Ecosystem for Augmenting Productivity, Income, and Sustainable Livelihood

A.M. Puste, S.K. Gunri, K. Jana, B. Ray Pramanik, S.K. Acharya, M. Dasgupta and T.K. Maity

Abstract Wetland has got a formidable role for maintaining the terrestrial and aquatic eco-dynamics, which in turn sustains critical ecological deliverables for sustainable development and environmental freshness. The northeast of India is endowed with 30% of total wetlands which has well been orchestrated with the life and culture, economy and ecology as well. All these wetlands are profusely fed during peak rainy season and as a result bounty of water gifted by nature has made the main river system, its tributaries, mostly in Indo-Bangladesh regions, a rich source of sweet water for this entire region. These are immensely resourceful for production of valuable aquatic food crops [deepwater rice (*Oryza sativa* L.), water chestnut (*Trapa*

A.M. Puste (✉) · S.K. Gunri · K. Jana
Department of Agronomy, Bidhan Chandra Krishi Viswavidyalaya,
Mohanpur, Nadia, India
e-mail: ampuste_bckv@yahoo.co.in

S.K. Gunri
e-mail: sgunri@rediffmail.com

K. Jana
e-mail: kalyan_agro@rediffmail.com

B. Ray Pramanik
ADA, Department of Agriculture,
Government of West Bengal, B-2/361 (LIG), Kalyani, Nadia, India
e-mail: binayrp78@gmail.com

S.K. Acharya
Department of Agricultural Extension, Faculty of Agriculture,
Bidhan Chandra Krishi Viswavidyalaya, Mohanpur, Nadia, India
e-mail: acharya09sankar@gmail.com

M. Dasgupta
Department of Animal Sciences, Faculty of Agriculture,
Bidhan Chandra Krishi Viswavidyalaya, Mohanpur, Nadia, India
e-mail: dasgupta_mrinal129@rediffmail.com

T.K. Maity
Department of Vegetable Crops, Faculty of Horticulture,
Bidhan Chandra Krishi Viswavidyalaya, Mohanpur, Nadia, India
e-mail: prof_tapanmaity@rediffmail.com

U.K. De et al. (eds.), *Inequality, Poverty and Development in India*, India Studies in Business and Economics, DOI 10.1007/978-981-10-6274-2_20

bispinosa Roxb.), makhana (*Euryale ferox* Salisb.), water-lily (*Nymphaea* sp.), *Colocasia,* or *Cyrtosperma* sp.] as well as vegetables crops in the contiguous lands, which remain so far overlooked or underutilized. These crops have got huge yield potentials and are highly remunerative, mostly preferred by rural and urban people in this region. This paper deals with a number of case studies commencing over last 15–16 years on proper utilization of waste wetlands in different agro-zones (new alluvial, old alluvial, and coastal and saline) involving wide sector of downtrodden, resource-poor to marginal farming communities. These research activities are carried out under the aegis of Government of India aided transfer of technology-based research projects, formulated with low-cost updating agro-techniques. The following improvised integrated nutrient management systems (organic, inorganic including micronutrients applied with proper dose and time) were executed for enhancing productivity and economic viability (exhibited even > 3.0-folds than that of farmers' practice) at sustainable level. The study reveals that this improvised farm practice is imperative to utilize these vast unused wetlands, particularly in north-eastern part with a focus on food, livelihood, engagement of household labors and ultimately, economic sustainability of rural people.

Keywords Agro-zones · Aquatic food crops-cum-fish culture
Economic stability · Integrated nutrient management system
Production system · Rural sustainability · Wetland and terrestrial ecosystem

20.1 Introduction

20.1.1 Global Climate and Agricultural Production System

The 143 million hectare of land under cultivation in India is basically a subject of monsoon weather and climate change over a protractile period. The onset of monsoon, the amount of precipitation and distribution, and the withdrawal of monsoon are of immense importance so far as production, productivity, and sustainability of Indian agriculture.

A transformation from a food-deficit nation to food-surplus economy of India has been indebted to Green Revolution, wherein a change of food production had been from 50 Mt in 1951 to 264 Mt in 2016. The mean cereal productivity has increased from 500 kg per ha to almost 2500 kg per ha. The export volume for cereal is also substantial with 15% of export earnings in the country. Moreover, agricultural growth also has a direct impact on poverty eradication and is an important factor in employment generation. Among cereals, wheat accounts for one-third of the total food grain production, while next important rice forms to about 43% of total and estimated total cultivated area 43 m ha (million hectares), which accounts 30% of the net cultivated area in the country.

Anthropogenic activities are affecting the global climate beyond doubt. The mean temperature for this region has risen approximately from 0.5 to 0.6 °C between the years 1990 and 2013, expediting a change in rainfall pattern, sea-level rise, and melting of snowlines at a faster rate for Himalayan regions. This is in compliance with the expected brunt of climate change. Agricultural production system is now also being changed their compatibility and sharing with this great diversity of non-congenial effect of the climatic situation, faces occasionally a huge loss elsewhere, which drastically affected the poor and marginal group of rural farming communities in most of the eastern part of this greater subcontinent. Improvised agro-technology (integrated farming system, INM in respect to nutrient and IPM (integrated pest management) in respect to plant protection, using of natural resources—land, water, and biodiversity), crops and cropping systems, multi-tier systems using aqua-terrestrial ecosystem, situation-specific suitable crop cultivars, government-level subsidization and moreover, combat at every trace of moments with the climatic change has reached to its saturated level, making productive in nature with compatibility and profitability.

20.1.2 Threats of Wetlands: Matter of Thought

Wetland ecosystem is always been facing the threats, comprising increase of biotic and abiotic pressures and perils, especially in underdeveloped and developing world. Biotic comprises (a) profuse siltation and weed infestation beyond its control; (b) unregulated discharge of wastewater from various sources like industrial effluents, surface runoff, etc., resulting in proliferation of aquatic ecosystem, which adversely affect flora and fauna; (c) random tree felling mostly used for fuel wood, causing soil loss that affects rainfall pattern in the periphery and moreover, loss of various aquatic species due to water-level fluctuation; and (d) in addition, habitat disturbing leading to loss of fish biodiversity and decrease in number of migratory birds elsewhere. Among the abiotic factors are (a) dereliction of productive areas due to encroachment, (b) continuous anthropogenic pressures resulting in habitat destruction and loss of biodiversity, (c) unscientific and uncontrolled dredging in the water bodies resulting in succession changes, (d) aquifers losing its depths especially during summer due to unplanned, drawing water for various uses, (e) water quality deteriorating from point and non-point sources due to causative factors, and (f) use of non-judicious use of agrochemicals in agricultural fields (fertilizers, insecticides, agrochemicals, growth regulating hormones, etc.) deteriorating wet environment, which is important.

20.1.3 Degradation of Ecosystem: The Major Causative Factors

20.1.3.1 Toxic Contaminants, Particulate Matters, and Acid Rains

There is a subtle relationship and interaction between man and environment. This relationship has already been distorted with the unwanted entry of toxic materials and particulates into different ecosystems and holons to jeopardize ecological functions and its efficacies (Anonymous 1995). This deterioration and ecological lethality are more pronounced in developing and underdeveloped countries. Thousands of toxic containments of various types, viz., inorganic, organic, and organo-metallic, have found their ways to our environment. Many of them highly toxic even at trace levels. Some have long biological half-lives and, consequently, will remain toxic for a long time. The extent of this contamination is so vast that the *food we eat, air we breathe and water-we drink* are suspected to contain a number of toxins.

A continuous interaction and functional osmosis amongst and between litho-sphere, hydrosphere, and biosphere are quite evident, keep on happening in a mutually inclusive manner to support the big ecological function. Due to different anthropogenic activities, indiscriminate, and disproportionate, the relationship has turned more fragile (Khopker 1995). Different gaseous emissions, liquid exodous, and hazardous particulates generated by thermal power plants, other industries including food and beverages, and so many are leveraging huge threats on eco-logical help and its productive functions (Chakraborty 1999).

Acid rain, the occurrences of which are increasing exponentially in areas heavily contaminated with gaseous emissions loaded with nitrous and sulfur oxides, is causing huge damage to different ecosystems functioning crop and animal health hazardous as well (Das 1999). The suspended particulates are also making an entry into different water and soil layers as an acidic rain to changing important char-acteristics of the pond-bottom soil as well as water characteristics in respective of land–water ecosystem. These changes are also affecting in situ agricultural pro-duction system in the fields including its plants growth and production of ichthiofaunal diversity under aquatic environment. In some cases, it reaches beyond its threshold level and makes vulnerable in its extreme points, unusable for organisms.

Nevertheless the conventional industries (small-, medium-, and large-scale) are contributing income and livelihoods generation across developing and underde-veloped countries, these are also the major sources of environmental degradation by violating/ignoring the regulations imposed upon through the government/ nongovernment and overall WHO's specifications. Major causes are focused on

(i) Industrial waste/effluents,
(ii) Agricultural chemicals, inputs,
(iii) Greenhouse effect,
(iv) Conversion of wetlands to agricultural lands and
(v) Over all mismanagement of wetlands.

These activities can disqualify a wetland's hydrology, water properties, and species diversity, and create an unhygienic situation for biotic and abiotic entity thriving in the ecosystem. Indiscriminate use of fertilizer and pesticides are driving toxic heavy metals, nitrates, etc. into the surrounding water bodies and ultimately, these toxic materials are entering food chains and doing menaces in the form of biomagnification.

20.1.4 Degradation of Coastal Ecosystem: A Threat

Indeed, diverse coastal lines sprawling over 7600 km in India and myriad of deltas scattering across Indian subtropics offers immensely productive ecosystem to sustain count of diverse flora and fauna. The coastal ecosystem of India is now running under the brunt of climate change and ecological impoverishment. Integrated coastal management (ICM) programs are all set to organize zone-specific interventions: (i) management of mangroves, (ii) coastal fisheries, (iii) integration of fish cum aquatic food crops and development of suitable models in situ watershed plans, and (iv) embankments possible to protect of any sudden flash flood, as safeguard. These are some of the imperatives to uplift village economical condition as the mounting pressure of these areas is posing a threat to the biodiversity including their lives and livelihoods of community people (Sinhababu et al. 1998; Puste et al. 2007).

20.1.5 Heavy Metals and Gaseous Emissions: Endangered to the Ecosystem

Heavy metal toxicity in wet ecosystem caused by different industrial effluents poses a serious threat to human beings and livestock farming system including health hazards. The available technologies as of date like, alkaline rainfall, ion substitute columns, electrochemical elimination, filtration and membrane technologies for heavy metal elimination, etc. are not economically viable and may generate unfavorable impacts on wet ecosystem as well (Rai 2008).

20.1.6 Wetland Management and Conservation in Different Agro-Climatic Zones

India is having bunts of agro-climatic zones wherein the water bodies and hyspheres play the most critical role to support agricultural production and livestock functions. Community-based extension approaches, ensuring both ownership and empowerment over this natural resources, are needed both policy and institutional restructuring. The nodal organizations and innovative extension institutions like ATMA (Agricultural Technology Development Agency), National Institute of Agricultural Extension Management (MANAGE), Farmers' Field Schools and KVKs (Krishi Vigyan Kendra), NICRA (National Initiatives for Climate Resilient Agriculture), and VRC (Village Resource Centre) are to go in an orchestrated manner. These will help building community water stewardship, water resource scouting, water auditing, and socialization (Egalitarian Access to Water Resources). The important assessment statement of Indian Institute of Management (IIM), Lucknow revealed that ATMA's extension approach has been proving to be very promising in execution of the reforms and thus the progress was extended further to other states.

20.1.7 Wetlands Has a Great Role for Ecosystem Maintenance

It is also to be noted that wetlands have a significant role for maintaining its biodiversity, comprised soil, water, biota, and their interaction. This vast wet environment of the carboniferous period, which has been continuously producing and preserving many of the fossil fuels for human civilization, functions as "*Nature's kidney*" of wet ecosystem of the world (James 1995), and it has a great role in maintaining

(i) Its ecological balance and refreshing,
(ii) Recharging groundwater and overall,
(iii) Sustenance of rural livelihoods.

The greater north-eastern parts of Indian subcontinent have chains of river system, so many tributaries, canals, and oxbow lakes, which are really important for rural agricultural–fisheries productive system, mostly in Indo-Bangladesh regions. Development of civilization and continued existence of human beings is inextricably connected with wetland ecosystem which sustained production and financial stability of millions of people. Moreover, wetland biodiversity is immensely valuable for the production of aquatic crops, naturally sustainable and economic viability of rural people including enrichment of biomass, which is nutrient-rich, effective for soil health and cultivation of arable crops in consequence (Puste et al. 2001a, b, 2004, 2012).

20.1.8 Resource-Based Aqua-terrestrial Ecosystem

Indeed, proper utilization of aqua-terrestrial ecosystem with suitable and updating farm technology, covering location-specific beneficial aquatic food crops, nonfood commercially viable crops under aquatic, and arable field crops including horticultural plantations under terrestrial or land system is really imperative and hence, a questionable and viable task today. It is thus possible to make it more productive through the full exploitation of land holdings, feasible for multi-cropping system and to extend all sorts of facilities (multi-tier cropping system, reuse of pond-bottom humus soil as a source of organic manures, etc.) in the different agro-zones of West Bengal (Ray Pramanik et al. 2013; Puste et al. 2011, 2012, 2013). Moreover, balancing of areas under aqua-terrestrial system is vital and effective for recharging of groundwater that makes balancing ecosystem in an area, life-saving irrigation to adjacent arable crops especially during dry periods, sustainable not only for productive but also non-vulnerable to climatic condition to a great extent.

20.1.9 Integrated Farming System (IFS) for Enhancing Productivity and Sustainability

Integrated farming system represents a complicated interwoven mesh of soils, plants, livestock animals, workers, farm inputs and environmental influences (Shekinah and Sankaran 2007). Among the different system variables, some of these are necessary to manipulate as per need of the area as well as system approach for making it more productive according to their preferences and aspirations. The synergistic effect could be achieved for sustaining productivity and profitability due to assimilation of different crops and other enterprises (animals, etc.). It resulting total contribution than the sum of their individual effects (Edwards et al. 1988). Indian farming communities are dominantly mostly small and marginal group of farm families have average land holding <2.0 ha. Hence, it is essential to integrate suitable enterprises at their optimal levels to capture the maximum benefits.

20.1.10 Our Goal and Sustenance

From pre-independence to its present decade, India has made major contribution and succeeding attainment in agriculture sector by increasing food production by about fourfolds. Many drivers of the system have accomplished this task, like policy, research, and extension activities, which supports a crucial role to achieving this sustenance and goal. Public and institutional extension activities (field-level demonstration, participatory rural appraisal, transfer of technology, information communication technology, farmers' school, etc.) played major role in ushering green revolution, even second green revolution in Indian agriculture.

However, considering huge agroecological diversity spreading over 127 agro-climatic zones and 15 regions in India, we need to have a high-resolution microplan, which will be effective for microlevel and resilient for region level. While frame working the plans, the issues like community mobilization, ecological deliverables, and resource ownership are to be considered and accommodated accordingly. Union Government of India mainly emphasized on road map through its national-level policies, situation-specific programs, and providing budgetary supports to the needing sector for their upliftment as a whole.

There is a need for work synergy and conceptual integrity between state organs and national-level functionaries. Similarly, an apex body like Indian Council of Agricultural Research (ICAR) at national-level supports the research and extension activities to evolve and functioning effectively 'Transfer of Technology (ToT)' models. This great job is mainly operated through its 650 KVKs (Krishi Vigyan Kendra's) spreading all over the country. State agricultural universities in different states and union territory also contemplate to develop extension models that suitable to take up transfer of technology in a befitting manner.

20.1.11 IFS—The Scientific Background—An Overview

Indeed, it is remarkable to present here that very limited information is available regarding the evaluation of these underutilized aquatic food crops other than rice [water chestnut or *singhara* (under the family Trapaceae) and fox nut or gorgon nut or makhana (under the family Nymphaeaceae) and other important aquatic crops] integrated with fishes (mixture of carp and air-breathing life fishes) in low-lying ecosystem. However, some studies were conducted and used enterprises successfully under combined and mixed farming system in different ecozones of the country as it is one of the pathways, which can be able to earn more monetary advantages due to its high marketable price at the time of harvesting/netting and these produces are mostly preferred by the rural and urban common people (energy-rich).

Admixing fish cultivation integrated with deepwater rice in waste wetland ecosystems is common for the utilization of food and total system productivity (Dutta et al. 1984; Bandyopadhyay and Puste 2001). Moreover, this scientific approach is also improving soil fertility by thriving on plankton and biomes, and adding nitrogen at soil profiles through fish excreta, enriched in consequence in the system (Brahmanand and Mohanty 1999; Puste and Das 2001a, b; Bandyopadhyay and Puste 2001). To realize the facts, studies on sole as well as integrated farming system were conducted on farmers' fields utilizing aqua-terrestrial ecosystem under new alluvial zone of state of West Bengal, India to find out suitable and optimize enterprise combination for sustaining productivity, income generating, and employment opportunity through cropping and related components utilizing all possible resources.

Keeping with this in view, a series of field works have been undertaken to address the situation-specific problem and prospects of aqua-terrestrial ecosystem with its full exploitation, magnitude and diversity of input use and natural sources of these greater areas of the regions (New alluvial, old alluvial, red and laterite, and coastal and saline zone).

20.2 Methodological Approaches

20.2.1 Land Holdings, Fragmentation, and Entitlement

It is to note that the marginality and fragmentation of holding stand as a barrier to ecologically sustainable resource management, especially in greater eastern part of the country (Indo-Bangladesh regions). For effective conservation and stewardship, we need to have collective farming in place. Collective farming, again, deserves a well-organized community mobilization through its different associated sectors in the society. Different water bodies are highly exploitable and being utilized for the enormous production system, agro-processing value-added enterprising, and generating income, making livelihoods that socially sustainable and food security for teeming rural populates. Need-based water monitoring system was developed in different agro-zones (new alluvial, old alluvial, coastal, and saline zones), utilizing skill personnel of water engineering for reorientation of existing system and making fruitfully for making its production potentiality.

20.2.2 Water Engineering and Modeling Approaches

The present paper is based on technological intervention, field monitoring, research and over all, extension ToT (transfer of technology) programs, wherein, kind of community ownership (SHGs, self-help groups; NGOs, nongovernment organizations; FS, farmers schools, etc.) has been incubated for intensive utilization of wetlands by implementing innovative aquatic enterprises (water engineering, aquaculture modeling, hydroponic system vis-à-vis enhancing production system and value addition of the different products) most suited in the giving ecosystems.

For appropriate and achievement of adoption of updating farm techniques covering agricultural—cum—aquaculture enterprising, a number of field trials-cum-modeling were emphasized and developed in different agro-zones of Indian subcontinent (in new alluvial, old alluvial, coastal, and saline zones, respectively), utilizing skilled personnel water engineering, water entrepreneurship, etc. The following system approaches were developed considering following objectives.

To diversification and diffused the result-oriented outcomes of aquatic crops-cum-fish culture practised in scientific and systematic manner following different agro-techniques to the common small to marginal fish farm sectors in different agro-zones through communication approaches, using variables like

(a) Cropping system and its enterprising system,
(b) On fish variables and its enterprising and
(c) On conglomeration using both the variables.

The participatory analysis was focused to use the extension and methodological approach effective in wetland ecosystem to choose best one through some need-based soil and water engineering aspects like need-based cleaning, excavation, renovation or some soil management (e.g., earth manipulation) for making it in the shape of watershed bodies or *bherri* system used for conserving and preserving excess rainwater during peak rainy months in different zones. This system can effectively be utilized for different agricultural-cum-fishery production system including maintenance of ecobalance under aqua-terrestrial ecosystem in the zones (Puste et al. 2007). Specific objectives were focused to find out zone-specific suitable agricultural production system which was further implemented in a large-scale at farmers' field as *'improvised farm demonstrations'* in the areas of: culturing of aquatic crops, integration of aquatic crops-fish-vegetables utilizing aqua-terrestrial ecosystem, their production economics including development of livelihoods as well.

20.2.3 Crop Culture

The crop culture itself as sole or monocropping and/or multi-nature under the umbrella of integrated farming system (IFS), the pathways for identical for boosting up crop productivity per unit area per unit time is the focusing object in rural areas. The diverse and complex farming system needs to be accommodated commercially viable wetland crops like semi-deep to deepwater rice, water chestnut or *paniphal*, makhana or gorgon nut, *Cyrtosperma*, *Colocasia* spp., etc., food-cum-ornamental crops (lotus, water-lily), nonfood commercial crops (mat-sedges, *Calamus*, shola-pith, etc.), and so many valuable aquatic medicinal plants, and their valuable products including quality products were emphasized greatly in the regions for increasing productivity and making them sustainable in nature. Thus, this broad spectrum research has modeled wetland-based IFS (Integrated farming system) for its subsequent application in another ecosystem, within India and abroad.

20.2.4 The System Economics

The unique approaches were emphasized based on the watershed plans through some manipulations in the different agro-zones of this subtropic. In addition, relative advantages of multi-tier mixed farming system were analyzed (benefit–cost ratio on the production system), which was evinced economically accessible to the resource-poor and marginal farming communities in the respective agro-zones. Benefit–cost was estimated to be >2.5, even >3.0-folds higher. This has contributed ultimately to sustainable development of the regions. This has gained more over the system through their value-added products produced from wetland crops, ornamental as well as income generating products produced by the women and aged communality of the rural areas. From study, it may be concluded that it is necessary to utilize this vast vacant water bodies including terrestrial or land or dyke or bund ecosystem of the country for production of food, livelihood, engagement of household labors and ultimately, economic stability of rural people for their economical development and sustainability as well.

However, a systematic field study was conducted during the last 15–16 years mostly at the farmers' field utilizing aqua-terrestrial ecosystem in the different agro-zones, viz., at new alluvial, old alluvial, and coastal and saline zone West Bengal, India. Adjacent dykes or bunds including land system along with border area were fully utilized covering seasonal vegetables including trailing types, banana, papaya, other valuable perennial tree plantations (coconut and other forest plantations), etc. The enterprises were selected based on the farmers' preferences, popularity and complementary nature of enterprises under aqua-terrestrial ecosystem of the area.

20.2.5 LFEY (Life fish Equivalent Yield)

For comparison among the crops, fishes, and other variables of the enterprises due to heterogeneous characteristics, life fish equivalent yield (LFEY) in respect to production (t ha^{-1}) was estimated utilizing the produce value at market after harvesting using the following mathematical formula:

$$\text{LFEY (t/ha)} = \frac{\text{Value of different crops / fishes / other enterprises (in rupee value,₹)}}{\text{Price of life-fishes/t (₹)}}$$

Average market price of all the variables was considered at the time economic calculation, so that it would be understood about their loss or profitability of the system. Initial soil samples were collected from the pond for determination of chemical properties, viz., organic carbon (0.587%), total nitrogen content (0.061%), available P_2O_5 (80.33 kg/ha), and K_2O (201.72 kg/ha), respectively, including post-experimental pond soil characteristics as per the standard method (Jackson 1973).

20.3 Results and Discussion

20.3.1 *PRA Exercise, Extent of Problem, and Framework in Rural Ecology*

While Indian agriculture is becoming highly vulnerable to brunt of climate change, it is facing the dual challenge of food security for more than billion people as well as ensuring inclusive economic growth for every one. The situation is further complex when more than 60% of rural people are depending on agriculture, a sector which is contributing less and less (13.6%) to the national GDP. It has been projected by IPCC (Inter-Governmental Panel on Climate Change) under the scenario of a 1 °C increase in nocturnal temperature, rice yield will drop by 15% and wheat yields by 20%, respectively. This would cause a decline in GDP by 1.8–3.4%. The agricultural production aspect is going to be affected in two broad areas of climate-induced impact: (a) direct effect from changes in temperature, precipitation, or carbon dioxide concentrations in the atmosphere and (b) indirect effect through changes in soil moisture as well as organic carbon.

It is equally important in the different corners of the country including in the different agro-zones of the study areas worked under new alluvial, old alluvial, and coastal and saline zone [S_1—Taldi (south 24 Parganas); S_2—Kalinarayanpur (Nadia); S_3—Nabagram (Burdwan); S_4—Ahiron (Murshidabad); and S_5—Mohanpur (Nadia) zones, respectively] of the state of West Bengal. This has been worked on the basis of soil–water relation and its effect under the wide situations of aqua-terrestrial ecosystem of its greater areas.

The problems were identified through PRA exercise (participatory rural appraisal), particularly to identify and magnitude of problems faced in the different agro-zones in greater regions of West Bengal, emphasized on different categories, viz., P_1—Mostly unused or waste in nature; P_2—Low-lying areas subject to waterlogging; P_3—Uncontrolled runoff sometimes making flush flood in the locality; and P_2—Soil loss as soil erosion through runoff water, respectively. However, among the different agro-zones and the specific areas, maximum deterioration and degradation were observed in Ahiron under Murshidabad district areas in old alluvial zone, while, comparatively better performance eco-friendly approaches were noticed in the areas of Kalinarayanpur under Nadia and Nabagram under Burdwan district of the state (Table 20.1; Fig. 20.1). It is advantageous to know the existence and situation prior to implement a development plan for proper utilization of the system as a whole for upholding productivity and livelihood development of the beneficiaries.

Table 20.1 Perception, vulnerability, and quantification on site-specific problem (%) through PRA exercise in different agro-zones of West Bengal

Sl. No.	Problems identified	Site-wise extent of problems				
		S_1-Taldi, south 24 Parganas	S_2-Kalinarayanpur, Nadia	S_3-Nabagram, Burdwan	S_4-Ahiron, Murshidabad	S_5-Mohanpur Nadia
1.	Mostly unused or waste in nature	20.8	16.7	18.6	30.7	18.4
2.	Low-lying areas subject to waterlogging	35.2	31.8	21.9	34.8	17.6
3.	Uncontrolled runoff sometimes flush flood occur	32.6	37.6	22.3	46.7	19.5
4.	Soil erosion	37.3	41.7	17.0	46.3	13.5

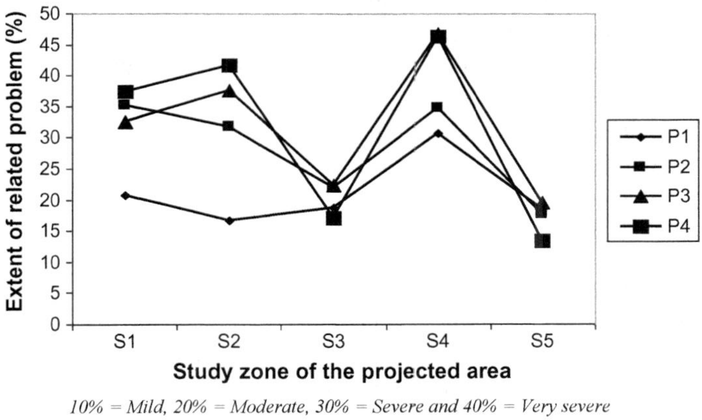

Fig. 20.1 Perception and quantification on site-specific problem (%) through PRA exercise

20.3.2 *Nature of Submergence and Changes of Soil Properties of Different Agro-zones Soil*

20.3.2.1 pH

Soil–water–plant–atmosphere is the imperative linkage, should exercise and prioritized in a developmental plan, more specifically if it is being a waste or unused areas. The base-level survey, sampling, data analyzing, and interpretations and course of action which are the basic information, is the task of pathways to be known or furnished by a planner as precautionary measures. Among the different soil properties, pH is one of the followings, the prerequisite was determined in laboratory and considered for taking prevention further for a developmental plan of actions.

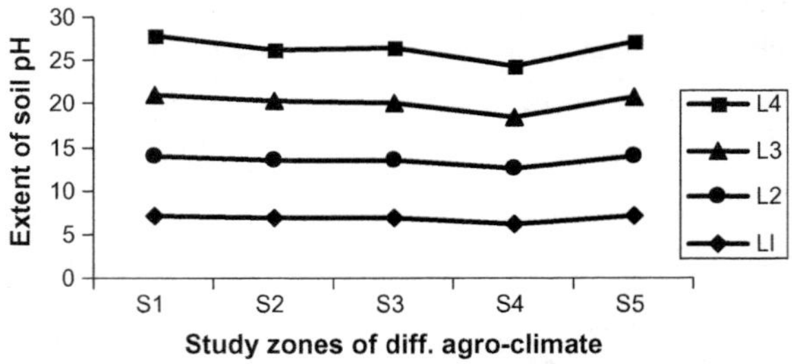

Fig. 20.2 Influence of submergence on soil properties (pH)

pH of pond-bottom soil at different water depths [L_1—Continuous flooding (permanent '*tal*' lands) of 2.5 ± 0.5–0.75 m of water depth; L_2—Continuous flooding (permanent in nature) of 2.0 ± 0.5–0.75 m of water depth, L_3—Flooding during rainy and drying during summer season (semi-permanent) of 1.5, and L_4—Flooding during rainy and drying during winter including part of summer (temporary) of ≤ 1 m of water depth to 2.0 m of water depth)] is the bench-level initial soil data, which were collected from the respective areas (of different agro-zones) and analyzed and interpreted accordingly (Fig. 20.2).

Decay or decomposition of organic wastes (farm wastes, green foliage, straw, roughages, stover, biomass, etc.) are the responsible for heat generating and conversion or changes the materials into decayed form due to microbial actions and thereby exudes or liberations of mild acids, resulted in changes of soil properties into acidic in nature. It happened so good in moist environment in aerobic situation, even it happens but slowly in anaerobic and/or in aquatic environment.

However, maximum low levels of soil pH of pond-bottom were noticed in Ahiron areas (S_4) correlated with comparatively shallow water depth with temporary in nature (Fig. 20.2), as it helps for sun-dried for a reasonable part of summer including last part of winter months. The soils of pond-bottom in the areas of Taldi under saline and coastal areas of south 24-Parganas (S_1) and Mohanpur under New Alluvial zone of Nadia district (S_5) were comparatively higher, might be due to comparatively dominated by base saturation and organic wastes and with more depth of water under low-lying situations. This probably happened due to the actions of man-made causes along with natural consequences in the different agro-zones of this greater regions. In most of the cases, water of said ponds under study was rectified with the use of lime ($CaCO_3$) at regulated intervals, prior to culture of aquatic crops integrated with fish variables.

20.3.2.2 Soil Organic Carbon

Soil carbon (C) is the basic characteristics of any soil and is effective as store house of the soil, which has a vital role for making productive and economic stability to the beneficiary group of farming communities. In the study, four types of water submergence in ponds in each four agro-zones [L_1—Continuous flooding (permanent '*tal*' lands) of 2.5 ± 0.5–0.75 m of water depth; L_2—Continuous flooding (permanent in nature) of 2.0 ± 0.5–0.75 m of water depth, L_3—Flooding during rainy and drying during summer season (semi-permanent) of 1.5, and L_4—Flooding during rainy and drying during winter including part of summer (temporary) of ≤ 1 m of water depth to 2.0 m of water depth)] were investigated and analyzed for knowing the nature and magnitude of organic carbon, the inherent capacity of the soil, which is congenial for growth and development of the phytoplankton in the aquatic body.

It visualized from the study that the presence of high level of organic carbon in pod-bottom soil was more in the areas following the trend of S_3—Nabagram (Burdwan) > S_2—Kalinarayanpur (Nadia) > S_1—Taldi (south 24 Parganas) > S_5—Mohanpur (Nadia) zones, and comparatively lower values observed in S_4—Ahiron (Murshidabad) under Old alluvial zone of West Bengal (Fig. 20.3). Likewise, possibility of the presence of more organic carbon in the pond's of shallow water depth than that of deep submergence, probably due to some restrictions imposed in the later category that favored in the former one. Use of these top 20–30 cm humus soil is the convenient practice of the local farmers, which is effective in arable crop cultivation in most of the areas due to its enrichment of this decayed biomass in sustainable crop production system.

20.3.3 Production Potentiality and Its Profitability Under Integrated System (IFS)

It is remarkable to note that dramatic changes were recorded irrespective of all the crop enterprises including life fish variables, which were practised in almost all the agro-zones of the regions (Tables 20.2 and 20.3; Fig. 20.4). Sole crop under composite farming system [*singhara*, fox nut, water-lily, *jal kachu*, etc.) and *lati kachu* or *taro* (*Cyrtosperma chamissomis*)] and life fishes [indigenous energy-rich life fishes including snake-head (shoil—*Channa striatus*; gajar—*C. marulius*; singi—*Heteropnuestes fossilis;* and magur—*Clarias batrachus*) maintained in

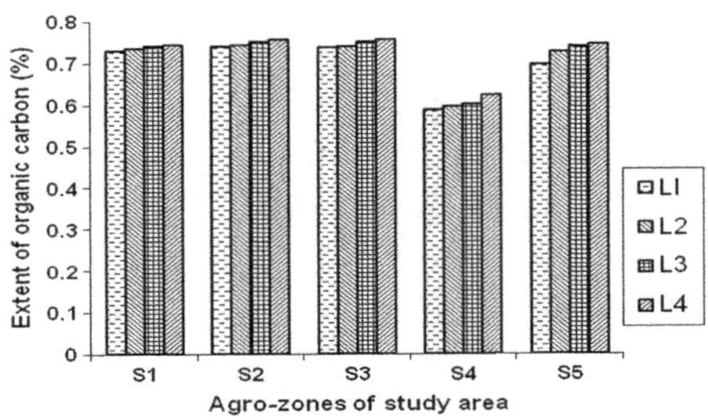

Fig. 20.3 Effect of submergence on soil organic carbon

Table 20.2 System productivity (individual and total yield in LFEY, t/ha), mean contribution of components to each enterprise of farming systems (average value of 3 years) in one of the centers (Kalinarayanpur under New Alluvial zone)

Farming systems (FS)	S_1		S_2		S_3		S_4		S_5		S_1	S_2	S_3	S_4	S_5	S_1	S_2	S_3	S_4	S_5
	WC	LF	MK	LF	WL	LF	Col	LF	LK	LF	Individual LFEY					Total LFEY				
FS_1 (WC + LF	1.241	2.262	–	–	–	–	–	–	–	–	0.105 ± 2.262	–	–	–	–	2.367	–	–	–	
FS_2 (MK + LF)	–	–	1.513	2.189	–	–	–	–	–	–	–	0.473 ± 2.189	–	–	–	–	2.662	–	–	–
FS_3 (WL + LF)	–	–	–	–	2.843	2.308	–	–	–	–	–	–	0.080 ± 2.308	–	–	–	–	2.388	–	–
FS_4 (Col + LF)	–	–	–	–	–	–	82.23	2.067	–	–	–	–	–	1.185 ± 2.067	–	–	–	–	3.252	–
FS_5 (LK + LF)	–	–	–	–	–	–	–	–	28.41	1.286	–	–	–	–	1.776 ± 1.386	–	–	–	–	3.062

WC, water chestnut; MK, makhana; WL, water-lily; Col, *Colocasia* (*Jal kachu*); LK, *lati kachu* (*Cyrtosperma* sp.), LF, life fishes and LFEY, life fish equivalent yield. Price of WC, MK, WL, Col, LK, and LF (t ha^{-1}) was considered ₹ 13,500 (WC); 50,000 (MK); 4500 (WL); 2500 (Col); 10,000 (LK); and 1,60,000 (t^{-1}), respectively

Table 20.3 System productivity and economic variability of different farming systems (average of three years) in two extreme agro-zones of West Bengal

Farming systems (FS) in integrated approach	S_2 (Kalinarayanpur, Nadia)		S_4 (Ahiron, Murshidabad)	
	Total LFEY (t ha^{-1})	B-C ratio	Total LFEY (t ha^{-1})	B-C ratio
FS_1 (WC + LF)	2.367	2.682	1.923	2.016
FS_2 (MK + LF)	2.662	2.986	2.127	2.218
FS_3 (WL + LF)	2.388	2.251	1.306	1.568
FS_4 (Col + LF)	3.252	3.125	2.229	2.423
FS_5 (LK + LF)	3.062	3.076	2.096	2.221

WC, water chestnut; MK makhana; WL, water-lily; Col, *Colocasia* (*Jal kachu*); LK, *lati kachu* (*Cyrtosperma* sp.), LF, life fishes and LFEY, life fish equivalent yield. Price of WC, MK, WL, Col, LK, and LF (t ha^{-1}) was considered ₹ 13,500 (WC); 50,000 (MK); 4500 (WL); 2500 (Col); 10,000 (LK); and 1,60,000 t^{-1}, respectively

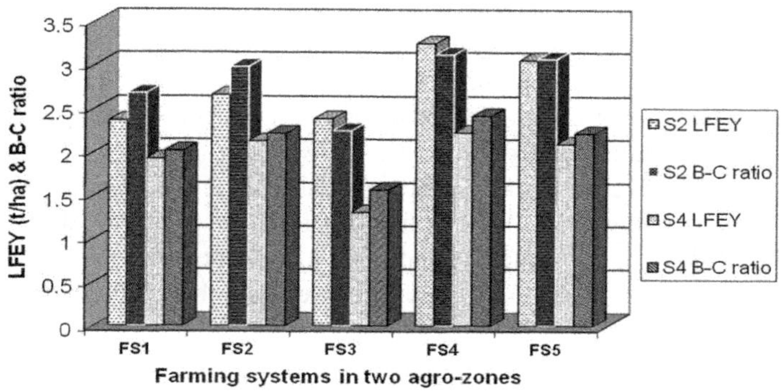

Fig. 20.4 LFEY and B–C ratio two extreme agro-zones

4:3:3 ratio were used under aquatic system] yield and their equivalent yield (t ha^{-1}) in terms of monetary conversion (LFEY) were greatly influenced due to zonal practised in the different situations of West Bengal.

There was a greater variation in respect to shared yield both of aquatic crops and life- fish under the integrated farming system (FS_1 to FS_5), their total yields in terms of LFEY. Among the different agro-zones, highest values of individual yield and total LFEY exhibited with Kalinarayanpur center (S_2) under new alluvial, whereas lower values obtained in Ahiron center (S_4) under old alluvial zone.

Monetary benefits had gone also in S_2 center (Kalinarayanpur in Nadia under New Alluvial), while minimum monetary gain was with the S_4 center (Ahiron in Murshidabad under Old Alluvial) of West Bengal, which might be due to more sharing value with the former than that of latter one.

20.3.4 Vegetables and Other Plantations in Adjacent Arable Lands

In aqua-terrestrial ecosystem, adjacent dykes or bunds or arable lands were effective and utilized through IFS system, practised in all the centers through the cultivation of seasonal vegetables (including leafy and trailing types), banana (dominated by female plants), papaya (both green and ripening type), and coconut and other tree plantations (valuable forest plants) were comparatively in elevated lands or dykes of the aquatic body, for total utilization of aqua-terrestrial ecosystem as a whole. Improvised agro-techniques like proper and timely manuring [inorganic (urea, single super phosphate, murriate of potash, suphala, etc.) and organic (neem oil-cakes, bone meal, etc.) in balance and suitable proportions] and biodegradable plant protection were followed as and when required by the crops/plants.

Production of seasonal vegetables, viz., leafy, peas, and beans type; cole crops; Cucurbitaceous and Solanaceous crops; root and bhindi or okra crops, etc. produced highest level of production system (19.83, 8.06, 17.98, 17.02, 19.68, 21.37, and 10.96 t ha^{-1}, respectively) or the average productivity of all vegetables of 16.41 t ha^{-1}, exhibited at Kalinarayanpur in Nadia under New Alluvial zone (S_2), which was nourished with optimum and integrated nutrient system with proper dose and in time. These were quite low values (15.07, 6.38, 14.07, 13.24, 14.45, 16.86, and 6.87 t ha^{-1}, respectively, or the average productivity of all vegetables of 12.42 t ha^{-1}) obtained in Ahiron in Murshidabad district under old alluvial zone of West Bengal (S_4), which might be due soil and other man-made causative factors (mostly uncared); almost these were 30.58–39.04% lower than that of previous situation.

20.3.5 Impact of Technological Intervention and Livelihood Development of Farming Community

Through studies on the beneficiary group of farming community, the areas were done systematically for knowing the impact/outcome of technological intervention and livelihood development with respect to before technological interventions (Fig. 20.5).

Condition before intervention

Cropping intensity (134.8%), ground water recharge (5.76 ft), and income were low; uncontrolled soil loss and runoff and lifestyle were not so good.

Condition after intervention

(a) **Crop Productivity**: It has been increased to the tune of 2.14 t ha^{-1} than the previous situation as like 1.46 t ha^{-1};
(b) **Cropping Intensity**: It has increased 68% (227.1%) due to increased number of crops and duration of working season;

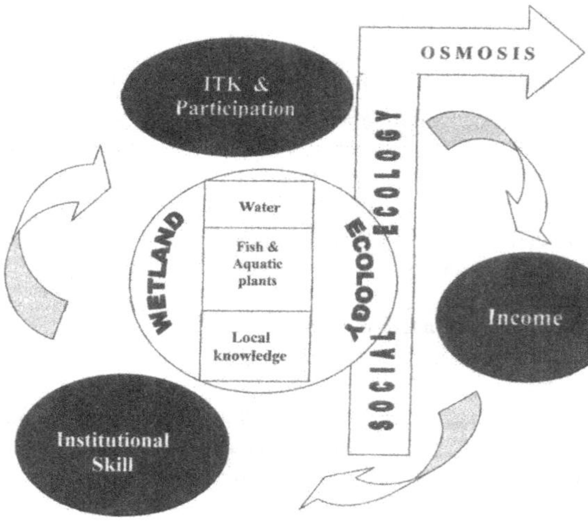

Fig. 20.5 Economy of IFS in wetland ecology: an empirical study on upliftment

(c) **Ground Water Recharge**: It has increased 31% (raised 1.78 ft) over previous situation due to controlling runoff;
(d) **Erosion Control**: Cleaning and excavation works increased storing of runoff water and controlled runoff;
(e) **Income**: Monthly income raised at about INR 3800/- than that of previous INR 2500/- system;
(f) **Benefit–Cost Ratio**: Benefit–cost ratio was changed remarkably from previous system (1.18) and raised to 2.35–2.64 adopting improvised agro-techniques on IFS on "*Rice-cum-fish culture-cum-vegetables*" at farmer's level; and
(g) **Livelihood Changes**: Owned a grocery shop for his unemployed son adjacent with his house due to more production as well as more out turn of the system.

20.3.6 Point of Convergence

20.3.6.1 Intervention and Osmosis: Social and Wetland Ecology

From the project sources, all sorts of technological interventions were introduced at the respective study zones and successive successful was gained in respect to (i) wetland ecology, (ii) crop including IFS ecology, (iii) maximization of production potential, (iv) water recharging at tried sources (surface, groundwater), (v) income and manpower generation, (vi) livelihood changes, and (vii) overall, environmental ecology (Table 20.4).

Table 20.4 A representation of the intervention and osmosis in respect to social and wetland ecology

Intervention	Wetland ecology	Osmosis	Social ecology
Economic production system	Suitable for various aquatic crops including fish culture	Income changes from Rs. 500/- to Rs. 1500/- per head	Need for generation for income
Water conservation measures, creating watershed basins, seepage tank etc. and terrestrial or dykes developed.	Water retentivity was there but not enough for the purpose	Cropping intensity and entrepreneurships developed	Need for irrigation to summer rice and live-saving irrigation to various arable crops
Makhana (*Euryale ferox* Salisb.) was included for economic production system	Different types of traditional aquatic crops but was neglected with poor agro-techniques	Social market for value-added mobility (popped-form) as an new income generation	New food for starch, nutritious
Water chestnut (*Trapa bispinosa* Roxb.) was included for more production system	Water chestnut with the system with poor management	Market developed as fresh fruit in absence of other fruits during the time and ground form as '*atta*'	New food item with enriched starch, carbohydrates, protein, minerals, etc.
Pani-kachu or *jal kachu* (*Cyrtosperma* sp.)	It was with their practice but with agro0technques, low inputs	Market developed as corm, stolons as vegetables	New food item with enriched starch, carbohydrates, protein, minerals, etc.
Intervention of energy-rich live fishes integrated with aquatic crops as IFS models	System was in the wetland ecology but with poor agro-techniques	Total productivity per unit area per unit time developed along with market accessibility	Foods from aquatic crops as well as fishes with the farming system enhanced, nutritious to the farm family also
Seasonal vegetables and other valuable tree plantation developed on the dykes	It was with the system but not in a systematic manner	More income generation from IFS in short as well as long term basis.	Developed IFS based on aqua-terrestrial ecosystem, enhanced total production system round the year

20.4 Concluding Remarks

Global environment is solely balancing with land, water, and its greater biodiversity. Among the natural resources, wetland has a key and pivotal role and most integral should be utilized wisely for mankind for its sustainability and their livelihood development. A greater wetland area, especially in north-eastern part of the country, is lying vacant, almost without cultivation round the year. This may effectively be utilized through the cultivation of valuable underutilized wetland crops, extinct fish genotypes, etc. with systematically following integrated farming system (IFS). This approach will able to utilize precisely aqua-terrestrial ecosystem as it is not only valuable for habitats but also supports and augmenting spontaneous income generation, which is the pathways for upliftment of resource-poor rural economy in the regions.

Keeping with this in views, initiation was undertaken during last 15–16 years utilizing the greater part of aqua-terrestrial ecosystem under new alluvial, old alluvial, and saline and coastal zone of West Bengal (India) to find out the suitable and optimize enterprise combinations in the integrated farming system (IFS) for enhancing and sustaining productivity, income generating and employment opportunity through cropping, and related components utilizing all possible resources. Results reveal that soil characteristics have greatly influenced due to different agroecological situations in the greater regions. Maximum benefits had gone in favor of integrated farming system, which combined popular and beneficial aquatic food crops integrated with life fishes under aquatic system and seasonal vegetables and other valuable plantations, which was possible to generate more income and employment opportunity sustainable for livelihood development and food security.

In addition, development of fertility status of pond-bottom soil has a greater effect to combat the vagaries of climatic condition of the areas. Over long run of the system for a considerable period, recycling of farm and animal wastes applying to cropping systems would be a vital source of plant nutrients, especially in this multi-tier agricultural production system utilizing aqua-terrestrial as a whole.

Acknowledgements The authors express their sincere indebtedness and gratitude to Indian Council of Agricultural Research (ICAR) and Department of Land Resources (DoLR), Ministry of Rural Development, Government of India, New Delhi for providing financial assistance; laboratory of Soil Science and Agricultural Chemistry and Department of Agronomy, Bidhan Chandra Krishi Viswavidyalaya (State Agricultural University), Mohanpur, Nadia (West Bengal), and the local farmers for conducting field experiments in the respective agro-zones of the state of West Bengal.

References

Anonymous. (1995). Forword message by Chatt, A, Director, Trace Analysis Research Centre, Dalhousie University, Halifax, Nova Scotia (Canada) quoted by Khopker SM (1995) Environmental Pollution Analysis, New Age International (P) Ltd.

Bandyopadhyay, S., & Puste, A. M. (2001). Effect of carp and fish feed on yield and soil nutrient availability under integrated rice-fish culture. *Asian Fisheries Science, 14,* 437–441.

Brahmanand, P. S., & Mohanty, R. K. (1999). Rice-fish integration: prospects. *Yojana, New Delhi, India, 43*(9), 11–12.

Chakraborty, C. S. (1999). Environment, evolution and man. In D. K. Basu et al. (Eds.), *Environment: Issues and challenges.* Academic Staff College, The University of Burdwan, West Bengal.

Das, D. K. (1999). Soils and environmental pollution. In D. K. Basu et al. (Eds.), *Environment: Issues and challenges.* Academic Staff College, The University of Burdwan, West Bengal.

Dutta, S. K., Konar, S. K., & Mukhopadhyay, P. K. (1984). Paddy and air-breathing fish culture: effect of supplemental feed on the growth and yield of rice and fish. *International Rice Research Newsletter, 9*(2), 23–24.

Edwards, P., Pullin, R. S. V., & Gartner, J. A. (1988). Research and education for the development of crop-livestock-fish farming systems in the tropics. *ICLARM Studies and Reviews*, No. 16.

Jackson, M. L. (1973). *Soil chemical analysis*. New Delhi: Prentice Hall.

James, E. J. (1995). Managing the wetlands and their watersheds. *Yojana, 39*(1 & 2), 43–50

Khopker, S. M. (1995). *Environmental pollution analysis*. New Delhi: New Age International (P) Ltd.

Puste, A. M., & Das, D. K. (2001a). Impact of air pollutant on the ecosystems in the vicinity of industrial areas of Indian sub-tropics. *Water, Air and Soil Pollution, 130*, 843–848.

Puste, A. M., & Das, D. K. (2001b). Optimization of aquatic-terrestrial ecosystem in relation to soil nitrogen status for the cultivation of fish and aquatic food crops of the Indian subtropics. *The Scientific World, 1*(S2), 130–134.

Puste, A. M., Mandal, T. K., Das, D. K., Dasgupta, M., & Ray Pramanik, B. (2012). Impact of industrial wastes and effluent on the wetland ecosystem and management options for productivity and sustainability in Indian sub-continent. In: *Proceedings of the International Conference on Industrial Waste Management and Process Efficiency (IWMPE 2012)*, (pp. 433–448). DUET (Dhaka, Bangladesh).

Puste, A. M., Ray Pramanik, B., Dasgupta, M., Maity, T. K., & Maiti, A. K. (2011). Integrated wetland management—A holistic approach for development of diversified farming system for production of aquatic crops and fishes for rural sustainability in Indian sub-continent. In: *Proceedings of the International Conference on Tropical Island Ecosystems: Issues Related to Livelihood, Sustainable Development and Climate Change, CARI (ICAR)*, (pp. 90–91). Port-Blair (India): A and N Islands.

Puste, A. M., Ray Pramanik, B., Jana, K., Roy, A., Sounda, G., Mondal, S. S., et al. (2007). Integrated coastal management—A holistic approach for sustainable development and economic stability of Indian subtropics. In *Coastal resource management* (pp. 9–24). Kolkata (India): Eastern Printing Processor.

Puste, A. M., Sarkar, P. K., & Das, D. K. (2004). Wetland ecosystem—A case study on fish-aquatic food crops diversity for enrichment productivity and economic stability for fish-farm families in Indian subtropics. In *Proceedings of the Twelfth Biennial Conference of the International Institute of Fisheries Economics & Trade (IIFET 2004 JAPAN)* held in TUMSAT, Tokyo, Japan, 20–30 July 20–30, 2004. IIFET, Oregon State University (USA): Theme: Aquaculture Economics and Management, Group 3 (pp. 1–8).

Puste, A. M., Mandal, T. K., Dasgupta, M., & Maity, T. K. (2013). Productivity, profitability and livelihood improvement through integrated farming system for new alluvial zone of West Bengal. *Indian Journal of Agronomy, 58*(4), 451–458.

Rai, P. K. (2008). Heavy metal pollution in aquatic ecosystems and its phytoremediation using wetland plants: an eco-sustainable approach. *International Journal of Phytoremediation, 10*(2), 131–158.

Ray Pramanik, B., Puste, A. M., Jana, K., Banerjee, K., & Dasgupta, M. (2013). Effect of integrated nutrient management and integration of makhana-cum-fish culture on soil and water characterization in wetland ecosystem. *Green Farming International Journal, 4*(2), 127–131.

Shekinah, D. E., & Sankaran, N. (2007). Productivity, profitability and employment generation in integrated farming systems under rainfed vertisols of western zone of Tamil Nadu. *Indian Journal of Agronomy, 52*(4), 275–278.

Sinhababu, D. P., Jha, K. P., Mathur, K. C., & Ayappan, S. (1998). Integrated farming system: Rice-fish FOR LOWLAND ECOLOGIES. In *Proceedings of the International Symposium on Rainfed Rice for Sustainable Food Security,* Cuttack, Orissa (pp. 203–222), September 23–25, 1996.

Chapter 21
Family Farming in Amazon: Solution to Food and Regional Competitiveness

Alex Rotta Romani, Flávio de São Pedro Filho, Jeoval Batista da Silva, Janilene Vasconcelos de Melo and Jayashree Patil-Dake

Abstract The present study aims at strategies for competitive farming with sustainability. The research is based on "Theory U." The study is of a qualitative nature, prepared through the Content Analysis Method, supported by bibliographical sources, to face empirically the strategy required to the sustainability with focus on competitive advantage. It is based upon three specific objectives. (1) To raise/craft the basic competitive strategies in the familiar farming activities (2) To analyze the operability of the strategies found in face of the perspective sustainability (3) To structure subsides to required innovation in socio-environmental sustainability with focus on family farming. It is observed that the adaptation of generators model of competitive advantage according to the theoretical concepts of Triple Bottom Line can direct the consecution of sustainable competitive advantages in the familiar farming activity.

Keywords Amazon · Business competitiveness · Family agriculture Innovation · Sustainability

A.R. Romani (✉) · F. de São Pedro Filho · J.B. da Silva
Research Group in Management of Innovation and Technology (GEITEC/UNIR), Federal University of Rondônia (UNIR), Porto Velho, Brazil
e-mail: alexromani_1601@hotmail.com

F. de São Pedro Filho
e-mail: flavio1954@gmail.com

J.B. da Silva
e-mail: jeovalbs@gmail.com

J.V. de Melo
Federal University of Rondônia, Porto Velho, Brazil
e-mail: janilene18@gmail.com

J. Patil-Dake
KPB Hinduja College, Mumbai, India
e-mail: js_patil2001@rediffmail.com

U.K. De et al. (eds.), *Inequality, Poverty and Development in India*, India Studies in Business and Economics, DOI 10.1007/978-981-10-6274-2_21

21.1 Introduction

Until the middle of last century, it was believed that natural resources were inexhaustible and renewable, requiring no concern related to natural extraction and transformation of the biota for development. With the industrial and technological progress, population growth and the consumer culture, the harmful effects of those practices reveal itself by the impacts on the environment. In this context, the term sustainability arises, and according to the World Commission on Environment and Development (WCED) it is the ability to meet present needs without giving damages to the satisfaction of needs of future generations.

Mankind begins to realize the need to changing of the current patterns of consumption and the consequent amendment of issues relating to care and maintenance of the ecosystem, in that sense all sectors of society have sought a balance between environmental impact and means of production, in order to demonstrate its potential customers, its concern and environmental responsibility as attractive requirement. Due to these questions, it is necessary a study that promotes discussion of sustainability strategies as competitive advantage generator element. In this sense, it is questioned the following: what are the epistemological conceptual elements for implementation of the required strategies for sustainability in generating competitive advantage in family farming?

To answer the question, it is proposed as a general objective to study competitiveness strategies in family farming and sustainability. This has support in three specific objectives: to raise the basic competitive strategies for family farming (1), examine the operability of the strategies raised in the face of sustainability prospects (2), and structure subsides for the required innovation in sustainability socio-environmental focusing on family farming (3).

21.2 Theoretical and Conceptual Review

The essence of the Theory U is to promote openness of heart and mind, aiming to generate a future marked by present actions in counterpart to the past. Study in Leão and Avelino (2014) characterizes the Theory U as sequence of actions that will depart from feeling the situation, observing the various aspects that may influence organizational changes, allowing reflection on the inner knowing, acting in order to bring something new to the inserted reality on a concept of organizational learning, where the rational is not the deepest source. It follows the journey proposed by the Theory U (Fig. 21.1).

Table 21.1 specifies the issues raised by the Theory U.

According to Leão (2014), Scharmer conceptualizes the Theory U as a theoretical support that allows you to learn about the future, with thoughts and previous judgments where the future submerges as it occurs by the construction process. It follows the journey proposed by the Theory U. The Theory U will support to lead

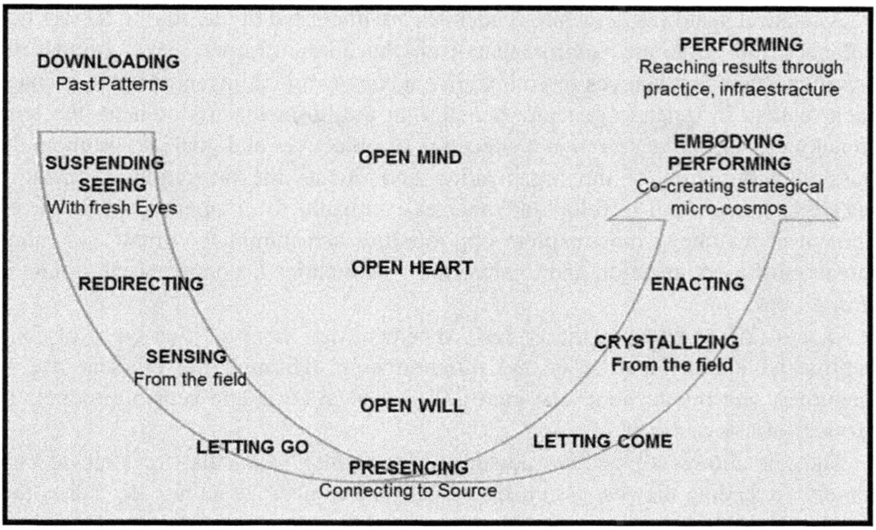

Fig. 21.1 The journey proposed by U Theory. A Jornada Proposta Pela Teoria U. *Source* Extracted from Leão and Avelino (2014), adapted from Scharmer (2010)

Table 21.1 Characteristics of Theory U

Instrument	Detailing
1. Open mind	1.1 Ability to suspend judgments and questions, it should see with new eyes the reality free from the chains of mental models. Seek the intellectual intelligence
2. Open heart	2.1 Ability to redirect the attention to the perception of feeling (seeing with the heart), visualizing the whole through other informational sources in the emotional field
3. Open will	3.1 Ability to let go, get rid of the mental models that cause delay and tune into the tuning into the future that you wish through spiritual intelligence

Source Prepared by the author based on Scharmer (2010)

and generate solutions to the questions raised, and guiding element of the knowledge production process.

21.2.1 Sustainable Competitive Strategy

In accordance with Minotti (2014), the strategy is a set of competitive changes that managers perform to achieve certain performance. For this author the strategy can be defined as one of the long-term business objectives, to be achieved through resources allocation in the scope of four visions of rational planning, learning, logical incrementalism and the very emerging strategy.

As states Orsato (2012) while academics are interested in identifying factors that influence the corporate environmentalism, the administrators seek to transform eco-investments on sources of competitive advantage, looking for ways to manage such matters in order to generate benefits. In the business environment, the term strategy can mean the search and execution of objectives and goals, to promote the mission and values of the organization and directs the allocation of financial resource, human and develops advantages compared to competitors. The development of a strategy must explore opportunities and minimize current and future threats of the organization and explore the potentialities becoming weak points in strong ones.

Orsato (2012) refers to the Porter's statement that there are two types of competitive advantage; low costs and differentiation. Through the efficient use of resources, one organization can gain advantages in costs and sell its products or services at a lower cost.

Thus, it allows competitive advantage by adding value that transfers to customers, exceeding the cost assumed to obtain the results; the author also states that in relation to the strategic conceptions, when developing corporate environmental standards it is possible to innovate and consequently value the product resulting in reduced cost and or implementing differentiation strategies. Porter says that to obtain competitive advantage, the organizations should have a clear strategy that enables to create a unique and valuable position, involving different activities.

21.2.2 Family Farming

The academy questions the applicability of sustainable strategies in family farming as a competitive advantage generator element. In this focus it is highlighted the many reasons why support family farming according to Altieri (2012): small farms are the key to global food security; they are more productive and retain more natural resources than large monocultures; They represent models of sustainability; They represent a sanctuary of agro-biodiversity of genetically modified organisms. Table 21.2 shows the basic differentiation between employer and family farming.

Due to the multiplicity of models and concepts there is not, therefore a general concept of framing and differentiation of what is or not family farming, the table guides and differentiates the family farming from patronal, making clear the favorable relationship of family farming in generating wealth in a sustainable way.

Family farming is seen as the main economic activity in many regions of Brazil due to its diversity of opportunities as employment and income. For this, it is necessary to guarantee access to credit and technological resources to the achievement of production and sustainable management of their properties and concomitant commercialization of production. Despite of contributing with more than 70% of the country's food production and be the economic base of about 9 to each 10 municipalities, keeping busy the productive rural landscape, the Brazilian family farming finds difficulty of adapting to the challenges of increased competitiveness of

Table 21.2 Models and main characteristics of family farming

1. Patronal agriculture	2. Family farming
1.1 Total separation of management factors and work	2.1 Management and work closely linked
1.2 Centralized organization	2.2 Production process driven directly by the producer
1.3 Emphasis on specialization	2.3 Emphasis on diversification
1.4 Emphasis on agricultural practices standardizable	2.4 Emphasis on durability of natural resources and quality of life
1.5 Predominance of wage labor	2.5 Wage labor is only complementary
1.6 Technologies directed only to the elimination of "ground" decisions and "moment"	2.6 Immediate decisions, appropriate to the high degree of unpredictability of the production process
1.7 Technologies mainly seek to reduce the work force needs	2.7 Decisions "in loco," conditioned by the specificities of the production process
1.8 Emphasis on the use of purchased inputs	2.8 Emphasis on the use of internal inputs

Source Lima and Silva (2012)

domestic and global agriculture. The family farmer usually produces the need for subsistence and sells the leftovers quickly without economic bargaining, once it does not have storage conditions, this way it undervalues its work.

In accordance with Galvão (2005) in Santos and Mitja (2012) in the Amazon region the family farming arises more characteristic shape than in other regions, constituting the basis where it is applied and the extraction of natural resources and food production, it predominates in this region family farmers in border areas and old settlement areas of colonization, producing temporary and permanent crops, beyond of extractives exploration, denoting a regional production base with traditional and local products.

21.3 Methodology

The methodology can be described as a set of methods used in conducting a research. According to Siena (2007), by method it is possible to understand the way, the form and the way of thinking. It is the way of approach in level of abstraction of phenomena. The set of mental processes or operations applied in the research.

This research has a qualitative nature, elaborated through the Content Analysis Method, based on bibliographical sources, in order to face empirically the required strategy to focus on sustainability in competitive advantage. In regard to the content analysis Bardin (2006) states, referred in Mozzato and Grzybovski (2011), be a set of communication analysis techniques through systematic means and objectives of description of the messages with the intention of analyzing the content and infer knowledge about the conditions of production and indicators. There is below the schema of procedures for content analysis (Fig. 21.2).

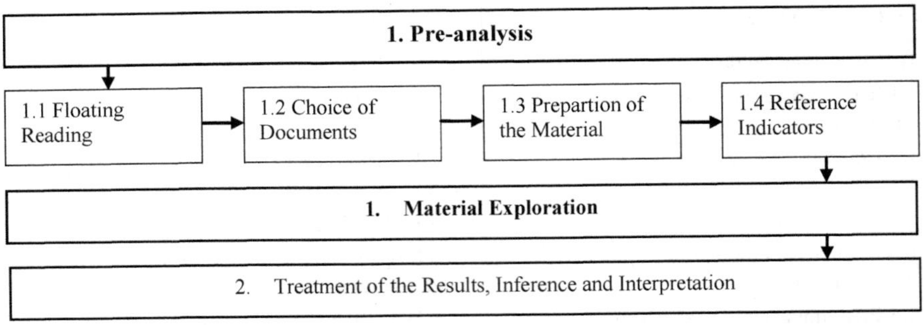

Fig. 21.2 Steps of analysis of contents. *Source* Prepared by the author based on Bardin (2009) through Mozzato and Grzybovski (2011)

Table 21.3 Description of the steps of content analysis procedures

Step	Detailing
1. Pre-analysis	1.1 Operational phase, documents were selected documents and analysis unit, beyond of formulation of hypotheses
2. Exploration of the material	2.1 The data were changed into information, within categories to the comprehension and later analysis
3. Treatment of the results	3.1 In this step the information were analyzed to subsidize technical inferences and conclusions

Source Prepared by the authors

Table 21.3 refers to the steps of procedures of content analysis.

Regarding the approach, the research is qualitative because it involves interpretation of the phenomena and the attribution of meanings, part of a process of reflection and analysis of reality. Concerning the technical procedures, the research is supported by bibliographical sources, due to the composition of the theoretical framework developed from published material such as books, graduation theses, master's, doctoral, magazines and articles.

The research included Brazilian articles that discuss the key thematic study such as sustainability, family farming and competitive advantage. The time gap of the work are publications in the relative time interval between 2000 and 2014, the selection was non-randomly through pre-analysis for thematic framework.

21.4 Innovation for Competitive Strategy Study to Sustainable of Farming Family

In this area is shown an analysis of the content covered by sampling selected through pre-analysis of publications, according to the methodology. Thus, it is concluded that the textual indicators linked to family farming and sustainability have been used more frequently than those related to competitive advantages, this is

Table 21.4 Theory U in family farming

Instrument	Detailing
1. Open mind	1.1 Suspension of judgment and questions to visualize new methods, processes, input supplies, production characteristics, logistics of acquisition and distribution and sales without the mental lenses that tie to the common practices that hind the effectuation of sustainable values with competitive values
2. Open heart	2.1. In his field, it should redirect attention to feel and visualize amongst the novelties interposed by the suspension of judgments of interior way and instinctive for a second way of analysis
3. Open will	3.1. At this stage, one should be able to get rid of the mental models that delay the changes necessary for evolution, by abandoning the traditional practices of family farming that stop the sustainable development in generating competitive advantages

Source Prepared by the authors

due to the difficulty of finding specific contents that approach sustainable competitive advantages for family farming.

For this it is inferred that there is an under-utilization of value-adding techniques to generate competitive advantage through sustainable principles in family farming in academia, in this sense from the Sects. 21.4.1–21.4.3 were answered the objectives of the research through the contents extracted from articles and available literature articles, which served as source for the realization of the content and construction of the technical instrumental analysis. Therefore, the elements of Theory U should guide the sustainable competitive advantage models as follows in Table 21.4.

21.4.1 Survey of Basic Competitive Strategies for Family Farming

This topic reports competitiveness strategies raised in the documents content analysis selected to give theoretical support to the research questions.

The value created is not summarily appropriate value, while the opportunity cost and willingness to pay define the value created, prices and costs define the appropriate value of production. The appropriate part of the farmer must be transformed into profit creating production value according to Brito and Brito (2012), Brito et al. (2012).

Bowman and Ambrosini (2000) in Brito and Brito (2012) state that the interaction with the customer, the difference between the willingness to pay the price and define the called surplus client, that is, the value captured by the customer. When generating greater surplus to its clients, it can then explore the asymmetry between its productions. The author makes use of Coff (2010) to report that the effects of competitive advantage on the performance will depend on

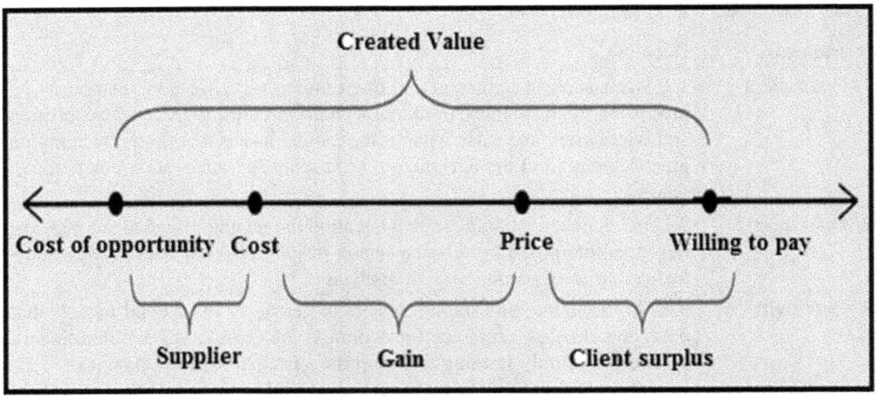

Fig. 21.3 Strategy to create value. *Source* Brito and Brito (2012)

Table 21.5 The strategy practice for value creation

Elements	Detailing
1. Supplier	1.1 It involves costs opportunities in a position to encourage the acquisition of raw materials at lower costs, such as seeds, fertilizers, machinery and others 1.2 They include the traditional costs of inputs purchased at an average price
2. Farmer	2.1 It composes part of costs of productive inputs acquisitions 2.2 In this part are defined the basis for stipulation of prices and competitive positioning
3. Client surplus	3.1 At this stage take place prospecting of generated opportunity costs 3.2 It evaluates the monetary disposal of the customer for the product offered
4. Created value	4.1 The junction of the above three factors define the value added to the product 4.2 The final step consists of verifying the acceptance of the product based on the value created, in order to check the consistency of the strategy implemented and its effectiveness as a competitive advantage

Source Prepared by the authors

decision-making factors of family farming management in equalize the moment of creation and monetization of the value created exemplified in Fig. 21.3.

It is possible to evidence on Table 21.5 the practices of value creation strategy for competitive advantage generator model.

Some consultants and academics have explored examples that suggest the advantages of assuming a socio-environmental behavior, but they do not clarify the situations in which these environmental eco opportunities may or may not generate results in a context. For that, it is displayed the following figure as a model for identification of competitive environmental strategies (Table 21.6).

The structure of Fig. 21.4 generates connections between economic segment that the company operates, its position, the types of market and its ability to acquire

Table 21.6 Detailing of the competitive environmental strategies

1. Advantage by costs	Detailing
1.1 Eco-efficiency of processes	Using production processes, technical and management according to environmental preservation precepts with focus on efficiency by identifying, understanding and management of processes
1.2 Environmental cost leadership	Obtaining costs advantage by costs requires effort, even harder in accordance with Orsato (2012) is to reduce costs and environmental impacts associated with the products at the same time. The idea is that with the reduction of costs the farmer can practice lower prices to compete in a niche market by price, or keep the average practiced increasing the profit margin for example
2. Advantage by differentiation	Detailing
2.1 Eco-differentiation of processes	Differentiation occurs when the eco-efficiency of processes reaches levels perceptible to consumers; at this moment the farmer should use these principles to build an image that distinguishes him from others, front of consumers
2.2 Socio-environmental brands	In this field the using of good ecological practices of structural processes as well as, production and the logistics ones to be used in the creation of a brand that links family farmers to a sustainable production unit and differentiated products and services

Source Prepared by the authors

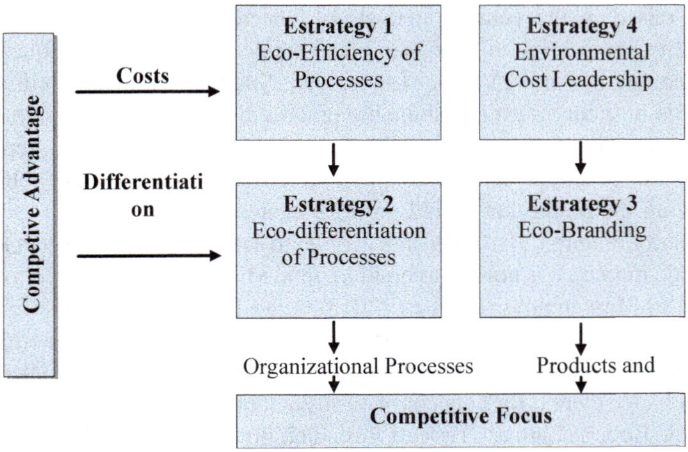

Fig. 21.4 Competitive environmental strategies. *Source* Adapted from Orsato (2012)

resources and launch innovative strategies that allow induce competitive advantage by cost or differentiation as the adaptation of the author.

It was identified in the analyzed content that competitive strategies can be classified into three categories: Operational Excellence, Innovation in Product and Relationship with the client according to Table 21.7.

Table 21.7 Categories of competitive strategy

Elements	Detailing
1. Operational excellence	1.1 It is applied in environments where the relation quality/price are determining factors of competitiveness. Where the superior operational efficiency solidifies the competitive position
2. Innovation in product	2.1 Creations of radically new product concepts for customers and specific market segments. This strategy favors the maximization of profits due to entry into niche not exploited by competing markets
3. Relationship with the client	3.1 Strategies oriented to meet specific customer needs by developing appropriate products and solutions to the current and future demands

Source Prepared by the authors

In competitive advantage, creation process is necessary that the farmer acquires the essential competences to perform his activity in accordance with the established strategy.

21.4.2 Analysis of the Operational Strategies Raised in the Face of Prospects of Sustainability

In this topic are presented the elements for the operation of competitiveness strategies raised in the content analysis of selected documents in the face of a sustainability perspective to give theoretical support to the research questions.

The literature in Porter, Van der Linde, Dier, Singh and Chirsmann discusses the key benefits in incorporating sustainable practices in maximizing profits, decrease costs and generation; it is as indicate Mascarenhas and Alex (2013) in reporting the generation of potential related to the value of credibility and reliability in strengthening the brand that would promote customer loyalty.

Souza and Cordeiro (2010) state that in order to achieve sustainable development in the domestic market, it is needed to build a tripod of sustainability linked to planning. According to Mascarenhas and Alex (2013) citing Barbosa (2007) the fundamental components to the sustainable development consist in obtaining economic growth, environmental protection and social equity, and being tacked these fundamentals to the paradigm change there is the conception of sustainable development from the precepts of the Triple Bottom Line or Triple of Sustainability as in Fig. 21.5.

The triple bottom line is a guide to the strategic adaptive in the generation of sustainable competitive advantage, where socio-economic and environmental factors are intrinsically linked and its alignment can promote sustainable development in various productive sectors including in family farming as shown in Table 21.8.

The interconnection of the three factors in a practical way generates a continuous sustainable development environment, where priorities are remodeled to meet the need of use of current resources without harming the existence and quality of life of future generations.

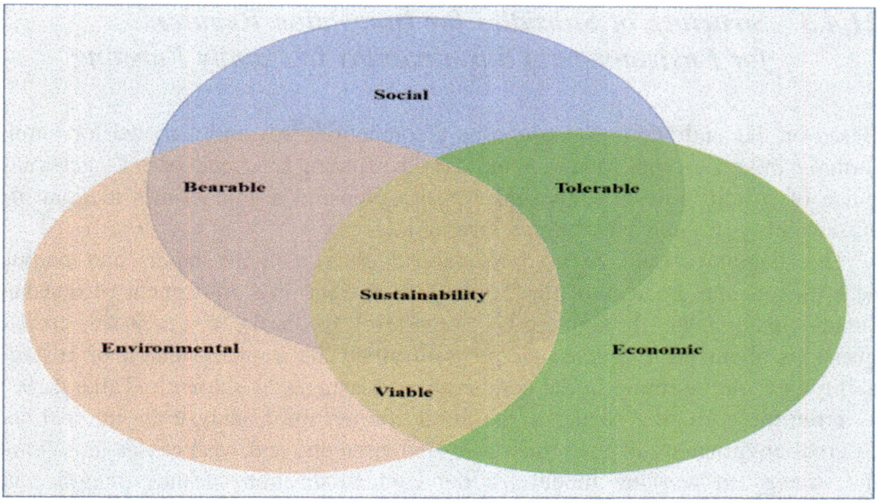

Fig. 21.5 Tripod of sustainability. *Source* Prepared by the authors based on Mascarenhas and Alex (2013)

Table 21.8 Aspects and detailing requirements for the triple bottom line

Aspect	Detailing
1. Social	1.1 Human capital should be respected and have their rights guaranteed, in addition it is necessary that communities around the area of cultivation and trade are not adversely affected in the short, medium and long term
2. Environmental	2.1 The environmental refers to natural capital in the case of the farmer can cite the soil, it is necessary to think about the impacts of short, medium and long-term and seek practices to reduction and equalization practices to ensure that future generations can enjoy fully of the current resources
3. Economic	3.1 It is the financial capital, where production occurs, distribution, purchase and sale of goods and services that move monetary values. In this aspect, it is important that the profit do not pass by the exploitation and irresponsible devastation of the environmental and human resources
4. Viable	4.1 Parameter of management that encompasses the economic and environmental dimension. The social aspect is ignored in this relationship
5. Fair	5.1 Harmonious relationship of social and economic nature elements. The environmental aspect is ignored in this relationship
6. Tolerable	6.1 Elements that promote interaction between the social and economic fields. The environmental aspect is not taken into account in this relation
7. Sustainable	7.1 When it reaches that level, it means that there will be a harmonious interrelationship between social, environmental and economic factors in which the current development does not compromise the existence of future generations

Source Prepared by the authors

21.4.3 Structure of Subsidies for Innovation Required for Environmental Sustainability in Family Farming

Based on the study done it is proposed a competitive advantage model for family farming linked to application of the Triplle Bottom Line concepts as generator guide of sustainability. In this sense, it was prepared a homeostasis diagram for sustainability in family farming as Diagram 21.1.

The diagram should be used to stablish criteria on the inputs and outputs according to the precepts of the Triple Bottom Line in a movement of constant strategic realignment through the post processing feedback, for this it was created questions about the discussed elements to guide the implementation of sustainability in family farming in the competitive advantages as shown in Table 21.9.

From these guiding elements, the family farmer must analyze the internal and external environment of his property to find strengths and weaknesses and define his strategy, a working model for the contextualization of the strengths and weakness is the SWOT matrix (Strengths, Weaknesses, Opportunities and Threats) that according to Romani (2013) allows to analyze a situation, market, policy, business, company among others, by identifying and organizing information characterizing the forces, opportunities, weaknesses and threats. It is a flexible instrument in terms of application that helps to organize functionally the diagnosis for decision-making as exemplified in Fig. 21.6.

Romani (2013) uses Ferrel et al. (2000) cited by Vilela (2007) to report that the strengths and weaknesses are internal and exclusives problems in conducting the analysis. The forces correspond to items that enable a competitive advantage. The weaknesses are related to organizational deficiencies that may have in the development or implementation of the strategy.

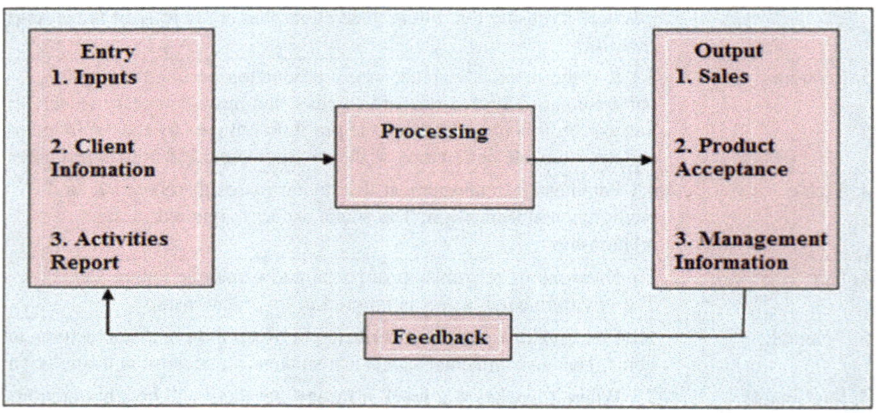

Diagram 21.1 Homeostasis diagram for sustainability in family farming. *Source* Prepared by the authors

Table 21.9 Detailed homeostasis diagram for sustainability in family farming

Entry	Social	Environmental	Economic
Inputs	Are the suppliers of input in accordance with the work law and value their employers?	Are the inputs produced to not degrade the environment impairing future generations?	Is the economically viable acquire input of that supplier?
Client information	Do customers understand the social concern of the farmer?	Customers understand and buy the idea of environmental protection presented in the products offered?	Are the customers willing to pay for the peculiarities embedded in sustainable production process?
Activities report	Do the activities performed meet the legal requirements and provide a healthy environment for employees?	Do the activities harm the environment and if so, what measures will be taken to restore?	Is the implementation of these activities economically viable?
Sales	Is the sale process appropriate to the current laws and satisfy the purposes for which they propose?	Will the sale process happen in a way to not degrade the environment harming future generations?	Is the value suitable for consumer willingness to pay for products?
Product acceptance	Will the community benefit itself of the offer of agricultural products with the concept of sustainability?	Will the sustainability concept linked to the products generate competitive advantage for commercial acceptance?	Is the value created by the customer surplus within parameters for market penetration?
Management information	Is the collected information in the community used to meet the needs of customers?	Are the information on sustainable performance of suppliers checked continuously?	Are the information on the acceptance of products in view of the value created modifiable?

Source Prepared by the authors

The author also states that the opportunities and threats are external issues that can affect. The opportunities are related to favorable conditions in the environment that can produce rewards, while the threats are related to conditions that may hinder the achievement of goals. With these modeling the family farmer must keep your mind open to new conceptions of work, have an open heart to redirect their attention to emotional perceptions seeking seeing all to feel the environment in which it is inserted, in addition to open will to rid of the mental shackles that impede the advancement of their practices and processes for value creation.

		External Environment	
		Opportunities	**Threats**
Internal Environment	Strengths	**Development**	**Maintenance**
		- What are the positive attributes of the internal culture of agriculture? - What is the level of knowledge of the Family in relation to the productive relation? - What is the advantage of the offered	- Is the families qualified and has knowledge to work in this niche market? - Are resources scarce? - Are the access to potential customers difficult?
	Weaknesses	**Growth**	**Survival**
		-Does the niche have potential? - Is the brand differentiation appropriate to sustainability? - Is the proposal innovative to market acceptance? - Are there needs of customers that can be exploited?	-Are there competitors in this market niche? -Are the government and industry regulations subject to change to prevent the continuing activities? -Is the local culture resistant to innovation?

Fig. 21.6 Suggestive model SWOT analysis matrix. *Source* Image free domain extracted via the web

21.5 Conclusion

In the recent past, there was no question in a relevant way the finiteness of natural resources that supported and subsidized the economic and social development of society sustained by the stimulation of consumerism attitudes. Over the time, these practices were being questioned by scholars who promoted studies and interviews to the new forms of development with environmental sustainability-oriented features.

The epistemological conceptual elements for implementation of strategies required for sustainability in generating competitive advantage in family farming activity can be done through competitive advantages models adaptations extracted from classical literature with the Triple Bottom Line Sustainability precepts, which models the sustainable development throughout the relationship of social, environmental and economic aspects.

The content analysis denotes that the indicators linked to family farming and sustainability have been used more frequently than those related to competitive advantages, this is due to the difficulty of finding specific content addressing sustainable competitive advantages for family farming.

In this sense it was raised the basic competitive strategies for family agricultural activities as the Strategy for Value Creation which works the interaction between suppliers, farmer, customer and the transformation of potential value; in other way it was identified the Environmental Competitive Strategy formulated by Orsato (2012) that generates connections between the economic sector where the farmer operates, his position, the types of market and his abilities to acquire resources and implement innovative strategies, that allow induce competitive advantage either by costs or through environmental cost leadership or eco-efficiency of processes is by differentiation through eco-differentiation processes or by the environmental brand consolidation. These factors raised should guide the farmer's market positioning that can be in operational excellence, innovation in product or customer relationship.

In regard to the analysis of operational strategies raised in the face of sustainability perspective, it is suggested that the operative models of competitive advantage must be suitable for the Triple Bottom Line precepts in the achievement of the advantages, where economic and environmental factors are only part of the sieve of sustainability, in this social model it also gains importance and creates a tripod to effectuation of sustainability.

The structuring of subsidies for the required innovation in socio-environmental sustainability it had been drawn up a homeostasis diagram for sustainability in family farming, which provides the questions for the implementation of sustainable competitive advantage. Taking into considering the entry of inputs, information of clients and implemented activities and outputs related to the sale of production, the consumer market acceptance, and the management information of the results within a social inquiry system, environmental and economic. For structuring these subsidies, it was generated an adaptive for family farming based on SWOT matrix, for the family farmer understand the internal and external environment in the execution of continuous improvement in order to achieve and maintain competitive advantages in the face the principles of sustainability.

References

Altieri, M. (2012). Agroecology: *Scientific basis to a sustainable agriculture*. São Paulo, Rio de Janeiro: Expressão Popular.

Brito, R. P., & Brito, L. A. L. (2012). Competitive advantage and performance: a value creation approach. *Journal of Contemporary Management*, *16*(3), 360–380. Available at http://www.scielo.br/pdf/rac/v16n3/v16n3a03.pdf. Accessed 8 October 2016.

Brito, R. P., Yang, D. J., & Brito, L. A. L. (2012). *Competitive advantage, creation of value and its effect on the performance* (p. 52). São Paulo: ERA, São Paulo.

Bowman, C., & Ambrosini, V. (2000). Value creation versus value capture: towards a coherent definition of value in strategy. *British Journal of Management*, *11*(1), 1–15.

Coff, R. W. (2010). The coevolution of rent appropriation and capability development. *Strategic Management Journal*, *31*(7), 711–733.

Leão, J., & Avelino, A. (2014). Scientific innovation for an institutional development: Case study at the Federal Institute of Education, Science and Technology of Acre—IFAC. *Dissertation (Master in Administration)*. Post-Graduation Program—Master in Administration (PPGMAD) of the Federal University of Rondônia—UNIR, Porto Velho.

Lima, O. C., & Silva, W. S. (2012). *Family farming: Analysis from the theoretical framework of the authors about the national family farming strengthening program*. Brasília: PRONAF.

Mascarenhas, M. P., & Alex, W. (2013). *Triple bottom line of sustainability: An analysis at the national companies producers of oils and fats*. São Paulo: REUNIR.

Minotti, P. F. (2014). Sustainability strategies: The environmental dimension in participating organizations of the clean development mechanism. *Dissertation presented to the Post-Graduation Program in Administration of the Paulista University*. São Paulo: UNESP.

Mozzato, A. R., & Grzybovski, D. (2011). *Content Analysis and qualitative data analysis technique in the administration field: Potential and challenge*. Curitiba: ANPAD.

Orsato, R. (2012). *Strategies of sustainability: When does it worth to be green? Quality mark*. São Paulo: EBAPE.

Romani, A. R. (2013). *Influences of the business compensation plan in satisfying the sales area employees. Work of course conclusion in administration at the Federal University of Rondônia*. Porto Velho: UNIR.

Santos, A. M. S., & Mitja, D. (2012). Family farming and local development: The challenges for an economic-ecologic sustainability at the Community of Palmares II, Parauapebas, PA. *INTERAÇÕES, Campo Grande, 13*(1), 39–48.

Scharmer, O. (2010). 'The Blind Spot of Institutional Leadership: How To Create Deep Innovation Through Moving from Egosystem to Ecosystem Awareness' presented in World Economic Forum Annual Meeting of the New Champions 2010 Tianjin, People's Republic of China, 13-15 September.

Siena, O. (2007). *Methodology of the scientific research: Methodology of scientific research: Elements for preparation and presentation of academic works*. Porto Velho: PPGMAD.

Souza, G. R., & Cordeiro, J. S. (2010). *Cognitive mapping and balanced score card strategic management of municipal solid waste. Management of production*. São Carlos: UNESP.

Chapter 22
Farm Growth in Northeast India and Its Effect on Poverty

K.U. Viswanathan and Anannya Gupta

Abstract Experience of growth in BRICS countries shows that one percentage growth in agriculture is two to three times more effective in poverty reduction when compared to one percentage growth emanating from non-agricultural sectors. State average of sectoral GSDP growth over 2008–09 to 2013–14 shows a recovery of 4.1% per annum as compared to 1.7% per annum during 2000–01 to 2004–05. Six out of the eight Northeastern states of India show higher than all India average performance during this period, viz. Sikkim (9.8%), Tripura (6.1%), Arunachal Pradesh (5.5%), Meghalaya (4.9%), Nagaland (4.9%) and Mizoram (4.3%). State wise analysis of various agricultural parameters and multi-dimensional poverty indicators revealed that each state has a unique relationship in terms of growth in agriculture and poverty. The hypothesis of high farm growth reduced poverty was true for Sikkim, Tripura, Meghalaya and Assam and true in the reverse direction for Manipur. High growth of agriculture was non-inclusive and hence could not have impact on poverty in Arunachal Pradesh and Nagaland. Mizoram with too many population in rural areas depending on agriculture had high farm growth and but increase in rural poverty. However, the state had only 0.094 MPI value in 2011–12. Overall, states with high GSDPA growth observed reduced poverty taking other parameters into account. States with high share of Non-Farm Sector (NFS) and Animal Husbandry (AH) in monthly income of agricultural household had improving rural poverty. Improving performance of agriculture needs to be focused upon reducing poverty, both incidence and intensity of poverty. Among agricultural inputs, irrigation needs to be prioritised, as in ground water resources in northeast India are under-utilized while blessed with sufficient rainfall, which offers scope to install a battery of shallow and deep tube wells to draw ground water during the Rabi season. Further, efforts are to be made to increase production and productivity of high-value crops. Northeastern states have

K.U. Viswanathan (✉) · A. Gupta
NABARD, Assam Regional Office, Guwahati, India
e-mail: ku.viswanathan@nabard.org

A. Gupta
e-mail: anannya.das@nabard.org

U.K. De et al. (eds.), *Inequality, Poverty and Development in India*, India Studies in Business and Economics, DOI 10.1007/978-981-10-6274-2_22

skill and raw materials to engage in self-employment activities, viz. weaving, pottery, cane and bamboo products, etc., and therefore, with the development of agriculture sector, NFS also to be stressed upon.

Keywords Farm growth · Poverty · Source of growth · Inclusion

22.1 Introduction

Endowed with abundant natural resources like fertile land, sufficient rainfall, rich bio-diversity and unique socio-cultural characteristics, North-Eastern Region (NER) of India offers potential for tremendous growth. The Region, constituting eight states namely Arunachal Pradesh, Assam, Manipur, Meghalaya, Mizoram, Nagaland, Tripura and Sikkim,[1] cover an area of 2.62 lakh sq. km. and population of 4.5 crore, constituting 7.9% of the country's total geographical area and 3.8% of the population, respectively. Among NER states there are substantial variations in geographical, demographical and socio-economic aspects. Arunachal Pradesh is the biggest state in NER in terms of area (32%) followed by Assam (30%), but 68% of total population of the region lives in the state of Assam. Consequently, the population density varies greatly from 17 persons per sq. km in Arunachal Pradesh to 397 persons per sq. km in Assam. The forest cover of the NER is more than 50% of its total geographical area, which ranges from 24% in Assam to 82% in Sikkim. More than 80% of the population lives in the rural areas and 20% in urban areas (Table 22.1). Development of NER is often referred as lagging, citing comparatively high poverty ratios, past incidences of disturbance in the social order and ascribing to its hilly terrain and associated physical and institutional infrastructure constraints.

Poverty, although defined as lack of adequate income, has several expressions like hunger, malnutrition, low access to education/health/other basic services and an overall exclusion in civil, social and cultural life. As per the latest estimates,[2] population below poverty line was 28.4% in the NER as compared to 21.9% in all India. In other words, NER had a share of 5% of poor population compared to its share of 3.8% in the total population. Rural poverty ratio was high at 31.2% as compared to urban poverty at 18.5%. As majority of the rural working population (varying from 56 to 83%) are dependent on agriculture, either as cultivators or as agricultural labourers, the performance of agriculture has a direct bearing on the poverty. Experience of growth in BRICS countries shows that one percentage growth in agriculture is two to three times more effective in poverty reduction when compared to one percentage growth emanating from non-agricultural sectors (GoI

[1]Sikkim joined the Indian union through a referendum in 1975 and was recognized as part of Northeast India in the 1990s.

[2]Planning Commission estimates based on Tendulkar Committee methodology.

Table 22.1 Profile of northeastern states of India

States	Geographical area ('000 ha) (2012–13)	Total population (crore)	Share of rural population (%)	GCA ('000 ha) (2012–13)	BPL population (2011–12) (%)
Arunachal Pradesh	8374	0.1	77.1	285	34.7
Assam	7844	3.1	85.9	4197	32.0
Manipur	2233	0.3	70.8	309	36.9
Meghalaya	2242.9	0.3	79.9	340	11.9
Mizoram	2108	0.1	47.9	116	20.4
Nagaland	1658	0.2	71.1	489	18.9
Sikkim	710	0.1	74.8	144	8.2
Tripura	1049	0.4	73.8	368	14.1
NER	26218.9	4.6	81.6	6246.911	28.4
All India	328,725.9	121.1	68.9	194,399	21.9

Source Land Use Statistics: Directorate of Economics and Statistics; Census 2011

2012a). Against this background, this chapter discusses agricultural growth in NER and its impact on poverty. Rest of the chapter is presented in four sections, viz. conceptual framework and methodology, performance of agriculture in NER, profile of poverty in NER vis-à-vis farm growth and conclusions and policy implications.

22.2 Conceptual Framework and Methodology

Impact of farm growth on poverty has been explored widely in the past. The benefits of farm growth reaches the poor by way of reduced food prices, increased demand for wage labour and opportunity for self-employment in rural non-farm ventures related to industry, business and services. According to Binswanger (1986), although, agricultural intensification may involve some labour-economizing innovations like mechanical threshing, new varieties of seeds and irrigation have allowed farmers to double- and even triple-crop the land, which has consistently increased labour demand. Several studies have indicated that increasing agricultural productivity in India was associated with the adoption of new technologies that increased demand for labour and majority of the additional labour used was hired rather than family labour (Lipton and Longhurst 1989; Hazell et al. 1991). Datt and Ravallion (1996) showed that in India rural sector growth has been instrumental in reducing poverty in both rural and urban areas, while economic growth in urban areas was not much effective in reducing rural poverty. Warr (2001) provided evidence that growth in agriculture in a number of South East Asian countries significantly reduced poverty, but this was not matched by growth in manufacturing. Gallup et al. (1997) showed that every 1% growth in per capita agricultural

Gross Domestic Product (GDP) led to 1.61% growth in the incomes of the poorest 20% of the population—much greater than the impact of similar increases in the manufacturing or service sectors. One of the disquieting features of Indian agriculture is the continuous subdivision and fragmentation of operational land holdings making the units uneconomical to operate.

Data used in the chapter are collected from secondary sources like Census 2011, Agricultural census 2010–11, Statistical abstracts relating to Indian Economy and States of India, CMIE, Indian Horticulture Database, 2013, Agricultural Statistics at a Glance, etc. For statistical analysis percentages, shares and Compound Annual Growth Rates (CAGR) are used.

22.3 Performance of Agriculture in the NER

22.3.1 Share of Agriculture in Total GSDP

With the growth of a country, the structure of the economy changes with lower share of primary sector in total GDP of the country. Analysis of the share of GDP from agriculture and allied sector (GSDPA) over 5-year period (2008–09 to 2013–14) shows that the theory holds good for India and NER states, except for Arunachal Pradesh, which observed marginal increase in the share of GSDPA (Table 22.2). In 2013–14 the share of GSDPA in total GDP of respective state varied widely across NER states ranging from 9% in Sikkim to 30% in Arunachal Pradesh. The share of GSDPA was more than the all India average of 13.94% in 7 out of 8 NER states signifying their dependence on agriculture. In 2013–14 NER states contributed 4% of agri and allied sector GDP in India with Assam alone contributing 56% of NER. In 2012–13 the share of NER in GCA was 3.2%, with Arunachal Pradesh having major share (69%).

During 2008–09 to 2013–14, national GDP recorded a growth of 6.7% per annum and 5 out of 8 NER states had grown above this national average (Table 22.3). Sikkim had a CAGR of 19%, which mainly attributed by growth in Industrial Sector. This is beneficial for long run sustainability of the growth process. It also marked 10% growth in agriculture sector, highest among NER states. Like the national scenario, most of the States observed relatively more growth in service sector than the other two sectors. Further, except Manipur and Assam, all NER states had higher growth rate in GSDPA than national average of 4.1%.

Table 22.2 Gross state domestic product from agri and allied sector in northeast India

States	Share of GSDP from agriculture and allied sector in total GSDP		Share in GSDPA in India (2013–14)	Share in gross cropped area in India (2012–13)
	2013–14	2008–09		
Arunachal Pradesh	30.31	29.79	0.22	0.1
Assam	20.73	23.36	2.25	2.2
Manipur	19.72	24.26	0.21	0.2
Meghalaya	15.92	18.58	0.27	0.2
Mizoram	18.07	21.74	0.13	0.1
Nagaland	25.39	28.71	0.36	0.3
Sikkim	9.48	14.4	0.07	0.1
Tripura	22.11	25.64	0.52	0.2
NER	20.59	23.66	4.02	0.1
India	13.94	15.77	100	100.0

Source CMIE—States of India—Gross State Domestic Product at Constant Prices: Base Year 2004–05: By Economic Activity (accessed on 30/06/2015)

Table 22.3 Growth of gross state domestic product from various sectors

States	Compound annual growth rate (2008–09 to 2013–14)			
	Gross domestic product	Agriculture, forestry and fishing	Industry	Services
Arunachal Pradesh	5.1	5.5	1.9	7.8
Assam	6.3	3.8	5.3	7.7
Manipur	5.8	1.5	−0.3	12.0
Meghalaya	8.2	4.9	9.2	8.7
Mizoram	8.2	4.3	2.9	11.1
Nagaland	7.5	4.9	3.8	9.7
Sikkim	19.4	9.8	33.2	7.5
Tripura	9.3	6.1	7.9	11.4
India	6.7	4.1	5.1	8.1

Source Calculated based on CMIE data base—States of India; extracted on: 30 June 2015

22.3.2 *Change in Gross Cropped Area, Net Sown Area and Cropping Intensity*

Production of agricultural crops depends on the expansion of area cultivated, i.e. net sown area, and the number of times an area is being cultivated, i.e. cropping intensity. Over a period of 9 years (i.e. 2003–04 to 2012–13), Net Sown Area (NSA) in India had reduced marginally (Table 22.4). Whereas for NER states as a

Table 22.4 Change in GCA, NSA and cropping intensity (000 Ha)

States	Years	Net sown area	Gross cropped area	Cropping intensity
Arunachal Pradesh	2003–04	201	254	126.4
	2012–13	216	285	131.7
Assam	2003–04	2753	3957	143.7
	2012–13	2811	4197	149.3
Manipur	2003–04	217	217	100.0
	2012–13	309	309	100.0
Meghalaya	2003–04	227	272	120.2
	2012–13	285	340	119.0
Mizoram	2003–04	98	98	100.0
	2012–13	116	116	100.0
Nagaland	2003–04	305	370	121.2
	2012–13	380	489	128.5
Sikkim	2003–04	78	121	155.1
	2012–13	77	144	185.7
Tripura	2003–04	280	283	101.2
	2012–13	256	368	144.1
NER	2003–04	4159 (2.96)	5573	134.0
	2012–13	4450 (3.20)	6247	140.4
All India	2003–04	140,708	189,661	134.8
	2012–13	139,932	194,399	138.9

Source Land Use Statistics at a Glance-State Wise: 2003–04 to 2012–13, Directorate of Economics and Statistics, Department of Agriculture and Cooperation, MoA, GOI
Note Figures in brackets are percentages to all India

whole it had increased over the same period, resulting in marginal increase in share of NER states in India to 3.2% in 2012–13 from 2.96% in 2003–04. Out of eight NER states, two states (Sikkim & Tripura) had decrease in NSA. Gross Cropped Area (GCA) had increased in all the NER states as also at all India level which was a combined effect of increase in NSA and cropping intensity in NER states and due to increase in cropping intensity alone at all India level.

22.3.3 *Status of Irrigation*

Among all the inputs, irrigation has most significant impact on agricultural production. Lack of irrigation also results in mono cropping or fallow land. In 2012–13, gross irrigated area as a percentage of GCA was a mere 10.3% in the NER as against all India average of 47.6%. The situation was all the more poor to notice that the percentage of irrigated area had reduced between 2003–04 and 2012–13 in NER

Table 22.5 Gross cropped area and gross irrigated area (000 Ha)

States	Years	Gross cropped area	Gross irrigated area	Percentage of gross irrigated area to gross cropped area
Arunachal Pradesh	2003–04	254	47	18.6
	2012–13	285	57	19.9
Assam	2003–04	3957	173	4.4
	2012–13	4197	160	3.8
Manipur	2003–04	217	40	18.4
	2012–13	309	49	15.7
Meghalaya	2003–04	272	82	30.3
	2012–13	340	125	36.8
Mizoram	2003–04	98	18	18.4
	2012–13	116	15	12.6
Nagaland	2003–04	370	104	28.1
	2012–13	489	92	18.9
Sikkim	2003–04	121	11	9.4
	2012–13	144	19	13.5
Tripura	2003–04	283	108	38.2
	2012–13	368	128	34.9
NER	2003–04	5573	584	10.5
	2012–13	6247	645	10.3
All India	2003–04	189,661	78,042	41.1
	2012–13	194,399	92,575	47.6

Source Land Use Statistics at a Glance-State Wise: 2003–04 to 2012–13, Directorate of Economics and Statistics, Department of Agriculture and Cooperation, MoA, GOI

as compared to an increase from 41.1 to 47.6% at all India (Table 22.5). However, 3 NER states, viz. Arunachal Pradesh, Meghalaya and Sikkim, had marked increase in the percentage of irrigated area (Fig. 22.1).

22.3.4 *Cropping Pattern*

During the period 2003–04 to 2012–13, there was shift in cropping pattern in favour of non-food crops like oilseeds and fibre crops at all India level, increasing their share in GCA from 25.1% to 28.4%. However, such shift in favour of non-food crops was marginal in the NER. What was obvious in the NER was area shift within food crops in favour of pulses, condiments and spices and more strongly towards fruits and vegetables. This reflects shift in cropping pattern as a result of the changing dietary pattern and demand for high-value food crops and can be gauged as slow transformation of NER agriculture from subsistence to market oriented (Tables 22.6 and 22.7). The share of NER states in the country in terms of

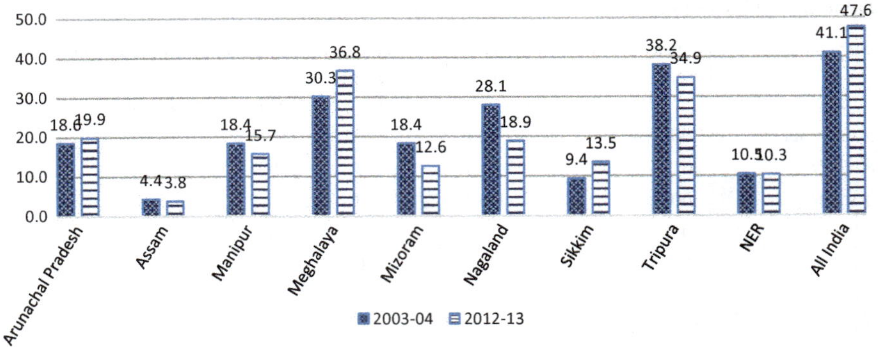

Fig. 22.1 Percentage of gross irrigated area to total cropped area. *Source* Land Use Statistics at a Glance-State Wise: 2003–04 to 2012–13, Directorate of Economics and Statistics, Department of Agriculture and Cooperation, MoA, GOI

area under fruits and Vegetables doubled (5% in 2003–04 and 10% in 2012–13). Shift in cropping pattern from food grain to high-value crops like condiments and spices and fruits and vegetables was more prominent Assam, Mizoram, Sikkim and Tripura.

Comparative analysis of share of area under food and non-food crops in gross cropped area, between two period of time, 2003–04 and 2012–13, shows that for India as a whole the share of non-food crops has increased and for NER it has increased marginally (Fig. 22.2). Further, among food crops, share of high-value crops (fruits and vegetable, condiments and spices and sugar) has increased for both India and NER.

Among NER states Manipur observed significant increase in share of non-food crop. Mizoram has experienced substantial increase in share of area under high-value food crops, which is accompanied by significant reduction in area under food grain. Other NER states like, Assam, Meghalaya, Nagaland, Sikkim and Tripura have also observed increase in relative share of area under high-value food crops.

22.3.5 Production and Yield of Agriculture Produce

Out of total food grain production of 265 million tons in 2013–14, NER states contributed 2.95% which had increased from 2.8% in 2003–04 (Table 22.8).

In 2013–14, excepting two states (Meghalaya and Tripura), all the NER states had lower than national average yield of food grains. Growth in yield of food grain from 2003–04 to 2013–14, reveals that 5 States, viz. Assam (2.7%), Arunachal Pradesh (3.5%), Meghalaya (3.3%), Nagaland (2.6%) and Tripura (2.4%) have shown above average growth rate of 2.1% at all India. However, Mizoram and Manipur, the States which had shown above average yield in 2003–04, experienced negative growth during this period.

Table 22.6 Area under food crops (000 ha)

States	Years	Cereals and millets	Pulses	Food grains	Sugar	Condiments and spices	Fruits and vegetables
Arunachal Pradesh	2003–04	184	7	191	1	7	21
	2012–13	210	9	220	2	10	20
Assam	2003–04	2628	115	2743	25	133	289
	2012–13	2550	141	2691	29	172	489
Manipur	2003–04	160	6	167	0	17	33
	2012–13	180	30	210	6	12	38
Meghalaya	2003–04	130	3	134	0	28	83
	2012–13	131	8	139	0	31	130
Mizoram	2003–04	70	5	75	1	9	4
	2012–13	31	4	35	1	19	58
Nagaland	2003–04	233	33	266	6	9	20
	2012–13	267	36	303	4	11	88
Sikkim	2003–04	65	7	72	–	32	8
	2012–13	60	6	66	–	27	43
Tripura	2003–04	261	8	268	1	–	6
	2012–13	259	8	267	1	10	73
NER	2003–04	3730 (66.9)	184 (3.3)	3914 (70.2)	35 (0.6)	234 (4.2)	463 (8.3)
	2012–13	3688 (59.0)	244 (3.9)	3932 (62.9)	43 (0.7)	291 (4.6)	939 (15.0)
All India	2003–04	100,513 (53.0)	24,458 (12.9)	124,971 (65.9)	4562 (2.4)	3195 (1.7)	9331 (4.9)
	2012–13	98,398 (50.6)	21959 (11.3)	120,357 (61.9)	5488 (2.8)	3312 (1.7)	9811 (5.0)

Source Land Use Statistics at a Glance-State Wise: 2003–04 to 2012–13, Directorate of Economics and Statistics, Department of Agriculture and Cooperation, MoA, GOI
Notes (1) '0' means area is less than 500 hectares; (2) blank space (–) denotes not available or no reporting of data from the States; (3) figures in brackets are percentages to GCA

In case of fruits and vegetables, although the area share had increased, the production share of NER states in all India declined from 5.9% in 2001–02 to 4.0% 2012–13 due to higher productivity levels in other States, resulting in lower growth in production of fruits and vegetables in NER (3.6%) compared to all India (7.2%) (Table 22.9). At all India level, growth in yield of fruits and vegetables was 1.6% per annum compared to a marginal growth rate of 0.2% in NER.

Table 22.7 Area under non-food crops (000 ha)

States	Years	Food crops	Oilseeds	Fibres	Total non-food crops	Gross cropped area
Arunachal Pradesh	2003–04	220	28	–	34	254
	2012–13	252	33	–	33	285
Assam	2003–04	3214	327	85	743	3957
	2012–13	3407	335	86	790	4197
Manipur	2003–04	216	1	–	1	217
	2012–13	265	44	–	44	309
Meghalaya	2003–04	245	10	16	28	272
	2012–13	300	14	18	40	340
Mizoram	2003–04	89	7	0	8	98
	2012–13	113	2	0	3	116
Nagaland	2003–04	301	62	4	69	370
	2012–13	407	68	5	82	489
Sikkim	2003–04	111	10	–	10	121
	2012–13	135	8	–	8	144
Tripura	2003–04	275	4	4	8	283
	2012–13	351	15	2	17	368
NER	2003–04	4672 (83.8)	450 (8.0)	109 (2.0)	901 (16.2)	5573 (100)
	2012–13	5230 (83.7)	519 (8.3)	111 (1.8)	1017 (16.3)	6247 (100)
All India	2003–04	142,129 (74.9)	26,226 (13.8)	9168 (4.8)	47,532 (25.1)	189,661 (100)
	2012–13	139,174 (71.6)	29,097 (15.0)	12,793 (6.6)	55,225 (28.4)	194,399 (100)

Source Land Use Statistics at a Glance-State Wise: 2003–04 to 2012–13, Directorate of Economics and Statistics, Department of Agriculture and Cooperation, MoA, GOI
Notes (1) 0' means area is less than 500 ha; (2) blank space (–) denotes not available or no reporting of data from the states; (3) figures in brackets are percentages to GCA

22.3.6 Distribution of Land Holdings

One of the major impediments to the growth of Indian agriculture is small and fragmented land holdings. The average size of operational land holdings in the country reduced from 2.28 ha in 1970–71 to 1.16 ha in 2010–11. In 4 out of 8 NER states, the average size of land holdings was more than national average, with Nagaland (6.03 ha) and Arunachal Pradesh (3.52 ha) having exceptionally high average where the majority of the operational holdings were concentrated in Semi-Medium and Medium categories (Table 22.10).

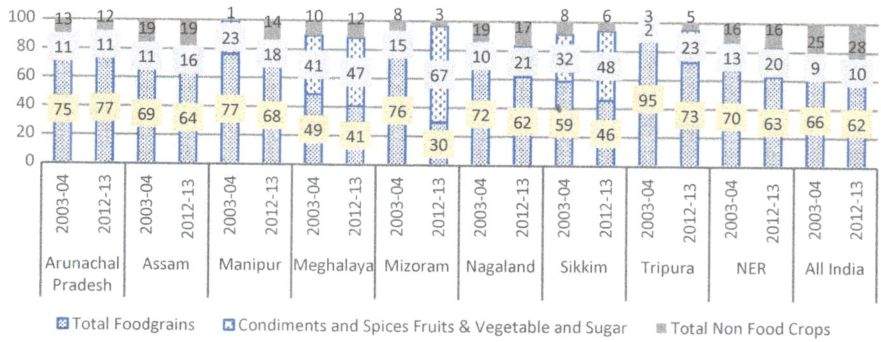

Fig. 22.2 Distribution of area under various types of food crops and non-food crops. *Source* Land Use Statistics at a Glance-State Wise: 2003–04 to 2012–13, Directorate of Economics and Statistics, Department of Agriculture and Cooperation, MoA, GOI

Table 22.8 Growth in production and yield of food grain

States	Production ('000 tonnes)			Yield (kg/ha)		
	2003–04	2013–14	Growth	2003–04	2013–14	Growth
Arunachal Pradesh	244.1	384.6	4.7	1277.3	1794.1	3.5
Assam	4035.0	5096.8	2.4	1471.6	1916.1	2.7
Manipur	391.9	490.6	2.3	2,355.2	1,745.4	−3.0
Meghalaya	233.8	320	3.2	1733.1	2387.0	3.3
Mizoram	139.4	72.8	−6.3	1853.7	1505.6	−2.1
Nagaland	409.8	624.6	4.3	1560.5	2017.8	2.6
Sikkim	99.9	102.4	0.2	1395.3	1576.7	1.2
Tripura	529.1	726.7	3.2	2120.6	2680.3	2.4
NER	6083.0 (2.8)	7817.7 (2.95)				
India	213,189.4	265,043.2	2.2	1730.0	2119.6	2.1

Source CMIE
Note Figures in parenthesis are percentage to all India

22.3.7 *Employment Scenario in Agriculture*

The percentage of rural working population depending on agriculture for employment was 72.3 at all India and 59.3 in NER. The lower percentage of rural working population in agriculture of NER was due to relatively low percentage of agricultural labourer. In all NER states, percentages of rural agricultural labourer in total rural working population are much less than the India as a whole. However, percentage of rural cultivators in total rural working population is higher than all India level in all NER states except Tripura (Fig. 22.3). One plausible inference from the employment scenario is that the agriculture in NER is mostly family labour-oriented leaving less scope for hired labour unless it is highly mechanized.

Table 22.9 Production and yield of fruits and vegetables

States	Production ('000MT)			Yield (MT/ha)		
	2001–02	2012–13	CAGR (%)	2001–02	2012–13	CAGR (%)
Arunachal Pradesh	191.0	532.0	9.8	3.7	4.9	2.7
Assam	4270.3	5488.9	2.3	12.3	12.8	0.4
Manipur	399.9	844.0	7.0	6.5	9.1	3.2
Meghalaya	231.0	553.3	8.3	7.5	7.6	0.2
Mizoram	349.4	500.7	3.3	7.7	6.6	−1.4
Nagaland	362.0	408.5	1.1	9.2	6.5	−3.1
Sikkim	94.2	61.6	−3.8	2.8	3.8	2.7
Tripura	805.3	1452.0	5.5	13.5	13.8	0.2
NER	6703.1 (5.9)	9841.0 (4.0)	3.6	10.0	10.2	0.2
India	113,547.6	243,472.0	7.2	12.6	15.0	1.6

Source Indian Horticulture Database 2013
Note Figures in parenthesis are percentages to all India

Table 22.10 Size of operational holdings in NER states

State	Average size of holdings 2010–11 (ha)					
	Marginal (<1 ha)	Small (1–2 ha)	Semi-medium (2–4 ha)	Medium (4–10 ha)	Large (>10 ha)	All
Arunachal Pradesh	0.57 (19)	1.37 (17)	2.76 (31)	5.54 (26)	13.86 (7)	3.52 (100)
Assam	0.42 (67)	1.38 (18)	2.69 (11)	5.14 (3)	Neg	1.10 (100)
Manipur	0.52 (51)	1.29 (32)	2.50 (15)	4.33 (2)	Neg	1.14 (100)
Meghalaya	0.45 (49)	1.33 (28)	2.76 (19)	5.88 (4)	Neg	1.37 (100)
Mizoram	0.60 (54)	1.27 (33)	2.40 (11)	4.50 (2)	Neg	1.14 (100)
Nagaland	0.50 (4)	1.15 (11)	2.60 (27)	6.17 (44)	17.68 (14)	6.03 (100)
Sikkim	0.38 (53)	1.18 (23)	2.45 (15)	5.33 (8)	12.00 (1)	1.43 (100)
Tripura	0.28 (86)	1.38 (10)	2.45 (3)	4.67 (1)	Neg	0.49 (100)
All India	0.39 (67)	1.42 (18)	2.71 (10)	5.76 (4)	17.38 (1)	1.16 (100)

Source Agricultural census, 2010–11, GoI
Note Figures in brackets are percentage of number of holdings

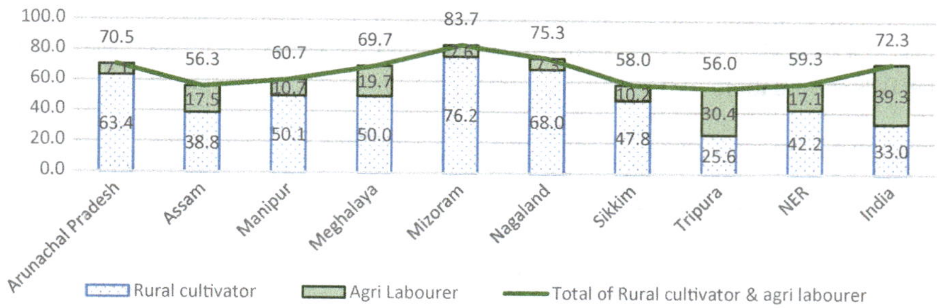

Fig. 22.3 Percentage of agri-labourers and cultivators in total rural working population. *Source* Agricultural Statistics at a Glance (2014)

22.4 Profile of Poverty in NER Vis-à-Vis Farm Growth

22.4.1 Head Count Ratio Measure of Poverty

Comparative analysis of Head Count Poverty estimated by Planning Commission for the year 2004–05 and 2011–12 showed in India percentage of population below poverty line declined from 37.2% in 2004–05 to 21.9% in 2011–12 (Table 22.11). Unlike 2004–05, in 2011–12 the poverty proportion for NER was more than national average. However, in 5 out of 8 northeast India states, the percentage of population below poverty lines was less than all India average in 2011–12.

In terms of total number of population below poverty line, Assam accounts for around 80% NER BPL population in 2011–12. Three States in NER, viz. Arunachal Pradesh, Mizoram and Nagaland had experienced increase in proportion of BPL population. In Arunachal Pradesh and Mizoram, though proportion of BPL

Table 22.11 Change in percentage of population below poverty line

States	2004–05			2011–12		
	Rural	Urban	Rural + urban	Rural	Urban	Rural + urban
Arunachal Pradesh	33.6	23.5	31.4	38.9	20.3	34.7
Assam	36.4	21.8	34.4	33.9	20.5	32.0
Manipur	39.3	34.5	37.9	38.8	32.6	36.9
Meghalaya	14.0	24.7	16.1	12.5	9.3	11.9
Mizoram	23.0	7.9	15.4	35.4	6.4	20.4
Nagaland	10.0	4.3	8.8	19.9	16.5	18.9
Sikkim	31.8	25.9	30.9	9.9	3.7	8.2
Tripura	44.5	22.5	40.0	16.5	7.4	14.1
NER	34.3	21.2	32.1	30.9	17.8	28.4
All India	41.8	25.7	37.2	25.7	13.7	21.9

Source Press note on Poverty Estimates, 2011–12: Planning Commission, July 2013

population in urban reduced, it was outweighed by rise in the proportion of BPL in rural area. On the other hand, Sikkim and Tripura observed substantial decrease in the BPL population.

22.4.2 Standard of Living of Average Agriculture Households

Monthly income and consumption level reflects the standard of living. In India, average monthly income per agricultural household during the period July 2012–June 2013 was Rs. 6426 as against monthly consumption of Rs. 6223 (Table 22.12). Per household monthly income was highest in Meghalaya and lowest in Assam and per household monthly expenditure was highest in Mizoram and lowest in Sikkim. Other than Tripura, all NER states had monthly income more than national average.

For India as a whole, income from cultivation accounts for half of the monthly income, whereas animal husbandry and non-farm sector contributing 12% and 8% of the income, respectively. The pattern is similar in all NER states except Manipur, Nagaland and Sikkim, where share of wages was more than cultivation. In Sikkim, 15% of monthly income comes from non-farm sources.

Table 22.12 Monthly income and consumption expenditure (Rs/agricultural household)

State	Net income					Consumption expenditure
	Wages	Cultivation	Animal Husbandry	NFS	Total	
Arunachal Pradesh	2076 (19.1)	6647 (61.2)	1310 (12.1)	836 (7.7)	10869 (100)	7109
Assam	1430 (21.4)	4211 (62.9)	799 (11.9)	255 (3.8)	6695 (100)	5766
Manipur	3815 (43.1)	2924 (33.1)	1563 (17.7)	540 (6.1)	8842 (100)	6490
Meghalaya	3776 (32.0)	6472 (54.9)	657 (5.6)	887 (7.5)	11792 (100)	6937
Mizoram	3655 (40.2)	4561 (50.1)	864 (9.5)	19 (0.2)	9099 (100)	7936
Nagaland	5393 (53.7)	3212 (32.0)	1384 (13.8)	59 (0.6)	10048 (100)	7285
Sikkim	3113 (45.8)	1696 (24.9)	980 (14.4)	1009 (14.8)	6798 (100)	5670
Tripura	2185 (40.2)	2772 (50.1)	311 (5.7)	162 (3.0)	5429 (100)	6922
All India	2071 (32.2)	3081 (47.9)	763 (11.9)	512 (8.0)	6426 (100)	6223

Source Key Indicators of Situation of Agricultural Households in India, NSS 70th Round, MoSPI, GoI, Dec-2014. Figures in brackets are percentages to total

Table 22.13 Deprivation in health and education

States	Infant mortality rate (per 1000 live birth)		Access to safe drinking water in rural households (%)		Rural sanitation coverage (% of hh)		Rural literacy rate (%)	
	2011	2012	2001	2011	2001	2011	2001	2011
Arunachal Pradesh	32	33	73.7	74.3	47.34	55.7	47.8	59.9
Assam	55	55	56.8	68.3	59.57	61.5	59.7	69.3
Manipur	11	10	29.3	37.5	77.5	87.7	67.3	76.2
Meghalaya	52	49	29.5	35.1	40.1	56.9	56.3	69.9
Mizoram	34	35	23.8	43.4	79.74	87.1	81.3	84.1
Nagaland	21	18	47.5	54.6	64.64	77.7	62.8	75.3
Sikkim	26	24	67.0	82.7	59.35	85.1	66.8	78.9
Tripura	29	28	45.0	58.1	77.93	84.6	69.7	84.9
All India	44	42	73.2	82.7	21.92	32.7	58.7	67.8

Source Economic Survey 2013–14; Ministry of Drinking Water & Sanitation, May 2012 Government of India

Gap in monthly income and expenditures determines the capacity of a household for investment. For India as a whole consumption constitutes 97% of income. In NER states the proportion varies from 59% (Meghalaya) to 128% (Tripura).

22.4.3 *Multi-dimensional Aspects of Poverty*

Poverty can also be described in terms of various socio-economic indicators, like Infant Mortality rate, Access to Safe drinking water, rural sanitation coverage, rural literacy, etc. In 2012 Infant Mortality Rate was highest in Assam and lowest in Manipur. In Arunachal Pradesh, the rate has increased than that in previous year (Table 22.13). The proportion of rural household with access to safe drinking water is highest in Sikkim and lowest in Meghalaya. Except Sikkim all NER states have lower proportion than India. Further, the proportion of rural household having sanitation coverage was highest in Manipur and lowest in Arunachal Pradesh. In terms of rural sanitation coverage, NER fared well than rest of the country. In terms of rural literacy, NER states (except Arunachal Pradesh) were above national average. Rural literacy was highest in Tripura (84.9%).

22.4.4 Multi-dimensional Poverty Index

Multi-dimensional Poverty Index (MPI)[3] is an international measure of acute poverty, complementing traditional income-based poverty measures by capturing the severe deprivations with respect to education, health and living standards. MPI value '0' reflects no deprivation whereas '1' reflects extreme deprivation.

In NER, six States had MPI less than national average of 0.283. Assam and Meghalaya had higher MPI than national average. The MPI is lowest in Mizoram and highest in Assam (Fig. 22.4).

22.4.5 Agriculture Vis-à-Vis Poverty in NER

The discussions on agricultural growth and its impact on poverty in NER states reveals that the generalized cause and effect relationship in terms of performance in agricultural sector and poverty are indicative but more or less conform to the hypothesis of higher agricultural growth reduces the poverty faster.

Sikkim observed highest growth (9.8%) in GSDPA in NER which had the lowest poverty ratio. Higher cropping intensity and higher proportion of area under high-value food crops were the major sources of farm growth in the state. Higher share of wages, AH and NFS in the income of agriculture household in the state was indicative of faster growing agricultural economy and exhibited a faster reduction in poverty ratio from 30.9% to 8.2% between 2004–05 and 2011–12. Tripura, registering second highest growth in GSDPA among NER states, had similar pattern of agriculture including increase in area under oilseeds. Major source of income of agriculture household in Tripura was cultivation which had contributed to reduction in poverty more significantly in rural areas. These patterns were absent in Arunachal Pradesh which had 77% of GCA under food grains with little crops diversification to high value crops. The state also observed increase in poverty, with lowest rural sanitation coverage and rural literacy and relatively higher MPI value of 0.274. Further, operational holdings in the state were more concentrated in medium and Semi-medium categories. Meghalaya, which had substantial diversification of agriculture to fruits and vegetables, showed similar correlation of high farm growth and low-poverty ratio like Sikkim and Tripura. Whereas Nagaland, which had same rate of growth in agriculture as Meghalaya, did

[3]The Global Multidimensional Poverty Index (MPI), developed in 2010 by the Oxford Poverty & Human Development Initiative and the United Nations Development Programme, uses different factors to determine poverty beyond income-based lists. It replaced the previous Human Poverty Index. The proportion of the population that is multi-dimensionally poor is the incidence of poverty, or headcount ratio (*H*). The average proportion of indicators in which poor people are deprived is described as the intensity of their poverty (*A*). The MPI is calculated by multiplying the incidence of poverty by the average intensity of poverty across the poor ($MPI = H \times A$); as a result, it reflects both the share of people in poverty and the degree to which they are deprive.

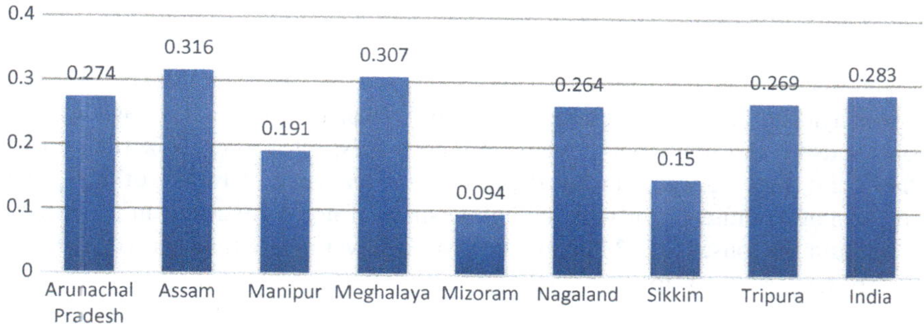

Fig. 22.4 Multi-dimensional poverty index. *Source* Oxford Poverty and Human Development Initiative (OPHI) Country Briefing June 2015: India

not experience reduction in poverty ratio, probably to be seen in the highly skewed distribution of land holdings towards medium and large farmers and consequently less inclusiveness in growth. In Assam, agricultural households had higher share and higher amount of income from cultivation which had experienced average diversification of cropping pattern to high value oilseeds, fruits and vegetables and growth of GSDPA at 3.8% which was reasonably well but lower than the all India average of 4.1%. The percentage of irrigated area was extremely low in Assam at 3.8% of GCA which could have constrained the growth of farm sector to less than potential. However, the impact on poverty was positive albeit marginally.

In Mizoram, although had good share of fruits and vegetables, the yield levels were very low and declining. The poverty ratio in the state was lower than the average at all India level and NER as a whole but had increased between 2004–05 and 2011–12 more sharply in rural poverty. The share of non-farm sector in the income of agricultural household was just 0.2%. Manipur had lowest growth of agriculture in NER and the highest poverty ratio. It had very low and declining yield level of food grains that occupied 68% of GCA.

22.5 Conclusions and Policy Implications

In the backdrop of the experience of growth in BRICS countries in terms of effectiveness of agriculture growth in reducing poverty as compared to growth in non-agricultural sectors this chapter examined effectiveness of agricultural growth in NER and its impact on poverty. State wise analysis of various agricultural parameters (viz. NSA, cropping intensity, irrigation, area, production and yield under food grains, high value crops and non-food crops, distribution of land holdings and share of agricultural labourer and cultivators) and multi-dimensional poverty indicators (viz. head count ratio, infant mortality, access to safe drinking water, coverage of rural sanitation, rural literacy, MPI, etc.) reveals that the relationship in terms of growth in agriculture (measured in terms of GSDPA) and poverty (measured in terms of head count ratio) was on the expected lines. The hypothesis of high farm growth reduced poverty was true for Sikkim, Tripura, Meghalaya and Assam. High farm growth in Arunachal Pradesh and Nagaland was non inclusive and impact on poverty was not on expected lines. Mizoram, on the other hand, had high growth but depicts overdependence of rural working population on agriculture sector with negligible share of non-farm sector in the income of agricultural households. Manipur showed the lower agricultural growth and high poverty ratio conform to the hypothesis but in inverse direction.

Agricultural performance has more impact on head count ratio than MPI. States with high farm growth, viz. Tripura, Meghalaya and Assam did not fared well in MPI values. Sikkim had exception which was caused by diversification of rural income in NFS and AH. Mizoram though had poor performance in head count ratio performed well in terms of lowest MPI. Both Arunachal Pradesh and Nagaland failed to channel high farm growth in reducing poverty, both in terms of head count ratio as well as MPI, due to non-inclusiveness of growth.

States with high share of NFS and AH in monthly income of agricultural household had improving rural poverty. States with relatively more number of populations earning livelihood from agriculture showed increase in poverty. States with higher ratio of GSDPA to GSDP have relatively high MPI values. In these states, relative share of area under food grain is diminishing and high value crops are increasing. Irrigation coverage in NER needs to be expanded as it will have positive effect in expansion of area under high value crop and positive impact in agriculture growth.

Improving performance of agriculture needs to be emphasized to reduce poverty, both incidence and intensity of poverty. Among agricultural inputs, irrigation needs to be prioritised. In northeast India, ground water resources are under-utilized while blessed with sufficient rainfall, which offers scope to install a battery of shallow and deep tube wells to draw ground water during the rabi season. Efforts are to be made to increase in production and productivity of high value crops. Northeast states have skill and raw materials to engage for self-employment in weaving, pottery, cane and bamboo products, etc., and therefore, with the development of agri sector, NFS also to be stressed upon. Instead of adopting one size fit for all approach towards poverty alleviation, state specific problems are to be addressed and benefit of comparative advantages of each state needs to be reaped.

References

Agriculture Census, 2010–11. (2012). Agriculture census division, Department of agriculture & co-operation, Ministry of Agriculture, New Delhi.

Agricultural Statistics at a Glance 2014. (2015). Oxford University Press: Delhi.

Binswanger, H. P. (1986). Agricultural mechanization: A comparative historical perspective. *The World Bank Research Observer, 1*, 27–56.

Census of India. (2011). Office of the Registrar General and Census Commissioner, New Delhi.

Centre for Monitoring Indian Economy Pvt. Ltd. (CMIE). (2015). States of India. Retrieved from: http://statesofindia.cmie.com on June30, 2015.

Datt, G., & Ravallion, M. (1996). How important to India's poor is the sectoral composition of economic growth? *The World Bank Economic Review, 10,* 1–25.

Government of India (2013–14). (2014). *Economic survey*. New Delhi: Oxford University Press.

Gallup, J., Radelet, S., & Warner, A. (1997). Economic growth and the income of the poor. CAER Discussion Paper No. 36. Harvard Institute for International Development: Cambridge, MA, USA.

Government of India. (2012a). State of Indian agriculture 2011–12. (2012). Ministry of Agriculture, New Delhi.

Government of India. (2012b). Background note and agenda for conference of state ministers and state secretaries in-charge of rural water supply and rural sanitation, Ministry of Drinking Water & Sanitation, New Delhi.

Government of India. (July, 2013). Poverty estimates for 2011–12, Press note on Poverty Estimates, 2011–12. Planning Commission, New Delhi.

Government of India. (2014). Key indicators of situation of agricultural households in India, NSS 70th Round, MoSPI, GoI, December 2014.

Hazell, P., Ramasamy, C., et al. (1991). *The green revolution reconsidered: The impact of high-yielding rice varieties in South India*. Baltimore, USA and London, UK: Johns Hopkins University Press for the International Food Policy Research Institute.

Ministry of Agriculture, National Horticulture Board, India Horticulture Database—(2013) (2014).

Ministry of Agriculture, Directorate of Economics and Statistics, Government of India. (2015). *Land use statistics*. Retrieved from http://eands.dacnet.nic.in/LUS_1999_2004.htm on July 15, 2015.

Lipton, M., & Longhurst, R. (1989). *New seeds and poor people*. London, UK: Unwin Hyman.

Oxford Poverty and Human Development Initiative (OPHI). (2015). India country briefing, multidimensional poverty index data bank. In *Oxford poverty and human development initiative*. University of Oxford.

Pocket Book on Agricultural Statistics. (2013). Ministry of Agriculture, Department of Agriculture and Cooperation, Directorate of Economics and Statistics, New Delhi.

Warr, P. (2001). *Poverty reduction and sectoral growth, results from South East Asia*. Canberra, Australia: Australia National University.

Chapter 23
Socio-Economic and Environmental Performance Across North-Eastern States of India

Rakesh Saxena

Abstract The Northeastern region of India consists of eight states—Sikkim, Assam, Arunachal Pradesh, Manipur, Meghalaya, Mizoram, Nagaland and Tripura. Their performance has similarities as well as dissimilarities under different socio-economic and environmental parameters. They have wide divergence in per capita income but by and large have low inequality in income distribution. The incidence of poverty in five of the eight states is lower than the national average. Six out of eight states have a lower infant mortality rate than the national average. Six out of eight states have a higher literacy rate than the national average. The Environmental Performance Index based on air pollution, water quality, forests, waste management and climate change varies from 0.43 to 0.75 across these states against a national average of 0.58. This chapter analyses the socio-economic and environmental performance of Northeastern states.

Keywords Income and environment · Growth and environment
Sustainable development · Environmental performance
Socio-Economic performance · Northeast India

23.1 Introduction

India is a lower middle-income country consisting of 29 states and seven Union Territories. Its per capita income was estimated as Rs. 67,839 for 2012–13 at current prices while about 22% of its population lives below poverty line (2011–12). There are wide differences in terms of different socio-economic and environmental parameters across different states and Union Territories of the country. The Northeastern region of India consists of eight states—Arunachal Pradesh, Assam, Manipur, Meghalaya, Mizoram, Nagaland, Sikkim and Tripura. This region accounts for about 8% of the total geographical area of the country and for 19% of the total

R. Saxena (✉)
Institute of Rural Management, Anand 388001, Gujarat, India
e-mail: rakesh@irma.ac.in

U.K. De et al. (eds.), *Inequality, Poverty and Development in India*, India Studies in Business and Economics, DOI 10.1007/978-981-10-6274-2_23

forest area but only for about 4% of the total population. This chapter attempts to analyse socio-economic and environmental performance across the eight states of the region as well as for the region as a whole against the national performance. The data available from different secondary sources has been used for analysis.

The second section of the chapter looks into the distribution of geographical area and land use in the region. The third section analyses the data available on demographic profile and health in the region. The fourth section assesses income and growth. The fifth section analyses inequality in income distribution through Lorenz ratios (Gini coefficients). The sixth section analyses the changes in the incidence of poverty. The seventh section analyses the housing conditions, basic amenities and ownership of assets to look into some additional dimensions of poverty. The eighth section analyses environmental performance and locates it in the context of economic performance. The ninth section does an exploratory correlation analysis between different economic and environmental indicators. The final section makes the concluding remarks.

23.2 Geographical Area and Land Use

We may first look at the share of the Northeastern region in the land use at the national level. As shown in Table 23.1, the region accounts for 8% of the total geographical area of the country. It accounts for relatively much larger proportions of the national forest area (19.1%) and the national area under miscellaneous tree crops and groves (17.7%). Due to this and other land use, the share of the region in the net sown area of the country is relatively very low (3.2%). It indicates limited opportunities for agriculture in the region. This situation becomes more contrasting when we look at the proportionate land use within the northeast region. More than half (57.3%) of the reporting area of the region is under forests while it is only less than one-fourth (22.9%) at the national level. On the other hand, less than one-fifth of the reporting area of the region is as net sown area compared to close to half (45.7%) of the reporting area being available for this purpose at the national level.

There are large variations in terms of land use across individual states of the region. Arunachal Pradesh and Assam are the two largest states accounting together for 62% of the total geographical area (GA) of the region. Sikkim, on the other hand, is the smallest state in the region with only about 3% of the total GA of the region. Tripura and Nagaland account for four to 6% each of the total GA of the region. Mizoram, Manipur and Meghalaya account for eight to 9% each of the total GA of the region.

Each Northeastern state, except Assam, has a very large proportion of its reporting area under forests, varying from 42% in Meghalaya to as high as 91% in Arunachal Pradesh. The percentage of the reporting area under forests in Assam is very close to the national average. Accordingly, the proportion of the net sown area is the highest in Assam (35.8%) and lowest in Arunachal Pradesh (3.8%). Mizoram

Table 23.1 Geographical Area and Land Use, 2012–13

S. No	Northeastern states	Geographical area (000 ha)	% of total GA of northeast region	Reporting area as % of geog. area	% of reporting area								
					Forests	Non-agricultural use	Barren & uncultivable	Permanent pastures & other grazing land	Misc. tree crops and groves	Cultivable waste land	Permanent fallow	Current fallow	Net sown area
1.	Arunachal Pradesh	8374	31.9	67.6	91.0	0.5	0.7	0.3	0.6	1.1	1.2	0.7	3.8
2.	Assam	7844	29.9	100.1	23.6	15.4	17.9	2.0	2.5	1.0	0.7	1.0	35.8
3.	Meghalaya	2243	8.6	99.9	42.2	4.8	5.9	0.0	7.3	17.4	6.9	2.7	12.7
4.	Manipur	2233	8.5	93.4	83.5	1.2	0.0	0.0	0.3	0.0	0.0	0.0	14.8
5.	Mizoram	2108	8.0	99.3	75.7	4.2	0.4	0.2	2.0	0.3	9.3	2.4	5.5
6.	Nagaland	1658	6.3	99.6	52.2	5.6	0.1	0.0	5.7	4.2	6.0	3.0	23.0
7.	Tripura	1049	4.0	100.0	60.0	13.4	0.0	0.2	1.3	0.4	0.2	0.2	24.4
8.	Sikkim	710	2.7	97.6	84.3	1.6	0.0	0.0	1.2	0.4	0.6	0.7	11.1
Northeast region		26,219	100.0	89.0	57.3	7.3	6.8	0.8	2.4	2.6	2.5	1.2	19.1
All India		328,726	–	93.1	22.9	8.6	5.6	3.3	1.0	4.1	3.6	5.0	45.7
% share of northeast region in India		8.0	–	7.6	19.1	6.4	9.2	1.8	17.7	4.9	5.2	1.9	3.2

Note The states are arranged in descending order of the total geographical area of each state
Source Government of India (http://www.indiaagristat.com)

is another state with a very low proportion of the net sown area (5.5%). In Sikkim, Meghalaya and Manipur, this proportion varies from 11 to 15%. In Nagaland and Tripura, this proportion is 23 to 24%.

23.3 Demographic Profile and Health

As in case of land distribution and use, there is a very uneven distribution of population across the northeastern states (Table 23.2). As per 2011 Census, the Northeast region accounted for only 3.76% of the total human population of the country. More than two-thirds of this population is confined to only one state of the region, namely, Assam. Sikkim, Mizoram and Arunachal Pradesh have the smallest populations accounting only for one to 3% share each in the population of the region. Nagaland, Manipur, Meghalaya and Tripura are in between with their population shares in the region as four to 8%.

While the population density of more than 300 persons per sq km in Assam and Tripura is close to the national average, it is much lower in other states of the region varying from mere 17 in Arunachal Pradesh to 132 in Meghalaya. All northeastern states except Nagaland have shown a positive growth in population during 2001–11. In Nagaland, the total population has decreased during the decade, 2001–11. While the overall decadal growth rate of the Northeast region is very similar to the national average, it varies from −0.6% in Nagaland to 27.9% in Meghalaya.

The sex ratio (number of females per 1000 males) of 960 in the region is higher than the national average of 943. It is the lowest at 890 in Sikkim and the highest at 992 in Manipur. Besides Sikkim, the two other states in the region with the sex ratio lower than the national average are Nagaland and Arunachal Pradesh. The proportion of the population living in urban areas is very high in some of the northeastern states like Mizoram (99.4%) and Manipur (64.9%). At the same time, it is very low in some other states of the region like Assam (13.2%), Sikkim (18.3%) and Meghalaya (23.6%). The average of the region in this regard at 22.4% is lower than the national average of 31.2%.

The average literacy rate in the region (74.6%) is slightly higher than the national average (73%). The rate varies from 65.4% in Arunachal Pradesh to 91.3% in Mizoram. The proportion of ST people in the region (27.3%) is very high compared to the national average (8.6%). In states like Mizoram, Nagaland and Meghalaya, this proportion is as high as 86–94%. The proportion of the SC population, on the other hand, is very low in the region (6.7%) compared to the national average (16.6%).

The Infant Mortality Rate (IMR) indicating the death rate in the age group of 0–1 year per 1000 live births is an important health indicator. The average IMR for the country has been estimated as 42. The average IMR is higher in Assam (55) and Meghalaya (49) compared to the national average showing relatively worse health situation in these states. In other states of the region, it is lower than the national

Table 23.2 Population, literacy and infant mortality rate

S. No	Northeastern states	Population, 2011 (No. of persons)	Pop. share in northeastR (%)	Pop. share in India (%)	Pop. density per sq km	Pop. growth 2001–11 (%)	Sex ratio	Urban population (%)	Literacy rate (%)	SC population (%)	ST population (%)	IMR, 2012
1.	Assam	31,205,576	68.6	2.6	398	17.1	958	13.2	72.2	7.2	12.4	55
2.	Tripura	3,673,917	8.1	0.3	350	14.8	960	29.7	87.2	17.8	31.8	28
3.	Meghalaya	2,966,889	6.5	0.2	132	27.9	989	23.6	74.4	0.6	86.1	49
4.	Manipur	2,570,390	5.7	0.2	115	18.6	992	64.9	79.2	3.8	35.1	10
5.	Nagaland	1,978,502	4.3	0.2	119	−0.6	931	39.5	79.6	0.0	86.5	18
6.	Arunachal P	1,383,727	3.0	0.1	17	26.0	938	43.6	65.4	0.0	68.8	33
7.	Mizoram	1,097,206	2.4	0.1	52	23.5	976	99.4	91.3	0.1	94.4	35
8.	Sikkim	610,577	1.3	0.1	86	12.9	890	18.3	81.4	4.6	33.8	24
Northeast region		45,486,784	100.0	3.8	175	17.1	960	22.4	74.6	6.7	27.3	–
All India		1,210,569,573	–	100.0	382	17.7	943	31.2	73.0	16.6	8.6	42

Note The states are arranged in the descending order of the total population of each state

Source Government of India (2014, July, pp. 217, 308–311)

NER Northeast Region, *IMR* Infant Mortality Rate, Sex ratio = Females per 1000 males

average showing a relatively better health situation in these states. The rate is the lowest in Manipur (10) and Nagaland (18). In the remaining four states, it varies from 24 to 35.

23.4 Income and Growth

23.4.1 Per Capita Income

The average per capita income measured through average Per Capita Net State Domestic Product (PCNSDP) was estimated as Rs. 24,143 for 2004–05 at all India level (Table 23.3). It grew to Rs. 38,856 in 2012–13 at constant prices (2004–05) indicating an average Compound Annual Growth Rate (CAGR) of 6.13% during this period of eight years. The highest per capita income for 2012–13 was recorded by Goa (Rs. 1,45,923) and the lowest by Bihar (Rs. 14,904) showing a vast difference in income across different states and Union Territories of India.

Sikkim has recorded the highest per capita income (Rs. 75,317) among northeastern states for 2012–13 and Assam the lowest (Rs. 23,448). Sikkim is counted among the high per capita income states of the country with fifth rank across the states and UTs in 2012–13. Nagaland is the distant second state among northeastern states in terms of per capita income, ranking 15th at all India level. Nagaland, Tripura, Mizoram, Meghalaya and Arunachal Pradesh may be considered together

Table 23.3 Per capita income and its growth

S. No	Northeastern states	PCNSDP at 2004–05 prices (Rs)		PCNSDP 2012–13 at current prices (Rs)	CAGR 2004–05 to 2012–13 (%)	National Rank[a]	
		2004–05	2012–13			PCNSDP 2012–13 at 2004–05 prices	CAGR 2004–05 to 2012–13
1.	Sikkim	26,690	75,137	142,625	13.81	2	1
2.	Nagaland	30,441	46,889	65,908	5.55	11	19
3.	Tripura	24,394	42,315	60,963	7.13	14	10
4.	Mizoram	24,662	40,930	60,836	6.54	15	12
5.	Meghalaya	24,086	38,627	59,513	6.08	16	14
6.	Arunachal Pradesh	26,610	37,051	78,145	4.22	17	27
7.	Manipur	18,640	23,996	36,474	3.21	25	28
8.	Assam	16,782	23,448	40,475	4.27	26	25
All India		24,143	38,856	67,839	6.13	–	–

Note The states are arranged in descending order of per capita income, 2012–13 at 2004–05 prices
Source Government of India (2014, July, pp. 172–173)
PCNSDP Per Capita Net State Domestic Product, *CAGR* Compound Annual Growth Rate
[a]Based on 28 states (no separate data for Telangana; seven UTs not included in ranking)

as the middle group of states among northeastern states with their per capita incomes ranging from Rs. 37,051 to Rs. 46,889 for 2012–13. Manipur and Assam may be considered together at the bottom of northeastern states in terms of per capita income. These two states, however, ranked above Uttar Pradesh and Bihar in terms of their per capita income at all India level.

Half of the northeastern states, namely, Sikkim, Nagaland, Tripura and Mizoram, had a per capita income above the national average while the other four states, namely, Meghalaya, Arunachal Pradesh, Manipur and Assam, had their per capita income below the national average. Sikkim has recorded an impressive annual growth rate of about 14% in its per capita income during 2004–05 to 2012–13. The only other two states that had a growth rate higher than the national average were Tripura and Mizoram. The annual growth rate in the remaining five states varied from 3.21 to 6.08%, below the national average of 6.13%.

23.4.2 Sectoral Contribution

The Gross State Domestic Product (GSDP) may be attributed to three main sectors, namely, Agriculture and Allied, Industry, and Services. At the national level, Agriculture and Allied, Industry, and Services sectors contributed 13.95, 27.27, and 58.79% to the Gross Domestic Product in 2012–13 (Table 23.4). Comparing these shares with those in 2004–05, it is clear that while the contribution of Agriculture and Allied sector to GDP has gone down, the contribution of Services sector has gone up. There is not much change in the percentage contribution of the industry sector at the national level.

At the level of northeastern states, it may be seen in Table 23.4 that the contribution of Agriculture and Allied sector to GSDP has come down uniformly in case of each state. Barring Sikkim, Meghalaya and Arunachal Pradesh where the contribution of Industry sector to GSDP has gone up, the share of even industry sector in GSDP during 2004–05 to 2012–13 has gone down. It is the Services sector whose share in GDP has gone up in case of all northeastern states except Sikkim. The contribution of industry sector to GSDP of Sikkim has gone up from 28.87 to 58.9%.

The Compounded Annual Growth Rate (CAGR) of the Gross State Domestic Product (GSDP) of Northeast region has been estimated as 6.73% which is slightly lower than the national average of 7.96%. However, the growth rate has varied across different northeast states from 5.52% (Manipur) to 15.46% (Sikkim). Only Sikkim and Mizoram have recorded a growth rate which is higher than the national average.

Table 23.4 Sectoral shares in gross state domestic product (GSDP)

S. No	Northeastern states	Sectoral share in GSDP (%)						CAGR of GSDP (%)			
		2004–05			2012–13			By sector			Overall
		Agri. & allied	Industry	Services	Agri. & allied	Industry	Services	Agri. & allied	Industry	Services	
1.	Sikkim	18.57	28.87	52.56	8.07	58.90	33.04	4.03	26.22	8.95	15.46
2.	Nagaland	34.75	12.88	52.35	26.27	12.71	61.03	3.90	7.43	9.68	7.60
3.	Tripura	25.07	24.25	50.69	24.33	20.29	55.37	8.02	6.03	9.62	8.42
4.	Mizoram	23.49	16.59	59.88	17.71	16.48	65.79	5.28	8.97	10.36	9.07
5.	Meghalaya	23.25	26.15	50.62	16.42	29.30	54.28	3.21	9.34	8.74	7.80
6.	Arunachal Pradesh	35.09	31.91	32.97	28.38	33.34	38.28	3.94	7.33	8.75	6.74
7.	Manipur	24.74	36.66	38.59	18.60	27.84	53.56	1.83	1.95	9.94	5.52
8.	Assam	25.57	27.54	46.89	21.53	21.59	56.88	3.51	2.60	8.35	5.77
Northeast region		26.09	26.52	47.39	21.25	23.44	55.31	4.03	5.09	8.81	6.73
All India		19.03	27.93	53.05	13.95	27.27	58.79	3.84	7.64	9.35	7.96

Note The states are arranged in descending order of per capita income, 2012–13 at 2004–05 prices
Source Government of India (2014, July, pp. 67–84)

23.5 Inequality in Income Distribution

Inequality in income distribution is measured by the Lorenz ratio (Gini coefficient) that can take a value from zero to one. Its value as zero shows perfect equality in income distribution while its value as one shows perfect inequality in income distribution. The estimated values of Lorenz ratio for northeastern states and India for the years 2004–05, 2009–10 and 2011–12 are given in Table 23.5.

The all India Lorenz ratios for rural and urban areas indicate greater inequality in income distribution in urban areas as compared to rural areas in each given year. These figures also show a rise in inequality in rural areas from 2004–05 to 2009–10 and from 2009–10 to 2011–12. In urban areas, the inequality rose from 2004–05 to 2009–10 but declined from 2009–10 to 2011–12. The same pattern is observed with respect to the comparison between urban and rural areas of individual northeastern states, except in the case of Arunachal Pradesh and Sikkim. In Arunachal Pradesh, the Lorenz ratios are found higher for rural areas compared to urban areas. In Sikkim, there is a mixed picture in this regard.

The extent of inequality in income distribution in each northeastern state, except Arunachal Pradesh, is lower than the national average. In Arunachal Pradesh, exceptions exist for rural areas during 2009–10 and 2011–12. In 2011–12, the lowest inequalities in both rural and urban areas were observed in Meghalaya, Nagaland, Sikkim and Manipur.

Table 23.5 Lorenz ratios for northeastern states and India, 2004–05, 2009–10 and 2011–12

S. No	Northeastern states	Rural			Urban		
		2004–05	2009–10	2011–12	2004–05	2009–10	2011–12
1.	Arunachal Pradesh	0.2401	0.2933	0.3345	0.2132	0.2991	0.3097
2.	Assam	0.1820	0.2199	0.2108	0.3010	0.3275	0.3447
3.	Manipur	0.1362	0.1591	0.1928	0.1488	0.1925	0.1988
4.	Meghalaya	0.1363	0.1703	0.1723	0.2403	0.2428	0.2278
5.	Mizoram	0.1665	0.1941	0.2434	0.2132	0.2283	0.2446
6.	Nagaland	0.1729	0.1814	0.1915	0.2136	0.2221	0.2277
7.	Sikkim	0.2358	0.2593	0.1927	0.2317	0.1861	0.1980
8.	Tripura	0.2034	0.1969	0.2074	0.2996	0.2876	0.2920
All India		0.2655	0.2758	0.2803	0.3475	0.3706	0.3673

Note The states in the table are arranged simply in alphabetical order
Source Government of India (2014, July, p.102)

23.6 Incidence of Poverty

The number of people living below poverty line has been estimated at 21.9% in India for 2011–12 (Table 23.6). This proportion ranges from 5.1% in Goa to 39.9% in Chhattisgarh. The average incidence of poverty in Northeast India estimated at 28.5% is higher than the national average. The incidence in northeastern states, however, varies from as low as 8.2% in Sikkim to as high as 36.9% in Manipur. Sikkim, Meghalaya, Tripura, Nagaland and Mizoram have a lower incidence than the national average while Assam, Arunachal Pradesh and Manipur have a higher incidence than the national average. In general, rural areas show higher incidence of poverty than the urban areas. However, there are exceptions to this like in case of Meghalaya (2004–05 and 2009–10) and Nagaland (2009–10).

The incidence of poverty has consistently declined in India during 2004–05 to 2011–12. In case of Northeast India as a whole, the incidence of poverty rose from 2004–05 to 2009–10 and declined from 2009–10 to 2011–12. Individually, it is only Sikkim and Tripura among northeastern states that show the consistent decline in poverty as shown at national level. The rest of northeast states show mixed pattern.

23.7 Housing Conditions, Basic Amenities and Ownership of Asset

Housing conditions, availability of basic amenities and ownership of assets show some additional dimensions of poverty. This section uses the information available on roof materials, sources of lighting, types of cooking fuels, sources of drinking water, availability of latrine facility and ownership of assets for assessing the relative position of northeastern states.

23.7.1 Roof Material

Normally, the type of roof material indicates the economic condition of a household. However, there may be exceptions when the choice of roof material is based more on considerations like earthquakes, type of terrain, climate, etc., than the economic condition of the household. Some available information on the use of roof materials is presented in Table 23.7. Out of the given roof materials, GI/metal/asbestos sheets and concrete appear to be stronger, more durable, more protective and more expensive. About 78% households in Northeast region have used these materials for roof making compared to only 45% households doing so at the national level.

Table 23.6 Percentage of population below poverty line

S. No	Northeastern states	Rural			Urban			Overall			National rank[a] 2011–12
		2004–2005	2009–2010	2011–2012	2004–2005	2009–2010	2011–2012 3.7	2004–2005	2009–2010	2011–2012	
1.	Sikkim	31.8	15.5	9.9	25.9	5.0		30.9	13.1	8.2	4
2.	Meghalaya	14.0	15.3	12.5	24.7	24.1	9.3	16.1	17.1	11.9	11
3.	Tripura	44.5	19.8	16.5	22.5	10.0	7.4	40.0	17.4	14.1	12
4.	Nagaland	10.0	19.3	19.9	4.3	25.0	16.5	8.8	20.9	18.9	16
5.	Mizoram	23.0	31.1	35.4	7.9	11.5	6.4	15.4	21.1	20.4	18
6.	Assam	36.4	39.9	33.9	21.8	26.1	20.5	34.4	37.9	32.0	22
7.	Arunachal Pradesh	33.6	26.2	38.9	23.5	24.9	20.3	31.4	25.9	34.7	25
8.	Manipur	39.3	47.4	38.8	34.5	46.4	32.6	37.9	47.1	36.9	26
Northeast India		34.3	35.6	30.9	21.2	24.6	17.5	32.1	33.6	28.5	–
All India		41.8	33.8	25.7	25.7	20.9	13.7	37.2	29.8	21.9	–

Note States are arranged in ascending order of the overall incidence of poverty in 2011–12
Source Government of India (2014, June, pp. 29–31)
[a]Based on 28 states (no separate data for Telangana; seven UTs not included in ranking)

Table 23.7 Percentage of households by predominant material of roof, 2011

S. No	State	Grass/thatch/bamboo/wood etc.	Plastic/polythene	Tiles	Brick	Stone/slate	GI/metal/asbestos sheets	Concrete	Any other
1.	Sikkim	5.8	1.0	0.3	0.4	1.1	68.2	23.1	0.1
2.	Tripura	11.8	0.5	0.5	0.6	0.8	81.4	4.2	0.2
3.	Meghalaya	16.0	1.0	0.7	0.4	1.7	69.1	10.3	0.7
4.	Manipur	17.5	0.2	0.9	0.5	2.0	74.2	4.7	0.1
5.	Mizoram	17.6	0.5	0.2	0.1	1.0	66.8	13.7	0.1
6.	Assam	18.6	2.1	1.0	0.1	0.8	74.2	2.9	0.2
7.	Nagaland	18.9	0.4	0.4	0.2	1.5	72.6	5.6	0.3
8.	Arunachal Pradesh	46.7	0.5	0.5	0.2	0.9	46.2	3.9	1.1
Northeastern region		18.4	1.6	0.9	0.2	1.0	73.4	4.2	0.2
All India		15.1	0.6	23.8	6.6	8.6	15.9	29.1	0.4

Note States are arranged in ascending order of proportion of grass/thatch/bamboo/wood etc
Source Government of India (2014, July, p. 328)
GI Galvanized Iron

At the level of individual northeastern states, Sikkim and Tripura are at the top in using these materials as 91 and 86% of the households, respectively, have used these materials for their roofs. The proportion of the households that have used these materials is the lowest at 50% in Arunachal Pradesh. It may be noted here that Sikkim and Tripura are among the top three northeast states in terms of least incidence of poverty while Arunachal Pradesh is among the bottom two northeast states in terms of highest incidence of poverty.

Compared to the above and other listed materials, grass/thatch/bamboo/wood/plastic/polythene, etc., appear to be less protective, less durable and less expensive. About 16% households at the national level and 20% in Northeast India have used these materials for their roof making. Sikkim and Tripura are at the top having only 7–12% of their households using these roof materials. Arunachal Pradesh is at the bottom as about 47% of its households have used these materials. Other notheast states are in between with 17 and 21% of their households having used these roof materials.

It shows that while a much larger proportion of households in northeast region have used the best materials for roof making compared to that at the national level, the proportion of the households at the other end using the worst materials is only slightly higher in northeast region compared to the national average. The use of better materials also seems to be positively associated with higher income.

23.7.2 Source of Lighting

Table 23.8 shows that about 48% households in northeast region use electricity as the source of light which is much lower as compared to the national average. Also, about 50% of the households in northeast region still use kerosene as the source of light which is much higher as compared to the national average. The use of renewable sources of energy like solar energy for lighting and the proportion of households with no lighting are extremely low at both the levels.

Across individual northeast states, the use of Kerosene is the highest in Assam where about 62% of the households use it as the source of light. Sikkim tops the list in terms of use of electricity as more than 92% households in the state use it as the source of light. Only about 7% of the households in Sikkim use kerosene as the source of light. The use of solar energy as the source of light is the highest in Arunachal Pradesh and lowest in Sikkim. While the proportion of the households with no source of light is close to 1% or less in all other northeast states, it is as high as 10.5% in Arunachal Pradesh.

It seems from the above comparisons that the level of income plays an important role in opting for better sources of light.

Table 23.8 Percentage of households using different sources of lighting, 2011

S. No	States	Electricity	Kerosene	Solar energy	Other oil	Any other	No lighting
1.	Sikkim	92.5	6.6	0.2	0.1	0.1	0.5
2.	Mizoram	84.2	13.5	1.3	0.3	0.3	0.3
3.	Nagaland	81.6	15.6	0.3	0.2	1.1	1.1
4.	Tripura	68.4	29.1	1.9	0.2	0.0	0.3
5.	Manipur	68.4	25.1	1.9	0.4	3.6	0.6
6.	Arunachal Pradesh	65.7	18.5	2.9	0.3	2.1	10.5
7.	Meghalaya	60.9	37.0	0.8	0.3	0.2	0.8
8.	Assam	37.1	61.8	0.8	0.1	0.1	0.2
Northeastern region		47.7	50.2	1.0	0.2	0.4	0.6
All India		67.3	31.4	0.4	0.2	0.2	0.5

Note States are arranged in descending order of proportion of households using electricity as the source of light
Source Government of India (2014, July, p.334)

23.7.3 Type of Cooking Fuel

The type of cooking fuel used by the households indicates the level of convenience in cooking as well as health and environmental implications. Table 23.9 shows the percentage distribution of households by the type of cooking fuels used by them. It can be seen from this table that the predominant cooking fuel in northeastern states is still firewood as about 72% households are reported to be using it. At the national level, on an average, only 49% of the households use firewood as cooking fuel. The use of firewood is reported to cause various respiratory and eye related health issues. The second most important cooking fuel is LPG which is used by about 20% households in northeast states and by about 29% households at all India level. LPG is considered as a clean and convenient cooking fuel. The rest of the households use other cooking fuels like crop residues, dung cakes, coal, lignite, charcoal, etc. Many of these fuels also create the same health and environmental issues as firewood.

Across different northeast states, Mizoram and Sikkim are the highest users of LPG and the lowest users of other cooking fuels including firewood. Their positions at the top seem to be a result of their levels of income, population and urbanisation. It was observed earlier that Mizoram is only somewhere in the middle of the list of northeast states with respect to per capita income, inequality of income distribution and incidence of poverty but at the top in terms of urbanisation (almost 100%) and at the bottom with Sikkim in terms of population. Sikkim, on the other hand, has highest per capita income, lowest inequality and incidence of poverty, and very low urbanisation. In the remaining northeast states, the proportion of the household using LPG varies from about 12 to 30%.

Table 23.9 Percentage distribution of households by use of cooking fuels, 2011

S. No	States	LPG	Firewood	Crop residues	Cow dung cakes	Coal/ lignite/charcoal/	Any other	No cooking
1.	Mizoram	52.6	44.5	0.3	0.1	2.2	0.4	0.1
2.	Sikkim	41.3	52.5	0.6	0.2	4.5	0.4	0.6
3.	Manipur	29.7	65.7	1.1	0.2	2.3	0.9	0.1
4.	Arunachal Pradesh	29.2	68.7	0.7	0.1	0.7	0.3	0.3
5.	Nagaland	20.0	77.9	0.8	0.1	0.6	0.3	0.2
6.	Assam	19.0	72.1	6.4	0.9	0.7	0.6	0.4
7.	Tripura	17.6	80.5	0.8	0.1	0.7	0.2	0.1
8.	Meghalaya	11.9	79.0	0.9	0.3	6.0	1.9	0.2
Northeast region		20.5	72.1	4.7	0.7	1.2	0.6	0.3
All India		28.6	49.0	8.9	8.0	4.4	1.0	0.3

Note States are listed in descending order of LPG use
Source Government of India (2014, July, p. 336)

23.7.4 Location of Source of Drinking Water and Availability of Latrine Facility

Availability of drinking water and latrine facility within or near the premises is a great convenience. As shown in Table 23.10, about 82% of the households in India have the sources of drinking water available within or near the premises while the rest of them have to fetch drinking water from the sources located away from the premises. In case of northeast region, the proportion of the households that have to fetch water from the sources located away from the premises is higher at about 22%. That is, the proportion of the people who face hardships in collection of water is higher in the northeast region.

The status about the availability of latrine facility is far better in northeast region compared to that at the national level. About 69% of the households in northeast region have latrine facility within the premises compared to 47% at the national level. Only 28% of the households in northeast region defecate in open compared to 50% at the national level. Within the northeast region, Assam, Sikkim, Arunachal Pradesh and Mizoram have relatively better access to drinking water. Mizoram, Manipur, Sikkim and Tripura have better availability of latrine facilities.

23.7.5 Ownership of Assets

The ownership of certain assets helps in communication, awareness and travel which in turn may improve the quality of life and livelihood. The ownership pattern of some such assets is shown in Table 23.11. The table shows that about 18% of the

Table 23.10 Percentage of households by location of source of drinking water and availability of latrine facility, 2011

S. No	State eastern	Sources of drinking water			Availability of latrine facility			
		Within premises	Near the premises	Away	Within the premises	Not within the premises		
						Public latrine	Open	Total
1.	Assam	54.8	26.7	18.5	64.9	1.9	33.2	35.1
2.	Sikkim	52.6	29.7	17.7	87.2	1.5	11.3	12.8
3.	Arunachal Pradesh	41.1	37.4	21.6	62.0	3.2	34.8	38.0
4.	Tripura	37.1	30.5	32.4	86.0	2.5	11.5	14.0
5.	Mizoram	31.2	46.7	22.2	91.9	1.5	6.6	8.1
6.	Nagaland	29.3	42.4	28.3	76.5	7.0	16.5	23.5
7.	Meghalaya	24.1	43.2	32.7	62.9	2.8	34.3	37.1
8.	Manipur	16.1	46.2	37.8	89.3	1.8	8.9	10.7
Northeast region		47.2	30.6	22.2	69.4	2.2	28.3	30.6
All India		46.6	35.8	17.6	46.9	3.2	49.8	53.1

Note The states are arranged in descending order as per source of drinking water within the premises
Source Government of India (2014, July, p. 332–333)

households do not own any of these assets at all India level. The proportion of such households is higher at about 25% in the northeast region. It is further higher at 31–36% in Meghalaya, Nagaland and Arunachal Pradesh. It is the lowest at 17–19% in Manipur, Sikkim and Mizoram. Regarding the type of assets, larger differences between the national average and the lower averages for northeast region are observed in case of the ownership of televisions, telephone/mobile and motorised two wheelers.

23.7.6 Overall

The northeast region enjoys a better status with respect to quality of roof material and the availability of latrine facilities compared to the national average status. The region has a lower status with respect to sources of light, cooking fuels, sources of drinking water and ownership of assets compared to the national average status. Across individual northeastern states, Sikkim enjoys the highest or the second highest status with respect to all the above parameters except the availability of latrine facility for which it has the third highest status. It is usually one of the lowest per capita income states, namely, Assam, Manipur, Arunachal Pradesh and Meghalaya, that has the lowest status with respect to these parameters.

Table 23.11 Percentage of households having assets, 2011

S. No	North-	Radio/transister	Television	Computer/laptop	Telephone/mobile	Bicycle	Scooter/motor cycle/moped	Car/jeep/van	None of these assets
1.	Manipur	54.4	47.4	9.1	57.5	44.6	19.8	6.0	17.2
2.	Sikkim	23.0	54.7	11.5	73.0	0.9	2.8	8.3	18.2
3.	Mizoram	33.5	55.1	15.2	72.7	4.3	13.8	7.3	19.0
4.	Assam	22.1	27.5	9.4	47.9	55.0	10.2	3.8	23.6
5.	Tripura	12.8	44.9	7.3	48.1	39.3	8.2	2.2	27.8
6.	Arunachal Pradesh	22.0	41.1	8.2	48.3	19.5	14.0	7.9	30.7
7.	Nagaland	25.0	37.9	8.9	53.1	7.9	6.3	7.8	32.3
8.	Meghalaya	25.2	33.7	7.6	43.0	13.3	5.4	5.4	35.8
All northeast states		23.6	32.4	9.2	49.3	45.6	10.2	4.3	24.7
India		19.9	47.2	9.5	63.2	44.8	21.0	4.7	17.8

Note The states are listed in ascending order of the proportion of the households owning none of these assets
Source Government of India (2014, July, p. 337)

23.8 Environmental Performance

The Planning Commission of India, now restructured as NITI Aayog, developed an index for estimating environmental performance across different states and Union Territories of India (Chandrasekharan et al. 2013). This index, known as the Planning Commission-Environmental Performance Index (PC-EPI), is based on five indicators, namely, (1) air quality, (2) water quality, (3) forests, (4) waste management and (5) climate change. There are a total of 16 sub-indicators under the above five indicators. The value of a single sub-indicator, based on deviation from the prescribed national standard or national average, varies from zero (lowest performance) to one (highest performance). The average score at any level is based on a simple average. The environmental performance of the above five indicators is shown in Table 23.12 for the year 2012, in decreasing order of the EPI across northeastern states.

As per the EPI, four of the northeast states, namely, Sikkim, Meghalaya, Mizoram and Assam, are ranked above the national average while the remaining four are placed below the national average. Sikkim indicates the highest EPI while Arunachal Pradesh shows the lowest EPI among the northeast states. Seven of the northeast states show better performance than the national average with respect to climate change and water, six with respect to air pollution, and three with respect to forests and waste management. Sikkim and Mizoram have the perfect score of 1.00 on air pollution. Though Arunachal Pradesh is the lowest placed northeast state on overall EPI, it scores perfect 1.00 on performance regarding forests.

It is very encouraging to note that Sikkim is at the top of northeast states not only with respect to per capita income and proportion of people above the poverty line but also with respect to environmental performance. On the other hand, Arunachal

Table 23.12 Planning commission—environmental performance index, 2012

S. No	State	Scores (0–1)					EPI (0–1)	National rank as per EPI[a]
		Air pollution	Water	Forests	Waste management	Climate change		
1.	Sikkim	1.0000	0.6933	0.6230	0.9333	0.4892	0.7478	2
2.	Meghalaya	0.8939	0.6544	0.4355	0.8718	0.4061	0.6524	10
3.	Mizoram	1.0000	0.6667	0.5071	0.4220	0.6280	0.6448	12
4.	Assam	0.9298	0.6536	0.4993	0.7643	0.3658	0.6426	13
5.	Tripura	0.5881	0.6667	0.7851	0.4008	0.3713	0.5624	18
6.	Nagaland	0.9608	0.6458	0.3677	0.4679	0.0378	0.4960	24
7.	Manipur	0.9048	0.6667	0.4601	0.0000	0.3740	0.4811	26
8.	Arunachal Pradesh	0.3333	0.3333	1.0000	0.0000	0.4885	0.4310	28
India		0.7984	0.6371	0.5508	0.6181	0.3175	0.5773	–

Note The states are arranged in descending order of EPI
Source Chandrasekharan et al. (2013)
[a]Based on 28 states (no separate data for Telangana; seven UTs not included in ranking)

Pradesh and Manipur are among the lowest three northeast states with respect to per capita income, proportion of people above poverty line and the environmental performance. Assam, which is also among the lowest three northeast states with respect to per capita income and proportion of people above poverty line, is placed relatively higher with respect to environmental performance. It seems there is positive correlation among per capita income, proportion of people above poverty line and environmental performance in the context of northeast states.

23.9 Income, Poverty and Environmental Performance

An exploratory correlation analysis is done between per capita income (PCNSDP 2012–13, 2004–05 prices), incidence of poverty (2011–12) and different components of Environmental Performance Index (2012). This is based on the cross-sectional data available across the eight northeastern states. The results are presented in Table 23.13.

The table shows a high negative correlation coefficient between the per capita income and incidence of poverty. That is, higher the average per capita income of a state, lower would be the incidence of poverty. While it seems somewhat obvious, it is not necessarily so as it also depends on the equality of income distribution. The negative correlation coefficients between the per capita income and the Gini coefficients (rural and urban) seem to have facilitated this. It is interesting to note that, in the context of northeastern states, the inequality of income distribution reduces as the average per capita income increases.

The table also shows positive correlation coefficients between the per capita income and different components of the environmental performance implying that as the per capita income increases, the environmental performance improves. These results of the northeast region do not seem to support Environmental Kuznets Curve hypothesis. This hypothesis is based on Kuznets curves (Kuznets 1955) that show an inverted U-type curve of inequality in income distribution with respect to per capita income. The Environmental Kuznets curves thus indicate that initially as the per capita income increases, the environmental degradation also increases but after a certain level of per capita income, an increase in income results in a reduction in environmental degradation. This hypothesis has been both supported and rejected by different empirical works (Stern 2004). In the present context of northeastern states, it seems that appropriate measures are being taken to improve environmental performance with rising per capita incomes.

With the above observations, one would expect negative correlation coefficients between the incidence of poverty and different components of the environmental performance. Interestingly, it is not so. The correlation coefficients are very low but positive for ‘Forests’ and ‘Climate Change’ indicating that the forests and the climate change do not necessarily deteriorate with higher levels of poverty.

Table 23.13 Estimated correlation coefficients between per capita income, poverty and environmental performance

S. No	Particulars	Environmental performance index, 2012						Poverty	Gini coefficient	
		Air pollution	Water	Forests	Waste management	Climate change	Overall	(2011–12)	Rural	Urban
1.	PCNSDP	0.1865	0.1789	0.1103	0.4776	0.0803	0.5115	−0.7675	−0.1436	−0.4640
2.	Poverty	−0.3228	−0.4949	0.1691	−0.7140	0.0070	−0.6627	–	–	–

23.10 Conclusion

As per the latest data available, Sikkim emerges at the top of the northeastern states with the highest per capita income, the lowest incidence of poverty and highest environmental performance index. It is also among the top northeastern states in terms of availability of basic amenities and services as well as the ownership of assets. It is the smallest state in the region in terms of total geographical area and population. A very high growth rate in its industrial sector seems to have contributed significantly to its better economic performance. Though, it rates low on environmental performance with respect to forests and climate change, its better environmental performance with respect to air pollution, water and waste management more than compensates to achieve the highest EPI in the northeast region.

On the other hand, Assam, Arunachal Pradesh and Manipur are the northeastern states that have performed low. These three states have recorded the lowest per capita incomes, lowest rates of economic growth and highest incidences of poverty. Arunachal Pradesh and Manipur have also recorded the lowest environmental performance indices. Assam, the most populous and the second largest state in terms of its total geographical area, has the lowest per capita income. Manipur, ranked in the middle of the northeastern states in terms of its total geographical area and population, shows the lowest rate of economic growth and the highest incidence of poverty. Arunachal Pradesh, the state with the largest geographical and forest area, has recorded the lowest environmental performance index.

At the national level, Sikkim, Nagaland, Tripura and Mizoram have recorded higher per capita income in 2012–13 than the national average. Sikkim, Tripura and Mizoram have also recorded higher rates of annual economic growth during 2004–05 to 2012–13 than the national average. Nagaland which had the highest per capita income in Northeast India in 2004–05 has lagged behind due to its lower rate of economic growth. Meghalaya joins the above four states in recording a lower incidence of poverty than the national average in 2011–12. Nagaland and Tripura slide down with Assam when it comes to environmental performance. That is, only Sikkim, Meghalaya, Mizoram and Assam record environmental performance indices that are higher than the national average. The northeastern states ranked from 2nd (Sikkim) to 26th (Assam) in terms of per capita income, 1st (Sikkim) to 28th (Manipur) in terms of CAGR, 4th (Sikkim) to 26th (Manipur) in terms of lowest incidence of poverty, and 2nd (Sikkim) to 28th (Arunachal Pradesh) in terms of EPI.

The exploratory analysis shows positive correlation between the per capita income and the environmental performance, negative correlation between per capita income and incidence of poverty, and also negative correlation between per capita income and inequality of income distribution. The incidence of poverty shows positive as well as negative correlations with different indicators of environmental performance. It suggests that the northeastern states should continue to focus on increase in income with an improvement in the environmental performance. It also requires a further deeper analysis between income and environment.

References

Chandrasekharan, I., Kumar, R. S., Raghunathan, S., & Chandrasekharan, S. (2013). Construction of environmental performance index and rankings of States. *Current Science, 104*(4), 435–439.

Government of India. (2014, June). *Report of the Expert Group to Review the Methodology for Measurement of Poverty*. Planning Commission, New Delhi.

Government of India. (2014, July 3). *Databook Compiled for Use of Planning Commission*. Planning Commission, New Delhi. Retrieved from http://planningcommission.gov.in.

Government of India. (2015). *Statewise land use classification in India (2010–11 to 2012–13)—Part I, II & III*. Ministry of Agriculture, New Delhi. Retrieved from http://www.indiaagristat.com/table/agriculture/2/landuse19502013/448932/7201/data.aspx

Kuznets, S. (1955). Economic growth and income inequality. *American Economic Review, 49*, 1–28.

Stern, D. I. (2004). The rise and fall of the environmental Kuznets Curve. *World Development, 32*(8), 1419–1439.

Chapter 24
Adaptability of Farmers in Assam Towards Extreme Climate Effects: An Empirical Investigation

Utpal Kumar De and Kamal Bodosa

Abstract This chapter tries to examine the adaptability of farmers with changing climatic and role of various factors in adaptation and crop diversificaty in Assam. Diversity of crops here is measured by Herfindahl *Index* (HI) at the farm as well as village level. Also the adaptation index (AI) is constructed using formula $AI = (\sum P_i * X_i)/n$, where P_i is the weight of *i*th adaptation; X_i. P_i is computed as the proportion of *i*th strategy in the gross number of adaptations followed by all the farmers in the area. Effects of different factors on the level of diversification of crops by the individual farmers and on the adaptability with the changing agro-climatic conditions are examined by the multiple regression of the type $Y = \beta X + D + U_i$. Here, Y represents either farm level *Herfindahl Index* (Diversity Index) or *Adaptation Index*. The results reveal that respondent farmers' education, their farm size, area of possessions and contribution of agriculture in family income have positive impacts on a diversity of crops as well as adaptation by moderating the adverse climate impact or avoid climate related disaster. Education is highly dominant for obtaining better knowledge and expediting technology adoption capacity of farmers in a better way to the changing climate.

Keywords Climate change · Adaptation · Crop diversification
Technology · Assam

U.K. De (✉)
Department of Economics, North-Eastern Hill University,
Shillong 793022, Meghalaya, India
e-mail: utpalkde@gmail.com; de_u@yahoo.com

K. Bodosa
Department of Economics, Kokrajhar Government College,
Kokrajhar 783370, Assam, India
e-mail: kbodosa@rediffmail.com

U.K. De et al. (eds.), *Inequality, Poverty and Development in India*, India Studies in Business and Economics, DOI 10.1007/978-981-10-6274-2_24

24.1 Introduction

Adaptation to the changing climate refers to adjustments to practices, processes and systems for minimising existing and/or future adverse effects of changing the weather and using available opportunities maximise benefits (Eriksen et al. 2011; Pouliotte et al. 2009). Local responses are very essential for adaptation and mitigation notwithstanding the fact that effective policy responses must reflect impacts and inter-linkages at the global level. Crop selection and diversification, date of planting, harvesting, tillage and fertilisation, etc., are some possible adaptation strategies to the changing climatic pattern. However, adaptability of farmers to climate change and appropriate cropping choice highly depends on their awareness level and gauging the emerging situation, which is very much dependent on their knowledge, access to information, training; extension services by external agencies regarding climate change along with the asset level, access to appropriate agro-technology and agro-infrastructure (IPCC 2007a; Anselm and Taofeeq 2010; Onyeneke and Madukwe 2010; Adensina and Forson 1995; Krishnamurthy 2012). Moreover, modern agricultural practices and technologies can play significant roles in climate mitigation and adaptation. This adaptation and mitigation potential are nowhere more prominent than in developing countries where agricultural productivity remains low and scarcity, susceptibility and food insecurity seems to be high; and the unswerving effects of climate change are expected to be particularly insensitive (Lybbert and Sumner 2010).

Assam is a highly weather-dependant large agrarian state in Northeast India dominated by small landholdings (average 1.2 ha; GoA 2012-13) with substantial agricultural diversity. Over the years, climatic conditions in Assam recorded gradual changes in terms of uncertain variations in rainfall, rising temperature and erratic humidity level. In recent years, the highest level of precipitation is observed in Assam (De and Bodosa 2014) either in pre-normal monsoon months of March–May or during post monsoon months of August–October, resulting in untimely and unexpected devastating floods. Flood is a common phenomenon of Assam and Dhemaji, Lakhimpur, Nagaon and some other districts are highly prone to frequent floods in the state. Moreover, both maximum and minimum temperature have been observed to be consistently increasing and the rate of growth is even more during winter months across the regions of the state. Rising uncertainty in monsoon rainfall and rising temperature have serious impacts on the pattern of agricultural activities undertaken by the farmers and their livelihood conditions as well. It thus necessitates appropriate preparedness and continuous adaptation in the crop and non-crop activities for the reduction in risk and best possible livelihood practice in the region.

Changing climate and extreme climatic behaviour like sudden floods, draughts has extensive impacts on the agricultural activities and its productivity which would compel rural farmers to shift their existing cropping pattern to reduce risk (Aufhammer et al. 2006; De and Chattopadhyay 2010). The performance of agriculture sector of any region is highly vulnerable relatively to the variability in local climate considerably across different locations rather than in global climate patterns that raise risk and uncertainty (IPCC 2007b; Ye et al. 2013). Under growing uncertainty, maintenance of agricultural productivity depends on the adaptability of the farmers with the changing weather pattern over the years. Farmers of the developing countries, especially in rural areas are supposed to be worst hit to the extreme climatic events like floods and draughts for the reduction in crop productivity generally in humid and sub-tropical regions that also happens because of intensified water scarcity (Adger et al. 2003; IPCC 2007a; Tanner and Mitchell 2008). Rural poor normally have limited adaptation choices including very limited options to diversify cultivation of crops. At the same time, they are more vulnerable than the rich farmers to agricultural disruptions and they lack access to improved technologies such as flood and draught resistant seeds varieties or crop insurance, etc. However, the majority of farmers are aware of the fact that greater crop diversity and mixed farming (crops and livestock) offers substantial protection against farming risk, including climatic hazard (FAO 2011). In order to get rid of such climate change risk or climate extremes continuous adaptation is inevitable. In the words of Kyte (2014), crop diversity is one of the paramount sources for agricultural adaptation and the foundation for future efforts to nourish the mankind. It is therefore, important to analyse farmers' perception and awareness about crop diversification as their adaptation actions followed towards climate change scenario in the region. Though there is several studies that have been analysed the process of diversification of crops along with the other resources to deal with the changing weather pattern, agro-technology and infrastructure for a sustainable agricultural growth (Krishnan et al. 1991; Bastine and Palaniswami 1994; Dale 1997; Hazra 2001; De 2003; Mehta 2009), the analysis of adaptation measures adopted by the farmers in response to changing weather pattern, different agro-technologies, risk and uncertainty on account of the climate extremes are rare.

This chapter, therefore, tried to explore the adaptability of the farmers towards the changing climatic conditions and extreme climatic in Assam. Also impacts of various factors including changing technological support, age, education and training, farming experience, the area under cultivation, income, access to capital, etc., on crop diversification or other adoption mechanism are examined by using a cross-sectional data collected from some sample villages of Kokrajhar and Dhemaji.

24.2 Materials and Methods

Multi-stage purposive sampling procedure has been followed to select the village. At first among the present 27 districts of Assam, Kokrajhar and Dhemaji have been selected purposively for the study. It is to be noted that, the district of Kokrajhar scarcely face extreme climate effect (except occasional draught), while devastating flood is a regular phenomenon of the Dhemaji district. In Kokrajhar three blocks namely Kokrajhar, Kachugaon and Debitola have been selected from its three sub-divisions. Also, Dhemaji, Bordoloni and Murkongseleck blocks have been chosen from two sub-divisions (Dhemaji and Jonai) of Dhemaji district. Three blocks are chosen as one advanced, one moderately developed and another backward, respectively, in terms of their socio-economic characteristics. Thereafter, three villages have been chosen from each district (one from each of the selected development blocks).

Considering the socio-economic characteristics (Table 24.1) like transport and communication, the presence of academic and administrative institutions, irrigation facilities, literacy rate, banking facilities, etc., in mind, we selected one advanced, one moderately developed and one backward village from Kokrajhar and Dhemaji districts as sample villages. These are Shyamgaon, Patakata, and Ubrijhora from Kokrajhar and Amulguri, Chumoni and Mahanpur from Dhemaji District (Fig. 24.1). From each of the selected villages, 50 sample households (total 300 sample farm households) are selected by using the method of simple random sampling without replacement. Data have been collected by direct interview using a pre-tested schedule, which includes questions pertaining to the socio-economic and demographic status of the families, utilisation of family labour and hired labour, uses of fertiliser, various agro-implements, availability of irrigation facilities, topology of plots, crops damaged by floods or other weather aberrations, perception of respondent about the diversification pattern, area allocated to various crops and outputs of crops, various measures adopted for saving crops from extreme weather (mitigation measures) or changes in cultivation practices to avoid extreme weather effects (abatement measures), etc. Also information are collected on educational achievement, experience, availability of family labour, farm size, proportion of income earned from agriculture, total family income, training, access to capital, technology, etc. Those are the potential factors accountable for bringing changes in the existing cropping pattern and influence farmers' adaptation. Descriptive statistics are used to understand farmers' socio-economic profiles, their overall reaction to climate change through cropping choice, various adaptation measures, etc. A sizable portion of farmers who cited cropping pattern changes as a response to climate change is considered to analyse the extent to which changing cultivation pattern has been perceived as an adaptation strategy.

Descriptive statistics are also used to examine farmers' perceptions concerning the impact of climate fluctuation on crop diversity and the technologies used by the farmers to adapt with the changing climate. Using primary data, effects of different factors on the extent of crop diversification of individual farmers and on their adaptability to changing agro-climatic conditions, is examined by *multiple regression* equation $Y = \beta X + D + U_i$. Here, Y represents either farm level *Herfindahl Index* (Diversity Index[1]) or *Adaptation Index*; X is the vector of explanatory variables and β represents the vector of coefficients. D is a dummy variable included in the regression that takes value zero in case of Kokrajhar (since the region hardly faces any flood incidence) and one in case of Dhemaji (that

[1]Herfindahl Index of diversity can be written as: $\mathrm{HI} = 1 - \sum_i^n (p_i)^2$, where, n is the number of crops grown and p_i represents proportion of area under ith crop to gross area under cultivation by the families.

Table 24.1 Basic characteristics of the sample villages

District		Kokrajhar			Dhemaji		
Sample village		Shyamgaon	Patakata	Ubrijhora	Amulguri	Chumoni	Mahanpur
Total number of HHs		98	85	64	96	70	88
Literacy rate (%)	Male	95	88	71	95	89	69
	Female	86	78	66	90	81	64
	Total	90.5	83	68.5	92.5	85	66.5
Distance from village to important places (km)	District H.Q.	5	35	40	8	30	56
	Sub-divison H. Q.	5	13	15	8	30	45
	Devt. block H.Q	2	15	20	8	15	45
	Market	2	2	7	3	4	8
	National highway	13	9	20	0.5	4	8
	Bus stand	2	9	7	0.5	5	8
	Railway Station	5	13	7	3.5	6	9
	Bank	3	7	8	8	5	8
Facilities available in the village	Electrification	Yes	Yes	No	Yes	Yes	No
	Faire orice shop	Yes	Yes	No	Yes	Yes	No
	Irrigation	Yes	Yes	No	Yes	No	No
	Mobile	Yes	Yes	Yes	Yes	Yes	Yes
	Land Line/WLL	Yes	No	No	Yes	No	No
	Internet/Wi-Fi	Yes	No	No	Yes	No	No

(continued)

Table 24.1 (continued)

District		Kokrajhar			Dhemaji		
Sample village		Shyamgaon	Patakata	Ubrijhora	Amulguri	Chumoni	Mahanpur
	Road type	Pacca	Gravel	Kacha	Pacca	Gravel	Kacha
Educational institutions	LP	Yes	Yes	Yes	Yes	Yes	Yes
	ME/MV	No	Yes	No	No	Yes	No
	HE/HSS/college	No	No	No	No	No	No
Classification of village as per development characteristics		Advanced village	Moderate village	Backward village	Advanced village	Moderate village	Backward village

Source Field Survey, 2013–2014
HHs Households, *LP* lower primary, *ME/MV* middle english/middle vernacular

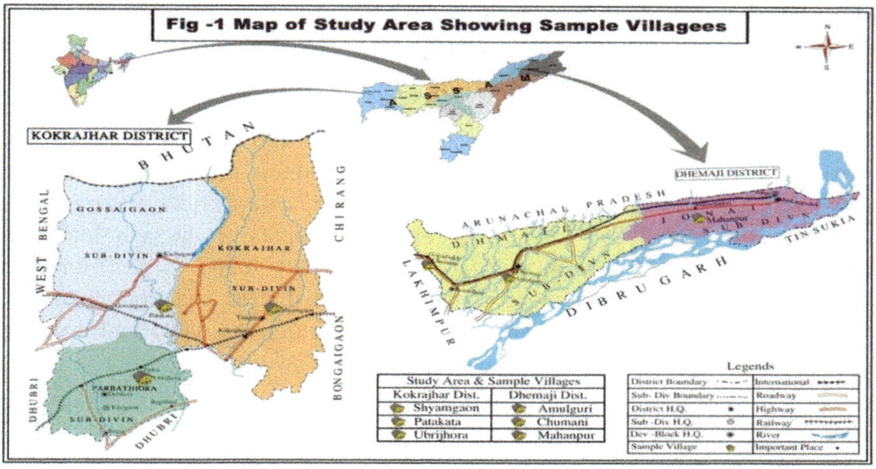

Fig. 24.1 Map of study area showing sample villages

observes frequent devastating flood almost every year). Crop diversity here is measured by *Herfindahl Index* (HI) and computed at the farm as well as village level.

Here, the adaptation index is constituted by using the formula AI = $(\sum P_i * X_i)/n$, where, n is the number of possible adaptation measures undertaken by the farmers in the area in accordance with their needs and capability, P_i is the weight of ith adaptation X_i and is computed as the proportion of ith strategy in the gross number of adaptations followed by all the farmers in the area. It is made to make the possible measures equally likely for all the individuals in the overall sample and AI takes values between 0 and 1. In the same way, technology index and infrastructure index is computed.

In order to analyse the impact of crop diversity on agricultural earning of the farmers in the sample villages the respondent families are divided into two groups on the basis of low diversity (with HI Index of diversity less than 0.5) and highly diversified farms (with HI Index of diversity more than 0.5). Thereafter, similar seven factors additive model is used to examine the impact of cropping pattern change on the agricultural yield as used by Minhas and Vaidyanathan (1965). The model may be written as

$$Q_{\mathrm{H}} - Q_{\mathrm{L}} = A_{\mathrm{H}} \sum C_{i\mathrm{H}} Y_{i\mathrm{H}} P_i - A_L \sum C_{i\mathrm{L}} Y_{i\mathrm{L}} P_{i\mathrm{L}},$$

$$\begin{aligned} \text{Or, } \Delta Q = Q_{\mathrm{H}} - Q_{\mathrm{L}} &= (A_{\mathrm{H}} - A_{\mathrm{L}}) \sum C_{i\mathrm{L}} Y_{i\mathrm{L}} P_{i\mathrm{L}} + A_{\mathrm{L}} \sum C_{i\mathrm{L}} (Y_{i\mathrm{H}} - Y_{i\mathrm{L}}) P_i \\ &+ A_{\mathrm{L}} \sum (C_{i\mathrm{H}} - C_{i\mathrm{L}}) Y_{i\mathrm{L}} \mathrm{P_i} + (\mathrm{A_H} - \mathrm{A_L}) \sum (C_{i\mathrm{H}} - C_{i\mathrm{L}}) Y_{i\mathrm{L}} P_{i\mathrm{L}} \\ &+ (A_{\mathrm{H}} - A_{\mathrm{L}}) \sum C_{i\mathrm{L}} (Y_{i\mathrm{H}} - Y_{i\mathrm{L}}) P_{i\mathrm{L}} + A_{\mathrm{L}} \sum (C_{i\mathrm{H}} - C_{i\mathrm{L}})(Y_{i\mathrm{H}} - Y_{i\mathrm{L}}) P_{i\mathrm{L}} \\ &+ (textA_{\mathrm{H}} - A_{\mathrm{L}}) \sum (C_{i\mathrm{H}} - C_{i\mathrm{L}})(Y_{i\mathrm{H}} - Y_{i\mathrm{L}}) P_i \end{aligned}$$

where, $Q_L = A_L \sum C_{iL} Y_{iL} P_i$ and $Q_H = A_H \sum C_{iH} Y_{iH} P_i$ represent total value of agricultural output {at average harvest prices (P_i)} of the sample villages in the low and high diversified farm, respectively. A_L and A_H are average gross cropped areas in the low and high diversified farm, respectively. $C_{iL} = (A_{iL}/A_L)$ and $C_{iH} = (A_{iH}/A_H)$ are, respectively, the proportion of area under *i*th crop to GCA in the low and high diversified farm groups and Y_{iL}, Y_{iH} represent yield of *i*th crop in the low and high diversified farm group. P_i is the overall average harvest prices of crops in the sample villages (2012–2013). The first three components on the right-hand side represent direct effects of area, yield and cropping pattern and the next three are interaction effects of area and cropping pattern, area and yield, and cropping pattern and yield. The last one is the interaction of all three, area, yield and cropping pattern.

24.3 Socio-Economic Profile of the Sample Families and Their Adaptation Pattern

This section examines the socio-economic-demographic profile of the sample farm households in the study area. It provides some background information for the agricultural diversification analysis followed and adaptation of new farm technology or agricultural practices through varied cropping pattern. Agriculture is the primary source of household income in the districts of Kokrajhar and Dhemaji. Also, a few of them have small businesses like hotels, restaurants, grocery and stationary shops, vegetable shops, etc. The differences in the socio-economic factors, infrastructure support, access to technology and the bio-physical factors and their effects on the adaptation pattern of farmers have been analysed subsequently.

24.3.1 Classification of Sample Farmers Based on Gender, Age and Education

More than 72% of the respondent farmers are male in the overall sample villages. However, the advanced villages like Shyamgaon and Amulguriare found to have lesser proportion of male workers as compared to the moderate and backward villages in both the districts. This variation of the male farmers may be due to the availability of alternative opportunities in the advanced villages (Table 24.2). Table 24.3 reveals that the highest proportions of farmers belong to the age group of 31–40 years and followed by 41–50 years. Very few farmers are found to belong to the age group of 21–30 and above 70 years. Educationally, majority of the farmers are found to be matriculate in all the sample villages (Table 24.4). However, there are a few highly educated farmers found in the sample villages except in Ubrijhora. Chumoni village recorded the highest proportion of illiterate

Table 24.2 Gender-wise distribution of respondent farmers in the sample villages

District	Kokrajhar				Dhemaji			
Gender	Shyamgaon	Patakata	Ubrijhora	Sub-total	Amulguri	Chumoni	Mahanpur	Sub-total
Male	36 (72)	47 (94)	46 (92)	129 (86)	44 (88)	45 (90)	45 (90)	134 (89)
Female	14 (28)	3 (6)	4 (8)	21 (14)	6 (12)	5 (10)	5 (10)	16 (11)
Total	50 (100)	50 (100)	50 (100)	150 (100)	50 (100)	50 (100)	50 (100)	150 (100)

Source Field Survey, 2013–2014
Note Figure in the parentheses indicates percentage of respondents

Table 24.3 Classification of respondent farmers based on age group in the sample villages

Age group (year)	Kokrajhar				Dhemaji			
	Shyamgaon	Patakata	Ubrijhora	Sub-total	Amulguri	Chumoni	Mahanpur	Sub-total
21–30	Nil	Nil	14 (28)	14 (9)	3 (6)	4 (8)	1 (2)	8 (5)
31–40	5 (10)	14 (28)	17 (34)	(36 (24)	6 (12)	13 (26)	13 (26)	32 (21)
41–50	22 (44)	22 (44)	9 (18)	53 (35)	17 (34)	10 (20)	17 (34)	44 (29)
51–60	12 (24)	8 (16)	8 (16)	28 (19)	10 (20)	8 (16)	11 (22)	29 (19)
61–70	9 (18)	3 (6)	2 (4)	14 (9)	10 (20)	12 (24)	7 (14)	29 (19)
71–80	2 (4)	3 (6)	Nil	5 (3)	3 (6)	2 (4)	1 (2)	6 (4)
81–90	Nil	Nil	Nil	Nil	1 (2)	1 (2)	Nil	2 (1)
Total	50 (100)	50 (100)	50 (100)	150 (100)	50 (100)	50 (100)	50 (100)	150 (100)

Source Field Survey, 2013–2014
Note Figure in the parentheses indicates percentage of respondents

Table 24.4 Classification of respondent farmers on the basis of education

Level of education	Kokrajhar				Dhemaji			
	Shyamgaon	Patakata	Ubrijhora	Sub-total	Amulguri	Chumoni	Mahanpur	Sub-total
Illiterate	1 (2)	5 (10)	10 (20)	16 (10.7)	6 (12)	16 (32)	11 (22)	33 (22)
Primary	9 (18)	14 (28)	13 (26)	36 (24)	11 (22)	10 (20)	8 (16)	29 (19.3)
ME/MV	12 (24)	7 (14)	10 (20)	29 (19.3)	6 (12)	9 (18)	10 (20)	25 (16.7)
Matriculation	20 (40)	16 (32)	14 (28)	50 (33.3)	17 (34)	14 (28)	11 (22)	42 (28)
Higher secondary	5 (10)	7 (14)	3 (6)	15 (10)	6 (12)	Nil	7 (14)	13 (8.7)
Graduation	2 (4)	1 (2)	Nil	3 (2)	4 (8)	1 (2)	3 (6)	8 (5.3)
Post graduation	Nil	Nil	Nil	Nil	Nil	Nil	Nil	Nil
Technical/professional	1 (2)	Nil	Nil	1 (0.7)	Nil	Nil	Nil	Nil
All villages	50 (100)	50 (100)	50 (100)	150 (100)	50 (100)	50 (100)	50 (100)	150 (100)

Source Field Survey, 2013–2014

Note Figure in the parentheses indicates percentage of respondent farmer

farmers (32%) to be engaged in agricultural activities, followed by Mahanpur (22%) and Ubrijhora (20%) villages, respectively. About 33–38% of the respondents are found to be cultivators in the advanced villages while more than 53% of the respondents are cultivators in moderate and backward villages. Thus, more is the backwardness of the village higher is the proportion of people engaged in agricultural activities (Table 24.5).

24.3.2 Sources of Income of the Sample Households

As per the distribution, share of agriculture in total earning is the highest and followed by wage earnings (service sector), business, livestock farming and labour works, respectively, in the overall sample villages (Table 24.6). Among six villages, per capita annual income of the households was the highest in Amulguri (Rs. 38,307) of Dhemaji and followed by Shyamgaon (Rs. 24,057) of Kokrajhar. This is because of the contribution of service sectors to those villagers. It is observed that proportion of income from agricultural sources is more than non-agricultural sources in all the selected villages except Shyamgaon. Contribution of non-agricultural sources to the total income is less in the under developed villages as compared to the advanced one.

24.3.3 Land Use Pattern and Area of Operational Holdings in the Sample Village

Another important characteristic of the survey villages is that the chosen farm families are found to be mostly in small (more than one hectare but less than four hectares), marginal (below one hectare) farmers category. Also, there is non-uniform distribution of cultivated area among farming households in all the villages. About 66 and 65% of the respondent farmers in Kokrajhar and Dhemaji districts, respectively, are small holders. However, more than 25% of farmers have land holdings between 30.0 and 75.0 bighas in Dhemaji district, while about 7% of the farmers in Kokrajhar belong to that group. It also indicates the presence of common land leasing practice in all those villages. The land holdings are not only small in size but also fragmented into many parcels due to sub-divisions on account of breakdown of the joint family system and law of inheritance (Table 24.7). The lease-out and lease-in phenomena are found to be more prominent among the marginal and small farmers (Table 24.8). Total operational holdings of the sample farmers in Kokrajhar district is 2115.5 bighas (about 283.62 ha), of which 11.70 and 3.45% are leased-in land and leased-out land, respectively. On the other hand, among the sample farms of Dhemaji district total holding is 3048 bigha (about 408.63 ha) of which about 2 and 1% are leased-in and leased-out, respectively.

Table 24.5 Percentage distribution of respondents in terms of gender & occupation

District	Kokrajhar				Dhemaji				Avg.
Gender	Shyamgaon	Patakata	Ubrijhora	Sub-total	Amulguri	Chumoni	Mahanpur	Sub-total	
Male	30.63	34.70	39.16	34.72	35.17	35.03	35.54	35.24	34.99
Female	32.39	34.70	38.78	35.16	37.59	39.84	36.14	37.95	36.62
Children	36.97	30.60	22.05	30.12	27.24	25.13	28.31	26.81	28.39
Total	100	100	100	100	100	100	100	100	100
Occupation	**Occupational distribution**								
Govt. service	5.63	3.01	1.52	3.40	7.93	2.14	3.61	4.32	3.88
Pvt. service	1.76	0.82	1.52	1.31	4.14	5.61	1.81	3.92	2.67
Businessman	8.10	3.28	2.28	4.49	10.34	6.42	6.93	7.73	6.18
Cultivator	38.73	58.74	62.74	53.67	33.45	53.21	56.33	48.49	50.97
Agri. labour	4.23	0.55	1.52	1.97	0.00	2.67	2.11	1.71	1.83
Dependents	41.55	33.61	30.42	35.16	44.14	29.95	29.22	33.84	34.47
Total	100	100	100	100	100	100	100	100	100

Source Field Survey, 2013–2014

Table 24.6 Percentage share of annual income from various sources by the sample households

District	Sample village	Sources of income						
		Agriculture	Business	Service	Labour work (Any)	Livestock	Oth. sources	PCI (Rs.)
Kokrajhar	Shyamgaon	28.28	17.75	47.60	0.86	4.03	1.49	24,057
	Patakata	56.13	6.39	30.57	0.40	4.14	2.38	21,940
	Ubrijhora	56.74	7.31	21.66	3.49	8.10	2.69	14,726
	Sub-total	46.10	10.72	34.94	1.20	4.92	2.12	20,241
Dhemaji	Amulguri	40.16	5.63	51.85	0.16	1.55	0.66	38,307
	Chumoni	66.96	6.46	19.42	1.74	3.73	1.70	25,042
	Mahanpur	41.19	12.50	35.58	1.57	5.75	3.42	28,445
	Sub-total	48.87	8.06	36.56	1.10	3.56	1.86	30,598
Average		47.81	9.08	35.94	1.14	4.08	1.96	25,419

Source Field Survey, 2013–2014
Note PCI represents per capita annual income

Leased on short-term contracts and substantial fraction of croplands would lead to fewer incentives for investments in soil conservation by the operators. However, owner farmers have more capacity to adopt new technologies frequently than owner-cum-tenant and tenants farmers (Habiba et al. 2012). Moreover, it is widely believed that ownership of land encourages adaptation of technologies like irrigation, application of fertiliser, etc. Farmers adapt their choice of farms' type and irrigation to their local climate that treats the choice of crops, livestock and irrigation as endogenous factors (Mendelsohn and Seo 2007c).

24.3.4 Cropping Pattern in the Sample Villages

Various types of crops have been cultivated by the farmers of the sample villages in different seasons. Generally, paddy, oilseeds, sugarcane, potato, etc., are grown abundantly in the study area and cultivation of arecanut, bamboo and banana has also been observed almost in all the villages. Though, sample farmers cultivate different food and non-food crops, we observe over 82% of area to be allocated for food grains (Table 24.9) for the last two consecutive years, i.e. in 2011–2012 and 2012–2013. It is also observed that the farmers in Dhemaji district are cultivating proportionately more food grain crops than their counterpart in Kokrajhar.

Rice is the predominant crop in all the six villages (like that of the state) comprising over 80% of the total cropped area (Table 24.10). Mustard is the second most significant crop, while share of non-food gains is still very less (merely 18% of GCA). This is an indication of very poor level of diversification and that towards relatively inferior crops with deficiency of basic inputs like irrigation, access to capital and modern technology.

Table 24.7 Distribution of respondents according to the size of operational holdings (in Bigha)

Category/size of operational holdings	Number of respondent farmers								
	Kokrajhar				Dhemaji				Overall total
	Shyamgaon	Patakata	Ubrijhora	Sub-total	Amulguri	Chumoni	Mahanpur	Sub-total	
Marginal (below 7.5)	23 (46)	1 (2)	16 (32)	40 (26.7)	2 (4)	2 (4)	10 (20)	14 (9.3)	54 (18)
Small (7.5–30.0)	26 (52)	43 (86)	30 (60)	99 (66)	36 (72)	28 (56)	34 (68)	98 (65.3)	197 (66)
Medium (30.0–75.0)	1 (2)	6 (12)	4 (8)	11 (7.33)	12 (24)	20 (40)	6 (12)	38 (25.3)	49 (16)
Large (75.0 and above)	Nil				Nil				
Total	50 (100)	50 (100)	50 (100)	150 (100)	50 (100)	50 (100)	50 (100)	150 (100)	300 (100)

Source Field Survey, 2013–2014

Note Figure in the parentheses represents percentage of the respondent farmer

Table 24.8 Farm operation under tenancy land of the sample farmers (area in Bigha)

District	Kokrajhar															
Sample village	Shyamgaon				Patakata				Ubrijhora				Sub-total			
Size/class (area in Bigha)	Cultivable land area	Own land cultivated	Leased-out to other farmer	Leased-in from other farmer	Cultivable land area	Own land cultivated	Leased-out to other farmer	Leased-in from other farmer	Cultivable land area	Own land cultivated	Leased-out to other farmer	Leased-in from other farmer	Cultivable land area	Own land cultivated	Leased-out to other farmer	Leased-in from other farmer
Marginal (below 7.5)	103	103	5	18	7	19	18	102	78.5	101	19	32	188.5	223	42	152
Small (7.5 to 30.0)	336.5	313.5	Nil	Nil	772	700	21	58	403.5	312.5	10	37.5	1512	1326	31	95.5
Medium (30.0–75.0)	36	36	Nil	Nil	199	60	Nil	Nil	180	150	Nil	Nil	415	246	Nil	Nil
Large (75.0 and above)	Nil				Nil				Nil				Nil			
Total	475.5 (100)	452.5 (95.16)	5 (1.05)	18 (3.79)	978 (100)	779 (79.65)	39 (3.98)	160 (16.36)	662 (100)	563.5 (85.12)	29 (4.38)	69.5 (10.50)	2115.5 (100)	1795 (84.85)	73 (3.45)	247.5 (11.70)
District	Dhemaji															
Sample village	Amulguri				Chumoni				Mahanpur				Sub-total			
Marginal (below 7.5)	13	13	29	24	12	12		5	42	40	2	32	67	65	31	61
Small (7.5–30.0)	642	703	Nil	Nil	451	446	Nil	Nil	516	484	Nil	Nil	1609	1633	Nil	Nil
Medium (30.0–75.0)	408	294	Nil	Nil	714	714		Nil	250	250	Nil	Nil	1372	1258	Nil	Nil
Large (75.0 and above)	Nil				Nil				Nil				Nil			
Total	1063 (100)	1010 (95.01)	29 (2.73)	24 (2.26)	1177 (100)	1172 (99.57)	Nil	5 (0.42)	808 (100)	774 (95.79)	2 (0.25)	32 (3.96)	3048 (100)	2956 (96.98)	31 (1.02)	61 (2.00)

Source Field Survey, 2013–2014

Note Figures in the parentheses represent percentage of the area to total cultivable area of respective sample village

Table 24.9 Distribution of GCA between food and non-food crops in the sample villages (%)

District	Village	Foodgrains		Non-foodgrains	
		2011–2012	2012–2013	2011–2012	2012–2013
Kokrajhar	Shyamgaon	88.28	87.48	11.72	12.52
	Patakata	83.57	85.37	16.43	14.63
	Ubrijhora	83.54	83.46	16.46	16.54
	Sub-total	84.70	85.41	15.30	14.56
Dhemaji	Amulguri	94.62	94.50	5.38	5.50
	Chumoni	82.30	82.09	17.70	17.91
	Mahanpur	89.72	89.50	10.28	10.50
	Sub-total	88.42	88.32	11.58	11.68
All village		86.95	87.17	13.05	12.83

Source Field Survey, 2013–2014

Other than food grains, farmers of the Shyamgaon village allocate relatively more proportion of GCA for the cultivation of potato (2.62%), roots (1.84%), chilly (1.41%) and mustard (1.36%) than that of other villages. Farmers of the Patakata village cultivate relatively more mustard (5.31%) and jute (2.49%). On the other hand, farmers of Ubrijhora village allocate more towards jute (3.71%), areca nut (3.42%) and sesamum (2.28%). Whereas; farmers in Amulguri allocate land for other than food grain crops, towards areca nut and bamboo as cash crops with 2.56 and 1.11% of total cropped area, respectively. Cultivation of mustard (5.14% of GCA) is significant in Chumoni along with tea (3.04%), bamboo (3.04%) and areca nut (2.63%). Similarly, farmers of Mohanpur village under Murkongseleck block cultivate mustard (on 3.16% of GCA), Bamboo (2.75%), and areca nut (2.47%). Most of the farmers in Dhemaji district utilise a part of their cultivable land for mustard, bamboo and areca nut. This may be due to the frequent occurrence of floods in rainy seasons that force the poor farmers to cultivate early some winter crops but less capital intensive and cultivate bamboo that can sustain in flood and protect homelands from the flood. However, for non-food grain crops, it is irrigation that is important, as many of these crops are highly water-intensive. Potato and chilly are grown mostly for home consumption like other vegetable crops by the farmers in the study area. All these above reflect the non-arrival of the Green Revolution technology at desired level and the rural farmers have not yet fully adapted to the modern methods of cultivation.

Another important feature of surveyed area is that most of the farmers follow single cropping system. The low incidence of double cropping is due to the prevalence of traditional and subsistence farming. It depends mainly on rainfall and there is very limited use of chemical fertiliser, irrigation facility, flood and pesticides control arrangements. However, out of 24 varieties of crops cultivated in these two sample areas, most of the farmers (62%) in Dhemaji district found less diverse in their cropping pattern, whereas farmers in Kokrajhar district are more diverse as compared to Dhemaji as they are growing relatively more number of crops (over 70%). The Herfindahl index also shows a very less diversity during study year across

Table 24.10 Area under different crops and their percentage share to total cropped area in the sample villages during 2012–2013 (area in Bigha)

District	Kokrajhar			Dhemaji		
Crop/sample village	Shyamgaon	Patakata	Ubrijhora	Amulguri	Chumoni	Mahanpur
Autumn rice	29 (5.63)	198 (18.60)	101 (19.20)	157 (15.14)	175 (14.38)	187 (19.06)
Winter rice	405 (78.64)	647 (60.79)	330.5 (62.83)	819 (78.98)	810 (66.56)	683 (69.62)
Summer rice	8 (1.55)	48 (4.51)	6 (1.14)	0 (0.00)	0 (0.00)	0 (0.00)
Total rice	**442 (85.83)**	**893 (83.91)**	**437.5 (83.17)**	**976 (94.12)**	**985 (80.94)**	**870 (88.69)**
Wheat	2 (0.39)	0 (0.00)	0 (0.00)	0 (0.00)	0 (0.00)	0 (0.00)
Gram	3 (0.58)	15.5 (1.46)	0.5 (0.00)	2 (0.19)	4 (0.33)	7 (0.71)
Tur	2 (0.39)	0 (0.00)	1 (0.19)	1 (0.10)	8 (0.66)	0 (0.00)
Pulses	1.5 (0.29)	0 (0.00)	0 (0.00)	1 (0.10)	2 (0.16)	1 (0.10)
Overall Food crops	**450.5 (87.48)**	**908.5 (85.37)**	**439 (83.46)**	**980 (94.50)**	**999 (82.09)**	**878 (89.50)**
Rapes and mustard	7 (1.36)	56.5 (5.31)	4 (0.76)	6 (0.58)	62.5 (5.14)	31 (3.16)
Sesamum	2.5 (0.49)	0 (0.00)	12 (2.28)	0 (0.00)	2 (0.16)	3 (0.31)
Linseed	4 (0.78)	5 (0.47)	0 (0.00)	0 (0.00)	9 (0.74)	0 (0.00)
Jute	3.5 (0.68)	26.5 (2.49)	19.5 (3.71)	0 (0.00)	2 (0.16)	0 (0.00)
Tea	0 (0.00)	0 (0.00)	10 (1.90)	0 (0.00)	37 (3.04)	0 (0.00)
Sugarcane	2 (0.39)	3 (0.28)	0 (0.00)	5 (0.48)	25 (2.05)	8 (0.82)
Arecanut	4.75 (0.92)	20.5 (1.93)	18 (3.42)	26.5 (2.56)	32 (2.63)	24.25 (2.47)
Potato	13.5 (2.62)	16.5 (1.55)	2 (0.38)	3.5 (0.34)	7 (0.58)	4 (0.41)
Chilly	7.25 (1.41)	4.75 (0.45)	3 (0.57)	0.5 (0.05)	2.25 (0.18)	0.25 (0.03)
Turmeric	1 (0.19)	3.5 (0.33)	1 (0.19)	0 (0.00)	0 (0.00)	0 (0.00)
Banana	0 (0.00)	0.5 (0.05)	1(0.19)	3 (0.29)	2.25 (0.18)	2.5 (0.25)
Bamboo	0 (0.00)	10.5 (0.99)	6 (1.14)	11.5 (1.11)	37 (3.04)	27 (2.75)
Onion	3 (0.58)	0 (0.00)	0 (0.00)	0 (0.00)	0 (0.00)	0 (0.00)
Brinjal	2.5 (0.49)	1.25 (0.12)	0.5 (0.10)	0.75 (0.07)	0 (0.00)	1 (0.10)

(continued)

Table 24.10 (continued)

District	Kokrajhar			Dhemaji		
Crop/sample village	Shyamgaon	Patakata	Ubrijhora	Amulguri	Chumoni	Mahanpur
Cabbage/cauliflower	1 (0.19)	5.75 (0.54)	0 (0.00)	0.25 (0.02)	0 (0.00)	2 (0.20)
Roots	9.5 (1.84)	1.5 (0.14)	9.5 (1.81)	0 (0.00)	0 (0.00)	0 (0.00)
Radish	3 (0.58)	0 (0.00)	0.5 (0.10)	0 (0.00)	0 (0.00)	0 (0.00)
Non-food crops	64.5 (12.52)	155.75(14.63)	87 (16.54)	57 (5.50)	218 (17.91)	103 (10.50)
Total	515 (100)	1064.25 (100)	526 (100)	1037 (100)	1217 (100)	981 (100)
No. of crops cultivated	21 (87.5)	17 (70.83)	17 (70.83)	14 (58.33)	16 (66.67)	14 (58.33)

Source Field Survey, 2013–2014
Note Figure in the parentheses indicate percentage of area to GCA and percentage of crop to total cultivated crops
Note The bolded values represents total of respective Rice and Foodgrain category

the sample villages of Dhemaji. Moreover, there is great variation in the pattern of diversification across the villages. For instance, Shyamgaon in Kokrajhar and Amulguri in Dhemaji are less diversified and Patakata in Kokrajhar and Chumoni in Dhemaji are more diversified in terms of Herfindahl index (Table 24.11). This variation is in line with the disparity in the share of income generated from the crop raising activities. However, some varieties of rice are found to be grown by the sample farms. From Table 24.12, it is also found that around 69% of the total sample farmers are agriculturally low crop diversified. Only 26% of the sample farmers in Dhemaji district are high diversified while in Kokrajhar district it is 37%. It may be due to the impact of extreme climate hazards (especially by regular flood) in the area. Another reason is the availability of farm land or farm size that constrained many farmers to diversify towards many crops and more equitably. The low-diversified 206 sample farm families have an average farm size of only 14.54 bigha, while only 94 high-diversified farm families have an average farm size of 24.95 bigha. Per capita income of those high-diversified families is much more than that of the low diversified families.

The regression result of Table 24.13 shows that both the index of diversity and total area under cultivation have significant positive impacts on the earning from agriculture. Significantly positive impact of dummy indicates that farmers in the flood prone area of Dhemaji earn comparatively more from agriculture. Also, a number of agricultural labourer available from the family has inverse effect on the agricultural earnings of the families.

Decomposition of variation in agricultural earning between 206 low diversified farmers and 94 highly diversified farmers reveals significant contribution of cropping pattern variation alone. Also area and area-cropping pattern interaction have significantly positive impacts but yield and yield-cropping pattern interaction are found to have adverse impacts on the variation in earning of the highly diversified farmers (Table 24.14). Despite having area advantage, due to low use of fertiliser and irrigation the highly diversified farmers are unable to take advantage of improved yields. They cultivate more varies of crops at the mercy of rain and diversified towards more inferior crops with less risk of failure. On the other hand, the low diversified farmers due to small area under cultivation have limited scope of diversity and choose relatively more remunerative crops and thereby receive the advantage of yield. The area-yield-cropping pattern interaction effect has also been negative. Whatever little wave of Green Revolution technology came to these regions was mainly concentrated to the limited number of large farmers that we did not observe among the sample farmers of either group. The technology did not spread over the large numbers of small and marginal farmers in the study area. Thus, whatever scope is available, despite low yields, the relatively moderate farmers have been able to generate positive cropping pattern effect through proper cropping pattern choice over the large small farmers.

Table 24.15 reveals that among the 24 most commonly grown crops, winter paddy has been the most adapted crop followed by bamboo in terms of its aggregate yields concerned to the poor farmer in study area. The yield of summer rice, pulses and tea was high to the better off farmers (High diversity).

Table 24.11 Herfindahl Index of diversity of area under crops across sample villages

District	Sample village	2011–2012	2012–2013
Kokrajhar	Shyamgaon	0.37	0.38
	Patakata	**0.61**	**0.59**
	Ubrijhora	0.57	0.56
	Sub-total	0.55	0.51
Dhemaji	Amulguri	0.33	0.35
	Chumoni	**0.53**	**0.53**
	Mahanpur	0.47	0.48
	Sub-total	0.45	0.42
All villages		0.49	0.49

Source Field Survey, 2013–2014
Note The bolded values represents the highest diversity observed in that particular village among the three villages of the respective districts

Table 24.12 Distribution of farmers as per high and low herfindhal index of diversity

District	Village	High diversified (0.50>)	Less diversified (<0.50)
Kokrajhar	Shyamgaon	6 (12)	44 (88)
	Patakata	32 (64)	18 (36)
	Ubrijhora	17 (34)	33 (66)
	Sub-total	55 (37)	95 (63)
Dhemaji	Amulguri	2 (4)	48 (96)
	Chumoni	21 (42)	29 (58)
	Mahanpur Pt-I	16 (32)	34 (68)
	Sub-total	39 (26)	111 (74)
All villages		94 (31)	206 (69)

Source Primary data
Note Figures in the parentheses indicate percentage to total

Table 24.13 Results of regression of per capita income from agricultural on relevant explanatory variables

Explanatory variable	Coefficients	*t*-stat	Significance
Constant	6155.647	6.252	0.0000
Total cultivated area	495.165	16.889	0.0000
Diversity index (HI)	4960.207	2.972	0.0032
Family size	−81.859	-0.686	0.493
D	1906.446	3.233	0.001
No. of family labour in agriculture	−1586.006	−7.997	0.0000
$R^2 = 0.658$, Adj. $R^2 = 0.652$, $F = 113.06$ (P-value: 0.0000)			

Source Field Survey, 2013–2014

Table 24.14 Contribution of various components to the difference in agricultural earning between the high and low diversified farm groups from their total cultivated area (at average harvest price 2012–2013) in the sample villages

Individual effects				Interaction effects					
Area	Yield	Cropping pattern	Sub-total	Area-cropping pattern	Area-yield	Yield-cropping pattern	Area-yield-cropping pattern	Sub-total	Total
48,898.74 (67.15)	−22,720.40 (−31.20)	42,666.96 (58.59)	68,845.3 (94.54)	30,551.97 (41.96)	−16,269.10 (−22.34)	−6007.83 (−8.25)	−4301.95 (−5.91)	3973.08 (5.46)	72,818.37 (100)

Source Field Survey, 2013–2014

Notes (1) Figure in the parentheses indicates percentage to total

(2) High Div. Family = 94 and total Cultivated Area = 2345.25 Bigha (24.95 Bigha per family), Low Div. Family = 206 and total Cultivated Area = 2995 Bigha (14.54 Bigha per family)

Table 24.15 Average crop diversity and yield in the low and high diversified farms in the sample villages

Crop	High diversity		Low diversity	
	Proportion of area	Yield of crops	Proportion of area	Yield of crops
Autumn rice	0.214	351.16	0.116	321.90
Winter rice	0.575	428.20	0.413	752.81
Summer rice	0.020	506.25	0.000	0.00
Gram	0.006	83.71	0.002	262.17
Tur	0.003	81.43	0.001	261.00
Pulse	0.000	288.00	0.001	209.50
R&M	0.052	80.49	0.015	91.83
Sesamum	0.005	84.18	0.003	87.53
Linseed	0.005	74.92	0.002	69.83
Jute	0.018	122.12	0.003	158.35
Tea	0.020	963.83	0.000	0.00
Sugarcane	0.012	2705.17	0.005	2645.71
Arecanut[a]	0.021	20082.47	0.026	20090.32
Potato	0.010	499.96	0.008	724.65
Chilly	0.004	383.76	0.003	363.49
Turmeric	0.002	395.25	0.001	441.33
Banana[b]	0.000	200.00	0.003	162.86
Bamboo[a]	0.026	1792.62	0.010	2653.55
Onion	0.001	307.00	0.000	480.00
Brinjal	0.001	348.00	0.002	425.05
Cabbage	0.003	550.40	0.001	627.64
Root	0.003	216.43	0.005	416.59
Radish	0.000	0.00	0.001	347.43
Average		24.95		14.54

Source Field Survey, 2013–2014
Note (i) Area in Bigha; Yield in Kg/Bigha, (ii) [a]Numbers in Bigha; [b]Bunch in Bigha

24.4 Use of Agro-technology by the Farmers in the Sample Villages

Technological progress takes place with the enchantment of human knowledge and utilisation of the same in production processes through research and practice. In rural areas of most developing countries, where land plots are small, capital is scarce and labour is abundant, introduction of heavy mechanical techniques is not suitable to the physical environment and that also cause more rural unemployment (Bezbaruah 1994). However, improvement in irrigation facility along with fertiliser is necessary to accelerate the process of diversification and thereby increase productivity. The pattern of adoption of different agro-technologies by the sample farmers are as follows.

24.4.1 *Use of Chemical Fertiliser*

Use of fertiliser is observed to be very low in both the districts. About 10% of the farmers in Kokrajhar district use chemical fertilisers for cultivation and among them 4% use in summer paddy and 3.3% farmers use it for winter rice, while 1.33% of them use for the cultivation of mustard (Table 24.16). Among different crops, the fertiliser application is more in modern varieties of paddy than in traditional varieties. In Dhemaji district, only 2% of the farmers use chemical fertilisers for tea and none for other crops (Table 24.17). Large number of farmers in Dhemaji do not use chemical fertiliser though use of chemical fertiliser is essential for summer rice cultivation. It may be due to the shortage of capital and lack of risk taking ability. Application of very low chemical fertilisers for seeding and sowing of winter paddy is conceived to be wastage for being washed out due to high precipitation and flood.

24.4.2 *Use of Irrigation*

In case of irrigation, it is observed that farmers of Kokrajhar district hardly use irrigation (Table 24.18). About 27% of the sample farmers use irrigation in autumn rice, 33% in winter rice, and 5% of them use it in summer rice cultivation. In sample area of Dhemaji district, irrigation is confined to a few crops and in limited areas. Such poor utilisation rates indicate that most of the crops are cultivated in un-irrigated area under rain-fed conditions. It is reported that a major section of farmers have opted for cultivation of different crops even under rain-fed condition without any irrigation, applying chemical fertilisers, and having pest and disease control measures. The cultivation of various types of crops was found on

Table 24.16 Percentage of respondent farmers using chemical fertiliser across the villages

District	Village	Autumn rice	Winter rice	Summer rice	Rape & mustard	Tea	Other crops	Total
Kokrajhar	Shyamgaon	Nil	10	2	Nil	Nil	Nil	12
	Patakata	2	Nil	8	4	Nil		14
	Ubrijhora	Nil		2	Nil	2		4
	Sub-total	0.67	3.3	4	1.33	0.67		10
Dhemaji	Amulguri	Nil	Nil	Nil	Nil	Nil	Nil	Nil
	Chumoni					6		6
	Mahanpur					Nil		Nil
	Sub-total					2		2

Source Field Survey, 2013–2014

Table 24.17 Percentage of respondent farmers using irrigation facilities across the villages

District	Village	Autumn rice	Winter rice	Summer rice	Mustard	Linseed	Jute	Tea	Potato	Cabbage/cauliflower	Other crops
Kokrajhar	Shyamgaon	6	98	2	Nil	Nil	Nil	Nil	2	Nil	Nil
	Patakata	74	Nil	12	2	2	4	0	4	6	
	Ubrijhora	Nil		2	Nil	Nil	Nil	2	Nil	Nil	
	Sub-total	26.67	32.67	5.33	0.67	0.67	1.33	0.67	2	2	
Dhemaji	Amulguri	58	86	Nil	Nil	Nil	Nil	6	Nil	2	Nil
	Chumoni	Nil	Nil					Nil		Nil	
	Mahanpur										
	Sub-total	19.33	28.97					2.00		0.67	

Source Field Survey, 2013–2014

Table 24.18 Percentage of respondent farmers as per adoption of HYV seeds across sample villages

District	Village	Autumn rice	Winter rice	Summer rice	Mustard	Brinjal	Other crops	Total
Kokrajhar	Shyamgaon	Nil	Nil	2	2	Nil	Nil	4
	Patakata	14	4	12	Nil	Nil		30
	Ubrijhora	Nil	Nil	2	2	2		6
	Sub-total	4.7	1.3	5.3	1.3	0.7	Nil	13.3
Dhemaji	Amulguri	Nil	2		10	2		14
	Chumoni	Nil	Nil	Nil	44	Nil	Nil	44
	Mahanpur	4	0		28	2		34
	Sub-total	1.3	0.7	Nil	27.3	1.3	Nil	30.7

Source Field Survey, 2013–2014

un-irrigated land mostly by traditional method because of the non-availability of irrigation facilities or non-functioning of existing irrigation facilities on regular basis. Many reasons are hypothesised for the low utilisation rates, such as shortage of labour, lack of proper distribution channels to carry water to the farmer's fields, and lack of suitable cropping pattern are probably the most plausible ones (Khound and Borthakur 1999).

24.4.3 Use of HYV Seeds

Table 24.19 reveals that limited sample farmers having irrigation facilities in Kokrajhar district (Patakata, Shyamgaon) cultivate high yielding varieties (HYV) of rice and a very few farmers use HYV mustard and brinjal for cultivation. Most of the other cultivated crops are of traditional varieties. In Dhemaji, only a countable number of farmers cultivate HYV paddy varieties or mustard on limited plots. Some farmers usually grow some special local varieties of paddy (e.g. Aijung, Ponkoj, Powalisali, Suwagmoni, Ketekijoha, Laxman, Borbora, etc.) for self-consumption. In such cases, previous home produced outputs are used as seeds and they apply seeds according to their traditional knowledge and experience and do not adopt modern farming techniques to a large extent. Survey data revealed that spread of HYV seeds and fertiliser usages by respondent farmers have been very low in the sample villages of both Kokrajhar and Dhemaji districts. It clearly indicates the slow pace of adoption of modern farming techniques in sample areas of Assam. Price and non-price factors including high cost of agro-implements, lake of irrigation facilities, access to credit etc. have been cited as critical determinants of technology adoption for the rural poor farmers in Assam.

Table 24.19 Distribution of respondents according to use of agro-implements (%)

District	Sample village	Traditional implements			Modern implements			
		Plough	Bullock carts	Harrow	Power tiller	Tractor	Oil engine	Sprayer and duster
Kokrajhar	Shyamgaon	100	Nil	10	66	18	6	78
	Patakata	100	8	28	30	58	18	66
	Ubrijhora	100	6	4	36	6	6	30
	Sub-total	100	4.7	14	44	27	10	58
Dhemaji	Amulguri	100	Nil	28	12	68	20	26
	Chumoni	98	2	40	28	48	14	38
	Mahanpur	100	Nil	12	14	44	8	30
	Sub-total	99	0.67	27	18	53	14	31

Source Field Survey, 2013–2014

24.4.4 Use of Agricultural Implements

Agricultural implements are necessary from ploughing to harvesting, irrigation, and spray of insecticides and several other related operations. So, availability and use of farm level assets like plough, bullock labour, machine work, agricultural apparatus and implements reveal the level of adoption of technology in farm operations. Most of the respondents do still follow the age old traditional methods of cultivation, depending on the primitive wooden ploughs, sickle, hoe, and their human and bullock powers. It is observed from the Table 24.20 that all the sample farmers extensively use traditional plough for the preparation of land. Farmers of Kokrajhar

Table 24.20 Distribution of respondent farm families faced crop damage in last five years

District	Village	Damaged by				Total number of affected farm Families
		Flood	Draught	Pests/Insects	Storms	
Kokrajhar	Shyamgaon	Nil	Nil	1 (2)	Nil	1 (2)
	Patakata	Nil	Nil	5 (10)	3 (6)	8 (16)
	Ubrijhora	Nil	32 (64)	4 (8)	Nil	36 (72)
	Sub-total	Nil	32 (21)	10 (6.7)	3 (2)	45 (30)
Dhemaji	Amulguri	41 (82)	Nil	Nil	Nil	41 (82)
	Chumoni	36 (72)				36 (72)
	Mahanpur	46 (92)				46 (92)
	Sub-total	123 (82)	Nil	Nil	Nil	123 (82)

Source Field Survey, 2013–2014
Note Figure in the parentheses indicates percentage of respondent farmer

district mostly use bullock carts and traditional type of harrows. Also, power tillers and tractors (own or hired) are used on a limited scale in the agricultural activities of the sample farms. However, comparatively, lesser proportions of these modern implements and machinery are used by the farmers of Kokrajhar than that of Dhemaji. These may be due to the larger size of land holdings of the farmers in Dhemaji than that of Kokrajhar district as observed in the previous section. Moreover, significant variation in the uses of different agro-implements by the farmers in the sample villages is observed. It may be noted that the marginal and small farmers have a dearth of money to buy power tiller, tractor, etc. But they can hire those implements as is observed in West Bengal, Punjab, etc., whose markets have not yet been developed significantly in Assam.

24.5 Measures Adopted to Mitigate Climate Risk in the Study Area

This section tried to focus on farmer's perceptions and adaptations strategy in the study area. The analysis provides information on the farmer's response to climate change and possible factors that influence their adaptation of strategies to moderate extreme climate impacts. Diversification of crops is one of the important adaptation measures where with the changing climatic conditions farmers can choose suitable cropping pattern over the periods of time to adjust to the changing climate and simultaneously maximise returns from agriculture in the respective region. However, geographical locations and socio-economic conditions have an important influence on the farmer's adaptability with the changing technology and climatic conditions in diversifying their crops. Sources of acquiring new knowledge or information about agricultural technologies and their cost effectiveness are important factors that also affect technology adoption. However, most of the farmers in the sample villages particularly the tribal farmers[2] are unaware of many programmes sponsored by the government to promote adaptation of new technologies. It may be due to the lack of dissemination of information or knowledge regarding agricultural techniques. These farmers being more tradition ridden and conservative are found to be less responsive towards the adoption of new agricultural technology. However, some farmers are ready to adopt new agricultural technology (as observed from foregoing discussions) but are not in a position to adopt the improved technology at the full scale due to certain socio-economic constraints faced by them in their daily life. Even then sample farmers reported that they have used some sort of modern implements on hiring basis with their limited capacity. Usually, the farmers also use both the modern varieties and traditional varieties of crops simultaneously depending upon the availability of seeds and capital.

[2]Since Kokrajhar and Dhemaji are tribal dominated districts and sample farm households are mostly tribal farmers in these districts.

Table 24.21 Distribution of respondent farmers according to the adoption of various measures to tackle the incidence of flood

District	Kokrajhar				Dhemaji			
Measures adopted/village	Shya.	Pata.	Ubri.	Sub-total	Amul.	Chum.	Maha.	Sub-total
Cultivated short period crops	Nil				12 (24)	20 (40)	18 (36)	50 (33.3)
Cultivated early					29 (58)	12 (24)	25 (50)	66 (44)
Cultivated flood resistant crops					3 (6)	9 (18)	3 (6)	15 (10)
Changed next crops					9 (18)	2 (4)	1 (2)	12 (8)
Diversified to other crops					2 (4)	Nil	Nil	2 (1.3)
Preserve seedling for sowing after floods					45 (90)	38 (76)	41 (82)	124 (82.7)
Total	Nil				100 (67)	81 (59)	88 (58)	269 (89.7)

Source Field Survey, 2013–2014
Notes Figure in the parentheses indicates percentage of respondent farmer
Shya. Shyamgaon, *Pata.* Patatkata, *Ubri.* Ubrijhora, *Amul.* Amulguri, *Chum.* Chimoni and *Maha.* Mahanpur

Experience of last five years by the respondents reveals that entire Kokrajhar district has never been affected by floods but rarely do they face draught (Table 24.21). Thus, no damage of crops due to extreme climatic hazards is reported by the farmers in the district as a whole. However, draught like situation damage some crops in southern parts of the district (Ubrijhora area) and damage of some crops of a few farmers due to pests and insects are reported for the last five years. On the other hand, farmers of Dhemaji district reported damage of their crops due to regular floods. Thus, farmers of Kokrajhar district hardly followed any adaptation measure to save their crops from floods and draughts in last five years as the farmers have not been affected by these climatic hazards severely in the past. On the other hand, farmers of Dhemaji district reported several adaptation measures to save their crops particularly from floods that occur frequently every year and at different times. Most of the respondents adopt early cultivation method and cultivate short period crops to avoid floods & harvest early. It is argued that timely preparation of land and plantation increase chances of survival of the crops (mainly winter paddy) from floods. Over 76% of the respondents preserve seedlings to sow again once the crop is damaged due to flood during the peak monsoon time (Table 24.22).

Table 24.22 Percentage of respondent farmers that changes their crop cultivation for different reasons from 1990 to 2013

District	Village	Reasons of changing to newer crops					
		Availability of HYV seeds	Reduction of risk	Earning profits	Lower cost	Weather resistance	Total
Kokrajhar	Shyamgaon	Nil	Nil	46 (92)	4 (8)	Nil	50 (100)
	Patakata	9 (18)	1 (2)	32 (64)	8 (16)		50 (100)
	Ubrijhora	Nil	1 (2)	47 (94)	2 (4)		50 (100)
	Sub-total	9 (6)	2 (1.33)	125 (83)	14 (9)		150 (100)
Dhemaji	Amulguri	Nil	7 (14)	27 (54)	11 (22)	5 (10)	50 (100)
	Chumoni		4 (8)	20 (40)	26 (52)	Nil	49 (98)
	Mahanpur		18 (36)	22 (44)	9 (18)	1 (2)	50 (100)
	Sub-total		29 (19.33)	69 (46)	46 (31)	6 (4)	149 (99)

Source Field Survey, 2013–2014
Note Figures in the parentheses indicate percentage to total

Farmers have reported to have changed their cultivation of crops (whatever possible) in the last two decades (i.e. 1990–1991 to 2012–2013) for various reasons (Table 24.23). Some farmers (18%) of Patakata village of Kokrajhar district have changed traditional varieties to newer crops due to the availability of HYV seeds, 83% of the respondents of the same district changed cropping pattern to earn more profit. Some of them cited lower cost of cultivation for changing cropping pattern. No weather resistant crop varieties have been chosen by the farmers of Kokrajhar district. On the other hand, risk factors (19.33%), earning profits (46%), lower cost of cultivation (31%) and weather resistance (4%) are cited to be the prime reasons for adopting newer varieties of crops during last 20 years by the farmers in the sample villages of Dhemaji district.

Table 24.23 Results of regression of diversity index (HI) on relevant explanatory variables

Explanatory variable	Coefficients	Std. error	*t*-stat	Significance
(Constant)	0.097	0.051	1.926	0.055
Education of head	0.020*	0.008	2.354	0.019
Family agricultural labour	0.028	0.007	0.210	3.800
Cultivation experience	0.001	0.001	1.049	0.295
Training	−0.023	0.046	−0.489	0.625
Total cropped area	0.008**	0.001	6.601	0.000
Income from agricultural share	0.001**	0.00403	3.060	0.002
Irrigation intensity	−0.00037*	0.000299	−1.231	0.219
Dummy variable	−0.131**	0.023	−5.762	0.0000
$R^2 = 0.354$, Adj. $R^2 = 0.336$, $F = 19.944$ (P-value: 0.00)				

Source Field Survey, 2013–2014
Notes ** indicate that the coefficient is significant at 5 and 1% level of significance

The above discussion and analysis of data clearly indicate that despite a number of constraints faced by the farmers in the study area; there is enormous scope to diversify their crops and adaptability varies across space with the changing technology and environment. Adaptation and disaster mitigation requires adequate knowledge, access to suitable technology, capital and appropriate policy measures. A failure in adaptation with the changing climatic uncertainty may lead to socio-economic disaster and jeopardise the livelihood security of the people particularly those who are dependent more on natural weather for agricultural activities.

24.6 Adaptability of Farmers' in Response to Climate Change

Agricultural adaptation to climate risk is a relatively new field of inquiry in Northeast India. On the basis of farmer's response to climate change and some other relevant variables, farmer's perceptions and adaptations strategy are examined for the study area. From the regression analysis as presented in Table 24.24 it is observed that knowledge of the respondent farmers; farm size and area of holdings and share of family income from agricultural activities are significantly important factors behind the diversification by the farmers. The coefficients of training to the farmers, and irrigation intensity are, however, not significant and that implies that crop diversity is hardly influenced by the training facilities and irrigation in the surveyed area. This may be due to the fact that training on cultivation of particular crops makes the farmers proficient on some specific crops and not on diversification needs. Also slowly growing irrigation facilities helped the small and marginal farmers to go for some staple food crops for food security and agriculture is still at subsistence stage.

Table 24.24 Results of regression of adaptation index (AI) on relevant explanatory variables

Explanatory variable	Coefficients	Std. error	*t*-stat	Significance
(Constant)	−0.043**	0.008	−5.248	0.000
Education of head	0.005**	0.001	3.368	0.001
Family agricultural labour	0.003	0.001	2.189	0.029
Cultivation experience	0.000454**	0.000167	2.724	0.007
Training	−0.005	0.008	-0.722	0.471
Total cropped area	0.001**	0.000194	2.839	0.005
Income from agricultural share	7.770e−005	0.00066	1.183	0.238
Irrigation intensity	6.727e−005*	0.00049	1.337	0.169
Dummy variable	0.090**	0.004	24.347	0.000
R^2 = 0.774, Adj. R^2 = 0.767, F = 124.265 (P-value: 0.00)				

Source Field Survey, 2013–2014

Notes *, ** indicate that the coefficient is significant at 5 and 1% level of significance

The regression results of adaptation index on various explanatory variables are depicted in Table 24.21. The table reveals that the level of education of the heads of households has significantly positive impact on adaptation. Education generally increases knowledge and helps farmer to gain adaptive capacity to the changing climatic conditions and use of appropriate agro-technologies. The size of the operational holding of the farmer (total cropped area), and years of cultivation experience also have significantly positive impacts on adaptation. The implication is that adaptive capacity of farmers increases with the increasing size of the land holdings and cultivation experience. However, training of the farmers is found to have no impact on adaptation. It may be noted that most of the training conducted by the concerned departments are basically held on how to raise crop productivity through the use of modern technology rather than on adaptation and awareness strategy towards climate change in Assam. Also, share of income from agricultural sources and irrigation intensity recorded insignificant effects on the climate change adaptation. That is, farmers are more adapted with the traditional way of cultivation under rain-fed conditions in Assam.

It is apparent from the aforementioned results that extent of holdings and learning level of the farmers are important factors for the extent of diversification and adaptation of crops with the climate change in different districts of Assam. This is in compliance with the results obtained by some other researchers not only in India, but in some other countries as well (Pingali et al. 1997; Mendelssohn and Seo 2007c; De and Chattopadhyay 2010; Anselm and Taofeeq 2010; Onyeneke and Madukwe 2010; Sahu and Mishra 2013). Moreover, the other agro-infrastructural variables like irrigation, training to the farmers, share of agricultural income, etc., are also important for agricultural diversification and adaptation. However, the nature and extent of variations of these variables for diverse crops and climatic conditions in different regions do not contribute in the same way.

24.7 Findings and Analysis

The above discussion reveals that in spite of many problems and limitations, the rural farmers of Assam manage to raise varieties of crops under rain-fed weather condition depending upon their availability of resources. One of the important factors hindering the proper utilisation of new farm technology is the dominance of scattered tiny plots (marginal and small in size) in the state. With such small and fragmented holdings, full utilisation of modern implements is not possible. The study established that due to small and scattered holdings, the farmers could not own the groundwater irrigation facilities (deep or shallow tube-well). Also, whatever irrigation facility is created not utilised at full potential. Uneconomic small and fragmented small holdings need to be grouped through land consolidation and cooperative formation.

As the average fertiliser consumption in the state is very low, the situation is not different in the study area too. Due to the scarcity of resources, the sample farmers cannot purchase the required amount of expansive fertiliser in time. Further, they are not aware of the recommended doses for different crops. Lack of irrigation facility and soil testing is also another problem of the sample farmers in using chemical fertiliser.

It is needless to mention that training of farmers on available modern technology can go a long way in accelerating the agricultural production and productivity. But, the respondents reported that they are not aware of the new knowledge and farm practices due to lack of adequate exposure from the agricultural extension centres. The farmers usually adopt the traditional variety of seeds whose average yield is almost half the yield of HYV. Existing irrigation facilities created in the study areas have many shortcomings. Although there are some STWs, it is difficult to extract the necessary water during *rabi* crops because of the high cost involved and no electricity. Besides, farmers of the sample area generally cultivate mustard, sesamum potato, gram and vegetable crops, etc., for home consumption with little commercial motive. Hence, due attention has not been paid on irrigation for better and efficient cultivation.

Most of the farmers are found to be risk averter and are sceptical in trying new varieties. It is also observed that farmers are not aware of the concept of crop planning and the effort of the agriculture department to train the farmers is inadequate. As expected in the traditional cropping system, thus crop diversification is limited as the farmers do not have suitable facilities and supporting agro-infrastructure. Lack of climatic change perception of the farmers in the study area of Kokrajhar is due to limited climate change effects in the area. Nature of adaptation with the changing technology and climatic conditions by some sample farmers of Dhemaji, however, proves that farmers are eager to adopt newer technology in their cropping activities to save their crops and moderate climate change impacts.

24.8 Concluding Remarks

The above discussion clearly indicates that despite a number of constraints faced by the farmers in the study area, there is enormous scope to diversify their crops and adaptability options with the changing variables of technology and environment. Cultivation of a large number of crops indicates the suitability of agro-climatic environment in the state. Majority of the farmers are small landholders and their income from crop and non-crop activities are not enough to meet their subsistence and they produce only a few specialised crops which are risk prone. Due to fluctuations in price and weather conditions; crop diversification becomes the need of the hour as a well-diversified agricultural economy unfolds many related opportunities. Moreover, soil fertility can be enhanced through crop rotation. It adds value through increasing total productivity and at the same time stabilises farm income by minimising the risk connected with single cropping system.

Furthermore, there is an urgent need for restructuring the existing crops sequences so as to make appropriate adjustment to changing weather condition in flood prone districts of Assam. Hence, emphasis should shift towards growing more *rabi* crops with assured irrigation support. There is ample opportunity for increasing the production of summer rice and short duration paddy in the sample area in particular and Assam in general. For introduction and popularisation of new crop varieties, adoptive and result oriented field demonstration may be encouraged. In the flood prone areas, short duration variety of paddy may be cultivated and harvested early to avoid flood damages. Adaptation options such as irrigation management and promotion of improved crop varieties are only viable if there is external support. However, there is a need to focus not only on technical aspects but also social dimensions such as perceptions of small-holder farmers. Government and policy makers should support farmers to generate long-term and location-specific adaptation strategies and therefore, major thrust should be given to the development of irrigation, easy reach of modern agro-inputs, provisions of location-specific and need-based solutions to support crop diversification in any type of land, e.g. plain land, lowland and upland, while management of irrigation, cheap and simple technologies, etc., innovative micro-insurance schemes can be another tool to help small-holder farmers to cope with climate variability and change (Patt et al. 2010).

References

Adensina, A. A., & Forson, J. B. (1995). Farmers' perceptions and adaptation of new agricultural technology: Evidence from analysis in Burkina Faso and Guinea, West Africa. *Agricultural Economics, 13,* 1–9.

Adger, W. N., Hug, S., Brown, K. Conway, D., & Hume, M. (2003). Adaptation to climate change in developing world. *Progress in Development Studies, 3*(3), 179–195. Available at doi:10.1191/1464993403ps060oa. Accessed March 15, 2003.

Anselm, A. E., & Taofeeq, A. A. (2010). Challenges of agricultural adaptation climate change in Nigeria: A synthesis from the literature. *Field Actions Science Reports* [online], *4*. Available at http://factsreports.revues.org/678. Accessed June 2011.

Aufhammer, M., Ramanathan, V., & Vincent, J. (2006). *Integrated models show that atmospheric brown clouds and greenhouse gases have reduced rice yields in India*. Available at http://www.pnas.org_cgi_doi_10.1073_pnas.0609584104. Accessed November 2014.

Bastine, C. L., & Palanisami, K. P. (1994). An analysis of growth trends in principal crops in Kerala. *Agricultural Situation in India., 48*(12), 885–891.

Bezbaruah, M. P. (1994). *Technological transformation of agriculture: A study from Assam*. New Delhi: Mittal Publications.

Dale, V. H. (1997). The relationship between land-use change and climate change. *Ecological Application, 7*(3), 753–769.

De, U. K. (2003). *Economics of crop diversification*. New Delhi: Akansha Publishing House.

De, U. K., & Bodosa, K. (2014). Crop diversification in Assam and use of modern inputs under changing climatic condition. *Journal of Climatology & Weather Forecasting*, *2*(2), 1–14. Available at http://www.editorialmanager.com/environsci/default.asp. Accessed February 2015.

De, U. K., & Chattopadhyay, M. (2010). Crop diversification by poor peasants and infrastructure: Evidence from West Bengal. *Journal of Development and Agricultural Economics, 2*(10), 340–350.

Eriksen, S., Aldunce, P., Bahinipati, C. S., Martins, R. D., Molefe, J. I., Nhemachena, C., et al. (2011). When not every response to climate change is a good one: Identifying principles for sustainable adaptation. *Climate and Development, 3*, 7–20. Available at doi:10.3763/cdev.2010.0060. Accessed March 2015.

FAO. (2011). Save and grow: A policymaker's guide to the sustainable intensification of smallholder crop production. Food and Agriculture Organization, The United Nations, Rome.

Government of Assam. (2012–13). *Economic survey*, Directorate of Economics and Statistics, Assam.

Habiba, U., Show, R., & Takeuchi, Y. (2012). Farmer's perception and adaptation practices to cope with draught: Perspectives from north-western Bangladesh. *International Journal of Disaster Risk Reduction, 1*, 72–84.

Hazra, C. R. (2001). Diversification in Indian agriculture. *Agricultural Situation in India, 58*(9), 409–418.

IPCC. (2007a). *Climate change 2007: Impacts, adaptation and vulnerability*. Cambridge: Cambridge University Press.

IPCC. (2007b). *Climate change: Synthesis report*. Contribution of Working Groups I, II and II to the Fourth Assessment Report of the International Panel on Climate Change, Geneva.

Khound, H. P., & Borthakur, N. (1999). The status and future needs of infrastructure, related to sustainable agriculture in Assam. Assam Agricultural University, Jorhat.

Krishnamurthy, B. C. (2012). The distributional impacts of climate change on Indian agriculture: A quantile regression approach. Working Paper 69/2012, May, Madras School of Economics, Chennai, India.

Krishna, M., Vasisht, A. K., & Sharma, B. M. (1991). Growth and instability in Kerala agriculture. *Agricultural Situation in India, 46*(1), 168–173.

Kyte, R. (2014). *Crop diversity is key to agricultural climate adaptability*. Available at http://blogs.scientificamerican.com/guest-blog/crop-diversity-is-key-to-agricultural-climate-adaptation/. Accessed May 2015.

Lybbert, T., & Sumner, D. (2010). Agricultural technologies for climate change mitigation and adaptation in developing countries: Policy options for innovation and technology diffusion. *International Centre for Trade and Sustainable Development (ICTSD)*, Issue Brief No. 6. Available at http://www.ictsd.org/sites/default/files/research/2010/06/agricultural-technologies-for-climate-change-mitigation-and-adaptation-in-developing-countriesweb.pdf. Accessed March 2015.

Mehta, P. K. (2009). Role of crop diversification in output growth in India: A state-level analysis ICFAI. *University Journal of Agricultural Economics, 6*(2), 1–18.

Mendelsohn, R., & Seo, S. N. (2007c). Changing farm types and irrigation as an adaptation to climate change in Latin American agriculture. Policy Research Working Paper 4161, Washington, DC, United States, Word Bank.

Minhas, B. S., & Vaidyanathan, A. (1965). Growth of crop output in India 1951–54 to 1958–61: An analysis by component elements. *Journal of the Indian Society of Agricultural Statistics, 17* (2), 230–252.

Onyeneke, R., & Madukwe, D. (2010). Adaptation measures by crop farmers in the southeast rainforest zone of Nigeria to climate change. *Science World Journal, 5*(1), 32–34.

Patt, A., Pablo, S., & Hess, U. (2010). How do small holder farmers understand insurance, and how much they want it? Evidence from Africa. *Global Environment Change, 20*, 153–161.

Pauliotte, J., Smith, B., & Westerhoff, L. (2009). Adaptation and development: Livelihoods and climate change in Subarnabad, Bangladesh. *Climate Change and Development, 1*, 31–46. Available at doi:10.3763/cdev.2009.0001. Accessed March 2015.

Pingali, P. L., Hossain, M., & Gerpacio, R. V. (1997). *Asian rice bowls—The returning crisis?* CAB International Wallingford.

Sahu, N. C., & Mishra, D. (2013). *Analysis of perception and adaptability strategies of the farmers to climate change in Odisha, India, 5*, 123–127, Available at www.elsevier.com/locate/procedia. Accessed March 15.

Tanner, T., & Mitchell, T. (2008). Entrenchment or enhancement: could climate change adaptation help to reduce chronic poverty? *Institute of Development Studies Bulletin, 39*, 6–15.

Ye, L., Tang, Wu, W., Yang, P., Nelson, G. C., D'Croz, D. M., et al. (2013). Chinese food security and climate change: agriculture futures, economics. *The Open- Access, E-Journal*, No. 2013–2.

Chapter 25
Dynamics of Forest Resources: Some Empirical Testing on Assam's Forest Cover

Gunjan Kumar

Abstract Unlike exhaustible resources, forest is one of the renewable resources having regeneration capacity. However the environmental effects of the deforestation as a consequence of rising consumption and economic growth is not ignorable. Therefore, it is essential to understand the dynamic behaviour of forest cover for their conservation and sustainable forest management. This chapter uses Pontryagin's maximum principle to formulate the optimal control path of forests. Mathematical softwares like MATLAB and Mathematica have been used to depict the behavioural trend of forests. Some empirical testing and calculations have been made by using the data of Assam's forest cover for illustrative purpose. However the outcomes are constrained by data availability. The chapter finds that any slight change in the stock leads to a change in the whole behaviour of the forest cover over time and there is a specific rate of regeneration and specific consumption/harvest rate for every quantity of stock, which may keep the stock of forests constant. A small decline in regeneration and a small increase in consumption may lead to notable deforestation. Impatience (discounting the future utility with higher rates) in planning may result lesser consumption and lower stock in future. Extraction of the rents from the renewable resources should be equal to the natural rate of growth of the resources and these rents should be invested in their regeneration wherever possible.

Keywords Forests · Harvesting · Stock · Regeneration

G. Kumar (✉)
Department of Humanities and Social Sciences, Indian Institute of Technology, Guwahati, India
e-mail: gunjan.kumar@iitg.ernet.in; gunjankumar26@rediffmail.com

U.K. De et al. (eds.), *Inequality, Poverty and Development in India*, India Studies in Business and Economics, DOI 10.1007/978-981-10-6274-2_25

25.1 Introduction

There is a growing concern for keeping the environmental resources and their quality intact. The developing concepts of sustainability have recognised the important roles of the forests as an integral part of the finite environmental resources. Forests are among such invaluable environmental resources which need serious concerns. The publication of the World Commission on Environment and Development (WECD, 1987) voiced new and urgent environmental concerns including deforestation and the loss of biodiversity. Continuous deforestation and the rising environmental problems are getting worldwide attention today. Arrow et al. (1995) explains that while empirical findings do indicate that economic growth may be associated with improvements in some environmental indicators, they do not imply that economic growth is sufficient to induce environmental improvement in general. The environmental effects of growth cannot be simply ignored. They further argue that indeed the Earth's resource base is not capable of supporting indefinite economic growth. Ecological economists argue for an approach which provides privileges to the requirements of the system above those of the individual. The peculiar behaviour of renewable resources (including forests) does not allow us to exploit them unlimitedly. The time has come for the forest conservation and sustainable forest management. Therefore, it is essential to understand its dynamic behaviour and make some approximate predictions.

Many ecological economists highlight one of the principles of sustainable development as: 'Harvest rates should equal Regeneration rates' with a concept of well-being of both the present and future generations. Economists often use Pontryagin's maximum principle to formulate the optimal control path of inter-generational equity. This chapter also uses the same to deal with forest stock which is a renewable economic and environmental resource. The aim of this chapter is to provide a picture of dynamic behaviour of forest. For the purpose of the chapter the case of Assam forest cover has been taken to obtain some empirical findings. Mathematical softwares like MATLAB and Mathematica have been used to fulfil the purpose, so that the study could be made more realistic and fruitful. The chapter attempts to provide an insight into the peculiar dynamic characteristics of forest stocks which may help in planning and management of forest resources while dealing with the problem of declining forests. In the subsequent section, a basic model of optimal control is presented which describes the case of renewable resources like forests. The case of Assam, a state in India has been discussed with empirical illustrations which are followed by a conclusion with policy implications.

25.2 The Basic Model

The basic optimal control model which a social planner is supposed to solve is:

$$\max_{c} \int_{0}^{\infty} U(c, s)\mathrm{d}t$$
$$\text{Subject to } \dot{s} = a * s - c$$

For notational simplicity, the time dependence of the variables is suppressed. 'a' denotes the natural growth of the resources and 'c' and 's' are consumption and stock of the resources respectively. Unlike exhaustible resources, renewable resources like forests have the regeneration capacity ($a > 0$). Assuming that the planner only concerns about the welfare from the consumption, and the function takes the form $U(c,s) = \ln c$, the equation to be optimised for a fixed time period 'T' is

$$\max_{c} \int_{0}^{T} \mathrm{e}^{-rt} \ln c$$
$$\text{Subject to } \dot{s} = a * s - c$$

The Current Value Hamiltonian[1] in this case is

$$\tilde{H} = \ln c + \Phi\,(a * s - c)$$

The two differential equations consisting optimal path of consumption and stock of resources take the form

$$\dot{c} = (a - s)\,c \tag{25.1}$$

$$\dot{s} = (a * s - c) \tag{25.2}$$

The stock of renewable resources which obviously includes forest stocks behave in the form of: $\dot{s} = (a * s - c)$. Hartwick's rule which is also sometimes known as weak sustainability approach states that 'zero net investment forever results in constant consumption forever' (Pezzey and Toman 2002). This rule implies that $\dot{s} = 0$ will keep the stock intact. The equation '$\dot{s} = (a * s - c)$' can be solved for the value of 's' and the resultant equation is

$$s_T = s_0\,\mathrm{e}^{(t - t0)} - \frac{c}{a}(\mathrm{e}^{a(t - t0)} - 1) \tag{25.3}$$

[1]Current Value Hamilton is the result of multiplication of both the sides of the Hamiltonian equation $\{H = e^{-rt} \ln c + \prod (as - c)\}$ by e^{rt} where r is the rate of discount. Equations (25.1), (25.2) and (25.3) have been found after solving the equation of optimal control by the author.

s_T and s_O are the stocks at time period '*T*' and at initial period respectively. When $\dot{s} = 0$, $s = c/a$; which indicates that in steady state for constant stock over time, stock must be equal to the ratio of the consumption and growth rate.

25.3 Case of Assam

Assam is a state situated in the north-eastern part of India between latitude 24007′ to 28000′N and longitude 89042′ to 96002′E (FSI 2005). This state has a geographic area of 78,438 km^2, which constitutes 2.4% of the country's geographic area. According to India state of Forest Report (2013) Assam's share in forest and tree cover with reference to India is around 3.48%. The forest cover in Assam has an area of 27,671 km^2 which is about 35.28% of its total geographical area. Table 25.1 shows the change in forest cover from 1987 to 2013 in Assam (Fig. 25.1).

The striking difference in forest cover between 1999** and 2001** assessments, as shown in the above table, is composed of two entities: difference due to technical factors and the real change in the forest cover during the intervening period between the two assessments done by the Forest Survey of India (Khataniar et al. 2012). These differences can be better represented in the form of a table (Table 25.2).

Net Real change in forest cover between the two years 1999 and 2001 is −123. Therefore, the average decline in a year is 61.5 km^2. Assuming 61.5 (for example) as a constant rate of harvesting/consumption (c) and taking 27,714 km^2 as the forest stock (s) in the year 2001 Eq. 25.2 can be written as

$$\dot{s} = a * 27714 - 61.5$$

By using MATLAB[2] software and through trial and error the value of 'a' has been found as a = 0.002219095042223 (approx.) which may keep the forest stock constant over time. A different value of the stock may change the behaviour of the forest cover over time and there is some specific 'a', rate of growth for every quantity of stock which may keep the stock intact in the future. Figures 25.2 and 25.3 depict this behaviour of forest stock.

In Fig. 25.2 the stock of the forest cover remains constant (27,714 km^2) over time, that is, $\dot{s} = 0$; but if the initial stock would not be equal to 27,714 km^2 the behaviour changes as shown in the Fig. 25.3.

With a higher initial stock (s_O > 27,714) the total forest cover area increases over time, even with the same consumption (61.5) and same growth rate

[2]**MATLAB** (**mat**rix **lab**oratory) is a multi-paradigm numerical computing environment and fourth-generation programming language. Developed by MathWorks, MATLAB allows matrix manipulations, plotting of functions and data, implementation of algorithms, creation of user interfaces, and interfacing with programmes written in other languages, including C, C++, Java, Fortran and Python.

Table 25.1 Forest of tree cover in different assessments (1987–2013) area in km^2

Year	Area in km^2
1987	25,160
1989	24,832
1991	24,751
1993	24,508
1995	24,061
1997	23,824
1999**	23,688
2001**	27,714
2003	27,826
2004–05	27,645
2006–07	27,692
2008–09	27,673
2013	27,671

Source State of Forest Reports, F.S.I*(2001–2013), *FSI: Forest Survey of India

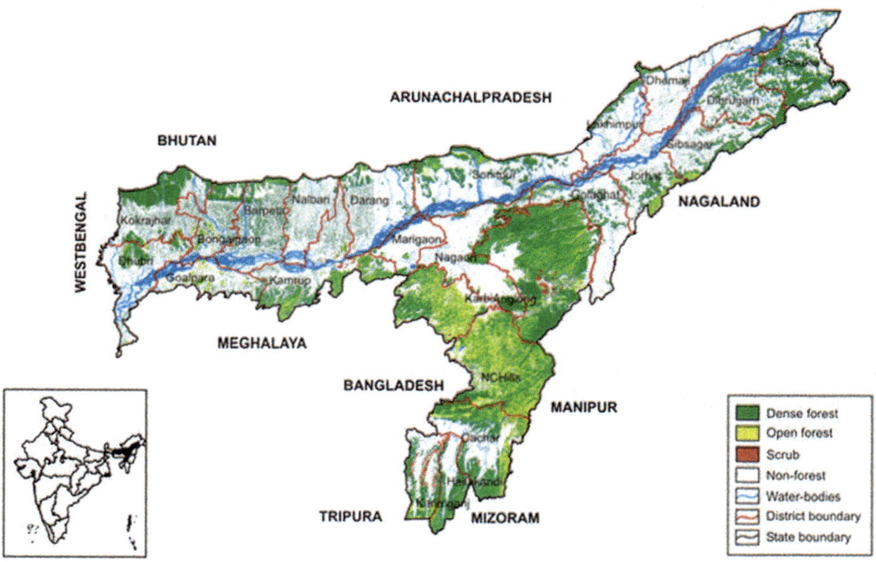

Fig. 25.1 Map of Assam and its forest cover. *Source* State of Forest Report, 2001 FSI

(0.002219095042223). On the other hand, the total stock declines with the same consumption/harvesting and growth rate, but with lower initial stock ($s_0 < 27{,}714$). Therefore, one can find the required growth rate or required consumption level which can keep the forest stock level constant over time for future generations. There is a specific 'a' and specific 'c' for each stock level, which can keep the stock of forests constant. There may be variation in the behaviour and the trend of the

Table 25.2 Change in forest cover between 1999 and 2001 assessments in km^2

1999	2001	Difference in forest cover			Net real change in forest cover
		Total	Due to technical factors		
			Delineated within forest cover in 1999	Additional forest cover captured	
a	b	$c = b - a$	d	e	$c - d + e$
23,688	27,714	4026	−1311	5460	−123

Source Khataniar et al., (2012)

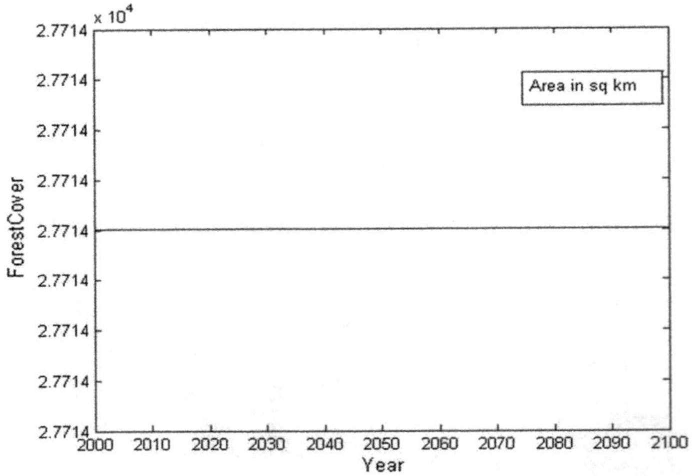

Fig. 25.2 Behaviour of forest stock with initial stock = 27,714 km^2

forest cover stock with different values of the rate of growth and the rate of consumption. For example, if the value of 'a', growth rate of forest stock would be ($a = 0.00221909504200 < 0.002219095042223$) or the value '$c$' would be ($65.5 > 61.5$), then the future trend is as depicted in Figs. 25.4 and 25.5 respectively.

A decline in the rate of growth of forest cover or a rise in consumption may lead to a lower stock of forests in the future. A rise in consumption may lead to a decline in the forest stocks, but it is not easy to control the growing consumption of the human population. On the other side, the growth of forest stocks through afforestation is also a long-term process.

One can find the value of 'a' and 'c' from the Eq. 25.3 using Mathematica[3] software. The equation may take any form depending upon the type of Utility

[3]Mathematica is a computational software program used in many scientific, engineering, mathematical and computing fields, based on symbolic mathematics.

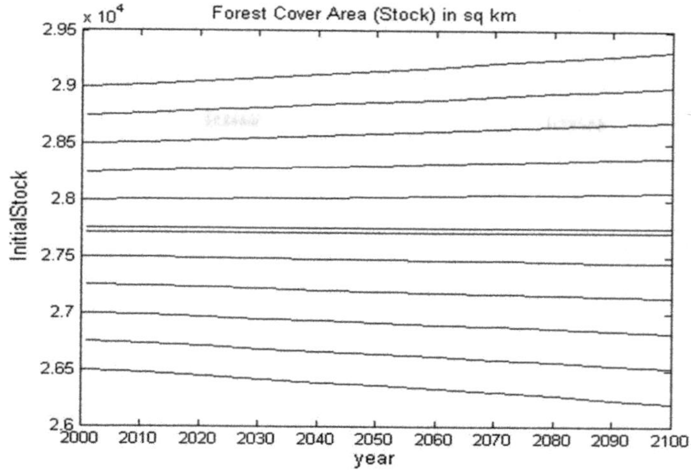

Fig. 25.3 Behaviour of forest stock with varying initial stocks

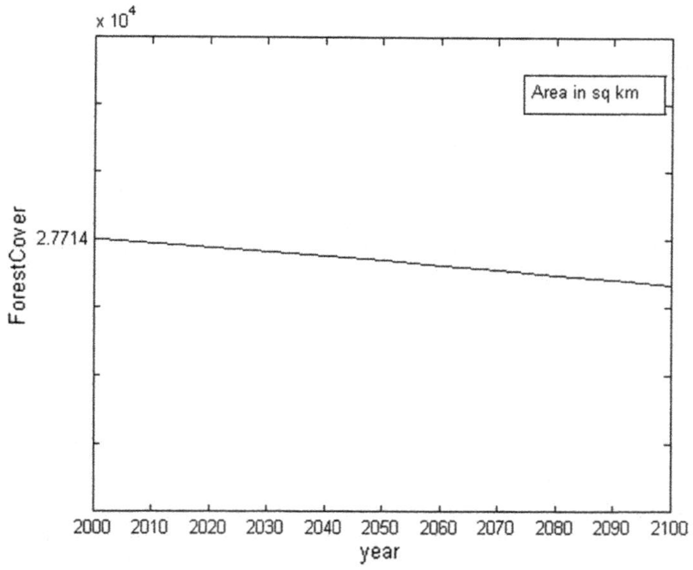

Fig. 25.4 Trend of forest stock with $a = 0.002219095042000 < 0.002219095042223$

function $U(c, s)$ used and the transition function of stock, $\dot{S}(s, c)$ which is constrained by the natural aspects. Therefore, Eq. 25.3 needs to be derived which is derived from Eq. 25.2 in this chapter for illustrative purpose. To get the value of 'a' and 'c', one has to provide the value of final stock (S_T), initial stock (S_O) and time period (t and t_0). The figures given below provide a comparative view of the trend

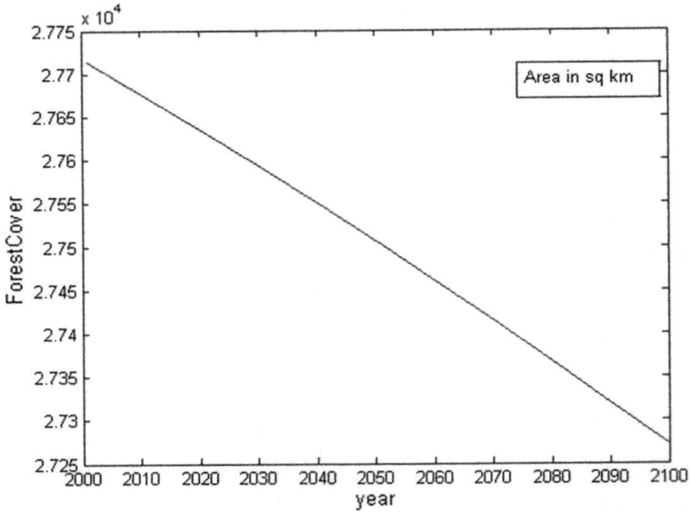

Fig. 25.5 Trend of forest cover area with $c = 65.5 > 61.5$

based on the value from the data shown in Table 25.1 and the trend obtained with the help of software Mathematica and Matlab for the period 1987–1999 and 2001–2013 separately (Fig. 25.6).

The trend depicted by the MATLAB software based on Eq. 25.3 and the value of 'a' and 'c' provided by Mathematica is similar to the original trend. Though the accuracy of the values cannot be guaranteed with limited data, but the trend of forest stock can always be established. Similarly to check the accuracy the trends for the year 2001–2013 have also been compared Fig. 25.7.

The trend is similar in both the cases except in the year 2003. The reason behind this difference is that the first figure based on the table is by the discrete nature, while the figure depicted by software is based on continuous time variable functions. But in both the figures for the period 2001–2013, the trend is to settle around the value 27,672. The rate of decline in the forests has become significantly lower in the period 2001–2013. This is due to the Supreme Court's ban order on all kinds of clear-felling in the north-eastern region from 1996 onwards, with a view to protect the remnant forests and some initiatives of plantation programme by government as data given in the website of the Department of Environment and Forests, Assam.

Now, the future trends of consumption and forest stock can be depicted using Eqs. 25.1 and 25.2. If the value of 'r' (rate of discount) is greater than the value of 'a' (rate of growth of the forest cover) which is more common in today's world the trend of forest stock will be as depicted in Fig. 25.8. The higher value of 'r' indicates impatience of the planner who values present more than the future. If the market rate of interest (6.68% = 0.0688) is used as the proxy for the rate of discount, and $c = 61.5$ km^2 per year as harvesting/consumption rate, the future trend

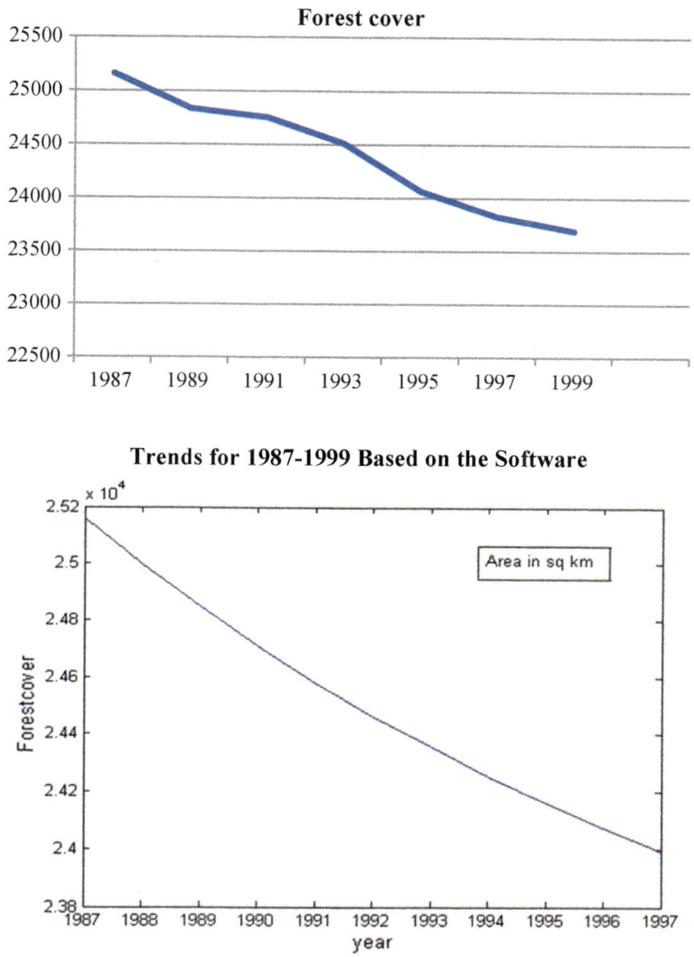

Fig. 25.6 Trends for 1987–1999 based on Table 25.1

for the Forest Cover of Assam with initial stock of 27,714 km^2 and rate of growth (a = 0.0022) can be depicted as in Fig. 25.8.

Impatience may result to low consumption and stock for the future. Therefore, to have a constant stock of forests in the future the condition $\dot{s} = 0$ must be fulfilled. In steady state $a*s = c$, which means the consumption or harvesting of the forests must be equal to the regenerated forest stock (growth rate multiplied by the existing stock). Further, when $\dot{c} = 0$, which means there is constant consumption, the rate of discount is equal to the regeneration rate ($a = r$). Thus, it is necessary to discount future utility accurately for effective forest planning and management. A small impatience may result faulty planning and management for future.

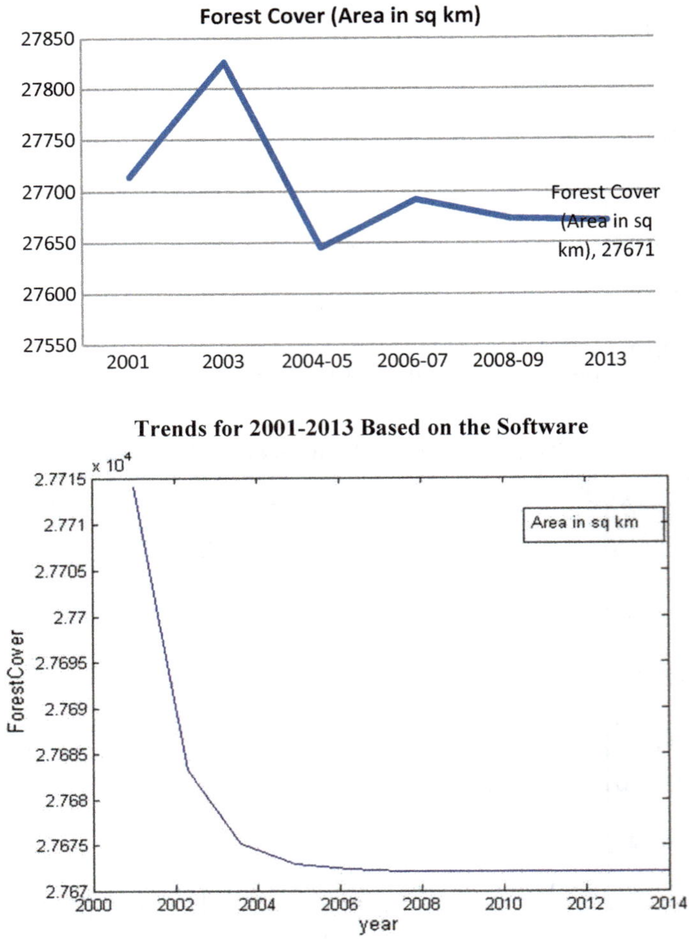

Fig. 25.7 Trends for 2001–2013 based on the Table 25.1

25.4 Conclusion

Sustainable development is a broad concept. Consideration of any single type of resources does not make the concept complete. The tradeoffs between present and future generation and between development and environmental conditions necessitate consideration of the constancy of the stock. Forests are an indispensable part of the environment and depict some specific behaviour. For the intactness of forest stock its extraction must not exceed the regeneration rate. A slight variation in regeneration and discount rates may lead to deforestation at a serious level. The

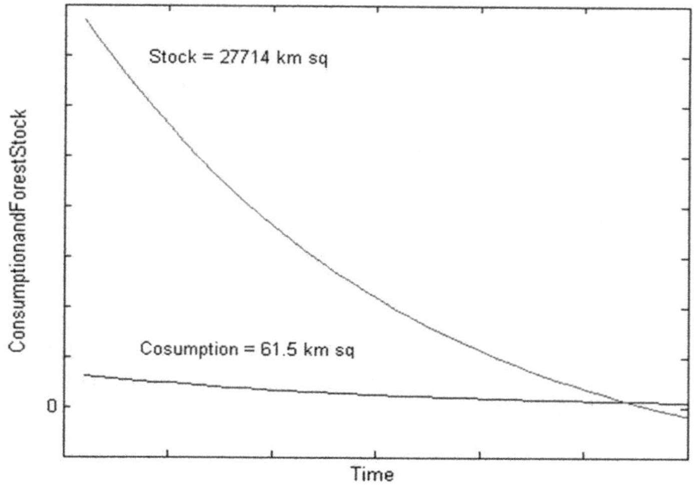

Fig. 25.8 Expected future trend

newly developed software[4] can be used to depict the trend going on and the required trend. The chapter has used the illustrations to describe the behaviour. The real figures are difficult to get unless there is proper data available for a long period of time. In case of availability of exact figures of forest stock and for an adequate time period, a picture close to reality can be depicted. On the basis of which forest planning and management can be done effectively. Extraction of the rents from the forest resources should be equal to the natural rate of growth of the resources and these rents should be invested in their regeneration wherever possible. Afforestation can be used as a tool to maintain the constant level of forests when consumption rate is higher than regeneration rate. But afforestation is a long-term process and its full success is not easily achievable. Therefore, controlling harvesting directly and consumption indirectly is better achievable on this ground. Better data collection for a long period of time may provide a chance to depict the future trend and present rates of regeneration and consumption. The behaviour of forests indicates the seriousness required in its management by planners and policymakers.

References

Arrow, K., Bolin, B., Costanza, R., Dasgupta, P., Folke, C., Holling, C. S., Jansson, B. O., Levin, S., Mäler, K. S., Perrings, C., & Pimentel, D. (1995). Economic growth, carrying capacity, and the environment. *Ecological Economics*, *15*(2), 91–95.

[4]The commands and steps followed in using software can be provided by author if required. One can refer to Economic Dynamics: Phase Diagrams and Their Economic applications by Ronald Shone, Cambridge University Press and MATLAB Tutorial books

Asheim, G. B. (2011). Hartwick's rule. Department of economics, University of Oslo. Retrieved from: http://folk.uio.no/gasheim/hr03.pdf. Accessed 4 April 2014.

Bretschger, L., & Smulders, S. (2007). Sustainable resource use and economic dynamics. *Environmental & Resource Economics, 36*(1), 1–13. doi:10.1007/s10640-006-9043-x.

Department of environment and forests, Assam. Retrieved from: www.assamforest.in/forestglance/assamForest-glance.php. Accessed 1 December 2014.

Farzin, Y. H. (2010). Sustainability, optimality, and development policy. *Review of Development Economics, 14*(2), 262–281.

Feenstra, T., Cesar, H., & Kort, P. (1999). Optimal control theory in environmental economics. *Handbook of environmental and resource economics* (pp. 1099–1107). School of Economics and Management, Netherlands organisation for scientific research (NWO) (No. 348cc100-2fb4-45b5-91ff-d0fa5120fe64).

GEO: Global Environmental Outlook-03, United Nations Development Programme. Retrieved from: www.unep.org/GEO/geo3/english/178.htm. Accessed 3 December 2014.

Hediger, W. (2009). Sustainable development with stock pollution. *Environment and Development Economics, 14*(06), 759–780.

India State of Forest Reports. 2001–2013. Forest Survey of India, Dehradoon.

Khatniar, B., Barua, A., & Talukdar, R. (2012). Dwindling forests in Assam, India: causes and remedies. *The Clarion, 1*(2), 154–167.

Pezzey, J., & Toman, M. A. (2002). *The economics of sustainability: a review of journal articles.* Washington, DC: Resources for the Future.

Shone, R. (2002). *Economic Dynamics: Phase diagrams and their economic application.* Cambridge University Press.

Chapter 26
Is Indian Agriculture Shifting Towards Feminisation? A Study on Recent Trend in Indian Agriculture with Reference to the Selected States of Northeast India

Banjul Bhattacharyya and Udaybhanu Bhattacharyya

Abstract Women are a key to development of rural areas through their contributions to sustainable agriculture and rural development, including food security. Present chapter is an attempt to realize women's status, including their unequal access to resources and their invisibility in statistics, in every aspect of agriculture all over India. Work Participation Rate (WPR) in agriculture is determined to study the gender biasness, if it exists, for all the states including the states of northeast. Access to land is also judged comparing the population as cultivator and agriculture Labour.

Keywords Faminisation · Gender biasness · Work participation rate

26.1 Introduction

Agriculture in India is the vertical backbone of the country and is regarded as the largest sector of the country's economic activity. Agricultural workers constitute by far the largest segment in the unorganized sector and their number according to 1991 Census was 74.6 million. In addition, a significant number, 110.7 million, are listed as cultivators (large, medium and small) of whom approximately 50% belong to the category of small and marginal farmers. Further, a significant number is engaged in livestock, forestry, fishing, orchards and allied activities. Small and

B. Bhattacharyya (✉)
Department of Agricultural Statistics, Bidhan Chandra Krishi Viswavidyalaya, Nadia, West Bengal, India
e-mail: banjul.b@rediffmail.com

U. Bhattacharyya
Department of Rural Development & Management, University of Kalyani, Kalyani, West Bengal, India
e-mail: uday.rdmku@gmail.com

U.K. De et al. (eds.), *Inequality, Poverty and Development in India*, India Studies in Business and Economics, DOI 10.1007/978-981-10-6274-2_26

marginal farmers work as agricultural workers in their spare time or in times of difficulty to supplement their meager incomes.

Since the early of sixtees of last century, the infusion of science and technology led to a paradigm shift in the agriculture in our country. It has brought in a massive increase of agriculture produces of India in terms of both value and quantity. Though the women work force of rural India is substantially engaged in the various agricultural activities, their role in agriculture has not been duly recognized so far. In developing countries, agriculture continues to absorb more than two-third of the female work force. In 1991, about 75% of rural female population belongs to the small and marginal farmers and landless agricultural labourers (Census Report) and interestingly, in 2011, the position has not been changed significantly. Like other developing countries, rural India is also witnessing a process that has now been described as *feminization of agriculture*.

Against this backdrop, the present chapter is a humble attempt to exhibit a realistic picture of the Agricultural population of the country with special reference to some selected states of Northeast India. Gender-specific study is made with the aid of statistical tools considering state-wise agricultural population data of India. The present chapter attempted to analyze the gender-specific participation scenario in Indian agriculture. The Work participation Rate (WPR) indicates the participation in agricultural work in respect of other economic activities. So, WPR is calculated and utilized to depict the gender-based participation in agriculture for all the states of India along with some selected states of Northeast India. Indices of participation are developed in respect of average WPR to measure the performance of the states. The effort has been given to assess the status of male and female cultivators in comparison with the agricultural labourers of different states in India. Percentage of Cultivators and agricultural labourers in each state of India were utilized to ascertain the gender biasness on access to land.

26.2 Materials

The data collected for the study are a secondary data source. The Economic classification of the population data over the states of India is recorded from the Statistical Abstract of India & Census of India for a period of 1961–2011.

26.3 Methodology

WPR, (Chatterjee and Ghosh 2002) is defined as the ratio of Economically Active Agricultural Populations and Total Economically Active Population as follows: WPR (Male) = EAMAP/TEAMP * 100, where EAFAP is Economically Active Agricultural Male Population and TEAFP is Total Economically Active Male Population. WPR (Female) = EAFAP/TEAFP * 100, where EAFAP is

Economically Active Agricultural Female Population and TEAFP is Total Economically Active Female Population. Systematic calculation of WPR is done from 1961 to 2001 for the states to study the discrepancy in gender-based participation in agriculture. The Average WPR is also calculated for all the states and is ranked accordingly. The percentage of cultivators and agricultural labourers present and their pattern of variation in post independence period is calculated and represented graphically. The graphical demonstrations based on gender are shown for all the states of India. It shows the occurrence of a type of workers in the states.

26.4 Results and Discussion

26.4.1 Work Participation Rate (WPR) of the States of India

The WPR considering gender impact has been critically analyzed for all the states over India. The result is presented in the table given below and represented by graphs (Fig. 26.1).

The result shows that the WPR in most of the states is increasing after independence up to 1991 census and then started declining. It is observed all over the country that female WPR is much higher in comparison with male but an exception is Punjab where the male WPR is much higher than female. If we consider a region wise study it can be clearly viewed that the southern region which comprises of states like Andhra Pradesh, Tamil Nadu, Karnataka, follows mostly similar pattern of WPR while Kerala shows different scenario. We can have a clear outlook that male WPR in Kerala is too low and with passage of time it is decreasing gradually. The decrease of WPR male in Kerala is noteworthy from 1991 and even decreased remarkably in 2001 whereas female WPR is increasing prominently since last decade. A similar pattern of the WPR for all the states of India is noticed. The average WPR calculated is shown in Table 26.1 and are ranked accordingly.

The highest average WPR among women is in Nagaland followed by Madhya Pradesh, Himachal Pradesh, Bihar and Rajasthan and the Lowest WPR among women is seen in Punjab followed by West Bengal. If a provincial study is carried out, it can be clearly viewed that Central India, i.e. Madhya Pradesh is doing well and excluding Punjab the northern region which comprises of states like Uttar Pradesh, Rajasthan and Himachal Pradesh have very high women participation rate in agriculture. In case of Western and Southern India, they follow a similar trend of participation but exception here is Kerala where participation of women in agriculture is lower as compared to other states in this region. The highest WPR is seen in Eastern region state, e.g., Nagaland but the WPR of women in the northeast region is quite scattered and does not resemble any prominent pattern.

The utmost average WPR among men is noticed and ranked for Bihar followed by Madhya Pradesh, Nagaland and Orissa. The male WPR for Kerala is also very poor and ranked below similar to that of the female.

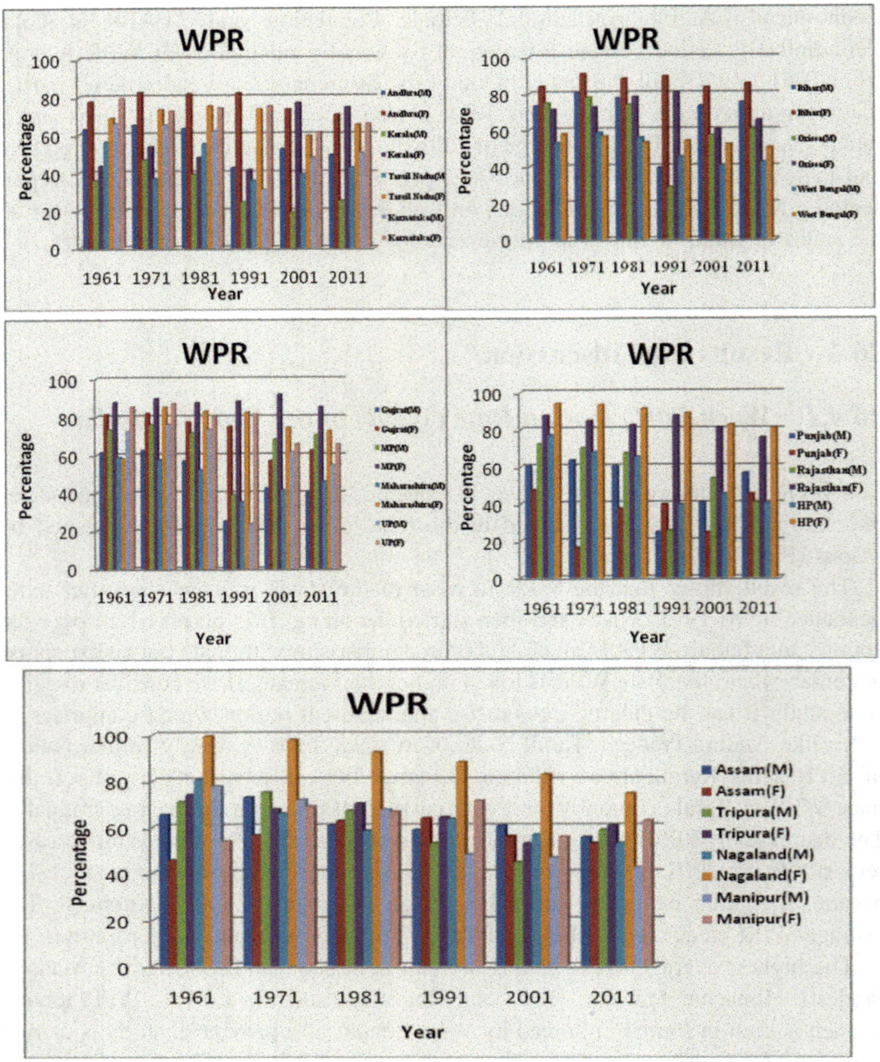

Fig. 26.1 Region-wise WPR in Agriculture. *Source* Statistical Abstracts of India and Census Reports

26.4.2 Cultivators versus Agricultural Labours

A Comparative scenario of Cultivators and Agricultural Labours with gender specification was critically examined by Bhattacharyya and Ghosh (2012) in their earlier study for a period of 1961–2001. In this work, the analysis has been extended to 2011 census data. The result is presented in Fig. 26.2. No remarkable change was observed. It has been revealed that the status of women as cultivators is

Table 26.1 Average WPR of India

States	Male	Rank	Female	Rank
Andhra Pradesh	55.91	9	77.95	6
Kerala	31.79	18	56.33	15
Tamil Nadu	44.28	17	69.20	12
Karnataka	53.72	12	71.27	11
Bihar	69.95	1	86.98	4
Orissa	62.24	4	71.45	10
West Bengal	49.35	14	54.05	17
Gujarat	48.19	16	72.68	9
Madhya Pradesh	66.52	2	88.46	2
Maharashtra	48.55	15	76.08	8
Uttar Pradesh	60.44	7	77.69	7
Punjab	50.96	13	35.12	18
Rajasthan	54.86	11	83.07	5
Himachal Pradesh	55.88	10	88.31	3
Assam	62.20	5	56.18	16
Tripura	61.52	6	64.84	13
Nagaland	62.87	3	89.02	1
Manipur	58.95	8	63.09	14

Source Calculated by authors

remarkably poor in comparison with a male for all over the country whereas women constitute a sizeable amount of agricultural labourers. From the study, it can be stated that male cultivators are more or less 40–60% higher than the female cultivators but exceptions are states like Himachal Pradesh, Nagaland and Arunachal Pradesh where female cultivators are comparatively higher. The percentage of female cultivators is extremely less in the States of Eastern region viz. Bihar, West Bengal and Orissa and in the case of Punjab both female Cultivators and Agricultural Labourers is to a large extent less in comparison with the other states although Punjab is a highly developed state in agriculture.

26.5 Conclusion

From the entire study, the scenario comes up is that if we consider the cultivators and also participation of agricultural labour, it is found that in both the cases male population are much higher than the female population in agriculture. Also, the declining trend of WPR in agriculture after 1991 is observed. This may be the indication of economic growth of different kinds of income generating opportunities after globalization. The fact behind it may be interpreted that among the Economically Active Community females are mostly engaged in farm work/agricultural activities but their land possession is very poor. The scope of

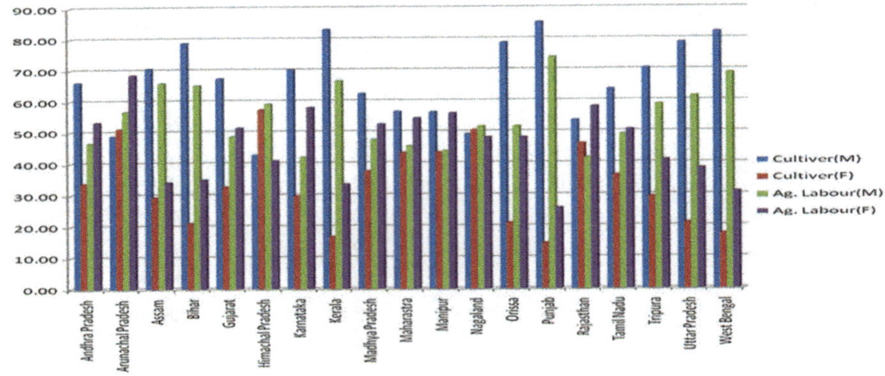

Fig. 26.2 Cultivators and Agriculture Labours (%) according to 2011 census. *Source* Statistical Abstracts of India and Census Reports

inclusion of female in other categories of Economic activities is much restricted than male. Key strategies are to improve women's access to land, credit, technology (agricultural research, tools and information technology), and extension services as well as adopting some technology suitable to women's work. Girls' education and making women visible in policy and programmes through leadership development, participatory planning methods are an integral part of sustainable development.

References

Bhattacharyya, B., & Ghosh, M. (2012). *Statistical analysis of Indian agricultural work force: A study on gender perspective* (1st ed.). Germany: LAP Lambert Academic Publishing.

Census of India. (1961, 1971, 1981, 1991, 2001, 2011). Retrieved from: http://censusindia.gov.in/.

Chatterjee, B., & Ghosh, D. K. (2002). *In search of a district development index*. West Bengal: SIPRD.

MIX
Papier aus verantwortungsvollen Quellen
Paper from responsible sources
FSC® C105338

Printed by Books on Demand, Germany